THE BMW STORY
A Company In Its Time

THE BMW STORY
A Company In Its Time

by
HORST MÖNNICH

Translated from the German by

Anthony Bastow and William Henson

First published in Great Britain in 1991 by
Sidgwick & Jackson Limited

First published in German in 2 volumes in 1983 and 1987
by Econ Verlag. Reissued in 1989 by Zsolnay Verlag, Vienna.
A revised version was published in 1991 as
BMW: A German Story in Pictures by Piper Verlag.

ISBN 0 283 06090 5

Typeset by Falcon Typographic Art Ltd., Edinburgh & London
Printed and bound in Great Britain by Mackays of Chatham PLC, Kent

for Sidgwick & Jackson Limited
18–21 Cavaye Place
London SW10 9PG

*Civilisation is a movement and not a condition,
a voyage and not a harbour.*

Arnold Toynbee

CONTENTS

the Rapp Works: 'BMW' – Enter a delegation – Friz's idea for
high altitude flying – A Bavarian way to someone's heart – It
is running perfectly – Test flight in Halberstadt – Reserve 2nd
Lieutenant Zemo Diemer.

Schleicher – Field inspection – How Friz makes a motorcycle out of the Helios and designs the R32 – Great moments in the life of an engineer – '. . . I suggested putting the engine transversely.' – A race with Stolle's Victoria in the Solitude – Schleicher's light-metal cylinder head – The R37 races ahead of all competitors – Gold for Schleicher (Six-day event in England in 1928).

The economy is the key – The greatest swindle in world history: inflation – Versailles and the consequences – The F 13 takes off for Stockholm – A lenient punishment for an industrial spy – In the background: Herr von Seeckt – Did the Reich army train the Red Army? – BMW aircraft engines from the military perspective – Experiences of an on-board fitter.

Jacques Montane's three miracles – The year 1923 – The greatest conjuring trick in world history: stabilising the mark – The balance sheet for 1924 – Mittelholzer's flight to Persia – Telegram from Cape Town in 1927 – The silver condor over Tierra del Fuego – Five world records for the BMW IV – Lindbergh crosses the Atlantic – 'Am flying, local traffic control permitting, over Greenland to the USA. Gronau.' – To hell with all Brandenburg's enemies! – Around the world – Water- or air-cooled, that is the question – 1928: Popp opts for the radial engine – The large oval area with walls.

South German car company under discussion – The masses and the car in 1923 – General Galliéni's taxis of the Marne – Popp's thoughts on the small car in 1924 – Co-operation contract with Mercedes, 1926 – Wunibald Kamm's SHW-car – Castiglioni makes out he's mad – Man in morning coat and bowler: Schapiro – The Gotha Railway Carriage takes on too much – Dr von Stauss: 'Go ahead and buy it!'

Dixi, I have spoken – From a peasant's son to an armaments industrialist in 1923 – When the engine was still under the driver's seat – A prophecy – Eight small cars on the Hohe Strasse – The Dixi throws off its mane – Bigger inside than out – International Alpine Rally, 1929 – 'No need to explain any further, salesman, sir!' – The grand design?

Why Opel declines a German car trust – Castiglioni leaves BMW – The time of the demi-gods is over – Easy come, easy go – Breakfast with Hermann Göring – Death without transfiguration.

A narrow ledge of freedom – Shared by airplane production – The feud between the star and propeller image (Mercedes/BMW) – Goodbye to the merger – Future face: the 326.

Henne's experiences on four wheels – 'Go ahead and try it out!' – Nürburgring, 14 June 1936 – The 328: answer to a protest – When it was raining gold medals – Calculation of a snob – The fiasco of the front axle on the BMW 320.

A farmer's practical advice – The motorcycle 'being' – Schleicher: motor conscience 'on test' – Why BMW introduced pressed steel frames – Stroke of genius: telescopic forks with oil dampers – Hitler asks: When are we going to get rear suspension? – Falkenhausen's solution: sliding tubes – Henne's absolute (and last) world record: 279.8 kph.

The Mille Miglia and four white BMW 328s – The Le Mans 24-hour race for the Grand Prix for endurance and speed – Why the Sarthe race track is one of the hardest in the world – Island with Irish law – Georg Meier from Mühldorf am Inn wins the Tourist Trophy for Germany (1939) – 'You won't make money racing motorcycles!' – Bavarian gendarme on Europe's race tracks – Out of the bend at 210 kph in Malmö.

The upside-down world of National Socialism – What Dahlerus lived through in the Reich Chancellery – No such thing as impossible – Ernst Udet's triumph and disaster – Lindbergh's warning in vain – Berlin-New York-Berlin in 45 hours – The He 111 worker bee – The plant in Allacher Wäldchen – Merger with Brandenburg Motor Works (Bramo) in 1939 – A State funeral – What did Udet know? – Milch versus Popp – von Hanstein's victory at Brescia (Mille Miglia, 1940) – 'That Popp must go!' – Supervisory board meeting, 1942 – Falkenhausen outside Stalingrad – BMW in the sights of Allied bombers – Things were not like that.

A Frenchman in Munich – Refusing to work on 14 July – The Ligocki affair – For posterity's sake? – The wooden bridge – Was it really sabotage? – RAM'S price control commission – Himmler's trade in humans: concentration camp inmates – The Ludwigsburg files – An SS sergeant major – A foreman.

BMW: Number Two on the blacklist – A secret robot command module – BMW 801 double-radial engine goes into production

PART TWO

The Tower

The Victors and the Vanquished 1945–1951

The Search for a Square Centimetre

At the beginning of the century, where our story begins, there is one thing which ranks amongst the finest achievements of science and technology – the internal combustion engine; a thing buried beneath the carriage seat, which moved four wheels without the previously harnessed power of horses. In a few examples, which crawled along rather than travelled at any great speed, it released a shudder of delight, not to mention displeasure, when people on public roads had to get out of its way; it was a discovery which had something unpredictable about it. Called then, as now, an automobile, we still avoid it – and the problems it creates. It has taken hold of life like an epidemic and remade cities to its own requirements. It has radically altered landscapes and transformed and redefined human habits and ways of thinking. Whether we enjoy it or curse it, we cannot deny its usefulness, and no one today can imagine life without it. Future historians, when coming to judge the twentieth century, will depict it as a monument more significant to the age than nuclear power or micro-processors.

Remarkably, literature, together with the arts and history, has only touched upon this phenomenon. Only the end-product is of interest, not its past or future. What do the annals of history have to say about a car factory, what information do they give about the driving forces at work at a time when the century underwent its changes, in the way that research tells us what went on in wars, what was discussed over general staff maps, what was secretly agreed in diplomatic intrigues? Technicians and engineers only ever appear as makers, as exponents of what can be made with historical forces – whose effects they put into motion and multiply, but never trigger off. Is not everything involving the marketing of technology affected by the economy? What does Ford's discovery of the consumer in bringing the car into the age of the masses in 1914 imply; what does General Galliéni's idea of sending soldiers to the front by taxi and thus changing the fate of France imply? A car is a thing to be used. Even when it inspires dreams suited to the force of epoch-making events, it is a subsidiary event and never a main one. This subsidiary event most clearly describes the upheaval we are currently experiencing: a class-based society transforming into one of mass-mobility, a society which no longer sees its life tied to one place, but as one constantly being caught up in the process of travel.

The development of the car has been determined by fashion, as the spirit of the times, bread and circuses, the spectacle of major races, as well as by sober considerations of profitability. It has a great past. Within a decade cars turn to heaps of rust, but the reasons for designers and consumers inventing and using them remain.

If witnesses are called for the short period of their development (not even a hundred years!), the archaelogist who excavates Etruscan graves seems more favourably placed than the historian of cars, who grew up with them and the internal combustion engine. I am referring not only to rust rotting sheet metal, but also to the desolation wrought upon the earth. In Germany production sites were destroyed by two wars, by bombs and dismantling and, in the case of BMW, dismantling down to the very last bolt. Anyone today who has ridden in a car produced in those bygone factories might well have believed he was in some kind of time-warp.

My book is based on hundreds of written records which I wrote down after speaking to people at BMW, and before I began the actual writing of the book. Foremen, fitters, engineers, designers, managers, secretaries, dealers and shareholders all told me what they knew, why and how such and such happened, and how they came to solutions which, once they were proved correct, resulted in their origin being forgotten. I learnt about how they came to the firm, about the times they spent together and about the reason for their leaving prematurely, if this is what they did. Strangely enough, and presuming their memories were not glorifying the past (this they all denied), they never told a lie; I checked every statement. Of course they could only recount what occurred in the way they saw it, but it was this that often made what they had to say as exciting as a detective story. It forced out facts which the official documents (business reports, minutes of meetings) either did not mention or only did so in passing.

I often wondered exactly what such obsessions revealed, and found it difficult initially not to be distrustful of any document with the 'official' stamp on it. This was natural enough. It hardly needs saying in the preface to my book that I felt I was more like a kind of detective than an author. It is only by comparing Report A with Report B, and then Reports A and B to C, that the whole composite picture comes into focus. This is what really matters. If you make allowances for what any human being omits or glosses over to protect himself, one comes to the vital ingredient for telling any story, which is 'approximation to the truth'.

The 'story' ahead of us is not an imaginary one – apart from that imagination which any author must use to fill gaps by adding two and two together. To avoid tainting or distorting those facts he must create 'bridges'. Here he is helped by the logic of usefulness. Events which lose their stitching can be sewn together again, thereby making what was happening behind the times clearer.

Occasionally I had the impression that I was grasping a lot with both hands before it escaped memory and could be put down in a story. Substantial parts of the book had already been written when I received a call from a group of demolition workers who had discovered several crates containing plate glass in the storeroom of the old administration building in Lerchenau Street (which had been rebuilt several times and was going to be pulled down due to its unprofitability). These were framed photographs from the thirties and forties. A kind soul had stopped the foreman from throwing them into the bin. They contained what I, like many others, had previously and unsuccessfully been scouring for – prints and sketches of those prototypes and mock-ups which were to ensure a successor to the legendary 335 car and which, in defiance of the ban, had been developed during the early war years – the 332 and the 337 – with all the design details which had remained only in the vague memories of a few technicians involved on them.

Those cars, prototypes and mock-ups from that time, may have (from our present perspective) not only nostalgic charm but technical value which is still worth something today. They are much more for me than that; they are the prime exhibits of the period, just like the people I questioned. Social phenomena, which I did not understand, can be discerned in them. Anyone admiring model ranges of a bygone age, anyone finding out how they came together, what effect they had, suddenly sees an image of what actually happened. This is reflected in the company which created them, which received and also put out 'signals from the time', and then, like them, progressed through the century as a piece of individual history. These were events in which the company took a hand, as well as the company being determined by the events, the former marking the epoch, in the same way as the epoch was marked by the company.

This may be the first time that a company has been described like this, when confronting its past. Companies are reluctant to put their history on show without embellishment of some sort. There may be rough patches which could be used by someone bearing a grudge who wants to cause harm. I have never understood this attitude. Striving, on the one hand, to leave their stamp on the economy they are not nearly as fearful as when they look at themselves in the mirror. What they were, they became. Simply putting out glowing descriptions called 'company history' provides little information.

The job remained, as an author, to write this story – history as illustrated by BMW. With the firm's readiness to understand itself through its past, even to accept and admit the 'rough patches', something had to come out of it which made the example, the model and the object of my activity a major task. I discovered this in the process. Where, I wondered, does this extraordinary fascination come from, this fascination which the car still has for the soberest and the most rational of men, who claim and feel to be enlightened as never before?

BMW was a kind of key to this.

On the map in front of me (to a scale of 1:50,000) the works took up little more than a square centimetre. What a unique opportunity it was for a writer to come to terms with his age by investigating, researching, penetrating this square centimetre; by setting the result, spatially, temporally and historically, in relation to the 'surroundings'; by making clear all that my square centimetre had involved, inspired and influenced, what it had 'emanated' and naturally what it had, retroactively, so to speak, absorbed from outside.

Does a thing called a 'Works' have a soul? People say: He was the soul of his business, she was the soul of her family. Of course a works does not have a soul, but a human being can be found to embody it. I was lucky enough to find such a man. He was an archivist, but much more than that.

He knew God and the world. His archives were a treasure-trove. Anyone needing spare parts for a vintage car came to him. He did not need to look anything up. He had everything in his head – right down to the colours of old models, their curious details, even their numbers, which would come to him before he had opened his dependable book.

From this man I gleaned knowledge which had already eluded time, and eluded my square centimetre. It was the same old song – anyone starting afresh sweeps away what is in front of him as he goes along, whether or not he notices, in rolling up his sleeves, how much his predecessor had done before, in having to make his mark. This begs the question as to whether he is forced to adopt new kinds of behaviour in place of old ones. This is the source of all intelligence; that is, the intelligence to learn from the lessons of the past to use the new techniques, knowledge and progress of the age better than others. This, in the end, is what it all comes down to.

Only a few people today know where the halo surrounding BMW engines comes from, and which, I am tempted to say, clings indissolubly to them.

No motor engineer in the research department containing over 3,000 personnel will be presumptuous enough to have it attributed to himself. He simply takes it for granted. Perhaps he will also reach for this book to discover in the end how a thing he works on can so convincingly dispel any illusion in the purchasers' minds. At least they are able to say where it comes from.

What is written here is what was. And also, what is. Both belong together. No present is conceivable without the past. Only by knowing the past can we discover who we are.

Horst Mönnich

PART ONE

Below the Sound Barrier

What he weaves, knows no weaver.
Proverb

Aircraft Engines at Oberwiesenfeld
1916–1922

Three Birth Certificates

Every biographer begins with his hero's date of birth. X saw the light of day on such and such a date ... the day, hour, even the actual minute of his first appearance interest and fascinate him. What was the weather like, what were people thinking, was there war or peace, what was just about to burst onto the scene, which king, president, ruler was governing? By eschewing astrology, which asserts that irrevocable cosmic conditions at the moment of birth determine everything which follows, the biographer is firmly convinced that he can define the salient life-lines of his hero from his very first moments of life. Hardly had he been born than Eulenspiegel fell into the stream as the wet-nurse carried him over the footbridge. Perhaps he would have been a completely different person without this shock? It all comes down to how you assert yourself, what forces fashion and mould you. Beginnings determine everything! So let us have the birth certificate, the time and place!

I am in a quandary when I try to find definite clues. The grass has long grown over what had previously been. Which of the certificates marking the birth is of any value? There are two, sometimes three – with widely differing dates, a year and a half between them!

I found birth certificate No. 1 in the company's register in the Munich District Court, Vol. 30, p. 78 Rge. Alt HRB Vol. 1 No. 123, where, on 7 March 1916, the court clerks had entered in copper-plate hand-writing:

Bavarian Aircraft Works PLC
The aim of the company is the manufacture and commercial marketing of aircraft and all associated machines, appliances and other items as well as the setting up of other ventures in any legally permissible form or the participation therein and in general the running of any company of this kind. The share capital is 1 million marks and is taken up by the following founder investors:
1 Albrecht Kiendl, bank official in Munich
2 Max Bürger, bank official in Munich
3 Ludwig Endres, as representative of the Machine factory Augsburg-Munich (MAN)

4 Herr Nadolny, lawyer in Berlin
5 Hermann Backstein, qualified engineer, Berlin
6 Gustav Otto, engineer in Munich

Under founding member No. 6 it was also remarked: 'Herr Otto brought to the new company the Otto Works he had previously owned, together with all assets and liabilities, and received the sum of 432,782.44 marks for it. He was further entitled to take up 100 shares at nominal value from Herr Albrecht Kiendl or his legal successor against cash payment, of which he did not avail himself.'

No word of BMW. However, anyone undertaking to discover BMW's origins would refer to 7 March 1916 as the real birthday: where once the Bavarian Aircraft Works (BFW) had had its workshops and assembly plants, BMW stands today at 76 Lerchenau Street (it was still known then as Neulerchenfeld Street) in Munich, on the edge of Oberwiesenfeld, later to be the Olympic site. So is Gustav Otto – the man who brought his aircraft factory to the Bavarian Aircraft Works, which was founded on that day – the founding father?

Not much can be said about birth certificate No. 2. It seems to tell a completely different story. Here the date is 20 July 1917. On this day, following a decision at a company meeting of a completely different firm, the Rapp Motor Works Co. Ltd at 288 Schleißheim Street, the renaming of the firm as 'Bavarian Motor Works Co. Ltd' took place. 'Following the departure of Company Director Karl Rapp', it adds laconically. However, the clerk entered this into the Munich register of companies on 21 July 1917. Here we see the name 'Bavarian Motor Works' for the first time.

This raises a new question. Is this Karl Rapp the founding father? There is no doubting the fact that it was his firm, which had now been renamed Bavarian Motor Works Co. Ltd, which undertook to produce: 'Land, sea and aircraft, cars and bicycles, car and bicycle accessories, vehicle parts, stationary engines for solid, liquid and gaseous fuels and spare parts and accessories for them.'

The above entry (and here I must call it my third date) was made on 5 October 1917 at the former Imperial Patent Office, where the trade mark, which was to protect all the above-mentioned and ensuing products, was registered; a propeller on a white and blue background carrying the initials BMW written round the edge.

The applicant, probably also the designer of this mark, was a certain Franz Josef Popp. As a new director of the firm, he had bought a large area of land north of Oberwiesenfeld on Moosach Street in that same year of 1917 on which to build a brand-new works.

The firm, the company now existed. A long birth indeed . . . What is still obscure, in particular, is the legal validity of birth certificate No. 1, which should and must be cleared up, even if it is at the expense of our story becoming top-heavy – a story where the car will only make its appearance much later on. But this pre-history only provides enough information about the forces that ensured that BMW did not immediately go under and that the records of one firm's founding would not be closed, unlike so many others which were closed shortly after they had been opened. Born into Oberwiesenfeld as a child of the war, in anything but happy times, my hero, who had appeared so indecisive, could take on life's adventure. In other words it could now fall back on the driving forces which would enable the technology of the time to break through.

A Place for Flying

If you look at the Munich city map, where Schleißheim Street passes through Milbertshofen in a north–south direction, you will see a green square spread out west of it like a flag on its staff. This is Oberwiesenfeld. The fact that even today it has managed to stay green under the onslaught of houses, dwellings, industrial estates, gasometers, railway lines and roads is due to one simple fact – the military (formerly the Imperial Bavarian War Ministry) owns it; and so tenaciously that there can be no doubt about the generals' environmentally protective role in choosing this treeless field as an exercise and training ground for their soldiers. The latter probably cursed the place.

In the pre-military age of 'Oweg' (as children called the large meadow) an Elector, the enthusiastic builder Max Emanuel from the Wittelsbach dynasty, had fortunately already prevented Oberwiesenfeld from being divided up. Of course it was his money. It was his plan to join up the residences of Dachau, Schleißheim, Nymphenburg and Munich by a network of magnificent canals. Although a thousand Muslim prisoners, whom the victorious Prince had brought with him from the Turkish War in 1688, had worked for twelve years on the so-called Turkish ditch (it had begun around the Georgenschwaige in today's Milbertshofen and continued as far as the palace gardens), this last section never saw a drop of water and was neglected. Since 'Upper Oberwiesenfeld near Munich' acquired a boundary to the east which suited the town commander very well, he could now move all the garrison's powder stores from the southern part of the meadow to the higher ground 'north of Marsbergel', which he thought expedient for safety reasons. This was all very well, until there was a huge explosion let off by chief gunner Stanislaus Schmitt, a failed student who blew himself up along with eight of his colleagues, probably as a result of 'conduct unbecoming to the NCOs in a first-line battery'.

> *O, my people,*
> *Look yonder to the Munich powder magazine,*
> *It's made a puff, it's made a bang,*
> *Heard as far as Regensburg,*
> *O look yonder, look yonder*
> *To the Munich powder magazine.*

They all flew into the air,
And found their own graves.
They found a dead foot at Starnberg
And a hand in the River Isar,
And mounds of entrails lay scattered all around.

Thus balladeers in Upper and Lower Bavaria long lamented the terrible event. Even the roof of the Frauenkirche was badly damaged! But this did not alter the way in which the military used the land. Its proprietors continued to defend it with cavalry and artillery, who were drilled here despite all attacks and petitions from civilians, without realizing that the danger to them lay not on the ground on the distant horizon, but somewhere quite different – the air. A Parseval airship landed there in 1909 at the mooring-masts which had been erected at Oberwiesenfeld by express military permission. This event was definitely to have consequences. The 'aviators' were there, and from now on were not to be driven out. They became unloved neighbours, even if the fighter-pilot Boelcke was later to describe fighter planes as the 'cavalry of the air'.

Yet it was due to the inevitable military nature of acquiring and defending land that Oberwiesenfeld stayed as it was, covered with sparse turf and exposed to the wind – an ideal exercise and practice ground which now, as the aviators had discovered, promised a future for military aircraft and, as a result, attracted people who would never have dreamt of settling there before.

'Look to the future! What is technology without it? Let's go to Ober-wiesenfeld and have a look at what we can do there!' was what many said; and little workshops shot up out of the ground like mushrooms at the edge of the exercise ground. Their owners, master metal workers, failed engineers, outsiders mad about flying, all believed in their genius and the great opportunity promised by aircraft and aero-engine manufacture.

This is where our story begins, with Oberwiesenfeld being used as an airfield, and if we take a big leap in time to the latter third of this century, over two destructive wars which set half the world alight, we shall find Oberwiesenfeld still a green plot of ground – hosting the twentieth Olympic Games, which brought together 'the youth of the world'. And we shall notice, on the edge of the ever-green area, high up on a four-columned tower which grew out of the ground at the same time as the Olympic buildings, a blue and white circle of rotating propellers with the letters BMW round the edge. Neither the military, when they annexed Oberwiesenfeld, nor the aviators, and certainly not the two engineers amongst the new arrivals, Otto and Karl Rapp, would have dreamed of Oberwiesenfeld's (totally unmilitary) uses in the same century as they lived when they founded their companies.

At the south-east corner of Oberwiesenfeld 135 Schleißheim Street was just behind the Stetten barracks, where the military name of Schwere-Reiter Street still reminds us of who held sway here. This was Otto's bastion, Otto's starting-point, from where he had tried to invade, or at least to share in, the

7

green square, if not on the ground itself, then in the blue and white sky above it.

In the 1970s there was little left of Otto's foundation apart from a depot for used cars – which had been tendered by a dealer with a Persian name – a few low workshops, which had obviously been bombed, perhaps built by Otto and cobbled together by someone. In front of this was now just a courtyard of puddles, old car-seats, delapidated buses. . . . On the fence there was a board belonging to a house-building company advertising private dwellings for sale on immediate discount. But surely the ashes of historical places radiate much more than this? Otto was here, I thought to myself . . . and a company of sweaty infantrymen on the march, laden with backpacks, divided up quickly and pressed themselves flat on the ground. In the sun's blinding light Otto's training biplane swooped about above Oberwiesenfeld and, fortuitously, over its exercise area. (Otto had immediately had a flying ban slapped on him by the military authorities which, after repeated efforts, was lifted; it nevertheless meant that he could never be entirely trusted again.) He is one of the engineers, to be found in the south-east of the field.

If we put a cross here on the map and write OTTO beside it, and if we do the same with RAPP in the north-east of Oberwiesenfeld at 288 Schleißheim Street (another man involved with aircraft engines, a man assiduously seeking customers and able to absorb one failure after another, who consistently strove to keep the creditors and customers happy), we can see the pincer that gripped Oberwiesenfeld in its jaws. Even at a time when one was competing against the other, Otto did not want to know about Rapp and, similarly, Rapp did not want to know about Otto. Both tried to steal each other's fire.

My pencil now wanders a little to the west, along Moosach Street, which is the northern boundary of Oberwiesenfeld, to the area which Popp had bought when the Bavarian Motor Works was already in existence. It should not concern us that a new name marks this place today: 'SÜD-BREMSE'. Let us put our third cross here and join up all three places, so that the field where everything happened, one which was to become one of the stories of the century, is marked out – the edge of an exercise ground with all its magical appeal; a place for flying.

The Son of the Inventor

The procession started off. In front of the hearse walked about 800 workers from the factory in nearby Mülheim, whose technical director had died. On both sides were skilled workers holding palm leaves. The sight of the deceased's only son and youngest offspring, an eight-year-old boy, gave a sombre air to the proceedings. He followed the hearse behind the priest, holding the hand of his father's lifelong friend and colleague, the Privy Councillor Eugen Langen. The midday sun shone brightly and cheerily upon the solemn procession.

This is how the *Rheinische Merkur* recorded an event which was important for two reasons. The first was that the engineer Nikolaus August Otto, who had died of a heart attack on 26 January 1891 and who had invented the so-called 'Otto combustion engine', had deserved only a slightly lower status than the great James Watt, the inventor of the steam engine. The latter's relief adorns the red sandstone front at 49 Heumarkt at the corner of Geyer Street, which now marked the starting-point of the funeral procession seen moving through the streets of Cologne, a procession 'so big as to be rarely seen in this city'. ('For like the man,' read the eulogy at the graveside, 'who first bestowed a constant power of life through the correct output of condensation in the steam engine, so was Otto first able to make the petrol engine viable through the correct timing of ignition and combustion.') The second was that 'this unique life of an inventor' (who from very modest beginnings, through unremitting application and genius, came to understand the properties of gases, in particular of mixtures and the requirements of a technically feasible small-sized engine) gave his son and successor little chance to take in, promote or even get an idea of his father's achievements.

'There is so much air in the world, and I can't get any of it,' the eight-year-old boy's father had lamented on his deathbed. Was this also to apply to the son? His mother had money and supported him until he left school. He studied engineering at technical high schools in Hanover, Karlsruhe and Munich. Munich! He missed the exam, changed to car making, and from that day on 9 May 1876 when his father had achieved some success with his four-stroke cycle, and the first working diagram of the Otto combustion engine had been demonstrated, he realised that there

9

was nothing fundamentally new to be done in the field, now that the car was plying the streets thanks to Daimler and Benz. Even the 'Bavarian Car Garage – Tuning and Repair Shops', which the young man founded at 72 Karl Street, Munich, could only be a temporary stop-gap, not a real business. Then, in September 1909 (in the same year as the first Parseval airship landed at Oberwiesenfeld), he stood on the race-track at Merheim in Cologne in a patient crowd which had been gathering there for days, looked up into the air ('there is so much air in the world. . .') and saw Blériot flying. He knew then where destiny lay.

In Germany at that time there was little development in flying. Why was that? Like everything in life, it was to do with convictions which people held and which, even if they were wrong or based on wrong premises, were not easy to dispel. Such a flimsy thing could not be trusted, even if it did work (lurching about in the air like a bird under one's own or motorised power), as Otto Lilienthal had demonstrated before the Wright Brothers when he had broken his neck. This was something for artists, perhaps. Not for good reason did insurance companies exclude 'tightrope walkers, animal trainers, acrobats and airship pilots' from their contracts, and the War Ministry ban its officers from taking free trips in balloons because they were 'too dangerous'. The experts believed that, in contrast to the dirigible airship, there was no military advantage to be gained from it; this was also the case for the economy, for transport and for anything 'useful' in terms of progress. The discovery of the airship (a gas, lighter than air, lifted it up; its engine was only needed for motion and direction) had put back the Wright Brothers' launch into the air, which was achieved by an engine little different from that used in cars. How was something heavier than air going to be able to fly? It wasn't!

Werner von Siemens wrote in a letter to Dr Fickert in Oldenburg in 1883: 'Aircraft will only be possible when powered machines have been invented which weigh no more than a fifth of the lightest machines now in existence, and which can convert at least 30 per cent of the theoretical power equivalent of heat energy instead of 5 per cent. Until then all aircraft will be a waste of time.' The following sentence appears in his memoirs: 'Inventors are always starting at the wrong end, and inventing aircraft before they have the power to move them.' He was certainly thinking here of Arnold Böcklin, the painter, who had sought in vain for half his life to transfer the mechanics of bird-flight to the kites and aircraft he had constructed, steadfastly believing that he would be lifted by the force of a head wind alone. Siemens had put his workshops and test field at Charlottenburg at his disposal.

Ten years later, nothing had changed and events moved from Germany to the 'New World'. There five men in the sand dunes at Kitty Hawk in North Carolina watched (on 7 December 1903) in an icy winter wind as 'a machine carried a man through its own power in free flight through the air and, without slowing down, moved parallel to the ground so as to land again without damage' (Wright Brothers' report). This first flight of a man by motorised power which took him 3 metres off the ground lasted

12 seconds and covered 53 metres. The problem of 'heavier than air' had been solved.

A good three years before, on 2 July 1900, the first rigid airship of Count Zeppelin had taken off from Lake Constance. The whole world followed the journey of LZ 4 over the Rhein falls, Lake Lucerne and northern Switzerland in awe, with the kind of amazement which not even the Echterdingen catastrophe (1908), when the airship caught fire and was completely destroyed, could undo. The old count had captured Germany's love and willingness for self-sacrifice with his Zeppelin, resulting in an immediate public contribution of 6 million marks to build a new one.

> And through the dawn-red gate, Count Zeppelin,
> You breathe horizons, in the glint
> Of eternal youth glowing around
> Your silver hair and wind-tanned face.
> You are a hero, young and hoary, who
> Like Abraham, believes only in God and the future.

This is how the poet Hans Brandenburg moved the masses in Germany when he wrote his effusive anthem. Enthusiasm prevailed, not for aircraft (although in France aircraft development was advanced not least for military reasons), but for airships. Germany believed that it was airships that would help them in their conquest of the skies, making them 'victorious over all other peoples'.

How great was the German mistake is shown by the report drafted by Captain Ferber of the French artillery when, in 1906, he advised the War Ministry in Paris to buy the patents for the Wright Brothers' aircraft. He stated that the time had come when industry had reached the high point required by aircraft technicians to build planes. It had become more than just a fascinating sport. This extremely swift means of transport was also destined to become a powerful weapon of war. 'I am thinking,' Ferber went on to say, 'not so much of the possibility of dropping missiles on the enemy's head every so often, but much more of the effective support of high command by employing countless squadrons of these airplanes.'

The commander-in-chief could at any moment receive accurate information as to the enemy's movements and advances. The government would enable their squadrons to cross over enemy-occupied territory and to send across the borders and observe the reserves and the hastily assembled support troops held there. 'This state of affairs will ensure victory,' Ferber concluded his report, 'as our old Montluc said: "When the opponent knows what the opponent is doing, the opponent will strike the opponent."'

This sheds some light on the background leading up to the conflict between 'lighter' than air (airship) and 'heavier' than air (aircraft) then being played out between nations.

As a tireless campaigner of flying and a pilot himself, Ferber's view maintained that the conflict 'would end to the latter's advantage', while Germany still continued to rely on the airship. As late as 1910 a spokesman for the War Ministry declared in the German Parliament that no planes would be procured, as the high speeds (at that time an airplane could do all of 70 kph) made reconnaissance impossible, there being only enough room for the pilot.

In October 1907 a German captain, Alfred Hildebrandt, travelled to Dayton in Ohio. He wanted to find out the truth: what was so special about the Wright Brothers' achievements? He visited the brothers' old father, the Anglican bishop Milton Wright, who told him his fears at having to watch his sons' foolhardiness (he had witnessed Orville and Wilbur Wright's longest flight). All right, the father might have been biased. But then he went on to interview in some detail a totally impartial witness, C S Billmann, the secretary to a banking institute. He also interviewed a dispensing chemist present at the time, and a workman, who had happened to come into the chemist's and had also seen the trial flight and was able to remember even the most trivial details. A master wheelwright, Henry Webbert, had seen the aircraft in his son's workshop and then outside, noticing how it had landed as softly 'as a turkey flying off a tree'. Finally, a German ironware dealer, Frank Hamburger, was even in the position of being able to illustrate his observations through diagrams and to name design details.

'I believe,' wrote Hildebrandt in the *Berliner Lokalanzeiger*, on his return in November 1907, 'that nobody can any longer seriously contest the existence of the first aircraft to have been put to the test. It is impossible that so many reputable people from different professions and ages could have got together to conspire for the sake of one inventor. They would have run the risk of contradicting each other in such a long "interrogation", which had been conducted according to strict, predetermined criteria.

'I am now of the view,' he continued, 'that now it has been demonstrated that flight is possible with airships whose weight is not carried by gas balloons, we must seriously turn our attention to constructing aircraft.'

But nothing happened. No less than air experts and specialists spoke of the 'American bluff' which Hildebrandt had been taken in by. This was the same man who later saw Wilbur Wright fly at Le Mans and was also present at Farman's first circular flight, and who now followed every achievement and immediately set about publicising it. All to no avail.

Characteristically, it was foreigners who collected their prizes at 'Flying Weeks', now fashionable in Germany, too. So when Gustav Otto, a prosperous young man, saw the Frenchman Blériot describe his circles above the Cologne race-track on that September day in 1909, he might initially have been fired up by the way in which the world had been running its own rings around Germany.

There is a picture of Blériot immediately after crossing the Channel on 23 July 1909. He is leaning on his machine, which had been badly damaged on landing, with his arms crossed gazing into the distance, to where he had almost touched the masts of the English fleet assembling on his approach to Dover. A Fleet Street journalist expressed the picture in the following way: 'New evidence of our civilisation's absurdity, that our first thought for aircraft is its possible application in war!' Indeed, Blériot's Channel crossing meant that England was no longer an island and that its *splendid isolation* was lost forever.

A German observer of the picture, Wolfgang Heinemann, saw it quite differently. For him, Blériot standing on the ramparts at Dover 'looked like someone gazing dreamily ahead of him, apparently struggling with the hardest part of all, his own spiritual excitement'. Although dazed and overwhelmed by the impact of one short half-hour, almost crushed, one could say, by too great a sense of euphoria, a true and profound awareness of the magnitude of his achievement emanates from his powerful and upright human form with his proudly crossed arms and that searing, intrepid look defying fate.

> With an instinctive pride unique to the human race, he senses the gigantic consequences of this one flight, this new victory for humanity, which gave Aubrun, a pilot of the Blériot school, good cause a year later to express the following memorable words: 'We depend not only on our machines and on the weather, but far more on the belief which humanity has in us, on that belief which is greater than the one we have in ourselves, that belief that sets us great and apparently insurmountable tasks and which drives us on to ever greater achievements.'

There is no doubt that Gustav was moved by similar thoughts. He, too, wanted to add new victories to 'mankind's victories', wanted to be there, to be able to apply a new invention that would be useful to humanity, in the way that aircraft would become *the* means of transport and conveyance of the future. He had no thought that it could be used as a means of destruction, as later happened. Highly gifted technically, enterprising, and having that naivety which easily and gladly overcomes contradictions because it assumes human goodness to be inherent in every human being, he no longer felt he was walking in his father's shadow. Quite the opposite. The latter's great invention, which had first brought the possibility of flying closer, spurred him on. His importance was acknowledged in whatever he tackled and achieved. His idealism came to the fore, removing any doubt that he might have had in himself and the job he was about to undertake.

He went straight to France from Cologne, and there acquired three Blériot monoplanes, as well as the right to represent Blériot in Germany. He started to teach himself flying in Munich, which resulted in one Blériot machine ending up in flames. He always managed to get back to earth safely, though. He raced ahead to found companies. And what didn't he found! He founded a 'Community Academy for Aviation' at the Puchheim airfield in Munich and the 'Central AGO (Aeromanufacture Gustav Otto) Workshops' at 72 Karl Street, Munich, where he undertook car repairs; he founded a company with the aviation pioneer Dr Alberti called 'Aeromanufacture Otto & Alberti' (proprietor Gustav Otto) and then the 'Gustav Otto Aircraft Works' at 135 Schleißheim Street, with thirty workers, which formed the kernel of all later developments and which would soon acquire an enviable reputation against the showy backdrop of the other newly-founded companies.

When Blériot crossed the English Channel from Calais to Dover, he certainly had no ulterior military motives. Nor had other French pilots such as Alberto Santos-Dumont, and Henry Farman and Léon Delagrange, the two biplane rivals, Hebert Latham and Léon Levasseur, the designer, along with the Germans August Euler and Hellmuth Hirth in Germany, and the Austrian Igo Etrich with his famous 'dove', although intimate circles knew of a secret contract at the French War Ministry. This had led in 1897 (!) to the construction of three aircraft, one of which, according to authentic reports, was said to have got some way off the ground – to about 250 to 300 metres. But that the Wright Brothers had intimated their intention very early on to Captain Ferber that they planned to offer their aircraft 'to governments primarily for military use' is undeniable. ('And if you think your government might be interested in it, then we would be happy to collaborate with you. . . .')

Even Gustav Otto was soon to make a similar offer. He sent it to the airship department of the Bavarian Inspectorate of Military Engineering and Fortifications. In it was written: 'My latest efforts are directed towards producing a passenger monoplane which can be easily assembled and transported, and which would therefore be particularly suitable for military use. This craft should thus be of special interest to the military.' But what did that mean? Flying cost money. Anyone involved in it ran high financial risks. (In 1911 a Blériot monoplane without its engine cost a fortune, i.e. 8,000 marks, while an Anzani engine, as fitted to the Blériot, cost 2,000 marks.) And wherever initiative and incentive could be spotted in people (enthusiam in sport, fashion, the desire for status, speculation, military foresight) then these were all used to advance the cause of flying.

Gustav Otto himself acquired Registration No. 34 of the German Airship Association in October 1910. With it he became one of the first aircraft directors in Germany, and when flying meant fighting (as an old military pilot expressed it: '1908 to 1910 – fought against prejudices; 1910 to 1912 – fought against the wind, the weather and the perversity of the inanimate; 1912 to 1914 – fought to win records for altitude, endurance and speed; 1914 to 1918 – fought to master the air against a world full of enemies') Gustav Otto was to be seen in the forefront of all these stages.

He was known as one of those 'daring young men in their flying machines', on account of being both a pilot and a flying instructor, as well as a designer of prototype planes (for own and outside accounts) and a manufacturer in the first Bavarian Aviation Workshops. In an application he pointed out with some pride that, after he had been able to compete 'so successfully at the last air shows in Berlin and Magdeburg with all the other German and foreign manufacturers', he should be allowed to carry out test flights on the exercise ground at Oberwiesenfeld. He got no reply. He applied again. Finally, on 3 March 1911, after a week-long silence, the Royal Bavarian War Ministry granted him 'permission, which may be withdrawn without notice, to use the south-east corner of the north exercise ground for taking-off and landing in his craft, and for flying over the exercise ground'.

Oberwiesenfeld was now his domain, and it was here, where one day the

Bavarian Motor Works would eventually find its permanent home, that the first hangars were soon to spring up out of the ground – two or three light wooden sheds, where undercarriages and propellers were to be fitted.

Here on the green meadow in front of the hangars, Otto Erik Lindpaintner, a Munich doctor and stepson of the painter Franz von Stuck, practised in his 'Racing biplane of the Lindpaintner type, built by the Gustav Otto Aircraft Works' for the great German cross-country flights – the Saxony flight, the round-Germany flight, the Swabian flight, the Bavarian manoeuvres, the cross-country Munich to Stuttgart flight, and the airshows at Chemnitz. As he related: 'We had neither a compass nor any other instruments on board, but simply cruised along over wood and stream with the aid of car maps at an altitude of between 100 and 200 metres. . . .'

This is where Adolf Rentzel took off for his World Passenger Record on 18 February 1912. As the newspaper *BZ am Mittag* wrote:

> While people were still disputing as to whether the flight by flying instructor A. Rentzel from the Gustav Otto Flying School in Munich with four passengers which lasted 9 minutes 8 seconds really should be treated as a German record, Rentzel settled the matter by taking off again last Saturday in his Otto biplane with four adult passengers, and staying airborne for 21 minutes 45 seconds. This time the passengers were the two Barons von Zastrow, Miss Conus and the mechanic Mr Enderlin. With the pilot they weighed 358.5 kilograms. . . . Rentzel took off from the Oberwiesenfeld Aerodrome after a run-up of approximately 150 metres and circle at a uniform height of approximately 140 metres. The landing was especially smooth. . . .

And this is also where Otto, with his mechanic/pilot Anton Baierlein, Lindpaintner and other aviation companies, prepared for the North Mark flight, which began in Kiel with demonstration flights lasting several days in the summer of 1912 and continued right over Schleswig-Holstein, with Flensburg as its most northerly point and Hamburg as its most southerly one. Letters testify to the primitive conditions and the strains which would make the company struggle to survive in adverse weather – letters which tell of the incredible optimism and courage of those young men who were also undoubtedly interested in the high cash prizes on offer, since these enabled them to carry on flying. Like Otto, the prizes allowed them to improve their machines or, indeed, simply to build them. En route Gustav Otto wrote to his fiancée Ada Haugg:

> We arrived on Saturday morning at 3 a.m. at the Kiel race-track. It was enveloped in fog, you couldn't see two steps in front of you. With weary limbs we parked up, and waited in a heavily-laden car, a Deutzer Bugatti. It got to 5 a.m., then 6; the first dare-devils took off despite the fog, and by six-thirty the slightly clearer weather meant that Baierlein wasn't going to wait a moment longer. Well, it's only a short stretch to Rendsburg, and we were hoping for the best. It was chocks away, and he was gone in a flash. The Deutzer was full of boxes and crates, and I went into the office (the

control room) to see if I could discover the pilots' whereabouts. I couldn't get a satisfactory answer to my questions from one idiot; and two telephone operators preferred to giggle and flirt with young lieutenants than worry about the precious lives of brave men. So I couldn't discover anything. A few paces from this comical telephone exchange in the control room, I found an annexe belonging to the newspaper *Kieler Neueste Nachrichten*. I ingratiated my way in, and quickly discovered the following: Caspar Tauber had got lost in the fog and his machine had been badly damaged while landing in a cornfield. Schmidt had landed on top of a tree; pilot had been unhurt, although the passengers had baled out, some minor injuries. Krieger had landed outside Schleswig. There was no news about the others.

Another anxious quarter of an hour. The phone rang. 'Rendsburg aerodrome here! Baierlein, Steffler, Horn and Krüger have landed safely, and gone on again to Schleswig.' Twenty minutes wait, during which I got in touch with Schleswig: 'Nobody has arrived yet, whereabouts unknown, thick fog.' Ten minutes later: 'Pilots arrived safely. Off again to Flensburg.'

Excitement increased by the minute. It struck 9 a.m. There was still no news; something must have happened. My mechanic Mebus and I drove off. The spare-parts crate stuck out of the car. The long propeller protruded, brushing the trees. I drove so furiously that the steering wheel rattled and the wheels jumped up and down. It did not matter, just as long as we got to those who were probably in need of help. Rendsburg came into sight. The password rang out: pilots passed over all right. The fine, large fjord of Schleswig appeared. I see Schleswig below me. Suddenly there is a bang. A rumble from the front wheel. A puncture! Mebus works away. I jump out of the car onto the passing milkcart of a peasant woman. It's now clip-clop to Schleswig, muggy heat, my thick car coat weighing me down, then a bar appears and I see the marvellous sight of two wires running off from white knobs into the distance. Hurrah! A telephone. I make an urgent call to Flensburg. The line is engaged. I try Flensburg again, and hear to my great joy that Baierlein has landed first in Flensburg at eight in the morning. I treck back to my broken-down car, still wearing my heavy coat in the oppressive midday heat, with pockets stuffed full of sandwiches and cigarettes for my mechanic Mebus.

On another occasion at Fuhlsbüttel air escaped from the front tyre. In the hope of getting a reasonable breakfast he and Mebus drove right up to his sister's front door (as she lived nearby), but 'as all the birds had flown, I had nothing else to do but sit down at the front door and write a poem about pilots, since the mood was nothing short of poetic'. In the evening at the banquet in Neumünster, as Baierlein was receiving his prize from the lord mayor, Otto recited his poem 'In the Name of the Pilot':

> *The crowd rejoices, the pilot longs for fame,*
> *He accepts the wheel of fate without fear,*
> *Today he is the vanquished, tomorrow the victor.*
> *In the bright sky above he blazes his trail.*

*He trusts the young force which impels him
And safely and tirelessly holds the controls,
When he fully masters the tricks of the wind
And brings the force of the air into his sway.*

*Up, up and away! so that gentle valleys vanish
And steep slopes lie harmlessly below.
He wants to experience man's greatest desire
And fly to meet his young fortune. . .'*

To his 'young fortune', his fiancée Ada Haugg, he wrote on 1 July 1912 from Altona:

From 7 a.m. to 9 a.m., on the last flight. How much there is to play for! At stake are 5,000 marks' worth of stage prizes and 25,000 marks' worth of orders from the War Ministry. My darling, our existence would be entirely assured. My hopes and disappointments depend on this event! You will learn by telegram long before this letter arrives. Above all, let nothing happen to my good, sturdy friend Baierlein who has slaved away so admirably. Hartmann smashed up his Wright machine; not injured. Krüger completely wrecked his Harlan machine; small superficial flesh wounds. Horn damaged his Schwade landing gear; pilot uninjured. König, a fine Munich pilot (who won the BZ – flight in the previous year and was personally better off by 50,000 marks), crash-landed in his self-made monoplane; suffered severe internal injuries and sadly died this evening in hospital. Baierlein suffered several engine failures but landed safely on the aerodrome by gliding down immaculately. At 5 a.m. the Argus mechanic arrived. Baierlein went immediately to the aerodrome, which is where I am driving to now. Must break off. . . .

Once the North Mark flight was over, Otto visited his family in Cologne on his way home. Everyone seemed happy.

Mama told me about her engagement, which had taken place on her first outing for seventeen years, when she had got to know my father, who held a senior position in the coffee-roasting company, Mertens & Co. This good old father had been taken to be somewhat mad when he came up with his idea for an engine, in the same way that no one in Cologne rightly knew today how to categorise the son. They congratulated me for decency's sake, but inside I felt exactly what my dear sisters thought. My sisters' legal representative, Justice of the Peace Herr Jüssen, congratulated me on my success and managed to shed a tear of emotion, which made me think he must be either a malicious person or a hypocrite. To cap it all, my former divinity teacher Herr Oberndörfer, that special friend of mine who made my life at secondary school such hell, met me on the way back. . . .

Back in Munich at Oberwiesenfeld, he quickly became the engineer again, full of ideas which he not only committed to paper but also produced. He transformed Lindpaintner's machine, made of ash wood, into one of steel tubes. The young doctor achieved success after success. The wings of his 'standard Otto biplane' could then be removed from the fuselage as a single unit in only a few minutes and carried anywhere lengthwise on the undercarriage, either by road or rail. His monoplane fitted with tailfins had wings which, in contrast to normal practice, were not fastened directly onto the fuselage, but had a gap in between. Deflected air was held up at the wings by the tailfins, with the result that both pilot and passenger, 'sitting with full protection in a covered fuselage', always had 'a clear and unimpeded view of the ground below'. His AGO-aero-engine (Aero-engines Gustav Otto), which Hans Geisendorf designed for him, had exposed pipework. It was squat, narrow, with very smooth covering surfaces, each cylinder being individually cast and thus immediately replaceable. To prevent the inlet manifold from icing up, it was made up of one casting with the cylinder and heated by the hot coolant in the cylinder, which made for an evenly distributed mixture and reliable ignition.

Otto had got himself noticed as early as 1910. A biplane (built in conjunction with the designer Gabriel Letsch), which had very small wings but whose direction and altitude could be significantly controlled by the pilot by means of a hand-wheel in front of his seat, took the world by storm. By 1912, offering the market thirty planes (twenty-four biplanes and six monoplanes), Otto was no longer an unknown. He did not miss a single demonstration flight or 'Flying Week', inspired wonder, and was not afraid of taking risks, as at Nordeney, where, according to the reporter, 'the flags on the beach at Wilhelmshöhe blew horizontally in the north-east wind and owner-captains in their airships measured a wind strength of nine metres. Seven times they took off and seven times they had to land again.' Then, on the next day, we found:

. . . Herr Gustav Otto, the pilot and inventor of the Otto biplane, owner of the Munich aircraft factory and proprietor of a pilot training school, climbing aboard with his passenger Herr Robert. As soon as he got into the pilot's seat, he spun the engine over. But it just wouldn't start. It first had to have the sand from the dunes cleaned out, at which point it started. The craft took off majestically, gained height, climbed and swung like a giant bird in magnificent flight. It swung in huge curves, higher and higher, now over the island, then over the North Sea, at one moment descending, and at the next ascending. He was followed by the young pilot trained at the Otto school, Robert Janisch from Paris, flying high in a Blériot monoplane. The reading on the altimeter showed him reaching the very respectable height of 700 metres.

Otto was also a shining representative of his craft. In December 1912 he got married. With his young wife Ada, he 'had his honeymoon in the air'. Anton Baierlein, his chief pilot, who was soon to win first prize in the subsequent 'Flight round Berlin', was the 'air coachman'. The honeymoon flight only went as far as Fresing and back for the benefit of the press, but Otto knew how to make the most of this story of year.

One thing Otto was not, though – a businessman. His father had been just the same. But whatever this modest man achieved, Gustav, the son, strove in vain to find a partner who was more than just a financial backer. Nikolaus August Otto had found his partner in Eugen Langen. And when the Otto engine had fulfilled what its inventor had in mind, which was to provide the same advantages to the small man, the trader, the artisan, as big business and the wealthy industrialist would experience through the steam engine, then there had been some hopes in the alliance between the 'scientific promotor' Otto and the 'financial promotor' Langen.

Naturally these are poor comparisons. The new century had quite a different feel to it. The great leap forward from the steam engine to the internal combustion engine had been made. Cars and planes had been born; and where is it written that the sons, however gifted, should continue what the fathers had devised and succeeded in? Here was a son who had all the makings in him, who would become successful (as we have seen), and yet was ultimately destined to fail. What was the reason for this?

Undoubtedly the partner which Gustav Otto, designer and pilot, found in 'the military' could not provide anything that a creative man demanded – trust, encouragement, clear-sighted motivation into what is technologically feasible, flexibility, a mutual responsibility for risks or perspicacity. Instead of these, almost every page in the old files in the Bavarian war archives looks like a petty war of attrition, in which Otto was worn down by the military authorities.

At first, everything went well. On 8 March 1912 Otto presented his biplane fitted with a 65-hp Daimler engine to the Bavarian Department for Airships and Powered Flight. There were encouraging nods as they found it '. . . made of German material throughout . . . very carefully assembled . . . stable, manoeuvrable, reached a speed estimated at around 80 kph, with sufficient fuel for three hours, one pilot and one passenger at 500 metres high within 12 minutes . . ., fully complies with the specified requirements . . . is (even) around 2,000 marks cheaper than the aircraft made by Euler and Albatros fitted with the same engine.'

The full flying squad issuing this amical appraisal in the Department of Airship and Powered Flight consisted of a captain (a cavalry officer), a lieutenant, a sergeant (in the Engineers), an NCO and ten lance-corporals and privates. Cavalry captain Count Wolfskeel von Reichenberg of the 1st Armoured Cavalry Regiment was in overall command, and as he had enjoyed training as a pilot at August Euler in Darmstadt, was the uncontested expert in the small company.

They and their later incarnation, the Royal Bavarian Flying Corps, were part of the Royal Bavarian Army, which from the start of mobilisation came under the order of the Field Marshal-in-Chief of his Majesty the Kaiser, but was otherwise answerable to the King of Bavaria. In certain fields of military aviation, the Bavarian Army remained subordinate to the Prussian Army. The Prussian War Ministry was responsible for their budget, defined guidelines for procurement, supplied information on firms and planes, with Prussia, in the final analysis, controlling mobilisation and commitment of air strike forces. It is easy to see why, aware of this dependence, the Bavarians only made a token effort to demand some freedom to control the administration of military aviation. How did they do this? Well, by conferring the procurement of military aircraft, for example, on a Bavarian manufacturer, namely Gustav Otto's aircraft factory.

But here a split opened up between the views of the War Ministry, who supported Otto, and the Engineer Corps Inspectorate of General von Brug, who did not like Otto. The latter's free and easy approach to the world (one which seemed innate to most young pilots) was simply not to his taste. He found it arrogant and inappropriate, because he suspected it of hiding carelessness, and carelessness meant downfall.

The Bavarian War Ministry was happy to have a Bavarian aircraft works 'on its doorstep'. But General von Brug wanted competition, 'competition in the market place can only be of advantage', even if, as the Ministry argued, the need for planes in Bavaria was so small that 'not enough profitable work could be guaranteed for two factories'. This aside, there were other complaints: that Otto could not develop newer, higher-performance models; that the small plant (this may have been closer to the truth) was not capable of complying with the ever-increasing demands of war. (For greater output, Otto had already founded a subsidiary, the AGO (Aviator Gustav Otto) Aircraft Works in the Johannisthal suburb of Berlin, to which he entrusted all business with the Prussian air forces – including contracts, repairs, and pilot training. This is where the AGO C1, a plane with double fuselage, rear-mounted propeller and two nose-wheels was developed for the navy; 600 machines of this type were built!) No, the General had a different view from the Ministry's and naturally from Otto's, whose whole approach did not suit him.

In his desire to remain independent of Prussia, von Brug had initially enthusiastically greeted the founding of the Otto Works as the first Bavarian aircraft company, and had granted Otto contracts for aircraft procurement and repair, and had even seen to it that the Bavarian Army participated to the tune of 60,000 marks in a rival aircraft factory planned by Prussia on the condition that Otto had a part in it. The rival concern was constantly postponed and finally never materialised. It had not been easy to prevail upon Otto. Someone or other amongst the Prussian authorities had something against him. Several Otto biplanes had crashed in the Prince Heinrich Air Race; the plane was viewed as such a design disaster that they even went as far as to deny that Otto had the ability to build military aircraft. To counter this, the Bavarians put the failure down not to the plane, but to the excessively short training of the Bavarian pilots.

When Otto now tried in vain to be a supplier to the Prussian Army (North German firms had in the meantime made every effort to capture the South German market by establishing subsidiaries), the Bavarian Army not only supported Otto's efforts, but secured his future by placing the majority of their own orders with him – seventeen of the twenty-three aircraft in 1912, and forty-seven (out of sixty-seven) in 1913 – which Otto had designed and produced.

All went well until von Brug started to openly champion the subsidiary of the Rumpler company in Munich, and Gustav caused a furore by reminding the Bavarian Army of his 'selfless service' which he wanted to continue exercising by making use of his family fortune. No, Bavaria did not need Rumpler who, in its opinion, was neither a designer nor a particularly co-operative supplier. A second firm would not survive in Bavaria, where a reliable workforce was very hard to find. This was proved by the collapse of 'Flugwerk Deutschland'.

Was this insubordination? In any case, von Brug no longer had any cause to spare Otto. If you browse through the pages of those files (which, incidentally, were seized by the Allies after the Second World War and left untouched in London before being returned to Bavaria) and read dispassionately of the 'records' which were moved up the bureaucratic ladder, records which were sometimes enlivened with comments, then you will see quite clearly which details were kept hidden, and how the arrogance and blindness of power comes through the many examples of writing embellished with official squiggles and bows.

High-handed commands were given as to who would fly, how flying would be done and whether, indeed, flying would even be allowed. Without any conception or knowledge of what was demanded in an emergency or what needed to be done, orders were made, sentences passed, directives issued, which, if they went wrong, apparently resulted in nobody having ordered them in the first place. The military proceeded in the same way with the economy, as if the name of the game were to show those calling themselves 'free' their actual dependence on others. Products which they had developed to the point of production were graciously accepted without anyone being in the least bit concerned about how they had been developed. If the products did not meet the (ever-spiralling) demands, they were simply put to one side, without thanks, payment, regret or justification.

Once, an Otto biplane crashed on a practice flight, killing the pilot and causing people to over-react against the aircraft. General von Brug wrote: 'We have moved towards evaluating our planes both from a static and dynamic point of view, and we are doing this independently of aircraft manufacturers, of which Otto is a typical example of ignorance. Otto is not and will never be an engineer destined to achieve anything. He lacks the qualities for that.'

On another occasion, after the outbreak of the World War, Otto was forced to take steps against the espionage of an 'expert' in his factory who thought he could pinpoint defects and shortcomings and whom Otto had accidentally overheard proclaiming (Otto could swear to it on oath): 'I will not rest until Otto is ruined.' Otto wrote to Captain Wilhelm Stempel in the Reserve Flying Squadron:

> The supreme duty of man is justice, by which I appeal to you in the hope that you, as an officer, will understand my jaundiced sense of honour and will know I can safeguard my threatened existence.
>
> I fight for justice, for the existence of many hundreds of families and for the honour of the name of Otto which my father made world-famous and which his son will not allow to be destroyed through intrigue.

It lies within the power of your captaincy to protect both you and me from a man who has only a petty selfish goal in sight, making him forget the great goal of serving the community in our Fatherland.

There will never be any differences between our idea of fulfilling our duty, if only you will give me some encouragement as before and not be paralysingly judgemental.

It was this paralysis which finally made him capitulate and abandon everything which he had exercised, instigated, built up and tirelessly invested with ever new ideas, everything which he had tested, along with the technical knowledge and understanding of flying which he had passed on (for example, to Udet whom he taught to fly at Oberwiesenfeld in 1914).

In August 1915, Otto fell ill and sought help in a Munich mental hospital. The aircraft inspectorate declared that a subsidy (demanded of the authorities by Otto's company bank, Martini and Simader) was out of the question, standing no more chance than the latest order placed for twenty-five aircraft against the corresponding deposit. It was finally stated that orders worth 3.7 million marks had been placed and paid for. Should the firm go bankrupt, the aviation department would be ready to take over the buildings as repair workshops. However, the military administration authorised another 300,000 marks, as by November Otto could no longer pay the wages and salaries at the old rate. ('No wonder', the authorities said; 'he also paid the highest!')

By the middle of February 1916 bankruptcy had been considered. The Darmstädter Bank, MAN and other industrialists now intervened and helped. A public limited company was to be formed with Otto's participation. But nothing came of it, and Otto agreed that if he were to receive so much for his departure, he could pay off his 'commitments'. Once he had fully recovered, he devised new plans. (After the war a bicycle with an auxiliary engine could be seen on the streets of Munich. Fitted to the front forks and handlebars, it drove the front wheel hub through a chain with a built-in clutch. With the drive de-clutched, it could be ridden like an ordinary bicycle. The whole thing was called a 'Flyaway'. It was built and named by Gustav Otto.) But the old zest had gone, even if the works he was next to found (producing fuses for grenades, petrol pumps and clutches) would employ 1,100 men by the end of 1917. Even this business had come to an end by the end of the war, and inflation ate up the rest of his fortune. On 26 February 1926 Otto shot himself.

What he had never imagined or expected, and would never know, was that the Bavarian Motor Works would refer to him as its founding father, that it would confer fatherhood on this failure at its fiftieth anniversary celebrations at a gala evening at the Munich State Opera. It points to 7 March 1916 as its birthday, the day when Otto's bankrupt aircraft works divided into a firm from which he himself broke ties at the very moment it was being set up. It would neither bear his name, nor be associated in any other way with him.

All this does not alter the fact that the Bavarian Aircraft Works would never have arisen without Gustav Otto, the son of the inventor Nikolaus August Otto. When, at the beginning of the twenties, BMW referred back to Otto's foundation, not only giving it a new name, but completely merging with it, it became not only right but a duty to claim him as its founding father, the man who had first created the conditions for life and survival at Oberwiesenfeld.

Founding father No. 2, Karl Rapp, would have doubted this. Granted there would have been just as little of BMW without him.

Rapp: Nothing but Worries

'The aircraft question is closely linked to the existence and development of the car industry', stated a prospectus from the Gustav Otto Aircraft Works, 'and I am here proudly able to honour the memory of my father, Dr N.A. Otto as the inventor of the four-stroke engine whose operating principle forms the basis of all present-day car and aircraft engines.'

Karl Rapp, that other engineer, who had settled at 288 Schleißheim Street, could not boast of such ancestry. We know little about him. He emerged from obscurity and disappeared into obscurity. In between there was clearly a man who went about his business of building and developing aircraft engines determinedly, even doggedly. He was not strikingly successful, unlike Lindpaintner, the young wealthy Munich doctor, with his Lindpaintner-type racing biplane (built by Gustav Otto's Aircraft Works), or the bold Rentzel (flying instructor in the Gustav Otto training school), all of whom praised Otto's name. It is very unlikely that Rapp did not make some comment, or at least turn up his nose, when the catch-word of Otto was mentioned. Only rarely was he to be found outside the 'hangars', as certain people rather grandly called those sheds which housed the planes. At any rate, this happened at least once when one of the spindly wire-boxes fitted with a Rapp engine was pushed over the road to Oberwiesenfeld. If it took off, Rapp offered up a couple of prayers, and returned to the workshop without waiting to watch it land. This was his field.

Rapp came from Daimler, which suggests solidity and perseverance, qualities needed to take over the technical management of Flugwerk Deutschland.

Founded in Brand near Aachen in 1912 (it is not clear why there) it drew its inspiration from an obsession which the artist Adolf Erbslöh from Munich had for flying, not unlike the one Arnold Böcklin had had a quarter of a century before. With a saint's power of belief and inspired by Leonardo da Vinci, Erbslöh had countered the thesis of 'anything heavier than air will not fly!' with the firm conviction that 'we only need an engine, and when we have it, we shall fly – even if it's on a barn door!' Inflexible, like all true idealists, with no regard to financial constraints (he did in fact have money which he unconditionally made available), he collaborated with like-minded people – Dr Oskar Wittenstein from Munich, a friend of

24

Blériot's, and an engineer called Veeh, who had already built a 95-metre airship fitted with Daimler engines and using the semi-rigid system. This triumvirate (Erbslöh, Wittenstein, Veeh) now built a motorised balloon or, to be more accurate, wanted to build it – with engines commissioned from Schneeweis in Chemnitz. Since these engines, personally designed by Herr Schneeweis, did not actually work, Philipp Dörhöfer, an engineer from Berlin who had opened his own consultancy business at 46 Clemens Street in Munich, was entrusted with checking the work at Chemnitz. His reports must have contained nothing but bad news – giving Erbslöh every reason to move the whole Schneeweis business (which was in debt to him) to the Isar; or, to be precise, to the former Riesenfeld bicycle works in Milbertshofen opened by Herr Ludwig Petuel many years before (today BMW lies on the Petuel ring-road). Shortly afterwards, Schneeweis left and Philipp Dörhöfer took over technical management, supported by a mechanic and a productive foreman. The business employed fifteen men in all. He himself completely designed the Schneeweis engines and new models were manufactured. How much they were worth is not known. Just as little is known about whether they had the desired effect. It was now no longer a case of sending up a motorised balloon, but proper aircraft. All that is known is that Dörhöfer, who was a confirmed pacifist, was one day summoned to the Royal Bavarian Government, to whom he had applied for a state subsidy. He was asked: 'How many bombs can be dropped from an aircraft like that?' He replied: 'From mine, none.' That brought the conversation to an end, as well as Dörhöfer's involvement with Flugwerk Deutschland. In April 1912 he left. Veeh, who had set up his own 'Airship Construction Veeh', involving co-ownership with Flugwerk Deutschland, also left the company, and took his airships to the Rhineland. 'My successor', as Philipp Dörhöfer was later to write about this early period to his son, 'was an engineer called Rapp. . .', as if he were saying: take note and safeguard it for the sake of future generations. 'BMW has its origins in the Schneeweis company at Chemnitz, which, with Veeh's airship manufacture and Flugwerk Deutschland, where my name was also listed, brought the Rapp Engine Works into existence.' Which brings us back to Rapp. Rapp, now established at the Munich subsidiary of Flugwerk Deutschland at 288 Schleißheim Street, where wooden buildings began to proliferate, sought, as a designer, to fulfil the conditions for an aviation engine as specified by the first Imperial Prize. Rapp planned a four-cylinder engine with an overhead camshaft which could produce 90 hp. This Imperial Prize, established by Wilhelm II from his privy purse, was designed (now suddenly recognised in 1912!) to counter the national danger which the German General Staff had noticed in France's military development of aviation. There they were already practising in squadrons, had over 234 military pilots (as opposed to fifty in Germany) and, with 24 million francs, had a budget four times higher than in Germany. 'The German aeroplane should be ready and capable at any moment of fulfilling what the hour of need may require of it, whether that may be vigilantly circling the skies in the hour of national danger, or as the latest means of modern transport and as a winged messenger of national industrial success, competing peacefully between nations.' It is these words that Prince Heinrich, the Kaiser's brother and himself an enthusiastic pilot, used in his call for action.

In six months a 'national appeal' collected all of 7.5 million marks. This enabled the hour of need to be answered with a 'test installation for aviation' on the Johannisthal Aerodrome near Berlin, where a small settlement of pilots had grown up and become a rendezvous for German, English and French pilots. Aviation engines built to the Imperial Prize specification, including the one from Karl Rapp, were tested on five test beds and thoroughly inspected. Each engine had to run for seven hours with its own propeller.

What Werner von Siemens had prophetically recognised and coldly calculated in 1883 was that an aircraft which was 'heavier than air', in contrast to an airship restricted to foreward movement only, can only fly when its engine has a sufficiently high power-to-weight ratio. French manufacturers had consistently put their plans into effect, going as far as to abandon conventional construction. This was shown by the famous Gnôme engine made by the Laurent brothers and Louis Séguin, which formed the basis for Blériot's and Farman's success. Euler swore by it, and Gustav Otto extolled its virtues in his prospectuses.

In the Gnôme engine, which was a rotary engine, seven cylinders fitted with cooling fins (ingeniously simple) gave off heat to the circulating air. The crankshaft was fastened to the aircraft and the propeller to the turning engine. In contrast to the uniformity and extreme quietness of its operation (it was often compared to a sewing machine), its one disadvantage was that it wore out very quickly, which radically reduced its operating hours. As mineral oils cannot tolerate petrol vapour, it had to operate with vegetable (meaning castor) oil, which was rare and very expensive.

It was perhaps not least for these reasons that the German designers remained true to the configuration developed from the car engine, and stuck to the water-cooled stationary engine. If its power-to-weight ratio was much lower than the costly Gnôme engine, which produced straight-line forces because of its high engine speed, which only an experienced pilot could correct through judicious and rapid counter-steering, then the stationary engine displayed operating reliability and durability, characteristics which were the ultimate goal for the German military authorities in an emergency – such as sending planes to fight a war.

Twenty-six contenders competed for the Imperial Prize with sixty-eight engines entered. Forty-three of them never got beyond the test bed. Only seventeen fulfilled the test conditions. No air-cooled engine passed the initial stages, least of all Karl Rapp's engine. The prize winner was a 100-hp, four-cylinder stationary engine made by Benz and Co., Mannheim (it had the lowest fuel consumption and the highest power-to-weight ratio). Daimler won the second prize with its six-cylinder engine, which had steel barrels, as well as fourth prize with a 70-hp engine fitted with inverted cylinders. Rapp was naturally disheartened. He had pinned his hopes on the 50,000-mark prize. But he pricked up his ears when he discovered that the winning engine had not been exhibited due to piston failure and buckling of several push rods resulting (presumably) from major vibration in flight testing. Why had it won a prize then?

Inevitably, there was failure all down the line, with the result that the firm was forced into receivership.

But Rapp did not give up. Even in the golden days of peace, when the war machine was already rolling, he founded the Rapp Motor Works with the Austrian consul-general Julius Auspitzer, and moved into premises at 288 Schleißheim Street. The entry in the register of companies for 28 October 1913 states the firm's intentions. Namely '. . .the manufacture and marketing of all types of engine, in particular, of internal combustion engines for aircraft and road vehicles, as well as the acquisition of the engine factory in Munich, previously owned by the company of Flugwerk Deutschland (in liquidation).'

But this engine factory had its headquarters at 288 Schleißheim Street. So Rapp had only symbolically left and rejoined where he had already been. With an initial 200,000 marks (Auspitzer contributed 130,000 marks and Rapp 70,000 marks, which he had somehow managed to rake together) he had acquired an old aircraft shed, with its still operating machine tools, from the bankrupt's estate. With all of six men, he went ahead with the building of a six-cylinder aviation engine. This was very similar to the failed model in its cylinder dimensions, and was still capable of developing 125 hp. And, of course, of winning the second Imperial Prize.

But, as is often the case in life, over-enthusiasm can lead to failure. In Lower Bavaria, the cost-conscious Rapp had acquired a collapsible hangar of the Oktoberfest type. He had it put up on an industrial estate, and set up his test engines there in a gallery. The six cylinders were no longer in a line. Rapp had simply built on two extra cylinders on the timing side to his tried and tested four-cylinder. The readings were quite amazing – 1382 rpm, 174 hp. There was only one insuperable problem – the engine vibrated. The vibrations being transferred to the aircraft components made it likely that the tailplane would break off, potentially (and with enough luck!) before take-off.

However much Rapp wanted it to be, the engine was not ready by the required deadline. Convinced that the vibrations had nothing to do with the asymmetrical arrangement of the cylinders, he sought in vain for the causes. The power-to-weight ratio and fuel consumption were still, respectively, far too low and too high. Rapp got too involved in superfluous details, and developed a V-8 engine, the subsequent RpIV, and even a twelve-cylinder engine rated at 300 hp – projects which were not appropriate to the size of the firm which, although called a 'Motor Works', really only had the equipment of a workshop, even if ten men were now working there. Yet the Rapp Motor Works, along with the Otto- and Pfalz Works (partly owned, incidentally, by Otto) were on the list of militarily important Bavarian businesses. And that means that if relations are stronger than good intentions, then success may come through the back door.

That this back door did indeed open can be put down to Bavaria's independence with respect to the Reich, and therefore with respect to the Prussian military administration. Armaments industries in Bavaria were certainly not owned by the Bavarian monarchy, but the Royal Bavarian War Ministry would see to it (as was the case with Otto) that they stayed in business. Heaven only knew how soon they would be needed!

They were needed more quickly than anyone had imagined. On 28 June 1914 the heir to the Austrian throne was murdered in Sarajevo. The German Kaiser still believed that Russia would not get involved, as there was no doubt that high-performance firms like Argus, Daimler and Benz were not in the remotest way capable of meeting the urgent need for aircraft engines at a time when an emergency was looming. (The Prussian War Ministry had rigidly stuck to its principle of not buying individual engines, but complete aircraft, whose development had been left to the aircraft industry. This again would have needed mass production runs in order to offset the high development costs. As it was, six-cylinder engines which had already been tested were being built throughout the industry.)

On 31 July, at a quarter to two, a first private announcement was made from Berlin to Munich by telegraph. Soon after came a second one, leaving no doubt as to the validity of the first. Towards two o'clock the telegram board of the newspaper *Münchner Neueste Nachrichten* announced: 'State of war in Germany!'

Sendling Street was almost free of traffic. Within a few minutes it was teeming with people. One of the passers-by who had read the headline suddenly began to run. People started looking around. Soon they were running from all sides to the headlines board. The news spread throughout the city with unprecedented speed. It even reached the outer suburbs.

Schleißheim Street was basking quietly in the midday sun. The tram squealed to a halt at the Cigonibad terminus. A man jumped off. From here there were still 150 to 200 metres over the Würm canal to No. 288; open land, hedges, sheds, an orchard, cabbage plots. The man (and with him the news) ignored all this. He had seen it all a hundred times before, and yet it seemed different to him. He was moving fast now; and so was the news. Had anything changed? Nothing. What should change? War! Well, Cigonibad would stay at the same place on the Würm. . . . Perhaps they would abolish the 'men only' days because there would not be any more men. Nonsense! It would all be over soon.

But if it were not, what would happen to the shop, Rapp's shop, the Rapp Motor Works, what would happen to me, Works Manager Otto Dümler? Perhaps as a result everything would now get into full swing. The signboard over the gateway was far too big for what went on behind it. Are we going to build? 'If we get the Imperial Prize, then immediately!' the boss had said. But who was now talking of the Imperial Prize? Rapp? He would not again once the news had sunk in.

'Boss! Boss!' shouted the man, a little out of breath from running. 'Where is the boss?'

From the courtyard he saw him go into the office. 'Boss!' But the boss did not hear him. Was he dreaming? Rapp turned round just in front of the house. 'Oh there you are, Dümler. Here,' he said, putting his hand into his jacket pocket, 'read this!'

Dümler read it. Rapp was holding out a telegram.

'An order?'

'What else?'

Dümler went numb. The order had come from the Prussian military command, requiring delivery of twenty-five large aircraft engines at short notice.

'Can we do it?'

'We must do it', Rapp said.

'Must is all very well. The mobilisation announced yesterday makes all trading agreements null and void.'

'Not with us. We are a "business vital to the war"!'

'Even in businesses vital to the war!'

But Rapp was no longer listening. He had gone into another room. Only now did Dümler remember why he had run so fast. The news! 'Herr Rapp!' he called after him, 'Herr Rapp. . .' Difficult, this man, he thought. Was there going to be war then? 'Proclaiming a state of war' was not quite mobilisation. Just as long there was no panic.

Saturday 1 August dawned. It was a day that might have been fashioned from gold, as if heaven were conscious of the historical moment which would be inscribed on the memory of humanity. Once again it was another bright and sunny summer day, such a day as had long existed during forty-four years of peace, just at a time when they were soon to disappear.

Towards 6 o'clock it was announced from the balcony of the newspaper *Münchner Neueste* that mobilisation had been proclaimed in Berlin. Cheers went up, people felt united. Then, that evening, a sea of people thronged the streets, making their way to the royal residence to hear the King speak. 'May God grant,' he said, 'that, as we march towards the enemy, victory will be ours. It is hard to remain calm in such moments. I have been trying to do so for days. But I know what my duty is, duty I have always performed. You must do the same . . . and now, God speed.' The crowd stood shoulder to shoulder from Rosental to Dult Street, singing patriotic and folk songs. 'It was a stirring scene,' wrote a reporter from the *Münchner Neueste*, 'when the first cavalry song rang out into the night: "Red dawn, you light my way to an early death". Hats flew into the air after other songs had been sung in praise of king and country. Then followed a short silence, as if the streets had been emptied of people.'

This was the almost idyllic beginning of what was to end with the deaths of millions of men who would slaughter each other in the line of battle, not counting the many others who would die of hunger, misery and disease. And at the same time the application of modern technology to the means of war started a hitherto unprecedented acceleration in the invention and manufacture of both weapons and systems of mass destruction, as well as of new engines (making aeroplanes fly faster and higher than those of the enemy), new production processes (to compensate for a lack of raw materials), new types of ships and their propulsion, totally new means of transport (tracked vehicles, tanks and electric vehicles), new medical techniques (for patching up mutilated bodies), and so on. 'Everyone who experienced it could choose what he most abhorred and what he most admired,' as an historian later wrote.

What was to come out of this and be tested would open up new perspectives and give insight into the future. Nobody could claim that mobilising human minds, which here would be urged on hand in hand with their extinction, would be directed at goals *beyond* the war, once it was all over, goals which were to be to the good to mankind. . . . Nobody could say that, whether he was a Rathenau who devised the planned economy in the Ministry of War Economy, or a small-scale engineer called Rapp who wanted to supply the front with a reliable aviation engine.

Rapp worked night and day with the people whom he eventually found amongst those exempt from military service, at a time when there was a continual flow of reservists to the barracks. He wanted to prove to the Prussian military command that his modest firm was at the forefront of engine building, and that he could do just as much here in Munich as the big companies of Daimler in Canstatt, Benz in Mannheim, and Argus in Berlin. The first delivery reached Berlin but, after thorough investigation, was rejected. The vibrations were too much! How were they to be got rid of between Munich and Berlin? Or was the answer to be found in the discrepancy between Prussian and Bavarian technical standards, the former not counting what the latter took for granted. For the Bavarian test engineers had not discovered any defects, neither had the Imperial Naval Office (to begin with), which wanted to equip flying boats with Rapp engines, nor had the Austro-Hungarian navy, which admittedly had no other choice than to work to the slogan 'better bad than nothing at all'. In any case, orders for these Rapp engines came from all these offices. Rapp fulfilled them (he had never had any complaints) and at the end of his first financial year on 30 September 1914, the books for the Rapp Motor Works showed a profit of 40,000 marks from the forty-six machine tools and sixty-one workers on the pay-roll.

The outbreak of war had saved Karl Rapp, or at least kept him from a second impending failure. He had indeed gambled everything on one card – to win that prize which was intended to entice Germany's aircraft manufacturers, to make up for the State's omissions. The dice had been cast, and sooner than expected.

There are certain events which cause human nature to go to pieces. Rapp had not gone to pieces. But was he up to it? He was a remarkable man, this Rapp, who drew inspiration from a constant sense of dissatisfaction with himself. Nothing worked out immediately for him, nothing went easily, and if anything did succeed, the euphoria never lasted. He would always demand too much of himself. This man, who doubted his own ability, would call upon others, while doubting in them too. Until one day there was a stroke of luck, although one not intended for him personally. In any event, he had caused it, had facilitated it as proprietor, had given it his name, his hopes, and his energy to the very end, almost like Otto. He had now discovered a new drawback – his new commercial director, who was all too capable of running the business for him.

This director was called Wiedmann. Was he unbusinesslike? Was he exposing others to blame? No. Did he throw in the towel too soon? Not in the least. And what about his entrepreneurial spirit? Unbeatable. Did he ever stop to reflect? No time for that. Did he seize opportunities? All of them. So what could he be reproached for?

Surely not for joining Rapp's as Julius Auspitzer's son-in-law with 17,000 marks, which Auspitzer had topped up to 43,000 marks? (The consul-general had a second son-in-law, Erich Laeisz from the famous ship-owning family in Hamburg, who had also been appointed a shareholding director of the Rapp company, but who acted purely as a financial backer.) Or should he be reproached for starting work at the race track, going bankrupt, moving to America and succeeding there?

In any case, in Rapp's humble opinion, Max Wiedmann, devoid of all sound commercial knowledge distinguished himself as commercial director by being able to buy in bulk, just when the firm's financial position was anything but rosy.

Particularly in the first summer of the war in 1915. Rapp's six-cylinder engine had been further developed, but he had not found success. Both an eight-cylinder engine and a twelve-cylinder engine, each in a V-configuration (the twelve-cylinder was simply the six-cylinder doubled) had also been unsuccessful. This brought Rapp almost to the point of despair.

This was not the case with Wiedmann, whose cheerful, optimistic nature radiated a power of persuasion which Rapp lacked when it came to winning over influential customers (of course, they were not to be found running down Schleißheim Street, but needed to be hunted down in much higher places), as well as financial backers for expanding the business base and building new plant; backers who enjoyed confidence on their side and were thus influential. Influence was everything. Customers would then come of their own accord. What Rapp had kept hidden, Auspitzer had long approved – that his son-in-law had concluded contacts which would involve the troubled firm in transactions of an international nature which could, and would, save everything, as we shall see. Even if the man getting it all going was someone best avoided.

The New Men

Indefatigably involved in everything that was new, this man laid a network of industrial acquisitions and bonds throughout Europe, in secret and without any obvious goal.

Described as one of the most dangerous, controversial and charismatic figures which only our age can produce, some called him a profiteer, a swindler, a cut-throat and a cheat.

Others saw him quite differently – as a man who never pushed himself forward, always staying in the background, and yet always helpful and reliable in an emergency. They said he was one of those people who benefited from the war, but without whom wars could not be waged.

Through his connections with Wiedmann (Rapp had already left and was all but forgotten now) he became BMW's financier. He was the Confidential Commercial Adviser. . . .

I still hesitate to give his name. Did he actually have one? There is no biography to trace the intricacies of his life. He was a balloonist, pilot, managing director, art collector, patron. Had he actually paid people not to mention him in reference books? I scoured Vienna for any trace of him. I could barely find a single one. Was he some mythological creature?

Yet in slightly yellowing company reports from one firm after another, in minutes from the supervisory board of this or that bank, in newspaper reports stacked away in archives, in bundles of correspondence carefully tied up and of no further interest to anyone, in despatches and communiqués from ambassadors in the metropolis on the Danube, and repeatedly (he could not stop this) in merciless Karl Kraus's *Fackel*, you will find his name mentioned over and over again.

The name I kept coming across was Cagliostro. Everywhere I encountered him, he was effortlessly pledging columns of figures or making transactions like some magician. The Italians called him Castimillioni. If he was involved in collapses, scandals, national crises, resignations, then he was called Castibillioni! If he were in two places at once, he would be Castitrillioni! He escaped, covered his tracks, disassociated himself from the person with whom he had just been. He returned anew, unknown, admired as Camillo Castiglioni. By trying to move and change the world (as he would have said himself), he only managed to scratch the surface. His possessions, which were so numerous that they would have taken weeks to gather together, were lost as quickly as they had been acquired – in no more time than it takes a rubber to erase a pencil mark.

Born in 1885, in a Trieste belonging to the Austrian state but populated by Italians, the son of a rabbi, he came to Vienna as a small-time car-tyre agent. Castiglioni had seized the day, realising that the war created many opportunities which in normal times would have left one worse off – the opportunities to change property-owning status and, above all, industrial ownership. Business cried out for men with quick insight, an ability to strike when the iron was hot, men who did not hesitate, because they knew they had nothing to lose and everything to gain, because they could see the way ahead.

He soon seized the opportunity, and rapidly acquired the Semperit Works, a rubber and car-tyre factory and, using this platform, found his way into car and engine manufacture, and then acquired Austro-Daimler and Puch, which he converted to mass-production. He just went on building. Then the aircraft industry took his fancy. Herr Wiedmann came along, they became friends, then Castiglioni appeared in Vienna before the Privy Councilors and General Officers as the representative of 'Rapp Motor Works Co. Ltd', for which he was paid a commission of 2.6 million marks for a single year, though for what, it is difficult to be certain. This was because Rapp's balance sheet showed a mere 1 million marks for the same period (from 1 October 1915 to 30 September 1916), which he had received for sixty-five aircraft engines with spare parts. In the meantime, the workforce at the Rapp Motor Works had increased to 370 men, and the number of machine tools to 114. Although fulfilling the orders left a lot to be desired, with further orders from Bavaria and Austria failing to materialise (complaints were raining thick and fast, the Bavarian military administration was not in the least bit satisfied with its new aero-engine works vital to the war, and only the Austro-Hungarian Navy retained Rapp), Wiedmann again bought in bulk, not realising that the Austrian military administration, which in future would allocate engines to its naval pilots, would also cease being a customer from autumn 1916.

Nothing now could really prevent the demise of the firm which had, in any case, only just managed to keep its head above water. This was good news for Castiglioni. He invited Auspitzer to his Viennese mansion, where he declared that he was prepared to take over Laeisz's and Wiedmann's shares and to raise the original share capital to 1.2 million marks. He was in high spirits. And why not? He had control of Austro-Daimler in Austria, which did not have enough capacity to supply more vitally needed aero-engines, of a type which Ferdinand Porsche, chief designer and general manager in Wiener Neustadt, had developed for Austro-Daimler as the most powerful aero-engine of its time (350 hp).

So what could he do? The job would have to be licensed out. To whom? The answer was close at hand – the Rapp Motor Works, whose reputation was tarnished, admittedly, but which had enough free capacity to take it over. Thus, all their difficulties would be solved, and (even if Castiglioni's general manager was to protest bitterly and threaten to resign, being against such intrigues) a further fee would be payable, which would exceed everything the business adviser in the Munich works had pocketed, since this involved a contract worth 10 million marks. (Just for the deposit alone of 7 million marks, Castiglioni raked in 1,848,000 marks.)

As the proverb says: 'Money asks no questions and tells no lies'. At a time when 'it was not armies fighting each other, but nation wrestling against nation, when the visible destruction at home was set against the blood-stained victim at the front' – as a confidential document in the flying squadron inspectorate expressed it – Castiglioni's stroke of genius seemed to be less a thickening of the plot than a revelation of the Janus face of war – one moment, sacrifice, the next, business. As was stated in the confidential document from Charlottenburg in Berlin on 31 July 1917 'to the management boards of all firms and factories serving the air corps':

> Just as the lance-corporal in the construction corps carries out his duties on 38 pfennigs a day without grumbling at the vital worker and his daily income of 20 marks; just as the non-commissioned pilot dices every day with enemy fire at 190 marks a month without so much as a glance at the test pilot and his monthly earnings of 6,000 marks; just as our young officers who shed their blood out of duty and self-sacrifice are on a fixed salary which does not even compare to that of a typist doing her dreary work on the home front; so I must earnestly request that no one sends me anything in writing to this effect at work, saying either 'that the firm could point to the fact that a major loss in interest will result should further deliveries of raw materials not be made on time,' or that the royalty from licences will only obviously be refused to preserve monopolies now and in peace time, and to prevent the river of gold effortlessly flowing from this appointment being exposed for all the world to see.

Is this why Rapp fell ill? Was this the root of the illness which consumed him – the need to conform and suffer in silence in the background, just so that the firm would stay afloat and could continue operating? What the respectable Rapp saw was shocking. Was it this that caused him to give up? Or was it the numerous defects in the Austro-Daimler 224 engines being built under licence? These caused a threat from the Austrian reception authority of a repetition of what had happened with the Prussian War Office at the start of the war; that the contract would be withdrawn. Was it further technical setbacks, meaning that the six-cylinder would not be ready and the Prussian air squadrons would change their loyalty, since they could not and would not wait any longer for its completion? The fact was that the commander of the Prussian Airforce, Major Felix Wagenführ, had personally put a ban on the Munich works, stopping it making the 175-hp Rapp engines, there and then turning the works over for repair jobs. Even if it were to remain capable of overhauling between eighty and a hundred Argus, Benz and Mercedes aero-engines a month. . . .

All these events, which had caused such pain to Rapp, even distorting his view of what had been successful, ensured his succession, preventing (almost against his will) what had been started and what had been created from perishing, despite all the setbacks.

The news that everything was going wrong in Munich got as far as Daimler in Untertürkheim where there was *one* man who clearly remembered Rapp – the engineer Max Friz. Working with aero-engines and obsessed by the same passion for engineering as Rapp, he had once worked alongside him at the drawing-board in the design department (we should remember that Rapp came from Daimler). He had now handed in his notice for a minor reason – Paul Daimler had, in fact, turned down his application because of a mere fifty-mark pay rise. This made Friz think that he would be just the person Rapp was looking for. So he wrote to him asking for a job.

This apparently did not make Rapp in the least bit enthusiastic. He wanted to design for himself, and categorically did not want any foreign Gods near him. As it was, building the Austro-Daimler engines under licence had made him feel detached from the drawing-board. So his answer was a definite 'no'.

But he did not stay there.

In October 1916 the Imperial Austro-Hungarian War Ministry invited both directors Rapp and Wiedmann to Vienna to entrust them personally with a major contract for 224 350-hp engines worth 10 million marks. They handed them the deposit, but on one clear condition – that a man enjoying the confidence of the authorities in Vienna should look over the Rapp Works in Munich and, if he felt positive about it, should take over supervision for manufacture.

On 29 November 1916 Franz Josef Popp, an Austrian Lieutenant in the Reserves and a qualified engineer, arrived in Munich. He had served as a volunteer in the Imperial Austro-Hungarian Navy for one year, had qualified from the Technical High School in Brno and, after a period teaching electro-engineering, had taken over supervision of production at the Austro-Daimler Works in Wiener Neustadt at the start of the war, while serving as a reserve officer. Popp was thirty years old. Versed in the arts (which was a form of escape for him) and used to being looked up to, he immediately moved to 288 Schleißheim Street. He could not believe his eyes; could these really be the Rapp Motor Works? Three miserable wooden sheds, machine tools which were more than a little suspect, and a morose, disgruntled boss. There was, however, one way in which it was different from all other works he had previously visited in his studies of the German aero-engine industry, such as Daimler, NAG (New Automobile Group) and Benz. Here was a workforce which assembled around Rapp like a cohort, and had the same determination as their boss – to put their all into fulfilling their licensing contract and so make the most of this last opportunity.

Popp was involved in this last opportunity in a remarkable and almost fateful way. In 1915, as a commander in the Imperial Navy at the Pula sea-plane station on the Adriatic, he had got to know both the needs and wishes of the Austro-Hungarian sea-plane squadrons and the Rapp engine, which was only in service here, since it was unsuitable on other fronts. He could not work out why. There were sea-plane pilots who swore by the Rapp engine. At that time tests had been suspended on a reconnaissance flying boat fitted with three engines, as the engine configuration had not come up to scratch. Looking for a remedy, Popp now suggested a 350-hp engine with twelve cylinders in a V – the very engine bearing Porsche's hallmark, and which an English trade journal had established, after a thorough investigation of enemy planes that had been shot down, as undoubtedly the best aero-engine of the Central Powers.

We know that Rapp then went ahead and built this engine. What we do not know is that Popp tested it himself in the new four-winged flying boat with the famous Austrian naval pilot, battleship lieutenant Banfield. Banfield, who was of English extraction, could claim to have scored the highest number of air victories on the Austro-Hungarian side and later became commander of the Naval Aerodrome at Trieste. As Ernst Heinkel, the builder of the large-scale W 13 sea plane, wrote in his memoirs:

> Here in Trieste, where you can hear the rumble of artillery on the Insonzo front, I often met him [Banfield] with Marine engineer Popp, who then became managing director of Castiglioni's Bavarian Motor Works. . . . Shortly before dinner Banfield and Popp would usually fly another short mission in a 'Hansa-Brandenburg W 13' to Monfalcone where they bombed Italian factories and got back around 8.30 p.m. Then we had dinner.

So did Popp ensure that Castiglioni got the contract? Without doubt, and the licence commission to boot. (But he had only got to know Castiglioni in Trieste in November 1916, on hearing him saying: 'It was a brilliant idea of yours granting Rapp the Austro-Daimler licence!' Popp stopped short. '*My* idea? Yes, I suppose you're right.')

Popp spent a week at the Works. Nobody knew what was going on his head. He had full access to all business papers, nothing was kept from him. Lying on Rapp's desk was the job application from Untertürkheim. 'Friz,' Popp said. 'Is that the engineer who hopes that his carburettor will be used to fly 4,000 metres higher than anybody else's?' He seemed to have heard something about it at Daimler, which nobody else there had taken seriously. Rapp nodded with disapproval and growled something to the effect that this was all he needed.

If this was a clear indication that Popp was happy about him, then he kept his thoughts to himself. He simply said: 'We'll take him on.' Rapp looked at him enquiringly. 'We?'

Then he became calmer. As new and unexpected as this 'we' was, could not the conclusion be drawn that Popp's report to Vienna regarding the solvency and prospects of the Rapp Works would not turn out as badly as had first appeared (in view of Popp's arrogant manner)?

On 2 January 1917, exactly at the time arranged, a tall man in a plain suit with a grey briefcase under his arm came into the unprepossessing dwelling in front of the wooden sheds at Milbertshofen in Munich where Rapp had his offices on the first floor.

'I am Friz,' he said to the young woman who was making out the wages. 'Tell your boss I'm here.'

'He's ill,' said the young woman, 'but Herr Popp will be right with you.'

Friz brushed the snow from his shoulders with his hat. The young woman wanted to take his coat. 'Don't bother,' Friz said, 'I'll just go and have a look at the workshop.'

A Turning Point

Long after birth certificate No.1, the Bavarian Motor Works left the Otto Works (Oberwiesenfeld, south-eastern edge) and were known throughout the world. In 1917 Max Friz joined the Rapp Works (Oberwiesenfeld, north-eastern edge). When the 'Rapp Motor Works Co. Ltd' changed its name in the same year, on 20 July 1917, to 'Bavarian Motor Works Co. Ltd', there was no merger (in spite of all subsequent announcements of a 'marriage' between the two works). The Bavarian Aircraft Works (previously the Otto Works) continued to coexist happily with BMW, well after the end of the war, right up until 1922; there then followed unification or, more exactly, the works 'overlapped' each other. BMW left its old building, the factory in Moosach Street, and moved into the Bavarian Aircraft Works, which ceased trading. We shall see the reasons for this later.

Historians mark 1917 as a major geo-political turning point. In what sense a turning point? In February a strike broke out at the Putilov Works in Petrograd (the name for St Petersburg during the war), which grew into a revolt, then an uncontainable revolution. In October the Bolsheviks seized power with all the huge consequences to come from a demand announced in the fanfare of the 'Internationale' and its desire 'to fight for human rights'. Elsewhere, the United States of America gave up its self-imposed isolation and entered the war. Even if the USA were to withdraw behind its borders again, Europe would be its domain from then on. It was to become a world power, right up to the southern shores of that 'dictatorship of the proletariat' which had proclaimed the end of Czarism in 1917, but which would soon bring forth a new czar.

For our story, too, 1917 acted as a turning point for that small corner of Oberwiesenfeld. It has a precise date.

On 9 January 1917 the German Kaiser took the advice of his admirals and generals and ordered 'unrestricted submarine warfare', which brought about America's entry into the war. (In a macabre way, this was to be repeated in the Second World War when Roosevelt used the attack on Pearl Harbor as a reason to intervene in the war.) As we now know, this led to Germany's defeat. Only Bethmann Hollweg, the German Imperial Chancellor, who was against unlimited U-boat war, saw what was happening and he was dismissed. The war machine rolled on. Entry 45 of a document drafted by officers, stamped TOP SECRET and signed by Major Siegert, Inspector of Air Squadrons, reads:

Charlottenburg 5; 3 July 1917
As America's entry into the war will be principally felt in the considerable reinforcement and increase of the already numerically superior air
capability of our enemies on the Western Front, the Supreme Command
has issued order No 1 58 034 op on 25 June 1917, under the Chief of the
Army General Staff for a significant reinforcement of our air capability.
Current monthly production of 1,000 aircraft will be doubled. The same
applies to fighter planes. There will be a similar increase in the other flying
groups.

You can imagine what effect this order had on Munich, where it reached
Popp under the seal of utmost secrecy. Specialisation in war industries,
strictest standardisation and increased production were all now required
and arrived just at a time when order books were looking very bleak.

Admittedly, there was still work under licence for Austria, but an attempt to
interest the Prussian military administration in ordering the twelve-cylinder
engine with its 350 hp had failed. Nobody needed such powerful engines. Only
a six-cylinder engine was required. What is more, the Prussian Inspectorate
for Air Squadrons had completely rejected all Rapp products. Their reports
between 30 October 1916 and 9 July 1917 do not once mention the name
'Rapp'. The Bavarian War Ministry let it be known, too, that it had no
further need of Rapp, despite the Reserve Air Department in Schleißheim
complaining that 'with the current demise of the Rapp Works, Bavaria no
longer had an engine factory'.

In the meantime, Popp had given up his secure job in Vienna at the
AEG-Union and had followed Wiedmann's suggestion of taking on the
technical management at the Rapp Works. But how was *he* to pull the
chestnuts out of the fire, to prevent the works going into liquidation or, if
it did not quite come to that, prevent it sinking to the level of a mere repair
and supply business for spare parts?

Popp stood isolated and alone. Herr Wiedmann was hardly to be seen
in the firm, preferring, as was laconically reported, to go about 'his
private pleasures'. What of Rapp? He had long since given up and retired
through illness. There was only one way out, and that was to remove
the tainted name of *Rapp* and found a new firm. This required much
more than painting over the firm's signboard. What was needed was a
new technical concept to remove the misfortune associated with the old
name. No sooner said than done. Rapp immediately left, and the *Bavarian
Motor Works*, with its white and blue propeller, opened its old, refurbished
gates, preparing itself immediately to receive a delegation, with a major at
its head.

'Immediately' is a relative term. The date set was 17 September 1917. The
delegation was of the view that this was the earliest date that it could meet
in its official capacity to inspect a works which was not yet two months old.

For Popp, the new works manager, those fifty-seven days since the founding of BMW were an eternity.

A lot of things happened inside the firm during this eternity. And Popp got very excited at the thought of explaining to the delegation and its major *what* had happened. Not the slightest thing had happened outside the firm. Silence from Berlin, Bavaria and Austria. BMW had been so completely ignored that when Popp now saw the gentlemen marching up, a shudder ran down his spine. As he walked across to the major (this was Felix Wagenführ, head of the Prussian Aviation Ministry, an extremely energetic gentleman who enjoyed a reputation for being considerably knowledgeable), Popp knew at once that this was no courtesy visit designed to placate any unjustified hard feelings. It was to tell him that orders would be accepted without argument, without explanations, without any 'ifs or buts'. At best, it amounted to an interrogation; Austrian charm had no effect.

So Popp listened seriously to what was not negotiable; it was simply a question of which firm to choose, Daimler *or* Benz.

Choose?

Yes. He said he was ready to manufacture parts and to carry out repairs for the aero-engines of either firm. Once he had decided which, a test would be made (only briefly, as they were in a hurry) using the machine stock to determine if it were possible.

If what were possible?

If Daimler *or* Benz could be reliably supplied.

Popp almost felt his blood boil. He could almost identify with Rapp. He thought of Pula, the young pilots as they swung back, with a sense of relief, over Brione, returning from submarine tracking and reconnaissance. What had kept them from the almost inevitable descent into the sea and certain death? It was the reliability of this engine which they depended upon to return safely. Defying all the ominous croaking which suggested that the engine was on its last legs, Popp had 'opted' for it, putting forward and concluding the licencing agreement with Rapp, without ever having seen where it was built. You can imagine his horror (or astonishment?) when he later saw the place. He had even wondered how he could leave the business and return to Vienna without losing face, until Friz had crossed his path. . . this Friz with his high-altitude gas theory. Why should it not be put into practice?

If the war in the air could have a decisive impact on the fighting at the fronts, then it all depended on the height which a plane could reach to fly over an opponent and shoot at him from above. The 'fighting' height of 800 metres, deemed to be scarcely feasible at the start of the war, had risen to 2,000, then 3,000 metres. At that point the technical limit had been reached, simply because engines just could not get enough oxygen from the rarified atmosphere *above* that height to enable efficient combustion to take place. An additional blower was no solution; it made the engine too complicated and, above all, too heavy. It lowered the power-to-weight ratio. The higher this was, the better the plane could climb (to reach a height of 1,000 metres, which initially required ten to twelve minutes, and now only four, output could in no way be affected). Friz's idea was to incorporate an inlet fitting before the carburettor, which would only open at 2,000 metres, but would remain closed when starting, taking-off and at low levels.

Rapp's scepticism was understandable. Experiments now? That's right, decided Popp, if only to allow Friz to rectify the vibrating six-cylinder. At which point Friz withdrew to a room off Riesenfeld Street, whose only furnishing was a drawing-board and a high-pressure stove; he had warned Popp that if he were not warm, he could not think, so Popp had wood and coal delivered to him. Three days later, Friz appeared again with the finished drawings in his briefcase. He was not particularly proud of the results – a new crankcase with the cylinders arranged in line. He really thought that he could have built a completely new engine, his *own* six-cylinder. As he looked at the wooden model he became more forgiving (the carpenter, fortunately, had at least indicated the spark-plug borings which Friz had forgotten in his hurry), and went to a foundry in Eßlingen run by an old friend, who ten days later sent eight castings by freight to Munich. And this was certainly worth his while! It resulted in an initial contract for 100 engines, and Friz got down to work enthusiastically, saying that the redesigned engine had already run for thirty hours on the test bed without any trouble, vibrations or crankshaft failure as before.

Faces were soon to fall. The licence to build Austro-Daimler engines had just been cancelled. The test run ordered by the Austrian authorities, which Popp himself had had to organise, had resulted in failure. It was all over.

'And what about *your* high-altitude engine, Friz?'

Friz had the plans for it in his briefcase. It had an oversized cylinder head which could develop high-altitude power of 160 hp at 3,000 metres, 'as against the present Daimler engine which only develops 115 hp at this altitude,' he explained.

'And what about the new Daimler IIIa?' asked Popp. 'Mine can develop between 20 and 30 hp more with almost the same construction and installation measurements,' Friz replied.

'Output on the ground?'

'200 hp as before.'

'And the engine doesn't blow up?'

'It stays throttled back. Consistent with its lighter construction, including its crankshaft, connecting rods, crankcase and so on, comparable in weight to a 160-hp engine.'

'And what is that?' Popp said, pointing to the drawing.

'A special high-altitude carburettor which actually works,' Friz explained to him in a few words. 'It allows me to obtain considerably lower fuel consumption, which until now would have increased at these altitudes.'

He then quoted the figures. Using 200 kg of fuel, it could achieve almost twice as much with a throttled back engine as standard flying of between four and five and a half hours with normal carburation.

Everything that Friz had put down on paper in May, when Popp handed over production to him, was now ready in a model housed in wooden shed 1 (which is the one Rapp had first acquired in Passau) – and it worked. The trick of getting 'it' running (Popp was convinced that this was little short of magic) was now to be followed by another trick – to get the high delegation and its head not just to walk around the shed, but actually go inside it.

The way to a man's heart is through his stomach, as the old saying goes. It was lunchtime. In the fourth year of the war this meant eating turnips. Popp, though, had managed to improve upon the turnips, and the sweet aroma of beef and horse-radish drifting out of the kitchen below and pervading throughout the house right up to the hall could now be smelt in the bare office. They were all standing there ready for hard Prussian-style negotiations when Popp invited them to have a little snack. Did the major hesitate? He did not. 'If it is no trouble, then with pleasure!' he said, turning to the others. 'All right with you, then?' The men nodded in approval, and Popp responded by opening the door and pointing to the workshops. This is what Popp had planned anyway.

And then along comes Friz, as if by chance, looking distracted. 'Coming with us, Friz?' And Friz would join them, following Popp, the Major and the others. This way, please, left, right, then left again. . . here we are! Popp looked at his watch. When others were chinking glasses (customary when concluding a deal), and as soon as their stomachs had been warmed by the horse-radish, he would give Friz his cue – high-altitude engine!

He would then appear defensive. 'Of course, Herr Popp, it's running perfectly. . . .'

'For how long?'

'Since six this morning.'

'That makes. . . uh. . . seven hours. How high are you now?'

'3,000, if the simulator is correct.'

'The critical height. Power output?'

'Throttled to 172.'

'How quickly do you think output will fall now?'

'A maximum of 20 hp per 1,000 metres.'

'Sure you're not wrong?'

Friz persisted. 'Well, only at an altitude of between 5,000 and 6,000 metres. Not below it.'

'Let's just hope the thing doesn't come crashing down around our ears! Excuse me, gentlemen,' Popp would now say, followed by, 'How's the food?'

Then came the inevitable pause, when an angel passed overhead. There was a clinking of spoons. Then came the equally inevitable question which the delegation head could not help asking: 'What were you talking about?' And Popp would come out rather nonchalantly with the nonetheless precise information: 'Major, gentlemen, Herr Friz has just come from the test bed. His high-altitude engine is no longer a fantasy. It's actually better than I thought. I hope that you'll have a look at it.'

That's how it should go, thought Popp, and the meal would begin. There are no minutes of the discussion at the table. Only a sketchy report that the delegation headed by Wagenführ altered its arrangements and wanted to inspect the miraculous engine. The delegation was more and more amazed as the claimed outputs were produced for all to see, in particular the high-altitude performance and the economical carburettor of the new IIIa, which they were convinced and excited by... the delegation extended its visit by several hours, during which there was no talk of repair work. . . .

It was already dark outside by the time they left the works. The very next day Friz was summoned to Berlin, where he had to justify himself after explaining his diagrams and plans in detail to the experts at the air inspectorate. They were still sceptical and asked hundreds of questions which revealed their surprise at how basically simple Friz's idea was. Why had no one thought of it before? Above all, why had Daimler not recognised it? Where was the catch? Only when all objections had been dealt with did they send Friz back to Munich with a trial order for 200 engines. That would certainly not be enough to live on. But the first models were able to be produced, new test-runs were completed on the test bed, right down to further detailed overhauling and painstaking examination (a process which was later to become standard procedure at BMW), and finally the IIIa was fitted in a Halberstadt biplane.

His test (the one which Friz had personally conducted) turned out satisfactorily. It also meant that there were to be difficulties in fitting the engine. This was said to have been deliberately delayed because no one dared fly the miracle engine until the intransigent Friz had forced himself into the co-pilot's seat, without his winter overalls and flying goggles, and defied the critics by flying. The altigraph, suspended between the struts so that it was always readable, had become unrecognisable at 3,000 metres. Friz's eyes were watering as the cold head-wind swelled his eyes. For whatever reasons, this first flight, which took place on 17 December 1917, had to be temporarily suspended.

The next day, they carried on from where they had left off. The altigraph showed an altitude of over 5,000 metres. ('Enclosed is a map with a photo of our first wonderful success in Halberstadt,' Friz was to write a year later to his father. 'On that occasion we improved upon our ascent by around 40 per cent with a record altitude of 5,000 metres!') But these figures still did not seem to satisfy him. Back in Berlin they were waiting impatiently for the results. But Friz wanted to know what his engine was worth, down to the last detail.

Christmas came. Friz spent more time in Schleißheim than back at home in Riesenfeld Street. Schleißheim was home to the No 1 Royal Bavarian Reserve Flying Corps, which had 2nd Lieutenant Zeno Diemer in its ranks.

Diemer was as competent as he was ambitious. He was twenty-one years old, an engineer by profession, and had served in Bogohl 8, the famous bomber squadron of the High Command, and had been one of the first pilots to fly at night.

Diemer, the pilot, and Friz, the designer, selected the RU CI 2643 aircraft, built under licence at the Germania Works in Leipzig, for the new tests. Fitted with a 160-hp Mercedes engine, it had given excellent service at the Flying Observation School in Schleißheim during continuous operation throughout the summer and autumn. Just before Christmas it was fitted with a newly

43

overhauled Mercedes engine producing 173 hp. With an overall payload of 230 kg on full tanks, Diemer then flew in it twice over the test-path at 3,500 metres from Schleißheim to Dachau and Nymphenburg and back. A real speed of 132 kph was measured. Now that the final comparative figures were available, the work could start.

The old engine-mounting struts could be kept, as the BMW engine had the same fitting dimensions as the Mercedes engine. Only the front engine frame had to be replaced. The crankcase on the IIIa had been made sturdier than on the Mercedes.

Only an expert could discover what was different inside the plane (on the control panel, which could now be read at a glance). There was a throttle lever for the high-altitude mixture which was coupled by a rod to a similar lever in the observer seat. Friz, flying as an observer, could operate the high-altitude carburettor himself by means of this lever. And that was not all. Using an additional air-line, which was connected to the inlet manifold and which ran to a changeover switch fitted at the observer seat, he could so regulate the engine at these previously unattainable heights that its output did not drop.

Two Reports

1 Report on test flights

The report by Reserve 2nd Lieutenant R. 'Zeno' Diemer on the test flights (with Friz, the designer, in the observer seat) reads, with its rationality and sparseness, like the log-book of intrepid seafarers, or an Amundsen at the North Pole. Diemer presented his confidential report to Commander Hochwohlgeboren of the No. 1 Royal Bavarian Flight Reserve on 10 January 1918. He wrote:

The first flight took place on Friday 28 December 1917, 4 p.m. As dusk was falling the ascent could be only carried out up to 4,200 metres. Propeller: Lorenzen D290, St. 200, rotating speed in the air with normal mixture 1,240, with altitude mixture 1,340. The engine somewhat vibrated at the lower altitudes and ran slightly irregularly. The more altitude mixture was introduced, the quieter it ran. It was very silent and satisfactory in every respect at 4,000 metres. On the ground the air temperature was a few degrees below zero. The temperature in flight and that of the coolant were not measured. The altitude mixture was applied between 1,500 and 3,000 metres with the aircraft's ascent speed staying constant up to 4,000 metres.

The second flight on 31 December 1917, 3 p.m. Propeller: Reschke, D 293, St. 185. Rotating speed in the air with normal mixture 1,200, with altitude mixture 1,300 rpm. Air temperature at 500 metres = −4; at 5,000 metres = −23° C. Coolant temp. 80° at 1,000 metres, 80° at 3500 metres, 70° at 5,000. Radiator was blanked off to about 30 per cent. The engine apparently used too much petrol on this flight, it laboured somewhat, and performance started tailing off above 3,000 metres.

Third flight on 3 January 1918 at 4 p.m. Propeller: Reschke, D 285, St. 185. Rotation speed in the air with normal mixture 1,250, with altitude mixture 1,340. Air temperature at 500 metres = −4, at 5,000 metres = −38°. Coolant temperature 65° at 500 metres, under 40° at 5,500 metres.

The radiator was not blanked off, the ascent test was suspended, as the coolant temperature was too low. The engine ran perfectly, the air was very gusty at various levels between 2,000 and 3,500 metres, with the result that the ascent speed was not even. The excessive fuel inflow on the last flight was due to residual pressure acting on the petrol still in the float chamber via the carburettor's overflow pipe, which was open to atmosphere. A fitting was mounted on this flight, so that any influence of the air flowing over the fuselage on the float chamber was made impossible.

Fourth flight on 5 January 1918, 10 a.m. Propeller Reschke, D 285, St. 185. Air temperature not measured, coolant temp. 65°. Rotation speed with normal mixture 1,280, with altitude mixture 1,370. The ascent test was suspended at 3,000 metres, because the engine took in too much fuel and the float constantly overflowed.

Fifth flight on 6 January 1918, 11.30 a.m. Propeller: Reschke D 285, St. 185. Rotation speed with normal mixture 1,300, with altitude mixture 1,400. Air temp. at 500 metres = −4, at 3000 metres 0°. Coolant temperature on take-off 65°, at 3,000 metres 90°. About 25 per cent of the radiator was blanked off. The test was suspended because the coolant got too hot. Right from the start of this flight the engine worked better than on all previous flights, running quietly and evenly, even when the throttle was suddenly opened, whilst on previous occasions, sudden revving up made engine stalling much more likely, due to excessive fuel supply. To counter the faults reoccurring in the regulation of fuel supply, the needle valve was made a few grams heavier.

Sixth flight on 6 January 1918, 12.30 p.m. Propeller as for Flights 2 and 3. Air temp. at 500 metres = −4°, at 3,000 metres = 0°, at 6,000 metres = −18°. Coolant temp. at start 65°, at 3,000 metres = 70°, at 6,000 metres 50°. Radiator not blanked off. The engine ran perfectly and evenly throughout the flight and left nothing to be desired. However, at 6,000 metres I had the impression that the engine could have done with rather more air. The height reached was shown on the barograph as 6,200 metres and on the altimeter as 6,400 metres. The aeroplane would have gone even higher had the crew not already been feeling the unpleasant effects of rarified air.

Results from the test flights and general verdict on the engine:

In contrast to all German engines previously used in flight, the BMW type IIIa represents a major step forward. Previous experiences show that it is completely reliable and serviceable for the front. One great advantage is that its installation almost fully coincides with the 160-hp Mercedes and so it can be fitted to all the airframes designed for this engine after modification of the foremost engine strut. This would make the craft fully serviceable for the front and an equal match or superior to enemy aircraft. Both in operation and in service the new engine requires almost the same treatment as the 160-hp Mercedes. The formations at the front will therefore get used to the new engine very quickly, assuming that more serious complaints do not appear in front-line operation.

From the dimensions of the propellers in use and the rotating speeds reached, the engine showed that it had more output in a height range of over 4,000 metres than the 200-hp engine.

Fuel consumption seemed to be very low. Precise measurements were not taken during the test flights.

Cooling: Results showed that for temperatures up to 0° the radiator designed for the 160-hp Mercedes was fully adequate; but a somewhat larger radiator should be specified from the outset for front-line operations and for warmer weather. The radiator blanking, which is adjustable from the cockpit, and the fitting of sensors in the cooling hose are vital so that revving up the engine after rapid cooling does not cause a surge in full power.

Following the favourable results of the test flights, I consider it vitally urgent in the highest interests of the Fatherland that everything should be done to supply large numbers of this engine to the front as quickly as possible. The Bavarian Motor Works are in a position to supply about twenty to thirty engines per month up to March 1918, and from then on to increase to about fifty, with subsequent production gradually reaching 100 engines. As these figures do not begin to cover the front's requirements, there is a need, in my view, to raise production of this engine type to the utmost by immediate and, if necessary, enforced issue of licences to efficient engine manufacturers.

Diemer

The ascent times reached in the January flights, although not given by Diemer, came out in a report by No.1 Reserve Flying Corps. They revealed previously unheard of figures; Diemer reached a height of 3,000 metres in 13 minutes 29 seconds, and 5,000 metres in 29 minutes, and the height of 6,000 metres in 49 minutes (overall from take-off). One month later Friz managed to break these records. 3,000 metres in 10 minutes, 5,000 metres in 20.5 minutes and, in a comparative flight using a fighter plane at Adlershof near Berlin, the BMW IIIa, fitted to a Western-front, single-seater Albatros DVa fighter, against the Mercedes D IIIa engines, reached an indicated height of 5,000 metres in 18.5 minutes (the Mercedes D III took between 29.9 and 36.3 minutes, the D IIIa 25.5 and 27.2 minutes). The BMW IIIa attained the height of 6,000 metres (which was not even recorded on the Mercedes engines) in 25 minutes.

All this may well have seemed like a miracle: 20 May 1917 – first draft designs; 17 September 1917 – test run on the work's test bed in Milbertshofen; November 1917 – 75-hour run of the IIIa without hitches (no abnormal wear). Outputs partially increased to 200 hp. Mean fuel consumption only 185 gr/hp/hr. Two engines delivered for installing in the Halberstadt CL II . . . as stated in the monthly report by the Prussian Air Inspectorate.

At the beginning of May 1918, less than twelve months after Friz had received the order, thirteen S II Fokkers fitted with the BMW IIIa high-altitude engine took off for their first sortie against the enemy.

For Popp this was all a long way off miracles, and only logically consistent after Wagenführ had given his approval.

It was consistent in that Zeno Diemer had received permission in January 1918 to fly with his now-famous RU CI 2643 to Prussia, so as to personally hand over his report on his flights to the Bavarian representative at the Prussian Air Inspectorate at Adlershof (how gratifying!). It was also consistent in that Friz, also ordered to Berlin, received an order from the Prussian military administration for 2,000 engines and the corresponding

47

advance could be laid on the table (how pleasant, honourable and inspiring!). It was also consistent in that 700 BMW IIIa engines could be built under licence by Opel, which had previously only built Argus engines; this was quite understandable, and yet it was anything but satisfying for Popp, just at a time when materials, machines, personnel and everything else were needed to increase production and to make products available in almost limitless quantities.

Why could it not have been earlier, Popp wondered? Because everything that could be seen as a stroke of luck in the combined efforts of production engineering, flying bravura, commercial acumen and major technical achievement by engineers and workers took place against the background of that decisive question as to whether there was any point in it, or whether it was not all too late.

2 My experiences with the BMW Type IIIa engine

In October 1918 Ernst Udet, Lieutenant and Leader of Fighter Flight 4 in the Richthofen Fighter Squadron, was sitting in his tent near Metz and writing the following report:

> We have begun to lose again the advance which we had gained over enemy fighter planes towards the end of 1917 through the Fokker triplane and the Fokker D VII. The D VII with the 160-hp Mercedes engine was technically an excellent machine, although its performance at 4,000 metres fell noticeably. I once had the opportunity to compare two Spads in flight, which my squadron and I pursued at around 5,200 metres. Both Frenchmen were considerably faster. They just carried on flying ahead, without worrying too much about us. The distance grew noticeably greater, and both were soon no more than two little dots spiralling away happily over the aerodrome.
>
> The overcompromised Mercedes was no longer up to competition in terms of speed, even at low altitudes, with the latest English twin-seaters such as the DH 9, DH 12 and the single-seater Sopwith-Dolphin. It was a depressing situation for us. The enemy now had greater superiority both in terms of the quantity and quality of his engines.
>
> During a summer leave in Munich I heard about a fantastic new high-altitude engine, which the Bavarian Motor Works were said to have brought out. It was said that it produced 160 hp with the same weight as the 160-hp Mercedes engine, but did not lose on engine power, even at high altitudes. By the time of my return, the rumour of this miracle-engine had even reached the squadron. As has been stated, the Richthofen squadron should first and foremost be supplied with these engines.
>
> We were stationed at Bougneux aerodrome during the push between Reims and Soissons, when the first BMW-equipped machines arrived at the front. There were initially twenty-two of them, of which eleven were destined for the squadron. There was general distrust, which

battle-hardened front-line troops always show to new things which have only been tested at home.

I quickly managed to 'wangle' (as we used to say) two of these new crates from our then commander, and used the worsening weather to have a thorough look at both aircraft and make them ready for the front. It only took test flights to reveal the great reserves of power hidden in the engine. The engine worked perfectly and had excellent throttle operation. On the same day I was shot down in my old Mercedes Fokker, parachuting out and landing safely just behind the front line.

On the next day I gave a BMW-equipped machine a first flight at the front, and noticed the enormous difference it had over the Mercedes Fokker. I needed only to fly at half-throttle if I was not to overfly or overtake my squadron. Its speed was considerably greater when pointing down, even at low levels, and rapidly increased over other planes at high altitudes. The machine was well-balanced at about 5,000 metres. Yet there was still a mass of power in reserve which could be very useful in an emergency. It is a comforting feeling to know in battle that such power reserves are available. The rotating speed remained constant up to 5,500 metres, and at this height the high-altitude mixture would make up an extra 60 to 80 revs.

My fighter flight attacked a Spad squadron and could soon claim one plane shot down. Thanks to its superior power, I felt confident enough to attack the enemy from below, a tactic which I often used.

As it was all too easy for me to become separated from my squadron, since my engine was more powerful than those in other planes which consequently could not keep up with me, I gave the second BMW-equipped Fokker to 2nd lieutenant Drekmann, who carried out many missions with me until his unexplained death.

We now generally flew over the front at about 6,000 metres, which other engines could not do, and stayed 10 or 20 kilometres undetected behind enemy lines. We almost always attacked by surprise, and with success. I particularly remember two notable victories over a couple of enemy reconnaissance planes.

On 1 July 1918 at 11 a.m. there were two of us at 5,800 metres over Longpont (south-west of Soissons). About 300 metres directly above us I noticed a French Breguet twin-seater which was just about to penetrate German territory. He had apparently seen us, too, since he swung round west again and flew back behind his lines. I pursued him, slowly catching him up. Instead of pointing down, the enemy climbed. He had not realised that gaining height was no protection for him any more. A few minutes later I was 6,300 metres up and about 100 metres behind him. I fired north-west of the wood at Villers-Cotterêts. A few seconds later the Breguet was in flames and spiralling downwards. The other time was very similar.

I was flying with Squadron 4 on 1 August 1918 at 4,500 metres patrolling the front. 1,500 metres above us a single French reconnaissance plane was returning from behind German lines. He was still about 4 kilometres from the front. I saw him and immediately applied high-altitude mixture. I quickly got my trusty, black-nosed Mercedes Fokker squadron in formation below and behind me, and tried to block this solitary traveller's way up. There was a strong west wind, so he could only move slowly. He apparently saw me at that point, because he turned away to the south-west. At the start, there was a great distance between us, which I slowly but surely reduced. I looked at the altimeter. We had just reached 6,000 metres. There was still 500 metres between me and the enemy. He started to get worried and was already zig-zagging to try and escape my line of fire. Until then I had not considered firing, being content just to notice that the distance was significantly shorter. Just before attacking I looked around again for my squadron. They were struggling along way down below me. About 2 kilometres, on the other side of the line, I took aim at the Frenchman, who was about 80 metres away, and at 6,200 metres I began firing. After the first shots, white smoke billowed from the plane, a sure sign that the fuel tank had been hit. His engine also seemed to be spluttering. A few more shots over 40 metres sent him spiralling down like a corkscrew. He was forced back over our lines by the strong west wind. At 12.15 p.m. he crashed at Muret et Crouttes and was burnt to death along with his co-pilot. Nothing, apart from a charred number, B 2710, was recognisable.

The BMW engines only needed a short time in service at the front to reflect a considerable rise in the squadron's fortunes: Captain Reinhard (20 victories), Lieutenant Löwenhardt (53 victories), 2nd lieutenant Kirstein (27 victories), etc., all achieved the majority of their victories with BMW engines. I myself had about 30 victories using the BMW engine.

The performances of my D VII Fokker No. 4253 fitted with a BMW IIIa engine are as follows:

0–2,000 metres in 6 mins
0–3,000 metres in 9 mins
0–4,000 metres in 12 mins
0–5,000 metres in 16 mins
0–6,000 metres in 21 mins

admittedly flying alone, without the squadron. When my squadron was later wholly equipped with BMW, I worked on about 22 to 23 mins for the squadron to reach 6,000 metres.

After 82 hours in service I had the engine overhauled during leave. Wear on the bearings and other parts was minimal. All that was needed was to lap in new valves and replace a few piston rings. When I returned to the front, I notched up on my very first day my 61st and 62nd victories over Metz with the same aircraft.

There is no question that the BMW engine proved to be the highpoint of aero-engines in the last stage of the war. Its only flaw was that it had arrived too late.

Udet
Lieutenant and Leader of Fighter Flight 4
in the Richthofen Fighter Squadron

The New Factory

Udet's 'too late' listed as the BMW IIIa engine's only flaw leads one to suspect that the First World War could still have been won by Germany if only everything related above had taken place a few months earlier.

There can be no question of this.

Troops which surrender (as Ludendorff, the First Quartermaster General, described the situation to the Kaiser) are no longer any use to their commanders; they disrupt their most carefully laid calculations and their action endangers all those divisions who have remained true to the cause. He was referring to the wholesale surrender of the 41st Division on 8 August 1918 at Amiens. The 'black day' of the German army, when the German front collapsed under an enemy tank attack, would still have been avoidable – with its last desperate offensive on the Piave, Austria could no longer prevent the collapse of the Danube monarchy, and it was no longer possible to ignore what was happening at home. Here the masses longed for peace, trouble was fermenting in the navy, which finally refused the order to leave port and embark on a 'mission of death' against England. This resulted in mutiny and revolution.

Above all else, what did the Central Powers think they could do to counter the shiploads of war material brought in from overseas, to counter the inexhaustible sources of raw materials available (and it was obvious what they *did* have available!) to the enemy? For the Germans, this was the stuff of dreams, meaning that planes could not be built, that copper and brass (vital soft metals for tanks, pipework and other fittings) had to be used for softening brittle iron, and that wooden discs had to make do for rubber tyres, and practice and training flights had to take place with low-quality mixtures instead of petrol. At the front German squadrons, supplied with top-quality fuel for only one day at a time, could not fly any lengthy missions; they often had to remain on the ground while swarms of enemy planes bombed the German positions. (On one occasion an American squadron recently deployed to the French front completely lost its bearings and inadvertently landed on an airstrip behind the German lines. The Germans gasped when they saw the equipment and machines. Nothing had been spared; one could almost say they had gone overboard in the pursuit of safety and ever greater performance. There was even a certain comfort. The subsequent report kept quiet about what the Americans had said when they looked at the German machines with their coverings made of artificial paper fibre – which at least contained steel wire inserts.)

Admittedly all this only took place in 1918. But had not those responsible seen the threat facing Germany much earlier on? Why could not the Kaiser, the generals, Parliament, the parties, even the ordinary man in the street from what he could judge in the newspapers, see it all a mile off, that everything contemplated would be in vain? The American entry into the war, with the mobilisation of a whole continent which would reinforce the exhausted Allied position, was guaranteed to get the Germans out. What was the good of having fronts that were holding out, and an 'Unbeaten Army' continuing to hold a country that had already been bled white, just in the hope and expectation of coming out of it all lightly?

Neither could anyone at Oberwiesenfeld in Munich shut his eyes to this. All Popp, the Austro-Hungarian immigrant, could do was stick to business, to *his* business. There had been no way back for him after that 21 July 1917 when he had changed the moribund Rapp Works into the Bavarian Motor Works Co. Ltd. And so it came about that the 'greatest aircraft works in Germany' were conjured up on Moosach Street, where Popp had bought 25 hectares of land just after founding BMW. The share capital was a full 1,200,000 marks which, rather than having the intoxicating effect of a dowry, actually inspired Popp with the foolhardiness of despair. A prospectus glowingly spoke of the new works as being resplendent in gleaming white, as having 'effectiveness, combined with perfect beauty of form', at a time when everything was already over.

In August 1917, when fighting on the front had been reduced to a war of attrition with no end in sight, the newspaper *Bayerland* presented the new BMW works to its amazed readers as the factory of the new man, which, so to speak, could also find expression artistically, in its tall chimney 'disguised as a beautifully composed water tower', and the halls in the administration building with their mosaics and allegories combining to form a kind of technical temple to the muses. This was a works designed in the middle of war for peacetime applications, where engines would be built not only in the interests of the safety and speed of aircraft, but also for other uses, such as 'for boats and agricultural appliances, especially the plough'. There was no mention of cars.

Anyone driving out to Moosach Street to look at the miracle works: the fully-illuminated, 220-metre-long machine halls, which could have their depth of 60 metres doubled at any time for increased peacetime demand; their tracks where production flow could be constantly observed; a 'second complex with a foundry, a hardening shop, an annealing furnace, a forge, a joinery arranged one behind the other' and the test beds for the engines; draughting rooms, rooms for the skilled workers, administration and working quarters, houses for manual and office workers, along with a smallholding having its own pig-sties (a hundred animals!), potato and vegetable gardens and swaying cornfields ('so that there is no loss in industrial production or in creative mental and physical power'); anyone seeing all this must have thought, however fanciful it sounded, of the tale of the emperor's new clothes – invented by the fool's imagination to dress the naked. Was all this a figment of Popp's imagination?

But admiration was already great when 1918 dawned, with the new works visibly developing and becoming a reality. The Germans wanted to be in Calais by the middle of March and in Paris by the middle of April, while the Allies only had one worry – not to arrive too late with their 18,000 tanks which, they believed, would flatten everything in their way, like dinosaurs.

As for life on the home front, this was expressed in the prosaic reports which went back and forth between the Bavarian War Ministry, the Airforce Engineering Corps and the Prussian procurement offices.

Rumours circulated in Munich of the imminent financial collapse of BMW (30 March 1918).

As the Prussian Air Inspectorate complained: 'Current production at the works is far too low, with only 10 out of the 25 expected and firmly promised IIIa engines being produced. Why is this? We ordered 2,500 aero-engines worth 60 million marks divided over two years, of which 12 million was paid in 1918. We have been promised 50 engines in April, 80 for May, 100 for June, 120 for July and 150 for August.'

'This is due to too few skilled workers being released from the front,' answered the 'Moba' (engine building supervision) official.

'What has happened to the 1,000 skilled workers whom BMW received in the year up to 1 March 1918?' asked the Inspectorate.

'Brand new, mass-produced aero-engines cannot be supplied within a few months,' said the engine building supervision officer, 'especially from a plant that is under construction. Fully-equipped factories need a whole year for that. In addition, the Friz engine has only just come out of the test stage. What you're asking from BMW. . . .'

'And how do you explain the discontent and turnover amongst the workers? BMW dismissed 140 workers at one go, some of them skilled!'

'There is a shortage of competent production engineers,' replied the officer.

'Then employ them. What exactly is going on in the works? We're sending you 2nd Lieutenant Britsch from the Flz. Inspectorate B Mak 2 Fighter to report back immediately after his investigation.'

Second Lieutenant Britsch of the Flz. Inspectorate B Mak 2 Fighter duly appeared, looked round the concern, analysed the situation, wrote down a few words – words of criticism, for sure. But he also saw the teething problems that the new works had to deal with.

There was no tramway between the new site and the old factory in Schleißheim Street, where work had to carry on until the individual production units had been fitted out 'over there'. The workers had to walk the distance; two kilometres, half an hour there, half an hour back.

The works had five cars in all, providing a shuttle service, with just a bicycle for the production supervisor. As a token towards fulfilling the greatly increased demands made by the commissioning authorities (which had led to a four-fold increase in the manufacturing schedule), a further car had been contracted, but no sooner had this been done than it was threatened with removal ('. . . the Bavarian Motor Works car was seen on Sunday, 17 February, at 7.55 p.m. travelling along Widenmayer Street in the direction of Bogenhausen; on Tuesday, 19 February, at 4.55 p.m. crossing Odeon Square in the direction of Ludwig Street; and on 20 February, at 9.10 a.m. crossing Station Square in the direction of Bayer Street. There can be no doubt that, at least on the evening of 17 February, the car was being used for non-official purposes . . .').

Severe disruptions in the production schedule could be put down to food shortages. The workers had been refusing to work more than eight hours for the past three days. Demands for more meat at canteen meals had been refused ('. . . even the meals today are intended to be more nutritious here than those served in other parts of Germany like Saxony, the Rhineland, etc.').

As for producing the engines, this was still hindered by a lack of materials for shafts and smaller wrought items, with the result that two BMW staff were constantly on the move to speed up deliveries of raw materials . . . and so on, and so forth. . . . Even sabotage occurred once; the oil ways in the drilled-out crankshafts had been filled in with filings and swarf – on the very day when, for specific reasons, a management directive was issued to the workshops to the effect that the oil ways on the crankshafts could only be sealed up on final assembly under the supervision of the fitters responsible. The suspect was dismissed on the spot, even if he had not done it intentionally. Sabotage could only have come about because he had been completely inattentive.

Britsch wondered if he should bother the inspectorate by giving his judgement on this or that 'person responsible' in other cases. Perhaps it would be better not to say anything.

He spent the whole night weighing up the pros and cons. Then he set about outlining the relationships throughout production and how everything was settling down in spite of the many failings. He gave a brief psychograph of each 'character'.

This is what he said about Popp: 'He should be an electrical engineer. The knowledge of engine manufacture and modern mass production which he brought to the management of the works which he took over at the beginning of 1917 were probably acquired as chief production supervisor of the Austro-Daimler company in Vienna. There are quite a few signs to suggest that this knowledge cannot have been all that thorough.'

He said about Friz, as chief designer: 'Already respected by the Daimler Engine Company as an excellent engine designer. He had designed the BMW IIIa engine which is the only reason why the flying corps is interested in the firm.'

Then came Hagemann, the works manager, who seemed to be the reason why mistakes had occurred in the firm's use of the facilities entrusted to it by the military administration. By facilities Britsch meant materials, manpower, cash advances – in other words, money. And so what was missing? 'A lack of vision and awareness in managerial decision-making and in human relations when dealing with his subordinates.'

His subordinates could certainly tell Britsch a thing or two about that. Their departments had, in the meantime, been taken over by grade A experts. At the top was the design office which, under chief engineer Hörauf, provided the pivot for all work procedures. All the work operations had to be ascertained and predetermined from here; the co-ordinated and scheduled production of all individual parts needed for assembly had also to be directed, together with informing workshop and purchase of the time-scales required for delivery of the parts, so that there was no break in continuous mass-production.

One can quite understand how this fascinated Britsch when he moved from materials testing at the aluminium and brass forge ('currently the most efficient section') to assembly, and then finally to fittings and tool manufacture ('entirely satisfactory'). On the way he got caught up in the pleasure of logical manufacture and continuity, which was inherent in the civilised variety that a factory like this provided, where it was easy to recognise that a machine's precision (together with the parts making it up) was a matter of life or death at the front. In particular, Britsch had worked on quality control, which 'was the most important element in parts production', implemented at three stages – external, parts and final quality control. He gave the following instructions to his department (as if he wanted to counsel them to adopt this principle so that the war would not be lost):

External quality control is carried out by so-called flying inspectors who check the machines during operation so that they can intervene on faults detected *before* the workpiece is damaged.

Parts quality control is concerned with checking the mass-produced parts after each operation, so that the producer of reject parts can be safely and irrevocably established.

Final quality control ultimately controls the *finished* part and, jointly with the design office and works management, examines whether parts not complying with prescribed tolerances could not after all be of some use.

This led to Britsch becoming the trustee of the works he was inspecting, and to him making practical suggestions:

The external and parts quality control have only been in operation for a short time, but have quite considerably reduced the percentage of rejects in the last few weeks, and will probably contribute daily towards better parts production. Final quality control, headed by foreman Stolle, has also shown considerable improvement in the last few weeks as a result of his indefatigable and expert efforts, and is continuing to improve by the day.

Stolle has been seconded to the firm on short term from Fea 2 (Reserve Air Corps), and it would be very desirable for the firm to be granted its request for his permanent transfer.

Next came the exact state of engine production (up to then 600 engines had been delivered, 140 engines were planned for September), the actual prime costs per engine were given (32,000 marks against the previously calculated figure of 26,000 marks, amounting to an additional sum of 3.6 million marks) and the size of the workforce – 1,744 personnel, which excluded office staff but included foremen. Productive work involved 1,198 of them, while 536 were involved in non-production work. The number of skilled workers in both businesses: 800. Situation as for the end of April 1918.

Forecast: normal production will be reached in two to three months.

One thing remained. It was not in 2nd Lieutenant Britsch's power to put it all into practice. That needed information from a higher level.

A Public Company is Founded

An item in the business pages of the *Frankfurter Zeitung* had intimidated the men. The report, perhaps put out as a piece of kite-flying (but who was doing the kite-flying?), revealed that the Bavarian banking institutions, which had only recently been very active in industrial financing, were absent from the group of banks formed under the control of the National Bank for Germany to convert the Rapp Motor Works into a public company. It was not clear if this had happened as a reflection on the personality of the company's top man, or for purely practical reasons connected with the varying assessments of 'Rapp Motors'. There was talk of 'Rapp Works' and 'Rapp Motors', but nothing of 'BMW'. The finger was pointed at Wiedmann, whose lavish lifestyle stuck out like a sore thumb for both the Bavarian banks and the higher military administration, as was shown in a confidential report by the War Ministry. The war had entered its fifth year. The ostentatiousness which Wiedmann displayed was inappropriate both to the seriousness of the situation and to the image of 'a leading business in the field', which was regarded by the military authorities as more of a military installation run by civilians than a private company. Whether that was true or not, it did not bode well for the future of the works. To put it in a nutshell: the playboy had to go. But how?

Rising to managing director because he held the majority of the share capital, Wiedmann showed he was responsible when only Popp was left running the business. Popp made it his business to know where Wiedmann's carefree attitude had taken him – that the financial basis which had been far too weak to allow the firm to function under its own steam had been offset by the high loans and bank credit which had all been swallowed up in the building of the new factory, with its now increased production facilities.

Conversion of a limited company into a public company was not only vital, but overdue and inevitable to all the shareholders (right up to Wiedmann). The only thing that was not clear was whether the public company would take over 'certain obligations towards the limited company's rights', when the latter went into liquidation. In other words, the customers were worried about the advances paid out, which in all amounted to 18,800,000 marks (11,800,000 marks from the Prussian fighter command, 7,000,000 marks from Austria); it was in fact possible (who could say?) that the limited company was already in liquidation.

This is what the men who met at the War Ministry on 19 July 1918 racked their brains over. They agreed initially to dispatch supervisory bodies from the Royal Prussian and Royal Bavarian military administration to BMW; on the one hand to keep the company going, and on the other to increase production to maximum output, and not least to monitor the continuing investments in the company 'to this end', and 'to file any petitions necessary for the company to reach the set goals'.

The works management, as was stated in the minutes of the meeting, were said to have already given their agreement, and were left in no doubt that counter-productive actions by the firm would result in the most severe sanctions. There were further conditions – Wiedmann was to resign as managing director, and any influence he might have on the commercial or technical activity of the company must cease forthwith. In the event that he did not agree to hand over his company to a legal official by 10 August, and make a full guarantee to comply with all the requirements made by the military administration for the continuation and further development of the works, then the sanctions available to the military administration (requisition of the business under wartime law) would come into force.

That meant nothing other than nationalisation or a military takeover.

But no one at BMW was going to be that easily upset, least of all man-about-town Wiedmann. BMW was a business, and not part of the military administration. And so, just before the deadline announced, things started moving. A telephone message taken down by the 'Air Corps Adjutant' at 12.30 on 6 August said the following:

To the Prussian War Ministry
   We are well on the way to founding the public company as desired, but cannot conclude negotiations. This is because both Captain Joseph and the Foreign Ministry here, to which Captain Joseph had referred us, and the War Ministry all declare themselves unable to name a price. We therefore request a statement of the highest settlement price by telegram, as all those interested in founding a public company currently have the necessary authorisation.
                                                                Bavarian Motor Works

Amongst these authorised men there were two that were missing, whom Popp had first of all contacted in his search for investors – Stinnes and Vögler. They were quite open in their reason for not wanting to participate – Wiedmann.

However, it did not actually matter that these men from the Ruhr were not included. The new investors, who had been summoned to the War Ministry, bore names which got them noticed. What they then thought up suggested that the Bavarian banks had given up their mistrust and that this boded well for the future. This was also possible for them in view of the considerable investments made by the National Bank for Germany and Berlin, represented by its director, Dr Hjalmar Schacht (2 million marks), Fritz Neumeyer in Nuremberg, where he had recently founded the Zündapp Works, and the

Austro-Hungarian Commercial Adviser Camillo Castiglioni from Vienna (both contributing 4 million marks), so that the total share capital amounted to 12 million marks.

The articles of association concluded on 13 August 1918 revealed that the limited company had sold the public company its entire business with all its assets, in particular all its buildings, furnishings, trade-mark rights and patents pending, together with all other rights and claims, including the right to continue the activities of the company, for 44,312,199.12 marks. 'The obligations taken over herewith amounted to 40,812,199.12 marks. The rest had to be paid in cash,' it said succinctly.

This happened at the very time when Ludendorff finally had to bury the thought of pushing the fortunes of war to Germany's advantage by a final onslaught. The German front, which had collapsed under the weight of 400 Allied armoured vehicles, could no longer be held from 8 August. Offensive action turned to defensive action and, in the absence of any reserves, they retreated back to the Schelde, the Meuse and the Rhine.

The entry of the new company as 'Bavarian Motor Works PLC, Munich' appeared in the register of companies in the middle of September. At this time there was no longer any doubt that the war was lost for Germany and its allies.

Wiedmann, who was given a golden handshake of 2 million marks, but who still held a seat on the new supervisory board, was not too disgruntled to be out of the firing line. The new board now welcomed Herr Wilhelm Strauss and Herr Franz Josef Popp, senior engineer, both from Munich. They were the ones who were now fully responsible for the company. The works, the new public company, was now running at full speed. But for how long?

But nobody actually asked this question. Now that BMW was given legal parity with a business known as 'Bavarian Aircraft Works PLC' (BAW for short), based not very far away in Neulerchenfeld Street, to the north-east of Oberwiesenfeld, there was no longer any chance of anyone speaking of the Rapp Motor Works when they meant BMW. This had happened time and again, presumably to prevent confusion with BAW. But this was not the kind of thing to affect Popp. He had invented the white and blue propeller, and the letters BMW surrounding it were attributed to him. It was to his credit that the firm had created the miraculous IIIa engine, uniting all the shareholders in a way which could not be rationally explained.

BAW, now a subsidiary of the Albatros Works in the Johannisthal suburb of Berlin, built aircraft (not aero-engines) and was not in any way connected with BMW, apart from the fact that, as the only Bavarian aircraft works after 1916, it was dependent on the Prussian military administration (medals had been lavished by the Bavarian War Ministry on the men responsible in Berlin, to keep their goodwill). BAW had produced about 200 new aircraft per month together with 30 they had repaired. This had meant that the firm had grown from the 500 or so employees at its founding in March 1916 (which was known to have started with Otto, who had nevertheless left immediately afterwards) to a workforce of 2,400 in Autumn 1917. Then, in November 1917, fire reduced the repair shops to ashes. They were never rebuilt. Shop after shop was closed down. The works hung on grimly and now employed only 370 men as the war came to an end.

'How big is that land over there, actually?' Popp asked Lynen, his production supervision officer, who was a professor at the Technical High School in civilian life, as they were crossing the courtyard.

'Too big,' said Lynen, '55,000 square metres.'

'But it's in a good position, directly opposite Oberwiesenfeld.'

'That's just why Otto went there,' said Lynen.

'Otto?' replied Popp. 'Oh yes, that's right. Otto . . . I never met him. Why, I really don't know.'

Of course, this dialogue never actually took place, but it could well have done. Soon after the end of the war Lynen went back to his chair, and drafted reports about the new BMW car and boat engine in which he recognised qualities which came up to the standard of the IIIa high-altitude engine as regards compression and wear resistance. At a moment when BMW actually ceased to exist, Popp was to remember those 55,000 square kilometres belonging to the very depressed BAW. 'Buy them,' he said to Castiglioni (this has been fully authenticated), as, in the troubled times of the post-war period, the latter had divested his entire BMW shareholding for reasons which were never clear. 'Buy them, and we shall put a new heart in the works – BMW.'

That was four years later, in May 1922. How BMW survived till then deserves a chapter in its own right.

The Misty Days of Peace

That November day came when the revolution crossed the Main and reached Bavaria. Thousands of sailors arrived in Munich not from Kiel but from the Austrian naval base at Pula (that was Popp's sea-plane station where he had come to know the Rapp engine), and surged through the streets with revolutionaries from the independent and main-wing socialist parties. They stormed the military prison and proceeded to the Royal Palace. Looting followed, shots were fired, and hand-grenades were thrown. By the night of 7 to 8 November, Bavaria's King Ludwig III became the first German prince to abdicate. The next day Prince Max von Baden, the last Imperial Chancellor of the old empire, announced the Kaiser's abdication in Berlin (which later proved premature). Ebert succeeded him as Chancellor, while at noon Scheidemann declared a republic from the steps of the Reichstag (on his own authority, as was later discovered). The Imperial headquarters in Spa witnessed a chilling scene.

Thirty-nine officers from the front, hastily summoned, were supposed to answer the question individually as to how the forces felt about the Kaiser; in plain words, would it be possible for the Kaiser to lead the forces in reconquering the homeland? The majority of the officers, twenty-three, replied no; only one officer replied yes, while fifteen abstained. As General Schulenburg said to His Majesty, Prussian officers had never betrayed their King and or let him down in any way. He also added that Prussian officers had never been allowed to vote for their King.

On the same day, Ebert had a secret telephone conversation with Ludendorff's successor, Groener, in Spa. Hindenburg was requested by the new Imperial Chancellor to stay in his job (in the name of the Republic!), so that the armies in the field could be led home in order. Did he know what he was doing? He knew full well. If Hindenburg had not remained, rivers of blood would have flowed. At the same time, however, he had reinstated the former Imperial bureaucracy, had confessed that nothing would work without it and had summoned the rest of the army to act as a core troop to come once again to the rescue of the empire.

On the very day when Kaiser Wilhelm II crossed the Dutch border, Matthias Erzberger signed the armistice at Marshal Foch's headquarters at the wood in Compiègne. At 11 a.m. on 11 November the weapons fell silent. The war was over.

It had cost Europe 22 million lives (if we include the reduced birth rate caused by the war). This does not include Russia, which suffered many more losses – in fact, 26 million. On both sides, the Central Powers as well as the Allies, this war had made everyone fully aware that everything had been at stake, and that a compromise to end it could never compensate for the sacrifices. The decision of history was accepted as definitive, even if it had long since been proven that it was not enforceable through arms, but only through applying military force on your opponent's economy (trade war, starving out Central Europe, etc.); in other words, through economic means. Both sides had known that victory, whoever carried it off, would be total, just as the war itself had been waged totally using the means available at the time. Germany had lost it. Could she expect leniency, insight, reason?

Popp knew full well that a peace that was not based on these things (leniency, insight and reason) could never bring real peace. No oppressed nation in Europe (where everything was interconnected) could ever renounce its own aspirations, unless it wanted to of its own accord. Technological development alone, which the war had so accelerated, urged people on, and no domination gained by other nations through dictated or artificial peace would alter anything. There were still hopes that a solution would prevent recourse to a new, and eminently possible, war. What were they based on? On having recourse to that international co-operation that had existed between technicians, designers and manufacturers, just as between pilots in the new world of flying; one only had to think to Johannisthal. That co-operation would doubtless exist again, once hatred, revenge and mistrust had subsided, all of which had been reduced to an obsession with national security. Unhealed wounds would be healed. Technology broke all chains, crossed borders, eradicated prejudices, and necessitated communication, solidarity, and exchange of ideas, whatever the political price. This was something that could be built on. But a barrier lay ahead – time. It was now all down to making up for lost time, until enough progress had been made.

Tactically speaking, that meant: do not speak about it, although always think about it. And do what can be done.

But what could be done? The first thing to do was to stop aero-engine production immediately. The customers, the Prussian and Bavarian military authorities, seemed to have got lost in the mist which covered the works and the town on those grey November days. The last monthly report of the Royal Bavarian Engine Building Supervision in Munich to the Air Corps in Charlottenburg, a suburb of Berlin, dated 8 November, stated:

The BMW IIIa has gone into production, while mass production of the BMW II (120 hp, for use in training) is about to start. The IIIa will have its high-altitude performance improved by increasing the bore and stroke by 10 mm each. Seven test engines of the BMW IV have been prepared for delivery; the first should be running in November. The BMW IV should be built under licence. The twelve-cylinder V-engine is designed to take a bore of 160 mm and a stroke of 190 mm and to deliver 370 hp at 5,000 metres. The BMW V should be running on the brake tester by the end of January 1919. . . .

If this sounded like a battle report from ancient history, where the messenger still reported what the Gods had long since annulled, then the first two announcements immediately after the armistice provided some information about the situation. The first came on 11 November 1918 from the Ministry for Military Affairs in Munich, as the War Ministry was then called. On behalf of his minister, Baron von Speidel let it be known that the country's requirements demanded that all State authorities, and especially the military authorities, provide supplies for the returning armies, and be resolute and unreserved during the orderly demobilisation taking place, while at the same time respecting the troops' state of mind and beliefs, for the good of community and State.

The officers' oath of allegiance up to now presupposed permission from His Majesty the King. An attempt to retain this was to fail because there was then no sign of His Majesty. As a further delay would have the most dire consequences for the country . . . Popp did not read any further. This was something for the satirical magazine *Simplizissimus*.

The second announcement, which could not fail to interest him, came from Berlin. Here the Council for the People's Deputies announced on 12 November (one day after BMW had completely stopped production), in a way that sounded like a guarantee, that the workers would not abuse the power which they actually held. 'The government,' stated the edict, 'would maintain orderly production and protect property from interference by individuals, as well as personal freedom and safety.'

Was this a denial of the revolution? If not, then it was a denial of civil war and anarchy. This would end the fear that the situation might result in a proletarian state (as in the case of the Soviet Union) rather than a bourgeois one. But Berlin was a long way off. From there, Bavaria, proclaimed as a Free State and, *de facto*, independent of the Reich (Kurt Eisner, Bavaria's new Chief Minister had announced to the Foreign Office that all political ties would be severed) could be regarded as abroad. What now?

The main customer for the Bavarian Motor Works had been the Royal Prussian War Ministry. The claim which BMW had made on the central authorities ran to 35.6 million marks. This included the entire installation costs of the works, the initial outlay for 3,000 aero-engines ordered, and an outstanding amount due in back payment for all the 600 engines already delivered.

The works' very existence depended on this sum. One worry which did not concern Popp was the possibility that Bavaria's government would *not* 'maintain orderly production', and would *not* 'protect property from interference by individuals, as well as personal freedom and safety'. The new Bavarian National Council, try as it might to consist of workers', soldiers' and peasants' councillors, was made up of Social Democrats, Democrats, the peasants' association wing of the old Landtag (State parliament), as well as members from all the business and trade associations – 'people's deputies', just like in Berlin. What else could they be?

Popp did not know what was going on in other German aircraft and aero-engine factories, as the collapse of the Reich loomed. He was a pragmatic man. His reasoning was simple. In whatever way things developed, what could prevent the factory gates being closed in front of his very eyes? If all the people working behind them were thrown out onto the streets, this could only increase the distress and confusion of the hard times around the corner, which in a town like Munich would be both intolerable and incalculable. Neither could this be in the minds of those who, after Eisner's murder, had proclaimed a soviet-style Republic, whose henchmen wore red armbands and old army coats. Several of them still wore spiked helmets or forage caps with the cockade torn off, as they stood on every street corner or prowled through houses, leaving no doubt as to who was in charge. As for their shoes, one had only to look at them to guess when they would fall off.

When man can no longer fly, he drives; and when he can no longer drive, he runs. And that requires shoes. Shoes can be made by machines. While all efforts were being channelled into the IIIa engine, Popp got BMW judiciously to invest in a factory making shoe machinery, whose products required, indeed demanded, the very highest precision work.

It was even more vital to ensure food production. As a result, Popp bought the licencing agreement for a motorised plough from the Karwa company ('A flick of the wrist brings the grab into operation,' was the caption under a picture which soon appeared in all the papers of the Free State showing an idyllic pastoral scene, a huge tractor with the letters BMW on the radiator (no propeller symbol), rear wheels as high as a man, with blades which could pull the plough through sodden ground).

But was that enough?

Well, there were thousands of parts lying around which could no longer be assembled for aero-engines. So Popp offered a quickly-developed car and boat engine (which the new factory had already announced in 1917 in its 'peace catalogue') to interested parties, and sold 1,000 of them for export, as such parties were fewer in Germany than abroad.

But all this, along with the office furniture and saucepans cast from cylinder heads, was no basis for keeping the works in production and the skilled workers being paid daily. But this was just what it was all about, the prerequisite for survival. Without skilled workers, the buildings of the factory, which were still expanding in elegant whiteness along Moosach Street, were not worth the powder needed to blow them up.

However, on 6 December 1918 the inevitable could not be forestalled a moment longer. In the general problems of the time, the announcement in the newspapers might have gone unnoticed. It read:

The Bavarian Motor Works has terminated all production. Until recently it employed around 3,000 workers, along with 400 office staff. The latters' contract of employment would, in most cases, run up to 1 April 1919, up to which time they would receive their salaries. At the last meeting of office staff, the following decision was taken: 'Those office staff affected by the closure expect the most effective representation by the Union of Office Workers on the Munich trades council to represent their vital interests which are now under severe threat. They trust that the elected representatives will take all appropriate measures to give back the closed works its economic role again, and to stipulate terms of employment appropriate to their professional status.' As we have learnt, it is the works management's intention in the foreseeable future to re-engage 25 per cent of the manual workforce and 6 per cent of the office staff.

It was clear that both sides, workers and employers, were skilled in the business of drafting resolutions; vague hopes were combined with demands, designed to ensure future rights, a future in which the conciliatory words of the management sounded like barefaced contempt. The supervisory board and the investor, even the ever resourceful Castiglioni in far away Vienna, who was never short of finding escape routes, no longer seemed prepared to waste time, money and effort in a hopeless cause.

Furthermore, anyone abusively accused of being a 'war profiteer' tried to rid himself of the odium connected with war production, armaments, complicity in all the misery into which Germany was catatonically slipping.

The decision to liquidate BMW was all but agreed.

It is not easy to penetrate the darkness of that period and visualise or understand what really happened. There are no extant documents issued by the war archives from 8 November 1918. It is like coming up against a brick wall. A single item found in the Bavarian War Archive reveals that the national authorities in Berlin had, at the end of December 1918, given the assurance to a Captain von Könitz, presumably negotiating for Bavaria, that the justified demands of Bavarian firms, including BMW, should not only be acknowledged but fulfilled as quickly as possible.

This handwritten document is dated 19 January 1919, leading to the conclusion that those millions which worried Popp continued to flow into BMW even during the closure. But nobody knows what happened during the company closure which lasted until 1 February 1919 (a date which was more accidental than predetermined), as no one knew how things were progressing. There is no record, no faded copy of any correspondence (which the Allied inspectorate might later have confiscated or which, if it had been left in the archives, might have been reduced to ashes during the incendiary bombing in 1945) to say what happened. On this occasion, too, the memory of those there at the time failed.

Even a frail old lady called Annie Hoffmann, whom I visited (she had been Popp's secretary and had spent a lifetime in his employ) could not remember much more.

'But something important must have happened,' I said. 'Look at this glossy prospectus, showing the whole works, the BMW IIIa high-altitude engine, "technically the ultimate in fighter aircraft engines" as it grandly says, now available for postal and transport planes. The BMW IV (five of them had been produced by the end of the war) is designed for high-speed post, overseas post and for record-breaking flights; and even the BMW V, 400 hp, maximum output 500 hp, which is recommended for passenger aeroplanes, for parcel post and transport overseas. . . . When was that? When had all that been produced? Engines for lorries, luxury cars, motorised ploughs, tractors, motor-boats. . . . When had all those been thought out, designed, built, tested, to guarantee [and here I quoted] "extremely low fuel and oil consumption, no overrunning parts, timing and drive shafts sealed to prevent dust entry, self-sufficient lubrication system with pumps for backfeed, clean oil and scavenging, five-bearing crankshaft . . .".'

'No idea!' said Frau Hoffmann, giving me a friendly look. How was she supposed to know now, if she had ever known then, a twenty-year-old girl who diligently wrote down whatever her energetic boss dictated, and who then immediately forgot. It was unreasonable to expect her to remember the year, let alone all those details, which not even closely-involved technicians could recall. All the same, I asked her: 'When did this wonderful prospectus appear? 1923, 1924?'

'Quite possibly,' she said, 'a lot was done, and a lot was planned, the most incredible things.'

'No,' I said, 'have a look here, look at what's printed here, minutely small, right at the bottom, almost invisible. It's the date. 1919! Nineteen hundred and nineteen! Either it was a massive bluff intended for the shareholders (although they would have known what was going on), or . . .'

'Or what?'

'Or it was simply the truth. And all those heart-breaking reports about the anger of the Allied inspectorates at German plants, including BMW and those at Oberwiesenfeld, were not true.'

'But they were true,' she said, 'only they were a bit later.'

'When?'

'Well, after this pilot . . . hold on, here's his picture.' She took an old photograph from the cabinet. I looked at it, and of course I knew who it was.

'Diemer?'

'Yes, after Diemer had won the world flying record.'

Settled at last! Diemer's world record, which admittedly was never officially recognised because a defeated Germany did not belong to the international governing body FAI (Fédération Aéronautique Internationale), was made on 9 June 1919. It was repeated on 17 June 1919 to make quite sure that the altigraph had worked properly. Diemer had taken off, secretly, so we're told, from Oberwiesenfeld with his DFW C IV (IV denoted the BMW IV engine developed from the BMW IIIa engine). He reached the previously unattained height of 9,760 metres in 87 minutes.

Of course, I knew that, I realised the significance of this flight, which has entered the annals of BMW as a kind of daring exploit. Red guards, so the story goes, had wanted to confiscate the machine and arrest the pilot, because they thought that a leading opponent of their party wanted to escape. Of course, nothing of the sort was true. The soviet-style palaver was long past, and everything took place quite legally.

What I did not know was *how* this event fitted into the sequence of all the other dates, after a deathly silence had fallen over the works.

When Popp again had the gates opened on 1 February 1919, he and his old team, headed by Friz, must have earnestly believed that the war and the post-war period would provide a smooth transition to peacetime. They were inspired by the thought that they had to get down to business again, to prove to the world that they were irreplaceable, that no one could do without them. They found the works just as they had left them, and made them flourish – to the amazement of the Hoffmann government which, admittedly, had quickly fled to Bamberg once the Bavarian soviet republic had been proclaimed. It was also to the latter's amazement.

For what was happening in the town also had the momentary capacity to shake the period to its foundations. The dictatorship of the proletariat had been proclaimed, 'a creation of independent compromisers and idealistic anarchists' as the *Red Flag* called it. The Spartacists also felt entitled to confiscate food supplies, bar entry to banks, disarm civil defence; the deputies of the soviet dictatorship demanded withdrawal from the Reich and union with Soviet Russia and soviet-style Hungary, and infiltrated barracks and factories. The BMW works remained unaffected by it all, although red guards patrolled there as well. The IIIa could still be built and the BMW IV was ready for mass-production! What could the Allied victors have to compare with the best aero-engine in the world? It was now being used for peaceful purposes, even to their profit. There were often trips to Oberwiesenfeld, where many questions were asked and many answers given. And then Diemer took the world record for flying! (He is supposed to have seen little more than a silvery haze up there; luckily he found enough oxygen, and he had found the sky above him rather black, or at least a very dark shade of blue.)

Eleven days later, 28 June 1919, the black sky that Diemer had seen above seemed to be descending and enveloping everything that had been dreamt of by designers and pilots on Oberwiesenfeld at 288 Schleißheim Street and on Moosach and Riesenfeld Streets, everything which BMW turned into reality.

The Peace of Versailles was signed by the German representatives, and article 198 of this 'Peace Treaty', which was no more than a dictated settlement, stated: 'Germany will not be allowed to keep air strike forces either on land or at sea as part of its armed forces.'

It was quite understandable that Major Siegert (the same man who had developed the American programme for the German aero-industry when the USA entered the war) should say: 'When we first read this article, we pilots stood round this monstrosity like children standing round a burning house, whose collapsing timbers had already killed the mother and father.'

What else had he expected? And what had Popp expected? Did he hope for some kind of agreement in which BMW's high aspirations (with Diemer's world record) would make an exception for the works amongst German aircraft factories? That the victor would be instructed to apply fairness, as shown in the rules of engagement which those opponents applied when relentlessly fighting each other in the skies during the last hours of the war, so that they could show they would not tolerate petty jealousies amongst competitors, hiding under the guise of military measures? Vain hopes, which article 202 of the Peace Treaty threw to the winds.

Following this, delivery of all military aero-equipment, apart from ever fewer exceptions, was required within three months. Popp discovered what this meant in practice, when he subsequently led the Allied inspectorate through the production hangars and off the catwalk (built for constant monitoring of the production line), as the gentlemen called out their orders to him through an interpreter – this one to be handed over, that one to be destroyed ... straightaway ... this minute ... (and what was officially handed over or destroyed throughout Germany amounted to 15,714 fighter and bomber aircraft, 27,757 aero-engines, 16 airships, 37 airship hangars, and millions of accessories and precision instruments).

What advantage was there in saving design drawings (which naturally also had to be handed over) in heating ducts running underneath the works? What was the good of keeping connecting rods used for making lorry engines as they could not be consigned to the cutting torch because there was not enough oxygen? (Why could not the connecting rods be put askew under the heavy press and bent? (This was later authenticated in a report by eye-witnesses.) This idea occurred to the Allied officers, but the BMW engineers made a template, laid con rods in it, brought the press hammer down, which resulted in a con rod flying out of the big pile and, thanks to the template, leaving it entirely straight.)

What good did it do? Article 201 prohibited Germany from manufacturing any kind of aircraft and engines, as well as associated parts throughout Germany for a period of six months with effect from 20 January 1920. So there was a ban on manufacture for much of 1920.

Make up for lost time, as far as possible ... think about it, but never talk about it ... do whatever you can. It was all very well saying these things, but the period had been so calculated that any company merely thinking about it would long since have stopped making payments.

What offered some kind of salvation was the shell; the shell of an impressive factory. But what was the shell of a factory without skilled workers? Those skilled workers were still there. What could be done?

This very question was being asked by an experienced foreman, the same man who had already caught the eye of the energetic 2nd Lieutenant Britsch in the quality control department. Martin Stolle, a man who before the war had learnt about engine manufacture from scratch, had trained with Métallurgique in Belgium and at a firm in Aachen, and had set up his own workshop in Feilitzsch Street in Munich. Through Otto and Baierlein, whom he often visited at Oberwiesenfeld, he came into contact with aviation, and when he was conscripted in August 1914 with his English-made Douglas (he was an enthusiastic motorcyclist, and received 1,100 marks for his Douglas, which shows how valuable an English machine was to the army at the time), he was soon transferred from the Carpathian front to the Reserve Flying Corps at Schleißheim. Here he was responsible for the daily requirements of maintaining 'ninety aircraft in the air' (he often flew in them, listened to the engines) and, without him having had any say in the matter, was 'loaned out' to the Bavarian Motor Works when these were still housed in the old Rapp Works. He had got to know Popp and Friz, the impressive Friz, who, from his place in the hangars on Moosach Street (which had been cleared out by the English), no longer had any idea as to what should or could be produced. Friz, as we have seen, had got down to designing and building an engine for lorries and for boats using the old remains of aero-engine parts which had stayed hidden in cellars, and which could still be turned to good use. That was all they had for the future.

One day Popp, Friz and Stolle drove over to Lake Walchen. An old Mercedes car from the director's fleet, which Stolle had dismantled and reassembled, needed to be tested. The desperate Popp then asked the question (Stolle remembered it quite clearly), without any of the ostentation which he subsequently showed as 'the General', but amicably, rather like speaking to an old mate.

'What are we to make? Things must go on, friends, what are we to make?'

Friz replied immediately, 'Engines for lorries and boats, of course. What else?'

Stolle shook his head. 'We must build motorcycles,' he said, 'they'll sell like hot cakes!' He told Popp how he had won third prize with his Douglas on an endurance race from Vienna to Munich over Whitsun 1914. He was thinking of the Douglas with its indestructible twin-cylinder engine.

'Good,' Popp said earnestly, 'I hereby place the order with you two . . . what am I saying? . . . with us all! . . . to develop this motorcycle engine, an air-cooled, horizontally opposed twin-cylinder.'

Friz, more embarrassed than enthusiastic, nodded. Stolle was ecstatic.

That was how motorcycle development began at BMW. Like every designer and engine builder starting with what he has at hand, Stolle stripped his Douglas (not his 1914 one; he had since acquired a new one) down to its individual parts and laid them out, down to the very last bolt, on Friz's design-room table. Each part was measured straightaway – crankshaft, connecting rods, pistons, everything.

Friz had made his aero-engines, as well as lorry engines and the boat engine with its inverter gear, all on his own. Nobody had ever (except in the most trivial things) had a part in it. He was now loathe, as Stolle suspected, to draw this engine, to have to draw it . . . not only to copy it, but to modify it, this time *not* on his own. When Stolle then went on to build from the drawings (resulting in six test engines), further modifications were necessary, which is what always happens when theory is put into practice. What came out of this was the M 2 B 15.

The first engine, carrying the number 25001, was then fitted into a Douglas frame. Stolle rode this machine on rough roads which could only be described as appalling, to the Victoria Works at Nuremberg. Here the engine was further tested (Stolle went home by train) and fitted in their own frame, and marketed as 'Victoria' with the BMW trade-mark on the crankcase. It lasted for two and a half years, although the M 2 B 15 engine, with its side valves, single carburettor and producing all of 8 hp (weighing, admittedly, only 31 kg), was far too weak to break the pre-eminent position of British motorcycles in Germany.

That Stolle, who left BMW in the middle of 1922, was to build for Victoria the first German horizontally opposed engines with overhead valves was just as unimaginable to him as it was to Popp, for whom the concept of motorcycles (until 1922) played only a minor role. But that was understandable. Everyone who could afford to rode a British machine, up to the time (and there was still competition from machines such as the sensational Megola with its five-cylinder radial engine running within the front wheel) when the new Victoria appeared with a BMW 500 cc engine improved by Stolle. (Stolle: 'It was a wonderful time, with the chance of driving along the roads at 80 kph. The engine ran very quietly. Each one was fitted with a butterfly on the exhaust which was always open when out on the main road, but which always stayed closed in built-up areas, something we had to be careful about.')

In Autumn 1921 Stolle twice succeeded in having the fastest time of the day at the six-day 'International German Road Race', and won first prize in the hill section at Königstuhl and at Karlenberg. ('With that we knew that we had built the best engine in Germany for the time.')

Such success had been anticipated. If you looked in the prospectus of 1919, there was still no mention of the M 2 B 15, and it could not be said to have brought BMW much, once it was running, except a certain fame, which the company could not live on. Orders from the Victoria were too small to keep the factory at Moosach Street running.

In short, Popp knew what to do; namely to credit Stolle with qualities that other people did not possess. This is not in dispute. Every banker, every economist liked looking further than he did, even if he was staring in the fog. Although he would have given up. Popp did not give up. Why was that? The answer was in the way his career developed. As a young engineer studying mechanical and electrical engineering at the Brno Technical High School, he had been entrusted at AEG-Union with the development of heavy electrical locomotives; at the time, the line through Mittenwald was under construction, a technical marvel. He made sure his work was not simply adequate, but superlative, so that he was allowed to be the first to drive an electric locomotive from Innsbruck to Garmisch (via Mittenwald) in 1912. One firm was involved in all this pioneering. This was Knorr Bremse AG, on whose compressed-air brakes Popp, as a test engineer, had carried out experiments.

He now remembered this company of Knorr Bremse and immediately contacted the Bavarian Railways Board (after he had discovered that his old acquaintance, Knorr Bremse AG no less, was to equip Prussian-Hessian Railways with air brakes in a ten-year programme) and acquired from Knorr Bremse the licence to build 10,000 air brakes a year for Bavarian Railways.

So Knorr Bremse moved in to Moosach Street under the sign of the white and blue propeller. The works would soon employ 1,800 men again, and BMW was once again happy at the merest idea of survival, even if it lived with a tear in one eye and a twinkle in the other.

Brake Intermezzo

'Now there are two of us who want to live off air,' Georg Knorr, the founder of that firm which now set the tone as the licencer in Moosach Street, had once said to a man who had become his tenant, and had the unusual idea of learning to fly using bamboo and sail cloth. This had taken place at Copernicus Street in Berlin on premises owned by Georg Knorr, as proprietor of Carpenter and Schulze, which had suddenly become too big for railway brakes. This was in 1894. The tenant, a boiler maker and manufacturer of fittings, was called Otto Lilienthal. Two years later, on 9 August 1896, Knorr pensively looked at the remains of the unfortunate contraption, with all its struts, which had been produced in the factory and in which Lilienthal had crashed to his death.

'Now there are two of us who want to live off air!' Popp, master of BMW and lord of a similarly largely unused, modern plant, was now similarly in a position to say to Knorr's successor, Herr J.P. Vielmetter, who controlled the destiny of the many branches established by Knorr Bremse AG and whose every yes and every no was final. He had said yes, and Popp had no doubt, in fact he knew, that the terms set by the Bavarian government for fitting Bavarian Railways with Kunze-Knorr brakes were linked to the commitment that they would also be built in Bavaria. What he did not know was that Vielmetter had more in mind than simply issuing licences for which there were no lack of offers and possibilities; in fact, the people at Knorr had an engineering firm at Frankenthal on their shortlist.

What had been the decisive factor in choosing BMW? Popp did not waste his time thinking about it; he was just glad. But was he not being too confident?

It certainly seemed that way, but this was how it was meant to turn out. The word says it all – brakes! Damn it, were not these brakes soon going to stop everything that he, Popp, and Friz, his chief engineer, and all the old technicians who had been able to keep up with brake manufacture, had put forward in the further development of BMW engines? Why did a works, which had been involved with the development and construction of aero-engines and could not give it up, have to get further involved with making compressed air brakes for railways? At least there was the M2 B15 running in the Victoria which carried the trade mark of the white and blue propeller. For the benefit

71

of Victoria, he wanted to bring the mystique of aero-engines down to ground level. Another matter was the four-cylinder lorry- and boat-engine, the M4 A1, which BMW had been able to sell with the unchallenged claim that it was 'the most successful design in modern times'. It ran in cabin cruisers as well as in buses, with customers such as the Bavarian Post Office, and benefited from all those experiences which could have been gained with understressed, high-compression aircraft engines. But what was the use of it all? Air brakes and in-house manufacture of BMW products came into conflict with each other, so much so that every BMW in-house activity stopped. Brakes had priority.

It was not just air that was lacking, but enthusiasm for carrying on at all. On the one hand, the firm was called BMW, Bavarian Motor Works; on the other hand, it was now fulfilling only Vielmetter's orders. Appointed to the supervisory board, he took over the chairmanship there and committed management, workers and office staff at BMW to producing his 'brakes'. How could he do that? Quite simply – he had acquired sole share ownership.

So was it true that Castiglioni no longer held this? Inexplicably, CC (his correspondence only ever bore these two initials) had sold off all his remaining shares in aircraft works shortly before the end of the war. Vielmetter had acquired, in addition to his own shares, all those interests in BMW from their owners dispersed throughout the land, so that he had become sole owner. Had all this been sold, or rather, flogged off (ostensibly for 28 million marks; 600,000 dollars!) to the main shareholder at Knorr Bremse, Vielmetter?

Inexplicable indeed. Who really did know the great magician? How often had his decisions appeared so contradictory and yet later proved to be right? Shrewd and clear-sighted, as when he had prophesied war, he had also assessed his own end, calculated the consequences and acted on the premise of not a moment too soon, not a moment too late.

By the time the revolution started, CC was aware, and yet unconcerned, of the danger, and had travelled to Brandenburg on the Havel. Here stood the Hansa-Brandenburg Aircraft Works, which he had bought in 1914 for the sole reason of enlisting Heinkel, who was chief designer there. He now said to Heinkel (this was how Heinkel remembered the conversation): 'Germany and Austria will be prohibited from building aircraft. All right then, but the victors do not know Germany. I know Germany. There'll be no peace in Germany. Planes will be built again. It will take a few years. But until then I shall get rid of my aircraft works. I cannot keep them if they cannot run, if you understand me. . . .'

Heinkel understood. On the next day the Hansa-Brandenburg Works were sold, and Heinkel himself accompanied Castiglioni by train (it would have been too risky to go by car, as the occupants might have been recognised and killed on the spot) to Berlin, where Hugo Stinnes approached Castiglioni in the 'Adlon' and called out: 'The Kaiser has fled! It's all over!'

On the same afternoon Castiglioni travelled to Munich, and next morning assembled the Bavarian Motor Works board, explaining that he had acquired all their shares (in addition to his, there were now Neumeyer's shares as well as those of the National Bank represented by Hjalmar Schacht since the founding of the public company), and moved back into the 'Continental' with two suitcases. As Heinkel reported what Castiglioni himself told him a number of years later, he burnt the entire contents, meaning all the BMW shares, for which he had simply had a small certificate issued to him, in the fireplace. It had apparently 'been all too much' for him. A day later he crossed Lake Constance for Switzerland.

Nothing was said to Popp, no instruction explaining the reasons behind Castiglioni's contradictory action. To wind up the material assets of one beast (the Hansa-Brandenburg Aircraft Works) in order to acquire the assets of another (BMW, aero-engine works) was then as clear as daylight to him – flying was over! The mystery was immediately solved when people suggested to Castiglioni that he did not regard the Bavarian Motor Works as an aero-engine factory any more, but as a works which was intact and would introduce motorisation, either on two or four wheels. This would doubtless start in Germany immediately after a lost war, resulting in Popp putting his old plans into practice. Could it be the case that now, in 1920, CC no longer believed that?

As someone brought up in Trieste with two loyalties (to Austro-Hungary and Italy), he had opted for Italy in 1919, where he had immediately acquired an influential position (as if it could be otherwise!) with the Fiat works, which under him had acquired shares in the Alpine Montan Company, Austria's largest iron-producing firm. At the same time, he established himself again at Austro-Daimler in Wiener Neustadt, whose products he wanted to bring to the German market, since the Austrian sales area was too small.

Naturally BMW had occurred to him, and Popp had taken over the overall marketing for Austro-Daimler cars in Germany, although he could not sell the six-cylinder ADO 617 type (with a capacity of 4.5 litres, 'one of the most remarkable cars in the early post-war years', as experts were later to declare enthusiastically) – it was too expensive. There was also not enough money for in-house motorcycle or even car production as Popp had in mind, and as long as Knorr Bremse was a tenant (a particularly solvent tenant!), there would always be a lack of facilities for manufacturing.

But that was no reason to dispose of BMW. Quite the opposite. As one of the first in Austria (like Stinnes, who had practised this in Germany), CC recognised the validity of devaluing one's own currency. He bought material assets wherever he could against large-scale credit from banks, so as to be able to pay for them with depreciating money. So was he now giving up *these* material assets in which he had invested so much, so that there was nothing left apart from money that he could receive for them?

But what was the point of pulling off such a coup? Popp seems not to have been informed, there had been no signs, so that the news hit him like a thunderbolt, with the added complication that he could have been an accessory. CC often made decisions on his own, and acted quickly, even if it was always predetermined. Distrust was not the reason why he should have deliberately kept quiet towards Popp. He had always sought Popp's advice, had trusted him. What makes a person keep a friend in the dark? Was it that he needed to make use of 'innocent dealings' in assessing new plans, so that he could be quite sure, sure of himself?

It was clear that Popp, despite being the new chairman of the supervisory board, demanding 'the fullest concentration on brake production', still managed to carry on building motorcycle engines, concluded new contracts to supply the Victoria Works in Nuremberg and even put forward the suggestion to the supervisory board that complete motorcycles or even small cars should be built. That was naturally rejected. Popp did not object, either, when he learnt that another project had been rejected, which was to build engines for the German car industry. Had he hoped for anything different? What had he expected to gain from it? What was the good of provoking the bull? Was it to wear down the contracted partner? He was the one who had the upper hand. It was useless.

No, Knorr Bremse and BMW were not to be reconciled, Vielmetter had known that for a long time.

Nineteen twenty-two had arrived, inflation was on the way up, on 2 January the dollar stood at 1,888, the mark was practically valueless abroad. What happened next revealed that Castiglioni's withdrawal in May 1920 (which may well have prompted him to sell BMW) was part of a single strategy – to propel BMW over the abyss which lay between war and peace, and to which countless companies (in which CC had considerable interests) had fallen victim. But he was attached to this company. I can no more prove this than I can disprove it.

In Vienna there was a count by the name of Sascha Kolowrat, a real man-about-town who knew everyone and everything, who had made himself known in the film industry (he had set up the firm of Sascha Film Industry PLC.) He was also an enthusiastic motor racing driver. As one of Porsche's friends (Porsche was the managing director at Austro-Daimler) he was, of course, also a visitor at CC's town house in Prince Eugen Street. Here he met Popp, who immediately recognised the possibilities contained in that small sports car which Porsche had designed for Kolowrat (a racing car with an engine size of only 1100 cc. Kolowrat had baptized it 'Sascha' and emerged the victor (for this small class) in almost every race, even in the most famous, such as the Targa Florio in Sicily. Popp ran his eyes over it. Was not this the car which, quite apart from its sporting qualities, was seen as a real miracle of speed, reliability and economy, especially in impoverished Germany? They had the vision. BMW could build it, could mass-produce it in place of the Austro-Daimler, which under Porsche's obsession with change (Castiglioni feared this like the plague) was certainly never going to be a mass-produced car.

Castiglioni pricked up his ears, when Popp suggested this to him.

'Mass-produced?'

'Mass-produced,' said Popp.

'And what about Knorr Bremse?'

'We'll leave them where they are.'

'What about BMW?'

'We'll buy them out. That means *you*, as the Commercial Adviser, will buy the firm, buy the name back . . .'

Castiglioni was silent.

'. . . And transfer it to another firm, which you will also buy.'

'And is there such a firm?'

'Yes, at Oberwiesenfeld. A stone's throw away from Moosach Street. In fact you know it. It's up for sale, since it's almost bankrupt. It's called BAW!'

'Start negotiating to buy it,' said Castiglioni (thinking at the same time how quickly the mark was falling).

'With Bavarian Aircraft Works?'

'And with Knorr Bremse, of course.'

Transplantation

Karl Kraus once said in the *Fackel* newspaper: 'One always has the feeling with Castiglioni that he could carry off Vienna in his aeroplane, that he could fly it to the stars and conclude a business contract with them.'

The people at Knorr must have had a similar feeling when Franz Josef Popp appeared at the headquarters of his current employer in the Lichtenburg suburb of Berlin and made an astonishing offer on behalf of Castiglioni. He, Castiglioni, wanted to buy BMW back.

What, were they supposed to give up their factory at 80 Moosach Street in Oberwiesenfeld and transfer brake manufacture to goodness knows where?

Popp shook his head. They would not have to give up anything. Everything would stay as before. There was only one thing they would have to give up – BMW.

But they said that BMW was Knorr Bremse, since it involved management, all the workers and office staff, all the halls and factory installations, every square metre of the 25 hectares including railway sidings, gas pipes and so forth.

The purchaser did not want any of that, or at least hardly any of it, Popp said; not a square metre out of the entire 25 hectares, not a stone out of a hall, not a brick out of the factory buildings, offices, and company housing which he, Popp, had once had built, not a piece of iron from the sidings, not a metre of gas piping, and so on, nothing except one or two things which would, it was true, only disrupt air brake production; except perhaps a few machines which had been used for building BMW engines or raw materials for them, equipment for the engine test bed and test runs, the hardening shop, when it was not being used for hardening tools within the company.

So everything had been settled then?

And as part of the forge and the aluminium foundry there would be three smelting ovens, two moulding machines; otherwise nothing. Castiglioni only wanted to buy BMW, the name, the symbol. With its patents pending, other patents, drawings and designs. And, of course, he also wanted certain people who were under obligation to the name, the sign, whose release was vital. Friz, for example, the designer, was one of them, as was he, Popp, along with the other member of the present board, Strauss, a few foremen and engine builders, a few dozen experts. . . .

76

They looked at him quite taken aback. So the basis for all this was something quite immaterial . . . 'It's really all to do with the name?'

Popp nodded.

'And what is it worth to the purchaser?'

'Here is the contract of purchase. The sum has been entered. You will see that Castiglioni is not mean.'

Indeed, Castiglioni had never been mean. Sometimes it was his style to throw money out of the window, but he had once said to Heinkel, when he was just starting out, that it would all come back of its own accord. Now he had risen to be master of an industrial and financial empire which would soon become difficult to manage. Did this 'style' have any power? Well, not on its own. BMW was a precisely defined mass in the galaxy of this empire, as it was later to prove, and CC knew exactly what he was doing. It would cost money, a lot of money, but it would repay itself.

He had offered 75 million marks for BMW, for the word, the symbol (the extras could be forgotten, though the men could not be, as they could not be found even for money). Out of this sum, 10 million was to paid by cheque immediately, on signature of the agreement. Popp had even brought the cheque with him.

So BMW left – with nothing but its name – the white and blue propeller, around which the famous letters were grouped, and with little more than a wheelbarrow-full of utensils, a few machine tools, parts from the hardening shop (which Knorr Bremse did not need for hardening their own tools), a few workpieces from the forge, half a dozen tables and cupboards from the design office, from the patent department and from the engine library. They went through the gate of the factory at 80 Moosach Street, which had now lost its name, did not look back, looked straight ahead of them, moved across to Milbertshofen and turned into the beginning of Neulerchenfeld Street.

Neulerchenfeld Street (which later changed its name to Lerchenau Street) at that time bounded a plot of land which, as a collection of cabbage gardens, old sheds and the occasional arbour on the left hand side, gloried in its own unsightliness, while everything on the right hand side was like the end of the world. For what spread out from there was an exercise ground with no trees or shrubbery, like all exercise grounds; this was Oberwiesenfeld, where generations of pioneers, artillery and infantry men had been slave-driven. Here, too, was where an airstrip had been, over which a man called Diemer had blazed the first vapour trails Munich had ever seen.

It was quite a while before a fence was seen. Behind the fence lay flat sheds, one as monotonous as the next. On one of them, which stuck out because it looked like an old barn, an inscription, which had been painted over several times, shone through. A trained eye could still decipher it: GUSTAV OTTO, AIRCRAFT WORKS. Then came quite an attractive, stone building with two floors and a protruding portal. Next to it was a gate with a name-plate hung over it. A man was in the process of painting over it. The old writing could still be clearly seen, showing how he had made an A (in the middle) into an M. He carefully removed AIRCRAFT and inserted the word MOTOR in its place. The whole inscription now read: BAVARIAN MOTOR WORKS PLC.

The most important part in the terms of sale between Herr Camillo Castiglioni (called the buyer) and the Bavarian Motor Works (called the vendor) was paragraph 11. This stated the following:

The vendor undertakes, in pursuance of the buyer's wishes, to change the firm Bavarian Motor Works PLC' in the shortest possible time and at a moment stipulated by the buyer, in such a way that the name 'Motor' disappears from the firm and that no name is adopted in which the word 'Motor', 'Motors' or similar is contained. They further undertake to ensure that no steps are in any way taken to prevent the buyer, or any company chosen by the latter, from adopting the company name 'Bavarian Motor Works'.

In the terms of the contract, the qualifying day was 20 May 1922. On that day, when the agreed sum fell due, of which, as we know, only 10 million marks had been paid, both vendor and buyer would have found it very unpleasant to glance at the exchange rates. Anger and shame counteracted each other. Inflation, however, had not yet peaked, not by a long chalk.

For a time the factory at 80 Moosach Street, where now only Kunze-Knorr air brakes were produced, had no name. In an extraordinary general meeting attended by F.J. Popp, who was still on the board (wound up ten days later in the register of companies), the decision was taken on 6 July 1922 to give the works the name of SÜDBREMSE AG. It is still called that today.

Things were going rather better for the vendor of the premises which BMW occupied – the Bavarian Aircraft Works. As early as November 1921, Castiglioni had acquired a majority shareholding there. In yellowing papers I have deciphered the following details: sale of the shares presently in the company's possession at an amount of 1,250,000 marks, at par and from 1,138,000 marks, shares held by Darmstädter Bank, to which were added 'as expected' the remaining shares at any amount of 612,000 marks held by the Maschinenfabrik Augsburg-Nürnberg (MAN). The sale was completed in May 1922. The sale price was 8 million marks (the dollar was at 250 marks), of which 1 million marks (= 4,000 dollars) was paid, the rest being written off to inflation.

On 5 June 1922 the capital was increased to 80 million marks at the AGM, and the decision taken to change the company name to 'Bavarian Motor Works Public Limited Company' (as entered in the register of companies on 17 July 1922). Company president Camillo Castiglioni, Vienna, was listed as the only shareholder. The 'company's activities' were agreed to be the following: 'Manufacture and marketing of engines and all vehicles thus equipped, as well as of accessories and all products in the engineering, metallurgical and wood industries.'

At the same time, 7 March 1916, the day when the Bavarian Aircraft Works PLC appeared in the register of companies, was set as BMW's founding date, with no acknowledgement made to Gustav Otto's contributions – simply because the area and the portfolio (what a beautiful word that is in the language of business!) had been taken over.

The Bavarian Aircraft Works would never have been founded if Gustav Otto had not existed. He was the son of the inventor Nikolaus August Otto, who created the four-stroke engine and with it triggered off a development which was to change the world and human life far more radically than any wars or ideologies – changes which can now be described because BMW had a part in them. Gustav Otto can confidently be described as BMW's founding father.

There, where in 1910 his biplanes rolled out onto Oberwiesenfeld from the first wooden sheds bearing the inscription 'Gustav Otto Aircraft Works', BMW finally came to settle.

A new phase was beginning.

A Deceptive Peace
1922–1933

Birth of the R 32

The customary view was that a young man after the First World War, especially if he came from a middle-class background, was either involved in saving the Fatherland (so taking part in the counter-revolution), or was caught up in the 'roaring twenties' during that extraordinary time between the Reichs. This was the time when there were never endless parliamentary debates, crises of government, no Ruhr occupation, etc., where millions were not starving, where inflation did not deprive millions of their savings and their last possessions, and where the future did not appear grey, but full of promise.

Of course, none of this is true. Neither was political involvement symptomatic of the times for a young generation which had escaped the war of its fathers unscathed, nor was the stereotyped image of the 'roaring twenties', in which people were heady with the joy of life, applicable. 'I hate politics and the belief in politics, because it makes people so arrogant, doctrinaire, hard-headed and inhuman,' Thomas Mann revealed in his *Thoughts of an Unpolitical Person* in 1918. And when he actively approved of republican democracy a few years later, then one thing was made patently clear to young people who still could not make up their mind where to channel their energies. Politics was out. 'We young students,' wrote Hannah Arendt, 'did not read papers at that time. George Grosz's caricatures did not strike us as satires but as realistic reports. We knew these types – they lived all around us. Were we to mount the barricades for them?'

They did not mount the barricades. Where did they go then in the search for reality, outside politics, which could offer nothing real? The technical high schools, for example, were full to overflowing. Was technology closer to reality than anything else? A young man called Rudolf Schleicher thought it definitely was.

He was a student at the Technical High School in Munich, specialising in mechanical engineering in his fourth year, aged twenty-five, and was close to taking his final exam. On a Friday evening at the Automobile Club (Friday evening was when they met), he happened to be sitting next to Max Friz, chief designer at BMW, who was said to be on the point of solving design problems which would make a drivable, saleable vehicle out of even the most unusable motorcycle. Schleicher, who was as tall as a tree and a head taller than Friz (who was not exactly short himself), involuntarily pricked up his ears when he heard Rudolf Reich, a racing driver he had befriended, say: 'By the way, Max, if you're looking for an assistant, this young man would like to be your man – but he cannot, because he carries his head rather high!'

Now for the first time, Friz had a good look at the 'young man', who could not have been much older than Reich, and enquired about his degree work, about his passions – which were motorcycles, of course. At this time Schleicher rode an English Douglas which was more home-made than original, and whose peculiarity of breaking away on bends he had tried to solve by changing the wheelbase and the engine's centre of gravity. 'So,' said Friz, 'does it work now?'

'Yes, it works,' said Schleicher. 'In a fortnight I'm taking it to Daglfing,' by which he meant the trotting course where the Munich Automobile Club organised races, which were already pulling huge crowds.

'Good,' said Friz, 'then start applying for jobs. . . . How silly of me, wait until you've got your degree. When will that be?'

Schleicher would have loved to have said 'Immediately!', but answered instead that he would have done all the theoretical work by the end of the year, and then he could come. He almost took it all back, when, on Friz's invitation a week later, he saw the site of his future work. What he saw took his breath away. Behind the administration building and another building made of stone, flanking the main entrance, lay a field. No factory, just a field, on which seventeen, single-storey wooden hangars were dotted, better described as sheds (which is what they were, old aircraft sheds) than workshops. A man called Martin Duckstein, whom Friz had taken as his right-hand man, explained to Schleicher in a gently ironical voice everything the latter did *not* see. They had now reached a spot where builders were just beginning to pour in the foundations around a number of closely packed sheds or, where this had already been done, to lay stones. Simply walling in the wooden sheds, Duckstein explained, would produce the main section here, a gigantic hall with a surrounding walkway which would simply be hung from the roof trusses so that production would not be disrupted. Once everything had been walled in, the partitioning walls would be knocked down, and everything would be complete! Then aero-engine production, component manufacture for motorcycle production, the automation area and complete gear-wheel manufacture would follow.

Schleicher rubbed his eyes. So this was the way things were going! All he had seen at first was air. Were they pulling his leg? No, the man taking him around seemed to be quite serious. A section of the walkway had already been hung as if from a gallows. 'Impressive, don't you think?' said Duckstein. Schleicher nodded. He could not have wished for a less impressive construction.

When he landed up again in the modest room called the design department, Friz started explaining, with the aid of the design sheet, that the 'test' (he meant the test department) would be housed on level ground (as far as was practical) – if anyone banged on the floor here, this would mean 'fetch the designs!' for the people below. This was to be the job of the future detail designer, i.e. Schleicher. Schleicher, who had greeted every remark with astonishment, now laughed for the first time. The designs could not have got very far, as the room was nowhere large enough to accommodate even a half-decent drawing board; in fact, he could not see one.

He only later discovered that Friz had made a virtue out of necessity – he was designing at home in Riesenfeld Street just round the corner, where he worked secretly in the guests' room, which no one was allowed to enter.

No, you get no marks for courage. But Schleicher liked the fact that everyone in his own way saw the primitiveness that was reigning here as a pioneer existence, and no one doubted for a moment that something extraordinary was being thought up. He also liked the fact that the people he had been thrown together with were all young – Duckstein in his early thirties, and a man called Sepp Hopf, a natural phenomenon in 'tests', who was a trained cobbler and could analyse the combustion noises in a cylinder head like a lung specialist listening to lungs, was not much older than Schleicher himself. Only Friz, who was approaching his forties, seemed rather sedate. They were all enthusiastic for their cause, even if they did not show it, a team giving the impression that something was being done.

Rudolf Schleicher, as a graduate from the technical high school, could not begin to imagine how much had already been done since they had moved there.

The huge mortgage had been paid off. Then there had been the 'Flink' motorcycle, with a single-cylinder, two-stroke engine which was a kind of predecessor of what is now known as a 'moped'. Gustav Otto's epicyclic-gear 'Flyaway' motorcycle, which plied the streets of Munich, was scarcely a competitor. They had also succeeded in transforming sheet metal and plywood (hoarded materials for building aircraft, which had escaped the notice of the Allied inspectorate) into tool cabinets and office furniture, and to offer them around BMW branches.

Included in the estate was an almost unsaleable motorcycle called the 'Helios', which was stored in considerable numbers in the wooden hangars. Homer tells us that the sun-god Helios rose every morning from a beautiful, quiet bay on the Oceanus. Friz, however, did not think that this motorcycle had much chance of matching the sun god; only a tightrope walker could ride it.

This had not cut much ice with Popp.

'We can't afford to throw away our assets. Either redesign this cycle so that it can be sold honourably, or we really will have to flog it off to tightrope walkers!'

That struck home. Infuriated at having to waste his skills on a worthless object (he, Friz, could end up by losing his reputation as an aero-engine designer), his thrifty Swabian nature was at odds with the designer in him, since there was no doubt that there was still a part of his own engineering work in the 'Helios', with which, God only knew, he had not been involved. Based on the aircraft building principle of 'have airframe, will fit engine!', the Bavarian Aero-engine Works had built the M2 B15 engine longitudinally (with V-belt drive to the rear wheel) into their 'Helios', as befitted the motorcycle frame which they had developed. This was the engine recovered by BMW for their Victoria.

An exciting week went by in which Popp only occasionally saw his chief designer. The latter was sullen, remarkably irritable, and only to be spoken to on sufferance. Popp recognised that this happened whenever Friz was on the point of abandoning everything, just when he was getting close to finding 'the answer'. This time was no different. Emerging from his cloister in Riesenfeld Street (Popp had kindly had coal delivered there again so that he would not be cold), Friz presented his salvation for the 'Helios' on a roll of paper. He insisted that nothing had basically changed, although he had to admit to having altered the frame and steering to the extent that the engine was now half correctly positioned, meaning that the whole thing was at least saleable and that no one need feel ashamed. He hesitated a moment. He was still harbouring something. A thought had occurred.

'A new engine?' asked Popp.

'A new motorcycle,' said Friz.

Schleicher had heard of that but had refrained from asking questions which obviously involved company secrets. Neither Friz nor Duckstein said a word, nor did Franz Bieber whom, as always, he met on Friday at the Automobile Club.

At that time, Bieber's place was at the other end of the table. He was the Club's sports director, and after the war had revived the ACM (Automobile Club Munich), which was then little more than a 'Munich Cycle Club' founded in the Bauerngirgl inn in 1904 as a kind of protective society for motorcyclists at a time when 'users and patrons' of cars mainly belonged to the 'landed and influential classes', while the motorcyclist, as a member of the deprived middle classes, obtained 'no decisive help from above', subjected, as he was, particularly by country people, to all sorts of difficulties, 'preferably in the form of beatings', as the Club's history relates. All that had now changed. . . .

Bieber, a racing driver like Reich, was more involved in freelance work for BMW than as a regular 'test driver'. For the benefit of comparisons, he had organised two annual meetings – the holding of the 'Club Championship between Moosburg and Landshut' and the other 'Race through the Bavarian Mountains', which Max Friz completed without any penalty points, three days after finishing his 'R 32' (as the new motorcycle was called).

In 1979, a full generation later, I visited Bieber in Garmisch. His house on Market Square was crammed with trophies. Protected under glass from the dust were cups and miniature reproductions of famous racing machines which he had ridden. The walls were covered with photographs, plaques of hill-climbing races and design drawings (Bieber held a lot of patents). From the window I looked out onto a crossing, where (before it had acquired tarmac and traffic lights) the 'Race through the Bavarian Mountains' had once passed over.

Bieber was by no means an old man. I had noticed a white car parked outside his house – it was not a BMW, but a Mercedes. He got into it as

I was leaving. It was a beautiful day in March, he wanted to travel through the Ötz valley to Obergurgl.

We had previously spoken about Friz. And, of course, about him, Bieber. And about the birth of the R 32.

Bieber said that a lot had been written about it which was both true and false. He said he had read almost all of it, and most of it was false; the little that was right being only of value inasmuch as it explained the phenomenon (and what a phenomenon it had been!) of a machine that they had suddenly come up with, which for over thirty, forty, fifty years (indeed, right up to today) had held up well in its basic design and proved itself resilient.

And, I interjected, had experienced all the stages characteristic of a great idea, from scornful dismissal to deep-seated scepticism, to which it, or rather Friz, was subjected, until its first world record won by Henne at the end of the decade.

'By then it was called the R 37 and was fitted with an aluminium cylinder head with overhead valves which Schleicher had made, the first BMW motorcycle engine with overhead valves,' said Bieber. It was essentially the original model from 1922 that he had first seen on paper when Friz had invited him to Riesenfeld Street, to that house still standing today where Kurt Deby, who had been works manager after 1945, now lives.

'I have been to see Deby,' I said. 'Was it the same house?'

'Yes. We went round there, it was winter. I remember it well. It was bitterly cold, although not upstairs – there was a cylindrical stove and a drawing-board as long and wide as a farm table. It almost completely filled the room. Friz was working at the drawing-board, which was covered with a sheet of paper, all smooth and white, a great, big piece of white paper as large as two bed sheets. There he was, drawing away, as if unveiling a monument, quite unceremoniously, and then he looked up at me. "What do you think?"

'Well, what could I say? Here was the whole new motorcycle on a piece of paper, from wheel to wheel, life-size. He had worked it out all on his own, and designed it down to the very last detail, every bolt, every spoke had been drawn in, in what must have been less than four or five weeks. It was quite different from anything else around at the time. The cylinders were mounted transversely; there was no chain, but a drive shaft, which was not new . . . but this isn't the time to go into all that. Oh, and, of course, a tubular frame, everything faired-in, engine and gearbox as one unit.

'We then compared it on the road with all the other possible types, with Friz also riding (he was a brilliant motorcycle rider, but no racing cyclist!). Then I tested an English machine, a trial model. I went for it, as people say nowadays. But as an old hand I thought I knew all about these machines, like this new one. And yet everything worked, even what I hadn't been sure about – Friz had managed to mount the transversely-opposed engine so that both cylinders had air blowing over them. One thing that really took my breath away was the "concept" of everything being logical, organic, simple. . . . It was amazing that something I could see in front of me on paper had not been on the road for a long time since. But would it work?

'Six months later "the thing" was all finished and ready to roll. I parked the English machine in the corner, and got on the "new" one. Friz rode on it, then I took over again. And so it went on, until another six months later it was ready for production.'

Technical history is as bare as a design drawing. It defies description, and we can only appreciate its existence and the creative thought behind it by an invention's effectiveness. Bieber's account reflected what he felt when he first saw Friz's design. He did not fully realise its significance until later when he rode the machine for himself, took it on 'test', and when it finally proved itself as the most successful motorcycle design in the world at the time. Long afterwards someone involved in technology, who was then still a young man and who was passionately keen to become a mechanical engineer, turned to Max Friz on his eightieth birthday and said: 'Whoever browses through the history of technology will soon discover an astonishing similarity to the development of a living organism. In both, there are lengthy phases of evolution, and then, quite suddenly, metamorphoses and major developments. Lucky is the engineer who has been able to inspire such a metamorphosis at a crucial moment. If one looks over Friz's life as a designer, there were at least four such crucial moments.'

Helmut-Werner Bönsch had praised him and enumerated the following: the 1914 Grand Prix engine (which won the French Grand Prix in a Lautenschlager, Friz's first 'feat' with Daimler in Untertürkheim); then the 1919 BMW IV high-altitude engine (with which Diemer won the high-altitude record); the 1923 BMW R 32 motorcycle; and, as the fourth vital moment, the 1926 BMW VI 12-cylinder aero-engine which, as a water-cooled engine, became the most widely built BMW aero-engine and introduced a new era in the conquest of the skies.

Are these grand words? I do not think so. Friz himself was too modest to claim them for himself. He never spoke about the ideas for his successes. Only once did he give voice to this thoughts, when somebody claimed that his first horizontally-opposed, twin-cylinder engine, as fitted to the R 32 (shaft drive, engine and gearbox combined in a flush-fitting block, tubular frame), had already been developed by Porsche working at Daimler, with Friz's assistance, and then had been left on one side as interest in motorcycle production had been abandoned.

Quite apart from the fact that Porsche had only joined Daimler in the twenties (in 1923 when Castiglioni showed him the door at Austro-Daimler in Wiener Neustadt), Friz, in his time at Untertürkheim, had never been involved in motorcycle engines. His brief report makes the position clear. Over and above this, it explains how an invention 'comes about', how it appears as a challenge, one which is often brought about through force of circumstance and which dramatically finds its way into the history books. Just as one thought leads on to a second, and one limb follows the next, one step inevitably determines the next step. I am doing this, I must do that, I am doing that, then this . . . until the rule that had determined everything up till then breaks down. No inspiration striking like lightning. A cause, an offence. This is my goal, here is where I start off from. Nothing in between should distract me; everything must tie in and be feasible. Advantages should not fight shy of disadvantages, and no disadvantage should outweigh an advantage.

Friz wrote:

In the Otto Aircraft Works [by which he meant the Bavarian Aircraft Works at Neulerchenfeld Street, which BMW took over] there had been small-scale motorcycle production in the management garage. As the operating capital supplied by Herr Castiglioni had largely been devalued by inflation, our workforce only had available the materials acquired from this motorcycle production and the materials of the 'Flink' and 'Helios' motorcycles for rebuilding BMW. Popp, as managing director, first commissioned me to rebuild the Helios motorcycle so that it would be saleable. As Herr Popp could no longer manage with the price of the M2 B15 engine at the Victoria works in Nuremberg, he said to me, 'Friz, we'll just make a few small steel tubes ourselves.' He commissioned me to provide suggestions for a new BMW motocycle.

Since we already had the 500-cc horizontally-opposed engine, this should be used. But as the rear cylinder in a horizontally-opposed engine gets too hot, which was the case in the English Douglas as well as the Victoria machine, I suggested mounting the engine transversely. To that was added a shaft drive, because even on a chain-driven machine, a pair of bevel-drive gears would have been needed. As we still had not got an established design office at the Otto Works, I saw through the design for the motorcycle in my house at 34 Riesenfeld Street. The design was often discussed with Herr Popp until its form was approved by him. Following from that, the motorcycle was designed in detail.

Three days after finishing the motorcycle, I entered the Race through the Bavarian Mountains on the cycle, which I completed without any penalty points.

To this he added: 'As we later discovered, the English ABC motorcycle also had the transversely-mounted, horizontally-opposed engine. Before our production, we had never seen or possessed an ABC motorcycle.'

It must have been a heavy blow for Friz when his motorcycle, after reportedly being thronged by fans and sceptics alike at the Paris Motor Show in 1923, should then fail at the very place he then (not without some trepidation) sent it to – to Stuttgart for the Solitude. Friz knew the course. He came from Stuttgart, and was aware that this was where it all mattered. He had had the racing machine fitted with special steel cylinders and overhead valves. Too hastily and inadequately thought out, the engine could not take it, and broke down with piston seizure. So BMW lost the meeting, and lost it resoundingly – all the more so (which might have lessened the disgrace) because it was not against any foreign competition that had escaped post-war problems and inflation, but against a German design, which had clearly proved to be superior, not least because it developed 4 more hp.

It was called 'Victoria', and the man who had built it was a BMW engineer.

Popp and Friz had reluctantly let him go, although he had wanted to. His name was Martin Stolle.

Being just as determined as he was sensitive, Stolle had no longer been able to put up with Friz's tutelage ('he wanted to do everything himself,' he told me as late as 1980), had fallen out with him ('because every innovation which I introduced was publicly attributed to Friz') and had joined a Munich precision-engineering company in 1922 with the instruction to build motorcycle engines. He was successful, with his very first test engine fitted into a Victoria frame, which straightaway produced a reading of 8 hp on the test bed, 1½ hp more than the BMW engine. So in July 1922 he went to see Avus in Berlin, at a time when the R32 had not even entered Friz's mind.

In Autumn 1922, somewhat earlier than planned, Rudolf Schleicher, a recently qualified enginner, joined BMW as a detail designer.

'I shall never forget the day,' he told me, 'when Friz brought in the drawing. He came in with a 2-metre-long drawing with the entire R 32 motorcycle on it. There, he said, you can now enter the specifications. Duckstein was in charge of that, but everyone was allowed to draw something. I did the cylinder head. . . .' Schleicher still believes today that the R 32 was only built because of Stolle and his competing engine, 'because when this engine proved to be better for Victoria, everyone at Nuremberg forgot about fitting the M2 B15. That was when BMW lost its main customer and could not find any more business other than for the complicated Helios.'

Schleicher threw himself into helping the R 32 to break through. Even as a rider.

'Fortunately or unfortunately, Friz did not let me ride in the Solitude. When the steel cylinders failed there, I was glad I had not gone along . . . although I was deeply upset. I had all kinds of successes, I had won every winter race from 1919 to 1923.'

He pushed his little black book, in which he had carefully recorded all the dates, races, successes and failures, to one side and laughed out loud.

'But, of course, I did not mind resting on my laurels a bit, until Frau Friz, who had been at every race, said to me, without consulting her husband: "Schleicher, *you* must ride next year!" Which is what I did, with Bieber and Reich . . . the three of us.'

That sounded very easy. But it was not so simple. Dates only reveal how far things have got when there is a struggle going on behind the scenes. A struggle for time, which no one had. Everyone knew that the next Solitude Race would be decisive, to show the superiority of Friz's machine or to give Victoria a lead which would be difficult to recapture.

The old dictum of the right man being in the right place at the right time fully applied to Schleicher and BMW's situation, when, as a trainee engineer under his instructors Friz and Duckstein, he realised that a new idea was vital to solve the dilemma. It was then that he got the idea which was to solve everything, and he told the others on 23 October 1922. That was the day when he presented his design diagram at the office. It showed a new cylinder head, the first light-metal cylinder head ever designed for a motorcycle, which had sealed and lubricated overhead valves. Time was now on their side.

Victoria was still superior over the next year – but only for a year. Schleicher had entered the winter race to Garmisch at the beginning of February 1923, with the road under snow and the thermometer reading minus 17 degrees, with the old steel cylinders ('Why?' 'Quite simply because the new light-metal cylinder head was not ready!'). He was first to Garmisch in a time previously considered impossible, of 1 hour 56 minutes. ('The fastest motorcyclist! The second fastest vehicle of the day – only one car went faster. From Weilheim on, I had left all the competitors behind with only wooden carts and level crossings ahead of me. Unfortunately, I could never open up the engine fully, fearing possible piston seizure, and so rode at three-quarter power, briefly making two stops . . . everything was warm, except my ice-cold face . . . The next day I had a clear run in the mountain section because I had started first, and I recorded the fastest time. . . .')

Three months later, on 19 May, the time had come for the Solitude! A racing engine with overhead valves, the M2 B36, specially developed for racing, had been fitted to all three BMW cycles, which Schleicher, Reich and Bieber took to the start. Schleicher's light-metal cylinder head settled the outcome. The BMW team won the three classes (it was still possible at the time to be mentioned in several classes!). In addition, Reich had the best time of the day. 'The new machine, called the R 37, developed 20 hp,' a report briefly stated. 'It pulled away from all the other competitors.'

This they continued doing at almost every race (the Schleizer Triangular Race, the Eifel Mountain Race, the Eilenriede Race in Hanover, the German Road Championship, the German Grand Prix, the Avus Race in Berlin), with the old triumvirate of Reich, Bieber and Schleicher and with Toni Bauhofer, Paul Köppen, Peppi Stelzer and all the other young men, whose passion it was to come out with new times Sunday after Sunday at different venues, in front of people squatting in ditches or sitting in stands on the home straight. They would suddenly leap up, as if electrified, when the favourites came roaring up, and would wave and shout as soon as they recognised man and machine. It was days like these, as if comets were flying past, which gave a new dimension to a rather drab existence, given how grey and poor it was, not to mention the general political and national despondency. 'Speed' was not the only explanation. Those aesthetics which an Italian Futurist had conjured up out of 'the beauty of speed' ('A racing car whose bodywork is adorned with huge tubes looking like fire-breathing snakes . . . a roaring car, which seems to run like a rocket, is more beautiful than the goddess Nike of Samothrace. . .') were actually much more down-to-earth, as expressed in the following words written by an Englishman in 1926:

> The most interesting machine by far in the whole competition was the German BMW, with its horizontally-opposed, twin-cylinder engine mounted transversely in the frame, with a fully enclosed valve mechanism, unitary construction, and shaft drive. After the toughest days in the field, we could not find a single oil leak, the machine was beautifully quiet, and

seemed to possess great reserves of power. From a design point of view, it is miles ahead of any British machine.' (Professor A.M. Low in the magazine *Auto-Cycle Union*)

It was Schleicher again who had inspired these sentences, exhibiting enough abandon to slaughter the holy cows of England – motorcycle building and motorcycle racing. As a private entrant, he and his friend Fritz Roth had ventured onto the island with their R 37 machines to take part in that toughest of events, the Six-day Race. By the time they noticed that they would probably not get through without off-road tyres, it was too late. They had not brought any with them. Scouring workshop after workshop, they kept coming up against the same answer – there were no off-road tyres anywhere in England. Whether by chance or design, they just had to accept it. They were almost laughed out of the race when they arrived at the start with low tyre pressures. When Schleicher crossed the finishing line, he had won the gold medal.

It was essentially still the same old R 32 which had deserved its gold medal and would again do so when, in 1929, in an attempt on the ground speed record when the open road was discovered to be a wind tunnel, the motorcycle was fitted with streamlining and a compressor. This was the machine on which Henne again beat the record in 1932, taking it away from the English with a top speed of 244.399 kph.

In the 'Cold Home'

The maxim 'The economy is the key' (inverting that Napoleonic statement that politics is the key) has been attributed to Walther Rathenau, the foreign secretary in the Weimar Republic, who was murdered by national extremists. What Rathenau had meant by that, as he saw salvation in the 'world union, leading to a complete community of production and economy', took no longer than the end of the decade to make itself known, when the world economic order collapsed. It hit Germany harder than any other country. The economy as the key proved to be a bitter truth, even the bitterest of truths, which the peace imposed by the victorious powers at the 'Peace of Versailles' ignored, just as much as the actions of the Reich Bank president, Rudolf von Havenstein, when, supposedly motivated by economic legitimacy, he flooded the country in 1922–3 with worthless paper money. At the time, price tags registered figures in hundreds of millions, as 300 paper factories and 150 presses worked day and night until the circulation of money and the range of goods for sale had become poles apart, and the balance of payments between Germany and the rest of the world had collapsed like a house of cards.

'The systematic expropriation of the German middle class, not brought about by a socialist government, but in a bourgeois state which had proclaimed the protection of private property on its banners, was an unprecedented event. It was one of the greatest swindles in world history,' the historian Arthur Rosenberg wrote about the inflation.

It is equally clear that industry, represented by men such as Stinnes and Castiglioni, was heavily implicated in this swindle, since it was such men who bought up assets, paid back their debts and charges with devalued money, and so created gigantic industrial empires, with the full complicity of the state. Industry got rich at the expense of the ever-shrinking real wages of its workers (nine or ten hours work were needed just to buy a pound of margarine!), at the expense of middle class savings accounts, government bonds and debentures, which had suddenly become worthless. Although the state denied this, it at least got rid of its internal debts at the cost of the middle class's trust – even if settling the external debt, which was very much linked to the word 'reparations', could not be contemplated.

Numbered amongst Castiglioni's possessions (which he would one day lose in the same way that he had acquired them) was, as we know, BMW.

However, anyone thinking that the financier of the Bavarian Motor Works, that legendary CC in far off Vienna, had dressed his favourite child, BMW, in silk and satin could not be more wrong. There was hardly anywhere in post-war Germany where things were more spartan than in Lerchenau Street in Munich. Economy after economy was made. And when they had to let a man like Martin Stolle go, then it ultimately all boiled down to the same reason why Daimler had given Max Friz his marching orders in 1917 – because he had asked for a 50-marks pay rise. By so doing, though, they had merely lost him to BMW.

What BMW lost in Stolle is difficult to assess. As a ninety-four-year-old man, whom I had looked up at Marktoberndorf in the Allgäu, he remembered having been very annoyed over the refusal to pay less than 100 marks in expenses which he wanted to have refunded for some trip. It was then that his resentment had bubbled up. It is almost certainly the case that Stolle's car, which created a sensation in 1925 at the Berlin Motor Show (it had a sliding valve engine and was the first car in the world with a box section chassis), would have helped BMW to build cars much sooner than in fact they did, when fully three years later it began duplicating through its manufacture under licence of the English Austin Seven.

But who has the power to predict the future? It was not a pleasure making economies (quite apart from the notorious meanness of the Swabian chief designer); economies were made because there was not enough to go around. Schleicher reported that the 'test department', which he took over, did not even have a simple welding machine, and that Friz had merely grumbled when he spoke to him about this: 'Why do you want one?' If humour was black, it did not come blacker. An article which I found in the newspaper *Münchner Neueste Nachrichten* also had no effect on the situation. It said in July 1923:

> A business of the importance of the Bavarian Motor Works should not fail to make its company report public, even if the AGM has taken place in Berlin. According to the balance sheet published in the Government Gazette, after subtracting 282.6 million marks for general costs and 105.9 million marks depreciation from the gross profit of 477.4 million marks, there was shown to be a net profit of 89.4 million marks. . . .'

A net profit of 89.4 million marks – but what did that mean at a time when the dollar (in July 1923) already cost 350,000 marks, a mark which had already spiralled into an abyss – and would carry on falling even lower?

On 31 January 1923, a thousand-mark note was still worth eight gold pfennigs. By the middle of July, two pfennigs, and by the end of July 0.5 gold pfennigs. By the end of September, a million-mark banknote was approximately equal to three gold pfennigs. By the middle of October 1923, 13 million marks were needed to buy a gold pfennig. In other words (as an observer at the time wrote), for a piece of paper guaranteed by the State, you could still buy a loaf of bread in the morning; at midday, a ropy cigarette; in the afternoon, a match; and by the evening, all it was good for was wiping your backside. Money, quite literally, burned people's fingers. Let's just get rid of it, was the motto of the day.

But this was not all.

I learnt more about the reality of those times from something I also heard from Stolle. At that time, the motorcycle, which had almost dropped into BMW's lap, had become a kind of last resort. In reality, Popp continued to think about aero-engines and hoped to revive them. All the activities in the design office, particularly those influenced from the desk where the boss sat, could not have hidden the fact that he had decided to start up again as soon as possible from where he had left off in 1918–19 when the ban on aero-engines had been introduced. Work was continued on land simply because they were banned from the air, as the terms of the Versailles Treaty laid down.

On the question of Versailles, the same Rathenau who saw the economy as the key, had the following to say:

> Anyone who thinks of Germany as a land of culture and education, of music and ideas, of two millenia of the rational and the emotional, even if they had nine lives, would brood and not be able to understand how a verdict can be issued to the world, a verdict made by human beings who think and feel, speak and understand, wake up and go to sleep, that this verdict, the word of death, is destroying our homeland, is depopulating our towns and burying our people. It is scientific murder, cold, wilful, premeditated, clinical, which is destroying the work of the past generation and the life of the one to come.

In contrast to such a black prophecy from a prosecutor, for everyday life in a small business muddling along like the one in Lerchenau Street run by Popp and Friz, the banal assertion remained that nothing was ever going to be eaten as hot as when it had been cooked. Not that anyone would have had any reason for doubting the seriousness of the victorious powers for implementing the conditions laid down in the 'Treaty' – the victors were always present in the form of an Allied inspectorate, which would regularly turn up unannounced to verify BMW. Violations were threatened with heavy fines or complete closure of the business. However, both the inspectors and those being inspected knew only too well that there were holes and gaps in the clauses of the Treaty. With one side being asked to be more Catholic than the Pope, and with the other side being forced to deceive out of a sense of professional honour, there grew up a kind of 'laissez-faire', a mutual complicity in which each side let the other side get on with it. This tended to act as an emollient, a phenomenon which came not from the defeated, but paradoxically from the victors themselves.

As always, life had proved to be stronger than paragraphs and penalties. Air traffic, which was going from strength to strength throughout the world, could not negate what Germany had discovered and developed in aviation (by necessity for military purposes, but which did not exclude a civilian application). Not for nothing had the signatory powers, in their jealous desire to beat each other to it, leapt upon the BMW IIIa aero-engine. It

95

was confiscated, copied, and its successor, the BMW IV, kept under scrutiny. There was also the example of the 'Prof. Junker's Research Establishment', founded in 1916, which had created the first all-metal aeroplane in the world, with cantilevered wings and supporting metal bodywork. This was the one, on its test flight during the war, that pilots had rather pejoratively called (in the jargon of the front) the 'metal donkey'. It had, however, become the precursor of a technique which would lead to light metal replacing sheet steel as raw material, and would prove seminal for aircraft manufacture throughout the world.

In June 1919, a few days after Diemer's (unrecognised) world altitude record with the BMW IV engine, and three days before the proclamation of the Versailles Treaty, an aircraft took off from Dessau, with Monz as pilot, which bore the German registration number 'D 1' (as a model from the Junkers Aircraft Works in Dessau, it had been given the description of 'Junkers F 13'). It was an unbraced, all-metal, low-winged monoplane with a five-seater passenger compartment.

On 28 June 1919 in the Hall of the Mirrors at the Palace of Versailles (where the German Reich had been proclaimed in 1871), the Peace Treaty was signed by the German Foreign Secretary Hermann Müller and the Minister for Transport and Colonies, Johannes Bell. A few hours later, the F 13 took off from Warnemünde for Stockholm, quite legally, as everyone had to admit, thus escaping the scientific death of which Rathenau had spoken. Two-and-a-half months later, the papers reported that the F 13, fitted with a Bavarian Motor Works 185-hp engine had achieved a new world record in Sweden with eight people on board. The 'first passenger aircraft in the world', baptised with the evocative name of 'Nightingale', had reached a height of 6,750 metres.

For Popp and Friz, who adhered strictly to the manufacturing ban, this success, along with Diemer's altitude record of 9,760 metres, would have been little more than cold comfort if both had not been party to common knowledge – that the United States of America had sent Mr John Larsen, their leading aviator, to Dessau to acquire a licence to build the F 13. As Junkers would not issue the licence, Larsen agreed the purchase of twenty-three of these aircraft. Built on neutral territory abroad, they were in fact delivered to America by August 1920, without violating the Treaty of Versailles, whose 'imposed peace' the USA had admittedly co-signed, but (in contrast to the other signatories) had not ratified. Only in 1921 did they conclude their own peace treaty with Germany, with all the rights granted to them by the Treaty of Versailles.

But that was not all. In Atlantic City, as was quite openly reported, 600 people were transported in the F 13 fleet on 1 July 1920. On the next day, an F 13 took off for Washington, where the leading figures from the US army, navy and post office had assembled, and again, three days later, the long-distance flight from New York to Omaha was accomplished in an F 13.

All this was underscored by simple considerations affecting US Airmail. The first eight Junkers aeroplanes put into service in 1920 had in fact considerably brought down the cost of postal deliveries within the huge land mass of America (New York-Chicago-Omaha and New York-San Francisco), since a gallon of fuel, which previously only gave 2.5 miles, now gave twice as much. An increased flying radius of 50 per cent, considerably lower maintenance costs, and the fact that German aircraft could pick up and transport two-and-a-half times as many mail bags had the world looking to America in amazement and shrugging their shoulders at the way the Versailles decisions had been circumvented in the process.

But in Germany, the ban on 'armed or otherwise armoured aircraft' was still in force, and arbitrarily adopted 'definitions' then ensured that German commercial aviation remained quite uncompetitive compared to foreign aviation, by deviously extending the ban on manufacturing and operating aircraft once it had expired on 5 May 1922. One of the thirteen British, French, Italian, Japanese and Danish officers forming the 'Air Security Committee' was responsible for checking all sites where flying had been re-established in Germany, to see whether, for example, the runways that were limited to 4,000 metres had been exceeded. They also had to check that the speed limit of 170 kph and the payload of 600 kg were not exceeded. What the committee actually did was legally-sanctioned industrial espionage, so that when there were 'amendments' (the payload was increased to 900 kg, and the speed to 180 kph), they always made a mockery of every established world regulation and ignored the developments which had taken place in world aviation (involving German designers and aircraft manufacturers), to a certain extent illegally, but for all the world to see.

In the meantime, an incident took place in Munich which set people thinking. A case came before the provincial court in June 1921, before a highly regarded audience from town and country which, day in, day out, filled the courtrooms, either out of curiosity or boredom. The charge, again, was industrial espionage (but this time *not* legally permissible).

That spring several thousand plans, diagrams and photographs, as well as technical calculations for aircraft, car, and boat engines had been stolen from the Bavarian Motor Works. The trail had led to 'St', an exceptionally gifted twenty-year-old technician, who had quickly risen in the company due to his competence, and who rather incredibly for his age called himself a designer.

The evidence was overwhelming. Searching St's house had brought to light around 1,000 drawings, the rest having disappeared. Where had they gone? St came straight out with it at the hearing. An organisation called 'United Settlers of the East' wanted to enable German workers to emigrate and settle in Russia – the Soviet government wanted to establish an aircraft and engine factory in or around Moscow, in line with communist principles. That was what the documents and design drawings had been needed for. St, who was politically naive and was proven not to be a member of any communist organisation, was to have had a leading position in the Russian enterprise, admittedly only when he could supply the materials. It was open to question how far his professional ambition had met with obstacles at Lerchenau Street. Nevertheless, he allowed himself to be persuaded, and spent months of painstaking work, in which every night, with two colleagues, he duplicated the plans and diagrams taken from the factory (he pleaded that the originals had been put back). And what about his colleagues? They had probably saved themselves; one was said to be already in Moscow. An expert estimated that just the design drawings found at St's were worth a fortune – they were so complete that they could have enabled production to start immediately. The verdict was interesting in that it appeared unusually lenient. The assertion by the defendant that he had not wanted to steal the drawings (in reality, they had not been stolen, but rather loaned out for copying) could not be refuted, pronounced the judge. Due to which the court could only condemn St for violating the law on unfair competition. St was sentenced to a year in prison, taking into account six months on remand, and a fine of 3,000 marks or a further 300 days in prison. Probation was refused.

It was an ambiguous case in that it had not been a normal theft. Industrial espionage! The word 'espionage' had been deliberately avoided, as if it were not appropriate here. And yet there was no question of it being anything else. Could not the stolen and copied papers also be regarded as 'secret' in the sense that they were items of classified information, since it was quite obvious that they were not available publicly and that aero-engines not only came under patent protection but also involved military interests? And yet there was no mention of treason. Why not, indeed? Was the court influenced by the fact that only recently in Berlin (6 May 1921) a German-Soviet trade agreement had been signed providing for the exchange of military supplies, inasmuch as Germany was permitted to under the Treaty of Versailles? Perhaps also the exchange of design drawings? In the end, had St done something off his own bat, so to speak, only in anticipation of what had now been made quite legitimate by the highest legal authorities in the interests of the Reich?

Anyone asking himself these questions was quite justified in doing so. It was also striking that those affected kept silent, and were not examined at all in the case. With such damages, they could have won claims for compensation. Against whom? A foreign power? Apart from the fact that evidence would have been difficult to offer, what was stopping them? Presumably certain connections with Bendler Street in Berlin where the Reich army, led by General Hans von Seeckt, had its headquarters. Other industrial companies enjoyed such relations, and why shouldn't they? Under the Treaty of Versailles, Germany had been granted a 100,000-strong army. An army needs weapons, and, as its leader, Herr von Seeckt had to see to it that weapons and vehicles, and even aircraft, were procured to consolidate and perfect his (small) military machine. Still within the framework of military limits imposed upon it, of course.

The Western Allies knew that it just would not succeed, because this framework was far too narrow. No powerful army could ever be built upon cardboard tanks and dummy canons, throttled back engines and blank cartridges. The Western Allies had drawn up the terms of the Treaty and monitored them with the same amount of success that they had in ignoring something else – that Seeckt was a realist. His enmity towards communism as a subversive force in the Reich had not blinded him. His co-operation with Russia gave him the one opportunity of attaining his goal of a modern army, which required the military limits imposed upon him to be circumvented.

On 18 March 1921, immediately after the end of the Russo-Polish War, Lenin made an official application to the German government for support in reorganising the Red Army. Thereupon Seeckt formed a secret section at Bendler Street, by the name of 'Special Group R', where the motivating force was principally Kurt von Schleicher who, ten years later, as the last Chancellor in the Weimar Republic, tried through coalition of the Reich army and the Trade Unions to prevent Hitler's rise. This came down to German help in building up Russian armaments and training the Red Army, for which, in return, Germany was to receive facilities for testing, even producing, weapons and training soldiers to use them. These were principally aimed at aircraft weapons which initially required pilots, flight mechanics and fitters to be trained in testing aircraft. To get all this going, a trading company was founded, under the innocuous name of 'Association for the Furtherment of Business Ventures' (in German, GEFU), which was allocated 75 million Reich marks by the government, while a 'Moscow Head Office' (ZMo) was set up in the Soviet capital. They linked up with each other through Russian authorities and German military offices independently of the German Embassy.

Assumptions that Germany at that time built up, trained, or indeed even created the Red Army and the Russian air force, in particular, are pure fiction. And so is the fact that BMW was said to have had a special interest in all this. In the years up to 1926 (these were the crucial years, as it was only following them that the ban on Germany's aviation was lifted) only a few BMW mechanics had seen the 'cold home', as the training grounds in Russia were called. Essentially they comprised the aerodrome at Lipetsk, lying between Moscow and Odessa on the Gryazi-Orel railway line, which the Russians had allocated to the German Reich army for training and testing. Here is where the prototypes built with difficulty in secret sheds in Germany were tested and German pilots and technicians trained. In return, German experts set up schools for aerial and tank warfare, giving the Reich army the chance to study more than just the theory of how to use weapons forbidden in Germany.

Everything was done in the strictest secrecy. A hundred fighter aircraft of the Fokker D XIII type, the best single-seater fighter at the time, were ordered in the Netherlands and originally destined for the active resistance planned in the French-occupied Ruhr. They were paid for by German industry with money from the 'Ruhr Fund', but little by little they were transferred to the Soviet Union. Operating under the code name of 'von Litz', the head of ZMo was a Colonel D. Thomsen (retired), who had worked as Chief of the General Staff for the Commanding General of Air Forces in the First World War. Lipetsk, the flying school, was known as the 'Scientific Research and Test Establishment for Aircraft'. Anyone visiting it, or belonging to its permanent staff, travelled (officially disassociated from active service in the Reich army) with a genuine passport, which, however, was issued under a false name and false job title on the Northern Express to Moscow, where 'von Litz' would meet them and send them on. On completion of training as a fighter pilot, as an observer or as a technician, they returned via Leningrad to Germany on Russian freight or passenger ships. Between the years 1924 to 1933 there were a total of 220 officers and officer cadets from the flying complement, plus between sixty and seventy men on the permanent staff.

If this figure appears modest, this training and testing for both men and machines in Lipetsk must be seen as extraordinary, compared with the very limited facilities that had to be so skilfully camouflaged in Germany under the Versailles terms. This justified all the elaborate schemes necessary to circumvent, as far as possible, border and customs checks for weapons and equipment. The port of embarcation for all goods was Szeczcin, with disembarkation at Leningrad. Particularly 'hot' material (as Air General Wilhelm Speidel reported after the Second World War) was even transported by small chartered sailing vessels right up to Kronstadt near Leningrad, often after eventful journeys. It was also difficult to overhaul the Napier Lion engines in the Fokker D XIII – that could only be done in England. The test planes did not need to take the sea route from Germany to Russia. From Rechlin they flew over East Prussia, Lithuania and Latvia to Russia, landing at the airstrip on Veliki Luki on the first leg of the journey.

So that no one was left in the dark, the instruction was given that GEFU (which was wound up in December 1926) was to carry out three tasks:

1 Establishing a Junkers subsidiary at Fili near Moscow to produce metal-bodied planes and engines, as provided for in the licencing agreement between the Junkers aircraft works at Dessau and the Soviet government.

2 The founding by Bersol PLC of a Russo-German joint venture to build a chemical factory to produce poison gas at Samara.

3 The manufacture of munitions for Germany under German technical supervision and assistance.

Whichever of these were completed, or fortunately not completed, lends one to suspect that Russia might have set up Germany as a military power after 1918. This is just as inaccurate as suggesting that those attempts at rearming, which the Germans concealed, had somehow (with Russia's help) laid the foundations for the Second World War, suggesting they were not simply for defence. Whatever was actually achieved under the camouflaging which concealed all the actions in the Reich army's Russian connection was, compared with the rearming in other European states (if not the whole world), modest to the point of being pitiful. Only the munitions contract was fulfilled. (This was brought to public attention when an oversight during the unloading of shells at Szeczcin in 1926 revealed their country of origin; Germany had only just been accepted into the League of Nations. This caused a bit of a furore, which was smoothed over without any politicians becoming involved.) Bersol proved a failure (fortunately, in retrospect). Nothing 'useful' was produced, let alone delivered.

There remained the Junkers subsidiary. It is worth mentioning because GEFU had imposed the condition on Junkers that it should involve the Bavarian Motor Works in work in Russia. Junkers declined, claiming 'the experiences of previous collaboration with BMW'. They claimed that after the war, BMW had refused to keep up aero-engine production. Bolstered up by Junkers's orders, they emerged much larger in 1923, from which date all the ill feelings stemmed. Another point was that the majority of the shares in BMW belonged to a foreign investor, Herr Castiglioni, and this alone made closer contact seem undesirable. ('The fact that Castiglioni would learn of the Russian venture and its repercussions via BMW was doubly disagreeable to Junkers in a political situation which was, in any case, uncertain, and even seemed dangerous,' was how the event was described in the files at the Foreign Office.)

The whole affair came to nothing. Production at the Junkers subsidiary (without BMW's involvement) was transferred to Russian ownership,

... and the Junkers Works at Dessau submitted a balance sheet for Fili showing enormous losses. This was naturally designed to obtain state compensation for the sacrifices undertaken 'in the interests of the Fatherland'. Checking the accounts revealed that there were discrepancies in almost all the figures, that none of the investment provided by the state had ever been anywhere near the subsidiary, and that now compensation was being demanded, even for those sums which had been used in Dessau. To put it mildly, it was a case of gross disloyalty. That quickly and categorically ended the spurious business relationship... (Otto Gessler in his book *German Military Policy in the Weimar Republic*)

An item from Bendler Street reveals how engine development was proceeding. It is dated 24 September 1923 and states:

1 BMW IIIa, 185/220 hp. Dry weight 308 kg. Permissible, short-term power increase through jets (as per Junkers), to 250 hp (even 270 hp). Silumin casing reduces the weight by 10 kg. Electron rejected due to latent fatigue.

2 BMW IV, 220/260 hp, six-cylinder, both bore and stroke increased by 10 mm over BMW IIIa = 160 × 190 mm. 5 engines produced by the end of the war.

3 BMW V, twelve-cylinder (2 × BMW IIIa) existed on draft at the end of the war; now abandoned. In its place:

4 BMW VI, twelve-cylinder (2 × BMW IV). Ground level output at nominal engine speed of 1400 rpm, 440 hp. Ideal ground level output 600 hp. Maximum output 520 hp. Constant pressure at around an altitude of 6 km. Bore 160 mm. Stroke 190 mm. Dry weight 550 kg. including 19.5 kg of coolant, hub 13 kg. Fuel consumption 140 g/hp (of interest to Junkers, Dornier, Fokker, Yugoslavia, Russia). Drawings ready by 31 December 1923. Two test reports by 31 March 1924 (possibly brought forward by 2 months).

5 BMW high-speed engine (projected), 480 hp. Maximum output 320 kg, 0.67 kg/hp. Design 5 months. Test production 3 to 4 months. 150 units per months delivered by the end of the war. Present output of 25 per month from workforce of 800; 50 per month feasible with 20 new machine tools.

What does this 'memo' reveal?
First of all, that Popp and Friz had not been sleeping during the ban.

Secondly, it revealed (the only information I found) just how far BMW had expanded by 1923 in Lerchenau as regards planning and development in aero-engine production.

Thirdly, it reveals the view from the chilly heights directed at BMW from the General Staff. A cool assessment of the state and performance of technology, its military application, possible quantities, time perspectives. No mention of plans, no comparisons, for example, between the possibilities of other countries to exploit German engineering expertise and those in Germany. (The Czech Defence Minister had just spoken to parliament about why the Czech-Moravian factories producing variants equivalent to the BMW IV engine would not be making use of the latter, despite their being 'brilliantly superior'.)

And, of course, there was no mention of the results which the 'cold home' could have produced. After all was said and done, had it really ever existed, or was it just an illusion, a rumour?

I asked all the old people connected with BMW whom I could track down. I eventually came across Hans Seufert, who had been an on-board fitter and whose work reports were in the firm's archives.

'I was then in the aero-engine department,' he said.

'So officially there was one?'

'Of course there was, but run at the same time as the motorcycle development section.'

'Why?'

He smiled. 'We were not allowed to build any large engines, only the BMW IV, and only that with express permission.'

'And this was granted?'

'Occasionally. For the Czechs, for example. They fitted their military aircraft with it, they were very keen on it. It was old hat to us, but it brought in the money.'

'And did you work on anything new?'

He did not reply.

'There was something, wasn't there? The twelve-cylinder, the BMW VI?' I prompted.

A shiver ran down him, fifty-six years after the event. 'You bet. A wonderful engine. I worked on it!'

'You did?'

He laid his stick to one side, ran his hand through his hair. 'Yes, me. It was all quite illegal. We did it secretly, we built it for. . .' and then he added, almost unintentionally, '. . . for the cold home.'

'For Russia?'

'It was never called Russia. Always the cold home. "Where are you going?" they'd ask. "To the cold home."'

'Did you ever go there?'

'Just on the first flight, in Johannisthal. That was where the VI was tested. We had to know if our calculations were right.'

'And were they?'

He nodded. 'They certainly were. The machine had only just landed, and then we flew as far as Staaken. That was enough. Then a man, I can still see it today, came running up to me. He was one of those who had to check the Versailles conditions. He was red in the face, and asked, as blokes like these were allowed to: "Why has the engine got exhaust pipes on both sides?"

'I replied (what else could I have said?): "Well, if the exhaust pipes were all on one side, then the air resistance would be greater, wouldn't it?"

'Then he looked at me (I stepped aside, coughed) and then he went off. Should I have said: "There's a twelve-cylinder in there"? They hardly ever knew what they were looking for, from a technical point of view, that is.

'Then we took out the BMW VI at our leisure, packed it in crates, and off it went. Not to Munich, though, but to the cold home.'

There was a pause.

'If people coaxed it out of me that we tested our Luftwaffe in Russia, then they'd all say: "Come off it!" But it was the truth!'

'But I thought you said you'd never been there yourself?'

'Only later, for engines in commercial flying, through my work at Dornier-Whale. I was the "Whale-specialist". The Whale was built in Italy near Pisa, and I went over there with the last one, to Sebastopol. That was in 1928. It was still called the cold home then.'

Flying Allowed Again

The Frenchman Jacques Montane wrote in 1928 that there were three miracles in his life – the miracles of the Marne, the German gold standard and German aviation.

If this sentence is not particularly good, it nevertheless clearly expresses that phenomena exist which defy rational explanation. Germany's return to the air was one such phenomenon. Ernst Heinkel, who himself played a major part in it, said:

> It was an indescribably turbulent time, but also a time of struggle, when people were likely to go under if they did not have the strength and courage to survive the hundreds of difficulties, bans and regulations, inflation and the absence of hard currency, and all the other technical and human problems. Anyone not tough enough went under. Anyone who did not work better and faster than everybody else was bound to fail sooner or later. It was survival of the fittest.

Is that it in a nutshell? Even the supposition, as expressed by the American Austin in 1924, that 'Europe knew of no country taking as many initiatives in aviation as Germany, which was only due to designers being so profoundly stimulated by the conditions imposed upon it by its enemies. . .', goes some way, but not far enough, to explaining this 'miracle'.

If we look at certain facts, their origins and effects, then we see that one thing will collide into another, trigger off one line of activities, while a third possibility is ignored for lack of opportunity. A man called Friedrich Christiansen turned up in Norway, drifting aimlessly around Europe like so many old war pilots, in his old Hansa Brandenburg W 29. He scoured the skerry coasts from the air looking for herring and sardines. The Norwegians were enthralled. Back home again (he now knew where aeroplanes could be used), he persuaded Heinkel to leave his home in Swabia and travel to Travemünde. That was where one of his old colleagues, Jupp Köhler, was already 'knocking together' aircraft for Norway. (He picked up the individual parts at Kranepuhl, which was the delivery point set up by the Allies for German aircraft to be handed over. He helped himself to what he needed, quite blatantly, under the very eyes of British officers.) Then

Clemens Bücker got in on the act. He had been taken on as a pilot by the Swedish airforce, and had been on the lookout for seaplanes for the Swedish Navy. On one condition – they had to be built on the wharf at Gashaga. But Heinkel designed them, secretly produced parts for them, and the He 1 was the start of numerous aircraft which Heinkel was now to build and in which the BMW IV was fitted (as in the HD 39 newspaper plane).

This is no isolated example. There were dozens of other such reciprocal arrangements. Anyone who has ever flown cannot keep his hands off the control column. 'I don't like human beings, but I do like what consumes them,' the flyer and writer Saint-Exupéry once said to his superior Riviere. Was it the same for Popp? What motivated him to take up aircraft engine building again, despite the fact that there were scarcely any sales prospects to make the whole thing profitable? Was it because the BMW engine had emerged from the war as the best? Or because people abroad took such a great interest in it? Or was it due to his designer Friz, who was always coming up with new ideas, and whom he did not want to disappoint? Was it because of those still operating aircraft factories which were crying out for power plants without being able to guarantee that they could pay for them? Whatever it was, BMW would now produce the BMW IV even if pedantic 'definitions' ensured that there were further restrictions once the construction ban had been lifted, meaning that the quantities involved would still be very small.

We have seen how this engine was appreciated everywhere it was delivered – in Holland, Denmark, Sweden, in the 'cold home' of Russia, in Czechoslavakia. (The Czech Defence Minister had declared in parliament that the 'brilliant superiority of the BMW engine in practice stemmed mainly from its operating reliability, simple construction, effortless operation, the ease with which it could be started, excellent durability and its high altitude performance.) Now this engine was also destined to conquer German aviation, which was now slowly picking up speed. With a continuous output of 250 hp and a maximum output of 320 hp, it provided a power plant which was itself easily adequate to satisfy the passengers' requirements for safety and comfort in heavy aircraft frames.

Popp was the last to imagine that technical high performance plus commercial acumen had created his 'miracle out of nothing'. That inflation (as paradoxical as this might seem) had a share in it was irrefutable. This was due to the fact that, while German industry was in the position of needing ridiculously small costs for wages and salaries, German prices on the world market could be lower than anybody else's, and so beat any competing offer. Was the miracle, in fact, a sacrifice offered up by the workers?

We should not ignore *when* they were asked to make this. Times had gone awry. There was the threat of civil war. Anyone who still had work, even if it did not give him much to live on, could at least make something out of what remained of hope – I am not redundant, I am needed. The following cartoon appeared in *Simplizissimus* in May 1923: an abyss, over which is hovering an angel with the huge skull and unmistakable features of Gustav Stresemann. He is seen protecting a plain honest German who is trying to cross the abyss, carefully feeling his way, step by step along the narrow footbridge.

105

The caption below reads: 'He's looking to the right, he's looking to the left – he will save me.' Viscount d'Abernon, the British ambassador in Berlin, wrote at the end of 1923 about the 'most turbulent and dangerous year for the continued existence of the Weimar Republic'.

> In the last twelve months from January, Germany has survived the following perils: the invasion of the Ruhr, the communist uprising in Saxony and Thuringia, the Hitler putsch in Bavaria, and the separatist movement in the Rhineland.
>
> Every one of these factors, if they had succeeded, would have brought about a fundamental change in the internal structure of the country or in its relations abroad.
>
> Any of these moments of danger, if they had not been averted, would have destroyed all hope of a general peace.
>
> Political leaders in Germany are not accustomed to the public offering them laurels, and yet those who have steered their country out of these dangers deserve more recognition than they have hitherto been granted.

D'Abernon was referring to Stresemann, the Reich Chancellor for 100 days. On his overthrow, Reich President Ebert said to his Social Democratic Party colleagues: 'Whatever has led you to overthrow the Chancellor will be forgotten in six weeks, but you will feel the consequences of your stupidity for ten years.' Stresemann, who then became Foreign Secretary, also brought about 'the greatest conjuring trick in world history'; that is, stabilising the mark and bringing the madness of inflation to an end.

But he would never have been able to steer the country through these dangers alone – as d'Abernon expressed it – if there had not been pockets of order and unwavering attachment to values, which were far from indestructible but which were nevertheless based on consequential ideas.

Popp wrote about his financial year of 1923:

> The current balance sheet for the profit and loss account using the mark = entries in marks, according to the legal requirements, following collapse of the currency in the past financial year, is completely worthless for determining commercial results. As a result, the board has refrained from extricating a profit out of the muddle of figures, and so cannot allocate a dividend. Only through the issue of gold marks from 1 January 1924 will it be possible to work out the results for the eighth year of business. Constructing our works is now completed and mass-production of all items is running at full stretch. We have achieved particular successes in the field of motorcycle production, just as aero-engine manufacture could be revived with good results. The contracts presently running leave us to anticipate full-time working till the end of the year.

The Bavarian Motor Works had successfully seen through that year of inflation which had proved so critical for so many companies.

The full success of the policies adopted can be read from the balance sheet in 1924. 'The turnover amounted to 8,495,913.10 marks and the net profit was 339,198.78 marks from which 300,000 marks was used for distributing a 10 per cent dividend. The remaining amount would be carried forward to the new accounts.'

On 18 December 1924 the Swiss pilot Walter Mittelholzer took off from Zurich in his Junkers A 20 fitted with a BMW IV engine on a flight to Persia. The Alps, the Taurus Mountains and the Persian Mountains, including the 5,670-metre-high Mount Demavend, glinted below him. After flying for forty-one hours (the BMW IV purred like a cat), Mittelholzer reached Teheran. Eighteen months later, on 24 and 29 June 1926, the same Mittelholzer, a lieutenant in the Swiss Army, established seven new records at Dübendorf in a Dornier Mercury, the new land aircraft of the Dornier Works, fitted with a 460-hp BMW engine. 'The achievements set by the new records point to the feasibility of transporting fourteen passengers from Munich to Sicily,' read the brief commentary.

This new engine, the BMW VI, had a double six-cylinder, V-configuration, producing 500 hp continuous output (maximum output of 750 hp). The connecting rods on one row acted as the main bearers for the connecting rods from the other cylinders which were joined on, above the bearing surface. So as to avoid increasing the overall length of the six-cylinder engine, the big end bearings were fitted with roller bearings. Friz had handled the design specification with masterly success. The balls on these bearings ran in direct contact with the hardened main journals and in the hardened eyes on the main-load-carrying big ends and the ball race, which consisted of four semi-circular sections, all enabling the bearing to be assembled over the individual crankpins and onto the journals once it had slipped over the big ends. Friz had thus avoided (and this was the only way) giving excessive weight to the bearing, and at the same time, produced a connecting rod in an aero-engine which not only gave maximum reliability but also the lowest maintenance costs. The other components, together with lubrication, had, like the BMW IV engine, been taken from the example of the old IIIa engine, meaning that lengthy tests could be dispensed with, and that the VI could go into immediate large-scale production.

Mittelholzer took off from Zurich on 7 December 1926, with it again fitted to a Dornier-Mercury airplane, and after ninety-seven-and-a-half hours in the air, flying over sea, desert and savannah, including numerous round trips over unexplored regions in Central Africa, reached Cape Town at 5 a.m. on 21 February 1927. The distance covered came to 20,000 kilometres. Apart from his mechanic, he had two scientists on board with all their equipment – cameras, dark room and instruments, together with sleeping facilities for the passengers and weapons for possible attacks.

He immediately sent a telegram: 'Cape Town, 21., 8.20 h. Bavarian Motor Munich. Congratulate your engines wonderful all through. Mittelholzer.'

The flight, carried out without any ground support, without the reliable weather forecasts of modern aviation and the benefit of radio telegraphy, conducted simply through the trust placed in the reliability of the engine and airplane and completed without any complaints, broke every conceivable record. 'Certainly,' stated a prospectus which was immediately drafted by Popp, 'foreign aircraft have previously achieved similar performances. But how many years' development have these engines had in flying operations? How speedily the BMW VI engine was developed!'

Popp's questions were justified. Sadness and scepticism were mixed with unmistakable pride. Admittedly, the good reputation of the BMW VI would soon bring in licence agreements with Japan once the Dornier Mercury had crossed the Caucasus as a fully-laden civil aircraft, and had covered 7,000 kilometres from Swabia to the Caspian Sea and back again at an average journey speed of 180 kph. It was unbelievable how this engine performed! On the Barranquilla-Bogota run along the Magdalena River, it carried out duties for the Sociedad Colombo-Alemana de Transportes Aéreos day in, day out. 'The engines 20 499 and 20 500,' the company reported, 'are now running up to almost 500 hours without any major overhaul being necessary. On the engine 20 499, valve lapping was only done after 350 hours, on engine 20 500, after 300 and 450 hours.'

In Tierra del Fuego and Patagonia Gunter Plüschow, the famous 'pilot of Tsingtao', ventured into completely unknown territories, and had penetrated unexplored mountainous regions in his HD 24 fitted with a 250-hp BMW IV engine. He had circled glaciers, surveyed virgin forests, and touched down in his 'Silver Condor' on lonely storm-beaten fjords. 'For six full months, despite the fact that the aeroplane never saw a hangar, a shed or a repair shop, but was exposed instead to surface water, pouring rain, the most violent storms, ice, snow and searing sun, in fact, every type of weather you can imagine, it was still capable of taking off at a moment's notice for the frozen heights.'

The BMW IV, fitted into the HD 39, which was a freight-carrying biplane with 1,000 small kg payload and chutes for newspaper bundles, had also received praise in the newspaper delivery service. 'BZ 1, our first newspaper delivery aircraft,' announced the *BZ am Mittag* newspaper at the end of 1927, 'has now . . . covered 100,000 kilometres in delivering newspapers, which is approximately equal to two-and-a-half times around the equator. The airplane was put into operation six months ago and has since delivered the BZ nationally, almost every day.'

The bulletin from the Fédération Aéronautique Internationale (FAI) was constantly proclaiming new records – records which drove pilots and firms on to ever greater 'world beating performances'. The individual record performance might not have proved very much, but the continuous establishment of such maximum performances said a great deal about the value and usefulness of an engine type. Werner Landmann, who had achieved the world record for continuous flight, with 21 hours 49 minutes as a young pilot for Albatros in 1914, captured five world records in 1926 in a RO VII Rohrbach flying boat fitted with BMW IV engines. Shortly afterwards, Hermann Steindorff, a former fighter pilot and now a works pilot at Rohrbach, achieved 22 'world beating performances' at Staaken with the BMW IV, which included continuous flying as well as speed and distance. ('Ever higher goals were set, and subsequent top performances achieved by other firms had to be outdone time and again. The demands became increasingly tough, until we were finally left as the overall winner in this peaceful competition. By "we" I mean the crew, my Rohrbach Roland aircraft and its life-force, my fine BMW engines.')

All these successes could not, however, hide the fact that foreign countries had meanwhile developed new designs, whose technical advances BMW could not keep up with. Research costs for a whole new range of engines were too high compared with the minimal sales potential. They consumed millions of marks which BMW did not have, at least not now, at a time when the Weimar Republic was experiencing a kind of spring, in which, mercifully, life was for living again.

An example of this was the problem connected with the reduction gear, which had almost made the designers, and even Friz, despair. An aircraft designed with a high payload needs an engine which can reduce propeller speed, particularly on take-off, thereby increasing its gradability. No facility in the world provided for such an exact machining of the gears that, when the engine output was high and the gears were subjected to extreme pressures, an even distribution of the loading could be applied as before over several gears. The solution came from France, where Farman had developed an epicyclic bevel-drive gear, comprising sun wheels each of which had three teeth resting on the three planet wheels rotating around them, without the need for a centering shaft. This drive gear (which BMW immediately acquired a licence to build) first made it possible to lift a flying boat of the size of the 'Romar', developed at the Rohrbach Works, by means of three BMW VI-U engines (with the combined effect of 750 hp maximum output per engine, and the low propeller speed of the Farman drive-gear enabling take-off).

On 21 May 1927 the chief correspondent at the Paris bureau of the *New York Times* cabled the following:

> At 10.20 this evening a white machine suddenly appeared out of the darkness in front of 25,000 excited spectators and began to descend in a gentle curve. At 10.24 the 'Spirit of St Louis' landed, and a thick cordon of troops and police and heavy steel barriers were necessary to protect the airplane and its pilot from the heaving masses as they surged like the sea against the barriers.

The world had not been so excited for a long time. This was the first successful trans-Atlantic crossing in an aircraft; non-stop, with no stopover, and not just over the shortest distance between the continents, but between New York and Paris. Two weeks earlier, the French pilots Charles Nungesser and François Coli had taken off from Paris to cross the Atlantic in the opposite direction – but in vain; they never arrived. The 'White Bird' went missing. Now Charles Lindbergh, a young postal pilot, had covered the 3,600 miles from west to east in 34 hours, alone, mostly at an altitude of 10,000 feet.

> The engine ran very evenly, and I did not feel tired at any time. I had the feeling that I was driving a car along a very wide smooth road, only I felt lighter and freer.
>
> Then it brightened up, and the clouds got higher and thicker. Some I flew over, while others I tried to dive under. They were hail clouds, and I could hear the hail drumming on the wings. This concerned me very much, and I debated whether I should not turn round. Finally I decided to stop thinking about whether or not to turn back.

109

Nobody doubted Lindbergh's daring, his flying prowess, or his luck. Lindbergh himself said about this that he wanted to settle an issue:

> They may call me 'Lucky', but luck alone would not have been enough. The situation in reality was that I had a machine which, after careful consideration, I believed was the most suitable for a flight from New York to Paris, and which I still think to be so. I had the one engine which I considered the best for this purpose, and I was equipped with the best instruments available for such an undertaking. That is why I made it.

Wolfgang von Gronau had experienced something similar when he had reconnoitred the North Sea in a flying boat. Gronau was head of the German Sea Pilots School at List on the island of Sylt, which he had had to develop without the 'proper procedures', as bureaucrats call them. Flight navigation, instrument application, all this had been ignored for years. There was not a single textbook; what there was had been partly written on site by people gathering together odds and ends – in the certain anticipation that the first scheduled trans-oceanic lines would be flown by sea-worthy airplanes. This was simply because the world comprised more water than land, which gave innumerable landing sites, providing the floats could resist the rough seas.

Consequently, flying boats had developed from hydroplanes, since the former could take off heavily-laden from a calm sea. Using two such flying boats of the Dornier Whale N 25 type, fitted with Rolls Royce Eagle IX engines, Amundsen set off from Spitzbergen on his first flight to the North Pole, but had only reached the 89th parallel when one of the engines failed, and he had to make an emergency landing on the ice sixty miles short of the Pole. Amundsen left his damaged machine behind, picked up the crew in his flying boat, and attempted to take off from the ice after he had abandoned all dispensible items, including all the polar equipment (the water channel was too short).

This Whale was now up for sale, as Amundsen was only prepared to undertake his next venture in an airship. As the Sea Pilots School on Sylt could acquire it cheaply, Gronau made up his mind to fit the 'Whale' with the most powerful German engines available (and that meant BMW VI engines), and fly to America.

In summer 1927 sensational test flights were undertaken by the Italian subsidiary of the Dornier Works at Marina di Pisa with two such BMW VI engines fitted into a Whale.

A newspaper article, which Gronau could not stop thinking about, stated:

> The Dornier Whale Flying Boat, which has long been fitted only with foreign engines, rose with an all-up weight of 5,850 kg in fifty-two minutes to an altitude of 4,800 m, but still a long way short of its maximum height. With the foreign engines and the same all-up weight, the maximum attainable altitude was only 3,600 m. The take-off time was around 20

to 25 seconds shorter than the Whale fitted with Italian engines. With an all-up weight of 6,700 kg an altitude of 4,250 m. was reached in forty-seven minutes, while the take-off specifications only required 4,000 m in sixty minutes. Even with this higher all-up weight, the take-off times were only two-thirds and often only a half of the time needed with other engines. For this, the engines maximum output was never once used. The speed tests with 6,700 kg all-up weight produced 202 kph at normal output, and 217 kph with the engine at maximum output.

With increased payload and an all-up weight of 7,600 kg, take-off was achieved in fifty-nine seconds at maximum engine output, and that in spite of a strong swell.

The report went on to mention that the test engines had been adjusted for normal output and not for maximum output, and that no reduction gear had been fitted, which (with a crankcase and pistons made from electron) would have considerably improved the output of the flying boat.

Of particular interest to von Gronau were the flight times recorded, showing that a Dornier Whale with two BMW VI engines took off on 22 July at '11.07 from Marina di Pisa and landed on the water at 14.26 on Lake Constance near Manzell, after the flying boat had reached an altitude of more than 4,600 m. over the Alps near Mt Spluegen. On 24 July the same flying boat took off from Manzell at 11.40 and landed at Kiel-Holtenau at 18.00.'

Gronau prepared his adventure with just as much secrecy as cunning. Lindbergh's flight had brought people to fever pitch. In spite of this, there was no chance of the Reich Transport Ministry authorising the flight. So Gronau only involved the Dornier company, which found a pretext for making fuel available in Iceland, Greenland and Labrador, as well as guaranteeing to meet the costs. As Dornier had to take the Shell company into its confidence, there were two accessories, quite apart from the Danish government, which had to approve these supplies, in view of the fact that Dornier had already built the Giant Bird DO X (which was in fact to fly to America, although this would never be officially announced).

Gronau took off in July 1929 for Iceland intending to fly further, but had to abandon his flight because of excessive fuel consumption. The speed was lower than he had thought, and the fuel stored in Greenland did not have a high enough anti-knock quality. So back he went. No one knew the slightest thing about it. In spring 1930 von Gronau had the Whale overhauled. As the rear engine no longer complied with safety regulations, a new one had to be fitted – which was easier said than done. The world was in the throes of the Slump, and there was only one BMW VI in the entire German air fleet. It was to be found, lying in pieces (for research work) at the German Research Establishment for Aviation in Adlershof, Berlin. Gronau complained that his entire training programme was ruined – and then received the engine from the Reich Transport Ministry to whom subsequently, on leaving Reykjavik and already en route to Greenland, he sent the following radio message (which was the first time the radio operator knew what was happening): 'D – 1422 to

Reich Transport Ministry Berlin. Am flying, local traffic control permitting, over Greenland to USA. Request telegraphic application for permission to land in both countries. D – 1422, Gronau.'

The flight to America was smooth, judging by all accounts, and without engine failure. Admittedly, the Whale lost its radio generator as it took off from Arsuk fjord on the southern tip of Greenland, but 'we had on board another petrol-driven generator. Some other instruments stopped working, but such minor problems were not going to stop us.' After ten days, on 26 August 1930, the old Amundsen Whale, the former N 25, touched down in New York, not to a ticking-off from the Reich Transport Ministry, but a congratulatory telegram for the 'well-planned and courageous flight'. It was accompanied by a gift of the deluxe edition of Kleist's play *Prince Friedrich of Homburg*. But why this gift exactly? In the Battle of Fehrbellin the Prince of Homburg, as the cavalry commander, attacked, against the orders of the Grand Elector, thereby decisively affecting the outcome of the battle in favour of the latter. Kleist's play ends with: 'To hell with all Brandenburg's enemies!' Brandenburg was also the name of the head of the aviation department in the Reich Transport Ministry. Was there more of a threat than an acquittal for insubordination in this statement of clemency? Gronau wanted to know more. No, replied the Ministry, alluding only to the words addressed by Colonel Kottwitz to the Grand Elector. Gronau looked them up. Kottwitz says: 'Sire, it is not the supreme law of the land that should move your general's heart, to which you should attach the initial of your will – it is rather the Fatherland, the Crown.' Gronau was surprised to find so much sensitive humour lurking in a government office in 1930.

Two years later when he went round the earth in a genuine seaplane, the new Whale, Gronau discovered the real reasons for his success, which he, like Lindbergh, had modestly attributed to his engines (this time, they were the standard fitting of the type VIIa BMW engines).

> Greenland and the Atlantic lay behind us. Canada with all its lakes had been crossed. Thanks to our two, totally reliable, BMW VIIa engines, we had reached the Rocky Mountains, that mighty mountain barrier rising to 3,000 m, which separates the country from the Pacific. . . Now came the hardest part of the flight – along the coast to Alaska and out across the North Pacific to Japan. My plan was to follow the stretch of the Aleutian Islands and fill up with fuel on the first and last of these.

Struggling in appalling weather and high winds, Gronau reached Unalaska, an inhospitable place, where he had to wait a fortnight for a steamer with fuel. The steamer had hit a reef in the fog, but at least now he had enough fuel to carry on flying.

'It's now or never, since any problem with the engines in this desolate place would be a real disaster! We met a storm shortly after leaving Unalaska, and realised that we were not going to reach our destination in a day.'

So the Whale skirted along the Canadian coast to a God-forsaken fur-trapping station, where Gronau found two drums of petrol which a ship had left in the previous year for him. He could now attempt the last leg of his Pacific crossing.

> Even if the smallest thing were to go wrong, and we were forced to do no more than turn round, the flight would have failed. For returning to the island would have meant, with the small amount of Shell we had stored there, that we would have been stranded. That would have been the end of everything.
>
> Our BMWs continued to drone away evenly, and our eyes often glanced across at the rev counter, the thermometer and all the other instruments. But all the needles gave us peace of mind, since they remained constant. Finally, after the long flight through the clouds and the fog, we broke through the veil, and the mountains of Kamchatka and the Kuril Islands appeared over the horizon – steaming volcanoes, grotesquely-shaped cliffs, larva glowing dark-red, or cold black. . . . That was the most difficult part over. Japan lay ahead of us.

By the time he got back, Gronau had covered 44,800 kilometres with only one mechanical problem en route. This occurred in the Bay of Bengal on the way from the Philippines to India ('a raging sea below us, full of sharks!'). The fault was incorrectly blamed by the press on the engines. A thermometer, not specified by BMW as original equipment, broke up in the coolant hose, and fragments of this thermometer damaged the water pump. This led to one engine breaking down. It was a difficult situation, as he was in a violent storm 250 kilometres from the nearest shore. But the engine still running kept the plane so securely in the air that an SOS signal could be put out and the Whale brought down smoothly onto the water.

In 1946 Popp reflected from his prison cell at Stadelheim in Munich on the facts of the case with which he hoped to prove to the Allied occupation powers, that BMW had directed the aero-engine production which he had started up again in the 1920s not for military purposes, but only for civil aviation, principally for commercial transport.

As we can read in his 'memorandum' which he was to draft shortly afterwards, he states:

> When I came into contact with the leading circles in the aviation industry during my visit to the USA in 1928, I was extremely impressed with their plans for the future, in particular with the successes they had had with the new types of aero-engines which had been developed for commercial aviation; above all, the air-cooled radial engine. . . After brief negotiations with the firm of Pratt & Whitney in Hartford, I succeeded in acquiring the licence to build their engines, the 'Hornet' and the 'Wasp', for the whole of Europe on very favourable terms. These were two nine-cylinder, air-cooled radial engines giving either 400 or 525 hp. Only the first five test engines of the Hornet had been produced at Pratt & Whitney, but my impression regarding the prospects of this design was so convincing that I gladly took this risk upon myself and was never to regret it. From that moment on, I enjoyed an ever closer friendship with the top people of

this American firm, which at the time was still relatively small, but which was to grow within a few years into the United Aircraft Corporation, the most important aviation company in the USA.

Popp then went on to speak about the two types of aero-engine, water-cooled and air-cooled, and to characterise their main differences in application:

The water-cooled engine, as was used during the First World War by all sides, proved to have considerable disadvantages for civil aviation after the war. The reason for this was that there was a switchover to developing air-cooled radial engines, first in England and then shortly afterwards in America, which corresponded exactly to the requirements of civil aviation. For military purposes, the water-cooled engine remained the preferred option because of its better output at high altitudes and because of its lower drag at high speeds. So within a few years the air-cooled aero-engine came to dominate civilian aviation throughout the world, while the military still hesitated as to how much consideration to give it.

Popp did not remain silent on the matter of subsequent developments, which were to show that the air-cooled engine had proved itself capable in all respects of meeting almost all the requirements of war planes, especially for bombers.

'Only the German military authorities,' Popp went on to say, 'which were heavily involved, as a study exercise, in preparing a future air force, rejected the air-cooled engine from the very start as unsuitable, in total ignorance of what technical progress had to offer.'

Popp's reflection is interesting on two accounts. Firstly, for the comparison that can be made with the years up to 1914 when Germany rigidly stuck to the virtues of the dirigible airship (lighter than air), to the point where the German War Ministry denied as late as 1910 that the aeroplane (heavier than air) could carry anyone except the pilot, thereby making it useless for reconnaissance.

Secondly (even if the intention of Popp's memorandum was to clear his company from the charge of being an armaments factory), he stated that BMW had little concern for the military, and vice versa. Even in 1930, when the League of Nations promised Germany the right to build up its own air force (whereupon the Reich army judiciously issued identical offers for tender to three German companies, Daimler-Benz, Junkers and BMW, for a water-cooled aero-engine of the latest design), Popp made it known that his licence agreement for the air-cooled engine was not forgotten.

He claims that there were witnesses who remember him saying that this development would prove him right. Just *how* right he was was proved by the transport plane 'Ju 52', fitted with a BMW 132 radial engine, which acquired an almost legendary reputation in the thirties. When Group Captain Udet took charge of the technical section in the Ministry of Aviation in 1936, he was to commission Popp in an attempt to correct the biased and, for him, completely wrong view of the Luftwaffe towards aero-engines, with the job of immediately acquiring a licence for a double radial engine – too late, as Popp was to discover; Washington had already banned Pratt & Whitney from further issuing licences.

We have jumped ahead somewhat and, like in a game of ludo, we need to go back to square one; with Duckstein, Friz's right-hand man, pointing out to the young Schleicher what would one day grow out of that field with its seventeen wooden hangars. Five years later, a factory was to stand there, complete with new production halls made of red clinker brick, 'a quality control station' for checking raw and finished materials at the goods inwards section, and, behind the raw materials store, which was so clearly laid out that only someone who was colour-blind could get lost (the materials were stored along colour-coded alleys), a machine tool hall housing 600 machines, each with individual drive, but with no direct- or intermediate-drive belts which the works in Moosach Street once had. The real hub was the main machine hall where aero-engines and motorcycle parts ran side by side in production-line type facilities. 'Can I grow a field of corn in the palm of my hand?' King Charles says in Schiller's *The Maid of Orleans*. Here at Lechanau Street on the edge of Oberwiesenfeld, it had all done just that – grown in the palm of a hand.

An underground passage led from the assembly halls to an oval area surrounded by high walls. From a distance it looked like a fortification. But anyone approaching it would hear a few whistling noises rising and falling in pitch above the even running of the test engines. Heads bobbed above the top of the wall like cannon-balls flying back and forth. Anyone climbing the wall would see the men on the other side running in motorcycles on a concrete track. In the middle of the oval area, sunk into the ground and thus below works level, the aero-engines raced at full throttle. Every engine, as an observer had once calculated, consisted of 4,500 parts. Once assembled, it came here to the test bed for its trial run. Then it was dismantled (a detached, two-storey building was built for this at the upper end of the oval), reassembled and again sent to the test bed for its 'final inspection'. The factory then employed 2,400 workers with 400 office staff in the administration buildings at the front.

In his speech at the BMW general meeting in April 1927, the chairman of the supervisory board, Dr Emil Georg von Stauss, spoke of the factory's duty to dispense with the remaining temporary arrangements, and restructure for rationalised production. The first consideration was for a new assembly hall for all engine building, which would have to be of such a size as to make small car production feasible, for which the company was developing its own design.

The assembly hall was ready. There was no sight of any small car production. No one seems to have given it a second's thought to the entire 200,000 square metres of field at Lerchenau Street.

Car Wanted

Anyone who knows anything about that darkest day in the life of BMW (9 December 1959, when the general meeting decided to liquidate the company) will also know the name of its presumptive heir. Flick, as the main shareholder in Daimler-Benz AG, had issued an ultimatum for the takeover of the Bavarian works which ran out at midnight, and everyone was betting on the fact that Daimler-Benz, 'Big Brother' and adversary (as BMW's love-hate relationship with them through the years might be interpreted), would pull it off in one go and make the Bavarian company into a kind of components supplier. This solution at least had the merit of taking BMW out of the hands of the banks, who would probably have broken up the BMW inheritance bit by bit and sold it off.

The rumour, which spread through the ranks of the excited small shareholders on that December day in 1959 as they gathered at the Exhibition Park at Theresienwiese, filled with despondent rage, turned out to be no rumour at all, but bitter reality. The leading figures from the Swabian car factory had already booked several suites in Munich hotels just to able to seize power the following day. The fact that it turned out otherwise does not alter Daimler-Benz's intention to add a plant to its own business, which should have teamed up with the Stuttgart works in the twenties, if things had gone according to the plans of a number of Daimler directors, in addition to Popp and his backer, Castiglioni. The plan was then, in 1925–26, to associate BMW to a joint venture between Daimler and Benz (which had not yet amalgamated), with the aim of creating a powerful car business in southern Germany. All those involved thought that this alone would be enough to maintain the high levels of quality which were found at BMW *and* at Daimler and Benz, even in times of crisis. Added to this was the argument that none felt strong enough on its own. The plan was designed, against a background of the major economic importance that the car was increasingly playing, to overcome the consequences of losing a war more quickly, in view of the fact that they were up against the car industries of the victorious nations. They also hoped to consolidate an industry and so have greater effect in countering short-sighted measures adopted by government (for example, cars were still taxed as luxury goods).

As early as 1919, when Count Kolowrat, the mad 'Sascha', had wheeled

116

out his racing car designed by Porsche in Vienna, Popp had had the idea of building this vehicle (with its unbeatable economy, speed and reliability) at BMW in Munich – instead of Austro-Daimler in Vienna. In spite of its sporting pretensions, it would find a perfect niche in an impoverished Germany. Indeed, this idea had persuaded Castiglioni not to get rid of BMW, although he knew that aviation had been the first casualty. With the possibility of mass-producing this car, he planned to help the works get back on its feet again.

In his 'memoirs', Carlo Schmid spoke of something strange he had observed when a demonstration crossed over Kings Street in Stuttgart on a beautiful December morning in 1918.

> Coming in the opposite direction and pulled by two fine black horses was a beautiful coach. Shouts went up, fists started flying, and things looked pretty desperate for the equipage. At the very last moment, the coachman managed to turn into a side street. Just minutes later, a heavy Daimler car went up the street, again going against the procession. Far from an outcry, this produced a general 'Ah!' of approval. Obviously the demonstrators saw the coach as part of a world from which they felt excluded, while they saw something in the limousine that was not far off what they could afford. Quantitatively, the car manufacturer belonged to one class, while qualitatively, the man in the coach belonged to an entirely different one.

What Carlo Schmid was referring to was only a hair's breadth away from Popp's philosophy that while the impoverished masses in Germany viewed the car as a luxury item, just like everybody else in the world, this certainly did not mean that they were abandoning their desire to own such a vehicle. The car, which was compensated for by the motorcycle, became (as it did after the Second World War) the ordinary man's dream for a better life, a dream which allowed hunger, deprivation, even human desperation to be forgotten in the trials and tribulations of a horrifying present.

Popp's intention of fulfilling the dream resolved him to sweep away the past. Car bodies could not be made from the plywood left behind by the Bavarian Aircraft Works. There was no point in jealously eyeing stocks of material which the car manufacturers had hoarded up in their amalgamated 'Union of German Engine and Vehicle Industries'. Bought in at prices considerably above those of the world market, they scarcely offered any chance to the proliferating car firms of establishing themselves competitively against mass-produced foreign models. In the early post-war years 131 makes of car appeared on the German market (a spring-like bourgeoning of cars), which were destined to disappear just as quickly as they had emerged. Amongst them was a three-wheeled car designed by Reinhold Böhm, of which twenty-five were brought out by the Mauser armaments factory at Oberndorf on the Neckar, powered by the BMW M 2 B 15 horizontally-opposed engine.

That was how the war had taken over the further technical development of the car, as it had done with the aeroplane. No private testing grounds, no testing to destruction could be contemplated in peacetime. Both of these had spurred

117

designers on to achieve technical feasibility and solve production problems. If the private car allocated to army staffs, which was nimble and robust over rough terrain, had still managed to preserve its feudal character, then the lorry, by contrast, had become the soldier's self-sufficient and indispensable aide as a beast of burden and traction for transporting supplies and pulling artillery. There was, in the meantime, no question of motorising troops to increase mobility and engagement, which could have decided the outcome of battles, as happened in the Second World War. Yet there was just one example in France in the early days of the war when the car did play a key role. It performed the first of those three miracles described by Jacques Montane, the miracle of the Marne.

Later the French called it the 'epic song of the taxis which saved Paris'. Indeed, one of those taxis of the Marne still stands today in the place of honour at the Hôtel des Invalides. It was one of the 700 of all that were available in Paris, mostly small Renault Coupés which had been requisitioned the day before and assembled on the square in front of the Hôtel. This was on 7 September 1914. General Galliéni, the commandant of Paris and commanding officer of the hastily assembled defence force, put five reservists in each of these taxis and transported overnight (and without lights) five infantry battalions, which could not have been done any other way. These 3,000 to 4,000 men thus reached General Maunory's embattled army fifty kilometres away, arriving at the height of the Battle of the Ourcq.

General Galliéni's idea of transporting entire units by car to the front (and so be quicker than conventional military wisdom allowed) was not only restricted to war, which had led to the motorisation of the army. Gallieni's idea went beyond the bounds of war, to demonstrate that the car was an opportunity for everyone to break the restrictions imposed on them by the prevailing conditions of life. If this moved the masses *unconsciously* (as proved by the demonstrators in Stuttgart, who waved their fists at the coach while allowing the Daimler limousine to go by), then it *consciously* prevailed over the ebb and flow of the many innovations put on the market. This was the essence of the 'People's Car', at a time when Hitler was in prison in the Landsberg fortress and the idea was far from his thoughts.

Popp was one of the first to 'transport' this idea, which he published in an article in the trade magazine *Motor* at the time of the Motor Show in December 1924. Here he categorically stated that an economical, mass-produced small car was feasible, and a market survey should establish in advance, firstly, what chances of success the plan had in itself and, secondly, just how far Germany could be motorised.

Years later, when Hitler (who had just assumed power) opened the International Motor Show at Berlin in 1933, he came across Popp on the BMW stand. To the latter's amazement, Hitler immediately started talking about the article in *Motor* (a magazine which he said he had always taken a special interest in), and about a further article which Popp had published on the same theme in February 1925 in the newspaper *München-Augsburger Abendzeitung* and in the ADAC news letter. As Popp later reported, Hitler had had all this at his fingertips, presumably because he had read about

118

it and reflected upon it at the fortress in Landsberg, since he said before leaving (and what he said was already 'irrefutable' in 1933): 'The car must not cost a thousand dollars, but only a thousand marks!'

Here at least, Popp admitted, was one reflection of his thoughts, which up to that time had produced next to no reaction in business circles, apart from one exception – which was the joint venture between Daimler and Benz in which BMW was supposed to be included. There was one man, above all, who not only shared Popp's views but had proposed them on many occasions. This was Dr Wilhelm Kissel, who had been head of purchasing at Benz and Co. in Mannheim from 1921 and then chairman and chief executive of the new joint Daimler and Benz company.

Both Kissel and Popp drew up a strategic plan for the merger. At first there were to be strict divisions between the companies: BMW would build only aero-engines and motorcycles; Daimler-Benz only cars, although BMW was to prepare manufacture of a small car. In England the small Austin Seven had gained so much ground, like the small Citroën in France and the famous 'tree-frog' Opel in Germany, that there was no time to lose.

This resulted in a proper contract, and we even know the date of it, despite its having been destroyed by the flames of the Second World War – 15 April 1926. Its goal was merger, and it first of all provided for the merger between Daimler and Benz. Just how seriously both partners took it was shown by the staff transfers – Franz Josef Popp was transferred to the supervisory board of the new company on the day of the merger between Daimler and Benz on 19 June 1926, and shortly afterwards Dr Wilhelm Kissel was put on the BMW supervisory board. This certainly could not have happened without Dr Emil Georg von Stauss (job description: 'Banker in Berlin'), who was chairman on both supervisory boards.

When a man has his eyes about him, he can (provided he is an honest man) serve not just two masters, as the Bible says, but also a third. Dr von Stauss was blessed with this gift. The maxim of Georg von Siemens, founder and for many years president of Deutsche Bank, when speaking about himself and his profession, was no less valid for Dr von Stauss as director of Deutsche Bank – whose business it was to invest wherever possible, which often involved considerable sums. 'The trick is not to rush headlong into the wall, but to use your eyes to find the door.' Von Stauss also felt that this German car trust planned by Kissel and Popp was absolutely vital to prevent failures. He saw the first step towards this as being the Daimler-Benz merger, followed by the incorporation of BMW. As Kissel and Popp trusted him, and he them, and because he could see as well as they could the virtues of building a small car, he felt able to say to Popp: Build it!

That was easier said than done, even if the money was now available. Porsche had already developed a one-litre small car for Daimler-Benz, which had even been built in thirty prototypes. It had nothing to do with Porsche's later 'Volkswagen', but had its four-cylinder engine fitted at the front in the 'orthodox way'. It was, to a certain extent, a miniature version of the large 8/38-hp Mercedes super-charged car, and Mercedes had decided against that. Why? Was it because, as a former Daimler director, Porsche had been against the merger with Benz and consequently had incited the new supervisory board against him? Probably not. (Castiglioni had once said to Herr von Stauss: 'You can take Porsche on . . . he is a brilliant man. But you will have to put him in a cage with seven locks. That's the best place to leave him to draft his engine designs. But he will have to pass his drawings through the bars so that, with luck, he won't be able to get his hands on the drawings or the engine again!') But it was not the development costs which caused the project to be abandoned; rather the reflection that it was better to stay with small numbers of large cars which guaranteed profit than to build a small car which would not be profitable – quite apart from the real risk that mass production would bring and the heavy investment associated with it.

'Build it!' Popp thought again of the model he had long since rejected. Friz had taken a centrally-mounted tubular chassis from a Tatra for it and powered it with an M 2 B 15. No, that was not good enough, either. But what was all this about the aluminium car which the car experts had extolled as a real step forward? The Swabian Iron and Steel Works SHW in Aalen-Wasseralfingen were working on it, and the aerodynamics expert Wunibald Kamm, a friend of Popp's, had designed it. It was very low and similar to the Lancia Lambda, and also very light due to its chassis, which was made of cast aluminium. It was a small car with front-wheel drive and a flat-twin, water-cooled engine giving 20 hp. Popp, with an equally enthusiastic Friz, was convinced that he had found 'his' car and concluded an agreement with Kamm and the Iron and Steel Works to participate in the further development of the SHW (as the car was called) right up to the production stage. Three prototypes resulted from this. They were chased up and down the Swabian mountains, which showed up their faults. As a whole, the car never met the individual promises made by its design features. Popp had to keep putting off his supervisory board, saying that better results were just around the corner. But it was all in vain. In July 1928 BMW finally abandoned the project at an extraordinary general meeting. At the same time, the share capital was increased from 10 to 16 million Reich marks. This meant looking around immediately for a new car design. It had to have the advantage of being ready for production.

In the meantime, Popp had been to the USA. He had visited the Ford Works in Detroit. What he saw there was not production in the German or European sense, but output of mind-boggling proportions. The supremacy of the conveyor belt, which put out a finished car every four minutes (just in the one hall that Popp saw), made him wonder where they would all go. The American continent was not infinite. By the end of May 1921, Ford had produced its five-millionth car and, with price cuts (which must mean reduced production costs, again resulting from rigorous rationalisation), had increased daily production to 4,000 cars. When would this wave reach Germany? Ford was already setting up in Berlin. There were not many who would have wanted to meet this scale of production – except with a small car which needed to be available yesterday rather than today. In discussions which he held in New York with the officials at the Henry Schroeder Banking Corporation, Popp confirmed that the chances for this were not at all bad.

They even let it be known that they would participate in BMW. Popp did not decline, but only thought: What a relief compared to Deutsche Bank, and Castiglioni.

Castiglioni! At the height of his powers, at the beginning of 1924, he had squandered a fortune estimated at between 5 and 30 million pounds sterling (still credited with an excellent press – he owned five newspapers in Vienna alone) by speculating in French francs to such an extent that the stock market crisis, as reported in an English article, dealt him a final blow. Finally he had to leave the country, relentlessly pursued by his adversaries. He had been president of the deposit bank which had collapsed. He returned to Vienna under safe conduct – with head held high once again – which he probably owed to the Italian government, as he was an Italian citizen and even president of the Banca d'Italia. Anyway, he was elected again as the chairman of the BMW supervisory board after he had temporally lost this post, and he was even attributed the unusual honorary title of 'President of the Bavarian Motor Works'.

It made it all the more incomprehensible that he was to dispose of his entire shareholding to the Berlin banker Max von Wassermann in 1925 when he had overdrawn the insignificant amount of 1.68 million Reich marks for Castiglioni, in order to buy it all back again a year later! What was behind all this?

'I have always bought when the others were selling, and always sold when the others were buying!' an old financial wheeler-dealer is supposed to have said when he was asked how he acquired his wealth. If the same were true for Castiglioni, then this was obviously due to the fact that, as one of the great exploiters of currency depreciation, he could only secure, maintain and increase his new assets if this depreciation continued. If conditions were to stabilise, these values would have to be secured and increased through self-financing productivity. If the old promoter, of whom it was said that he could hear the grass grow, had stepped aside, was this because he had seen that things could not go on as before? Or did he merely want to create unrest so that nothing would go wrong while he waited to see what would happen to 'stabilisation'? When Wassermann's bank suggested increasing the share capital at BMW by 5 million Reich marks so as to finance expansion of the plant at Lerchenau Street, sudden heavy demand for BMW shares showed up those who knew what was what, and CC immediately stepped back in. Perhaps he merely anticipated what nobody else had sensed, i.e. the Slump, which would sweep away everything that was not secured in granite.

We do not want to attribute him with powers of clairvoyance. Castiglioni could not help noticing a man whose rise had been no less spectacular than his own – Jakob Schapiro. He observed him more closely at a time when his attempt to consolidate his own quickly acquired wealth was running up against obstacles. Schapiro had been born in Odessa and then, like Castiglioni, had gone to Vienna, before moving to Berlin, where he started up a driving school and then a car dealership, mainly in Benz cars. His cast-iron principle was that he bought them with credit that was extended until it was only worth pfennigs, but which could always be traded in for assets –

panels, tyres, shares, and preferably ordinary shares in the Benz Works. This uncompromisingly direct approach, which was not far off swindling with all its tricks and subterfuge (which honest business people were not up to), had not only made him the owner of his own business which bore his name, but also secured him a place on the company board, with almost fifty per cent of Benz shares in his possession.

Alfred Neubauer, for many years in charge of racing at Mercedes, reveals in his book *Men, Women and Cars* how Schapiro bought 200 chassis from the Benz Motor Works in the Rhineland one day, and had them bodied at his own works in Berlin: 'Suddenly finished cars appeared on the market which were 3,000 marks cheaper than similarly-sized vehicles from established companies. From the outside you could not tell that they were fitted inside with cheap, poor-quality panels. A year later Jakob Schapiro was already the main shareholder and sole representative for Benz and Co., Germany's oldest car company.'

On one occasion he met this man at the Berlin Motor Show. He would never forget the way Schapiro stood in front of his four-litre Benz car in a morning coat, his bowler hat pushed back a bit over his head, arms akimbo, with a fat Brazilian cigar between his lips.

He said to Neubauer, 'Herr Neubauer, I'd like to see anyone do what I've done: come to Berlin seven years ago with just a few pairs of braces and end up owning Benz and Co. like me!'

At first Schapiro, fearing the end of his influence, put up bitter resistance to the proposed Daimler-Benz merger (the first hurdle for Kissel and Popp in their plans for a south German car company). Then, when he discovered the advantages, he became its proponent. As it was, no one had been able to stop him entering the new company's supervisory board (and BMW's supervisory board). He was upset by BMW's plan to build cars as well, and opposed it. Until Castiglioni made it clear to him that several firms involved with cars in which Shapiro had invested, and whose future was not very rosy, were in a position to achieve increased turnovers as suppliers to BMW. Was Castiglioni thinking here of the Gotha Railway Carriage Company, which Schapiro had recently acquired? Schapiro had certainly thought of it (over everything else) – and gave his consent.

Then things got worse. Success had evaporated (the German car industry was in a dire state) in the bitter struggle for power in 1928, in an economic climate that had changed from five years before, when inflation had allowed absolutely everything to anyone who 'did not follow the herd, but made it on his own'. Schapiro had affiliated the Gotha Railway Carriage Company to the Zyklon Works, exercised a leading role at NSU, and had also acquired the Chillingworth Presser and Extruder Works in Nuremberg. Withdrawing at the moment a firm has broken even could not be done without getting your fingers burnt, in the same way that it would be difficult to sell a complete shareholding abroad without being noticed, even if you had wide-ranging contacts.

Once before, when Schapiro had tried to dispose of his Benz shares to Belgian banks (this was in 1923), one man had known how to prevent him, a man who eventually became a staunch opponent. Now, at a time when Schapiro wanted to pull off the same coup (this time with Daimler-Benz shares), his adversary learnt of it in sufficient time to thwart his dealings on the stock market.

This man was a banker, and director of the Deutsche Bank, chairman of the supervisory boards at Daimler-Benz and BMW. His name, as we know, was Dr Emil Georg von Stauss, a man who had always kept a watchful eye on the wily speculator, who pulled no punches and got what he wanted from his tricks.

When autumn 1928 had fallen over the country and the car BMW was supposed to build was nowhere near a reality, von Stauss told Popp: 'Go ahead and buy it!'

What Popp had to buy was not just a car but an entire factory. The car, a small car, was there ready and waiting, had proved successful and had shown that it still had something to offer. It was a foreign make produced under licence. The factory, which had acquired the licence, was, in spite of the success, on the verge of bankruptcy. It, or rather its owner, had 'taken on too much', as the expression goes. It was the Eisenach Vehicle Factory, a subsidiary of the Railway Carriage Company in Gotha which had its main office in Eisenach, and it belonged to the Schapiro concern. The car was called the Dixi and was provisionally the last product of a whole generation of cars bearing the same name. In reality it was nothing other than the famous Austin Seven, whose licence the Eisenach Vehicle Factory had acquired.

Popp immediately went there.

Below Wartburg

The concepts of discontinuing and launching something new are closely interconnected in the car industry. When Heinrich Ehrhardt, the founder of the Eisenach Vehicle Factory, gave up the chairmanship of the supervisory board in 1903 due to business problems, and left his works, he concluded his defence, so the story goes, with the word 'Dixi', like those Roman orators who brought their orations to an end with the set phrase: 'Dixi et salvavi animam meam' – 'I have spoken (meaning it was my duty) and saved my soul (meaning my conscience is clear).' If Ehrhardt, Clerk of Works (provided we are to believe he actually said this), had known anything about the deeper significance of the word, he could not have sensed what it meant for the future of his works, which he himself did not think had one. 'Dixi' was in fact the name given by his successors to the new cars which were to make Eisenach famous and enable it to flourish over a quarter of a century.

In 1896 Ehrhardt, the son of a Thuringian peasant who was to become a leading armaments industrialist in Düsseldorf, founded the Eisenach Vehicle Factory. With a contract issued by the Procurement Office, he wanted to build (in a place where there were ample skilled workers, and where he could help his impoverished home region at the same time) 'private petrol-engined cars' alongside bicycles, military vehicles, gun-carriages and other military equipment. Acquiring a licence from the French firm of Décauville, and thereby saving him costly and time-consuming development work, was to make this possible. As the third German factory after Daimler and Benz, he was immediately able to begin mass-production of a car.

Indeed, 307 Wartburg cars which still had a de Dion-Bouton engine under the driver's seat rather than under the bonnet, rolled through the gates of the factory at Eisenach. But the costs (only a year later the share capital which had been raised from 1,250,000 to 2,700,000 marks had to be increased by a further million) soon exceeded all profitability, which could not be offset by gold medals and victories in road and long-distance rallies, let alone by the occasional visit, where words of praise were uttered, from the Grand Duke of Saxony-Weimar-Eisenach, complete with retinue. Why, the Clerk of Works might have wondered, didn't he just stick to his cobbler's last (meaning military contracts) and rely on what he had invented himself? In fact, Ehrhardt had thought of quite a few designs. Working with the engineer

Conrad Haussner, he had developed a 'pressing and extruding method for producing seamless hollow sections', the so-called 'Ehrhardt process' which is still used even today for producing steel sections. He also developed a rail-guided saw, as well as a chainless hill cycle, for which he had thought up a kind of transmission shaft. Above all, he is credited (though experts continue to contest this) with being the inventor of the recoiling-barrel gun, for which contemporaries called him (with no little respect and certainly no mockery) the 'little cannon king'.

But who can look into a man's soul? No sooner had Ehrhardt pronounced his 'Dixi' and left Eisenach than he continued to build the Décauville car, now called the 'Ehrhardt-Décauville' at Zella St Blasii in Thuringia, the home of his manufacturing business, as if showing that Eisenach was no longer the right place for this. Did he perhaps only want to show to the men back there that the old Ehrhardt did not give up so easily? It was, of course, connected with the fact that his son Gustav, who had left Eisenach at the same time, now had the chance of making his own way in car building. So why should the licencing agreement, which Ehrhardt was so much a part of, lie fallow and not be used? Anyway, he continued to build cars, and cast an eye across to Eisenach. At first, he was sceptical, then amazed. Finally, he was admiring. No, Heinrich Ehrhardt could be at peace with his duty and conscience, which had demanded that he leave. The company he had founded lived on.

And how it lived on! Not least of all because of the 'Dixi', that secretive and magical-sounding word (even for technicians who were no Latin scholars). This was the name used on the very first two models which appeared in 1904 at the International Motor Show in Frankfurt am Main: the S 6 and the S 12. The 'S' came from Willy Seck, one of Germany's most famous designers, who had been specially recruited. His designs, taken over and further developed by his successor, Georg Schwarz, were based on use of a modular system throughout, providing an uninterrupted range of engines from 1.2 to 5 litres, even offering a 7.3 litre engine fitted to the 'luxury limousine, which was also available as a sports car and landaulette'. In spite of a succession of owners, cars brought Eisenach fame and fortune.

But there was trouble on the horizon. Eisenach, now called the 'Eisenach Vehicle Factory', a subsidiary of the Gotha Railway Carriage Company, had to balance the losses suffered at the parent company, and the old privy councillor Kandt, left in power as the only member of the board since 1902, immediately knew how to do this. As the number of activities carried out in Eisenach was continually increasing, while falling in Gotha, he transferred whole product ranges to Gotha: production of oil-burning engines, manufacture of fire-hoses and lorry building. But none of it did any good. The firm was not saved by the ever greater investments made in Gotha, but only got deeper into debt. By 1926 bankruptcy loomed.

And then along came Schapiro. In the 'process of building stronger companies', the Gotha Railway Carriage Company joined the Schapiro group of companies, with Eisenach also coming under new control, thereby landing itself with new worries on top of its own. These were the Zyklon Works at Mylau in Saxony, which Schapiro had also incorporated. Zyklon had developed a 40-hp six-cylinder car, seen as a wayward child in Eisenach, but which Schapiro still held out some hope for. With an engine capacity of only 2.3 litres (which should have the effect of encouraging sales due to high road fund taxation in Germany), this car would now be built and sold as the 9/40-hp Dixi, although the high quantities planned for it did not materialise. In fact, the engineers in Eisenach 'preferred' to develop a 3.5 litre car with 60 hp (completely disregarding the market and its cry for a people's car), which ended up less of a wayward child than a stillborn one. Bankruptcy seemed inevitable. What was to be done? There was just as little time for a new, in-house design as there was money, which would, however, just stretch to a licensing agreement. And so Schapiro came to the same decision as Ehrhardt had done when he began car-building at Eisenach in 1896 with the licence agreement for the French Décauville.

This time the owner's eye fell upon an English make, a small car which the Austin Motor Co. in Birmingham had been building since 1922. It was called the 'Austin Seven', which, despite its rather spartan look, had become Britain's most successful small car.

A convoy of lorries laden with a hundred Austin Sevens rolled into the yard at the Eisenach Works in July 1927. An eye-witness, then an apprentice, who helped with the unloading, was not wrong in telling me (as he struggled for the right words to describe what it was like and the effect it had had on him and the other workers):

'It was like a blood transfusion. We all got back into the swing of things. Everyone had the feeling that this was it! The factory had completely gone to the dogs. A few Englishmen had already arrived in advance. They had brought with them design drawings for re-equipping the machine tools. I worked in the bodyshop. The car was really tiny; we only realised just how tiny when we saw it at first hand. But that was just it! Everyone immediately fell in love with it. Somehow everyone knew that Eisenach would not close down and that it would carry on.'

It was now Popp's turn to stand in front of this car. This was on 28 September 1928. Although 7,000 of these 'small Dixis', as they were affectionately called, had meanwhile been sold in Germany, the blood transfusion had not been sufficient to save Schapiro. He was forced to sell.

On 14 November 1928 the contract was signed between Hoppe and Cleinow on behalf of the Gotha Railway Carriage Company, and Popp and Voigt on behalf of the Bavarian Motor Works. Everything took place quickly and without any hitches. The Gotha company received 200,000 Reich marks in cash and shares in BMW to a nominal value of 800,000 Reich marks, for which Castiglioni, as president of BMW, guaranteed a rate of 250. In exchange, BMW took over a liability of 11 million marks shown on the right-hand side of Eisenach's last balance-sheet. The book value of the Eisenach Vehicle Factory, along with properties in Berlin and Stuttgart, amounted to 4,996,487 marks. Naturally BMW acquired all rights and patents pending, drawings and designs, 'in particular thereof also the trade-mark Dixi', as was stated in Paragraph 6, and also the personnel employed at the Eisenach Works (Paragraph 13), 'if they are prepared to do this'.

Most of them were prepared.

On the day the contract was signed in Eisenach, the German Foreign Minister, Gustav Stresemann, gave a press conference, at which he said:

'I would ask you to take as a basis for your judgements, as regards the economic state of Germany and other questions associated with it, the fact that we in Germany have lived on borrowed money over the last few years. If we were to be faced by a crisis and the Americans were to withdraw their short-term loans to us, then we would be bankrupt. What we raise by taxes goes to the very limit of what a state can conceivably do. I do not know where the money for new taxes will come from. Statistics show how much the cities have needed, how much industry has needed, how much foreign money we have accepted just to keep ourselves going. Not only are we militarily disarmed, we are also financially disarmed. We have no resources left.'

The days which followed this bleak report heralded further warning signs. There was turmoil in the iron and steel industries in Rhineland and Westphalia − strikes for higher wages, lock-outs, attempts by the government to mediate, which failed to satisfy anyone, economic recession with ever decreasing tax revenues due to the rising numbers of unemployed. In December 1928 there were almost 2 million registered unemployed, and by January 1929 there were close to 3 million. In February the figure rose to 3,229,871 unemployed, who were obliged to stand in front of the offices during an exceptionally cold winter and appreciate how the whole social security system no longer worked, and that if the dams were to break, then living standards would fall even further. This was how things continued until that 'Black Friday', 24 October 1929, when banks shut down on Wall Street.

The crisis had come, the Great Depression, which gripped the whole world. It broke over Europe like a storm tearing off roofs and, at its destructive height, raged in the very place where there were no longer any roofs − Germany (as Stresemann had prophesied less than a year previously).

But the Hohe Strasse, Germany's famous trade route, which ran below Wartburg Castle and linked Frankfurt on Main straight through Thuringia to Halle, Bautzen, Görlitz by Breslau (which is now called Wroclaw, whose inhabitants are unfamiliar with the Hohe Strasse, which was originally known as the Via Regia), was the venue for a sight in 1929 which made people forget their troubles. Eight small cars of indescribable simplicity and grace (given one can apply grace to a machine-made product, people would gladly have jumped into the seats next to the drivers) were to be seen chugging along. What were the eight men doing in their eight cars? Well, they were running them in, listening to gear-boxes and back axles for noises, driving their vehicles to a parking place in the middle of the wood, jumping out, opening the bonnet behind the radiator (which bore a centaur with flowing mane), and adjusting valves and oil pressure with their spanners while the engine was warm (the real reason for their journey), based on the noises they had heard. They would start up the engine and listen. Then they would climb back into their seat and chug back along the Hohe Strasse. They objected to the word 'chugging', because this was when they picked up speed (some of them getting up to 80 kph). This time they went in the opposite direction, back to the yard at the Eisenach Works where the next eight cars were already waiting for them. Every Dixi went through this procedure, come winter, come summer, and once it had accomplished its running-in test, drove off against the economic tide that we have just spoken about.

It had a 3/15-hp, water-cooled, four-cylinder engine, an electric starter motor, its chassis was made by rivetting together easily-manufactured pressed rails and a pressing running to the front which held together engine, radiator and front suspension. With the exception of its left-hand drive and the symmetrically fitted engine, it was the spitting image of its archetype, the Austin Seven, its English brother.

This was how its virtues were extolled to people:

The DIXI is the car for national and local government offices, commercial travellers, building contractors, architects, traders, engineers, government employees and sales representatives.
It is very cheap to run.
No need for you to rely on the railway.
It can avoid delays.
You can reach your furthest customer with ease.
It will enable you to forge close contacts with your customers.

The DIXI is the car for doctors, lawyers, solicitors and priests.
It is indispensable for professional people.
It reduces to a minimum time spent en route.
It stands ever ready for private or business use. It is extremely reliable and is so easy to drive that you will be tempted to take the wheel yourself.

The DIXI is the car for gentry and farmers.
It has the additional ability to handle bad roads. Compared with the horse and trap, it has the advantage of only running up costs when in use.
It is suitable for any type of terrain.
For the same reliability, it is cheaper to acquire and maintain than large cars.

The dictum 'irreplaceable', which then rang out from the Thuringian Forest, was accompanied by figures able to beat anything comparable. The purchase price was 2475 marks, running costs over a 100-km journey were all of two marks. Coupled with this it was 'within one's means'. This was no luxury vehicle for the aristocracy, no 'designer' sports car; it was a utility car for motorists who could not afford the larger touring cars, but who equally were not interested in motorcycles. The Dixi combined two things – mechanical integrity *and* customer expectation – that secret greatness which any design must have to be successful.

But Popp immediately saw what had to be improved. The poor road holding, which was due to axle problems, could be solved. The defective brakes, with the footbrake only working on the rear wheels while the handbrake did no more than 'retard' the front wheels, could also be solved. But it would be harder to remedy the spartan exterior and interior – that could only be done by widening the body. An enquiry was sent to a Monsieur Lucien Rosengart at Neuilly-sur-Seine – Can you help us? Certainly, Rosengart wired back, since, after taking a licence agreement on the Austin Seven for France and Belgium, he had already widened the bodywork and covered it with a more modern, lighter, artificial leather, without altering the chassis. With Rosengart's help, the German Austin Seven, called the Dixi, was altered in the following way – the running boards were removed, larger side and rear windows and new front seats were fitted, along with cable-operated brakes to all four wheels, and a completely restyled radiator, the running centaur with the flowing mane now replaced with the white and blue propeller and the initials BMW.

Under the slogan (which raised many a smile) of 'bigger inside than out', Popp presented this Dixi DA2 (DA being short for German Version) at the new BMW showrooms near the Berlin Zoo at the end of July 1929 as a convertible with retractable windows and an all-steel saloon using a woodframe chassis (basic bodywork supplied by Ambi Budd). At this point, the laughing stopped. At the first attempt, the standard production model won the 'International Alpine Rally' which lasted for five days and went over all Alpine passes. Treated with pitiful disdain at the start, it was now being prophesied (after the team of Buchner, Kandt and Wagner had safely completed all the rounds in their magnificent victory) that 'What Ford did for America, the BMW Dixi will do for Europe'.

The *Deutsche Automobilzeitung* (which was highly unlikely to eulogise without due thought) got positively carried away when it said:

> The Bavarian Motor Works took over the Dixi, and produced the improved Dixi as a BMW. Yet it must be considered a new make. It took part in the Alpine Rally and amazed the whole motoring world by giving a performance which left everyone flabbergasted. In the three groups and eight classes with engines from 500-cc to 800-cc, the BMW 748.5 cc engines beat them all hollow!

The reporter kept starting again as he tried to document the event:

> The BMW victory would have defied even the tales of Rabbi Akiba! In such a difficult contest, which the 1929 version of the Alpine Rally indisputably was, the only make of car giving its team the best time over 2,500 km dotted with Alpine passes . . . did so with engines having a capacity of 748.5 cc! A best average speed of 42 kph was maintained plus 'reserves of speed' which were definitely there.

Then he described the mountain sections with the best times for the BMW cars in their group: 'On the Jaufen, Buchner had the best time of 25:42 in his BMW, on the Pordoijoch, Kandt had the best time of 14:06 in his BMW, and the BMW team undercut the overall required time for both mountain sections of 44:33 with 39:58 (Buchner), 42:07 (Kandt) and 42:58 (Wagner).'

He paused for breath again. 'What an advertisement! Priceless. . .' he extolled.

> The new BMW has shown itself to the whole world at a stroke! From now on, the factory need make no further claims as to how good the little car is, what it can offer and all the other things said in the sales brochures to prospective customers. They need look no further than the remarkable success in the Alpine Rally, thereby dealing with the business between the factory and the potential customer in the most courteous way: 'No need to explain any further, salesman sir! I know everything! Any car which wins the Alpine Rally so convincingly is the car for me! Wrap it up and send it to my address!'

It then occurred to him to quote Shakespeare in conclusion: 'Thrift, thrift, Horatio!' This did not mean that the sensational victory by BMW in the Alpine Rally was like hitting the jackpot. Far from it! Hitting the jackpot is a matter of chance.

> The Bavarian Motor Works, in bringing out the small BMW car, left nothing to chance; on the contrary, they put their all into it. As the facts prove, no stone was left unturned. Anyone who understands the huge number of factors involved in creating a new model of car which can be safely put on the market will not fail to recognise this. The factory can proudly say that we have succeeded in our grand design!

The grand design? Popp had immediately lowered the price. The two-seater now cost 2,200 marks, the four-seater 300 marks more, meaning that the BMW 3/15 hp now considerably undercut the comparable Hanomag 3/16 hp (2,800 marks), and was now not much more expensive than the small Opel, against which the main thrust of the sales campaign was principally directed.

If Ford had made its Tin Lizzy all in black ('You can have the car in any colour you want, provided it's black'), then Opel in Rüsselsheim had coated its small car, modelled on the small Citroën and shaped at the back like a boat's stern, in green, that garish, eye-piercing grass green, which immediately earned it the name of 'tree-frog'.

By 1928, after further price cuts and technical improvements which finally made it into a four-seater saloon, this tree-frog, with its 42,741 units sold, had captured 37.5 per cent of entire German car production.

No, BMW was by no means out of the woods. This fact also emerged from a private discussion which Herr von Buttlar, the company representative in Berlin, had with Becker, the head of Siemens Aviation, in the summer of 1929, in which he indicated that 'a rather large number of BMW shares could be acquired at a comparatively low rate'. Buttlar was keen to have his firm appear in the most favourable light possible. The publicity generated by the newspapers over its poor financial situation was exaggerated. The takeover of the Dixi car factory was admittedly a heavy burden, but business with aero-engines and motorcycles (the latter having seen last year's turnover double) was good. He also said that the firm had found new business, such as the recently concluded large-scale contract with Russia for 200 of the 600-hp engines (twelve-cylinder BMW VIs). In addition, Dixi had profitable contracts for many years to come, supplying the government with mortars, vehicles, tractors etc. In an emergency it would thus be possible to discontinue Dixi car production.

Herr von Buttlar intimated that Becker might suggest to Herr von Siemens the advantage of contacting Herr von Stauss, who was on the supervisory board of both the Bavarian Motor Works and Siemens. Herr von Stauss would certainly be more than ready to explain the true position of the Bavarian Motor Works to Herr von Siemens and provide him with the evidence that acquiring BMW shares (which Herr von Buttlar calculated was only temporary) carried no risk to it at all.

Then BMW, racked by doubts as the first signs of the crisis were being felt, offered the Eisenach Works, acquired less than a year ago, as a production site to the Ford management streaming into Germany. They declined. The Lord Mayor of Cologne, a certain Konrad Adenauer, had already succeeded in getting Ford interested in a more attractive site in the suburb of Nordhafen which had docking facilities for ships of up to 3,000 tons. Moreover, it lay near the industrial region of Rhineland-Westphalia.

Herr Castiglioni from Vienna

Fear and respect of the people at Rüsselsheim had by 1928 materialised into an adventurous plan in Castiglioni's head. The famous headquarters of the Berliner Disconto-Gesellschaft bank, whose leader, Gustav Schlieper, had connections with the Opel family, and whom Castiglioni asked for a discussion, gave me some information about it with a page from Schlieper's diary:

> Headquarters, 28 April 1928: Herr Castiglioni from Vienna, who has been here for a few days, visited me today and was intent on discussing the following matter. After he had mentioned, as usual, that he was continuing negotiations here with Herr Oscar Wassermann, Herr von Stauss, Herr Gutmann of the Dresdner Bank, and Herr Goldschmidt of the Danat Bank (presumably to do with Daimler-BMW), he went into great detail about the poor state of the German car industry, with all the companies having a terrible time, except for Opel which was doing extremely well. The situation would certainly force the firms outside Opel to consider at least merging, although it would be much better if Opel joined in. Herr Castiglioni indicated that in the meantime discussions had been going on for quite some time between the financial backers behind the individual companies (except for Opel), with a view to producing a merger between Daimler, Adler, NSU, BMW, NAG, Presto, Brennabor, Hansa-Lloyd and Magirus. This would involve between 100 and 150 million marks, together with at least an additional 100 million marks for modernising and restructuring, in connection with which certain promises were thought to be forthcoming from America. The main difficulty beside the financial question was industrial application, bringing into doubt in the first place even BMW's managing director Herr Popp, and even Herr Castiglioni. Herr Castiglioni now tried to give me a detailed description of the advantages this would have for our friends at Adam Opel in not standing somewhat apart from this grouping, but getting fully involved in it.

At this time, Castiglioni, the man who could hear the grass grow, did not yet know that Alfred M. Sloan, the president of General Motors, was thinking of co-operating with an established German car maker – instead of the assembly operations which GM, Chrysler and Ford had previously gone for in Europe, and especially Germany. His choice fell on Opel, whose owners had long since brought in production-line methods, which Popp had admired in Detroit, for faster and cheaper production in their factories in Rüsselsheim. (Admittedly, as a feasibility study by GM in Rüsselsheim reported to their president, the Adam Opel Works had reached that stage of development which was comparable with what it had been in America in 1911. But working practices were flexible and new models were easy to put into production.)

In December 1928 the Opel Brothers changed their family business into a public company. But it was difficult to work out what that meant when the stamp on the company notepaper read: 'Until the German balance of payments is in the black, we would ask you kindly to visit and supply us only in German vehicles!' Yet in March 1929, just three months after Opel had placed large newspaper advertisements saying: 'Anyone not having the tact and responsibility to buy a German car shares the guilt for renewed inflation and its devastating consequences!', the American General Motors Corporation acquired 80 per cent of Opel shares!

So the German car trust, which Camillo Castiglioni had dreamt about, was finally off the agenda. And was it the same for Castiglioni? In the business section of newspapers was the brief remark: 'Camillo Castiglioni left the supervisory board of BMW in October 1929. His shareholding of 5 million Reich marks was taken over by the banking consortium backing BMW, and involving the Deutsche Bank, the Danat Bank, the Disconto-Gesellschaft bank and the firms of Hagen & Co. and AE Wassermann.'

What was behind it, what had happened to cause Camillo Castiglioni's final fall will probably remain forever a mystery. Castiglioni never spoke about it. He refused to see reporters, just as he refused to allow Emil Ludwig to write his biography, despite the latter asking him twice. Denials from his own company (purchase of the Dixi Works had not produced any losses, and falls in the value of BMW shares had been kept to manageable proportions) should be as little believed as press reports which were linked with the usual attacks made by the right-wing press against him as a Jew, a wheeler-dealer, and a profiteer from inflation – all against a man who (as he later admitted with some embarrassment) had undeniably been a friend of Mussolini.

But this much can be established; namely that Castiglioni had to mortgage his BMW shares to the Deutsche Bank in Berlin because of heavy financial losses (malevolent tongues claim that he suffered them on the gaming tables in Monte Carlo). The shares were then quoted at 250. The Deutsche Bank took them up at 180. As General Motors had taken over control of Opel, and Ford was concluding closer ties with the IG Farben Dye Trust, the stock market immediately reacted nervously. BMW shares slumped. (It was every man for himself, as acquiring Eisenach and Dixi production was now shown to have been a failure. This took away the safe basis surrounding Milbertshofen, meaning that aero-engines and motorcycles, even when they are held to be the best in the world, could no longer guarantee the nest egg which up to now every BMW share had been worth.)

When the rate reached 134, the bank demanded an 'additional payment', as it is called in the language of the stock market. Castiglioni declared that he could not cover all the difference, yet he paid one million, followed by another 800,000 marks. However, this was not enough for the Deutsche Bank. Hurrying from door to door in Berlin, the quick-thinking, never-say-die CC climbed aboard his private plane (to the sound of clicking cameras) and flew to Vienna, in order to invite the great American financier, Otto H. Kahn, for breakfast in his town house in Prince Eugen Street. (The press noted it, but the shares did not go up.) Soon afterwards, La Scala from Milan, directed by Toscanini, was making a guest appearance in the Austrian capital. As a friend of the arts, Castiglioni boarded his plane, threw a big party. All Vienna said how fabulous it was. The whole event was said to have cost 10,000 dollars.

A confidential report dated 18 June 1929, which was issued from Vienna and went to the French Foreign Minister, said:

> The facts are strange, and Herr Castiglioni's denial is not convincing. There is a definite crisis, as revealed by the figures. . . There is talk of a contract affecting deliveries abroad, and of the profits that have been syphoned off, which Castiglioni will have to pay back again. But what kind of profits could these be which have to be paid back and are connected with deliveries abroad?. . . Even the greatest sceptic cannot help thinking that not only the fame, but the very reputation of Herr Castiglioni, is under threat . . .
>
> But a crisis in the Castiglioni business, which would have led a few years ago to financial difficulties, today will have much less serious consequences. . . The time of the demi-gods is over. Anyway, the skill with which this financier knew how to 'turn things round', and with which he had already recovered from his insolvency in 1924 after his adventurous speculations when our franc was falling, leaves one to suppose that his situation is not completely hopeless.

But this supposition was wrong. CC's situation *was* indeed hopeless, at least when it was announced that a consortium led by the Deutsche Bank and the Disconto-Gesellschaft bank had bought up all Castiglioni's BMW shares. We would soon learn how many these were. If Herr von Stauss spoke of 5 million, then estimates put it that CC had at his disposal a further 3 million 'tactical votes' from helpful companies, bankers and private individuals. However, a one-year moratorium to realise all Castiglioni's estate (his office building called 'Majestic' in Vienna, his private mansion with all its *objets d'art*, and other buildings, as well as his estates and his stud-farm in Hungary) could not be kept. And so he disappeared, the man who had always regarded BMW as his soundest possession (a view which BMW would never have objected to), never to be seen again.

Had not his nose always been able to tell what was in the air? His fine sense of smell for what was economically and politically feasible had never let him down. He had always managed to get things in the right place at the right time, as the popular expression goes. Despite getting himself hopelessly tied up in a knot, in which business and adventure had become extraordinarily intertwined (his knowledge about the practices, possibilities and limits of power had always shown itself equal to his love of risk-taking), he had always remained a realist, in spite of his habit of over-indulging in money and possessions. He was a realist in both a European sense and as a Jew.

On 5 September 1929 Aristide Briand, the French Prime Minister, first brought up the question of Europe at the General Assembly of the League of Nations, with the plan of a federal association with full sovereignty for all the member states. (Castiglioni, as an Italian living in Vienna and Berlin, felt himself a European.) Immediately after the speech, the Greek Professor of International Law, Nikolaus G. Politis said to Briand: 'Your proposal comes too soon and too late. It is too soon, because the nations have not yet been through the great European crisis which is about to break. It is too late because European euphoria is over.'

How right he proved to be was shown by events in Germany. Barely four weeks later, Stresemann, Briand's friend and ally, died. Not only did the Slump break over the country, but Hitler arrived on the scene.

And Castiglioni left, perhaps not unhappy that everything had turned out the way it had, both for himself and BMW.

Did he ever come back? Heinkel related in his memoirs, *A Stormy Life*, that he met him on a further occasion in Berlin in the early years of the Third Reich:

He was coming out of breakfast, which he had just had with Hermann Göring. Or, more accurately, from an evening reception held the night before at the Italian Embassy, to which, as a famous Italian, he had been invited – with Göring as the new minister. The breakfast was only a follow-on from this reception. The first signs of the National Socialist policy of anti-Semitism were already on the horizon. The Italian ambassador had apparently considered it a special pleasure to introduce Göring to the millionaire Castiglioni.

But something quite extraordinary happened. Göring shook Castiglioni by the hand. He said: 'Are you Castiglioni? Do you know who I am?'

'No, Excellency.'

'But I know who you are,' replied Göring, within earshot of everyone. 'I once worked in Stockholm as a representative for the Bavarian Motor Works. A long time ago. I tried to obtain an order from the Swedish government for aero-engines, but I did not succeed. I came back to Berlin a year later, and heard that in the meantime twelve aero-engines had been sold to Sweden. I wrote to BMW saying that I had started the ball rolling, and that I was entitled to at least 30,000 marks commission. But the Bavarian Motor Works replied that they were sorry, and that this commission had already been paid to another representative. I had no money to go to court. However, one day I met a friend who told me: "Listen here. There is a generous man owning or co-owning BMW – Camillo Castiglioni. If I were you, I'd write to him. Perhaps you'll get your money from him."

'I wrote, and within a fortnight received 30,000 marks. Do you remember me now?'

Castiglioni still could not remember the event. Too many men had passed through his life. He had received too many begging letters.

'Excellency, I still don't quite remember it,' Castiglioni replied.

'But I remember it all too well,' said Göring. 'Please do me the pleasure of having breakfast with me tomorrow.'

Castiglioni took up this invitation. He met Göring, accompanied by several representatives from the American press who brought his attention to the anti-Semitic demonstrations which had just taken place. Göring, though, replied: 'It was an accident, a misfortune. It won't happen again. Herr Castiglioni, when I was young my best friends were Jews, and they always treated me well. I wouldn't dream of harming them.'

'But Hitler is anti-Semitic,' protested Castiglioni.

To which Göring replied: 'I'll talk him out of that. Just leave it to me.'

Castiglioni told that story at our last meeting before the catastrophe of the Second World War, adding: 'I believed this Göring would do what he said. But I know human nature. He's well-meaning, but lazy. I'll take my leave of you now, as I am leaving Germany forever. I understand you have to stay, but from what I see, it's all going to be a disaster.'

There were rumours that Castiglioni, who then went to Switzerland and founded a bank in Milan, is said to have become friends with Tito after the Second World War, and to have arranged a loan for him from the Americans of 40 million dollars (via the Export-Import Bank of Washington), against promises of expenses and commissions. This was denied by the Italian Foreign Minister. But he can probably be credited with having taken Tito to court when the latter failed to pay the agency commission, and was able to enforce the Italian court's verdict in his favour by repossessing Italian property in Italy.

A denial here, a denial there. In 1957 he even denied his own death. He wrote to Professor Wolfgang Zorn in Munich to say he was still alive. On 18 December 1961, at the age of seventy-six (as *The Times* informed its readers), he did die, in Rome.

The Going Rate for a World Going Bust

It was a day like any other, a Thursday, 24 October 1929. No one could predict how unsettled the weekend ahead would be – neither in Munich, Eisenach, nor in New York. It was only in the evening that concern was voiced when Wall Street realised that an extraordinary accumulation of purchase orders was up against a number of sales offers which bore little or no relationship to each other. This realisation was substantiated the next day and was ultimately to go down in the history of the stock exchange as 'Black Friday'. Share values plummeted, crashed. The alarm was raised, but to no avail. No one knew how to counter this disaster, which, like a natural catastrophe, exploded the myth of 'prosperity for ever' which America believed in as wholeheartedly as it did in God.

The catastrophe was complete by the following Tuesday, a day which could only have been described as blacker than black, when 16.5 million shares changed hands on Wall Street.

'The ticker,' as it was called by Robert Nöll von der Nahmer, 'spent several hours with the share values showing a negative value. In all the drugstores and hotel lobbies where ticker-tape machines were to be found, the ruined small shareholders arrived to establish just how their unsecured investment and share values were falling by the hour.'

The New York Stock Exchange, at times not dissimilar to a boiling kettle, had meanwhile become a place of fear and damnation, as witnessed by Charles Michell, president of the large National City Bank, who 'wandered aimlessly without hat or coat, with hair all dishevelled, through the stone caverns of Wall Street, which was filled with seething masses. . .', or as one observer described, 'a nation has speculated away its entire annual income'.

The bad news from America had alarmed Popp, too. Was there any reason for panic? In the last few days the BMW share value had not significantly recovered. Admittedly little more than 7 per cent could be paid out as dividends, due to the high bank overdraft resulting from the purchase of Eisenach. This was so even though turnover had increased and would now reach a better-than-expected figure of 40 million. Last year it had been 27.2 million, with 14 per cent in dividends!

In spite of this, the news was not reassuring. What was being played out 'over there' would doubtlessly affect Germany first. Customer demand had been exhausted, the 'boom' was over, there was no 'Prosperity for ever'. Fear held centre stage. How could it have come to this? As it had become the major creditor to the European countries, the USA had doubled its industrial production since the end of the war. Popp himself had been to see it. Large, even the largest businesses, had materialised which were capable of developing the most modern, rationalised production processes – as were required, in turn, for any mass production which the market (given the size of the American continent) effortlessly absorbed.

It was pointless to consider doing the same in Europe – what with its very different sales potential, lack of capital and shortages of raw materials unknown to the American economy. Export surpluses and foreign currency revenue made it possible for the American economy to obtain credits at any required level, and if the boom forced up share values, then shares would simply be run off 'like soap, simply because money could be made by producing and selling them'. All this meant that if a few people thought it was too good to be true and pulled out, a market crash was inevitable.

The question was now down to what extent this figure of 'prosperity' had been inflated. Did the sudden release of pressure (in itself quite understandable) mean that everything had to fall in on itself so undramatically? But this is precisely what happened, namely that the banks, as share values had fallen below their minimum value, would call in their credit, first in America, then in Europe, and not least in Germany where they had been restricted to short term, in the understandable expectation of imminent crises. What Stresemann had forecast had now come about. With deficits running into billions, and with already over 3 million unemployed, the situation was too fraught for there to be any hope of avoiding the disaster.

That BMW, used to bad times, should withstand the blow may, primarily, have been due to the robustness of its Dixi, which admittedly was selling sluggishly, but had kept its purchase price as one of the five cheapest cars in Germany. The advertising department had tried to make it desirable to its clientele by claiming that it was 'like a lady, having all the qualities you expect when driving a small car'. What the eloquent copywriter meant by this when he promised 'to satisfy their needs in the most perfect way possible, with its 0.75-litre, 15-hp engine', came out in a brochure with the baroque title of: 'ELEVATED from the ordinary, run-of-the-mill cars, the BMW, BIGGER INSIDE THAN OUT, is a miracle of German precision engineering', as indicated by the fact that: 'The steering is effortless, even in the daintiest of hands, and the individual controls have been so spaced that no sweeping movement counter to natural grace is required to drive the vehicle.' And naturally it appealed to their sense of adventure, evoking that less than happy moment when a wheel needs to be changed: 'No outside help is at hand. The lady will just have to fend for herself. In such moments she will find it twice or three times as pleasant that her little car has been built so small and light, making no excessive demands on her physical strength. The feeling of independence, which has been so powerfully shown by modern women, requires freedom of movement, and is satisfied in the fulfilment of unrestrained self-assurance.'

A calculation of the running costs provides an historical proof of the way people lived. This shows that a sales representative in his BMW 0.75-litre, 15-hp (the name Dixi had already been dropped), covering 100 kilometres a day over an estimated 300 working days a year, thereby doing 30,000 kilometres, could fully compete with the train on costs, the latter 'requiring to transport one person at a rate corresponding to the transport costs of between two and three people in the BMW car' – quite apart from all other considerations such as comfort and independence.

1	Fixed costs:		
a)	Garage hire (on average)	RM	240
b)	Tax	RM	106
c)	Third-party insurance	RM	120
		RM	466
2	Variable costs:		
a)	Repairs, approx 5 per cent of car value	Rm	110
b)	Cleaning implements	RM	10
c)	Tyres	RM	180
d)	Petrol, approx 6 litres per 100 km, with 1,800 litres @RM 0.40	RM	720
e)	Oil, approx 0.12 kg per 100 km, with 36 kg @ RM 1.5	RM	54
		RM	1074
3	Cost per kilometre:		
	Group 1	1.53	Rpf
	Group 2	3.58	Rpf
		5.11	Rpf

There was only the purchase price in addition to this which, after a down payment (BMW had introduced this in April 1929), could be settled in twenty-four monthly instalments of 107 marks (a monthly interest charge of 2.83 marks!).

The outcome of all this, against a background of 17,000 German firms going under (the biggest being the leading German textile company, Nordwolle, which collapsed with debts of 100 million, followed by the Danat Bank, which had investments in the former, to the tune of 40 million), Popp could cautiously proclaim in 1929, with 5,390 cars sold (6,792 in 1930): 'Producing the BMW small car has been so carefully calculated that after-sales and warranty costs do not reach a thousandth of turnover!' Admittedly the turnover fell from the level of 1927 and about 700 workers had to be laid off at Munich and Eisenach. While the Slump, with its armies of unemployed and destitute farmers in the USA, moved towards its height, accompanied by hunger and indescribable misery; while Britain abandoned the gold standard in September 1931, devaluing the pound by nearly 40 per cent and thereby openly declaring Europe's bankruptcy – since maintenance of the gold standard had been the basis of Great Britain's hundred-year-long tradition as banker to the world; while all this happened, BMW's cycle business (lynch-pin no 1) proved to be almost crisis-proof. In aero-engine manufacture (lynch-pin no 2), the Pratt & Whitney radial Hornet engine, whose licence Popp had acquired in America, continued in production for Junkers and Messerschmitt aircraft, even if cuts in state funds for aviation had led to reduced orders.

Yes, Friz had even developed a rather smaller five-cylinder radial engine for sports aircraft, which was successful on Round Europe Flights in 1930 and 1932, producing strong demand for it. Even the Dixi (lynch-pin no 3), continually criticised for its rigid front axle and its internal space – which had not increased one iota in spite of its advertising slogan ('bigger inside than out') – had undergone a complete transformation.

In an effort to give it a markedly sporty appeal (for all those who could not forget the Alpine Rally, and wanted to imitate Buchner on the Jaufen or Kandt on the Pordoijoch), the Dixi DA 3 was created as a sporting twin-seater with a drop-down windscreen, tapered tail and running boards, and was christened the 'Wartburg'. With its 18 hp, it went faster, but not because of any of these attributes, nor because it ran on a mixture of 60 per cent petrol and 40 per cent benzole (which simply meant that it had a different smell). It cost 3,100 Reich marks and fewer than 400 examples were produced.

Next in the BMW Dixi range was the DA 4. Duckstein, who had meanwhile become chief designer at Eisenach, and had developed it in a few weeks, giving it a spacious body and a 'swinging-arm axle' (even if that was only a spring assembly mounted transversely, whose multi-leaved ends fitted into the main axle components, each of which held the stub-axle on either side). This would enable the car to counter any bounciness in the ride, but which it did not do due to its short wheelbase. The wider bodywork was even more out of proportion with the car's track – at 1,030 m it was still too narrow. The press was admittedly enthusiastic, stating that the suspended axle had kept pace 'with the latest designs'. Test reports, however, complained about 'the poor directional stability and indifferent cornering'. So what was new? There were a total of 56,000 new registrations in 1931 – and 300,000 deregistrations. In spite of this, the DA 4 reached 3,668 examples, obviously leaving 'excess capacity' at Eisenach.

In order to make use of this and to ensure it was crisis-proof, Popp decided to build a commercial vehicle which was to be a three-wheeled platform truck with a 200-cc single-cylinder engine. This would be built at Milbertshofen in series with the motorcycle engines. The customers, who were small traders, rushed out to buy this 'thing'. Its load surface was at the front, with the driver sitting behind. Its peculiarity was a shaft-drive with a trailing rear arm, and (for quick wheel changes) a rear axle anchored only on one side. If the power plant was not up to heavy loads then there was a 400-cc version available.

Getting round and getting out of things (in total only 600 examples of the 'thing' were built) – such were the inventive ideas which, nevertheless, could not deny the hardship from which they originated. And to which Popp had to bow, whether he liked it or not. And then something happened which was apparently ridiculous, quite incredible. At a time when all the staff at Munich and Eisenach had taken a 10 per cent pay cut, Popp, acting on his own (perhaps everyone thought he was mad), gave the order in December 1931 to design, develop and build a completely new car in the shortest possible time; meaning that work would have to be divided – the engine in Munich (designed by Friz), the chassis in Eisenach (designed by Duckstein), while he would leave the bodywork to Mercedes designers, which led him to place an outside contract with Sindelfingen. 'Genuine Bodywork made in Sindelfingen' read the prospectus, whereby BMW again got closer to Daimler-Benz in the terms of that joint-venture contract which was going ahead, as planned, to the second stage.

The resulting car left behind every aspect of the Dixi's past: twin-tube frame, rear self-aligning axle, smaller but wider wheels, and an engine now with 20-hp at 3500 rpm fitted with overhead valves operated by a side-mounted camshaft through push-rods and rockers. It ran incomparably more quietly than its Dixi predecessors and had really blossomed into a proper car in terms of visibility, comfort and styling. It even went so far as to incorporate quite secondary features, such as a speedometer which had a roller behind glass, rather than a needle, to indicate the speed, an idea which was as sensible as it was ultra-modern.

In January 1932 Popp went to Longbridge in Birmingham. Sir Herbert Austin received him. Popp had all the design documents in his briefcase and was keen to discuss them. The licence agreement made with Eisenach was for a ten-year period – up to 1937. Even England, racked by the Slump, had nothing to give away. Yet Austin could appreciate the situation (in fact, what Popp was presenting to him was no longer his Austin Seven) and waived the terms of the contract with effect from 1 March 1932.

That was a load off Popp's mind. It did not bear thinking about the licence fee, if it were to be levied on the new car. He still did not know how he would see through the pricing for his vehicle. He knew only one thing: 'Unlike a more prosperous America, we cannot solve our crisis through money, but only by the more rigorous application of better ideas. Therefore we cannot retain antiquated car designs, concealing them by piling on suspect additional minor innovations, and thereby build ever cheaper large cars as America does. No, we must . . .'

Yes, this is what we must do, he thought (and why not admit it, even if it was a bit unpleasant): 'We must make our small cars more attractive without increasing running costs, these being the only deciding factor for our customers.'

He paused, made a note of these sentences and looked through the train window. Ice floes were drifting down the Main, people were standing in front of a level crossing, there was a protest march, red flags . . . How will you do that, you fool? he heard himself saying, as the express went through Stuttgart.

He would have preferred to get out, to bang down Austin's concession on worthy Herr Kissel's desk. No, there was no time. He could always tell him by phone. Sindelfingen flew by, then the goods station. He looked over in its direction. Weren't those beautiful wooden frames being loaded, onto

141

which the people of Sindelfingen knew more skilfully than anyone else in the world how to fit the panel skins? How many were now leaving each day for Eisenach? Ten? Ridiculous, a hundred per day were possible, were essential. And how can a fool like you reach that goal?

'That goal,' he went on to note, 'can only be reached by following new types of design. The new BMW will prove it. We have not only abandoned the antiquated, we have just as consciously guarded against pursuing misguided ideas in innovation, style and luxury. . .' Yes, that was it, in a nutshell. 'Advances in design can only be found through simplification and greater clarity in construction. Only through these means can we master the dynamics of motor vehicles and meet increased demand.'

When the train drew up in Munich, Friz was there standing on the platform. He told Popp that the car was causing unexpected difficulties. Popp replied dispassionately that the only difficulty was that the 3/20 could only be presented four weeks after the licence had expired. Austin had insisted on that. When would that be, Friz asked cautiously.

'On 1 April,' said Popp, handing him the contract and notes which he had written down on the journey. Friz glanced over them.

'What is this?' he asked 'An April fool's joke?'

'Perhaps,' retorted Popp. 'Perhaps it's also a programme which will at last mean we can make real progress in cars. Proper cars.'

'Good,' said Friz, 'I shall hang it on the wall in the design department.'

'You can save yourself the trouble. Anyone working there who does not already know that has no business to be there. I shall inform the press, like this, with these very words.'

And so it happened. With these very words: 'Unlike a more prosperous America, we cannot solve our crisis with money. . .', Popp appeared on 1 April 1932, at the moment when the 3/20 was ready (the '3' indicated the tax rating based on horse power – 250 cc engine size = 1 horse power rating; the '20' was the real horse power), in front of a radiator grille of the first 'real' BMW with its propeller logo. He then announced the intensity with which his firm would pull itself out of these troubled times; not by resigning, nor by going under, but rather by accepting the challenge and following a new path. This is what it said in the prospectus: 'Anyone cruising through town in the new BMW car or, with four passengers, comfortably maintaining the average speed on the open road of cars that are twice as powerful, will have the feeling of owning a large vehicle.'

None of this seemed to disturb big brother Mercedes-Benz. And why should it? The cheapest Mercedes-Benz was still two and half times dearer than the most expensive BMW, with both cars standing peacefully next to each other in the showrooms of Mercedes dealers in Baden-Baden, Gleiwitz, Ravensburg and Ulm. There was no sign of any competition. It was quite a different matter whether the new car, which no longer wanted to be a small car, had any chance of reaching large sales volumes. This could only be done if it could compete on price with DKW, Opel and Hanomag, the popular makes of small cars. It would have to go into mass production, which was impossible due to insufficient money for investment. There was also the question of whether the 'ordinary man in the street' was still in a position to have a car. Popp had been anything but sarcastic when asserting – and publishing – a year before, that the bus, as the leading national vehicle, was the only economic solution possible. Quite a few had laughed about that – quite unjustifiably, as Daimler-Benz had long been a very successful bus manufacturer. No, the question was something quite different. Whether those categories of customers who could be described as prosperous would still be able to afford a car tomorrow. That was what it was all about. Emergency decrees had already started to be issued, the unemployed were forming themselves into armies and marching either as Nazi stormtroopers or in the Red Front.

'We were under extreme pressure,' Popp was later to recall. 'The Slump would soon come to a head, annual production in the German car industry had fallen to 40,000 units and closures, recovery plans and bankruptcies were the order of the day. Who would be the next in line in this collapse?'

There was a sense of hopelessness behind the fine words. It was a vicious circle – there was no money for investments to introduce mass production which could offer the product at a desirably low price; and there was no customer who was in the position to acquire it, even given its low price.

In 1914 Henry Ford had only been able to sell his inexpensive car because the introduction of the eight-hour day at the Ford Works had enabled salaries to be increased, thereby making the workers into customers. Had it only been, as his opponents claimed, a 'dirty capitalist trick'? Ford had discovered the consumer in his own workforce. As soon as increased production allowed it, he immediately lowered prices. This was the way in which he surprisingly quickly transformed advantages (which he made sure were passed on to the consumers) into advantages for himself, for his factory and for his company. He had nothing against profits. He was only against them when they did not help his plants stay in production, did not provide for their expansion or his own independence. Who could doubt that he had paved the way for a new socio-economic structure, that by doing what he did he had made a bridge between trade and industry which benefited not only a few but everyone? Even American farmers had first been brought out of their isolation through motorised transport. In some senses Ford had brought the market to their doorstep.

But who in the world recognised and comprehended that the policy of keeping wages high and prices low, and of making the workers into producers *and* consumers was the achievement of the century, in fact was the real revolution, in that it genuinely altered the social structure?

Like a dried-up river bed, the German economy, deprived of its credits, shrivelled away. Instead of supporting it through public spending (which required the courage to run the budget at a loss), the Brüning government adopted the opposite, namely deflation. The days of high inflation, whose shock effect was still felt in every politician's bones, were still too close for any of them to even think of suggesting putting new money into circulation. So it governed by emergency decree, further limiting production and consumption, and trying to control the situation through spending cuts. Yet this was soon to result in 36 per cent of all Germans (more than 23 million people) having to live off the state.

What was to be done?

'Unlike a more prosperous America, we cannot solve our crisis through money, but only by the more rigorous application of better ideas. Therefore we cannot retain antiquated car designs. . . .'

The words had died away. Popp remembered them. As did his partner at Daimler-Benz, Kissel. Since neither firm, Daimler-Benz nor BMW, could see themselves able to put up even the first instalments for the mass-production planned by both firms, should they now split up? Should they forget the Dixi's successes in all its versions and give up any thought of it? There was no point in trying to compete with a mass-produced item against cheap, American designs. So the venture turned to 'engaging the strength of German engineering skill against the purely commercial approach of these foreign factories'. These were Popp's exact words.

Kissel's were simpler: 'Headlong into quality!' What he meant by that emerged from one of the model programmes drawn up by both firms, which would extend from the largest and dearest small car right up to the large-sized car, leaving no demand uncatered for. The detail of this was that Daimler-Benz would develop a four-cylinder small car with 1.3 litres (offering two versions: engine at the front or at the back), while BMW would develop two other models – a four-cylinder with 800 cc and a six-cylinder with 1200 cc. Tests would reveal which models would go into production. Dr von Stauss had agreed to the necessary funds.

There were other hopeful signs. On 4 September 1932 the Reich President issued a decree for 'economic regeneration'. Was that the ray of sunshine which Stresemann had promised? Indeed, the depths seemed to have been plumbed, things were looking up, according to none other than the one and only 'Führer', who had claimed that he would stand or fall by 'mobilising discontent' and who now seemed to have missed his chance. 'The period of disastrous economic recession may be said to have ended,' was reported shortly afterwards by the Institute for Economic Research. The number of people finding work was indeed increasing after unemployment had reached the 6 million barrier in January 1932. Renfro Knickerbocker, the American economic journalist, wrote at the end of that year after travelling through Europe's depressed regions: 'The shrouds have left Europe's living-rooms, and the nurse is feeding the patient with broth. There may yet be a relapse, but things are unquestionably on the mend.'

Henne and his Victory

That things were looking up was certainly the case on 3 November 1932 for a young man from Munich by the name of Ernst Henne, but that was for quite different reasons. Wearing white overalls and a strange crash helmet, which tapered to the back of his neck, he had just been lifted from a triangular piece of sheet metal stretched between the wheels where protruding cylinder-heads to the right and left indicated the presence of an engine behind it. His hands let go of the handlebars, which were as steeply bent as a ram's horns, and Henne collapsed onto the grass, tearing off the leather protectors which reached up to his elbows. Here in Hungary, on the main road from Tata, where the land was as flat as a pancake, the grass was still green. This was when he first heard the time people were shouting to him – 244.399. So he had raced through a kilometre in less than fifteen seconds, meaning that he had achieved the highest speed ever recorded for a motorcyclist and had thereby broken the world record held by the English since 1930.

How much time does a man need to cover a thousand metres? Henne knew without having to think – a walker takes 15 minutes, a brisk walker 10 minutes, the world record for running was 2.236 minutes, the touring motorcyclist 1 minute, and he, Henne, the world record motorcyclist had now done it in 14.7 seconds! With what? With a 750-cc BMW. And with the obsession that he, Henne, and BMW could grab the world record using a compressor, which supplied a greater fuel-air mixture than would normally go into the cylinder. No, not that, there had to be something else. . . . As he was not an employee, but worked freelance in the racing team like a sailor who has got himself signed up, he had access to the 'King' without having to climb the ladder of seniority. 'Mr dear Herr Popp. . .' Popp reacted slightly sceptically as was his wont: 'But Henne. . .', but then decided to give the green light anyway.

That something else had not exactly been new – the entire world swore by streamlining. Paul Jaray, the Zeppelin designer, had developed a streamlined car, and Franz Kruckenberg was in the process of putting a streamlined 'something', which he wanted to power with a BMW aero-engine, on the rails. Circumventing air and becoming streamlined was, to use a pun, already in the air – but no one had yet thought of applying it to a motorcycle. Perhaps it was all due to Rudolf Schleicher, who had discovered Henne on his Astra in Monza; Henne, said to be calmness personified, a man whom high speeds made still more composed; Henne, the ace. Schleicher had accompanied him on all his races and victories, advising and supporting him: at the 'Race around Lake Constance'; at Karlsruhe, where he won the German Motorcycle Championship in all three classes of 500, 750 and 1000 cc with both the fastest lap and the outright best daily time; the Solitude Race which then still had the long lap running around the Solitude Castle. In 1926 he had covered the distance of 267 km in 3 hours 7 minutes 34 seconds at an average speed, considered impossible, of 92.6 kph! And so on and so forth. . . .

But Schleicher was no longer with BMW. He had gone to Horch, not out of obstinacy, but because Friz had ordered him to break off certain tests. He had decided to leave on the spot. There was nothing else he could do. The test he had to give up was connected with the 'compressor' idea. As the British and the Italians were in the process of outstripping BMW with their super-charged machines, Schleicher, wanting to measure the engine's load-bearing capacity, had tested it on the bench with compressed air which he ran straight into the engine. It failed. Failed? A year later Friz himself began tests with a new compressor, where, without further ado, he installed a French 'Cozette' supercharger on the horizontally-opposed engine – which subsequently satisfied Schleicher (but to no avail) as he worked far away from Munich for Horch in Zwickau, where he had been given control of the 'research and development' department.

What was a supercharger? Basically, it was nothing other than a vane pump driven off the engine, which sucked in the fuel-air mixture through the carburettor and forced it into the cylinder. The difficult part was coping, at such higher engine outputs, with the high mechanical and thermal stresses on the pistons and the cylinders, especially at the top of the rev range. The answer lay in the right materials and manufacturing tolerances. So there was no problem! Friz had fitted the supercharger horizontally above the engine-and-gearbox unit, so that it could be driven by an oil-bathed chain off the crankshaft. As a result of this, Henne, with his mind on the world record, had withdrawn with Hopf, known as the natural phenomenon for 'tests' (the skilled cobbler had been Schleicher's right-hand man, and this prompted Schleicher to come along as well), to his own 'test station', a shed off Kidler Street in Munich. Henne had his BMW franchise in the nearby stone building.

'Hopf got stuck into the engine, and I got to work on the chassis . . . the handlebars. . .' he said to me when I visited him in the self-same Kidler Street fifty years later, back on site, so to speak.

'The handlebars had by then acquired a certain notoriety,' I interjected, but Henne was not listening. Instead he said that he had spent all his time thinking about how and where he could help the wind 'be on our side instead of against us. My aim was to get round it wherever possible. Of course, this depended on weight, too. The machine should not be too heavy (anything dispensable was left off). It had also to be stable and, above all, not have anything, even a tube or a piece of metal, sticking out into the airflow, as this would produce eddies. The cowling was built simply with metal-cutters, pliers and rivets, working with the naked eye, in the absence of slide-rules or any knowledge of aerodynamics. And my wife designed my racing outfit. On our honeymoon we went from Paris to Arpajon, where the English were making their world records. So she knew what it was all about.'

Henne went over to a chest of drawers and pulled out the top drawer. There lay his racing outfit. He said he had recently slipped it on, and it still fitted like a glove. He quickly pushed the drawer back – indeed, the years seemed to have had no effect on him. We both cast our minds back to the time when I was at secondary school and made a pilgrimage to the Marienberg Triangular Race at Zittau. I remember tearing up to the track with the crowd shouting excitedly: 'Henne! Henne! There he is!' and watching him coming towards me like an oblique line on a blurred photograph. Behind sandbanks I had shouted 'Henne!', too, but he had long since gone by. Yet I thought I had clearly made him out, just like in magazine pictures!

Then he took me to the window, and pointed down to a yard, as if the shed with its pit could still be seen beneath that jumble of workshop and showroom roofs; the pit where Henne would be faring the frame, shaping the handlebars to an aerodynamic curve, wrapping sticking plaster around them, and lacquering the frame.

'For me,' he said then, 'the extraordinary thing about the R 37 was that it was the very first machine which had overhead valves that were fully enclosed. Where all the valve gear had previously run in the open, it was now protected from dust (dust destroys the very heart and soul of an engine) and was also fully waterproofed under its cover, meaning that there was no need to use an oil can every so often to lubricate the rocker shafts. I had wanted Schleicher to take the dust-proofing as far as the cooling fins, where there was naturally still a need for an air-flow, thereby making the machine wind-proof or, at least, wind-deflecting and streamlined; with myself as the rider in all that. Then, when I thought we had got half-way there, we looked for a stretch of road which could act as a wind tunnel, so to speak (the concept was only thought up later), complying with the strict conditions laid down in London for the world record. We set off, Franz Bieber, regional sports director of the German Touring Club, and a few friends, to take some measurements, and we surveyed (topographers and surveyors helped us) all the potential straight sections around Munich (which were largely flat), until we found the right one – the main road to Ingolstadt between milestones 15 and 17, where there was a bend immediately followed by the level crossing at Lohhof, with its barrier constantly going up and down. But the turning mark was on this side. There'd be no difficulty making it here, I thought to myself.'

The six-metre-wide road was not very even. In comparison to Arpajon, where the Englishman James Baldwin had reached 200.500 kph on a 1000-cc Zenith-Jap, it was a joke. Lined by metre-thick embankments, with avenues of trees running right up to the edge of the road, it went through pine woods, groups of houses, through open fields with potential windbreaks and clusters of trees. Then finally, beyond the bend at Lohhof, there began a thick deciduous forest. Henne had calculated that this was where he could still exceed the 200 kph barrier when, right in the middle of his preparations, the news broke that Bert le Vack, the 1924 world record holder, had snatched the record back. Where? In Arpajon, of course. At 207.530 kph he had outdone the world record (this was on 25 August 1929), which Baldwin had established just a year previously, by 7 kph (it had taken five years prior to Baldwin to be 7 kph faster!). Henne remained calmness personified.

And 'made it with no difficulty', even though the front wheel jumped out of one of its mountings on his thirteenth test run. (Henne rode on with the good old bead tyre screwed onto the rim with wing-nuts, as he still did not trust the recently introduced wire-braced tyres.) The tyre pressure was simply increased to around 4 bars, so that the beads would press harder onto the rims, giving the feeling of riding on solid wheels. Henne kept the machine under control as he tore across to the other side of the road on full power, with the front wheel almost at right angles to his machine, and turning past the avenue of trees as in a slalom, he came to rest after covering the two kilometres at 210 kph – safe and sound to fight another day. He broke the world record a few days later, on 19 September 1929 – at 216 kph. Newspaper photographs showed that at this speed he had often had both wheels off the ground.

World records presuppose a kind of nervous hyperactivity. With practice sessions, top-secret test dates, disturbing news from the previous record-holder's camp, and with the intentional announcement of quite specific expectations, whereby enumerating the dangers for man and machine releases wild speculation about success and failure, the record itself frequently becomes a farce.

Henne's world record, which was a national event for Germany and a breakthrough in BMW's bid to become a world marque, was a farce for other reasons: the FIM (Fédération Internationale Motocycliste), which, as an international governing body, ensured that the regulations for establishing records were kept, insisted on a passage which prescribed that the measured kilometre covered in one direction had immediately to be completed in the other direction. This had actually happened, but the other way round, because the imperial mile was always measured at the same time. Now, acting more royally than the king, the decision was taken not to acknowledge the 220 kph for the measured kilometre, but only to allow the time measured for the imperial mile, which at 216.5 kph was admittedly still 9 kph above the previous best time in the world. As a result, Henne had not conquered eight world records (because of the high costs, records are always attempted for all classes), but only four, meaning that records with the 500-cc machine had not even been considered.

A year later, almost to the very day, on 30 September 1930, Henne outdid the new world record for the measured kilometre which the Englishman Wright had in the meantime established. Henne had ridden at 221.539 kph. And this was on a 750-cc BMW machine, while Wright had done his 220.990 kph at Arpajon on a 1000-cc OEC Temple.

That a deadly duel was just about to begin (after all, Henne's lead, with which he had brought the world record back to Germany, was only half a kph) must have been clear to anyone who knew the English – and who knew Henne. He had in the meantime taken to the ice in pre-trials on Lake Eib near Garmisch, with special tyres fitted with 3-cm long steel studs. Henne rode at 160 kph at a temperature of minus 4 degrees. Then in Sweden, on the Oestersund, at considerably lower temperatures (the thermometer read minus 14), he prepared, with face wrapped in scarves, to take on the international elite of ice racing. BMW had developed a special racing machine. In the contest against the Swede Manger and the Belgian Milhoux (old pros on the ice), he fell off. Henne got caught up in the ruts which his competitors' studded tyres had cut into the ice, flew off the bike and slid 500 metres along the ice. But he refused to give up, starting again and achieving a record time (another world record of 198.2 kph). Everyone congratulated him. Naturally he was rankled by being so close to that magic figure of 200. Back to the start again. He was just getting near the magic barrier when he again slid in a rut, shot off the track and fell over, spraying clouds of snow over the wide, unswept icy surface of the lake. He came back almost cheerfully, unscathed, got off, took the scarves off his face: 'Anyone considering that 198.2 is not a good time should go ahead and break it. I won't.'

And no one did break it. But on 6 November 1930, six months later, Wright broke Henne's 'land' speed record at Cork in Ireland, dashing through the measured kilometre in 14.8 seconds (at 242.568 kph) and with it outdoing Henne's world record by 21 kph. The duel was just beginning.

Perhaps all this raises a smile. Were world records so important? Was it not ten times more sensible and sporting, and was it not also harder, to race man to man and come up with a best time for the day, to win a Grand Prix, or an Eilenriede or Avus Race involving the world's elite, rather than simply to achieve a speed record travelling like a bullet over a dead straight track? This is what Henne said to me on the subject:

'It is difficult to compare them. For whom did I achieve these records? Naturally, one does it for one's country – showing that we Germans are just as good as the English! And certainly not for a tyre factory, for their "fastest tyres in the world!" Not for a Bosch magneto, "the most reliable in the world", not for any "world record oil which will never let you down!" Or for BMW or any other make because they build the fastest motorcycle in the world (this was actually my BMW). No, of course not, I didn't do it for any of them. I would never have risked my neck for any of them. And certainly not to determine factors which were important for mass production at a time when they could only be ascertained by record attempts on the open road. And definitely not to have the name "Henne" known to all for a certain period as "the fastest man in the world on two wheels". Just to have things working right again was enough to flatter me – who could avoid being flattered by that?

'The urge came from somewhere else. You see, in racing you're competing against another man, pitting yourself against him. Speed records bear no comparison. To break the ultimate limit you have to project yourself into the void, where no one has been before, to conquer the unknown, by venturing into what is completely uncertain. That's the thrill of it for the masses: is he going to come back? But it's no thrill for me. I go beyond the frontier. All to be proved, of course. But you'll find that in other places, too. Well, I found it here, more by chance than design, because speed makes me cool, calm and collected. I put more strain on my nerves at every record attempt than in any of the hardest races. But I discovered more. Perhaps an illusion, or just curiosity. Every new discovery is soon forgotten. That was when I gave up. I had no regrets.'

The fortune of a racing driver depends, first and foremost, on his readiness for action, his courage, discipline and a sixth sense, without which everything else is valueless. His sixth sense directs him, lets him make lightning calculations, tells him when he can increase speed, and when he has to reduce it, so that he can handle any critical situation which external factors (weather, track conditions, other competitors' driving) can impose upon him at any time. Yet even this sixth sense will not be sufficient if anyone claiming to have it is not at one with his machine. The unity of man and machine is not a question of faith. The racer must know the 'thing' under him as well as he knows himself, must have fathomed the engine's soul, and must have mastered the technology which transmits mechanical power, with all its merits and pitfalls, beyond mere understanding, to the very point where it reaches the subconscious.

Henne, whom Schleicher had initiated into all the secrets of design details, making him fully conversant with them, always picked up something with every new machine entrusted to him. This had come about through the interrelationship of man and machine, and through his experiences as a rider (among them were some very practical pieces of advice). His life had been spent either in the racing team or out on 'test', and he trusted BMW in the same way that BMW trusted him. It was no wonder that he also had a close affinity with Schleicher. So it was all the more painful that he was having to do without him now, when all his attempts to regain the world record came to nothing. It was as if he had crashed into an invisible wall.

At the beginning of April 1931 he made an attempt on Wright's world record on a new stretch, the wide, dead-straight Neunkirchner Allee near Vienna. Admittedly, he took the measured imperial mile off Wright, and he achieved almost half a dozen class records (500 cc, with side-car over 750 cc and 500 cc), but he did not reach the land speed record, only managing 238.250 kph, although he did achieve a new world record for the class above 750 cc.

Henne's association with BMW reached a stage where, as someone versed in private business arrangements, he put down a 'second leg' as a BMW dealer. The sales literature grew to be a kind of mirror of the stock market, of how things stood with BMW. He found figures a burden. 'Henne achieves world record' was synonymous with an immediate increase in motorcycle sales – and 'Henne falls off' with an equally instantaneously registered collapse in sales. The Slump at its height left business after business bankrupt. BMW could, as we know, hardly complain about falling sales since the start of the Slump. Now they were falling. There were redundancies. It certainly looked alarming. Popp was not yet wringing his hands, but when Henne now came across him, his face looked more sombre than friendly. He did not say: 'When are you going to get the record back?' It was much worse than that. He did not say anything.

So now Henne avoided any chance of encounter. All his new attempts to win back the old glory for BMW failed: at the beginning of 1932, with an improved, 'souped-up' 750; and in the following April, when (during further assured improvements in class records) he even got his side-car wheel into the sand beside a dry summer road, started to flounder, and crashed, resulting in the test being abandoned.

Henne was unable to remember the precise sequence of events when he came to talk about it, other than that he had to crawl to Popp. He still recalled the exact words which he had said to the 'King': 'Either you bring back le Vack from England now. . .' (he sounded off: and let him ride for me so that at least one Englishman gets the record back for BMW) . . . 'or I shall go to Zwickau and bring Schleicher back to you.'

Popp immediately decided upon the latter, whereupon Henne jumped on his motorcycle and roared off to Zwickau. There he was lucky enough to be able to persuade Schleicher to return. As it was, Henne had to admit, this piece of luck was bound up with the fact that things were going too badly at Horch for them not to release Schleicher. Soon afterwards, Horch was swallowed up in the large Auto-Union, where Schleicher would have found it just as easy to leave of his own accord.

Arriving triumphantly back in Munich in a V8 Horch trial car (always one to combine the useful with the necessary – here on a test run), Schleicher rolled into Lerchenau Street (he could still see it today) with a small case beside him on the open-air seat for the meeting with Popp.

There may well be no immediate connection between Schleicher's come-back and that almost military scene on 3 November 1932 beside the main road from Tata, when the Governor of Hungary, Admiral Horthy (in full military uniform, with the German and Hungarian national anthems ringing out, and salutes by top military personnel and local police), came up to Henne and congratulated him on the land speed record. The fact that countless small details go into making up that little bit extra, which is what it is all about (a principle which Henne, as a racing driver, applied), could be put down to the contribution Schleicher made. With Hopf he had developed a new multi-plate compressor, which Henne found fitted to his racing machine as he went up to the start. Henne was convinced that it was this new supercharger which made him superior. It was clear, and not only to Henne when Horthy congratulated him, that since Schleicher's return to the company, things were going to get better at BMW.

Schleicher had also done something to the motorcar engine, and with it anticipated a development from a purely design point of view which, now that Hitler was in power and the situation in the car industry would change from one day to the next, was to take BMW away from making cars for the people towards quite different horizons.

It was Popp and not Schleicher who had given the rallying cry for this. It was his proposition that a new BMW car must hide more power under the bonnet than was apparent from the outside, which had triggered it off. It was called: *Six Cylinders*.

He insisted that the car must have six cylinders, when the designers Friz and Duckstein told him that the new car planned by Popp would be perfectly all right and just as good as before with four cylinders, without having to abandon the outer dimensions of a small car. Popp was adamant. He wanted six cylinders. He gave three reasons. Firstly, a car for him only really started with six cylinders. He was so used to the Austro-Daimler, and he kept having the intolerable thought of sitting in one of his own cars without six cylinders. Secondly, the Slump had brought with it the situation where small cars had penetrated a clientele which a car manufacturer found ever harder to please. Would the Dixi satisfy them, even in its 3/20 version? These people wanted a faster, more flexible and elegant car without having to give up any of the economy, solidity, ease of maintenance (not having a chauffeur), and all the other advantages offered by a small car. But did they not also wish to be able to show through their cars just how hard to please they were? And wasn't it also true that they were prepared to pay a little extra for their requirements, and would not settle for anything less than other people (who were obviously less intelligent), who had chosen something like the big, new Horch twelve-cylinder to show their awareness of what was elite? Thirdly, BMW had to lead the field. That had been the case with aero-engines – world record! It had also been true for motorcycles – world record! And as their first line of business, the car should not be forgotten.

But how was this to be done in the shortest possible time?

Popp had not the slightest intention of playing his people off against each other. On the other hand, time was pressing. No sooner had the rallying cry been given than Friz set to work, in the absolute certainty that he had the answer. From his last experiences with aero-engine production (the aero-engine had remained his preserve), he planned to produce the six-cylinder engine with an aluminium block and thereby develop a true power plant. Over at the design department at Eisenach, Duckstein, driven on by the ambition to show the great Friz in Munich what he could do, swore by a cast-iron block, which was cheaper and much easier to produce for mass production, insisting that it only needed three main bearings. Schleicher had not been idle either and had spent some time thinking about this, without exchanging ideas on it with his masters Friz and Duckstein. That was not his business. He stuck to 'testing' and had enough to do with Henne and his world record, which was there to be beaten.

It was now the summer of 1932, and the design plans lay on Popp's desk. He was not happy with either set. One, he calculated, would come out far too expensive, and the other. . . no, it might be all right for Opel to be so cheap, but not BMW. Schleicher was called in.

'What's your view on it?'

Schleicher looked at the plans for the first time. He liked Friz's design.

'But. . .' said Popp, 'it's impractical, far too expensive. And what about the other one?'

Schleicher hesitated. Duckstein's ideas had inspired him, had always done so. He had learnt and profited most from him. Yet he said: no, the cheap version was certainly not the worst, but, he explained, the mechanics would be too temperamental. No BMW design!

'So how would *you* build the six-cylinder?'

'According to the American design principle,' replied Schleicher. Cast-iron block, 1.2-litre capacity and instead of a new carburettor, which would take too long to develop, quite simply fit two (no need to worry about the cost – a Solex carburettor then cost a mere 7.5 marks!).

'Then build it,' said Popp, 'under one condition. . . .' He named it, and Schleicher agreed, even if he did not know who that 'first-rate expert authority' was who was to give advice on all three engines.

Schleicher asked if he could also set a condition.

Popp looked somewhat surprised. Schleicher said that a new six-cylinder engine would be useless if fitted to a chassis which was constantly twisting. Suspension and handling qualities would never be right, however quietly the engine ran. He admitted that he did not have any time and was not, in any case, the right person to do anything to the frame. But he knew a man who could. He was called Fritz Fiedler, and at present (like Schleicher himself, until very recently) was to be found at Horch.

'Can we get him away from there?' asked Popp.

'No sooner said than done,' said Schleicher.

He knew what things were leading up to; that Audi, Horch and the Zschopau Motor Works would merge into the Auto-Union (in fact the general meetings of all three companies would sanction the merger in Chemnitz on 29 June 1932, which was also voted through by Communists and National Socialists in the Saxon Diet, as it was the only way to prevent 8,000 workers being made redundant – just at the Horch factory in Oberschlema alone).

One man's meat is another man's poison, as the proverb goes. Fiedler packed his bags at Horch, unpacked them at BMW in Munich, and immediately started work on the tubular frame. And Schleicher set off for Sindelfingen to see Daimler-Benz (with plans in hand), as stipulated in Popp's condition, with Max Friz, the official head of the Munich design department and Leo M. Glass, his counterpart at Eisenach. They were accompanied by a lorry carrying the chassis developed by Fiedler.

This episode was later to be called the 'Judgement of Paris'. The role of Paris, whose judgement is said to have unleashed the Trojan War because he handed the golden apple to Aphrodite as the most beautiful of the three goddesses, was played by a very down-to-earth man who had determined the type of technical progress to be adopted by Daimler-Benz. He was Hans Nibel, an undisputed expert, whom even a man like Porsche would take his hat off to. Nibel had the plans for the engines laid out in front of him and gave his verdict, as the three originators held their breath in anticipation (Glass was here representing the designer Duckstein), to Schleicher's engine, which had immediately produced 34 hp on the test bed in Munich. While praising the engine he had reservations about the bodywork, which Popp wanted to have built in Sindelfingen, as before. Nibel was an advocate of channel frames. No, this tubular frame with its high cranking at the tail was no good. The three candidates kept quiet, apart from saying that they would pass it on to Fiedler.

The new car was designated the BMW 303. It was fitted with the tubular frame, which Fiedler had developed for it – high-cranked at the tail and tapering at the front as allowed for by the engine. The six-cylinder engine with a capacity of 1173 cc produced 30 hp at 4000 rpm. The front axle was fitted with additional wishbones underneath, and the rear axle had longitudinal, semi-elliptic springs. Mercedes again produced the coachwork – a wooden-framed body with panels stretched over it. Fiedler's mark was on the radiator grille. He had given it a slightly sloping shape and had rounded off the corners to reduce air drag, which, in itself, resulted in the so-called 'BMW kidneys'.

The car was 200 kilogrammes lighter than any comparable model, it ran as smooth as silk, it had 50 per cent more power than the four-cylinder 3/20, and was fitted with central pressurised lubrication which would supply grease to all ten lubricating points on the chassis, simply by operating a foot switch every 50 kilometres or so.

When the 303 was presented at the International Motor Show in 1933, nobody guessed that a whole model range would stem from this car, that Schleicher's cast-iron block with top and bottom sections made from one casting would turn out to be the cheapest and sturdiest configuration; even that it would remain essentially unaltered for over twenty years in versions from 1.2 litres up to 2 litres (and in a four-cylinder version right up to today). Initially it was available in only three prototypes, which had turned out rather awkwardly.

The three cars stood in marked contrast to the official poster of the Motor Show, which, in the view of *Motor Kritik*, the trade paper of the intrepid and feared engineer Ganz, was an inexcusable blunder:

> What a gentleman to behold – so good-looking, so like a film star, and as sublime, that only fabulous riches could bring him about. His steel-grey, penetrating eyes are directed towards the next Grand Hotel Palace, and genteely ignoring the lady, who is hopefully his wife, sitting next to him in his car. She knows that she is a refined lady, and wants people to look at her discreetly. She is sitting inside the car with slightly misty eyes, looking dispassionately over to the eroticised menfolk. Short-hand typists find it chic. Motorcyclists wander away empty-handed.'

The critic, who openly admitted coming to Berlin by motorcycle, must have known this.

'Joking aside,' he then said, remembering that cars and motorcycles were piling up in garages and sheds facing an uncertain future, with scratch marks on number plates because their owners could no longer afford to pay their taxes, 'joking aside, this current show which appeals to people's snobbish instincts is a mistake, because it is now more than ever appropriate to prove that the motorcar is anything but a luxury object. It is something one or two luxury cars cannot alter.'

Without doubt, the 303 *was* just such a proof. What did it matter, then, if the Reich Chancellor, who did not miss the opportunity of personally opening the 'International Motor Show', managed to avoid visiting the non-German stands? Was it perhaps the result of concentrating thoughts too intently on national concerns, as the *Motor-Kritik* tactfully suggested, or simply a mistake in management?

The article was written on 11 February 1933 when that German Reich calling itself the Third Reich, or presumptuously and blasphemously the Thousand-Year Reich, was all of twelve days old.

Reason Covers her Face

The fact that only twelve days since his seizure of power seemed enough time for him to turn his attention to something apparently as unimportant as opening a motor show, proved that Hitler was firmly in the driving seat. It also showed how important it was to combine his favourite project of *national car ownership* with the desires of the masses, whose support he needed. To supply the new state immediately with the glitter and glamour of the car, as he planned to do, was just the opportunity which the international forum of an annual show like this one provided, enabling him to appear in the ermine coat of a statesman and show the world just how radical his social thinking was and how he was tackling his thousand-year task. And so it was that on 11 February 1933, Reich Chancellor Adolf Hitler, in the presence of six Reich ministers, the presidents of all the motoring organisations, as well as the managing directors of all Germany's car companies (the Slump had decimated them to five), and even in the presence of Franz Josef Popp, announced a four-point plan for national car ownership. The four points involved:

1 Removing state interests in road traffic from the present transport arrangements; 2 gradually reducing taxes; 3 undertaking and completing a major road-building programme; and 4 developing motor sports facilities.

These four proposed measures sounded as sensible as they appeared utopian. Anyone reflecting on them for any length of time, especially the experts, would find them unexciting and even hackneyed. This was because people employed all round the car industry had been working on each of the four points in one way or another over the last few years, and had tackled them, inspired by hope, only to see the Slump push all this intense activity into the background. There had even been talk for some time of the motorways which would join up the entire German road network. The plans lay fully worked out in the drawers of the Reich Transport Ministry.

The only surprising thing was that they were all now cemented into a single plan. Anyone listening to the speech given by Hitler to economic experts and major industrialists (Hitler was then asking for financial support for his party and getting it) at the Industry Club of Düsseldorf, could not help remembering what this Herr Hitler, before he had become Reich Chancellor, had said: that there was only *one* basic solution to the present economic dilemma. According to Hitler, this was based on the premise that collapsing

156

economies had always had the collapsing state as their precursors, and not the other way round, meaning that there could not be a prosperous economy until there was a thriving, powerful state around it. He made an analogy to Carthage, claiming that the Carthaginian economy could not have existed without the Carthaginian fleet, its trade, or its army. This, he stated, was also the case in modern times where, when life was getting increasingly hard and people's interests had all been wrecked, there could be no economy without the rock-steady, wholly decisive political will of the nation behind it.

Anyone remembering it would have been left in no doubt that putting the four points into practice was, so to speak, a piece of cake for anyone planning to change not only Germany, but the world. But who remembered it, and who, with hand on heart, could claim to have read Hitler's *Mein Kampf?* It referred to everything that was now about to happen.

Before it begins, I must just take another look at the year 1930 which, from today's perspective, can be described as the real turning point, a change in the times, and not just in a political sense. When the Nazis won their spectacular election victory in September (they returned to the Reich Parliament with 107 members), it took place against a background of other profound changes. These found expression technologically, in what was later to be called the 'second industrial revolution', while in the natural sciences the 'dawn of the atomic age' was breaking. Culturally, however, there were no new developments in the so-called fine and applied arts, developments which brought about an awareness of its own existence through hope and experimentation. Ortega y Gasset says of this existence in the twentieth century, in his book *The Rebellion of the Masses*, that we regard 'the crowd *per se* as being in possession of the institutions and appliances created by civilisation'.

Remarkably, Ortega noticed this in the midst of the upheaval (his book, *La Rebelión de las masas*, appeared in 1929), while any further change or transformation of such a fundamentally and previously unknown nature can only usually be recognised from an appropriate distance, perhaps indeed only from a distance of half a century. Only then can an historical observer perceive what happened, even though he might have been present at the time as an eyewitness. It was only fifty years later, in the BMW museum, that I could appreciate it.

Hans Wichmann had given the title 'Turning Point 1930' to the exhibition which he had mounted there, assembling every piece of evidence from all walks of life (architecture, technology, films, theatre, literature), such as books, posters, items of clothing and household objects, and ranging from the design of famous cutlery, such as that of Andreas Moritz, to the smile of Greta Garbo, from Max Planck's experimental table and the first television pictures to Franz Kruckenberg's rail Zeppelin, from the first traffic control system using flashing lights, right up to the pictures documenting Albert Einstein's meeting with the Indian philosopher Rabindranath Tagore in Berlin in 1930, where they discussed the existence of truth that was independent of human existence. Amongst the treasures was also a small car marketed throughout the world and produced in many of its countries – it was known as the

'Rosengart' in France, the 'American Bantam' in the USA, and the 'Datsun' in Japan. In England, however, where it originated, it was called the 'Austin Seven', and in Germany the BMW 3/15 was produced under the name of 'the little Dixi'.

This collection, squeezed into a space of 1,000 square metres, clearly revealed the common denominator of all the exhibits as a secret source from which they seemed to stem. It was as if the originators, artists in the widest sense (writers, architects, artisans, playwrights, directors, producers of posters, copywriters, graphic artists, couturiers, gold and silversmiths, photographers, banknote compositors, along with physicists, town planners and so forth), had met, before starting work, at a world congress where, in determining and discussing the worldwide 'newness' of their time, they had brought together movements in style and forms of expression as a single entity. This was, of course, mere fantasy.

But it was undoubtedly true that worldwide communications must have come about which involved an interweaving of a New Objectivity ('New Living', 'New Photography', 'New Lens') with that well-articulated desire (which had been influenced by these principles) of the masses, who were striving to create a *new* world that was far removed from provincialism and narrowness, and who wanted to contribute to all the results gained from technology and natural sciences. The explanation for how such an 'interweaving' could have come about was now to be found in these 'results' – in the entirely new phenomenon of world travel which arrived towards the end of the twenties, enabling not just individuals but 'masses' to be carried from capital to capital, from continent to continent, across the oceans, by sea, land or air. In 1927 alone, 10,000 ships went through the Suez and Panama Canals and the DO X giant flying boat built by Dornier in 1929 housed 169 passengers in its 'quarters'! News technology had also been similarly refined and perfected by 1930 (the first overseas radio links were made in 1927, while five years later, 64 permanent teleprinters were established in Germany with a range of 20,000 km), making the word 'news' synonymous with 'brand-new'. Alfred Braun's moving report of Stresemann's funeral in October 1929 reached every house by radio, and electric reproduction technology had already replaced the gramophone horn and transfered the liveliness of music onto record in a way that made you feel you were in a concert hall.

All this had the effect of 'a whirlpool drawing in humanity' (Wichmann). Thomas Mann, however, spoke in the same year of 1930 of the 'primitive democratic crudeness of the fun-fair' which went round the world and made the adventurous development of technology responsible for this crudeness, 'with its triumphs and catastrophes, noise and sensation when a sporting record is achieved, the adulation and excessive payment of stars who attract the masses, and boxing matches with million-dollar fees held in front of large numbers of spectators'. Yes, humanity seemed to be on the loose, 'like a group of school children let out of the humanistic and idealistic school of the nineteenth century.'

With this he was already aware of what was coming to an end and what was just around the corner, from the 'Salvation-Army-type behaviour, mass hysteria, mob rule, hallelujas and dervish-like repetition of monotonous slogans, to the point where everyone was foaming at the mouth. Fanaticism had become the principle for salvation, enthusiasm had become epileptic ecstasy, and politics the opium of the masses in the Third Reich, or a proletarian eschatology, while reason covered her face.'

Emotive words? Reality would prove him right. In Russia Stalin had taken power in 1929, and had immediately started wholesale liquidation of everything which a European-minded elite had in mind as it tried to communicate to the people the 'New' it had formulated, and hopefully to be found in the 'new society'. Isolationism, confinement to national borders, blind determination to sever communication was the answer. Germany was soon to follow the same path. 'We will soon find ourselves between two great powers, the United States and Russia. Then you will see that it is vital for us to create a United States of Europe,' Aristide Briand said, and circulated an extensive brief to governments in May 1930 entitled: 'Memorandum on the organisation of a system towards federal union.'

Twenty-six governments replied to this with reservations, some raising a legitimate 'if', others a 'but', showing that they had not understood a single thing about the situation. The reply of the German government was totally negative. It would be pointless wanting to build a new Europe which did not stand up to present developments. In other words, Europe and Versailles were incompatible for Germany, so the answer was no.

Hitler could almost have written these words himself. And, indeed, had he not done so? Briand's passionate appeal for the unification of Europe before the assembly of the League of Nations in September 1930 coincided with Hitler's electoral success. When Briand heard this, he said: 'I am the Nazi's first victim.'

The great Frenchman and European would admittedly have had some difficulty maintaining that the isolation of existing or potential dictatorships (causing a breakdown in communication and world solidarity that had existed up to 1930) could not happen in such a free country as France. This country, fearing its security, began in that same year of 1930 to build the most powerful system of fortifications ever seen in Europe. This was the Maginot Line, the symbol of an isolationism which clearly negated everything which man had dreamt and hoped for in a 'world of reason'.

The year 1930 was in fact the turning point, around which time pivoted. When Brüning, the hapless Reich Chancellor of those last few years of the Weimar Republic, later admitted that he was '100 yards from the finishing line' when he gave in or was forced to give in, it made him realise that any democratic attempt to improve the situation was already doomed, and that (to quote Thomas Mann again) reason had long since covered her face.

We shall see how technology made its particular peace with Hitler, so to speak, though admittedly only for as long as the general peace held. The fact that technology enabled Hitler to wage his war turned out to be a gradual process which, to the extent that Hitler identified himself with Germany, and Germany with him, also involved BMW. It was the undoing of the

Germans getting mixed up with Hitler. When they saw what they had let themselves in for, it was too late. Too late to appeal, too late to turn back, too late to repent, too late to prevent or merely alleviate the catastrophe which Germany, and everyone in that country whatever they might have done to accelerate or retard it, had decided upon.

In essence, BMW was the mirror image of German existence, German thought, desires, emotions, aspirations and abilities; it was the possesser of all those virtues attributed to the Germans – diligence, resolve, strength, ingeniousness, steadfastness, the German insistence on the best, as well as all the vices for which the Germans are feared and hated – arrogance, self-righteousness, overestimating themselves while underestimating others, unreasonableness to the point of presumptiousness, lack of foresight, obsequiousness.

All these qualities condemned and enabled BMW to live with Hitler, and to perish with him. It also made it possible, on the other hand, for a completely new life to rise up from the rubble.

A Thousand Years are not like a Day
1933–1945

National Car Ownership

When Wolfgang von Gronau was received by President Herbert Hoover in the White House after his world-beating flight in 1930, the secretary remarked on his departure that his visit must have greatly interested the President as they had considerably exceeded the usual time for such a reception.

In October 1934 Gronau was again in Washington, where the general assembly of the Fédération Aéronautique Internationale was in session. Gronau was representing the Aero Club of Germany, whose vice-president, a Herr von Höppner, had meanwhile to go abroad due to remarks he had made criticising the government. Hoover had left office. His successor wanted to see the delegates. They were presented to him individually at the White House, and he had a few kind words for each of them. When it was the turn of the German, Wolfgang von Gronau, the face of the thirty-second President of the United States hardened. The stony silence was broken with the single words: 'Good morning'.

The thirty-second President of the United States was in a wheelchair. He had come to power at almost the same time as Hitler, and his name was Franklin Delano Roosevelt.

> Franklin Roosevelt took over a state with an economy which had collapsed because of democracy, and I came to the head of a Reich which was in complete turmoil, again due to democracy.
>
> The United States had thirteen million unemployed, Germany had seven million, with a further seven million on short time.
>
> In both states the public finances were in ruins, and the decline of general economic activity seemed almost impossible to check. At that moment, the United States and the German Reich began a development about which posterity will find it easy to make a conclusive judgement on the validity of the theories.

Hitler spoke these words which, in this excerpt, still appeared moderate (otherwise his speech was a masterpiece of demagogy, false accusations and arrogant comparisons), to the German Parliament on 11 December 1941 when, a few hours before, inspired by the Japanese attack on the American fleet at Pearl Harbor, he had declared war on America and, by so doing,

163

had expanded the European war into a world conflagration in which both he and the German Reich would perish. His prophecy (that posterity would find it easy to make a conclusive judgement) was therefore not without some sinister irony, the kind which history sometimes likes before preparing itself to become the courtroom of the world.

Yet we must wonder what prompted the German members of parliament to leap out of their seats and cheer when Hitler said he had just served the American chargé d'affaires with his passport. Had the entire German people become so blinded that they could not see what was real?

In his speech, in which he described the New Deal legislation, that economic programme developed by Roosevelt, as the greatest failure which any man had ever suffered, while National Socialist Germany under his, Hitler's, leadership would record a huge increase in living standards, in economic, cultural and artistic activity and so forth, the 'Führer' reproached Roosevelt time and again for not understanding Germany and the political landscape of the Reich.

At least he was right about that. With Hitler's accession, Germany and the World (and not only America, headed by Roosevelt, whose era – until his death – remarkably mirrored his opponent Hitler's, which ended in suicide seventeen days later) were divided, and people in *one* world began to live in two.

'Heil Hitler' was how Popp immediately signed the first letter he had written to Kissel after the 'seizure of power', and 'Heil Hitler' was how Kissel returned the greeting. Were they Nazis? Not in the least. He apparently used 'Heil Hitler' as a matter of course, as if he had always done so, and as if greetings like 'Good morning' or 'Hello' had temporarily become symptoms of decline. This was how one German citizen greeted another on the street when raising their arms, when a band of Hitler Youth, or a troop from the scouts, marched down the road behind their swastika or black runic flag to the banging of troopers' drums or the flourishing of trumpets. The traffic would come to a halt, cars would hesitate cautiously. The teacher would say 'Heil Hitler' to his class in the morning (to the same scouts in front of whose flag his hand would be raised). 'Heil Hitler' was the greeting that market women would use when selling vegetables, what the car mechanic would say when he crawled out from underneath a Mercedes or a BMW and explained to the customer that there was something wrong with the gearbox. Without grumbling, smart workers could be seen going cheerfully and amiably to the maypole, men who were still communists and who still showed the clenched fist. They would see the words 'workforce' and 'works manager' together, as if there had never been any class struggle, and they would hear HIM say: 'We want to go to the worker and the farmer to teach them that there can be no German life without the German spirit, and that they must all join together to form one large community – spirit, brow and fist, workers, farmers and citizens!'

Had they all gone mad? The company director, who let his factory premises be decorated with the symbol from the Labour Front, a gear-wheel surrounding a swastika; churchmen who now no longer appeared as Protestant

Christians but as 'German Christians'; then the nuncio, who concluded a concordat allowing Pope and Reich to live in harmony; the conductor who declared Beethoven's Ninth Symphony to be the story of German destiny; German women who had been ordered not to smoke and went about in sandals dressed, according to the most recent research in folklore, like the Teutonic women in museums?

No, they were not all mad, they were quite normal, unlike a few people who were deemed to be mad, such as Otto Wels who made a speech against the 'Enabling Act', like Martin Niemöller, a real 'stick-in-the-mud', who still could not understand, even in a concentration camp, that his place was no longer in the pulpit, that a 'new time' had dawned with the battle cries: 'We are not citizens, farmers, or workers. Smash down the barriers, comrades!' The people who were mad were a few subversive writers whose books had always been kept locked away in the glass-fronted cabinets of the bourgeoisie, long before Hitler arrived, and the 'cowards' (as the Party called them when they threw their books on the fire) who had fled abroad. A few local politicians, who had spontaneously packed their pens and pencils and vacated town halls, did well to join the Party quickly, even if it was not what they wanted. The very fact that no one would 'buy' their change of mind was another story altogether, as was the fact that some of their faces still betrayed their lack of involvement when they would not believe that things were getting better and better, when they would not see that the unemployed were disappearing, that motorways were being built, that purchasing power was increasing, and that people were heaving a sigh of relief and could not care less if trade union offices were closed, that the press could no longer write everything they wanted, that there were labour camps for the 'die-hards' (the word 'concentration camp' only appeared later), and that Jews were forced to live outside the community.

But were people really so unconcerned? Did they really heave a sigh of relief? Anyone delving into the question would be hard put to find an answer.

Germans who had fled abroad reported that the first three months (after 30 January) were the hardest of their lives. They said that there had been a 'total revolution', and a complete levelling out and extinction of class differences. There were only farmers and small shopkeepers left, who were treated as the masters of the lower middle class (the view of Count Hermann Keyserling to 'Harry' Count Kessler, who noted this down from Paris in his diary). And the spirit, as represented by intellectuals, artists and writers who no longer mattered, had completely lost its significance. As something which the petty bourgeoisie had always wanted, this seemed like the ideal situation for them; 70 per cent of the German people were said to be all for Hitler, and closed ranks behind him. Hitler, though, from his handwriting and physiognomy, could be said to have had pronounced suicidal tendencies, to be a person with a strong death wish, who incorporated an essential feature of the Germans – an infatuation with death, whose constantly recurring motif was unremitting despair. In a situation such as this, the Germans could feel nothing less than completely German, in their admiration and longing for a futile death and self-sacrifice. They sensed that Hitler would lead them again to this unremitting despair, and so to a grandiose destruction. They were inevitably fascinated by him.

This analysis, which is as gruesome as it is true (how true would be revealed twelve years later), still does not explain how that self-inflicted limitation, which the Germans greeted with such frenzy, could occur. This reached its peak in a concept taken from technology and later to be known as 'Gleichschaltung' (the co-ordination and unification of the laws passed by the Nazi government in 1933), which systematically robbed a people of its constitution, taking away its parliament, abolishing its Reich president, extinguishing the federal nature of the Reich, turning the state apparatus into a party apparatus, expunging justice ('what is right is judged on what the people need'), consolidating the army, and placing the whole of Germany (by invoking the famous Article 48 of the Weimar constitution) under a state of emergency which would last until the bitter end, allowing no basic rights, and having only the fateful words of State Lawyer Carl Schmitt as its leitmotif: 'The Führer's will is law.'

The chronicler recording contemporary history at BMW did not differ in his opinions on the events from the leading article writer in the *Völkischer Beobachter*: 'With the dawning of 1933, the German people, and its industry, trade and commerce, experienced the most powerful impetus which they had ever owed to one political action. The name of this Chancellor arising from the creative German people, Adolf Hitler, would never be forgotton, as he took over leadership of the nation on that historic morning of 30 January.'

There is the customary deference, all right. But if we think that it was unavoidable, then we become a bit suspicious when the article continues:

> This radical change born out of a political philosophy goes far beyond the bounds of the purely political, because the drastic change of attitude, in the national rebirth of our fatherland, was too overpowering not to penetrate even the most outlying reaches of our national life, not to be expressed in all its different manifestations; this was just one of the essential findings of the National Socialist revolution, namely that politics should never be an end in itself, but only an objective for the human will to express itself through every action, whether big or small.

Who ordered the chronicler to write such things, to enter such simple-minded nonsense into the historical records not of a propaganda ministry but of a company archive – the 'Party'? No, they had other things to worry about. So who then? Well, it was the writer himself who took it upon himself to enter into the 'spirit of the times', as everyone did; not out of fear, but in the conviction that he had to be faithful to 'the New', and that he had to prove that he was not yesterday's man if he wanted to have his say. Later a red pencil would cross out these sentences, would erase the worst of this nonsense. Yet this would not be without a certain comic irony, since this same uneasy attempt which had inspired the writer to fall in with the prevailing mood of the times, now inspired correction, so that only what was defensible should be left in. But what, in the end, was defensible?

166

When the Nuremberg Trials came to session in 1945, Brigadier-General Telford Taylor pronounced the following devastating words: 'Without the co-operation of German industry and the Nazi Party, Hitler and his party members would never have been able to assume power in Germany, and the Third Reich would never have dared to plunge the world into a war.'

But did this damning indictment really describe the complex reality of the Third Reich?

On 20 February 1933, Dr Hjalmar Schacht invited leading industrialists, bankers and businessmen from the Ruhr to the German parliamentary president's mansion in Berlin. Hitler and Göring were present. Hitler said that the private sector could no longer be maintained in the age of democracy; it could only come about when the people had grasped the essential idea of authority and personality. Everything in the world which economic and cultural life had created as positive, good and valuable was due solely to the importance of personality. If defence of enterprise and its political administration were handed over to a majority, then it would be irretrievably lost.

What was meant by majority was clear, as was the meaning of personality. But what was meant by: 'We must not forget that all cultural values have to be introduced more or less forcibly'? Did that mean violence? Against whom? But no word was made of an intended dissolution of the trade unions, nor anything said of the elimination of the Jews, and, moreover, nothing of what was once called the 'irrevocable manifesto' with which Hitler had won over the masses – nationalisation of trusts, profit-sharing in large companies, 'local government ownership of department stores and low-cost sub-letting to small traders', land reform and 'abolition of the rates'. (In actual fact, there was nothing in all this that could justify the appendage 'Workers' Party' on the full party title, nor was anything ever carried out, apart from, admittedly, the promise to 'deal with' Marxism, and of course to 'build up' the armed forces.)

After the meeting, Dr Schacht went around with hat in hand and collected 3 million marks, and on 2 May the supporters of Robert Ley, later to lead the Labour Front, forced their way in to every trade union office in the country, confiscated its files, appropriated its bank assets (more than 100 million marks) and locked up the trade union leaders who, only the day before, in an attempt to maintain industrial peace, had ordered their members to take part in the May-day processions, which had now been renamed 'National Labour Day'.

It should be mentioned here that by the time Ley's action had started, leading industrialists from the Confederation of German Industry meeting at Carl Friedrich von Siemens's residence in Berlin had decided to establish immediate contact with Theodor Leipart, leader of the 'German Trades Union Congress' and Tarnow, its economic expert, with the aim of preventing a last-minute collapse of the 'historically created organisations of employers and employees as poles for social equilibrium'. After they left, they discovered with horror that both men were already behind bars.

This is the way things continued. What effect did a missing signature have (for example, at the bottom of that famous petition by leading industrialists to Hindenburg asking him to make Hitler Reich Chancellor)? It simply encouraged Dr Schacht, later to become Hitler's Economics Minister, to comment in a letter to Hitler on heavy industry that it fully deserved its name, 'because it is so leaden-footed when it comes to decision-making'. What effect did old Emil Kirdorf's break with Hitler have, when he, the 'Wotan of German heavy industry' and loyal vassal of the Führer, defended his Jewish friend Paul Silberberg, President of the Cologne Chamber of Commerce, and castigated, in a letter to the press, anti-Semitic incitement as a crime? ('The dagger thrust at this valuable human being has now reached me as well. It is now my hope, my confidence, that I will come to know a new, unsullied Germany yet.') What was Friz Thyssen's warning that he would withdraw still worth, when this man, who had brought about Hitler's rise by paying out millions, resigned from his post on the Prussian Council of State when hordes of stormtroopers threatened the regional government president in Düsseldorf, Carl-Christian Schmid, with death and forced him out of office because his wife was Jewish? To say nothing of that telegram which Thyssen sent to Hitler immediately after the outbreak of war, the only German member of parliament to do so: 'I am against the war!' Even internment in a concentration camp (after he was recaptured attempting to flee Germany) and confiscation of his fortune took nothing away from the guilt of having got involved and failing to resist, even if he was to profess ten times over that it had all been in the interests of the company to whom he was answerable.

Popp was no hero either. On photographs showing visits by the Führer to the works, he appeared neither bored nor particularly enthusiastic, in view of the honour that the head of state had shown to BMW by his visit. Neither was he especially humble in the company of prominent figures and vassals. His pride, which was difficult to overlook, was confined to his products; people coming to BMW (even the Führer) were not bringing glory to BMW but only to themselves. There was nothing to conceal, nothing to gloss over. He knew what this man wanted – results. Successes in racing, records. Every race that was won added to Germany's glory, made the Germans stronger, showed the world who was really the boss, in spite of all the scorn heaped abroad on the 'Führer and Reich' and the new 'industrialised nation', by which they meant the German workforce. New designs, recognisable by the high-pitched whining of their superchargers, appeared on the race-tracks of Europe, where they won victories, flew the flag, to disappear even before the German national anthem and its Nazi counterpart, the Horst-Wessel-Lied, had fully died away, but only to reappear next time round, where they again came out top. The Germans were coming! Nobody else seemed to know whether they were coming or going. There should have been amazement, respect – or at least surprise.

The second thing Hitler wanted was the people's car. Did the Führer know that he, Popp, had designated the bus as the only economic solution justifying the term 'people's car No 1'? He had never forgotten a thing, Popp was to say to him smiling, when he reminded him: 'But that was under the previous

Reich, my Führer. Things are completely different now. Industry will build *your* people's car, *your* Volkswagen!'

'At what price?'

'I stick to what I said before when you, my Führer, were still in prison at the Landsberg Fortress. 30 hp = 1,000 dollars. That makes 4,200 marks!'

'Industry, dear Popp, does not fully appreciate what lies behind Newness – namely, its social function. A thousand marks, no more, no less!'

'Führer, even Corps leader Hühnlein, whom I spoke to on this matter, agrees that price is not feasible.'

'But I think it is. Industry creates problems through fear of competition. I shall stamp this out. Porsche has all the technical answers. Just the price has to be worked out – and the factory. I shan't wait much longer.'

Whom was the Führer addressing? It was going to be a tricky business, to say the least. On the one hand, the German car industry was not allowed to appear as a saboteur (after all, it was the first to profit from the upturn in economic activity), but on the other hand, it had to fear for its own small car designs, which would not be able to resist, in the long run, a state-built Volkswagen in which competition had been ruled out. Even mid-ranged cars, which the market valued, would then be threatened, such as the car which Daimler-Benz (in a 1.7-litre 170-V version, aimed as a utility car) and which BMW (in a 2-litre version, emphasising its sporting qualities) wanted to develop in their joint venture. What would happen if Opel and DKW, essentially small car manufacturers, had their bid accepted and built Porsche's design with state subsidy?

The Volkswagen was a directive from the Führer. There was nothing you could do about it. What had been established was that Porsche's design, the main features of which had already been laid down in 1931 and the first prototypes produced at NSU (rear engine, fully swinging half-axles, lightweight construction, central tubular frame, engine and final drive as a unit, giving greater passenger space), had been applauded by the Führer, apart from the price, which even Porsche had estimated at 1,550 marks. It seemed out of the question to reduce it to 900 marks as Hitler required ('It *must* be possible to offer the German people a car at a price costing no more than a middle-range motorcycle used to'). So anyone wanting to solve the problem was faced with having to square the circle, leaving the Reich Association for the German Car Industry (RDA), which the Führer had decided to entrust with carrying out the plans, under the obligation of: 'furthering car ownership among the German people, on the basis of shared responsibility, by employing the leading forces in the automotive world, with all the means serving the good of the German people'; and offering bits of advice here and there, until they finally thought that they had found the answer in the materials that were going to be used. Popp and Kissel protested; that was like receiving the bill without having looked at the menu. It was, of course, feasible to put pressure on materials suppliers, to make them lower their prices accordingly, but not to prevent them from passing on their losses in correspondingly higher materials prices for all the other cars (which would naturally spell ruin for everyone). Fortunately, the majority realised this. 'That also meant,' as Popp was to say later, 'that the last chance to solve the problem of pricing had gone.' What was to be done?

The role of the RDA, which certainly must have fought hard not to condemn its members to a lingering death, remained, by all accounts, contradictory to the point of spitefulness. Some said that Hitler, by commissioning the Reich Association to solve the problem, had knowingly asked for trouble (which meant forcing industry to abandon profits and finally comprehend their social duty), while others claimed that the RDA would have liked nothing better than to present the world with the proof that Morgenstern's dictum 'what must not be, cannot be!' could also be turned on its head, to 'what cannot be, must definitely not be!', to give reason to a dictatorship. As to what was really going on behind the scenes, how everyone changed places, whether anyone at all had knowingly tried to delay the project (either by supplying Porsche with completely inadequate means for building his prototypes, or by subjecting the test-runs to the most trivial criticisms) need not concern us. It would only have concerned us if there had not been any information about the behaviour by which a dictator makes demands on individuals and whole groups – including BMW – within the group formed by the car industry.

Hitler wanted to establish his authority down there with the masses by realising his social utopia of the Volkswagen, and simultaneously show people abroad what his true social thinking was. He could expect the car industry to meet him not in enmity but in gratitude. Had the car industry not flourished, had he not approved subsidies to two large German concerns, Daimler-Benz and Auto Union? The money was not a pittance, after all (in 1933, each received a million marks). Had he not abolished car tax, and ensured that foreign imports had been almost totally wiped out through currency controls, while greatly encouraging car exports through subsidies?

His patience came to an end in 1937 when he announced at the opening of the Berlin Motor Show (with obvious anger in his voice) that he had taken the 'irrevocable decision' to free the economy surrounding German transport, 'one of our people's greatest industries', from the uncertainty of international competition by putting it on a solid, secure and, above all, self-supporting footing. (Why, he did not say. Was there anyone in the audience who was also thinking of war?) Hitler continued – in any case, there could be no doubt about it – and now came the open threat: 'Either the so-called free economy is capable of solving these problems, or it is not capable of existing as a free economy. . .'. The National Socialist state would under no circumstances capitulate either to the idleness or the narrow-mindedness, still less to the ill will, of individual Germans.

At this time Popp was working on the Volkswagen project (whose delay had caused Hitler to become so worked up) more than anybody else. The reason for this was to be found in a note found amongst his papers.

'At one of these discussions (in the Reich Association of the German Car Industry), in which we again raised the question of materials and wage costs, as well as other costs, it occurred to us (here Popp meant Kissel, the managing director of Daimler-Benz, and himself)

170

to review the overall costings from the tax point of view, and so to examine the percentage which taxes represent in the price of a car. This consideration was to turn out extremely fruitful; it was just what we had hoped for.

We immediately got people to do the calculations in our companies, and we unanimously came to the conclusion that 25 to 30 per cent of a car's production costs at that time in Germany were made up of taxes. Further work revealed that about 20 per cent of the list price was taken up by distribution costs.

This enabled a new picture to emerge for the costings – car production costs alone amounted to only 50 per cent of the list price! Here was where Kissel and I saw the key to solving the price question. Since the costs for the Porsche car had been established in all previous calculations at between 1,400 and 1,500 marks, a price of 1,000 marks must be perfectly possible when a reduction of production taxes and distribution costs could be carried out.

From these thoughts, Kissel and I formulated the following solution:

1 The Labour Front would become the sponsor of the Volkswagen Works, because in it was a union of all those for whom Hitler wanted to create the Volkswagen.

2 The Labour Front possessed enough capital to set up the Works so that neither the existing car industry nor the banks would be called upon financially. (Here Popp made the suggestion that industry should provide the factory with all its patents and rights free of charge.)

3 To maintain tax exemption, the Volkswagen Works would have to be set up as a public utility, meaning that it would be non-profit-making. However, this would not mean any loss in tax revenue for the state as the great increase in car ownership resulting from the Volkswagen could be expected to provide increased tax revenues out of the overall economy.

4 To make savings on the majority of the distribution costs, the Labour Front undertook every aspect of marketing through its many branches, meaning that the profit margin within distribution costs could also be abandoned.

Popp suggested that the Volkswagen Works should be established in Nuremberg, the city used for National Party Rallies. The reason for this was that visitors to the Rallies could collect their Volkswagens immediately after the event. That avoided the need for a sales network. Was there irony in this? As it was, Kissel and Popp were convinced that they had found the answer which would be proved right, not only from a manufacturing, but also a political point of view. It all now boiled down to convincing Dr Ley and winning him over.

The Reich trustee for labour in Bavaria, Kurt Frey, was the appropriate intermediary, because he had a lot of influence with Dr Ley. Popp knew him as a reliable man, and had always been able to speak openly with him about problems in the car industry. Frey took up the proposals with great interest, asked Popp to set his and Kissel's thoughts down in writing (Popp did this immediately with two documents on 24 and 25 June 1936), and came back to him just a few days later. Yes, he had managed to speak to Dr Ley, who had immediately shown interest but had declared that the 'Scientific Institute of the Labour Front' would first have to pronounce on it, and this would take a bit of time.

In the meantime Hitler had become impatient on the Volkswagen issue, which had been dragging on now for some time. Trial cars had been presented to Hitler by Porsche and Werlin, Hitler's friend and subsequent director of the 'Company for Volkswagen preparation', and had been given his approval.

The RDA now had to make a decision, but did not know which one. An immediate meeting was vital. It was called on 27 July 1936 at Koblenz. Everyone realised how critical it was.

Popp reported:

Kissel and I had a long discussion before the meeting, and after careful consideration, agreed *not* to put our proposal before the debate, to avoid counter criticism, until we knew of Dr Ley's position. But we then decided to inform Werlin, to win him over to our way of thinking, because he seemed to be the right man for solving this problem, given his close association with Hitler. To do this, I agreed to travel back with Werlin from Koblenz to Munich, when I put forward our proposal to him.

Werlin was very impressed and immediately declared that this way must be given a chance, as all his own considerations on how to solve the puzzle had drawn a blank. The next day I sent him carbon copies of both my letters to Kurt Frey with a short covering note, dated 29 July 1936.

And then some odd things started happening. Firstly, Kissel and I heard nothing more. Then on 30 October 1936 Kurt Frey passed on the long-awaited statement from the 'Scientific Institute for the German Labour Front', which issued a devastating verdict on our proposals and refused to burden the Labour Front with a task which Hitler had set the car industry.

The RDA, however, had not been pressurised during all this, although its technical committee continued to work on the cost question. Test runs continued to take place, but all the pressure seemed to have been taken off now.

Kissel and I now considered further steps and informed Dr von Stauss, who brought up our proposals at a BMW supervisory board meeting at the beginning of June 1937, where he declared himself ready to intervene to win over Hitler. My letter of 11 June 1937 gave Herr von Stauss a further brief description of this project.

Meanwhile, I had discovered that Dr Ley had put this project forward in a memorandum to Hitler as the only solution to the Volkswagen, and had received Hitler's wholehearted approval!

Kissel and I were out of it now. At the end of May 1938, the foundation stone of the Volkswagen Works was laid, with the Labour Front starting massive sales propaganda which would soon result in more than 400,000 customers.

The Birth Certificates

The trade mark for the Bavarian Motor Works was registered at the Imperial Patents Office in the middle of the First World War

A prospectus from the Rapp Motor Works

The first mention of the Bavarian Aircraft Works

Franz Josef Popp is appointed

The memorandum of association of the public limited company, 13 August 1918

The Men who made History

On 29 November 1916 Franz Josef Popp, a qualified engineer and reserve lieutenant in the Imperial Austro-Hungarian Navy, joined the Rapp Motor Works in Munich

The engineer Max Friz came from Daimler in Stuttgart in 1917. He had applied to Rapp. Popp employed him

The subscribers to BMW's share capital: Camillo Castiglioni, an honoured businessman in the Austro-Hungarian empire

The honorary Doctor of Engineering and Privy Councillor, Fritz Neumeyer, head of the Zündapp Works

Dr Hjalmar Schacht, director of the German National Bank

Above: A man in his thirties: Gustav Otto, pilot, flying instructor, designer and entrepreneur

Below: 1916: the boss in front of one of his test beds *(foreground, right)*. One of the few pictures we have of Karl Rapp

Below: Gustav Otto was full of new design ideas. Lindpaintner's machine, with its initial construction of ashwood and glue, was braced with metal tubes. Lindpaintner flew from success to success

Ernst Udet in front of his Fokker D VII No. 4253 with its BMW IIIa engine. With it he rose to an altitude of 6,000 metres in 21 minutes and achieved 30 victories

9 June 1919: Zeno Diemer *(centre of picture)* shortly before his world record altitude flight, during which he reached 9,760 metres with a BMW IV engine. On the far left is the designer Max Friz

Austrian Marines in the
Rapp Motor Works carrying
out final inspection on
engines built under licence.
Left of picture: Austro-
Daimler engines. *Right of
picture:* Rapp's six-cylinder
engine

The propeller on its blue and
white background, which
Popp had registered as the
trade mark for BMW in 1917

Above: BMW motorised plough: '. . . a flick of the wrist brings the grab into operation . . .'. Potential customers were asked to refer to the Munich branch of the Youth Movement

Below: BMW everywhere – visions from prospectuses of 1921

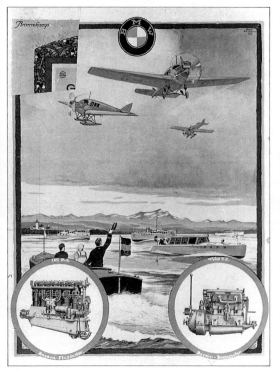

The Dornier military 'Whale', built on the wharves at Marina di Pisa, taking off for Sebastopol

D-142 with BMW engines in the harbour at New York

Due to its superior power-to-weight ratio, the air-cooled radial engine gained general acceptance at the beginning of the thirties. In 1931 a Ju 52 with three BMW Hornet engines won the race across the Alps for the Bider Cup

The First BMW Motorcycle

The BMW R 32, the first motorcycle of the
Bavarian Works, built in 1923, with a
transverse, horizontally-opposed engine,
shaft drive, double-guide tubular frame,
500 cc, 8 hp

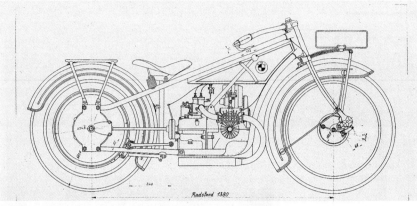

The 'Helios', redesigned by
Friz

On the Solitude Race. From
left to right: Franz Bieber,
Rudolf Schleicher, Rudolf
Reich

The First BMW Car

'The Bavarian Motor Works took over the Dixi and produced the improved Dixi as a BMW.' The yard at Eisenach

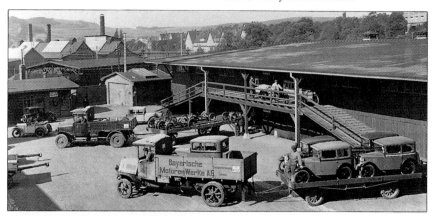

Spare wheel on the roof: even the German Post Office would not give up the little Dixi – they used it as a parcel van

The winners of the Alpine Rally. From left to right, at the steering wheel: Max Buchner, Albert Kandt and Willi Wagner at the reception in Eisenach

Reich President von Hindenburg inspects the BMW stand at the International Car and Motorcycle Show at Berlin in 1931

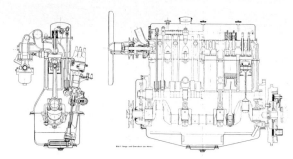

Above: Longitudinal and transverse cross-sections of the six-cylinder engine designed according to the American principle

Left: Fritz Fiedler designed the tubular frame for the BMW 303

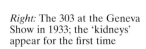

Above: Engine designer Rudolf Schleicher

Right: The 303 at the Geneva Show in 1933; the 'kidneys' appear for the first time

Above: The new '326' car, called the 'Flagship', the sensation of the Show, presented to the Berlin Motor Show on 15 February 1936 and inspected by Hitler. The kidney-shaped radiator grille, which the Ihle company in Karlsruhe had introduced for its Dixi variants, now gave BMW cars their distinctive appearance

Cars from the modular system: BMW 326 saloon

BMW 326 convertible

BMW 320 (its forerunner was the 326)

Racing after Records

'Acceleration' as a main design idea: the BMW 2-litre sports car 319/1, which Frazer-Nash overtook, together with the 315/1, at the Eifel Race on the Nürburgring in 1935

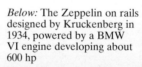

Left: Schorsch Meier winning the Tourist Trophy. Jock West, seen congratulating him, was second. Both on BMWs!

Right: Ernst Henne on his 500-cc machine chasing the world record: like a torpedo

Below: The Zeppelin on rails designed by Kruckenberg in 1934, powered by a BMW VI engine developing about 600 hp

Politics and History

Men amongst whom there were still communists, showing the clenched fist. The 'workforce' at BMW's Munich plant for the opening of the Winter Collection Works in 1936 at the works site

From left to right: Popp, Hitler, General von Blomberg, Commander-in-Chief of the Wehrmacht, and Air Commodore Erhard Milch, Secretary of State at the Reich Air Ministry

Aero-engines were the order of the day. They were built by large-scale production at the Allach and Milbertshofen Works

BMW Engines Deployed in the War

Above: 'It's as if an angel were pushing!' The Me 262 'lightning bomber', which was supposed to be everything: fighter, night fighter, interceptor, reconnaissance plane and bomber

Below: The X 4 on test

Above: 'Bring your equipment into the shelter, 'cos the bombs are coming down helter-skelter!' Do not let your important tools and equipment be damaged by air raids

Below: Allach: the camouflaged works in the forest

Right: On 1 May 1943 the Bavarian Motor Works received the designation 'Model armaments factory'

Below: Watch-tower, sentry posts, electric fencing, barbed wire . . . Camp sheds for SS prisoners, who were also 'allowed' to work for people, Reich and Führer in Allach

DER FÜHRER

ICH VERLEIHE AUF VORSCHLAG DES REICHSORGANISATIONSLEITERS DER NSDAP UND LEITERS DER DEUTSCHEN ARBEITSFRONT SOWIE DES REICHSMINI-STERS FÜR BEWAFFNUNG UND MUNITION

DER BETRIEBSGEMEINSCHAFT

Bayerische Motorenwerke Aktiengesellschaft
München

DIE AUSZEICHNUNG

KRIEGS-MUSTERBETRIEB

DIE AUSZEICHNUNG ERFOLGT IN WÜRDI-GUNG DES HERVORRAGENDEN EINSATZES UND DER VORBILDLICHEN LEISTUNG DER BETRIEBSGEMEINSCHAFT IM RAHMEN DER DEUTSCHEN KRIEGSERZEUGUNG. MIT DER ÜBERREICHUNG DIESER UR-KUNDE ERHÄLT DIE BETRIEBSGEMEIN-SCHAFT DAS RECHT, AN IHRER FLAGGE DAS KRIEGSVERDIENSTKREUZ ZU FÜHREN

BERLIN, DEN 1. MAI 1943

Below: Inmates from the Dachau concentration camp working on final quality control, measuring cylinders at Allach

The End of a German Dream

The BMW Works at Milbertshofen in
Munich were substantially destroyed by
American and British air raids in the
summer of 1944

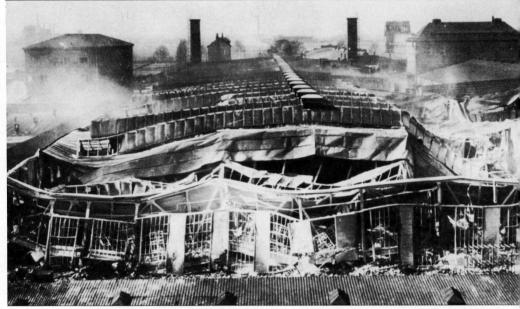

If things had gone just as Popp had depicted here, then what was all the fuss about? Dr Ley and comrades (as Popp went on to say) simply overlooked the crux of the Kissel-Popp idea, namely the problem of tax relief and distribution. They preferred to work out the price on a very simple calculation – the Volkswagen weighed 600 kg, one kilogramme of car cost 1.5 Reich marks, therefore the overall cost was 900 marks.

If Volkswagen, working to this formula, had been forced, like any other business in the private sector, to declare itself bankrupt, and if it did not owe its existence to Kissel's and Popp's financial wizardry (Kissel only had a small number of the first Volkswagens built at Daimler-Benz, resulting in, according to Popp, 'serious defects in the design being weeded out'), then this was a clear indication that Hitler's social utopia as a political issue in 1938 still only played a minor role. In contrast, he had plans in which putting a dream of the masses into practice only acted as a camouflage, revealing the extent to which the Führer was still thinking about peace.

If the Volkswagen idea suddenly complied with strategic military consider-ations, which nobody (apart from one man, the Führer himself, whose will was law) had had cause to think about before, then, like motorways which were to serve as future deployment bases for military units, money was no object.

So it was not surprising that the second expansion stage of the state works on the Aller, estimated at an annual production of one million Volkswagens, as well as the car city which was later to be christened 'Wolfsburg' (at the time it was still called 'KdF [strength through joy] Car City'), should no longer concern Kissel and Popp. Both had real worries on their minds, as Popp said:

> . . . since the pressure for rearmament was taking ever more monstrous forms, and no works was spared Hitler's decisions. Orders came thick and fast, forcing all factories to expand, while intrusions and regulations, particularly on the part of the Aviation Ministry, took on increasingly more intolerable forms from the point of view of running a private sector business and being aware of one's own individual responsibility for the future. Actual management for factories passed gradually into the hands of public officials who made their own arrangements, unconcerned about the futures of the factories, and, above all, making them run up huge debts.
>
> In such circumstances, Kissel and I could no longer pursue our plans for the merger of the two companies, as private car manufacture no longer formed the centre of our activity. But we were clear about one thing – that its time would come again, since setting up a car-manufacturing company in southern Germany would be even more pressing once we had stopped rearming.
>
> Then war began.

Is it really to be believed, as Popp subsequently protested, that Kissel and he had seen war as impossible, practically up to the last moment? One of those copies of *Germany Report* which the party faithful of the banned Social Democratic Party of Germany (Sopade) smuggled abroad, spoke of the mood at BMW in May 1934: 'Discussions are held in secret. But everyone knows war is coming.'

Did the worker know more than his managing director?

It was well-known that Popp attached as little importance to meeting people below as he did to those above. He was a timid man, always aware of his distance, almost unapproachable. There was no doubt that he loathed everything connected with 'the Party', as well as with 'the People', the very way in which that party appealed to such people. When he went home for lunch and came back, he managed to escape being noticed (the gateman had to make sure the coast was clear, and woe betide him if it weren't!). He had an almost manic fear of people. No one entered the inner sanctum, unless asked to do so. But if the reason for this was not simply a reprimand, then Popp was open-minded, quite unlike anybody else – affable, understanding, fair, never showing any mightier-than-thou attitude, and always keen to make the matter in hand, and not himself, the centre of discussion. He never showed the slightest trace of arrogance.

Having no respect for directives, he entirely avoided giving directives himself – except when someone deviated from the 'BMW concept'. There was no question of anyone remaining in the inner circle if he abandoned the original premises of this fundamental idea, by insisting that 'quality' should be sacrificed in the pursuit of 'quantity', or if personal issues were responsible for a lowering of standards. There was no way, absolutely no way, in which anyone could speak to Popp about this. Except for one man, Popp's private secretary, Schweppenhäuser. ('He was a refined man, for whom I had a lot of respect,' Hans Seufert said to me. He was the fitter on the Whale, a man who had travelled half way round the world for BMW and who on his return to Munich was told to report to the 'General' first.) Schweppenhäuser always listened to everything Seufert said, but would then always say: 'Now go in there and tell everything to Herr Popp, just like you've done to me!' According to Seufert, this was not only in relation to technical matters, or the details on engine development which had particularly interested people (navy, army and air force engineers from the contracting countries), but also the criticisms they had raised on faults, and any suspicion of these they may have shown. Popp always wanted to know how he, Seufert, had been treated either in Sebastopol, in Marina di Pisa, or in Stockholm; if he had felt all right, how he had been accommodated, and if he had managed on his allowances, and so on. Then there were always the questions about the climate, the way people felt and lived in the respective countries, and what they thought about Germany.

Nobody knew what he himself thought about these things, and what criteria he employed. It was similarly unclear how he got his information on the 'broad perspective' of things (he was always exceptionally well informed, as shown by his astute decision-making). Of course, much came up from the shop-floor, giving clues to the overall situation. This was the case with the metal-worker Lang. As an SS man and fanatical Nazi even before Hitler's accession, Lang acted unscrupulously against the Free Trades Unions, and straight after 30 January became leader of the first cell of the National

Socialist Factory Cells (NSBO) in the company. There was nothing that could be done about it, with Popp never having met the man until then. But he could hardly have remained in the dark on the question of the arrests of some of the works officials from the 'Free' Union, instigated by Lang. These were men held in regard by the workforce and also known to be reliable by the 'General'. Lang had them taken to the Union building where two of them were roughed up. We do not know if Popp protested. If we suppose he did, then he did little more than fire a shot in the air. In the meantime, Lang had left BMW and, perhaps due to his action, had been named ward leader for the Labour Front in the metal-working section, making him unassailable. Until his successor on the works council discovered that there were 2,000 marks missing from the company benevolent fund. Lang had misappropriated them. Now *that* was something that could be reported. An audit on Lang's financial conduct in his new office brought further irregularities to light – 10,000 marks missing. As a result Lang was forced out of office, with both Party and SS expelling him.

The mention made in the *Germany Report*, which had prosaically recorded Lang's case, stated: 'There was amazement amongst those in the know that Lang had not been prosecuted.' Was Popp one of those in the know? When I spoke to one of the works councillors, who had by then been demoted, but was reinstated after 1945, and for whom Popp had put in a word at the denazification court, he told me that he did not know one way or the other. He went on to say that this was a time when, with Popp having as little desire as anyone else to get his feet wet, no one would have wanted to play the public prosecutor of his own free will, certainly not an entrepreneur. As the 'master of the house', the latter could have done anything he wanted in his business, even Popp. There was no way anyone from outside could have seriously done anything to him, were it not for the fact that by getting to the bottom of things 'outside', he would have attracted unwanted attention. So he let sleeping dogs lie.

'Popp had got things going at BMW with the help of Castiglioni, who was of Jewish extraction. Popp had a resident doctor, who was also Jewish, right up to my time. This created certain difficulties,' I was told by Krafft von Dellmensingen, who joined BMW in 1938 as an articled clerk and later became head of the legal department. 'But he also worked with men who were freemasons, which the Nazis certainly knew about. He came from the liberal, Austrian bourgeoisie with its rather Pan-Germanic sentiments, from a family which had already had some success. He spoke frankly. I quote word for word: "We had to build these aero-engines, otherwise we could never have financed our motorcycles and cars!" On the other hand, there was scarcely any chance of delving into his innermost thoughts. Popp's style, when he summoned someone to him, had always been to give a lecture – and this exactly conveyed the Popp he wanted to show publicly. He had never spoken in emotional terms about himself, something which might have given people the opportunity to say: "That's just what he would do! Just like him!" Even his lectures, delivered with plenty of gestures, had always been carefully controlled. He was a great showman, placing an almost exaggerated emphasis on his outward appearance, the way he presented himself and how he shook hands. Everything was designed to show everyone he was "sovereign", even people whom he must have known would not have been impressed. Countless remarks were attributed to him, which were then circulated even amongst the chosen few. His proudest remark came when there were problems with the aero-engine, and Herr Milch, whom he could not stand (he only really liked Udet), had been critical of him. He blurted out to Milch (who was, after all, a Permanent Secretary, and who made it to Field Marshal): "I made the best motorcycle in the world, I made the best car in the world. There is no earthly reason why I shouldn't make the best aero-engine in the world, too!" Popp had made another remark to the effect that the cars he built always had to be a bit better than other people's. On another occasion he said: "We must build fewer cars than the others want, cars with cavernous boots." In a reference for one technician he wrote: "The man is incorrigible. He steadfastly believes that cars are inextricably linked to technology." Even the finance people laughed, now and again rather sourly, when he said: "A car factory needs to earn only enough to keep its board well fed."

'Popp was no National Socialist. The word seemed alien to him, cobbled together, badly designed. But as he was the inventor and father of BMW and, aside from his family life, as he had nothing other than BMW and the goal of leading BMW to even greater fame, he had made many political concessions. Goaded on by his own theatrical temperament, he had now and again acted more forcefully than was necessary. Consequently, he stood for the people who never had an opportunity to talk to him personally and, above all, trustingly. In any case, he never got the impression in the presence of such a person that the latter was just waiting to denounce him to the Gestapo. These were the kind of people who, as co-promoters of National Socialism, even as Hitler's devoted followers, now appeared inside industry. This meant that from 1938, the year when I got to know him, up to his departure during the war, the Nazis regarded him as a man who was quite unreliable, only kept "up there" through the support of Udet (who was also no Nazi), a man who had a Jewish doctor and, as I have already said, a man who associated with freemasons. He also never "followed the crowd" for the sake of it, never wore a uniform (not that he could have, as he did not belong to any Party grouping), and was viewed by a small circle (which itself rejected the National Socialist state) as more of an opponent of National Socialism than as a friend. Popp's problem, indeed his crucial problem, was how to present himself to the outside world in every aspect of his true thoughts, showing where his motivations came from.'

Krafft von Dellmensingen concluded with the remark that he had never heard Popp make any emphatic comments about Hitler in conversation, or talk about successes in the war, etc. – never. But that was no answer to the question of why, on the other hand, he had gone along with it all.

'Just imagine him marching through BMW with Hitler, all dressed up! Why? The same question was levelled at Krupp. Could the answer be found in the response: this has nothing to do with me, I just make needles? But just who was making needles? BMW was producing aero-engines!'

Schweppenhäuser's successor as secretary was Fritz Trötsch, who, because of his experience abroad and knowledge of foreign languages, became BMW's first export manager. I learnt from him that when 'something like that' (meaning the Lang affair) happened, it was not a lack of civic duty which had resolved Popp never to cross that bridge before he came to it. Not wanting to know was simply his way of doing things. The humdrum had never interested him. There had never been any friendly questioning ('Well, Trötschi, what are they saying out there in the country?'), no fishing for information ('Does X or does Y know about the business?'), no secrets in telephone conversations with his *equals* ('Yes, put him through, Frau Hoffmann!') such as Herr Kissel, Herr von Stauss, Herr Haspel. (Haspel was the manager at Daimler-Benz's Sindelfingen Works whose house in Heumaden Popp often visited as a guest, and where his daughters also met their future husbands, Paul Heim and Richard Seaman, the racing driver, who were both employed at Daimler-Benz.) All he ever spoke about was arranging appointments, production figures, design details, accounting matters, conveying wishes to people at home, sending his warmest regards to the man's wife, etc. There was no question of any conspiracy, no chance of making a pact with the powers that be.

Are we supposed to believe that this man did not know where things were heading?

Top and Bottom

Anyone who knew Germany's role at the League of Nations would not have been surprised that Hitler immediately showed the world what was what in foreign affairs. There it stood as a loser, an anachronism, as even its former enemies had to admit. Without recourse to war or the benefit of military might, the Reich could only make cautious diplomatic steps in its attempts to remove the intolerable burden of Versailles. These were not without success, but also not without setbacks, producing a revised way of thinking which, unfortunately, reality did not bear out. This could only be to Hitler's advantage. Admittedly, the British politician Ramsey MacDonald made a proposal for disarmament in March 1933, followed by Roosevelt in May, as he directed his proposal to forty-four nations to abolish all offensive weapons. These included bombs, tanks and heavy artillery. The Führer had immediately taken this up with a major speech on peace, in which he stated that, without further ado, Germany was prepared to destroy not only the few weapons it had retained (provided that adjacent countries did exactly the same), but also to enter into a solemn and binding non-aggression pact. Germany was not thinking of aggression, but of its own security, and it had no desire to Germanise foreign peoples. 'The French, the Poles, etc. are our neighbours, and we know that no historically conceivable process can change this reality. . . .'

The world was delighted, the President of the United States (according to a report from his secretary sent to the official German news agency) was 'very enthusiastic that Hitler should agree to these proposals'. It was all the more incomprehensible, therefore, that the second version of MacDonald's disarmament plan in Geneva on 9 October 1933 should not only tone down the March proposals but also see the Allies insisting on a lapse of at least eight years before reducing their levels of armaments *vis-à-vis* Germany's.

Five days later, Hitler declared that, as parity had been refused to Germany, the Reich would be leaving the disarmament conference and the League of Nations. He immediately dissolved the German parliament, announced a referendum (about whether it had been right for him to withdraw from Geneva) and entrusted General von Blomberg, the Reich Defence Minister, with an instruction (secret and yet intended for the ears of the world) to put up armed resistance should the League of Nations apply sanctions.

Was all this just bluff? There was no way any armed resistance could have occurred.

As regards aviation, a 'Reich commission' had been created as early as 2 February 1933, headed by Göring, which was changed into a 'Reich Aviation Ministry' on 5 May. Göring's department, chaired by the former director of Lufthansa, Erhard Milch, who had a less than Aryan pedigree but was now a Permanent Secretary and Göring's deputy, was made up of old officers from the Reichswehr and of engineers. The 'modesty of the Reichswehr period' still applied to it, as well as the limitation on the latter's technical imagination created by the Allied bans. It confined itself to what was tried and tested, and felt uneasy when contemplating anything new.

There was the Dornier Whale under conversion to a reconnaissance sea plane, the DO 11, which had been designed as a bomber for the Reichwehr; there was the three-engined Ju 52 which, at the third International Air Meeting in 1932, starting from Zurich and twice crossing the Alps, had proved to be unbeatable with its BMW engines as far as air safety, economy and pay load were concerned. (With its top speed of 240 kph and a range of 1,600 km, it could conceivably become a temporary bomber.) There was also the Heinkel He 49, a biplane capable of 325 kph powered by a single BMW 750-hp engine, available as a single-seater fighter plane, together with a few other similar Heinkel designs, which could be used militarily for 'short-range reconnaissance' or 'artillery observation'. These, for the most part, though, were still at the test stage, like the He 60 sea reconnaissance plane with its BMW 600-hp engine.

And that was about it. To speak of a 'Luftwaffe' was pure bravado, even if all these planes built under licence were in mass production at all available aircraft plants, where, as Heinkel reported, the mixed production methods using steel, wood and material coverings caused relatively few difficulties. The problems were to be found more in aero-engine manufacture, where there was a total lack of skilled labour needed to satisfy demands 'which had shot up overnight'.

'When I think of the Siemens engines supplied in 1933–4 for my He 46 reconnaissance plane,' wrote Heinkel, 'it still makes me shudder. They produced such vibration throughout the whole machine that the pilot often had difficulty reading the instruments, and Köhler [Heinkel's closest colleague] only spoke of "shaking falcons" when the He 46 was mentioned.'

BMW, as an aero-engine manufacturer of international reputation (Wolfgang von Gronau had made the BMW engine almost a legend by the end of his world flight), was given a key role.

Those air-cooled radial engines called 'Hornet' and 'Wasp', whose licence Popp had acquired in 1928 'on highly favourable terms for the whole of Europe' from the Pratt & Whitney Company, Hartford, Connecticut, USA, had been explicitly developed for commercial aviation. With a lower weight than water-cooled engines of comparable output, they had proved themselves (with roughly similar thermal properties and no greater fuel consumption)

179

to be not only the latters' equal, but in many ways their superior. They were much quicker to warm up, more reliable (as there were fewer things to go wrong), simpler to service (requiring no special maintenance) and, as regards repairs and overhauls, which took twice as long on a water-cooled engine, were cost-effective into the bargain.

(For those *au fait* with technical terminology, the Pratt & Whitney engines were fitted with steel cylinders capped by bolted, shrunk-on light alloy cylinder heads, into which the aluminium-bronze valve seats had also been shrunk-fitted. The crankcase was die-cast from duralumin and consisted of two halves. Inside were a crankshaft built up from two pieces, solid-eye connecting rods, fully enclosed valve gear, balanced filling of each cylinder using a rotary blower, and all auxiliaries fitted behind the engine away from the elements.)

The 525-hp Hornet engine went into large-scale production at Milbertshofen in 1929, while the smaller Wasp models, with 450 hp, and the Wasp-Junior, with 300 hp, were brought over made-up from the USA in small quantities. The fact that BMW also started producing its own designs for the Hornet (Friz had small five-cylinder versions for sports planes developed to take part in the round-Europe flights of 1930 and 1932; these were the BMW X and the BMW Xa, which had continuous power outputs of 51 hp and a maximum power of 54 hp) only went to vindicate Popp's decision to build under licence. This saved him the development costs for an in-house engine, which, with the very limited sales opportunities at the time, would have made funds very hard or, indeed, impossible to raise. This did not take account of the savings on time which would have been required. Germany was too poor, the world's technical lead too great, for him not to step in quickly.

His decision to stop manufacturing water-cooled engines would later be used as proof that BMW would have nothing to do with 'rearming'. But it was more by good luck than management that in 1936, when air force armament really began, the manufacture of modern fighter planes was based around water-cooled engines of between 1,200 hp and 1,500 hp. This meant that the air-cooled BMW engines with only half as much power had to be discarded for fighter planes. No, this card, which Popp (understandably) played as a trump, was not taken, for one basic consideration regarding the future of the works – if BMW had in fact produced large numbers of water-cooled engines in the contracts issued by the Reichwehr, as Daimler-Benz and Junkers did, then the plants at Milbertshofen and Eisenach would have immediately expanded beyond measure – and to what effect? Without doubt, to become nothing other than an armaments factory with a strict ban on all other activities. They would have had to abandon motorcycle and car production, as well as any thought of working in the private sector (meaning civil aviation), increasing exports and producing engines needed in cargo planes (designated by the military for commercial operations). To have stopped this happening right up to the outbreak of war was to Popp's credit and, without doubt, stems back to that licencing agreement for the radial engine in 1928. The fact that this would personally involve Popp in a life or death struggle in the clash with Milch was something he sensed as little as anyone at the start of the Third Reich, with its mind on war and Germany's destruction.

In 1933 the famous He 70 'Blitz' appeared in the skies. Fitted with the old, reliable BMW liquid-cooled VI engine, it was the first European transport plane (a few weeks after the American Lockheed 'Orion') to pass the 300-kph limit. On 21 February it achieved a phenomenal new speed record at the hands of Captain Werner Junck. Carrying a payload of 500 kg, it reached 348.162 kph for a distance of 100 kilometres. Further records followed which had previously been held in France, and twenty-eight of these He 70/BMW with their elliptically-shaped wings, new engine cooling and retractable undercarriage, entered service as transport planes on German Lufthansa's high-speed routes. It was only right and proper to Göring and Milch, who were still disguised as civil officials in the Reich Aviation Ministry, that BMW, as almost the only German manufacturer of aero-engines, was building these exclusively for transport planes. Thus any measure potentially able to create an air force could at any time sustain an objection from the signatory states to the Versailles Treaty, which still included the Reich. Typically enough, that first German air fleet, in the absence of any military value it may have had, was called a 'Risk Fleet'. BMW, with its brightly-polished plaque, while taking the odd risk here and there, had nothing to do with rearmament.

In the meantime the Pratt & Whitney Works had further developed their nine-cylinder radial engine. Following discussions with the German Lufthansa, Popp immediately acquired this new version as well, which, as the '132 type', was to make aviation history. In variants running from A to N the '132' would be built up to 1942 with ever new 'development features'. Aircraft fitted with the BMW 132-L engines had speed-adjustable propellers providing previously unknown climbing capacity. In contrast to 'direct' engines (whose propeller sat directly on the crankshaft and so turned at the same speed as the engine), the BMW 132 H type had epicyclic gearing fitted between the propeller and the crankshaft, which provided for a reduction in crankshaft output speed. Increased engine speed did not automatically mean increased propeller speed, providing for much greater output. An airplane fitted with the BMW 132 Dc and its reduction gear governing propeller speed could reach 625 hp in continuous output at 2,100 rpm at an altitude of 3,800 metres.

How peaceful it all sounded, when the establishment by Lufthansa of a regular service over the South Atlantic was described in BMW papers:

The post is first taken from Berlin or Stuttgart to Seville in a Heinkel He 70 high-speed aircraft fitted with a BMW VI engine. There a Junkers, fitted with three BMW 'Hornet' engines, takes over the post and carries it to Las Palmas, from where it is transported on the third day to Bathurst. Here a Dornier 'Whale' flying boat with two BMW engines is already standing by to carry the load across the ocean to Natal on the Brazilian coast. The South Atlantic has seen the first floating airbase in the world for which the 'Westfalen' had been converted. There the Dornier 'Whale' made a stop-over for refuelling, so as to cover the second part of the ocean leg. At Natal the planes from the Condor Syndicate, also fitted with 'Hornet' engines, took over the post.

A grandiose picture. Who could deny it? At the 'crossroads of Europe's airways', airlines stretched out from Germany in all directions – to London, to Paris, to Spain, to the Balkans, to Poland, all providing regular air transport for passengers, luggage, freight and post, just as they did for Finland, the Scandinavian countries and the Soviet Union.

> There is hardly a stretch on which BMW engines, either water- or air-cooled, are not operating. The Junkers Ju 52, which today is the most widely used plane in the German Lufthansa, is only fitted with three air-cooled BMW 'Hornet' engines. And the latest advance, the introduction of high-speed routes, carrying passengers from Berlin to Hamburg in 50 minutes, from Berlin to Frankfurt am Main in 85 minutes, from Hamburg to Cologne in 75 minutes, and from Cologne to Frankfurt in 35 minutes, is based not least on BMW VI engines fitted to the Heinkel He 70 high-speed planes, able to operate at 370 kph. It was these planes which established no fewer than eight new international speed records last year.

If this was all undeniable, then it was also advertising, simple product advertising, quite separate from political propaganda. Anyone wanting to make a living had to portray himself as good, even in times like these. And, in times like these, what exactly did company reports reveal with their offerings of spartan figure work, dividends, depreciations, numbers employed, salaries, profits, losses?

Anyone reading the first company report issued on 29 May 1933 would not have found much that was new. Next to the usual details dealing with the previous financial year was a text which reported that the positive repercussions of a general improvement now affecting the German Reich had also been registered in BMW AG's balance sheet. How courageous it was for people in 1933 to speak about 1932 like this:

> With the consolidation of political conditions through the national govern-
> ment and the intention announced by its leader to strengthen the economy,
> especially in its automotive industries, the requirements for a return of
> confidence have been created. The first few months of the new financial
> year have already shown a marked increase in activity. We particularly
> welcome the establishment of a Reich ministry for aviation. It will give
> to German aviation what other countries have long enjoyed, and which
> our development work has been directed towards achieving for the past
> ten years. . . .

There you are then – the usual bowing and scraping, the imperative proclamation. Anyone who has read this far should read a bit further. Here he will see that, in relation to the year before (1932), the workforce had increased by 1,500 to 4,300 office staff and workers, and the 5 per cent dividend which the directors had been able to pay to their shareholders in spite of a fall in turnover to 19.1 million Reich marks did not come from manufacturing profits, but 'first and foremost from licencing fees for products built abroad'.

Abroad? People were taken aback. What did that mean? It meant nothing other than that they were living off people abroad.

Suddenly everything was ambiguous. The homage which had just been proclaimed was nothing but wrapping paper, and the declared gratitude a cunning tribute to refer to the real matter at hand. And what was this? The company management said it quite openly, with the kind of reverence and generosity that demonstrated their strong confidence 'for the future profitability of our company and providing support in the efforts of the national authorities to regenerate the German private sector'.

So that was it – the private sector! Not mentioned in so many words, but impossible to ignore. Hands off! The balance sheet and company report for 1933 (submitted in 1934) betrayed in great detail how skilfully the board could hide the real issue between the lines, showing that they would render unto the state what was the state's: but, in spite of that, wanted to remain independent, within the private sector, free of spoonfeeding by the state!

We have (therefore) consistently supported the measures taken by the Reich government to combat unemployment through our own initiatives. Entirely confident of ultimate success and the lasting improvement in the German economy, we have fully reinvested the allowances from depreciation and, over and above that, directed the considerable sums created through expanding orders to the recovery of our Works. Access to funds for building is essentially intended for a community centre for our workforce, which is to serve them in the future as their own home so that they may realise the theory of 'Strength through Joy'. Increased car production has made the appropriate completion of our stock of machine tools necessary . . .

900,000 Reich marks, equating to a 6 per cent dividend, have been paid out to shareholders. 100,000 Reich marks have been paid out on 'welfare projects' – the assistance funds for our workforce.

This was as far as BMW portrayed its role in the early years of dictatorship.

There was another reality to be found on different paper. The fact that it reported the truth can be in as little doubt as the fact that the directors at BMW were striving to write between the lines, even on glossy paper.

Here there was nothing between the lines. In the same financial year, 1934, when the company report referred to a further increase in turnover of 192 per cent on last year's, and commented on the important event of the aero-engine business being taken out of the main company and set up with a full profit and loss account as the 'BMW Aero-engine Company Ltd,

Munich (with a share capital of 7.5 million Reich marks, put up entirely by BMW), the *Germany Report* from its head office, exiled in Prague, included an article about BMW in May-June 1934:

The Bavarian Motor Works (BMW) have now doubled their workforce. The business is still expanding. The number of aero-engines ready for delivery has gone up by 50 per cent, and is to be increased by up to 150 per cent. In addition, armoured motorcycles with side-cars are now being built. Machine guns have been planned for the side-cars. The workforce in various departments now has to give a written undertaking not to speak about what it does in the company. Three shifts are now working in almost all departments, while elsewhere there seems to be no limit to the amount of time worked. Sixty-five hours per week is by no means exceptional, and there is again strong demand for special skills.'

Germany, it said in another part of the report, now has at its disposal (this was April-May 1934) an enormous number of aircraft. A considerable number were not produced with state funds. Since the spring of 1933, communities, associations, firms and private individuals had been induced to sponsor aircraft. This has largely taken place.

The machines have been standardised, and are of the same type. Only a few are ready to be flown. The majority have been completely knocked down and stored in sheds. But within a short space of time, simple assembly will be all that is needed for Germany to increase its level of operational aircraft many times over. At BMW three large production halls have been built for a workforce of 2,000. The reason given for these buildings was a Russian order for 5,000 aero-engines.

(Which cannot have been a pretence – the German Reich under Hitler continued to comply with the agreement made by Seeckt for German military assistance to Russia right up to 1935.)

The *Germany Report* went on to say: 'There are secret discussions going on. Everyone knows that a war is coming.' And: 'The workers no longer want to hear anything much about the Nazis, although the whole city knows that BMW is the best company in the NSBO [an organisation which had already been dissolved in state-owned companies because, in the view of the Party, it was already National Socialist].' The workers also no longer needed negotiators, decisions being made by the head of personnel to whom they had to turn in all relevant matters (that was the same process as in government offices, where works committees had been dissolved for quite some time). In June the anonymous reporter, following meetings by the workforce, announced that they could no longer be held at Krauss or Maffei owing to poor attendance. This led to the introduction of the so-called call to duty, in which every member of the workforce had to be present. This was similar to the 'duty training courses'.

At the start of June 1934, the workforce (3,800 at the Milbertshofen plant) had to sign a declaration stating that, in compliance with his duty of silence, no worker 'could stay in any other part of the company from the one where he worked, with any such violation resulting in immediate dismissal. This will be so strictly enforced that even workers standing around at the entrance to another hall and glancing inside will be given a warning.' In spite of this, news leaked out in August 1934 that the so-called machine-gun spigots on the crankshafts of the aero-engines built by BMW (their function was to synchronise the machine-gun's firing through a rotating propeller so that bullets could be shot within the propeller's circumference) had recently all been removed. Was this a deliberate leak to feign peacetime production? The answer to this cannot be proved, only guessed at.

The workers were now monitored not only by the official security force dealing with accidents, fires, etc., but by an unofficial one, assigned to counter-espionage, whose members remained obscure, apart from its leader, an engineer called Bauer. He was well known for dispensing on-the-spot dismissals if two or three workers were caught having private conversations at their workplace, or if anyone made the slightest error or otherwise appeared less than totally reliable (grounds for this could even be refusing to buy the winter assistance badge). Bauer also ensured that the company register for dismissals carried the entry: 'Not suitable for BMW.' Individual departments were systematically infiltrated by people whose job it was to find out what the workers were thinking and pass on their observations. 'More often than not, such an informer had to turn to other people, so it quickly got around who the spy was, which brought all political discussions to a hasty conclusion.' As salaries (as was emphasised time and again) were good in comparison to other branches of engineering, the mood of the workers at BMW was less bitter, and people fell into line. When engineer Bauer rummaged through all the lockers and had all the toilets thoroughly searched (as happened in March 1937 when he was looking for leaflets said to have contained foreign radio broadcasts about Spain), the delegates of the admistration office declared that they had never seen such a leaflet anywhere in the works. Terror and spying led to nothing other than the National Socialist German Workers' Party appearing increasingly as the enemy of the workers.

It was not the state but the Party itself which meddled in everything, which involuntarily resulted in its becoming the scapegoat for anger and ill-humour. An example of this at BMW in Munich (December 1935) was when 'the disruption in production brought about by a drop in orders was used to explain a cut in wages'.

The source of this news reported:

When the workers had been laid off and wanted to report to the employment exchange, they were told that they had not left BMW's employment but had simply been laid off for a short period. They would receive benefit. There were three reasons for this procedure: 1 The 1,700 workers not entered on the unemployment register did not appear in the statistics; 2 BMW made sure that it kept its qualified workers; and 3 reinstatement could be used to lower salaries. Upon re-employment, the earlier wages for these workers were cut by between 8 and 14 per cent.

Or in Eisenach, where piece rates had remained the same since 1933, but with such poor-quality raw materials being delivered that not even the best skilled worker could manage to attain output at 1933 levels, it was reported:

So as to be able to offload the blame for poor materials supplies, there were penalty deductions everywhere. The best skilled worker could not manage properly without handing over something in the way of a penalty. The penalty deductions were considerable, and amounted on average every week to 4 Reich marks. There were workers who got away with only 3 marks in deductions, but there were others who had 6 marks deducted each week. The average earnings based on piece work, before penalty deductions, were 43 marks a week. On top of these penalties was a deduction for tools. With poor quality raw materials, tools wore out that much quicker. This was also borne by the workers, who had to pay between 1 and 1.5 Reich marks a week for tool replacement.

And what did a worker at BMW in Munich earn, where piece rates were also in operation? The *Germany Report* stated:

There are three piece rates, A, B and C. Women are paid the C-rate. The starting rate for unskilled workers is 56 pfennigs, qualified workers receive up to 1.22 marks per hour, and the best of the skilled workers such as operators of circular and automated grinders commanded 1.3 marks. Semi-skilled workers earned 1.08 to 1.10 marks. In contrast to former times, tool makers, repair mechanics and cutters only earned between 80 and 90 pfennigs. Previously they were the best paid workers in the company.

So it was no wonder that (as observed in Munich in December 1937) the Party members in the Works had become very cautious. 'If you did not know otherwise, you would not think from their present behaviour that many of them were members of the Nazi Party before the seizure of power.' Even the fear of denunciation was not as strong as before. 'It was often the case that an SA man would barge his way into a discussion, which carried on as if nothing had happened. When the SA man then went away, people were no longer as worried as before. "He won't say anything, even if he knew what we were speaking about." That would settle the matter.'

What could the Party do about this? It could refer to the fact that work had been created, a situation dealt with in the *Germany Report*:

It is difficult to say anything against this argument, as the workers do not ask about the purpose of their present work. They only see the fact that there is more work and there are fewer unemployed about than before. Naturally, there are countless numbers who will not let themselves be influenced, as they know where it is all leading to. But they are in the minority, and so inhibited in this repressive state that they cannot do much against the system, other than indirect resistance.

As it was, the special efforts made by the leading figures in the Nazi Party towards the workers showed that the situation was starting to get critical, and that the Nazi bosses no longer felt so safe with the workers. They knew very well that the workforce was not for the system, and that this was the major danger area for the Third Reich. Wages could not be raised, although prices went up every day. So 'Socialism' had to be done in another way. The employers were spoken to nicely, since it was they who were left to finance the 'beauty of work' through holiday allowances, maternity allowances, and setting up 'Strength through Joy' works funds. In other words, this was an attempt to establish all kinds of welfare provisions which would cost employers a fraction of what they would have to pay if wages were increased in line with the general level of prices. Coupled with this were the complaints certain employers received, and the bureaucracy in companies. This was meant to give workers the impression that there was constant concern about their welfare, that the conscientious worker would be promoted and there were really no grounds to complain about bad times. Moreover, there was an attempt to intimidate employers, who did what they liked in their businesses, as there was no one about who could seriously do anything to them. To a certain degree, the workers let themselves be passified by such antics. However, the employers could not care less. It was a cunning game which the Nazis played designed to play off one stratum of the people against the other.

And what was the worker's relationship to Hitler? I looked at the photograph showing Hitler, accompanied by Popp, standing in the yard at BMW and surrounded by workers. Are they 'workers' or just selected officials? Dr Ley, who was also there and whom the Führer had described as his 'greatest idealist', had his big day by general interpretation. He did not see a flock of 'yes' men in contact with HIM, but rather unsullied German workers who looked to Hitler as to a friend whom they could implicitly trust, far above the mistakes, failings and bullying of the rank and file. (You can't make an omelette without breaking eggs. Yes, the Führer could not be everywhere at the same time, could not do everything himself!) On the other hand, had he not given them new courage to face life, as well as wages and bread? Had he not freed them from the shadowy existence of ants, had he not created prestige in the world, had he not created pride? Did they not take trips on the 'strength through joy' ships on Norwegian fjords, sun themselves in Malta, relax from the daily grind in company hostels between the Alps and the North Sea? No scoundrel could shout that one down, no bigot can convince you, Führer, that this worker did not know what he owed you. Click! The camera had it all on record.

In the *Germany Report*, the anonymous source painted another picture, although not one outspokenly anti-Hitler. There was a communal reception at BMW before the election, as everywhere else on Friday (April 1936), to hear Hitler speak, at which the Gauleiter Wagner also appeared. [Gauleiter: Senior Nazi official in charge of a 'Gau', an administrative region.] Wagner had noticeably bored the workers with his speech. They all saw in him the typical bully-boy. Everything in his behaviour expressed brutality. By contrast, the majority always listened to Hitler with interest. When Wagner spoke, almost everyone felt he could have stayed at home, as he only made matters worse. At 4 o'clock all the workforce had to go into the large machine shop. Everything was so orderly, so like a barracks; something the workers were not slow to tell each other. 'Some day soon, things will change,' was often heard, 'but we can't do anything about it now.' No applause greeted Wagner's speech. Just a stony silence. Even after Hitler's speech, people simply listened to the cheering in the loudspeakers, without joining in themselves. Only when the works branch of the SA struck up the Horst-Wessel-Lied did some people join in, but only those in the front rows. In the back of the hall, the workers stood behind their machines and did not seem to bother about what was happening at the front.

Seven months later, in December 1936, the observer commented on a recent speech by Hitler:

> In the last third of the broadcast, there was suddenly great applause from the loudspeaker, which went on for longer than usual. The workers at once dashed to the gates and demanded to be let out, now that the speech was over. The gatemen were taken by surprise, by the crowds running en masse towards the exits. Even windows were opened, people forcing themselves out of them as if they were fleeing.

Fleeing from what? One could well ask. According to an illegal report smuggled out about the mood 'on the shopfloor', about the same time Göring had made a secret speech (on 17 December 1936), to industrialists and leading civil servants, which contained the answer. As the trustee of the 'Four-Year Plan' (the four years which Hitler had demanded from the people 'for reconstruction' had just expired), he demanded the immediate application of all resources throughout the economy. No restriction on rearmament was planned. There was only victory or destruction. 'We are in a time just before the final conflicts. We are already mobilised and at war without a shot being fired.'

That was the reality, even if it was only fully recognisable (for the people at the top and bottom) behind the scenes; even if the entry of German battalions into the demilitarised zone of the Rhinelands that same year in March still had not opened the eyes of people in Great Britain and France; and even if both these countries shared the view of the mass of the German people, despite Hitler officially announcing 'the annulment of the German signature to the Versailles Treaty' on 30 January 1937. They all believed that, given all his bluffing, Hitler would never resort to war. Anyone holding a key position in Germany had not the slightest doubt about that.

Did Popp hold a key position? What was certain was that Milch, at the Reich Aviation Ministry (the RAM), was making a determined challenge to him. It was equally certain that he was striving for it, even if from quite another area. His love, his drive, his passion were in cars.

And so he made a proposal which was as reasonable as it was bold. It was both cunning and touchingly naive. He made it to the head of the technical department at the RAM, who had just ordered an increase of between 60 and 80 per cent in the capacity of aero-engine factories. This took place at the beginning of September 1938 when European capitals were buzzing with Hitler's threats towards Czechoslovakia, making war seem imminent. His opinion (as he wrote in an express letter on 5 September 1938 to General Ernst Udet, then at 4 Pommersche Street, Berlin) was that aero-engine factories could not be increased to this extent in the foreseeable future, as both machines and, more importantly, skilled workers were lacking. The solution to the problem of such a large increase in aero-engine production was only to be found 'if factories producing goods not necessarily vital to war, underwent a wholesale conversation to aero-engine production'.

Right in the next sentence, Udet discovered what Popp was thinking about – 'the car industry in general' which, because of quotas in iron and steel, was now only working to between 60 and 70 per cent capacity. If just one of the car factories were turned over to aero-engine production, the iron and steel quotas released could be allocated to the other car manufacturers who would then immediately be in a position to make up for the missing car production because they themselves were only working to two-thirds capacity.

In an apparent gesture of national generosity, was it Popp's aim to put his own car production at the disposal of the state? Far from it.

If I suggest the Opel company as the first choice for this, this is initially because I believe that Opel is capable of building, at a rough estimate, between 500 and 1,000 aero-engines per month, and can do this in a shorter space of time than any other factory. The second reason comes from my war experience. I would like to remind you that when the BMW IIIa engine proved its excellent qualities in the war, the Aviation Inspectorate immediately commissioned me to build this engine in large numbers. However, I recognised that in circumstances similar to today, this was impossible, and suggested that Opel built them under licence. This is what happened, with the outcome that within four months Opel had set up mass production of the BMW IIIa in the most appropriate and successful way. If the war had continued another year, Opel would have then become the largest German aero-engine factory.

And its plant should now make it largely possible to take on aero-engine production in a very short space of time, as components for aero-engines had not essentially changed much. (How tempting and logical! And, of course, under licence from BMW. Some things do not change, even if Popp had not expressly mentioned it.)

What's more, if Opel were to give up car production in Rüsselsheim, then the number of skilled workers required would be available. Increased aero-engine production would require an additional 10,000 to 20,000 skilled workers, who could be found nowhere else. As regards the US majority shareholding in Opel, some form of nationalisation would have to be found. Even the Americans would find it impossible to keep 40 per cent of German car production in American hands in the long term.

It was clear that Popp had not forgotten the ultimate aim behind this idea,

189

when he stated that 'for the other German car manufacturers to reach that strength so important from the point of view of the economy, as they were faced with very difficult times due to the KdF-car (Volkswagen), could in fact be called killing two birds with one stone.'

A few days later Popp sent a carbon copy of the letter to Milch, then Permanent Secretary and his adversary in the RAM, suggesting to him that the transaction would best be carried out by the Hermann-Göring Works (in Salzgitter). Due to the amount of capital required, the private sector was highly unlikely to be able to handle it. In this case the Steyr car factory, which happened to be part of the Göring works (Austria had in the meantime been incorporated into the Greater German Reich), could immediately be turned over to producing double-radial engines. There was little future in car building there, and overcapacity in the German car industry now made it desirable to undertake this transfer.

So is this the way Popp would have got one unloved competitor off his back, and at the same time been freed of the burden of rearmament? Naturally, none of this happened. There was no time for either Udet or Milch to be able to go into his proposals or to refute them before Czechoslovakia's fate was decided – without war. At the Munich agreement Britain and France granted the Führer and Chancellor of the Greater German Reich, Adolf Hitler (if only to keep the peace!) annexation of the Sudetenland and entry into Prague. This was the last time they would be deceived. In preventing Hitler from quickly and comprehensibly losing a war for which Germany was not in the least bit prepared, they were only letting themselves in for one a year later, when Hitler launched his attack, setting Europe alight, and bringing all the cunning of a Popp to build cars (instead of aero-engines) to nought.

Kit Games

Let us look at two pictures. The first is of a young lady in 1930, standing in front of her Dixi with its soft top, her right foot elegantly resting on the running board of her dream 'People's car'. (Text: 'The BMW Works subscribe to the view that even a lady fully possesses all the qualities required to drive a car'.) The other picture is of that 'dream' car, of which the chief stylist, Paul Bracq, built just two examples in 1972, at a time when people were dreaming of never-ending progress, and just before the oil crisis – the BMW Turbo 'from inside out'. (Text: 'With its rubber crumple zones, the bodywork has the harmonious shape of a second skin being stretched over the occupants, an absence of sharp edges which are threatening and therefore dangerous to pedestrians and cyclists. One might almost say that the engine has been digested by the bodywork, and that our highest goal has been achieved – to put ever more human and less aggressive bodywork on to four wheels.')

When we compare the pictures and their texts, what do we find that is so striking about them? Probably that the automobile, which had previously been a tasteful object for a lady, one she could innocently indulge in, would exhibit characteristics forty years later which were more reminiscent of a bullet than a vehicle, in which humans could move around without endangering themselves or others. It must have seemed as if the designer were mocking when he claimed that his goal was to put ever more human, and less aggressive bodywork on to four wheels – with a top speed of 300 kph!

Nobody who builds cars for their utility value (and who builds cars if not for that?) can do without concepts which reach out *beyond* redeemable reality. This is how Bracq's Turbo is to be understood. Quickly concluded upon at the end of the sixties, and equally quickly superseded by the reality of the seventies, it remains the reference point for technological utopias, without which 'progress' is unthinkable.

How far the mass-produced car lies *below* the upper limit of technological dreams, or technological feasibility, is determined by reason, traffic conditions, justifiable costs, the game of supply and demand, and, at a calculated guess, the question as to who one is and what one wants.

Let us examine the period between the two pictures; between the Dixi, which could not become the utility car, as this is what the Volkswagen would become under dictatorship (but only just in time, before the outbreak

191

of war!), and Bracq's Turbo, we can see a modular range of six-cylinder cars which were the hallmark of the entire epoch. Their reflection could still be glimpsed in the sixties with BMW's 'New Class'. It was the 'dream' cars of the thirties which led the way, such as the 328 with its leather straps across the bonnet, and the Mille-Miglia streamlined car of 1940. To many they seemed like the fulfilment of Marinelli's futuristic manifesto of 1908, in which he saw the magnificence of the world enriched by a new beauty, the beauty of speed: 'A roaring car which seems to run like a rocket is more beautiful than the Goddess Nike of Samothrace!'

But it was not with the Goddess Nike of Samothrace, but rather with his own Frazer-Nash, that a man from England drew his comparisons. In August 1934 he was looking at the speedy new design of the 1.5-litre BMW sports car which ran alongside, then behind, and then invariably just in *front* of his team through the Alpine passes. Starting out from Nice, amongst 127 cars (eight-cylinder Fords, Delaheys, Talbots, Hotchkisses, Singers, Triumphs and the German makes of Adler, Wanderer, Opel and DKW), it proved to be the clear winner in its class. The comparison was to have its consequences.

At one time the Dixi people had been to Austin in Birmingham looking to acquire the licence for the Austin Seven as there was no other comparable small car in Europe for them. Now the Englishman, HJ Aldington by name, managing director of the Frazer-Nash Company and even a noted racing and rally driver, crossed the Channel to go and ask Popp about acquiring the licence to build the 1.5-litre BMW car in England.

'I was extremely surprised,' he wrote frankly and fairly (as only the English know how when they are enthusiastic about something) in an extensive article in which self-interest was far from his thoughts. This appeared in the leading British car magazine, *The Motor*, on 18 December 1934 and said:

> These cars have acquired an exceptional reputation in Germany and throughout Britain, because, to all intents and purposes, they are perfect, totally reliable, and blessed with unbeatable road-holding. The car has steering and suspension which many drivers can only dream about. It is very fast (especially in the two-seater sports version), extraordinarily comfortable and gives the feeling of absolute safety on any road surface and at any speed.

The contract was far-reaching. BMW delivered practically the whole car in its individual components – bodywork, chassis, engine (there was a lower rate of customs duty for these, while complete cars were heavily taxed), and Frazer-Nash assembled them true to original design, right up to the right-hand drive, with the inscription Frazer-Nash BMW around the propeller. As an example of Anglo-German co-operation lasting right up to the war, it proved a tremendous success throughout the British Isles.

It proved an equally great success with Aldington, a cool-headed business-man, with the end result that it was unnecessary to offset the new German design by an equivalent, in-house one. That would not have been impossible in itself, although it would have taken a lot of time. But Aldington could not do things which were not in his nature, such as simply imitating something just because it is successful. Then came something which could not be copied. It was the principle, the manufacturing principle behind the car.

What did this consist of? Certainly 'acceleration' and not 'speed' was the main design idea, which BMW pursued in model after model. When the tester of the *Deutsche Automobilzeitung* wrote admiringly in 1935: 'The 1.5-litre BMW accelerates in third gear from 10 to 60 kph in less than 10 seconds!' then this was due not only to the increased engine capacity from 1.2 to 1.5 litres and to the 34 hp which the engine now produced, but also to its 'lightweight' construction.

The saloon, in fact, weighed only 850 kilogrammes (the sports model, only 700!), in contrast to the 1,100 kilogrammes usual for this class of car.

How had BMW managed this? The extraordinarily advantageous power-to-weight ratio equalling 24 kg/hp (a value which otherwise was only to be found in the most powerful cars) had been achieved either through thrift or because it had been designed that way, and the so-called kerb weight had been kept to that of the 1.2-litre car. The light and rigid tubular frame, which lowered the centre of gravity to such an extent that tight corners could be taken without compromising safety had not changed in the least. This was also the case with the independent front axle, and the rigid rear axle mounted on two longitudinal springs, as well as the excellent steering geometry characteristic of wheels individually steered by the rack-and-pinion system.

What today seems impossible, namely to have a new car model planned, tested and built within twelve months, was then the norm. If the number of types and years are added together, then BMW needed considerably less time. This was quite odd if you considered that planning, designing and testing took place in Munich, while prototype manufacture and series production were in Eisenach. There was no 'research and development office' (something every car plant now has) with its army of technicians, let alone any computers to do the calculations, any automation to turn the lathes, or market researchers to produce forecasts. Of course, there was a check on materials, there were laboratories, quality control checks and analyses to prevent poor quality work and eliminate failures. They also ensured absolute reliability as required in the manufacture of aero-engines, for which BMW was famous ('No aeroplane stays in the air if the engine cuts out!'), reliability which was passed on to cars and motorcycles. The fact that this would never have been possible without the training of staff skilled in airplane manufacture sheds some light on the secret, as far as manufacture and mass production are concerned (even allowing for the fact that they did not have electric conveyor belts as other German car factories did).

In the forefront (in planning, designing and testing) there were three men who supplied the necessary information. There was Popp, the businessman, planner and motivator; then Fiedler, a designer who conceived of the car as a whole, who always kept his designs at the cutting edge of lightweight construction and always sought the best solutions, and who found his *raison d'être* at BMW; then there was Schleicher, the engine specialist, *the* man in 'tests', who did not think much of inspired 'forward leaps', preferring to slow down and pause, while pushing forward everything that was logical with the kind of uncanny accuracy which the clearance required by pistons in cylinders has. He was a man fighting for fewer designs and more time, acting rather like a personification of the mechanical conscience of the company.

All three men mutually inspired each other with ideas, even if these led them a long way round. Through constant analysis of the market and of technology combined with the ability to react quickly, these ideas brought about that concept which was later to be heralded as a revolutionary yet simple idea – the modular system. Once before, a firm not unknown to Popp had put its trust in it and found it to be successful – the Dixi. That was a long time ago, before the First World War. Two ranges of engine, respectively initialled S and T, had then provided the Eisenach works with a multiplicity of types, enabling the customer to choose the one for his purposes, without having to be disloyal (once would be enough!) to his beloved make.

There is no doubt that from the outset Popp had had this system in mind when he created his six-cylinder; the very system which did away with off-the-shelf production, even with the 'threat' of a 'people's car' on the horizon. More explicitly, so that the company would not have to expand, the manufacture of 'off-the-peg' items was abandoned, obliging customers to stay with the same tailor in future. We shall see how, with help from Fiedler and Schleicher, he succeeded in achieving what other people could only dream about – and this despite a spectacular setback at the start.

The year 1934 had, from a financial point of view, gone much better than the previous year would have led one to suspect. The company report announced an increase of 192 per cent. If the car business could only claim a modest part of this increase, BMW, with a slight improvement in market share from 4.5 to 5 per cent, was nonetheless number 5 among German car makers – after Opel (with 33.5 per cent, the outright leader), the Auto Union (17.9 per cent), Daimler-Benz (here market share was still considerably lower due to the Slump) and Adler, where their market share had fallen from 10.3 to 8.4 per cent. Overall in 1933, BMW had produced 5,832 vehicles, and with 5,322 new registrations from this production on German roads, Popp had every reason to be satisfied. But, as Schiller puts it, 'eternal union cannot be woven with the forces of destiny'. Suddenly there was no demand for the 303.

Where had they gone wrong?

The sales staff claimed that with its six-cylinder engine, there were no customers for the car. Those it could find mourned the demise of the four-cylinder, which was no longer good enough for the Dixi, even if it was called the AM 4. So what *was* good enough for them, asked Popp? If the body is the problem, then all right, we can take the one from the 303. And if the engine is not good enough for them because they are determined to stick to their four-cylinder, we'll bore it out and give it back to them. What do you think that will produce, Schleicher? He had said 22 hp. Well, that means a new car, Popp had said. Two for the price of one. A single body, engine A with six cylinders, engine B with bored-out four cylinders, giving us not only a 303 in addition to the 309 (as we will call it), but also, to a certain extent, a kit from which we can draw off further models.

In fact, the 'new' car (launched at the same time as the AM 4 was discontinued) started well, being more economical than its stable-mate, although it had only half as much acceleration as the latter, and was less than quiet on the road. To take the sting out of any criticism, it immediately acquired the nickname 'the car with the suspended engine'.

What was meant by that can be gathered from the BMW papers:

> The time which pushed the four-cylinder engine to one side is over. Today the whole engine and gearbox assembly on highly advanced four-cylinder engines is mounted on a rubber suspension so that the mechanics need apply no force to their properties, which are, on the contrary, allowed to vibrate around their centre of gravity as nature intended. This feature not only prevents this vibration reaching the chassis, but converts it into useful mechanical work through the springing of the active rubber suspension along the centre-line. [BMW was using the original Chrysler two-point suspension!]
>
> It is strange when you get a good grip on this suspension-mounted BMW cylinder block. The whole mechanics seem to sit so loosely in the chassis. You can almost wobble the assembly inside the chassis with your hands. With the engine idling under an open bonnet, it starts to jig about at certain (very low) speeds. The amazing thing is that the chassis remains unaffected and stable, with the four-cylinder engine pulling away smoothly and jolt-free even at the lowest engine speeds. So you can enjoy the simplicity and practicality of a four-cylinder engine in the new 0.9-litre BMW, which behaves almost like a high-quality six-cylinder.

We do not know if Popp agreed with this. But he had to accept that there could be no talk of sales success with 'his' 303 (Eisenach produced only 3,200 examples in all), while this four-cylinder, available as a touring car with soft top, as a saloon and as a convertible, found a niche in the market.

In the meantime Fiedler had set about being his own man at BMW – which Horch had always stood in the way of before – designer, inventor and experimenter all rolled into one. He started improving BMW's own image.

The idea of a 'single body' had long since lost its appeal to him. So he transformed it, by making greater use of glass, expanding the interior, producing rounder lines and doors which opened forwards, thereby providing easier access, all of which bore little comparison to the old 303. The engine capacity had, as it was, been increased to 1.5 litres, suggesting a completely new car with its 34 hp. Popp was delighted. With a sloping windscreen, smaller running boards and, last but not least, its 'light weight', the 315 was now ready (it was called the 315 after the last two digits of its engine capacity in decilitres). This was now the third car in the BMW 'kit', enabling them to establish that they had built a completely modern car which, with 'a weight of only 800 kg flew along and over the road without any strain or noise at 100 kilometres per hour'. It cost 3,750 marks and if it was unashamedly conservative, it still begged the question as to what BMW meant by it. With

195

their constant preference for radical solutions (as borne out by shaft drives and horizontally-opposed engines in motorcycles, which had become the trend-setters for the 'German School' of motorcycle design throughout the world), the car's designers also pointed to the new ways in which it had been designed, despite having only just put into practice solutions which could justifiably be called technologically and economically faultless. An example of this was the vehicle frame. Made out of thin-walled steel tubes with a diameter of 90 mm which were electrically welded (weld spots were arranged in the direction of the material's grain), it was an extremely light and, at the same time, rigid frame, the like of which could not be built in any other way to such a high technological and economic standard.

When I looked in on Schleicher in his farmhouse at Thanning near Munich forty-five years later, we talked about the method of lightweight construction. I suggested that it was not for reasons of design, but rather for the need to save materials (raw materials were in short supply, and Hitler's autarchy [economic and industrial self-sufficiency – part of the early Nazis' radical thinking] was to come later) that the decision was taken. In some ways, this was making a virtue out of a necessity.

I said: 'When the legendary 328 later appeared on the race tracks, its lower weight gave it the decisive edge over heavier cars.'

Schleicher retorted: 'But there were already many "light" cars among them. No, the main feature of the 328 was its tubular frame chassis. It was torsion-resistant. And on top of it was the engine with its light-metal cylinder head and three down-draught carburettors. It was *this* combination (above all, the better road characteristics from the tubular frame, making BMW the leading sports car firm) which provided the lead, not the lower weight.'

'And who was responsible for this tubular frame?' I asked.

Without a trace of embarrassment in his voice, Schleicher replied: 'I had the basic idea. I had already started with frame stiffeners at Horch . . . sometimes the doors would fly open on the road!'

Hitler's real thinking has revealed in 1934, when he showed that right was only right when it served Germany's purposes. Murder was committed, hundreds of state-sponsored murders, for which the so-called Röhm Purge provided one such opportunity, when former and potential opponents of the regime were cold-bloodedly eliminated. The nation kept quiet – either because they were misinformed and truly believed in a counter-revolution and the right of the Führer to be able to eradicate it, or because the Reich President, at the end of his life, had now legitimised what 'in the name of the people' was no longer his will, but Hitler's alone. The fact that there was no dissent against him and the state (whose highest authority he now represented, following the death of Hindenberg) was patently clear to any intelligent person. Popp must have felt relieved when, a few days before Christmas in the historic year of 1934, a document of some importance, concerned with company law, lay on his desk. This was the memorandum of association for a separate company which was to trade under the name of 'BMW Aero-engine Company Ltd'.

After spending many hours persuading the supervisory board into making this rearrangement, Popp was then able to isolate the BMW parent company from any state intervention for its airplane production, an intervention had already become a matter of course in airplane production in view of the imminent announcement of the Reich's military sovereignty. So there was a narrow ledge of freedom – the state would have no say wherever and whenever matters concerning car and motorcycle development in the company were on the agenda. Popp was determined to exploit this, but was careful not to give himself any illusions. He who orders, pays, as the saying goes in Bavaria. And he who pays, calls the tune. And so he should, once he took into account circumstances which could not be changed.

This showed that, as the technical aspects of producing engines for vehicles and planes were brought ever closer, overlapping had become inevitable.

Next to Hall 20 (208 metres long, 45 metres wide), in which aero-engines were produced in lines off the conveyor belts, was Hall 19 (126 metres long, 57 metres wide), handling all motorcycle production. Close by was Hall 17 which, although not much smaller than Hall 19, was concerned only with production of aero-engine cylinder blocks, with equipment for liquid oxygen and arc welding. It was similar to Eisenach where, as there was less space about than in Milbertshofen, a brand-new aero-engine plant was to be put up outside the town in the so-called Dürrerhof area, whose management would be entrusted to Max Friz. This meant that it would remain associated with the old works within the city limits. The test installations for heat treatment, metal inspections, hardness testing using Vickers equipment, X-ray equipment for testing the magnetism in materials, spectrographic information provided by photometric densimetering, in short, everything demanded by the most modern technology for producing aero-engines brought about a situation which was also of benefit to vehicle production. In addition, it became policy that the latter's final quality control (a cost item which amounted to between 5 and 6 per cent of the overall price) was shared by airplane production. This facility, tacitly provided by the state, was not inconsiderable, since it ran into millions. Popp had once dreamt that when everything was back on the right track again, he would sell off the old Eisenach works completely (a load of old iron, he thought; any reasonable offers considered). Now that Dürrerhof was no longer state property, it should be able to take over all the available aero-engine production from Milbertshofen, leaving Munich to build only motorcycles and cars; especially cars.

In the meantime, down on the 'race track' which, for some unknown reason, was what the production line was called, where the old Eisenach vehicle works, now BMW, was situated, that sports car which had 'extremely surprised' Aldington was going into production. The works had a railway siding, and only the initiated knew that car bodies no longer rolled in from Sindelfingen, but were sent to Eisenach from the bodywork company of Authenried in Darmstadt.

Had there been trouble between BMW and Daimler-Benz? In a letter to Dr Kissel, dated 14 November 1934, Popp referred to a conversation they had had in Eisenach and repeated what had been on the agenda – that there was no point in renewing the contract of co-operation 'because good relations are entirely maintained through our reciprocal seat on the supervisory board and through our common chairman of the board, privy councillor Dr von Stauss. If this were not the case, then the mistake can only be ours, which would make any contract of co-operation redundant.'

So this was how the sparring began, with Popp, too, becoming more vociferous. The contract concluded at a time of very detailed discussions about a merger between the two companies had not materialised in many of its points (quite apart from the unsuccessful merger). There had even been obstacles placed in its way. He went on to explain why: 'It has come about through changes in the manufacturing programmes of both our companies, which have resulted from the market situation and the consequent changes in competition and design circumstances.' If neither partner were able to maintain the terms of the contract, due to internal and external pressures, what was the point of extending it? At the same time, he believed (and here he fired a salvo or two) 'that considerable evidence of co-operation had been forthcoming on our side in the past three years which, however, had not been repaid in kind to us by several members of your company'. Now he was really in the thick of things, complaining that Sindelfingen's prices were too high: 'You were always promising me price reductions with the very clever proviso that the more attractive I make the rates to you, the less BMW will think of producing its own bodies or of looking at other competitors. On this point I would finally ask you to be a bit more accommodating towards us.'

Whereupon Kissel immediately relented, and even went as far as to thank him (Popp had complained that this was the first time he had been thanked) for the fact that BMW had placed quite considerable orders for aero-engine parts with his company, to the tune of 5 million Reich marks (as Popp had made a point of noting), and said that he, Kissel, was well aware of the value attached to the bodywork business that had been given to Sindelfingen. He asked him, however, not to overlook the fact that 'using bodies made by ourselves could give your make of car a reputation in itself and greater worth than you could have found by using another make'. He was also fully aware that sales of BMW cars had been greatly helped by having bodies made at Sindelfingen. In addition, as regards sales of BMW items, such as six-cylinder cars, in Daimler-Benz subsidiaries, Kissel had shown his resolve to settle these differences as quickly as possible. (Popp had complained about falling sales, especially in areas where Daimler-Benz had the sole franchise, which had had a direct influence on reduced six-cylinder sales.)

If such a squabble might imply that relations between the two partners, who had once jointly planned to set up the leading car company in south Germany, were beginning to break up, then, as can easily be shown, it was not Daimler-Benz which wanted to part from BMW, but rather Popp who was sailing against the current. Did he have such a tail-wind that he thought it better to weather it out alone?

A year later, in autumn 1935, he set out with Fiedler to see his partner in Untertürkheim. Fiedler had the design for a large car in his briefcase. A new two-litre car had joined the 315 model. Called the 319, which Schleicher had raised it to 45 hp, again by boring out. As a critic wrote, this two-litre 'took off like a shot from walking speed, and could reach its top speed of 115 kph in a very short space of time.' Yet it broke a price barrier (it cost 5,200 marks), which made its slogan sound hollow: 'Not often in the history of car production have designers truly been able to claim: *No more changes need be made!*' Even the production of 3,000 units a year had no effect on what Popp knew, namely that the modular system, from which this car also stemmed (with its sports version 319/1), did not produce *more* than five types. One had to aim higher, if the claim that BMW designs were always years ahead of the state of technology was to remain inviolable.

And Fieldler's technical imagination had already captured on paper what Popp was planning – this was the larger car, a precedent for future developments, which had an aerodynamic, all-steel body developed from the most recent wind-tunnel data, a body which, in essence, no longer needed a chassis. (However, for safety's sake, Fiedler was to fit a panel frame underneath.) It was also fitted with torsion bar suspension recently patented by Porsche, of which historians were to say that it represented the last major mechanical invention of the technological age (it cost licencing fees, but never mind), together with a completely new gearbox, with an overrun clutch on the bottom two gears and synchromesh on the top two gears. This made gear changes very silent and smooth. It had a 50-hp engine, of which only one thing could be said: some things never change. No further developments were needed.

Popp stubbornly rejected the initial calculations, making the project seem unfeasible (he had calculated that the starting-up costs would be one million marks), as if it were all absurd theorising. He had decided to build this car and no other – with less money. But even he did not know how. All he knew was that BMW would break into the top range with this car.

And how would Daimler-Benz fit into this now? Well, as before, Sindelfingen was to build the bodies (the quarrel had been buried). Nobody could do it better. Moreover, Popp thought it only fair to obtain his partner's opinion when contemplating this step into the 'design unknown'. In spite of all the frustration involved, he once again saw what it was that lay at the heart of the planned merger of star and propeller – the possibility of a unique constellation in the future development of the car, whose past had ties with both firms, on the one hand through Gottfried Daimler and Ernst Benz, and on the other with Nikolaus August Otto and his son Gustav. But how did things stand now? Faces were filled with consternation. All-steel bodies were not built at Sindelfingen, never had been (of course, they were later) – quite apart from the absence of suitable production technology. They said that they did not want to supply a product which would inevitably be seen as competition, which until then (all right?) had not been the case.

No, it was not all right. Popp was completely taken aback. Fiedler put his design drawings back into his briefcase. As they approached Munich, it dawned on them both that this was the break. Goodbye to the merger. There was no doubt about it, and even Father-of-all von Stauss, with the chair on both boards, would not be able to clear up this conflict of interests now. All those protestations of co-operation had been nothing more than face-saving devices.

Telegraphic confirmation: the bodies would be delivered by the firm of Ambi-Budd, Johannisthal, Berlin, a specialist in all-steel bodies. So now nothing stood in the way of producing the new car.

On 15 February 1936 Adolf Hitler opened the International Motor Show in Berlin. In his speech, broadcast to all car plants and equipment manufacturers throughout Germany, he rejected the view that a small car (and he prophesied that the day was not far off when three or four million Germans would own their own small car) would force larger models out of the market. The opposite was true, in that there was ample evidence that the cheap model not only made car ownership popular, but gradually increased demand for more expensive models.

Really? Hitler's words inspired scepticism rather than encouragement in Popp. BMW had been relegated from number 5 to number 7 for 1935's registrations. And this was despite the fact that, due to the range on offer, they had never sold so many cars before (8,769 – Popp had the exact figure at his fingertips).

There was the new car, called the '326', the 'flagship', thronged by crowds of inquisitive onlookers, *the* sensation of the show. It had given BMW its future face (the crowd sensed it, Popp knew it), on condition that the future provided economic redemption.

Despite its proven and new technology, its narrow, aerodynamic radiator grille (which emphasised rather than covered up the hallmark of its 'kidneys'), and the elegance of its lines which flowed way past the sweeping mudguards into a steeply-raked tail without sharp corners or edges, it had one disadvantage – at 5,500 marks it was too expensive. Who would want the 'old' models now? Who could afford the new one? Two questions which said more than Popp would like to admit. For there was no time to build a new, reasonably priced model *below* the 326 (smaller but similar).

And time, now, was the real issue.

Numbers and Names

Time was also the issue for one man who had already decisively influenced the fate of BMW once, when he was pushed out onto the starting line at the Nürburgring, wearing white overalls at the wheel of a similarly white sports car (he always appeared in white overalls at his races). The date was 14 June 1936, and anyone knowing this man, who was calmness personified, would have understood the bad memories he now had to suppress as he surveyed the forty cars waiting for the starter's gun beside and behind him (he was on the front grid).

It all came back to him: on the lowest section of the Nürburgring, just behind the Breitscheide Bridge, was the Junek bend. Anyone pulling through it and accelerating out of it hard knows the danger – the slight left-hander before reaching the sharp Bergwerk right-hander. This left-hander concealed a bump. It was now two years ago (but he remembered as if it were yesterday) that Ernst Henne, taking it on the inside, had immediately applied full power to avoid 'jumping'. No sooner had the engine picked up than its superchargers cut in (a potential and still unsolved defect on the new 300-hp supercharged Mercedes). Turf, slope, uprooted trees. Henne, sliding off the track, ended up unconscious, with a fractured skull, severe bruising, and a few broken ribs, in a stream, from which a farmer, collecting snails in the neighbourhood, pulled him out. A few weeks later, barely recovered, he achieved a measured 294 kph in the Coppa Acerbo in Italy, ahead of Caracciola, again for Mercedes in a Grand Prix car. His strongest rival was Guy Moll, a twenty-year-old, the fastest and boldest driver in the Alfa-Romeo team. The southerly wind, the infamous Scirocco, was blowing. Moll overtook Henne at 275 kph, moved too far out to the left without touching him, left the track, and ended up fatally injured.

After the Coppa Acerbo had been restarted (he had only been lying fifth in the race), misfortune struck again for Henne – in the Italian Grand Prix at Monza. This time it was not serious. In one of those artificial bends which drivers call 'chicanes', he touched the back of the car in front of him. The oil cooler sprang a leak and he had to abandon the race. The last upset was at Gyon near Budapest, a track he knew inside out, where he achieved a record-breaking time of 300 kph in the new, hard-top, 3-litre Mercedes which had the coupé body. (Caracciola was out in front in the open version.) The car began to float, but Henne was just able to catch it, steer it out of trouble and brake. When he was lifted out at the end of the measured section, he was in a state of shock. Such were the experiences Henne had had up to now on four wheels. This man, who had previously only ridden on two wheels and broken world records in doing so, had had enough. (Finally, in 1935, he had improved upon his own motorcycle record, made at Tata in Hungary, to 258 kph on a stretch of motorway between Frankfurt and Darmstadt on a supercharged 750-cc BMW.)

In the meantime, Schleicher had persuaded him to chance his luck again on four wheels. No one could offer him a Grand Prix, or a supercharged car. No, it was a mini compared to the 'real' ones. But mechanically speaking, it had grand pretensions. Fiedler had had a light-metal cylinder head made for it. Just look at it, Henne! And Henne did look at it – an overhead-valve, six-cylinder engine with a removable cylinder head (he took it off the model and held it in his hand – light, very light, not at all like cast iron!). Then he scrutinised the valve gear, with its overhead, inclined valves driven by push-rods and rockers from a block-mounted camshaft. It was highly refined. The push-rods via rockers first operated the inlet valves, which were much larger than before, while the exhaust valves were each driven by an oblique cam-follower between the vertical push-rod on the camshaft and the rocker on the valve. The crankshaft had four, white-metal plain bearings. There were three down-draught carburettors with choke, and a large, oil-bath air filter with metal mesh. It also had an oil cooler, in front of the radiator, which could dissipate the higher thermal stresses common in racing and long motorway journeys, while the coolant temperature (just look at the row of slats fitted to the radiator grille) could be adjusted by hand. With a compression ratio of 7.5:1, engine output was about 80 hp at 4,500 rpm, this being the 'running speed' which provided for 135 kph at continuous power and 150 kph at maximum power. The 'hot' version, standing ready for Henne, naturally had more to offer. How much more, asked Henne? Schleicher smiled, saying that he did not exactly know, but had seen the test results – and the chassis.

To keep the heavy sports car sufficiently light (it weighed 810 kg), Fiedler had fallen back on the tubular steel design of the 319 and created a double-flitched frame (with tubes of 90 mm diameter). He had had the bonnet, fastened with two leather straps, together with mudguard parts and other items, made from aluminium. Light, torsion-resistant, safe and fast – safer and faster than anything they had previously built on four wheels. So go ahead and try it out! said Schleicher, somewhat unnaturally, but with confidence, although, like all prototypes, the car had only been tried on second-class roads in the absence of an in-house test track. This had been from Munich to Eisenach and back again, sometimes on bumpy cobbles and other times on smooth asphalt roads (430 kilometres each way). These kilometres were broken up by towns which they knew with their eyes closed, towns covered by engineers, designers, business people and couriers. Taking six hours there and six hours back, this was an endurance run with a short mechanical inspection at either end, and a few hours' sleep. They were always able to combine something useful (internal mail, exchange of personnel) with the main job in hand, which was to establish technical data, wear resistance, modifications to the body and the mechanics.

Well, Henne had 'tried' it out. This car was almost *too* beautiful, he thought. It smelt of Russian leather (that was the straps), and had turned everyone's heads when he had ambled along like one of the gentry or a spoilt little rich boy, or cruised along the Kurfürstendamm. Then he accelerated, with foot hard down, soon reaching the south curve, noiselessly drawing away from the pack of fellow drivers. My car noiseless, he thought, noiseless in the midst of this hell of howling engines? Yet the engine could hardly be heard, and barely a minute later the car flew past the pits on the back straight. He forced himself into the lead over other 2-litre sports cars in Hatzenbach valley and the labyrinth of bends on the Nürburgring. And no memory inhibited him. (Junek bend, the gentle left-hander with the bump before the sharp Bergwerk bend, the stream, the snail gatherer. . . .) Nothing could disturb him now, or inspire him with caution or defiance.

A quarter of a million people had gone to the Nürburgring that day. An eyewitness, Ernst Rosemann, reported:

Loudspeakers announced: 'Henne is leading all the other sports cars on the Karussel bend!' A lot of kilometres have to be covered from the carousel to the starting line. Thousands of eyes were trained on the advance announcer who reported from Döttinger Hill: 'Now the driver is entering the long home-straight.' Again Henne's race number came out first. Seconds went by. Then it emerged, the little white car, quickly and safely passing the stands – so safely that it almost seemed slow. But what did slow mean here? It meant 160 kph, the speed the BMW effortlessly roared over the concrete track. So much for a few seconds! Henne was still in the lead. He came into view again on the back straight, just when his closest rival was passing the stands. Second lap! There was another count, the loudspeaker could be heard from the Karussel bend, the marker board went up on Döttinger Hill, showing that Henne was gaining ground. In the meantime, the smaller sports cars had naturally been lapped. Two BMWs were contesting the lead. The German make was also able to assert itself here. Rose and Krings (two men from the Rhineland) were leading the field.

There was no change on the third and fourth laps. With a stop-watch it became apparent that Henne's lead was increasing all the time. But then, what was that? In the middle of the field of racing cars, a sports car pushed itself in. Was it Henne? Quite correctly, he had started two minutes later than the racing cars. Henne had already caught up on the racing cars, with the first supercharged sports cars now way behind him. The naturally aspirated BMW was faster than the supercharged cars!

They were now entering the last and decisive lap. But it was all over bar the shouting! Ernst Henne's white BMW car emerged from Döttinger Hill, in sight of the chequered flag. He raced along the straight once more, took his foot off the accelerator, braked and came to a halt. Ernst Henne had won the Eifel Race in a BMW, a resounding victory in this major race. His average speed had been 101.5 kph, covering the 140-km race with almost split-second accuracy, without there being the least threat to his chances. He had beaten the supercharged sports cars and had been faster than various racing cars.

The car was called the '328' (presumably in line with the 'pattern'), and it was the answer to a protest. This was because Fiedler had designed a convertible for the 326, that bone of contention with Daimler-Benz. He did not want it to be known simply as a variant, but to be acknowledged as a new model in its own right. So it was given the designation '327' without anyone realising that this car, with more elegance than sporting pretensions, in spite of its soft top and its headlights faired into the bodywork, would antagonise that section of the clientele which expected more from BMW than simply the production of 'beautiful' cars, even if they were practical and unquestionably innovative. No, this convertible was not the anticipated sports version of the much admired 326, and certainly not the successor to the unforgettable 315/1 sports car which Aldington had taken back to England.

A car factory registers customer disaffection like a seismograph. Popp, who had been no less taken aback by the lack of interest in the 327 than he had been over the high price of the 326, interpreted this disaffection correctly. Nothing would be more dangerous than to risk the sports reputation which had so recently been won in rallies around the Alps and Germany, and nothing could be more self-defeating than a utility car which, while being highly appreciated, remained unsaleable on account of its price. And so the 328 emerged in an incredibly short space of time, under project 'Roadster', which admittedly made no profit for BMW in the remaining years before the war, but acquired a reputation as the fastest production sports car in the world.

Consequently a second car emerged under the objective 'within the means of the middle class', to be designated the '320', a slimmed down 326.

Only 462 examples of the 328 were produced, yet wherever it appeared its path was paved with gold medals, first prizes and best times. At its very first appearance in England, Frazer-Nash (Aldington had immediately acquired the licence) won the British Tourist Trophy in it, quickly followed by the Brooklands Race. It won Grand Prix in Finland and Bucharest, as well as the Brighton Trial, together with the major hill-racing competition in Germany, and at La Turbie in France. It again took the Tourist Trophy, and was preparing (this was in 1938) to take part in the famous Italian Mille Miglia. Translated that meant the 'thousand miles of Brescia', which, with the 'Le Mans 24-hour Race', was one of the most feared of all endurance races, but whose victories commanded the most sought-after trophies.

This 328 cost a small fortune – 9,000 marks.

The 320, on the other hand, (with its 45 hp from a single carburettor and two doors instead of four), was crucially to cost only half that – 4,500 marks; a clear thousand marks less than its larger model, the 326. Although there were external similarities, it had not simply been produced through pantographic reduction. Fiedler had put all his ambition into designing a model with its own features, in spite of the real need to make savings. He wanted to make this car as advanced as possible with a 'self-supporting' structure, whereby the body was no longer bolted to the chassis but welded to it. As trials took time (almost as much time as a new design – about a year, Fiedler estimated) an intermediate model would have to fill the gap. In fact, he and his fifteen-man design team succeeded in formulating it from the modular system in just a few weeks – a four-seater convertible to be mounted on the chassis of the 319. The latter's engine (with two carburettors) was also fitted to it, yet its 'refined *and* sporting' qualities were unmistakably new (leather seats and soft top!) so that it could be brought out, not as a variant of the 319, but as a model in its own right called the '329'. In the next twelve months 1,179 examples emerged from Eisenach, while feverish activity went on on the 320, on which the firm's hopes for a breakthrough into mass production rested.

Was Popp also hoping for mass production? From the outside it would seem so, as the marketing people were pressurising him, telling him that they needed the affordable car. But in his heart, he had stayed loyal to his old opinion and remained stubbornly silent when Fiedler and Schleicher returned from a study trip in the USA in 1936. There they had looked around Ford and Chrysler, especially their production technology, and were now reporting to him, as he invariably asked them to do, on what had most impressed them. Even the statement that car manufacture was only worth it if high quantities were involved was greeted in silence. It was only when Fiedler said that there was no way that even BMW could avoid mass production, based on what they had seen over there and on the need to keep Germany competitive, adding that producing a 1,000 cars a month was quite ridiculous, that Popp showed his displeasure by exclaiming, 'What do you mean, ridiculous?' He said that he had not sent them to the USA just for that. He knew it all, and it was old hat.

'If I build a thousand convertibles a month and earn a thousand marks from each,' he reckoned, 'I would much prefer that than to build ten thousand a month (presuming everything went according to plan), and to have earned no more than a million at the end of the year.'

'And yet didn't he approve the 320?' I asked Schleicher, who was telling me about the event as if everything had only just happened.

'Yes, he did!' replied Schleicher. 'It was *he* who had wanted it, not us! *That* annoyed him, especially since he was on our side. It was just that he did not want to admit it. It was only much later, during the war, that he admitted to third parties just how right his technical managers had been, in spite of his opposition to them. It was only because of historical circumstances, which no one could have foreseen, that *his* calculation (at least to some extent) had proved right – small quantities, exclusive, not cheap, one model followed by another.'

'Look here,' said Schleicher, 'I've even copied it out. You wouldn't believe it. In February 1936 we brought out the 326 and the convertible, the 327. In August, the 329. A month later, the 328. Then, ten months later, in 1937, the 320 appeared on the market, and barely a month after that, in August 1937, the 325, the army vehicle, a completely new design – five gears, four-wheel drive and four-wheel steering (the rear wheels steered, so that you could turn it on the spot). Good, it was a job, but everything had to be designed, developed, tested until it could be built . . . and it was built!'

'I've heard a lot about the cars of those years,' I said. 'Reports about the 326 and 328 and later the big BMW, the 335, were almost legendary. Anyone having a car like that, anyone who could afford it, sang its praises. Nothing was said about the 320.'

'A real mix-up, that one,' said Hans Fleischmann, the archivist and cataloguer at BMW, a man who had the technological history of the company at his fingertips, and to whom I was grateful for not being up against some kind of impenetrable 'magic mountain'. He had accompanied me to see Schleicher in Thanning. He added that the museum's cellar still had an example of it. He could walk past it without so much as blinking.

'Why?' I went on.

Fleischmann said dismissively: 'It's a number, no more, no less. At least for me. There are numbers and names at BMW which are connected with models. You can forget the numbers.'

'But this number was built in 4,185 examples,' I said, referring to the table.

'But what does that mean? Mass production was not what it had been intended for.'

'The car was soon to be forgotten, too,' Schleicher said. 'Principally because Popp did not have the capital to make it in any larger quantities. That aside, it had failings. . . . It was my job to look into them. There were constant breakages on the front suspension. We had taken it over from the 319 but the 320 was much heavier and the front suspension was not up to it. That cost the company a lot of money, around two million marks. Thousands of vehicles had to be recalled, which obliged Fiedler to fit the expensive front axle from the 326. We tried to keep this after-market fitting secret. Well, these things happen. No car company is immune.'

'How did Popp take it?'

Schleicher laughed. 'He was not angry at all. He looked upon it as a completely new car, with an already expensive suspension being even more expensive. It was called the "321" and had its own premiere in three versions at the Berlin Motor Show in 1938, I believe. At that time, what people now call marketing was not the deciding factor for BMW.'

'And what was the deciding factor?' I asked.

'Reputation. You could say we were overrun with records. We were still a small company in terms of motorcycle and car production. Should we reach for the stars and gain a reputation for production? That would have been beyond all our capabilities. In my management of the test department, cars were, to a certain extent, only incidental. My main activity, in amongst all Popp's and Fiedler's model mania, was the motorcycle. And that had been far from idle.'

The New Saddle-Horse

A letter which a farmer wrote to BMW in 1930 referred to an R 62 which he rode almost every day and in all weathers:

> I acquired my motorcycle as a replacement for a saddle-horse, as I could only use the horse to a limited extent, and even then not all the time. On acquiring the machine, I realised that I would not be able to ride over the field, as I could with my horse, but thought that even if I was bound to use roads I would still be able to get round my estate and check on my workers, who were scattered far and wide.

Since buying it, he had covered 41,000 km in fifteen months. 'Nowadays there are no longer any ditches or bad roads to hold me back, and if anyone wants to see how easy it is to take a BMW across newly-ploughed fields, stubble and meadows, etc, then I am more than ready to roll up on my "saddle-horse".'

Only his workers were not happy with the machine, as they did not know if he was in town or would soon come back, they were never sure . . . on the other hand, they were glad to be given a lift when he needed an extra person and had to bring someone from elsewhere on the estate.

> My wife, who is seventy-six, still works on the farm. From time to time, when I can, I try and save this woman the considerable walk to the fields. I am not exaggerating when I say that this woman is my best pillion rider, and whenever I drop her off after we have done a hundred kph, all she says to me is: 'That was just great!' I can say in all good faith that if a farmer keeps a BMW instead of a saddle-horse, he will be more than satisfied, and will soon see that his new 'saddle-horse' is much more than just a replacement, it's a major asset to his estate.

The new saddle-horse, which one man here discovered for himself, may explain the fascination which motivated a Friz, a Schleicher and a Hopf to apply ever improved designs to an essentially different means of transport from that of the car, quite apart from the speed records and desire for simple sporting pleasure. It was more than just a simple transfer from four to two wheels. It meant nothing less than being fully conscious of a being which comprised both man *and* machine. Man and machine, which were linked to each other in a unique way, formed a pair; the former inconceivable without the latter, which carried him to a destination that he would not have been able to reach on his own. The latter inconceivable without the former, by whose help it first moved and received its will, driven by the rider's arms and legs. Nothing was what it seemed, and if Friz's ingenious R 32 was praised for having established landmarks in design, and for having sensibly transferred car features such as twin-tubular frames, unified engine and gearbox, and shaft drive cleverly transferred to two-wheel transport, then that was only true for the outside. In essence, the two were quite separate.

On the question of the engine alone, this 'saddle-horse', having little in common with the car, imposed stricter demands. It had to be light, it had less space, and cooling was a problem. There was no comparison in terms of frame construction, suspension and power transmission, because the centre of gravity as a relation to wheel-base was almost twice as high as in a car (which led to quite different values for accelerating and braking), and because the rider, fully stretched both physically and mentally, quickly got tired in the unfavourable relationship between suspension components and the mass of the bike, which was only cushioned by the tyres. It bore no comparison with the car in production terms, either. With the requirements for maximum profitability, only limited numbers of each model could be produced in line with customers' individual needs. This did not inhibit the designer. Far from it; it kept him on the move, fired his imagination, with questions like: What can be improved? What can be simplified in production? How can style be coupled with simplification, so that a whole is formed by the merger of shape and substance? Nothing was 'eternal', everything was in a state of flux, with defeats, insults and setbacks counting for little when another of those 'quiet' victories was attained. It was a technological breakthrough, whose real worth was not to be found in the establishment of records, but in the new nuance applied to the life of the motorcycle 'being'.

Schleicher had embarked upon that course, which in all modesty was inherent in the verb 'to seek' rather than the verb 'invent'. He was one of those 'seekers' who had helped the R 37 to acquire its light-metal cylinder head with overhead valves, and when he won the gold medal at the Six-day Race in England, an ambition had been fired in him which was to accompany his further 'finding' over the next decade. This ambition drove him on and guided his designs. It was to bring back to Germany the crown which England, the classic country for motorcycling and motorcycle sport, had long since regained and had no intention of giving up again.

This ambition bordered on presumption, if one considered that the technological advance enjoyed by the English was virtually unbeatable.

Great Britain had always set the tone. By the time Friz had succeeded in that challenge on the R 32, with a design which had prompted one Englishman to say that it was miles better than any British machine, Matchless had already (by 1923!) brought out a production machine with an overhead camshaft. Such admired and, at the same time, awesome makes, as Norton, Brough-Superior, Douglas, Rudge, Triumph, BSA, Ariel, Sunbeam and Scott had made sure that the English reputation of possessing the technology of tomorrow had left little chance for any other country to appear more than just a backwater.

BMW could also say a thing or two about that.

In 1930, when Schleicher returned to BMW from Horch, all the sports interests had been stopped. Not that things were going badly. The 500- and 750-cc BMW supercharged machines were practically unbeatable on fast roads, but the admittedly slower but much more agile English ones pulled away from them out of the bends, and riders such as Köppen, Henne, Bauhofer, Stelzer, Gall and Soenius could only look back on past successes (no less than ninety-one first prizes) with an air of resignation. Only Henne struggled on doggedly to win the absolute world record. No sooner had he succeeded than it would be taken back from him by someone like Wright or Fernihough.

In 1929, following frame fractures, pressed-steel frames were introduced (bolted and riveted, but not yet welded together) which were admittedly durable, but made the R 11 even heavier than it already was and, as connoisseurs stated, made a scarred, sheet-metal object out of Friz's unique creation. (Schleicher's pet theory: 'We had too little experience with hard-soldering . . . we built "sleeved" frames. They fractured on the soldered joints and not on the sleeves. . . . We should have employed people from motorcycle construction who knew how frames were hard-soldered. The English had twenty years' experience in producing impeccable, hard-soldered frames. We only produced good frames when we went over to welded tubular frames in 1936, using clinker-free arc-welding. That enabled us to design something quite different.')

And so Schleicher designed the R 5, a motorcycle which dwarfed all its predecessors, and which was so new that it broke the mould, as the old R 12 had done in its time. It had a strengthened tubular frame, of the type still built today, and, based on the 24-hp in the R 5, easily coped with a three-fold increase in engine output. As early as 1932, when the R 11 was remodelled into the R 12, Schleicher had developed telescopic forks 'straight from the drawing-board', which were unprecedented in this particular form, being fitted with oil-filled dampers.

Celebrated as a stroke of genius (which, indeed, it was), they went into production on the R 12 model in 1935, providing a lead for which even the English did not withhold respect.

'And when are we going to get rear suspension?' This question, asked by Hitler in 1935 as he passed the BMW stand at the International Motor Show, had filled Schleicher, as he generously admitted, with embarrassment, almost consternation. The English had long had it, and once it had been proved that telescopic front forks gave a machine road qualities at the very edge of what was at all feasible on an unsprung-frame design, Schleicher had had rear suspension developed based on the English Norton model. The job was conferred upon Alfred Böning, one of his most experienced designers. Although nothing was abandoned from this version, Schleicher decided upon an idea which Alexander von Falkenhausen, a young designer in his team, had come up with on his own. His solution (sliding tubes for housing the drive shaft and the springs at the frame ends) had the advantage of keeping the frame rigid. A test machine was built, and Falkenhausen, who also went in for racing, took it out on the race-track. There was nothing else left for him to do. The works team of Peppi Stelzer and Wiggerl Kraus did not want to try out the new rear suspension, because it was *too* new. And Schleicher had said to him: 'You've got to try out what you yourself have designed!' Falkenhausen did so and took part in the exhausting International Six-Day Race at Füssen with the works team. He worked all evening, still quite fresh, while the works drivers fell off their saddles, thoroughly shaken, tired, aching and exhausted. They wanted the new suspension now, too. Victory after victory on BMW machines fitted with it confirmed for Falkenhausen the superiority of his invention – in the Hungarian Grand Prix, the Swedish, the Dutch, not to mention the German, which BMW won. Even the Irish Grand Prix fell to a BMW machine with rear suspension, and naturally Henne's new, supercharged 500 BMW was fitted with it, even before it was taken over into series production.

It was on this machine, which was almost completely aerodynamic, that Henne once again improved on his absolute world record (then 256 kph) along the motorway between Darmstadt and Frankfurt, achieving the incredible speed of 272.006 kph. Schleicher had replaced the previously common system of operating the valves via push-rods with a König shaft drive, and had had cylinder heads made out of resilient bronze, whose high copper content made for even better heat dissipation.

The vehicle itself looked like a torpedo, having a domed, transparent, plastic panel at the front and small stabiliser wheels at the sides, whose struts could be retracted inside the body, like on an aircraft. Henne had to drop these stabiliser wheels down at just the right moment when starting and stopping (not too late, not too soon), so that he would not fall over. But Fernihough was already preparing to counter-attack, breaking Henne's record on a 1000-cc Brough-Superior-Jap at 273.2 kph, a record which he was to lose shortly afterwards to the Italian Taruffi on the Bergamo motorway. His machine was also fully faired-in, and he managed 274.18 kph, giving Henne the signal to enter again with a 500-cc BMW whose streamlined body had meanwhile been tested in the wind-tunnel and improved with tail-fins, which were designed to obviate the fearful 'juddering'.

On his last ride, Henne found it almost impossible to drag his machine back onto the track after it broke away like a bolting horse. In a week set aside for attempts on records at the end of October 1937, with both Fernihough and Taruffi present, simply nothing went right. Even Taruffi broke off his tests. It was not only Henne who was desperate – Schleicher was, too. Agonising days followed. It was already November. Would it be best to give up? Forget the fairing, decided Schleicher. He removed the 'Zeppelin fins', he lengthened the tail, and fitted deflective edges on the ends of the stabilising fins. Every day before dawn, Henne raced his mount along the Munich-Salzburg motorway through Hofolding Forest and got his confidence back. Everything seemed to be going well now.

Then, on Sunday 28 November 1937, things were ready. It was already snowing. The Frankfurt section, which had been checked by car at four in the morning, was free, right down to a few ice patches which were easily got rid of. Henne was lifted onto his machine at around eight. He started up, and retracted his stabiliser wheels. Then came the Mörfelden exit (this was where Rosemeyer was to have a fatal accident just six months later). Henne felt the terrible juddering in the machine, and checked it – there was no comparison to the last time. He opened up fully, and went into the 'Measured Kilometer'. The timekeepers recorded 278.853 kph. He turned round, and on the way back broke the magic barrier of 280 kph, giving a mean value of 279.503 kph. He had achieved the absolute world record, which was to stand for fourteen years. The first words that Henne said when he was told his time reminded Schleicher of that ice racing in Sweden (even then he was just below that round figure): 'That was pretty good, wasn't it?' Then he went to his wife, who had accompanied him to all his races.

She had never tried to talk him out of, or into, racing. She had never wasted a word on the risk he was taking, and the risk she took being with him. He had the definite feeling that her presence pulled him through, that she was there when he started, and would be there when he came back, whether he would succeed in crossing that barrier beyond which no man had travelled, or whether he would fail. That was other people's business, the firm's, not hers. But it was no one's business to guess where his sense of safety, his staying power, his courage came from. Now he had once again succeeded, succeeded like never before. But for how much longer?

'And so I said to her,' Henne concluded his story in Munich, where I was visiting him in Kidler Street, over the yard with the old workshop where everything had begun, 'I told her something I had decided upon beforehand, something I was to stick to, I told her: "That was my last race."'

'How old were you then?' I asked.

He thought for a moment. 'Thirty-three, or thereabouts.'

'And you never regretted it?'

'Never.'

The Heydays

BMW's heydays began with Henne's absolute world record in 1937 (which Fernihough tried in vain to regain five months later when he was killed doing 270 kph in Gyon in Hungary). Those were the days of splendour before the lights went out. They evoked something like European euphoria, at least where nations met to compete in sport and technology, and where national colours were the features distinguishing countries of origin, countries of origin having world-class names and concepts. The place in Italy where they met and competed was Brescia. In France, it was Le Mans, and in England, the Isle of Man, that island in the Irish Sea which awarded the TT (Tourist Trophy).

How unimportant nationality was amongst drivers can be seen by the team sheet for the four white BMW 328 sports cars which started out in the night of 2 and 3 April in Brescia, among the 150 cars in the XII Mille Miglia. In the first car were Prince Schaumburg-Lippe from Germany and Count Lurani from Italy; in the second car, the Englishmen Fane and James; in the third car, the Germans Richter and Dr Werneck; and in the fourth, von der Mühle and Holzschuh, again Germans. The thousand miles (1,621 kilometres) went first to Bologna (the first control). From there, covering the entire width of the Italian boot, they made two huge loops in a figure of eight. In the south, through Florence, Pisa, Livorno, along the Via Aurelia through Tarquinia to Rome, and in the north, after repeated crossing of the mountains, through to the Adriatic Sea and on as far as Venice and Treviso. Then they passed through Vicenza and Verona, before returning to the starting point at Brescia.

Schleicher was now sitting on the Piazza dello Vittorio, wrapped in blankets. It was April, and the mist was thinning over the Po valley. Although calm on the outside, inside he was scarcely able to bear the tension, waiting until the first message came through by telephone (this was after 234 kilometres): 'All four arrived in Bologna. Splendid times. Richter is dawdling a bit, but nothing serious.' BMW had entered the 2-litre class, in which there were only four other cars – a Riley, an Aston Martin, a Fiat and an Alfa. The Alfa dropped out in the Abruzzi, as the others had already done in Rome, leaving the field almost wide open for the BMWs.

But would all four of them make it? The drivers, spending 13 to 15 hours at the wheel (if they did not relieve each other, as leading drivers like Fane were reluctant to do), had to contend with all manner of obstacles lurking behind steep bends on the narrow roads through the villages (a dog crossing the road, stones falling off overhangs), not to mention the early morning mist in the valleys, the dust covering the gravel roads which suddenly replaced metalled ones, and squalls off the sea. In addition, the Italians lost the advantage they had of being at home and knowing the route with their eyes closed. Even if they were generous with their tips, no one can memorise the positioning technique for taking corners sharply for the thousands of bends which had to be taken, even if he has already driven them on trial runs. The art needed to master all this was set against the imponderable nature of whether every possible technical failure could be ironed out in the cars' production. In reality defects were *bound* to occur on an endurance race like this where brakes were just as important as acceleration, road holding, visibility, not to mention gearboxes, axle layout and carburettor settings. If they did not occur, it would be a miracle.

And yet just such a miracle occurred. There had been no problems until one cylinder failed, forcing Richter to continue determinedly driving on five 'pots', although this did not stop him keeping up with the leaders (at an average speed of 115.6 kph, as was later established). And so they made it, sticking close behind one another like watch-dogs, as they conquered the Apennines with its hairpin bends and passes rising to 900 metres, joining the Via Emilia effortlessly and almost cheerfully as they left Rimini. ('Such pulling power, speed and reliability, I wouldn't have thought it was possible!' Prince Schaumburg-Lippe was later to say, and Fane, on arriving first, acknowledged that he would have liked to race like that every Sunday.) At Bologna they turned off to the right, towards Venice, when suddenly a Lancia Aprilia travelling at 90 kph ran onto the footpath, probably due to driver fatigue, rolled over and caused a bloodbath amongst the spectators. There were plans to call the race off. Fortunately they heard nothing of this, and had already passed Mestre and were racing on, past the Venetian lagoon, drawing on every ounce of power in their machines, as they moved along the recently built Brescia motorway towards the finish. They were the fastest naturally-aspirated cars in the race, faster than the French Delahaye in the leading formula class, whose track record the previous year was an average of 121.6 kph. This year the winners in the XII Mille Miglia, the fastest ever, were Pintacuda in the open class, with an Alfa Romeo at 129.6 kph, and in the 2-litre class, the BMW team of Fane and James with an average speed of 119.7 kph. Just behind them came Prince Schaumburg-Lippe and Count Lurani. At tenth and eleventh in the overall classification were the two other BMWs. Victory in its class, victory for its team, and (what Schleicher found more satisfying than anything else) BMW had won the Prize for Overall Consistency.

It was quite a different matter at Le Mans. Anyone setting out to discover the meaning of fear (like the boy in Grimms' fairy-tale) would experience it here. The race took place every year in June, from 4 p.m. on Saturday to 4 p.m. on Sunday – in other words, right through the night. Anyone wanting to win the Rudge-Whitworth Cup awarded here had first to qualify in two consecutive years. He could win nothing in the first year. If he succeeded in achieving a minimum performance by the end of his second 24-hour race, calculated on a formula using engine capacity, then he could take part. But what conditions he would have to endure! His car was not allowed to be push-started, and could only be started again after a pit stop using an electric starter motor. If that failed, vehicle and driver were disqualified.

If a headlight flickered during the seven hours of night, or a light, even a brake light, did not come on (if only temporarily), this meant immediate disqualification. Any liquids, whether fuel, oil or coolant, could only be topped up every 24 laps, i.e. after every 324 km (all filler pipes were sealed and their use was monitored by course stewards, no matter how long it took). If a participant pulled out of his pit by so much as a metre, then he had to drive on, and was only allowed to stop again after completing another lap. If he stopped just once during the race (even when he was so far ahead that he was assured of the cup), he would be disqualified. No cars without boots could enter, and only spare wheels from these boots were allowed at tyre changes, which, for once, were allowed as often as required. The last lap (half of all the participants generally did not even get that far) had to be driven in a maximum time which was reset at every new race. So there was discontent right from the start.

Pedantically arranged according to their engine capacity, the cars stood in front of their pits and opposite the drivers. When the starting flag went down, they had first to prove that they could run, so that they could reach their cars. They then jumped into their seats and raced off, wildly, with no regard for the other competitors (provided the engine started), showing a nervousness as great as in the final sprint in other races.

The actual race was lethal. Its greatest danger was the monotony of the route, the long hours of night driving, the infamous early morning mist around the Sarthe, the constant cloudbursts which almost invariably occurred in every race. Pile-ups (the smallest lapse of concentration, or a minor technical failure could cause them) were part and parcel of these races, with deaths and injuries commonplace. (In 1955, eighty-eight people died here, and over a hundred were injured.) What did BMW hope to find here? Well, the 'Grand Prix for Endurance and Speed', even if it was so hated, and even if those who were inviting applications looked like real sports sadists and bureaucrats, still had a value which no large-scale car company believed it could ignore. This was either for reasons of publicity, or because of the quite exceptionally high durability demanded by the Sarthe course. Anyone ignoring it counted for nothing – exceptions proved the rule. Auto Union and Mercedes were, as often before, not on the starting grid in 1939 for unknown reasons. And so 'Le Mans' belonged to the most important of all world-class trophies at the time, whose technological *raison d'être* was also subject to constraints which would not only produce 'armaments' and 'war'.

'For the first time,' the BMW papers said, 'the famous NSKK-team [National Socialist Driver Corps] took part this June in the 24-hour race with three BMW cars.' So was it done out of duty, at the behest of the highest sporting authorities, in the Reich, so that Germany would not be absent? It almost seemed so, with Prince Schaumburg-Lippe, the 'NSKK Lieutenant' (as entered in the team sheet), sitting there in his aerodynamic covered cockpit, which had been specially bodied for Le Mans and fitted with a higher axle ratio than the other two, standard, open-top 328 sports cars accompanying him in the marathon. It was clear that this car would be the fastest of the three. But Schleicher, who had stayed in Munich this time, would never have imagined in his wildest dreams what it was capable of. His feat was to cover 3,188.4 km in the 24 hours (including all stops for changing drivers, filling-up and changing tyres), which gave an average speed of 132.8 kph. The previous record at Le Mans for the 2-litre class had stood at 120.7 kph and no driver in the world had been able to reach such a high performance even in the 3-litre class. All three BMWs went through in 5th, 7th and 9th positions in the overall placings, far and away the winners in the 2-litre class. Lap after lap they steadfastly pursued their goal, producing a result which, with a 50 per cent drop-out rate in this race as well, had only been achieved by one other make before in the sixty-year history of Le Mans, with the three cars that started reaching the finish.

Although several other race tracks in Europe awarded the prize of a Tourist Trophy, none compared to the 'Senior TT', which England advertised every year. Nothing in motor sport could match this trophy. Since the day when the Marquis des Mouzilly St Mars founded it as a challenge trophy in 1906 (in the style of the time, it portrayed Hermes, the God of trade, roads, wayfarers, thieves, sleep and dreams, on a winged wheel), it had remained the exclusive possession of *one* nation, namely, the English. That was until 1939, when a certain Georg Meier, born in Mühldorf in Bavaria, appeared on the Isle of Man, disputed the English right to it and carried it off.

Admittedly this did not cause the collapse of a world empire, but anyone aware of what the 'Trophy' meant to the British will understand that their handing it over must have seemed like a fall from grace. This was because the supremacy which had made England the Mecca of motorcycling sport was principally attributed to it. The reasons for this could, like so many other things in that country, be explained by history. Law-abiding and conservative as the British are, they did not like to deviate a hair's breadth from tradition. At a time when the island empire was competing with the Continent in every field, it must have seemed particularly painful to be restricted to twenty miles per hour on the road. At the same time, there was still an old law in force guaranteeing access to all highways and byways. It was thus illegal to close road junctions, for instance, to organise motor competitions, meaning that racing could never take place in England. Any racing enthusiast, whether spectator or participant, had to go abroad.

With the founding of the Tourist Trophy, the Marquis des Mouzilly St Mars remedied this ill. In fact he managed to kill two birds with one stone by, on the one hand, liberating his compatriots (within the confines of the law) from an intolerable piece of legislation, and, on the other, by helping a picturesque, but poor region to prosper and become internationally famous.

Irish law held sway on the Isle of Man, one of the small islands lying off the west coast of England, whose inhabitants made a reasonable living from agriculture and livestock. The island even had its own constitution. (An assembly of nine members and the House of Keys formed the legislative body in conjunction with a Lieutenant-Governor appointed by the Crown, and laws were only valid when they had been promulgated by the Tynwald Court, which had been the custom from time immemorial.) This island, about 20 km wide and 50 km long, had a range of hills running down the middle, through which an almost ideal circular course ran, encompassing coasts, hills and valleys. Despite a large number of bends, there were now and again short, straight sections with hump-backed stretches. This inevitably led people to the idea of organising what could not be organised anywhere else in England, i.e. races, specifically motorcycle races.

The first race was held there in May 1907, and the Tourist Trophy was first awarded to touring motorcycles. Naturally, an Englishman won it, benefitting here in front of his compatriots from that incentive which the British needed for them to do the best they could (and which they had always lacked when competing on the Continent, this being not the least of the reasons why they so often failed to win). It now became apparent what it really meant being here, on one's home ground, able not only to practise just before the race, but also to have time to become familiar with a stretch which demanded cast-iron toughness from man and machine, a toughness unlikely to be found on any other circular course.

After initially limiting each lap to 15 miles (gravel roads, blind bends, smaller inclines), in 1911 the organisers dared to include the hills on the island and extend the course to 37½ miles (i.e. 62 km), which, with further developments, made the route both faster and more dangerous. When Meier practised here for the first time (that was in 1938 when he had just won his first race for BMW at the Eilenriede near Hanover), Gall, the German champion in 1937, crashed, landing up in a stream from which Meier pulled him out. Bad luck (or was it good?) then saved Meier from racing in the 'TT'. A sparkplug broke up at the start; he took to the road but could not finish. When he appeared for a second time in 1939 (they were out practising), Gall, who was much more experienced, came off again, this time with fatal results. With this weight on his mind (BMW had wanted to withdraw its riders and abandon the meeting), Meier went off to the start on that Friday, 16 June 1939, on the insistence of the highest sports authority in the Reich.

At 11 o'clock, the race started. It was sunny, there was a gentle northerly wind, and the track was dry – ideal conditions, not quite what the signs had reckoned when they said: 'This way to the seats where the greatest sensations and the most dangerous crashes can be expected.' The practice weeks had been marked by rain, icy winds and a fog on the hills, with Gall's death another reminder of the risks of the course. Yet the people flooding onto the island from 6 a.m. onwards were not motivated by the thrill of watching an artistic lethal game, but simply by wanting to witness something which had become a national institution, to be present when England fought to keep the title (this would be the 33rd time). Many were regular visitors. Spread about over the length of the course, holding stop-watches and pens to record times and placings, they were a unique group of spectators. The course could not be seen in its entirety, with only those at the start and finish able to read the stage results given on large boards. Catching any glimpse of their favourites racing past every half hour, their imagination reconstructed what must have taken place on the sections they had not seen; and whenever anything dramatic happened in front of them, it was seen as a stroke of luck which made their blood freeze. Starting off at 20-second intervals there were seven aces whose silhouettes stayed on their retinas until they flew by again half an hour later. No 1: Daniell on a Norton; No 10: Stanley Woods on a Velocette; No 17: F.L. Frith on a Norton; No 28: Mellors on a Velocette; No 35: Jock West, British, on a BMW; No 49: a complete unknown, Meier, Germany, on a BMW; and No 51: White, the ace of aces on a Norton.

The race lasted three hours or, more exactly, two hours fifty-seven minutes and nineteen seconds, a time which the victor would achieve, and three hours and eleven seconds, a time achieved by the third fastest. The others are of no interest.

Nobody would have suspected that number 49 would achieve a commanding lead a full 14 seconds ahead of the rest of the field at Ballacraine, the first control point. Then, spectators in Ramsey, and in the hills, recorded a lead of 22 seconds. Number 49 was going incredibly quickly. Yet they still thought that Woods would win and if not him, then Frith. He went through Ramsey in 1 minute 55 seconds, ahead of Woods. And yet appearances are deceptive. Meier, only starting from eighth, had covered the first lap with a lead of . . . (they had checked it, and it was true!) 52 seconds, and Jock West, the other BMW rider (who at least was British!) was, as he passed the pits on his second lap, 5 seconds faster than Woods, the best Englishman. Until Meier completed this second lap with the board showing that he had covered the distance at an overall speed of 90.75 mph, which was only four and two fifths seconds slower (a matter of fractions) than the absolute track record which Daniell had established the previous year. Now the two BMW machines were in the lead, and by the fourth round it was practically all over, bar the shouting. What followed was by now typical of the clockwork precision of BMW. Meier, the German, held the lead lap after lap, followed by Jock West, his British stable-mate. Neither was concerned about what was happening behind them, however exciting that was for the spectators. At the start of the last lap, Meier even took the liberty of pulling into the pits and wasting twenty seconds asking how things were going. There was no doubt about it, he would be the winner; which, indeed, he was. At the finish, the cheering crowd surged round him, along with Jock West, who came in second (with 2 hours 59 minutes 39 seconds).

Forty years later, Schorsch Meier, as he was known to the world (he confessed to me that only his wife addressed him as 'Georg') remembered the Tourist Trophy like this:

'Imagine what the route was like: 60 kilometres long, ordinary main road, very uneven, very hilly, up to 700 or 800 metres above the sea. That had already made the carburettor setting go wrong. But the worst thing was all those bends. But until you know this stretch by heart, you've got to spend at least . . . well, the English say they spend years practising . . . I practised in March in 1938 and then in June just before the Trophy. I arrived from the Eilenriede, that's the Eilenriede near Hanover, I'd just taken part in my first race, my very first race, I mean, the first one I had won – I had had no experience at all on my machine. And then it was off to the TT! BMW told me I should get to know the route there. There was no thought of winning . . . well, perhaps later. Anyway, it could not do any harm. So I got to know the route, was not as quick as the British. That was when Gall crashed in practice. Perhaps you know that it was me who pulled him out of the stream. He looked half-drowned. We both went to start the race, and then a sparkplug died on me. Right at the start. That meant I could start, but not carry on. The thread had torn away . . . Bad luck, I suppose. Or perhaps it was good luck? Anyway, immediately after the TT race, I went to Spa (Francorchamps in Belgium) to the European Grand Prix, and won it! My second race, and already the Grand Prix! Then I went to Holland, won there, to Italy, won there. This was all in 1938, my first year of racing, when I became German and European champion. Being the European champion then was the same as being the world champion today, because the courses were the same. And then, of course, along came Auto Union (that was where Bernt Rosemeyer had been killed in a crash), and said: "Well, blow me if this isn't the man for us! If he can race motorcycles like this, let's try him out in a car." So they wrote to me, and I thought: Well, who doesn't want to be in Formula 1 (nowadays it's called Formula 1, then it was just car races)? "All right, then," I said, "I'll have a go."

'We carried out some tests at the Nürburgring on 9 November. I remember it well, it was my birthday – and they offered me a contract. Then came the moment of decision. What should I do? On the one hand, I had hit it off so well in my first year with BMW, while on the other, I could have joined Auto Union racing as an up-and-coming driver. There was also the money side to consider – motorcyclists had always been the poor relations of racing car drivers.

'So I went to BMW, to the manager Schleicher, and told him the story. He was naturally very sad, and said: "Yes, Herr Meier, you won't make money racing motorcycles!"

'"But some more money would help, Herr Schleicher," I said. So we agreed, and in 1939 I raced BMW motorcycles one Sunday and Auto Union racing cars the next. Then came the TT, and BMW had (apart from Karl Gall) no ace rider. And they asked me, and I said: "Yes, if Auto Union will let me go. . ." Well, they did let me go, and I went across to BMW.

'As everyone knows my colleague, Karl Gall, fell heavily on the first practice day and died of his injuries a day before the race. Then Hopf, the BMW team manager, took me aside. He said that they could no longer accept responsibility for my decision to start. Then I said that I had come across here with Karl, that as racing cyclists we had both known that our lives were a bit on the line, just a bit, I said, so I started. In practice, I had been the fastest practically every day, and the British did not think that I could keep it up for seven laps because I would have to ride flat out for three hours, and this meant that I wouldn't be able to keep it up.

'We then had our own telephone line, which we had laid to Ramsey, about 30 km away, and when I had completed the first lap, the people at the start and finish had telephoned to our extension on the route. That Meier sure is damned fast, they said! So I knew how fast I was going. That was when I was more than 50 ahead. More than 50 seconds, can you imagine! Then I said to myself that they weren't going to catch me today, now that I had got more than 50 on the first lap. On the second lap, I got more than 80 ahead, and at the same time, a sign from the pits: "Watch out! Slow down!" But I just kept on going without pushing myself to the limit, and was leading by three minutes at the end. Of course, this was a great success for BMW and for me. And the British have never forgotten how a foreigner on a foreign machine won the TT for the first time. And as for me, it was the greatest moment of my career.'

Meier was not yet 29 years old when he won the Trophy. When the people in his home town of Mühldorf had asked him: 'What do you want to be?' he had always replied: 'Either a racing cyclist or a gendarme.' He was quite serious. When, at the age of seventeen, he applied as a semi-skilled mechanic to be a racing driver at NSU and received a very polite rejection, he actually did become a gendarme (with the Bavarian traffic police in Munich). He could not be faulted on anything in his job, except that he always attracted attention for the wrong reasons on country roads – he rode too quickly. Words may have been voiced in high places about things which were not seen so charitably below ('My captain always used to say: "Here comes mad Meier!" when I roared up!'). It was all part of that great talent which was now asserting itself. In 1933, Meier was commissioned to the three-man police team for the '2,000-km rally through Germany' (a kind of German Mille Miglia, involving the elite of motorcycle racing). The race started at Chemnitz. Meier said:

'There was general laughter when we appeared in our First-World-War outfits – in our leathers, which we used to clean with boot polish. But it was all pretty hollow laughter . . . It had rained all night, and then we had fog in the Teutoburg Forest. But that was to my good fortune, because I was a bit of wild dog; fog had never bothered me. Even if I saw a red light in front of me, I would say to myself: the road must go straight on, so I'll just carry on flat out. Then I discovered in Baden-Baden that I had arrived four hours too early, and that I was the fastest motorcycle rider taking part. All I had was my 400-cc BMW, with the BMW works team, and there I was, up against the DKW and the NSU people.'

That was the beginning. Winter rallies, East Prussian rallies, six-day rallies followed. And every time, the team of Forstner, Linhardt and Meier proved to be the fastest. They were soon called the 'Three Ironsides', not because of their police helmets, which they wore to each tournament, or because the three of them showed iron resilience ('They would always drive on, even if they only had half a handlebar'), but because they worked together as a team 'cast from a single mould', as they ploughed through the countryside. Silver prizes and gold prizes were won. These provincial policemen were transferred to the Wehrmacht, becoming sergeants, and later staff sergeants. They were victorious in all cross-country rallies, with Schorsch Meier becoming the

German Army champion in 1936 and 1937. All of a sudden (due to Henne's illness), he was selected for the German national team to take part in the International Six-Day Rally to be held this time in England. The team only used BMW motorcycles – two solo machines and a machine and side-car. In the final race at Donnington Park, Meier rode the fastest time, winning the Gold Medal on a standard 500-cc BMW machine, and the papers, English papers, wrote: 'Why is this man not already on a BMW racing machine?' Then Schleicher stopped vacillating and the staff sergeant in the German Wehrmacht, still officially assigned to the test department at Wünsdorf in Berlin, reported back to the BMW works team at Munich. 'Either a racing cyclist or a gendarme.' He had never dreamt that he would become both. Soon his home was on all Europe's race tracks, Sunday after Sunday.

When he had won the TT, he travelled to London with the cheering from the Isle of Man still ringing in his ears. Trötsch, BMW's export manager, and SS General Kraus from the NSKK, naturally in uniform, accompanied him. The morning papers were out on display in the hotel where they spent the night. Meier was struck by the headlines on the front page of the Daily Mail: 'NAZI SOLDIER WINS TT'. Trötsch and Kraus went out to flag a taxi down. When Meier was about to get in, the driver drove off, cursing. He wasn't going to pick up any German swine, he said. This episode etched itself into Meier's memory. There was no doubt about it, he was a staff sergeant, he was a 'Nazi soldier'.

And suddenly he realised just how much the world had changed around him, while he had been spending his time at race after race, notching up victory after victory, always with the start and goal in sight, and the rumble of racing engines in his ears. It had so changed that a nation like Britain, whose fairness and sportsmanship he himself had experienced on countless occasions and could vouch for, now found it impossible to tolerate having to hand over a trophy of national importance (which certainly embodied its own self-esteem) to a country which appeared to it as trouble-maker number one in Europe. A country which was now blindly and madly attacking and trying to destroy the worth and existence of not only the British Empire, but also the peace of the world. But this country, this people, were his. Georg Meier's identification with all those people who, as 'The Germans', were responsible for Hitler, and with all those people shouting out 'One people, one Reich, one Führer', could not be denied.

What could he, as an individual, do about it?

Schorsch Meier's intention to make 1939 the year of his victories was predetermined before he entered the TT. What was now to follow the race, or what he made follow it, was (if you consider his biography up to the present day) something which seemed to go hand in hand with a secret rage, which drove him to give the world quite a different picture of the 'Germans' from the distorted, hate-filled and propaganda-filled one of the taxi-driver, whom he could not consider (once he had thought about it for a moment) to be the typical Englishman, in the same day that the latter would see him as the typical German.

The following Sunday Meier drove in the Belgian Grand Prix for Auto

Union. This was the race where Popp's son-in-law, Dick Seaman, had been fatally injured. It was pouring with rain. Meier slid off the track at a bend, into a ditch, jumped out of his car, ran back to the bend, and saw Seaman go past; only to see him being pulled across, the car overturning and bursting into flames. He ran up, but got there too late.

The week after, the French Grand Prix took place, at the circular course at Gueux, Reims. Meier again took part, but only came second. The reason was given in the article in *Motor und Sport*:

> When the ironside sergeant stopped at the pits to fill up and change tyres on lap 23, some petrol overflowed and was set alight by a carelessly discarded cigarette. In a second, Meier's car was engulfed in flames. There was commotion amongst the spectators in the stands. Meier succeeded in freeing himself from the burning car and putting out the fire with a foam extinguisher. Although the brave driver had suffered burns to his hands and arms, he immediately jumped back into the doused-down car to continue the contest. This brave, heart-stirring behaviour was rewarded with a special round of applause from the spectators. The ironside sergeant only went for treatment after the race, and after he had received his congratulations.

A week later, he was again astride his 500-cc supercharged BMW in the Belgian Grand Prix at Assen. His main competitor was Serafini on a Gilera. Meier came in first, winning the prize.

A fortnight later, he was back in his car again for Auto Union in the German Grand Prix at Nürburgring. He was lucky in practice when he took a bend too fast, spun round and slid into a ditch, but escaped uninjured. He was unlucky in the race when the front brakes failed, forcing him to pull out.

The following week, at the start of August 1939, he was again up against Serafini, this time in the Swedish motorcycle Grand Prix at Malmö. He came off. This is how Meier described it:

'I had raced off and was, I think, seven seconds ahead of my main rival, Serafini, on the Gilera. I would certainly have won the race if I had not been stuck behind someone. Then I pulled out at full speed, i.e. 210 kph, and spun over a few times ('for 80 metres,' it said in one report, 'he flew like a ball through the air'), landing up in a clover field, with the bike beside me. So I had a look around, and thought to myself: "Well, that's it, then." I wanted to stand up, but once on my feet I felt something wrong in the small of my back. So I lay down, the medical team picked me up, and it turned out I had bruised and cracked the seventh, eighth and ninth vertebrae. I arrived at hospital in plaster, seven months in plaster. There they discovered that I had broken my back, my foot, my arm, and even a wrist which I had broken before, and which was still stiff. I also had slight concussion. That's what they told me. The only thing I noticed was that things weren't quite in the right place; I had no idea what concussion was. Later I was brought back to Germany by plane.'

If you weigh up the good with the bad, then it was clear that Meier's bad luck was always good luck. No more so than now. 'Just imagine what would have happened if I had not been cut down in Sweden. I would have marched off with my comrades on 1 September against Poland, and later against Russia. After spending seven months in hospital, I wouldn't have been able to march anywhere. So it was decided that I should be sent to Paris. And guess where? To Admiral Canaris, first as a driver, and then as head of the Abwehr transport section [Abwehr: German Military Intelligence]. That was to stand me (and BMW) in good stead when I joined the Yanks at Allach when things were all over. But that's another story.'

Aeroplanes, Aeroplanes, Aeroplanes

A last glimpse of German living conditions under Hitler was presented to the free world at the 1936 Olympic Games. If the propaganda, 'fellow-travelling', mass hysteria and that getting-in-on-the-act, which was either ironically or seriously meant – all of which were hidden behind excellent organisation – if all this were removed, then (as the saying goes: 'We'll see who's who!') the picture remains of a people who had prospered under Hitler, had let themselves be led by National Socialism, but had in no way been entirely consumed by it. A modicum of reason seemed to have been preserved.

However, to appeal to this modicum of reason, as Thomas Mann did in his famous and moving radio addresses to the Germans from Switzerland and California (this we learnt only later), was completely futile. Since the daily press had undergone its 'Gleichschaltung', the Germans were not informed about actual events in the world, but only the interpretations of editors who received their instructions from the Propaganda Ministry via so-called 'Green Letters'. News and commentary were synonymous.

On 10 August 1939, the American correspondent accredited to Berlin, William S. Shirer, wrote in his diary: 'What an isolated world the German people live in! You only need to look at recent papers.' Shirer had just returned from a short holiday which he had spent in Washington, New York and Paris. On the way back, he had bought papers in Switzerland from Berlin and the Rhineland to read on the train. They quickly took him 'back into the distorted world of National Socialism, which was so different from the world which I have just left, that it might as well be on another planet'. He noted in his diary:

> While everyone else in the world has the view that Germany is about to break the peace, saying that Germany is threatening Poland, etc . . ., the newspapers here in Germany are giving quite the opposite impression. The Nazi newspapers are claiming that it is Poland which is endangering peace in Europe, it is Poland which is threatening Germany with armed invasion. WATCH OUT, POLAND! read the headlines in the *Berliner Zeitung*, and underneath: REPLY TO POLAND RUNNING AMOK AGAINST LAW AND ORDER IN EUROPE! Or the headlines in *Der Führer*, a paper from

Karlsruhe, which I bought in the train: WARSAW THREATENS DANZIG
WITH BOMBARDMENT – INCREDIBLE PRODUCT OF POLISH MEGALOMANIA!
Can the Germans really believe such lies? one wondered. All you had to
do was speak to them. They did believe them.

And two weeks later, he noted:

At midnight, on my way to the radio station, I bought the Sunday edition
(27 August) of the *Völkischer Beobachter*. There stood in giant letters right
across the whole of the front page: ALL POLAND IN WAR FEVER! 1.5 MILLION
MEN MOBILISED! UNINTERRUPTED TROOP TRANSPORT TO THE BORDER!
CHAOS IN UPPER SILESIA! Naturally there was no word of any German
mobilisation, although Germany had already mobilised a fortnight ago.

What Shirer could not note, because it was not in any German or foreign
newspaper, was what had taken place in the Reich Chancellery that same
night (26–27 August 1939). A Swedish friend of Göring's, Birger Dahlerus,
who had undertaken to try and save the peace at the eleventh hour, had
flown with Göring's message for the British government in London, and
had returned with a letter from the British Foreign Secretary, Lord Halifax.
Göring considered this letter so important that he immediately drove with
Dahlerus to the Reich Chancellery, which was in darkness at around
midnight; Hitler had already gone to bed. Göring had him woken up. Hitler
took Halifax's letter expressing Britain's repeated wish for a peaceful solution,
but took no notice, preferring to describe in long tirades his futile endeavours
to reach an understanding with Britain, finally asking the amateur diplomat
for the latter's view on 'that strange island and its strange people' whom he
could not understand.

Dahlerus describes this discussion in his book *The Last Attempt*:

Hitler listened without interrupting, and then suddenly leapt up. He
became very agitated and on edge. He paced up and down, saying,
as if to himself, that Germany would not be beaten . . . He suddenly
stopped in the middle of the room, stood still, and stared aloft. His voice
sounded gruff, and he was behaving quite abnormally for a human being.
He spoke in clipped sentences: 'If war comes, I shall build U-boats,
U-boats, U-boats, U-boats, U-boats.' His voice trailed away, and at the
end, we couldn't follow what he was saying at all. Then he pulled himself
together, raised his voice, and as if he were speaking to a large audience,
shouted: 'I shall build aeroplanes, aeroplanes, aeroplanes, and I'll destroy
my enemies.' He seemed more like a spectre to me then than a real human
being. I had stared at him in surprise, and now turned round to see how
Göring was reacting. But none of this had the slightest impact on him.

That Göring remained unmoved was probably due, initially, to the fact
that this was not the first time he had experienced such outbursts from his
lord and master. Moreover, he may really still have believed that he could
'save the peace' with Dahlerus's help, something which could only happen
if Britain rescinded its assistance pact with Poland. (In fact, Dahlerus flew

to London with an offer from Hitler containing six points, which he could recite by heart. Point 6 went: 'Germany will be bound to defend the British Empire.' He returned again to the British capital at 4 a.m. on 30 August, where the Foreign Office told him that there would not be a second 'Munich', and that they were not going to have the wool pulled over their eyes again by Hitler and Göring.) Göring's undoubted intention not to let a war break out (at any rate, not now) was based on the fact that, even if he believed as strongly as Hitler in the principle of 'there's no such thing as impossible!', the Luftwaffe was still nowhere near adequately equipped, something which he, more than anyone else, knew only too well.

Göring had told the inner circle (it must have been around the time that military service was reintroduced, i.e. 1935, when the Luftwaffe, an already 'open' secret, had officially become the third service in the Wehrmacht, after the Reich army and Reich navy): 'We must thoroughly rearm, so that others fear us, and so that we can achieve our aims without war. If, however, war comes, it must be a lightning war, because if it lasts more than three months, we are done for. The Luftwaffe must prevent that.'

Göring was fully aware where the trouble lay in the Reich – especially what advances civil aviation in Germany had made technically *vis-à-vis* the rest of the world. He knew how much time new developments required to create a powerful Luftwaffe (a lightning war could not be waged purely on bluff, whatever interpretation he gave to that). With these technical guidelines established in the Reich Aviation Ministry, 1934 stood out as the year in which Popp went to Milch and put forward the following: based on his good working relations with the USA, he had very accurate information as to the extent of technical progress in relation to the increasing demands for safety, speed and comfort on commercial aircraft. This had led to the construction of huge aeroplanes which required correspondingly more powerful air-cooled engines – fourteen and eighteen-cylinder double-radial engines with outputs of 1,200 to 1,800 hp were no longer beyond the realms of possibility. He had now received a licencing agreement for the air-cooled, double-radial engine, the 'Twin Wasp' (nominal output 915 hp), and that was with the express approval of the US government, an indication that, in spite of all the gossip, America did not doubt Germany's peaceful intentions in the slightest.

Milch, after first covering himself by conferring with his engineers in the RAM, curtly rejected it. His reasoning was that for military aviation, which was now the major priority, the double-radial engine was quite unsuitable and the capacity of the German aviation industry was, for the time being, far too small to be able to absorb new designs for civil aviation as well. Popp contradicted Milch, reminding him of the time when he, Erhard Milch, as head of Lufthansa, had been the only one in Germany to buy at least a small quantity of Hornet engines from him. Neither the Reich army ministry nor the Reich Transport Ministry, looking after German civil aviation, had shown the slightest interest at that time, although Popp had risked almost 2 million marks on setting up manufacture under licence. 'That was in 1928,' was all Milch said, and stuck to his 'No!', even when Popp went ahead with the purchase of five double-radial engines, and had them tested on the benches at Milbertshofen and delivered to the Technical Section of the RAM. Despite admitting the extraordinary success of their endeavours, the answer was still a firm 'no'.

Two years later, in 1936, Ernst Udet (the same Udet who had written about the BMW IIIa high-altitude engine in 1918 when it had been fitted to his planes in the Richthofen squadron: 'Its only flaw was that it had arrived too late!') took over the Technical Section in the Reich Aviation Ministry. And he was horrified, quite horrified about the 'totally wrong, biased view of the RAM on the question of engines'. He knew Popp well, and he had felt a close affinity with him since 'those long-passed days'. Until 1924 Udet had lived in Munich, where he had his own company, 'Udet Aircraft Manufacture', at Ramersdorf, and he had then become a stunt pilot, travelling from town to town for aerobatic displays. Whenever Popp looked out of his window across to Oberwiesenfeld, his mind always conjured up 'Ernie' as he came shooting down from the sky and picked up a ladies handkerchief lying on a small table with a hook fastened to the outer edge on his Fokker's wing. If the gates on a hangar were open, Ernie would roar through them, and immediately hang in the air as an instantly recognisable spot in the white sky, from which he would finally loop down wildly and, ignoring the runways, come to a halt on the green grass. Encouraged by Göring, he felt like 'going over to America and seeing what was going on there'. At the Curtiss-Wright Works in Buffalo, he discovered the nosedive, which was to have far-reaching consequences. Amongst the most feared aspects of German air warfare in the Second World War was the Ju 87 dive-bomber, which the pilot, guiding the underslung bomb to its target, could bring to a few hundred metres above the ground (depending on the kind of weather, target or anti-aircraft guns) and then gain height again through automatic interceptors to continue normal flying. There was also Udet's famous Jericho device, two sirens fitted to the left and right of the fuselage and driven by a wooden propeller, which spread real terror over the battlefield with their wail, not to mention the whistles fastened to the leading surfaces of the bombs.

This Udet, first made group captain and then head of the Technical Section, had once said to friends, not taking things as seriously as they actually were: 'At times you've got to make a pact with the devil, for aviation's sake, provided he doesn't have you for dinner. . . .' Udet immediately implored Popp to make good the missed licenced opportunity, i.e. the one refused by Milch with Pratt & Whitney. This time the answer of 'too late' came from Popp's lips – Pratt & Whitney did not hang around once the US government had refused to approve the issue of a licence. So how were things going? Well, they were going nowhere. Ordered now to undertake the development of BMW's own double-radial engine, Popp knew only too well what Udet also knew – that it would take five years to put it into production, time which could not be made up if war was really on the agenda. ('As you know, my dear Herr Udet,' Popp wrote on 17 July 1941 to the Luftwaffe Director of Armaments in Berlin, 'if your predecessor in office had complied with my urgent requests to be allowed to develop a double-radial engine, then today's engine, the 801 type, would not only recently have gone into production, but would have done so in 1934! Unfortunately I then had to pursue the development of large water-cooled engines, just like all the other firms, which was a complete waste of effort.')

A year after Udet took office, in 1937, Lindbergh was visiting Germany. He was probably the most famous pilot in the world after crossing the ocean in his 'Spirit of St Louis', and Göring had given instructions to show him everything there was to show. He also visited the Heinkel Works in Marienehe and Rostock, and there, over coffee in Heinkel's garden, Lindbergh, a colonel in the American Air Force and a good friend of Germany's, said to Heinkel: 'Things should never come to an air war between Germany, England and America. Only the Russians would profit from that.' Heinkel then had nothing to hide. He had just fitted a plane with the same BMW VI engine which had helped the Heinkel Blitz He 70 to its speed records in 1933, a plane with space for ten passengers (just as Lufthansa had wanted) and multi-engined for safety reasons. However, that did not mean that it had to be three-engined. Heinkel had rejected this principle with some boldness, and had shown that the middle engine only meant a waste of space – with one engine less, the twin-engined machine remained entirely operational and manoeuvrable in spite of everything. This was the famous He 111, at 345 kph one of the fastest commercial aircraft in the world for its time and class. If Popp was later to claim that everything had been fostered at BMW to serve the development of civil aviation, then it was still undeniable that this airplane could also carry bombs. There was certainly no getting away from the fact that the He 111, when fitted with three machine-gun berths and a full-view cockpit (in 1939, 1,340 He 111s were built for the Luftwaffe), was to become one of the most famous and reliable of German fighter planes.

Popp drew up in his memorandum three precepts which were to apply to any country, including Germany:

1 Only specific rearmament, which is consciously designed for expansionist attacks, is a war crime, and not rearmament for defence.

2 Armaments are only systems which can be used as a comprehensive means of waging war, and not individual elements.

3 Production of armaments during a war does not make a factory into an armaments works. That is determined by what the works produced in peace time.

Two figures reveal what Popp understood by 'peacetime production'. In 1938, Lufthansa could announce 17.7 million kilometres flown on their routes and 5.3 million kilogrammes of mail carried, the largest quantity in its history up to the Second World War. In its scheduled services, it was using the four-engined Focke-Wulf FW 200 and the Ju 90, which, for the first time, had forty seats and was as comfortable as an express train, and which, with a range of between 1,600 and 2,000 kilometres, had a cruising speed of between 350 and 400 kph. Its four air-cooled radial engines, each with an output of 880-hp for cruising and 1,000 hp for take-off, were of the BMW 132 H type, while the Focke-Wulf 200 used four BMW 132 Dcs.

On 10 August 1938 at 19.59 hours, Captain Alfred Henke took off from Staaken, Berlin, in the Focke-Wulf 'Condor' D-ACON on a transatlantic flight, which was officially billed as an attempt on the long-distance record, flying over Newfoundland and the St Lawrence River to Floyd Bennett Aerodrome near New York, and returning to Berlin after 45 hours, at 10.01 hours on 14 August. All the European radio stations and the National Broadcasting Corporation had running reports on the flight, whose take-off had been kept secret. He flew at a height of between 2,000 and 3,000 metres (at that time, there were still no pressurised cabins), and on the outward trip maintained a average speed of 255.499 kph. When the machine landed at Tempelhof, it was pouring down; yet half Berlin had turned out and lined the route the crew would take to Aviation House. This flight resolved the question of 'land or sea planes' over such long stretches of sea, in favour of land planes. At the end of November, Henke took off in the same machine for Tokyo. He covered the 13,844 kilometres in 46 hours and 42 minutes with three stopovers in Basra, Karachi and Hanoi. Time in the air came to 42 hours and 18 minutes.

'We must thoroughly rearm, so that others fear us, and so that we can achieve our aims without war,' Göring had said, 'but if it comes to war, then it must be a lighting war. . . .' When war did break out, or rather, when Hitler wanted it to break out, the Luftwaffe was initially equipped with fighters and Stukas, but not with sufficient bombers which, with their carpet bombing, would play a decisive part in a lengthy war. (The He 111, which Heinkel himself called a reliable, easily-maintained 'worker bee' was unable to reach the fighting in the West and around the Mediterranean due to its limited range and, as late as 1941, had been technologically superceded despite all the development work applied to it and the fitting of more powerful engines. The fact that by 1944, four million man-hours had been spent on it in the design offices, as Heinkel himself declared, trying to increase its range – in vain, as it turned out – showed that there was no suitable replacement for it.)

This basic failing was the central theme in all the measures taken by the Reich Aviation Ministry, as they tried to adapt air forces geared for lightning war (with their limited ranges) and to reverse their inferiority shown in the Battle of Britain into their former uncontested air superiority (which would never be recovered).

Popp's assertion in 1948 was therefore not wild speculation. 'If BMW had then, in 1934, gone ahead with production of the double-radial engine, then there would not have been the serious allegations laid against BMW and me after the outbreak of war. The German air fleet would have been perhaps 50 per cent bigger at the outbreak of war, with a corresponding increase in the number of bombers and fighter-planes, with Britain probably experiencing the same terrible devastation which Germany was later to suffer.' One cannot help feeling that Milch's rejection and inadvertent help to the Allies must have produced an unpleasant feeling in the writer, as it was he who was forced to put this head on the block for failures which were entirely due to Göring and the RAM.

At a time when 'armament' was not yet associated with 'war', Popp's stubborn refusal to step up production of purely military engines, indeed, to give priority to aero-engine manufacture at BMW (as the RAM demanded), led to his removal as head of aero-engine production. In a letter which Udet subsequently wrote to BMW on 17 June 1939 (which was not unlike the first one which he had written to the firm from the front as the leader of the Richthofen squadron in October 1918), he gave 'final technical responsibility *vis-à-vis* the Technical Section' exclusively to Franz Josef Popp, managing director and qualified engineer. This appointment was followed up by the BMW board on 12 October 1939, when it also conferred 'senior technical directorship' and 'full responsibility' in the company on Popp.

This seemed like rehabilitation. However, by September 1939, the engine was nowhere near ready, and Popp wrote in his memorandum:

As a result an increasingly bitter campaign started against BMW and myself because there was no way of complying with the absurd demands made by the Aviation Ministry, either in testing or producing the engine. The (then) overhasty mass production led to unforeseen difficulties, because there was also no way of finding the necessary capacity outside the company. This meant that by no means all the relevant undertakings to the Aviation Ministry could be fulfilled.

Popp's suggestion of 'state-owned factories', which he had already previously put forward to the RAM, corresponded (although he could not have known about it at the time) with the establishment of so-called state-owned 'shadow factories' in Britain. The British aviation industry had refused to undertake anything required of, and wholly subject to the state. Milch rejected Popp's suggestion, but was to return to it in a modified form. This was when, in 1936, Milbertshofen received the instruction from the Reich Aviation Ministry to give up development work on water-cooled engines, and confine itself to producing air-cooled engines. Popp had been proved right. This is what he had long been fighting for, and now it was official. At the same time, the RAM called for 'strict rationalisation of the German firms involved in aero-engine production, as there were always at least two firms competing for the same line of business. For large, water-cooled engines, this meant the firms of Daimler-Benz and Junkers, while air-cooled engines were made by the firms of BMW in Munich and the Brandenburg Motor Works (Bramo) at Spandau in Berlin (previously known as Siemens Engineering Ltd), which produced the air-cooled Bramo 323 Fafnir, while BMW was still building its nine-cylinder radial engine developed from the Hornet licence.

The RAM's concern about producing this engine involved BMW in offering to build a second plant which would leave Milbertshofen as a 'reserve factory' in the event of war. The new factory was to be camouflaged and built underground. Initial thoughts were centred on the Isar meadows, then sites were looked for in the Ebersberg Forest, while consideration was also given to the woods behind Grünwald and near Peißenberg. The choice finally fell on Allacher Wäldchen, which was not too far away from Milbertshofen. In the middle of the hill forest, the halls could be set out 50 metres apart (as stipulated by one condition), and a person was specially employed to come and catalogue (even number) the trees, checking to see they were all still standing once the factory was up.

Beyond the three-metre broad land there was nothing but trees, and the test stations (horseshoe shaped, and not openly arranged as at Milbertshofen) had soundproofing, which was supposedly designed to contain noise within a hundred-metre radius. (However, a Munich doctor by the name of Gillmer was later only too keen to sell his little castle at Karlsfeld, to the north of the site, to BMW precisely because of the noise made by aero-engines on test. It was here that the 'millionaire farmer' Hauser Lenz had had his own drive off the Dachau road built before the turn of the century. It still stands today in all its gingerbread glory, along with its scorch marks in the hallway, which were made not by vandals, but by the charcoal fires on which GIs barbecued their steaks in 1945.)

The Allach Works, which Popp always described as the 'Reich Works' or, at best, the 'extended workbench from Milbertshofen', was used for the time being as a repair shop and then, as planned, for assembling and testing the engines in the BMW 132 K-N series. They were brought to Allach from Works No 1 (Milbertshofen) on low-loaders, where they were run-in and then subjected to several hours of continuous running, before being taken back to Works No 1 where they were reassembled and prepared for delivery. In all, this involved about 600 workers. Until a man called Kries ('Dr Kries, production manager; I'm in charge round here!') appeared at Allach on 3 September 1939 (the war was only three days old) with plans approved by the RAM and issued for production, and met a farmer ploughing his field on the west of the woodland site. He went up to the farmer and said that he could go home because work was going to start on a new plant there as from tomorrow. He did not say that it would involve production and assembly halls, a full dozen heavy-duty test beds, two generator buildings and the usual disparate collection of administration buildings, canteens and so forth, providing a four-fold increase in the size of the 'Old Works' in Allach (as they then came to be known). There was no talk of camps – dormitories, labour camps, concentration-camp huts, and brothels. In fact, the plans did not go much beyond a few hatched-in 'settlements', although it was obvious that men and not ghosts would work in the gigantic halls. All these men, wherever they were taken from (there were 13,115 of them in 1943, and 17,313 a year later), needed a roof over their heads.

The plant in Allacher Wäldchen, founded on 16 October 1936 by BMW PLC and its subsidiary, the BMW Aero-Engine Co. Ltd, was first of all reregistered as the 'Aero-Engine Factory Allach Co. Ltd', whose share capital was soon to be sold to a company based in Berlin and owned by the Reich. This 'Aviation Office Co. Ltd' immediately signed possession over to another subsidiary owned by the Reich, the 'Aviation Establishment Co. Ltd', after striking the old designation off the company register. Heaven only knew how and why all this happened. As it was, the Allach Works, which were then still under construction, were bought back through the subsidiary of BMW AG from this Aviation Establishment Co. Ltd, Berlin-Schöneberg, Am Park 12, in a contract drawn up by the solicitor Dr Walter Neye, (business address Berlin-Charlottenburg), as item No 6 for the year 1941 on the title deed scroll dated 7 November 1941. The purchasing company was none other than the aforementioned Aero-engine Co. Ltd based in Munich. It now combined, as its name suggested, all the aero-engine interests of BMW, having set a purchase price. This was 30 million marks advanced as investment credit by the German Aviation Bank PLC, a sum therefore issued by the Reich but which BMW AG were to pay back by the start of 1945 down to the last penny (something of subsequent importance due to the terms of ownership contested by the Americans). This meant that everything belonged to the company (therefore, to BMW as a public limited company), which also owned the 'Eisenach Aero-Engine Factory Co. Ltd', also founded on 16 October 1936 as another subsidiary – a new aero-engine works set up at Dürrerhof and managed by Max Friz.

The last piece of development work before the war was the most interesting – BMW merged with the 'Brandenburg Motor Works', known as Bramo, at Spandau in Berlin. The merger, preceded by a joint venture agreement in the middle of 1938, was based on sound technical considerations. Urged by the RAM to go over to higher numbers of cylinders, BMW had developed a 14-cylinder double-radial engine, the BMW 139, out of the 132 engine (with which Henke had flown to New York and Tokyo in his Focke-Wulf 'Condor'). At the same time, the Brandenburg Motor Works were working on a 14-cylinder double-radial engine, the Bramo 329. On 30 September 1938, all current engine developments were stopped at both works – to the benefit of an epoch-making new power plant, the BMW 801, for which the RAM had already placed orders for mass-production by the end of December 1939.

There was no question that the merger between Bramo and BMW was in direct contravention of the principle of competition fostered by the RAM, which always entrusted two firms with the same jobs and made them compete against each other. Popp could take the credit for having broken this. The cause of it was provided at a meeting held at Karinhall on 8 July 1938, to which Göring and Udet had invited representatives of the aviation industry. The Reichmarshall, in taking into consideration the forced expansion of the Luftwaffe, had demanded limitations in the types of airframes and engines being developed and produced, explaining that not every firm could build equivalent types in mutual competition. Popp himself described what then happened in a letter to Lucht, engineer-in-chief at the RAM, dated 8 February 1942:

After the meeting, the Reichmarshall spoke to me in the presence of the Director of Armaments, asking me what suggestions I could make about limiting types and concentrating development within the engine industry.

I explained that, right from the beginning, I had had his current ideas in mind, and for this reason had already given up making water-cooled engines, as I felt that the two remaining firms of Junkers and Daimler were perfectly capable of solving all the problems associated with them. In this way, I had prevented the series-production of a third engine in the power-range of the DB 601 and the Jumo 211, which would have been called the BMW 117.

I further explained that there was just enough time to comply with the

Reichmarshall's order with regard to the development of new air-cooled engines. Both companies of BMW and Bramo were involved in developing a modern, 9-cylinder, 14-cylinder and 18-cylinder engine of equal power. If this design was carried through in common, then the type limitation required by the Reichmarshall would be feasible, with a considerable saving in lead time, human resources and enormous development costs. This concentration was bound to have the same technological advantages both in the industrial and military fields.

Popp's pleasure must have been almost tangible when he got his own back on his old adversary, Milch (without actually mentioning him by name), as he continued:

> I further declare that in my opinion the battle cry for necessary competition has been stressed by government offices and this is just the reason for the multiplicity of types which the Reichmarshall has described as intolerable. My view is that a wealth of experience of this type exists both in German airframe and aero-engine manufacture, making such internal competition quite unnecessary to produce high-performance technology. There is only one competition for the German aviation industry which is of any importance and will prove decisive (competition which can give us no greater incentive) – and that is foreign competition!

This led to the Reichmarshall and the Director of Armaments ordering 'the necessary steps to be taken immediately in order to bring about co-operation on air-cooled engines between BMW and Bramo as quickly as possible'.

The Brandenburg Motor Works (Bramo) had only taken over the aero-engine activities of Siemens Engineering Co. Ltd in the summer of 1936. The latter had been reconstituted as Siemens Aero-Engine Production from the electrical business Siemens & Halske three years earlier.

The first trial flights by the Siemens company went right back to 1908, when airships, as well as replicas of the Wright biplanes, were built, but without great success. It was only after 1914 that this branch of the business became important again – with rotary engines for fighter planes, which were designed according to a principle then revolutionising aviation, namely the Gnôme principle. The same experiences which led BMW to produce its high-altitude IIIa engine (rotating pistons are limited in their performance through the centrifugal force of the cylinders rotating around them) had led, by the end of the war, to the high-altitude engine Sh 3 with fixed cylinders. As with BMW, this development had come too late, leaving hundreds of engines to be dismantled. And again, just like BMW, the company was convinced of the importance of radial engines after development had been stopped in the post-war years. ('As we were the only company producing air-cooled engines,' stressed CF von Siemens in 1927 in an internal memo, 'so we were convinced that we should not give it up completely, out of general consideration that Germany would at least remain able to develop this technology.')

Two years later, the head of Siemens & Halske Aero-Engine Works, Herr Becker, held a conversation with the Berlin representative of the Bavarian

Motor Works, Captain von Buttlar, about the possibility and usefulness of co-operation, 'given that in future we would only have air-cooled engines and the Bavarian Motor Works would only have water-cooled engines in their product range'. Herr von Buttlar declared, as was to be expected, that it was too late for this now that his firm had acquired, through its own means, the licence to build the American 'Hornet' engines of 500 hp, and that it would soon be bringing this engine onto the market.

As with BMW, Siemens had stuck with the air-cooled engine throughout the thirties and were still convinced of its virtues in 1936 (even after Bramo had been founded as an independent company). By this time, aero-engines were out of place in the production facilities of the Siemens group (due to the quite personal conviction of Carl-Friedrich von Siemens). He declared to the general manager of Gutehoffnungshütte iron and steel company, Paul Reusch, in September 1936:

> Internal combustion engines do not really belong to our activities. The aero-engines were left over from our development work on electric motors and petrol engines for cars. I never had the intention of remaining in aero-engine manufacture in the long term, because, as I have said, it does not belong to our activities. Due to rearmament, we have been compelled by the Aviation Ministry to expand this production, which we have done, to a not inconsiderable extent. Junkers, Daimler and BMW are so much further ahead. Demands from the Aviation Ministry have risen so much that I no longer feel bound to invest further sums in this branch which is not in our line of business. Furthermore, it is my view that it is devoid of any long-term, economic prospects. As a result, I have hived off the aero-engine factory into a separate company, the Brandenburg Motor Works, in which the Reich will also make further investments. In any case, certain difficulties arose here, because the Aviation Ministry was making ever greater demands for expansion.

Amongst these difficulties was the construction of the so-called 'Forest Works', which the RAM was demanding of the armaments industry. For all his struggling, Siemens could not prevent such a 'Forest Works' going up in 1937, this being at Basdorf in the Marches, north of Berlin, between Oranienburg and Bernau, where an area of forest almost 300,000 square metres was acquired. Here, as happened at Allach near Munich for Milbertshofen, was where the 'extended workbench' for the Spandau Works was set up, which, after initial engine assembly, let Basdorf carry out all the subsequent processes such as running-in, reassembling and final testing.

So this is how things stood when the BMW Aero-Engine Co. Ltd and the Brandenburg Motor Works Co. Ltd announced at the end of 1938 that they had decided to merge their development work on air-cooled engines with immediate effect and equal participation, which in practice amounted to a division of responsibilities as both development facilities in Munich and Spandau were kept fully operational. Yet it was only two months later that a common marketing company, the Aero Motor Export Co. Ltd was founded.

Already, by the beginning of January, Udet had ordered (because the Reich had given him the means) the first stage of expansion at Zühlsdorf. Still allocated to the Brandenburg Motor Works, the name of Zühlsdorf was mentioned for the first time. (Zühlsdorf, whose aero-engine works, legally linked to the Basdorf works directly opposite, would later be run under the name of 'Niederbarnim Aero-Engine Works Co. Ltd', producing a monthly output of 300 large engines from two shifts of 10 hours.) For the time being (January 1939), only 150 engines of the Bramo 323 type were planned, in conjunction with the Spandau works, yet the secretary (the letter must have been dictated and typed up afterwards) inserted the words 'or successor' after 'Bramo 323'.

At the end of September 1939, with the war already a month old, the 'Bramo shares still owned by the Siemens group' changed hands 'as they had continuously urged us to do' – as Popp was later to remind the RAM in a historical survey, which mentioned the sales price of 12 million marks paid by BMW to acquire them.

'We undertook this purchase with a heavy heart. . .' Popp continued. And went on to assure them that the Bavarian Motor Works had never conducted a policy of expansion by buying up other companies in all the twenty-five years since he had founded and subsequently managed it. He had always represented the viewpoint that he was only interested in the 'flesh of our flesh and blood of our blood'. 'When we acquired the Eisenach car factory 13 years ago and merged with the Bramo aero-engine factory 2 years back, it was only because of exceptional circumstances, which more or less forced us into it.'

As Popp was putting these words to paper, he had good reason to clarify 'some other misunderstandings in another area'. These involved the confusion caused by the interlinking parts of the company, and the high-handedness of chief engineers at the associated works. Popp was therefore once again spending time on improving the BMW group. He wrote:

> The parent company is BMW AG, having three subsidiaries which are the Aero-Engine Cos Ltd in Munich, Eisenach and Spandau. These three subsidiaries are wholly owned by BMW AG. Thus there is no state interest in any of them. The founding of the limited companies was only done as a cover, otherwise there would be no limited companies. The public limited company (the AG) would continue to run aero-engine production under the name of BMW AG, as it had always done. In practice, then, the three limited companies are only of importance for company law. Internally, there is only one company, and that is BMW AG, whose three limited companies are, in practice, only sub-divisions, just like car manufacture, motorcycle manufacture and military equipment manufacture. As has happened with almost all companies in the past few years, we have merged the AG with the three subsidiaries through a holding contract, thereby consolidating all the accountancy work.
>
> And this is not all. So as to provide united development not only for human, but for spatial resources, engine development has been concentrated in Munich and equipment development in Spandau. In this way we are only establishing the same condition which exists with Daimler,

Junkers and every other company which is concentrating development and top management in one place, something that is so self-evident, it needs no further explanation.

Popp then declared frankly that the top management for the whole company and, by extension, the subsidiaries of the AG would be the board of the AG. 'As I am the managing director and chairman of the board of the AG and, at the same time, chairman of the directors in the three subsidiaries, I am, in both a legal and actual sense, the first representative for our company to the outside world. Internally, I have immediate control of all the technical departments, and all technical managers are therefore subordinate to me.' This was a legal position which was underlined by that order pronounced on 17 June 1939 from the Director of Armaments to the Privy Councillor von Stauss as the chairman of the BMW supervisory board, 'whereby managing director Popp exclusively has the final technical responsibility *vis-à-vis* the Technical Section'.

When 'full responsibility' was transferred to Popp, he took over a monstrous organisation running from the works beside the Julius Tower in Spandau (Bramo), with its branches at Zühlsdorf and Basdorf, through the old vehicle factory at Eisenach, and Dürrerhof, on to BMW at 76 Lerchenau Street, Milbertshofen, and out into the Allach Forest with its hidden 'shadow factories' – and soon all those outposts, bases and repair shops in Nazi-occupied Europe. These started in Vienna, going through Paris, Bitschweiler and St Dié in Alsace, Lodz in Poland, then called Litzmannstadt, and on to Denmark, Norway, etc. Their job was 'provisions', not to mention storage operations, which were set up, quicker than expected, in Immenstadt, Kempten, Kaufbeuren, Landshut, Stefanskirchen, Bruckmühl and Kolbermoor in Upper Bavaria. They all carried the name of BMW, Bavarian Motor Works, and whether they were producing cylinder liners, crankshafts, valves, oil coolers, exhaust systems, engine cowlings, oil pumps, mixture governors, propeller adjustment fittings or normal, everyday, standard parts, up to complete aero-engines and in-house machine tools, all of them were working not for peace, but for war; not for Popp's war or for Germany's, but for Hitler's.

Udet's letter, which led to Popp's 'full responsibility', was destroyed in the flames of the Second World War and today is only known by its date. It must have contained something of the hope that he, along with men like Popp, could succeed in keeping control of the huge organisational apparatus of his Technical Section in the face of imminent events (which, everyone knew, would not suit Udet at all).

Two years later, when the war against Russia had not been won in eight weeks, as Hitler had expected, Udet, burdened with the guilt that Göring and Milch had put on him for the failure of the German aviation industry, broke down at work and shot himself. 'At times you've got to make a pact with the devil, for aviation's sake, provided he doesn't have you for dinner. . . .' Now Udet had been had for dinner, and the day was recorded: 17 December 1941. Hitler ordered a state funeral.

The next month, in January 1942, Popp was 'relieved of his position of trust' by Milch. The official reason was lack of foresight and operational incompetence, 'even on the question of transferring motorcycle production from Munich to Eisenach', as referred to in a subsequent board meeting which dealt with Popp's case. But this was just the tip of the iceberg. An 'inventory of the problems', which Fritz Hille, Popp's successor, read out at that meeting, went right back to 1933 and German rearmament – 'when the Bavarian Motor Works were predestined to remain the leading firm in the field of aero-engine production, both in respect of liquid-cooled, as well as air-cooled, engines'. This was correctly acknowledged as the root of the quarrels between Milch and Popp, but it somehow all sounded different from Hille's point of view.

As a result, the firms of Daimler-Benz and Junkers gained a lead in the area of liquid-cooled engines, while BMW fell behind, since the latter was principally involved with air-cooled engines. Based on its licencing agreement with Pratt & Whitney, it was confident of being able to make use of the progress made by this firm. It had then proved impossible to sustain further development through the company's own resources and endeavours, firstly because the development facilities at BMW were far too small, and secondly because there was a lack of sufficient experience and knowledge. So time had been wasted in trying to institute in-house development work, which, to date, had proved impossible to catch up on. Even Max Friz's replacement as head of aero-engine development in Munich (this was in 1937!) by a director called Sachse had not altered anything, nor had the merger with Bramo, which had nothing at all to do with commercial considerations or removing a competitor, but was designed to concentrate both companies' resources in rationalised operations for standardised production. This should all have had a positive effect on manufacture, something which Popp failed to achieve, especially as it led to the construction and commissioning of the Allach works right in the middle of war, with all the difficulties associated with that, while Daimler-Benz and Junkers were able to set up mass-production works in good time before the outbreak of war thanks to their timely development successes.

Was that the case? Certainly, if you consider that the 'inventory of problems' was compiled somewhat biasedly (i.e. without Popp), and that no effort was spared to view every event (exclusively) from Milch's point of view.

Things looked somewhat different from Popp's point of view. In replying to the criticism that in the past few years BMW engineers working in design had not 'been invested with glory' (in contrast to the successes of companies building liquid-cooled engines), he pointed out to Lucht, engineer-in-chief at the RAM, the unfairness of this charge. He wrote to him on 1 August 1940, saying:

As you know, we began designing 12-cylinder, liquid-cooled engines in 1929–30, while we only received instructions to design a double-radial engine in 1936. We then spent four years working on the engine. If our design capabilities are to be judged in this way, then the question needs to be asked as to how far design on the liquid-cooled engines had got after four years, i.e. in 1933–34. I feel able to say that after four years development work, the liquid-cooled engines were nothing like ready for production, while we are now already mass-producing the air-cooled engines.

That had been Popp's argument up to now.

It would be advisable to look at the other point of view: whether it was desirable to keep the leadership and command structure in the company firmly in BMW AG's hands. And that was now increasingly being put in doubt.

As early as spring 1941, Udet (as reported by Hille in his 'inventory') had seen fit to appoint Werner, a board member at Auto Union and member of the Industrial Council, to the task of investigating BMW production. BMW had obtained a probationary period with respect to this, although there had already been threats of appointing a commissioner.

Was that right? It was, but it was a longer story than that, one which needs to be told if we are to understand its conclusion. As he explained in a letter to Popp on 15 February 1941, Udet had been drawn into a dispute – as a referee – which, within the company, began adversely to affect all air force rearmament. It involved the 800 and 801 aero-engines, which had both entered the design stage at the end of 1938. One of them was being designed by Bramo in Spandau as a single-radial engine, and the other by BMW in Munich as a double-radial engine. The problem now arose over the failure to harmonise their individual components, a situation which Popp remained unaware of and which was now making series production of the 800 engine doubtful for April 1942 (it had long been expected at the front). Without informing Spandau, or even the RAM, Popp had consequently, with his usual arrogance, entrusted Max Friz at Eisenach with the design of a simplified, 9-cylinder radial engine to be built from BMW 801 parts, and he now presented this design to the RAM as ready for production (as a replacement to the highly expensive 800 engine which would never go beyond the pre-production stage).

The report from the department LC 3 of the Reich Aviation Ministry stated:

> The fact that company management, without even speaking to the appropriate men in the development departments at Spandau and Munich, wanted to force the Section into a decision to cancel work on an almost fully developed engine, only to bring an engine still at the design stage into production within the available time by April 1942, can only be described as criminally negligent.

As a result, there was nothing left for Udet to do as Director of Armaments (following the dismissal of the works manager Wolff in Spandau and the immediate transfer of the chief designer there, Bruckmann, to the RAM), other than to arrange a 'non-partisan and factual examination of the feasibility for redesigning a simplified 800 engine'. As he stated in his letter to Popp, this had resulted in 'the complete inability to comply with the lead times as well as the technical requirements made in the initial proposals'. He went on to say in the letter: 'I believe that I have always been loyal and especially co-operative towards you, based on our acquaintance over the years. I found it all the more displeasing that, in a letter last December to Herr Wolff, you should take the liberty of criticising my measures and how I have handled industrial policy, something I would not have expected considering our mutual relationship.' (Popp had openly told Wolff, who immediately revealed these comments to the RAM upon his dismissal, that he, Popp, had found the RAM's entire development policy to have been misguided over many years, especially the fact that the leading firms developing aero-engine production were repeatedly given the same work running in parallel. Taking a wholly objective view of any new product from German aero-engine factories over the last seven years, it would have to be admitted that, with the right organisation, this could all have been achieved in much less time, with far fewer men and much less money.)

'My dear Herr Popp,' Udet now replied, 'if anyone has taken risks over the unification of our air force armaments, it has been me. To a considerable extent, I had your interests in mind, too. Certain product lines must run in parallel, and you realise better than I do the advantages of healthy competition.' He went on to say that the enquiry into the 801 matter had led him in the last few days to the worrying conclusion that 'almost all your engineering colleagues, in Spandau and in Munich, get on well with each other, but do not feel they are colleagues enjoying your closest confidence, but simply employees of your board. They do know my management principle and would not hold it against me if I took the liberty of bringing your attention expressly to this point.' He concluded: 'The responsibility entrusted to me now makes it vital that I consider very carefully, from the present supply situation, what measures must be taken by the Section to improve the position in the short term, and rectify matters.'

It was clear that relations between Udet and Popp were not what they once were. And when an old friend of Udet's, Dr Ammann, employed at BMW's aero-engine plant in Munich, was asked by Udet to give him some inside information as to who 'was behind Herr P. in this whole business', the deep sense of insecurity which had taken hold of both men became clear. (Udet wanted to know what was what, and discovered that Popp himself ruled the roost, because he genuinely believed that he could judge everything much better than the people actually responsible, whom he regarded as mere pawns.) 'The real reason for these difficulties,' wrote Ammann to his 'dear Udet', 'was that Herr P. had the impression that he could judge all these things with complete expertise and authority, whether they were development matters or the production planning department inside the company or the Section.'

Anyone who had ever had anything to do with Popp and knew him only slightly could confirm this. The fact that Udet now had to get information 'behind people's backs' (this man who loathed intrigue), did not conjure up the image of the man whom Popp had trusted and still trusted now (despite the fact that relations were rather strained between them). This was shown when he openly revealed his annoyance to Udet with the complaint that 'a very unpleasant situation could arise through the intrusion of personal and misguided points of view on the part of my subordinates at BMW and with the misinformation these gentlemen propagate'.

It was another document which proved to be the straw that broke the camel's back – Popp's refusal of Milch's categoric requirement that the car test department should immediately be turned over to aero-engine production and that motorcycle production should be transferred from Milbertshofen to Eisenach. 'I refused this,' Popp wrote later, 'because it was obvious to me what the outcome of the war would be, and car and motorcycle production guaranteed the only hope of saving BMW after the war.' But could he really believe this? It was, admittedly, more than just a defensive statement directed at the Allies. A captain of industry like himself could not fail to know that the Reich, as things stood then, was neither willing nor capable of granting dispensations. Certainly, BMW was a case in its own right, and had always been so – and if that is what Popp wanted to prove, then he failed to fully understand his counterpart; a man who was determined to keep a tighter rein on his own Technical Section, where, for example, department LC II 2 had stopped work for three years on engines which the neighbouring department LC II 1 (aircraft development) needed for a new aircraft under construction. If Milch did not act now and 'pull out all the stops', then his credibility would be lost for ever.

Remarks he made after the Popp affair confirmed the worst to him. 'We do not say no, but rather no, then yes, then no, then yes. Then we ban it altogether. People do it all the same. That is twice as bad; first we order something stupid to be done, and then we don't carry out the order.' Hille, an ambitious man, who was acceptable to the powers that be and who had admittedly, as Popp's successor, always put up with this, was also more amenable to Milch and his demands than to his boss. After the high-level reorganisation carried out at BMW on 16 October 1940, Popp was made responsible for 'ensuring general co-ordination of the engineering interests in the overall company'.

Popp might well have wondered what that all meant. Well, what did it all mean? It was pretty unlikely that someone who had shown the cunning he had could play tricks on the war economy and (either out of spite or injured pride) get away with showing to 'those up there' what was appropriate and what was not. No one could deny the fact that the command economy, which the war, like every war, had demanded, was only reasonable, if not essential. What it should not do is stifle individual initiative, as nothing could be done without that.

Did not the people up there know that? Hille did not doubt it for a moment. The Reich gave financial support, the private sector was not abolished, and BMW had not been nationalised. Even an otherwise fastidious officialdom had understood that and was open to discussion.

Immediately after the outbreak of war, when the economic council for the motor vehicle industry forbade all car manufacturers from selling and delivering motor vehicles, dispensations from the OKH (Army High Command) enabled Eisenach to sell around a thousand vehicles of the 321 and 326 models to people who had the so-called 'red corner' (special driving licence) on their number-plates. People turned a blind eye – if spare parts, which would otherwise have rusted away, produced a car, then all right, it would have to run.

At Milbertshofen, the R 75, developed as an off-road cycle with drive to the side-car wheel and eight forward and two reverse gears, could not be built quickly enough, while Eisenach, where the lines were still running, looked after the 1,470 jeeps required by the Wehrmacht. But for how much longer? Would they perhaps carry on running, without stopping, straight into peace? Wait a bit, be patient, but always be on your toes! When work was over on the jeeps, when defective aero-engines in need of repair had had their time at Eisenach, and when engine cowlings were built instead of car bodies, then any car production, even as a side-show, was utopia, and only the development work (which went on at Munich in the strictest secrecy) needed to guarantee successors to the 'large' BMW 335, was of some comfort to the initiated. In 1939 Fiedler had designed the 332, a four-door saloon with low-slung, rear mudguards, a steering-column gear lever, and 'self-supporting' body with three side windows. Somewhat later, with the body designer Peter Szimanowski, he produced that streamlined '337' which was fitted with air-channelling ducts under the front wings for extra wind deflection (just like the BMW hard-top racing cars which had won at Le Mans). Some consolation, to which an event happening in the middle of the war (which motor sport and BMW helped to arrange and make hearts beat faster) also contributed.

The lightning campaign against Norway had just ended (and with it, the fear that Swedish iron ore supplies to the Reich would undergo cut-backs which would be disastrous for Germany), when the Mille Miglia in Brescia again invited Italian, French and German cars to take part in peaceful competition. What a ray of sunshine! A new Mille Miglia (the last one had been in 1938) right now, in the middle of the war! The circular route was no longer the old one; it was now faster and more dangerous, made up of ten laps of a single section closed to traffic and running for 165 kilometres from Brescia, Cremona, Mantua, then back to Brescia. BMW sent two hard-top and three open sports cars over the Brenner Pass (under their own steam, which in itself prompted admiration). The company had had particularly light, streamlined bodies built for both versions, made from a special alloy of aluminium and magnesium at the Italian bodyworks of Touring, who also worked for Alfa. With their light weight (650 kg; the body only weighed 42 kg) and their increased engine output (5,500 rpm produced 135 hp), the word immediately went out, no sooner had they reached Brescia, that BMW had as good as won the 1,000 miles in Munich.

What happened then took everyone's breath away. Huschke von Hanstein, with Bäumer, in one saloon, and Count Lurani and Cortese in the other saloon took the lead right from the start. When they went through Cremona, they were measured at 180 kph, von Hanstein achieving the fastest lap at 174.102

kph (the fastest Alfa covering it at 164.844 kph), and it was only with difficulty that the large, French three-litre supercharged Delange cars (driven by Italians, as France was then at war with Germany) managed to make a stand against the BMW cars. With an average speed of 166.723 kph, von Hanstein/Bäumer were overall winners in all classes, and when one considered that the Alfas raced in a higher class than the BMW sports cars, then the victory was overwhelming (the team prize was also won). The next day, 29 April 1940, Popp received the following telegram from Mercedes-Benz: 'My dear Herr Popp! Allow me to offer you my sincerest congratulations on the supreme victory won yesterday in Brescia by your cars against the fiercest foreign competition. You and the whole German motor industry can be proud of this brilliant result. Best regards and Heil Hitler! Yours, Dr Kissel.'

It was pointless to dwell on this pride. Just reading the quantities (and Popp knew them well!) which BMW was still allowed to deliver in the autumn of 1940, after the fall of France, read almost like an obituary:

321 saloons – 47	326 convertibles – 17
321 convertibles – 29	327 convertibles – 28
326 saloons – 60	335 convertibles – 6

Together with 14 cars for the fleet, this produced an overall figure of only 201 cars, even if the successes which the R 75 achieved on all fronts as the standard-issue motorcycle to the Wehrmacht, prevented the good old name from falling into oblivion. What would be left, once the war was over? The mere act of contemplating peace then could have cost someone his head.

In spite of this, Popp persisted in his refusal to give up vehicle production and, as Milch had demanded, to transfer 1,000 men from all sections of the company to aero-engine production. A letter to this effect, which Popp had sent to Berlin unknown to Hille, dropped (to use military jargon) a bombshell. Heinrich Krafft von Dellmensingen, head of the legal department at BMW, described to me the occasion he had found himself with Hille.

'The telephone rang. Hille picked it up. It was Milch on the line. He was shouting so loudly that Hille, even if he had been able to hide his consternation, was quite unable to stop anyone overhearing the curses. "That Popp must go!" Milch was shouting in Berlin. Perhaps Hille was not too concerned that I overheard everything, that I could say it was not he who had brought about Popp's downfall, so that he could become his successor. For that is what he had now become. "Have you seen this letter?" Milch asked. "No" answered Hille, "for some peculiar reason, I haven't!" He genuinely had not. Popp had once again acted alone, as was his wont, regarding the Technical Section as a sub-division of BMW. Yes, that was it.'

That was that – Milch now had an easy job. Using a decree from Hitler outlawing any planning of future peace activities and threatening the severest punishment for any such involvement, he now accused Popp of sabotage, even threatening him with imprisonment in a concentration camp (going as far as to mention which concentration camp – Tilsit). But Dr von Stauss, in his capacity as supervisory board chairman, stepped in to protect Popp.

Popp could not be persuaded to 'turn his talents' to another branch of the economy or industry, or anything else on the home front, so he went into retirement. His pension was not ungenerous. Yet he stayed in his country house at Buchenbichl in Untergrainau as if he were sitting on a powder-keg – the threat of investigation by the military police, initiated by Milch, continued to hang over him without any charges being brought against him. This was almost part of the general madness which had broken out during the death-throes of the Nazi state, with the man who had made BMW into BMW attributing no special importance to the whole affair.

Incidentally, looking coldly at the situation on the board, the backlog in engine deliveries was nowhere near as great as the RAM would have people believe when they claimed this was the real reason for sending Popp into the wilderness. Out of the approximate total of 4,000 engines to be delivered, the company was only in arrears by 100, or throughout the 'BMW circle', including Spandau, by 166 engines. This corresponded to about one week's production. If one considered that in Munich alone, 1,400 skilled workers had had to join the front, that machines, tools and special plant of vital urgency had been delivered late, that production schedules were constantly being altered, and that any attempt at planning development and mass production had no chance of being maintained, then it was all a fuss about nothing. If the customer were now to hold this against the works (namely, against Popp, although any mention of him was now forbidden), then there were no reasonable grounds for them to do so.

Yet the order to lay the blame on Popp seemed to have gone out because a few leading technicians (as was admittedly the case in other German firms) were subjected to military police investigations because of delays in production. And that was not all. Due to a minor mistake committed by a development engineer, the RAM had threatened the management and the whole supervisory board of BMW with withholding their profit percentage fee. A letter to this effect was held back by the Ministry at the last minute, after the board had explained that all orders involving development work had been agreed with the Section. If any guilt had to be apportioned at all, then it would only apply to Messrs Popp and Sachse, as the former had been entrusted with overall technical responsibility with respect to the Reich Aviation Ministry, and Herr Sachse (who had been dismissed in the meantime) special responsibility for the 801 engine.

It was inevitable that Herr von Stauss, the supervisory board chairman, and someone who certainly did not like such language, should take note of this and other business when he opened that supervisory board meeting which hinted at establishing a truce. This was at 12.30 p.m. on 29 July 1942, held in conjunction with the ordinary general meeting in the conference room at the Munich branch of the Deutsche Bank. Amongst others sending their excuses were Kissel and Popp, who had been invited pro forma so that they could answer any possible criticisms. This was now unnecessary. The assembled heard that the size of the workforce at BMW (without the partially state-owned plant at Zühlsdorf/Niederbarnim) had increased from 35,700 on 31 March 1942 to 37,600 by the end of June 1942 (not including the company employees now recruited by the Wehrmacht). In Alsace the 'Bischwiller Foundry and Engineering Factory' granted to the Bavarian Motor Works by the head of the civil administration at Strasbourg had been legally acquired. This was situated at the entrance to the Thur Valley at the foot of the Upper Vosges, and dated back to Popp's time. Its acquisition would now solve the considerable bottle-neck in tool and equipment manufacture for the company's own workshops.

The company's total turnover in the second quarter of 1942 amounted to around 122 million RM, 40 million RM higher than the first quarter, and 32 million RM above the annual average of 1941.

The picture from all this was of a 'company with excellent investment and cash-flow', which corresponded with the figures given by the Trust report. There was no mention in it of any serious complaints, and nothing was said of the contribution made by Polish, Russian and French prisoners-of-war to the proceeds, or whether they were included in the overall workforce figure. In fact, they were entered statistically as 'workforce'. Lists still intact show that for Allach alone, the figures as at 1 October 1943 (with figures in brackets as at 1 October 1944) were: workers from the East and Russian prisoner-of-war – 865 (1,340); SS prisoners – 490 (700); concentration camp inmates – 1,480 (5,500). All were then entered as 'wage earners', being paid at an hourly rate of 0.88 RM for semi-skilled workers, 1.10 RM for skilled workers, and 1.30 RM for piece-rate workers. This was admittedly only paid to the wage earners if they were foreign workers. Concentration camp inmates and SS prisoners did not see a penny. The respective offices collected the money in their sole capacity of supervision and 'care', in strict division from any works responsibility (not only at BMW, but throughout the Reich).

There was also no mention of the fact that the transfer of motorcycle production (which Popp had rejected) had gone ahead from Munich to Eisenach – 'in accordance with plans', to use an expression as befitted Field Marshal Erhard Milch, now the real master of the BMW house. As Schleicher had also voted against the transfer and, as Hille stated, had started plotting dangerously (the normally very reticent man had publicly said: 'But that is madness!'), he was forbidden entry to the works for nine months from 13 April 1942, so as to 'temporarily annul his major managerial powers', as Schleicher noted in his diary.

What were these 'major managerial powers' based on? Presumably on fear of Schleicher's unwavering way of continuing to pursue technical developments which the war had stopped, even when this was forbidden. While Popp was in charge, he had become skilled at this and, in order not to rely solely on motor sport, had secretly used budget funds for a 3.5-litre car design, which Alexander von Falkenhausen had planned brilliantly. It was to be the 6-cylinder sports car whose engine, fitted with an aluminium block and two overhead camshafts, only weighed 140 kilogrammes, and, following initial test results of 120 hp at 6,000 rpm, was ready for series production. If it was more or less an open secret that this '318' engine existed (along with secret work on the 332 and 337, whose 31 prototypes just could not be swept under the carpet), then further secret projects could at best be stopped by Schleicher's temporary exclusion.

So Schleicher went off. A few days later, Hitler spoke in the Reichstag. A secret status report from the SS security service (no 279 of the 27 April 1942) refers to this, stating: 'The Führer left a strong impression when he asserted that it was the battleground in Eastern Europe which would decide the outcome of the war and, furthermore, that it had been decided last winter.' Although both assertions contradicted each other (one acting as a prophecy, and the other as an established fact), Hitler was right. History was to validate the assertion that this war had already been decided 'last winter' (as Hitler had said, although the result was not for, but against, Germany), namely in 1941 near Moscow, and not just 1942–43 at Stalingrad. Stalingrad was only necessary as a portent to show the entire world the full extent of Germany's defeat, which Franz Halder, after his dismissal as Army Chief of General Staff, attributed to Hitler's 'pathological over-estimation of his own power and criminal under-estimation of his enemy's'.

The engineer Alexander von Falkenhausen might also have had an inkling of this, when he was detrained at Kharkov station at the end of August 1942. Now freed from the uncertainty as to whether he would get there or not (partisan attacks, ripped up tracks, train derailments and the like had cast some doubt), he wheeled his motorcycle and side-car, an R 75 which he had designed himself, out of the railway carriage, checked to see that there was no damage, and joined the other vehicles in the convoy to which he was assigned. This was a group of civilians which the OKH (Army High Command) had invited to acquaint themselves with conditions at, or just behind, the front. These conditions involved recurring shortages in vehicles, jeeps, and motorcycles, which industry could not fully explain. Engineers from Opel and Steyr, people from Bosch and the accessory industry, designers like Falkenhausen, to whom a man from BMW after-sales service had been assigned, had started out a week previously on the journey from Berlin, to sort the matter out quickly. The convoy was led by a major (his Knight's Cross showed that he had had experience on the front) who now flagged everyone down, unfolded his card, and said: 'We have reached our departure point. Our destinations are determined by two positions which, when we left Berlin, must have seemed uncertain. Yesterday, units of the 6th Army reached the Volga north of Stalingrad; this means that the route upstream is now open to Moscow. And for three days now, the swastika has been flying on Mount Elbrus, the highest peak in the Caucasus.'

Then the the small contingent set off, shrouded in clouds of dust, like all the troop columns in front of them, which had moved into the great arc formed by the Don and from which they were never to return. Soon there were no more firm roads, no trees, not even bushes to offer shade. The sun blazed down from the sky, the tyres started to gleam. Here and there were villages behind small hillocks, following a small river-valley which ran steadily from north to south. Most of them were empty, but houses had not been destroyed. Their inhabitants had followed the retreating troops of the Red Army with their cattle.

Forty years later, Falkenhausen was to recall this journey, which was to prove the strangest in his life: '. . . we would follow the daily progress of the front, spending the night in tents on the steppe. . . We crossed the Don and moved on towards Stalingrad, calling upon the field workshops which had to work in the most primitive conditions directly behind the front line. There we scrutinised the machines in detail, and asked after the troops' experiences. My assumption was right. The machines broke down in the bucket-loads of liquid mud which flowed over the engine and were sucked into the low-lying air filter. The mud got into the engine. There was often no oil left in the sump; only something that looked like sand. And the same happened to the front forks, which at that time had no rubber sleeves for protection. The reality of it was that in bad weather on the short section from detrainment (Kharkov) to the front (about 200 kilometres), the machines had already had it, and were no longer operational. Not a single person brought them back. The field workshops had absolutely no spare parts, while there was a huge parts store in Kharkov which never issued any. The difference between the privates out there at the front and those back at base was glaringly obvious. The latter were die-hard bureaucrats, while the troops were trying to make one machine work out of ten broken down machines. We then got as far as Seti (20 kilometres from Stalingrad, as it was then called). Although we thought it would be a push-over to take Stalingrad, we needn't have bothered. The Volga had already been reached! And from there we could have crossed the Kalmyk steppe into the Caucasus, or at least up to them. Apart from punctures, there were no problems. . . The front in the Caucasus ran along the Terek. From there we went back through Rostov, along the Sea of Azov and were entrained at Mariupol.

'The new high-mounted air filter, screwed onto the tank, worked perfectly on my machine. But the improvements (despite working day and night on them, and immediately changing the series) had next to no effect for Russia. Nothing was the same after Stalingrad.

'All the machines sent to the East went missing; at least, nobody heard of them again. But we had good reports from Africa. The new R 75 acquitted itself admirably in the desert. But much worse than the dust was liquid mud. I remember one day in the rain – it was terrible.

'The clay was so thick that the wheels got stuck against the mudguards. For a motorcyclist, that could have been quite dangerous. You just couldn't let yourself get left behind. We were civilians without identity cards. Anyone getting detached from the group would be put on the spot by the field police. And there was no firm front on the steppe. Only scouting parties. You never knew what was happening.'

'And I will break the pride of your power, and I will make your heaven as iron and your earth as brass.' So says the third Book of Moses 26:19. Not even a man like Popp could have predicted the force with which this would happen, now that Germany was to discover the dark meaning of these words for itself as it entered its third year of war. With his knowledge of America, Popp had often warned about the latter's limitless reserves. Yet they were to surprise even this man who, from his exile, had only one thing on his mind – that BMW should survive the war.

The events of the war had been played out at some distance from the homeland. Now, after Hitler's declaration of war on America, they moved nearer. While the British attacked at night, carpet bombing not only industrial installations but also residential areas, the American bomber groups appeared by day. Town after town was engulfed by them. In 1942, 41,400 tons of high explosive had fallen on the Reich; in 1943, this had increased five-fold to 206,000 tons. In 1944, 1,202,000 tons of incendiary, high-explosive cluster bombs had fallen, destroying households, offices and industrial plants, turning human beings into living torches and making those who did escape with their lives homeless.

Munich suffered its first attack on the night of 4 June 1940. It passed off lightly. Only in the autumn of 1942, when high-explosive, incendiary and cluster bombs rained down over Munich, causing the deaths of 143, did fear come to the fore. The fate of other German towns could no longer be dismissed, nor could the ever worsening news from the Eastern front, from Italy, and from the Mediterranean area. On 25 May 1943, Goebbels noted in his diary:

> The night attack by the British on Dortmund was totally devastating, probably the heaviest meted out on a German city till now. The reports coming from Dortmund are atrocious. . .Industrial and armaments installations have also been heavily hit. . .There are between 80,000 and 100,000 homeless. . .The population in the West is slowly becoming ground down. . .29 July: Last night the heaviest attack yet took place on Hamburg. . .involving 800 to 1,000 bombers. . . [Gauleiter] Kaufmann gave me an initial report. . . he spoke of a catastrophe that would seem to be of unimaginable proportions. We were here confronted by the destruction of a city of one million people which has probably never happened before in history. . . He (Kaufmann) spoke of around 800,000 homeless wandering around the streets shocked and dazed. . . .

It was only a question of time before it was the turn of Munich, as the 'capital of the movement', and BMW.

At the beginning of the war, giant camouflage nets had been stretched across parts of the town, such as the Prince Regent Street near the House of German Art (as if the purpose of the exercise was to show what needed to be protected and what did not). The nets were covered with artificial green foliage. But it was still easy to make out BMW from the air – paintings on the roofs on the production halls were meant to give the impression of suburban houses; nothing but tiny, quaint houses inside little green gardens, with red brick roofs, surrounded by trees which never changed colour or lost their leaves. Their aim was described in a confidential 'US report on strategic air offensive':

The Works were situated in Oberwiesenfeld, a suburb of Munich in the northern part of the city. They stretch over a rectangular area of 92 acres. In all there are 52 buildings covering a surface of 1,156,000 square feet. Around 50 per cent of the buildings are used for assembly, whose interruption would greatly or wholly endanger production. The buildings are made of different materials – some are made of wood and brick, others of concrete and steel. The plant has a railway siding and a highway. There is an adjoining airport. Electricity is taken from conventional sources in Munich. No power is produced in the plant itself.

On the Allach Works, it says:

It lies in Allach, a small suburb north-west of Munich. It covers an almost square area of 235 acres. The north-eastern corner is cut off by a highway, which gives the complex the impression of having five sides. There are 29 buildings in all, covering a surface of 1,500,000 square feet. The buildings are variously laid out, most of them being made of concrete and steel. There is a very large 'bomb-proof' bunker-like building for engines. . . The plant is connected with a siding and a road. Electricity is taken from sources in Munich.

This shows that cool-headed fascination with the actual object (human beings are not visible to bomber pilots) was the rule of the day in the battle of 'technology against technology'. Did the 29 buildings with 1,500,000 square feet covered by machines and the engines produced by these machines gaze fearfully at a sky that would bring ruin? No, they did not; it was people, not robots made of iron and steel, who were running below in fear of their lives. The whole aim was to destroy these people, to make it impossible for them to continue working on weapons which were in turn designed to destroy those who were releasing bombs from up above! Because this was the whole aim, it was inconsequential whether these people were called Popp or Hille, whether they sat in the boardroom or were conscripted workers – who came from all over the world and were crammed into camp huts, separated from their families, French, Rumanians, Slovenes, Greeks, all going to work every morning 'voluntarily'. Did it really matter whether they included Russian prisoners-of-war or people from the SS punishment squads who, guarded by the SS, hoped to find in Allach some hope of survival; or those pitiful figures who, as detainees of the Dachau concentration camp satellite, belonged to that 'procession of shades' which went from Ludwigsfeld across the bridge spanning the road to Dachau every morning and evening, from the camp to the plant, from the plant to the camp? No, none of this mattered.

But for just four Russian prisoners-of-war, No. 119 186, No. 178 715, No. 2992 and No. 120 814, Sergei Guryev, Nikolai Alexeyev, Alexander Boiko and Ivan Boschenov, it did matter. They would willingly have continued running for their lives with the other fellow-sufferers. Yet they had been 'requested to get in touch with the deputy Abwehr officer at BMW Works II in Allach, called Fischer' (this emerged from the files at the state police regional headquarters in Munich) 'for deployment on work in the Dachau concentration camp at the headquarters of Stalag VIIa in Moosburg [Stalag = fixed quarters for prisoner-of-war groups]'.

The reason for their transfer was 'systematic sabotage'. In order to produce items for barter, such as rings, armbands, cigarette holders and the like, it was established that they had unscrewed parts from machine tools, switched plates on test beds, etc. (according to a secret memorandum from the works management), in particular it was claimed that they 'had stolen the high-value material found over an engine, namely a chromium-nickel steel with 10 per cent nickel, 20 per cent chromium and 1.5 per cent tungsten, which would be very difficult to acquire with the present state of materials supply'. Interrogations, it went on to state, had revealed that the Russian prisoners-of-war were perfectly aware of the consequences of their actions, admitting themselves that such an offence in a Russian armaments factory would have resulted in them being shot immediately by the political commissar for the works. They found that the punishments inflicted on them up till then (maximum of seven days' strict detention) were ridiculous, describing them as 'a chance to have a good sleep'. The memo finished with the words: 'We hold the view that shooting a few saboteurs from the assembled camp workforces would bring these acts of sabotage to a speedy end.' So the order was given to introduce the necessary measures so that proven acts of sabotage and theft would be punished by death. This was signed by the works management.

I asked Krafft von Dellmensingen if he knew of the incident. He said that this was the first time he had heard of it. But he admitted that it was irrefutable that (after an edict to protect the German defence forces which, to his knowledge, had been enacted in November 1939) even Germans had been punished by death for proven acts of sabotage similar to the ones mentioned here.

'By a court of law?' I asked.

'Of course,' he said, 'inasmuch as it was possible to talk about courts of law (there were not any others) for this kind of case within the framework of National Socialist justice.'

'Were there any reasons for the Allies to spare Allach,' I asked next, 'because they knew of prisoners-of-war at Works II (not only Russians, but prisoners-of-war in general) and, above all, of concentration camp detainees?'

Krafft said that it was difficult to judge. He said that Allach had always been covered by a smoke-screen when the air-raid warning sounded, though he did not know how much could be seen from above. There had been rumours that the Allies had *not* bombed Allach for other reasons (in view of the repair shop which the Americans were later to operate in conjunction with BMW). But he had had his doubts about that. He clearly remembered that Allach had once been subjected to carpet-bombing, when bombs had not fallen on the works, but to the north of them, on the same plot of land. He then looked at a map showing the inaccurate carpet-bombing, where bombs had been released either too soon or too late. This seemed to have been more of a mistake than anything intentional.

However, the report of a detainee, Hermann E. Riemer, stored in the archives of the concentration camp memorial building at Dachau, states:

Every so often there were nights when the shed seemed like a madhouse, nights when the British bomber squadrons were carrying out their attacks on Munich and the Bavarian Motor Works. If daytime raids caused pandemonium amongst the mass of people crammed together who were not allowed to leave the sheds for fear of shrapnel, then the night attacks turned a crowd of five hundred men into wailing, screaming, raging beasts.

No more than 200 metres from the shed stood a heavy anti-aircraft battery, which sent a constant stream of volleys into the night sky. The air trembled, the earth shook, and the shed swayed. The shrapnel rained down incessantly onto the concrete roofs (a troubled mind might well have believed the world was coming to an end), but that was only the start. The story got worse when the British answered the night-time volleys from the anti-aircraft fire. That was when the bombs screamed down, right next to our block, and gouged huge craters in the gravel. Each time the shed seemed to jump, and the echo of five hundred detainees, fearing for their lives, mixed with the whistling of shrapnel and soughing of pebbles exploding from the bowels of the earth. The level-headed amongst us had soon found out, though, that in spite of the apparent danger, the episode was relatively harmless. The foreign squadrons were always deployed longitudinally to the camp, so that, as far as one could judge, it was impossible to hit the sheds. In fact, by the end of the war, not a single bomb had fallen on the camp at Allach.

Mark you, that was only on the Allach-Ludwigsfeld camp. That lay on the far side of the road to Dachau, crossed by the notorious wooden bridge outside the works site. It may very well have been spared from Allied bombs because it formed a satellite of the Dachau concentration camp.

'We won the air war against Germany through muscle-power rather than brain-power. We stifled them through the sheer weight of our airplanes,' wrote US Senator Albert D. Thomas, Chairman of the Aviation Committee, shortly after the war. He based his impressions on what Allied scientists and engineers had discovered (after Germany's occupation) in laboratories, test stations and industrial plants serving the Luftwaffe. 'Your air force,' he admitted, 'was superior to ours at the start of the war and greatly superior by the end. If we had had to delay our invasion of Europe by six months, we would have lost the war due to your superiority in the air. Before the war, we were told that the American air force was the best. During the war, we were told that it was the best *and* the greatest. It was not the best, just the greatest. It was muscle-power, not brain-power.'

Whatever anyone may think, the fact remained that when this muscle-power appeared over Munich, Oberwiesenfeld and over Allach, and brought its power into play, it was no longer just a matter of 'only an unspecified number of targets' being hit (as happened on the first air raid on BMW made by the Royal Air Force on the night of 9 March 1943). The 'US report

Works 1 Oberwiesenfeld

Raid No	Unit	Date	Number of aircraft involved	Number of bombs dropped	Tons
1	RAF	1./2.9.40	1	7	2
2	RAF	9./10.3.43	226	270 HE	329
3	15th	9.6.44	37	207 HE	104
4	15th	13.6.44	138	1397 HE	371
5	8th	11.7.44	975	11939 HE	1839
				8303 I	287
6	8th	12.7.44	1117	5288 HE	1330
				5500 I	1397
7	8th	13.7.44	592	2498 HE	627
				3810 I	818
8	8th	16.7.44	35	1386 I	69
9	8th	31.7.44.	565	2863 HE	785
				2539 I	639
10	15th	22.9.44	75	744 HE	187

Works 2 Allach

Raid No	Unit	Date	Number of aircraft involved	Number of bombs dropped	Tons
1	15th	9.6.44	117	7176 HE	215
			27	135 HE	68
2	15th	13.6.44	56	302 HE	151
			24	648 I	33
3	15th	19.7.44	28	280 HE	70
4	8th	21.7.44	79	512 HE	120
				1189 I	80
			35	214 HE	54
				120 I	30
5	8th	31.7.44	108	? HE	?
				1065 I	266
6	15th	12.9.44	91	359 HE	180
7	15th	22.9.44	26	300 HE	75
8	15th	23.9.44	44	248 HE	62
9	15th	7.1.45	?	1505 HE	?

Key: HE = high-explosive bombs
I = incendiary bombs

on strategic air offensive' gives detailed records of the attacks in 1944 made by the 8th and 15th American Air Force squadrons (see opposite).

To sum up:

Material damage was caused both by high-explosive bombs as well as through incendiary bombs and was very considerable. Damage to the larger buildings mainly resulted from explosions. Fire damage was a great deal higher at the Oberwiesenfeld works than at the Allach works. In the period from the first heavy air attack on the Oberwiesenfeld until the end of the war, production of BMW 801 aero-engines for the whole of Germany amounted to only 75 per cent of projected output. This was principally due to the air raids on the Munich works.

Research work by the intelligence service of material damage was essentially correct. However, the information from the intelligence service about losses in production was limited in all cases.

Even what the intelligence service obtained elsewhere was not overwhelming, and was probably common knowledge to any outsider:

Due to its research and development work on aero-engines, turbines and rockets, the Oberwiesenfeld works were of great importance for Germany's overall aero-engine production plan. It supplied all the other BMW works in Germany with plans and relevant data. It supplied test engines to all the BMW works involved in mass production, as it did to numerous BMW test stations, to the Reich's research departments, to Junkers, and Focke-Wulf (engines), to Henschel in Berlin and to the Brink Iron Works in Hovelhof (rockets).

All this was undeniably true. But if that ultimately meant that it could be definitely assumed that 'the works, had they not been damaged by air raids, would have been in the position, through their experiment work, to set up large-scale production of rockets which could have posed a serious threat', then this was quite wrong. There were a number of people at BMW who would dearly have wanted this, but, to quote Brecht, things were not like that.

A Dark Chapter

He said that things had turned out all right for him compared to the fate of his comrades. Every day prisoners, including French ones, were delivered to the works. They were marched from their camp, accompanied by German soldiers who then handed them over to their respective foremen. In the evenings they were picked up again and brought back to their various camps. In contrast, he could go to work just like any other ordinary worker and go back home in the evening, which meant his shed on Leopold Street, where the French conscripted workers of the class of 43, and other Frenchmen, including a number of volunteers, were housed. He could even go out.

Go out where?

Wherever he wanted; to city-centre bars, to a concert (which he would have liked to have done more often if it had not been for his shabby clothes), or to visit a church where he could meet priests.

German priests?

Yes, amongst others. He also met French ones, who, as members of Catholic Action like him, had volunteered for work in Germany to support their compatriots.

Was this legal?

Of course not. They had kept quiet about being priests. Only the Bavarian clergy knew of this, having promoted gatherings so as to come into contact with French priests who were prisoners of war. They had celebrated mass together in the camps and even gone as far as having spontaneous and communal outings, which were far from safe (as they were certainly not allowed officially), to places like Wolfratshausen or Schäftlarn (where prisoners also worked), and even once getting to Garmisch on a Saturday afternoon or a Sunday morning. Sometimes, they would only venture a walk in the woods, where they would practise doing good deeds like boy scouts. He had joined the Christian boy scouts at the age of thirteen, where he acquired a boy scouts belt which he wore buckled over his work tunic. On arriving in Germany he had immediately become the spokesman of a small group whose members, along with other Frenchmen, belonged to Catholic, Protestant or political associations back at home, or even just to a sports club, and who simply behaved better than other people, kept up their morale, resisted German pressure and remained 'true' Frenchmen.

Did he feel like a deportee?

Definitely, he said, because he had come to Germany against his will, forcibly, even if there had been an agreement between the French and German governments whereby the class of 43, meaning all young men born in 1922, were to be conscripted, based on the so-called 'relève' (army intake), for work in Germany. In return for this, a French prisoner-of-war was supposed to go back home, which naturally did not happen. Looking at it from a different perspective, France was an occupied country with no military service, this being replaced by the STO, Service du Travail Obligatoire (Compulsory Work Service).

Had he been able to choose where to work?

At home, he had been working in a garage repairing German lorries (or should have been, since he did not do much there), when he was called up for a medical inspection. Two days later, he received notification that he was going to be sent to BMW. ('There were a few wise guys,' he added, 'who did not go, and used the two days to make themselves scarce. Then there were real Charlies like me who just went along.') When he then got caught up in the amorphous mass, with all the different types of people – intelligent people as well as fools, thieves and criminals, who hoped to escape punishment through volunteering – above all, those people who accepted this kind of captivity and were completely passive, then he realised that it would be the end of him if he just stood idly by. This was how he, a Catholic anarchist, became a kind of ringleader in the camp, inciting his compatriots not to be too keen about putting themselves forward for the Germans.

At work? How had this come about?

Oh, he said, let us take M. Morisi. (He had to install heating, ventilation and water in workshops, where the new double-radial engine, the one with 28 cylinders, was supposed to be tested.) He was a very quiet worker who went about things deliberately slowly at work, carried out every chore in a methodical way, taking twice the time, and if anyone tried to hurry him up, he explained that he was doing his work conscientiously, for the benefit of the company, the plant.

And did they buy that story?

For a time, yes. Then they threw him out.

When had this been?

At the beginning of December, after barely nine months in BMW. He then went to Zella-Mehlis in Thuringia, to the firm of Kerpatz, which produced drilling machines and the like for, amongst others, BMW in Eisenach. There the food was better, but supervision was worse, because he had been assigned to a slave driver who did not let anyone get away with anything. On the other hand, he had a good friend at Zella-Mehlis, who was also in Catholic Action and who was so involved in it that he ended up in a concentration camp, where he died. Two years previously, the Pope had described him as blessed by the Holy Spirit. His name was Marcel Callot.

He paused. No, Morisi had not been born a hero. Yes, at the time when he still trusted his document and the clause in it setting the length for his compulsory work at twelve months (which was never mentioned again), he had naively, or even cunningly (depending on your viewpoint), gone to his works manager a few days before 14 July, and declared to him that, as the Germans wanted co-operation between themselves and his people, they had to respect the fact that France had a National Day. This was why he requested permission to stay away from work on that day, and not just him, but all the French in the camp. Naturally he was refused and, in spite of persisting in his request, he got nowhere. But on 14 July, he was the only one to stay in his shed while the others went to work. This is what he said:

'I stayed there until someone from works security came and kicked the door open and said: "Is Morisi here?" I, as Morisi, replied: "No, he's not here", and the security man, whom I did not know and who did not know me, then went away. As for me, I went to the English Garden, and then back to work quite normally the next day. A few days later, I received written notification that a third of the daily rate would be deducted from my wages.'

Fourteen years later, in 1957, Morisi had to go to Munich to conduct a report for a car magazine, and went to BMW. Although he was no collector or fan of old, yellowing documents, he had kept the statement of punishment and brought it along. He asked after the man who had signed the warning, but he could no longer be located. He then read out, to general amazement, what was on the slip: '21 July 1943. To Herr Morisi, Henri, Department 3279, Squad Number 58014. First warning. On 14 July you were absent from work without permission. I am thus issuing you with a strict warning with respect to this defiance of duty, and I am imposing upon you a fine to the value of one third of the daily rate. This amount will be deducted from your next wages, and given to the German Red Cross. Bavarian Motor Works. Signed. . . .'

Morisi asked jokingly how they still viewed this, saying: 'Well, what do you say? (he could still manage a bit of German). Can I claim the money back?' Everyone burst out laughing. Including him.

This was all told to me by Henri Morisi, who was by then 67 years old, and employed by Alfa Romeo as a publicity manager and test-driver (he had picked me up from Charles de Gaulle airport in the latest Alfa Romeo saloon), as we drove to Villiers-le-Bel, to his little house in Avenue P. Curie.

'I can tell you another story to match yours,' I said.

'About a conscripted worker?'

'About a conscripted worker or, as they were officially called, a foreign worker, although he did not have a third of the daily rate taken away from him. He recently wrote from Brazil, requesting that the company give him a work certificate, presumably for his pension. So the files for Ligocki were dug out (they did exist, believe it or not), which was when I discovered what had happened to him, and to BMW because of him.'

'Go on. Where did he come from?'

'His personal papers had him as an ethnic German. Born in Poland, and allegedly taken to Paris by his parents at the age of seven months.'

'Allegedly?'

'Somebody had added that to his personal record. It never ceases to amaze me what you can find in files.'

'You're right, there,' said Morisi, 'that's why I don't like keeping them.' He laughed. 'But go on, you've got me hooked now.'

Ligocki, Simon, had certainly been no special case. Allocated by transport, as was stated on his recruitment form, he was barely nineteen years old when he started at BMW in October 1942 as an engine fitter. He came from France (home address: St Germain-en-Laye, Dept Seine et Oise), claimed to have Polish nationality (born in Ostrzeszow, known as Schiltberg in German) and was treated as a foreign worker. He received an hourly rate of RM 0.88, plus a bonus of RM 0.10 for his work at the test bed, where it was particularly noisy and stressful. Not far away was Riesenfeld camp, where he lived. The first piece of information about his subsequent fate is given by a change of activity (he was now entered on the form as 'Ethnic German'), and the second piece of information was a wage rise; it was tiny, barely 4 pfennigs per hour, plus 10 pfennigs, as already granted on his test bed bonus. The reason for this was increased enthusiasm brought about by a change of work.

In the meantime, he had even gone on leave (to visit his family), although this was only allowed to a bachelor after one year's work. After presumably spending pleasant days with his parents, he returned via Paris on 29 April 1943, only to be inexplicably absent from work without permission ten days later in May. He was issued with a strict warning, and after discussion with the secret council, fined three days pay, followed by a second warning in November for avoiding duty – this time it was 11 days which he took off work without authorisation. A fine of 4 days pay, and so it went on. What was happening to Simon Ligocki? Increased enthusiasm was countered by permanent absence from work without permission! On one occasion, a check was made on hospital files – Ligocki, Simon; 8 Sonnen Street (where he had moved). No record to be found. Until the trail finally re-emerged, thanks to the head of the health centre at BMW, who wrote the following to the defence officer at Works 1 regarding Ligocki, Simon:

The above-named has been persistently skiving off work for three months. He blames an old injury which left him without part of his little finger on his left hand. He wears a large dressing put on by himself. His arm is in a sling. He has never been to see me. He claims to have been to numerous private doctors. As the man only came to us for the first time today, we were not in a position to help him previously. We need to establish how he can stay away from work for months on end without a validated card, and how the wages office can issue medical certificates to private doctors. It would also be interesting to know what the young man has been living on. I suggest that the man is apprehended and held until these questions have been answered. It should be stressed that he is not unfit to do the relevant work.

To this text, which resembled a police statement more than a medical report, the Abwehr officer had added succinctly, and almost humanely, in his own hand: 'L. has not committed any crime. His application for release is being processed.' Later (the application had then gone to the work office which refused it), we learnt that Simon Ligocki had lost the four fingers on his left hand and one finger on his right hand, this occurring during rescue work following an air raid on Munich (Sonnenhof) in the spring of 1943. We also learnt that he wanted to return for duty in France (as far as this was still possible in view of his mutilated hands).

In the meantime, the unfortunate applicant, who had been pronounced fit for work again, was being sought by the works management. First at the Sonnenhof camp, whose administration informed them that he had gone to see his brother at Donaueschingen. However, this was denied by his brother, who had just arrived in Munich looking for him, whereupon he was immediately interrogated.

Where was Ligocki? And what was he? Was he a hero, who had lost four fingers from his left hand and one finger from his right hand for Führer and People (an example for all foreign workers, now exceeding a million, without whom things would have ground to a halt in the Reich), and who was reportedly rewarded at every possible opportunity by the works management with active service decorations and special leave? Or was he a malingerer, a man who had inflicted injuries upon himself, and was simply fed up and wanted to get away? Or was he perhaps just a homesick young man who wanted to see his girlfriend?

We will not find an answer until we come to the train approaching Metz, where 'civilian worker Ligocki' (as he was now called), in breach of his contract of work, fell into the clutches of the Secret State Police (Gestapo), probably trying to escape home. In any case, the commander of the security police and the security service covering the Lorraine, Saar, and the Palatinate, Section IV (and that was the Secret State Police) informed BMW in Munich that the defendant had been put in custody for remedial work and re-education for 21 days, which he had already served. The company was asked to come and collect him, because if they did not do so by such and such a date, the work refugee would be made available to the regional employment office in Saarbrücken for further deployment. Signed on behalf of . . . . Then came the charge which the personnel department at the Bavarian Motor Works had laid against L., when he appeared before the Honour and Disciplinary Court of the Munich-Upper Bavaria Gau of the German Labour Front. There was no mention of the honour of having lost four fingers from his left hand and one finger from his right hand for the cause of People and Fatherland, and German rearmament. The fact that L. had stayed away from work a number of times (in the end, continuously), defying all warnings and threats of severer punishment, had, so to speak, cleared up the problem of itself. And that was the end of the matter.

'I have always said,' commented Morisi, who had been listening intently, 'that I was lucky. It all depended on where you were allocated to work, and what the boss was like. If he could get on with you, or if you could get on with him. Naturally, the one who got me did not want to go to the front. So he had to make sure that the work got done, neither too quickly, nor too slowly, as either could land him in trouble. The first would mean that he was expendable, and the second that he would be in trouble for not being up to it. So the rules of the game were this: if I helped him to keep the balance, that was all right. If I was over-passive, he ran the risk of being relieved of his job and being crucified, as the expression went. He knew that I knew that. And I knew what was in store for me if a slave-driver took his place. Our fates were in each other's hands. But who's interested in that today?'

Morisi pointed to a pile of old letters and photographs which, in anticipation of my visit, he had managed to dig up and display on the small mahogany table where we were sitting.

'This is the first time I've taken out the punishment notice in a long while,' he said. 'I don't know if I shall ever read it again after you have gone.'

'If you were a German and you lived in Germany,' I replied, 'you would have to do this. Just so that you could prove you had a clean slate – in terms of what was happening then. Did you know about the concentration camps, M. Morisi? As a Frenchman, you don't need to answer that question. But you were in Germany, you were no more than ten kilometres from a concentration camp, the notorious Dachau. I can hardly believe that, as a conscripted worker, you did not see, speak to, or know anything about concentration camp inmates working practically next door to you.'

'Of course I knew about them,' said Morisi, 'because I saw them every day, small groups of them. They were assigned to excavation work in Milbertshofen. They looked like starving zebras in their striped pyjamas. They were guarded by the SS, never left alone for a minute, making it difficult to slip a piece of bread, which we had set aside for them back at our camp, to any of them.'

'Did you tell German priests about this, did you ask them why they put up with this, why the Church did not step in?'

'I went to the priest in Milbertshofen, many times. Once we found him very ill in bed. He was holding his hand over his face, covering his tears with his hand, lamenting and calling out in fluent French: "What is to become of Germay? Where is the country going?" I did not need to ask him. If he had been able to do anything, he would have done it long before.'

When we got into the car again to catch my evening flight back home, I asked Morisi my last question, which was not an easy one: 'Do you think it was possible that over there in Allach, even if you yourself were not there, a foreman, working with concentration camp inmates (someone instructing them, supervising them on the machines and in daily contact with them), could not have known about the atrocities which the SS perpetrated on them *after* work, every evening, every night?'

Morisi took his hand off the ignition key and leaned back. It was only after a while that he seemed to understand what I had asked him. Then he said, as if speaking more to himself than to me: 'It is difficult. I don't want to condemn anyone who knew about it, though the foreman knew, of course. Neither he nor any manager in charge of work allocation, nor people whose little houses were near the camp and saw the inmates going to work and being led back every day, accompanied and beaten by their thugs, could justifiably claim they knew nothing about it. No, no one can say people were not part of it. But on the other hand, it was quite understandable. Anyone witnessing

an execution would find it difficult to admit it and say: "I was there." Look,'
he said, turning to me, unconcerned to find me looking at my watch, 'faced
with such stark, direct questions, where only two outcomes are possible, a
human being blocks off certain associations, because he is trying to survive,
to struggle with himself. That may also give some clue to the response: "Knew
nothing, nothing at all." Just look at the difficulties we French have trying
to cope with the past. Even we don't seem to be able to bring the Algerian
War to an end. I don't want to gloss over anything, to trivialise anything
that happened in Germany. True enough, there was a war on . . . and, for
instance, the SS were always associated with concentration camps, although
the SS guarding the camps were not the same as those fighting on the front.
Everyone knew that, but didn't want to make the distinction. Everything in
the past works its way down to the present, and I don't envy young Germans
having this past, because wherever they go, questions are thrown up about
their fathers and grandfathers. In asking me this question, you've taken a
weight off my mind. If you hadn't asked me, I would have been depressed in
some way or other, because memories came flooding back. Do you believe me
when I say that now, and forty years from now, I am glad *not* to be a German?
And why? Simply because I don't have to say that I knew nothing.

'My mother always used to say to me: "If you are a good Christian, then
you will forgive, but never forget." As a conscripted worker, I am lucky that
I'll never be in a position where I'm forced to forget. My time then is a part
of my life. Why should I forget it? Hasn't it made me what I am today?'

A few days after this conversation, I drove out to Allach. It was as if
everything had been brought forward in time. What I saw to the left of
the road to Dachau (mainly industrial buildings which had once been
Works 2) only evoked vague images in the search for clues as to where
the footbridge might once have been over the road. I turned off right at
the sign 'Ludwigsfeld'. It was here, and nowhere else, that the site where
the concentration camp outbuilding had been must have extended.

'Five hundred years later found me travelling along the self-same road. . .'
Friedrich Rückert's *Chidher* poem says. But after no more than fifty years,
I thought, Chidher would himself have been unable to find a grain of soil
which could remind him of the camp which had once stood there in all its
wretchedness. With a sketch in my head, which a former inmate had sent to
me, I headed for a housing estate which might have been the roll-call area,
trying to get it to tie in with a delivery hall which MAN had put up for its
heavy vehicles.

It suddenly occurred to me that Morisi might allow himself to read the old
bundle again, before stacking it away for good. And I thought about what
was marked on all the legal files of political prisoners in the Soviet Union
– Lev Kopelev had chosen it as the title for drawings which he had made
as an eye-witness to the looting, rapes and murders committed by his own
troops and comrades – 'For posterity's sake'.

For posterity's sake. . . . Those reading what follows may well choose to
dwell upon this.

The Allach-Ludwigsfeld satellite had consisted of nothing more than a few old barracks which had once served as stables and accommodation for a cavalry regiment – a barn door at the front and one at the back as entrances, the walls panelled with planks, strips on the joints with enough gaps in them to see what the weather was like. 'Lights had to burn day and night in the main area because there was no natural lighting.' That was how an inmate described it.

Overall, there would have been about thirty buildings (most made of wood, but a few of stone) which gradually filled a huge rectangle. It was initially divided into two, then three, areas fenced off from each other, with a communal area for roll-call where wooden scaffolding was occasionally mounted which served, with its cross-beams, as a gallows. The Jewish compound was at the back, again strictly fenced off from all the other inmates. The whole site was surrounded by electrified barbed wire, with watch-towers at the corners. Again fenced off, and secured by a chain of sentry posts, ran the 'chemin entouré de barbelés conduisant à l'usine BMW' [the road surrounded by barbed wire leading to the BMW factory], as the French inmate Henri Gayot (inmate number 102435) described this path in a drawing which he made for posterity.

> In the harshness of the searchlights, the column started marching, headed by the proud and upright sergeant-in-charge, an ex-Foreign Legionnaire, who was about forty-five years old. As he spoke French quite well, they had to take care not to drop any careless words in his presence. The prisoners followed, marching in step, five abreast, accompanied by the SS guards and their dogs.
>
> On the orders of the camp commandant, we went through the camp's large wooden gate, climbed up some wooden steps a bit further on, which led to a railway line, along which we walked for a few hundred metres, until we went down some steps on the other side of the embankment. Still five abreast and with arms linked, we entered a road with fencing around it, with SS troops and their dogs standing on both sides. After about 1,000 or 1,500 metres we reached BMW.

This was how the French doctor Dr Laffitte (in his book *Allach, Kommando de Dachau*) described the daily trip to work. Another inmate expressed the same thing in the following way: 'A funnel marked by barbed wire through which we were driven to our workplace like sheep into a pen had been built from the camp to BMW.'

What went on over there in the 'pen', where the inmates were taken in the morning and handed back to their tormentors in the early evening, was work in two types of activity – work for construction companies, who were putting up bunkers, new buildings and roads for BMW (each one named after the contractor, including the dreaded building commando unit, the 'Dyckerhoff Commando Unit'), and work for BMW itself, where the inmates, trained in Hall 2003, worked for the most part on producing cylinder heads.

The inmate Marcel Rivière recalled; working for Dyckerhoff meant dying quickly: worn out by the infernal carrying of heavy cement sacks; laid low by the cold (some nights the thermometer fell below -27 degrees Celsius); by hunger (two litres of clear soup and 200 grammes of bread a day); beaten to death; or as victims of accidents (such as falling from scaffolding due to attacks of vertigo). The commando units in the factory were less fearsome. Divided up into various gigantic concrete halls (including some bunkers for air raid protection) which (two kilometres from the camp) were in the midst of the pine forest, the inmates worked with a minimum of eagerness, as can easily be imagined, for the good of the Bavarian Motor Works (BMW) producing military equipment (gearboxes and aero-engine parts). At least they had the invaluable advantage of being protected from the vagaries of the weather.

And a fellow-sufferer of Laffitte's recalled:

There were random checks on large-scale production, which were carried out by inmates. A German civilian was in charge of final quality control. Every controller had his number stamp so that he could mark items for which he was responsible. The production line ran at a very considerable rate, especially on day shifts (there were also night shifts running from 6.20 p.m. to 6.20 a.m.). Our comrades who did the checking were subject to supervision by the same personnel – SS, sergeants-in-charge, German civilians – who enthusiastically competed against each other. To drop or to destroy a work-piece, however unimportant it was, or to lose a tool, immediately resulted in severe punishment, often justified by the charge of 'sabotage'.

A third inmate, Riemer, who worked in the cylinder-liner department, confirmed this:

There were a few, fully-automated lathes, which made the preformed, rough liners from steel blanks in an incredibly short time. From there they came to me along a conveyor belt, and I sent them to the gaping jaws of an electrically-heated revolving oven, where they were heated to 900°, and then immersed in an oil bath. The cylinders were put in the oven on tilting stands and were carried by an electrical feeder through the heat for over forty-eight minutes. Now and again, a cylinder would fall off the stand while it was being rotated or would get stuck somewhere, or perhaps would even tear out the heating element, making an expensive repair necessary. It was even worse when the oven was out of action for a few days, and if there was a break in the supply of cylinder liners, then production down the line was disrupted.

Although there was little an inmate could do when such a disruption occurred, he still had to pay dearly for it. Two of my predecessors on the oven were unlucky with the cylinders. First they had not noticed the problem, probably because of their technical inexperience, and when they did notice it, perhaps did not have the courage to report it straightaway.

The foreman in charge of the department then accused them of sabotage, and both were publicly hanged in our camp, after the same fate (as I learnt on this occasion) had been meted out to a French comrade.

The reports were undeniable, their cynicism understandable when they stated that people had worked for the good of BMW with a minimum of eagerness, but at least with some protection against the weather. The fact was that the company benefiting from this dubious good was still, legally speaking, a limited company in the private sector, but in reality was part of the Reich's armaments machinery, not receiving its orders from the board, but carrying them out for the Reich Aviation Ministry. Whether it wanted to or not, was quite another story. This was also true from what Krafft von Dellmensingen, the head of the legal department at the time, told me; which was that industry, here represented by BMW, had explicitly given priority to recruiting German workers for its contracts, or trying to keep its established workforce of German origin. But as the war progressed, that had simply proved impossible, as skilled workers were withdrawn by the Wehrmacht and sent to the front as soldiers. Only the highest qualified, practically irreplaceable technicians were left in the firm, and other workers had to be acquired for the simpler jobs resulting from increased capacity in aero-engine production. The accusation that these 'foreign workers' (conscripted workers, prisoners-of-war, concentration camp inmates) had been taken on and deployed with particular alacrity, because they had been 'cheap', meaning that the firm had been able to get rich through lower wages or, better still, no wages at all, and so increase its 'profits', was not only utterly wrong, but quite slanderous.

'There was a price control commission at the Reich Aviation Ministry,' said von Krafft, 'with which BMW worked exclusively as the issuing authority. The price inspectors regularly came to Munich and checked all the costing documents for aero-engine production down to the last detail. Of course, wages made up a not inconsiderable part of these costs. If they had been lower, by employing non-German or Jewish workers, than those for German workers (who were usually professionally trained and had their better performance rewarded correspondingly higher than trainees without any qualifications), then the profit would be set correspondingly lower by the price inspectors, because wages were added on to the overall costs according to specific statutory regulations. There could be no question at all of any extra profit created by lower wages.'

Back to the reports by the inmates. If mere damage to a machine, just as likely to be caused by skilled hands as by those of an inmate, could be interpreted as sabotage, resulting in death (as Riemer wrote, there was no investigation, simply a report; the accused was never allowed to defend himself), then it was no longer a question of deploying labour in order to fulfil production quotas after the widest possible interpretation of all the regulations and requirements. It was murder. If there were stories (bringing relief with them) of how German inmates still knew how to defend themselves (for instance, if their machines suffered damage, they would inform the commando leader first, and *then* the section foreman, generally meaning that the latter's report, even if he made a fuss about it, ended up going nowhere), then Poles, Russians, Greeks, Frenchmen, Belgians or Dutchmen had little chance of escaping with their lives if they did not speak German (and only a few did).

Riemer:

> The day was long and the rations bad enough for what the work required. There were more and more cases of people collapsing at their machines. If a comrade did not immediately rush to help and switch off the machine, then this might have resulted in a damaged work-piece and an inmate promptly being served with a charge of sabotage by a resentful foreman, with the last act of the tragedy being played out on the gallows. And there was no standing on ceremony when it came to the non-German comrades. Admittedly, not all the foremen at BMW were slave-drivers. There were some amongst them who had their hearts on our side, even if they dare not let it show. Just a wink was often enough to show our complicity, and quite a few cigarettes and loaves of bread were secretly slipped to us by well-meaning hands.

There are villains and angels in every society. The foreman who brought about a death sentence through his report would deny that he was amongst the villains, since he would claim only to be doing his duty. But what did that mean, doing one's duty? Fulfilling a production quota can lead to a greater breach of duty than endangering it through a little humanity. The first requires a little courage, and the second a lot. Courage is not every one's strong point. But were there reasons for considering punishments like the ones mentioned above as justifiable within the framework of some kind of law? No, there were not.

It was only in the eighties, almost half a century after the events, that the background to how conscripted workers were deployed in the Third Reich's war economy became known and discussed in public. The earlier belief that the disclosure of mass murder at Auschwitz, Majdanek, Treblinka and all those other sites of horror had put an end to the revulsion of human extermination proved to be wrong. But what had the programme for exterminating the Jews – the extinction of a people, an entire race – as was decided at the Wannsee Conference in January 1942, to do with conscripted labour? Well, nothing more or less than the fact that in the third year of the war, the extermination of able-bodied Jews was by no means stopped. On the contrary, it was pursued – through work. This is precisely what concerned SS Reichsführer Heinrich Himmler, the keeper of the Party's Grail, as he liked to be known, when he presented Hitler and the Armaments Minister Speer with the proposal to set up production sites for war materials inside concentration camps. This was no humane gesture. He was simply working from the premise that there was some value hidden in the 'vermin' (these being Jews to him) which, if they could be exploited for their ability to work, would benefit the German war economy. Hitler approved. And Speer, faced with an ever diminishing German labour force, was delighted, and (in compliance with Himmler's plan of producing munitions and weapons directly in concentration camps) arranged for the armaments industry to stay in private hands and for concentration camp inmates to be deployed on site, outside concentration camps. This was how the murder of the Jews was stopped, or rather how not all of them were indiscriminately sent to the gas chambers – there was some kind of selection process. The able-bodied were sent to armaments, while the others were sent to the gas chambers.

Those selected were then deported. They were often young people of between seventeen and twenty who had been rounded up in raids in the 'General Gouvernement', as parts of Poland were then called, in Hungary and in other countries in occupied Europe, and transported to Auschwitz, where they waited, like everyone else, for the treadmill of death. They were deported, in many cases with their fathers, to the various concentration camps in the Reich, while their mothers and younger brothers and sisters stayed behind, to end up in the gas chambers. (At the same time, in March 1943, Hitler's governor in Poland, Frank, with unparalleled cynicism, called out at the main railway station in Krakow to 'voluntary' Polish slaves: 'You are now travelling to Germany, and I thank you for this. As a token of the fact that you are the one millionth worker, I hereby present you with a gold watch. It's yours, take it. Workers all, travel now to the great German Reich and return refreshed and happy to your homeland in the General Gouvernment. That is my wish, that is the wish of the area government to you. I wish you all a pleasant journey!') In the meantime, the deportees, for whom the 'pleasant journey' consisted of having escaped Auschwitz, were distributed to the concentration camp satellites, where they were guarded just as closely as before by the SS, in order to be able to collaborate in the German victory through day and night shifts in industrial plants.

This was the case at Allach, as well. Entrusted to the SS, who were paid by the firm for each inmate (not only for guarding and feeding them, but also for exterminating them through work, this being in line with ideological consistency, but unbeknown to industry), this camp, amongst hundreds of similar satellites, was no worse, and in some ways rather better than other, smaller ones. Working for BMW and situated within the environs of Munich, the satellites were to be found, as stated in reports, at Mühldorf, Kaufering, Kempten, Rothschwaige (that being a labour camp under another jurisdiction, namely the Todt Organisation), Kaufbeuren, occasionally Trostberg, and Markirch in Alsace, where, however, the inmates were no longer in the charge of the Dachau concentration camp, but the no less notorious Natzweiler camp.

According to the last report which, with typical German thoroughness, the Dachau camp issued as late as 25 April 1945 (the Americans marched in only four days later), the following numbers of inmates were listed for Allach (referring here to the satellite) without any details for the commando units:

I Allach = 8,970 male inmates
II Allach = 1,027 female inmates

An average workforce of 3,800 inmates is given for the 'Allach sub-commando unit – BMW, construction and manufacture, established on 19 March 43, last mentioned 15 April 45', also belonging to the Dachau concentration camp.

Other figures, partially corroborated by the staff statistics already given, speak in 1944 of 3,300 foreign workers, of whom 300 were women, about 3,000 prisoners-of-war (predominantly Russian), around 700 SS prisoners (members who had committed offences), as well as between 3,000 and 5,500 concentration camp inmates.

The information that the number of all those employed at Allach had increased from only 1,000 men in 1939–40 to 5,732 men in 1941, and then through the following years up to 17,000 in 1944, is entirely credible. The claim that there were 22,000 working at Allach by the end of the war is also not to be dismissed out of hand, because Allach acted as a reception camp in the last days of the war, containing people who had never been there before.

Working on a tip that further material about Allach was still to be found at Ludwigsburg, I went there, to Schorndorfer Street, where the offices of an authority called ZENTRALE STELLE (central office for administering justice in the prosecution of National Socialist crimes) were housed in a former women's prison. This was where investigations were conducted, in connection with the Allach concentration camp satellite, against a certain E., who had perpetrated his inhumanities as deputy camp commandant under the head commandant, the SS lieutenant Jarolin, executed by the Americans at Landsberg in 1945. There were statements from former inmates about the 'limping devil', as he was called in the camp, about the conditions there, as well as about the work itself and the 'cases of sabotage' which were punishable by hanging. From wherever they had been traced, from Haifa in Israel, Warsaw, Jelenia Gora, Kielce, Krakow, Ostrów Wielkopolski, and Myslenice in Poland, in Ratibor (now in Poland and known as Raciborz), to Cleveland and Los Angeles, USA, and from courts in Germany providing official help, they all testified under oath. What I read took my breath away.

For it was now no longer a question of the acceptability of measures in war time for press-ganging human beings into work, regardless of where they came from. Neither could it be justified any longer by some kind of morality, or the fact, as Cicero claimed, that laws fall silent in war time (*Silent leges inter arma*). It was a question of crimes committed on innocent people; those committing them had only been able to do so because others, receiving the proceeds of slavery, kept quiet, either because they knew nothing about the crimes (was that likely?), or because they were fortunate enough not to have anything to do with the camps, only feeling responsible for what directly concerned them – work, production figures which had to be reached, and self-preservation.

Yet it is scarcely conceivable that anyone who knew of these crimes did nothing to stop them, to stem them or, by overcoming all his fear, at least to protest against them. It is inconceivable that all those meeting the murderers every day, in the form of SS guards in the production halls, from the ordinary worker to the foreman, from the foreman to the branch manager, had simply buried their heads in the sand when it came to the ignominious treatment meted out to the inmates over in the camps. It is inconceivable that the technical manager of Works 1, Zipprich, a man of unimpeachable personal integrity and moral courage, and, as his closest colleague in production planning, Monn-Weiß, assured me, a 'technical ace' and thus indispensable to BMW, would not immediately have gone to those in charge on hearing of an outrage, would not have put them on the spot and personally assumed full responsibility for it, the punishment for which ranged from immediate dismissal to arrest. It is inconceivable that he would have just sat back if he had had the slightest idea of the following: that SS sergeant major E. had shot two sixty-year-old Jewish inmates because they had asked for easier work; that in the winter of 1943 he had pronounced the death sentence on ten inmates who had stolen potatoes, who were then hanged in the camp under his supervision; that, after catching a Czech political prisoner writing a leaflet, he locked him in a bunker for some considerable time, after which he had him stand for days at a time in his summer clothes, regardless of the rain and snow, beside the entrance gate, finally dousing him with cold water from a hydrant and killing him; that he mistreated a Polish inmate who was too exhausted to work, before having him stripped naked and dealing with him in the same way he had dealt with the Czech; that he fired along the rows of prisoners at head height, killing those not standing in line (this happened with an inhabitant of the town of Znyn called Kaszmarowski, whom he fatally wounded, as witnessed by Wladyslaw Lenski); that three further inmates were hanged on E. 's order – a Russian, who had picked up an apple, a sergeant-in-charge from Hanover, who had refused to beat inmates, and a Polish inmate from Swiece, offence unknown; that in the autumn of 1944 he had the whole workforce of an annealing oven, consisting of about a dozen French inmates, hanged for alleged sabotage; and that he would frequently tear the cap off an inmate's head and throw it out into an open space, whereupon the inmate, then trying to retrieve his cap, would be shot by an SS man (who would be financially rewarded and given extra time off work). Explanation: shot while trying to escape.

These were certainly not all the offences E. was charged with (proceedings against him were abandoned on grounds of ill-health, including schizophrenia), and made up only a fraction of what the Ludwigsburg files contained.

I read aloud some of the charges on the list against Eberl and the so-called acts of sabotage to a foreman who had spent his whole career at Allach (apart from postings to Markirch and Trostberg). I said:

'If there was no way to make decent human behaviour prevail, then it is quite clear that the SS, obviously using work instead of gas as a means of extermination, were actually sabotaging their own orders. Instead of deploying able-bodied Jews for final victory and keeping them fit for work, they kept alive the idea of "vermin" as the only way to behave. By virtually stopping inmates from being put to work, they ironically and quite idiotically brought about exactly what would have been punishable by death amongst inmates, i.e. sabotage. Nobody intervened, preferring simply to assert that training the inmates cost money, time and effort, that they must therefore be treated well, so that the capital invested in them through training would be paid back (there was a war on, after all!). Instead of that, the aim was to beat them, literally with intent to take revenge, straight on course for organised sabotage! The inmates were forced to give up the idea that simply doing work satisfactorily was a way to survive.'

The foreman had listened in silence. Then he said that this was the first time he had heard of this. He was horrified, shattered even. If there had not been the court seal at the bottom, he would not have believed it. He knew nothing of the concentration camp satellite, the camp at Ludwigsfeld near Allach. Only foreign workers had been in his section and he had got on exceptionally well with the Russian prisoners (certainly at Basdorf and Zühlsdorf near Berlin where he had also been temporarily posted). Sometimes when he passed the halls where inmates were working, he would see them in their striped clothes. They had to take their caps off when passing SS guards posted at the exits on concrete bunkers, thereby revealing their shaved heads. Sometimes things would flash through his mind. But there was nothing he had 'suppressed' (or so he claimed), given that the word had only recently been around. At most, he had felt fear, fear because if he had been a bit cheeky (as he tended to be) when speaking about the political situation, his superior might have had it in for him. That he avoided this was explained by the fact that he had been put on reserve the very day he had received his call-up papers. If the slightest thing had become known about him, he would have had to go to the front. So everyone had tried to do their work to the best of their ability. Let us say, then, as he finished speaking, that he had known just as little or just as much as the entire German people had. In other words, nothing. For example, it was hardly likely that radio broadcasters would announce on the morning after the Wannsee Conference that the decision had been taken to liquidate the Jewish race. What we could not explain was how this happened. We knew nothing. Hitler's order No 1 (the foreman had read it only recently, and it had greatly interested him), Hitler's order that everyone should know only enough about the task entrusted to him to carry it out, and that he should keep quiet about even that if he valued his life, had brought about a situation where people had only an inkling of the eerie events taking place in the country; an inkling which that 'procession of shades', fortuitously glimpsed as it crossed the wooden bridge over the road to Dachau every morning, reinforced in men's minds. Anything outside this inkling was pure conjecture, and who would risk communicating their conjectures when the issue at stake was death?

Below the Sound Barrier

On 1 October 1945, the order was issued from the headquarters of the military government in Munich to the lord mayor of the city at the city hall instructing that the BMW factories 1 and 2 lying within the city limits should be razed, i.e. levelled to the ground. In addition, all the factory installations (meaning, as the dismantling lists later showed, every machine down to the very last bolt) were to be packed in crates ready for shipment.

BMW was on the Allies' blacklist, comparable with the leading war criminals on trial at Nuremberg, where Göring was as the prime defendant. BMW was second after the I.G. Farben Dye Trust amongst those industrial companies charged with having been most responsible for the disaster that befell Europe and the world. Why?

In 1939 the head of development at BMW, Helmut Sachse, had reported to representatives of the RAM and industry at the UFA Palace in Berlin on an ingenious idea which had found its way into the new 14-cylinder, double-radial, fuel-injected BMW 801 engine as a 'command module'. What would a pilot make (when in aerial combat) if he had to adjust all the functions individually, especially in a multi-engined plane? Undoubtedly, a mistake. The designer Heinrich Leibach had now created a kind of robot with his 'command module' which brought together all the control facilities in an easily exchangeable block. If the charging-air pressure and engine speed had been chosen, then all the other control values governed by these would be automatically set and remain set until the respective maximum pressure had been reached. If the command module was somehow damaged in combat, then the engine or engines would not be put out of use.

In addition, the new BMW 801 double-radial engine was the first German aero-engine to be delivered by the manufacturer as a complete power assembly, including engine, engine fittings and installation fittings – from the propeller spigot to the mounting ring. The aircraft manufacturer was thus spared the difficult installation tasks involved in designing the cowling and the air ducts, arranging and accommodating the oil cooler, as well as many other considerations. This made it possible, in practice, to remove the damaged engine and refit a new one in twenty minutes.

Sachse, who had been engineer-in-chief at the RAM before going to BMW, had not been telling stories or making cheap promises. In fact, the command module, which performed mechanically what electronics would make possible just a few decades later, was a technological marvel, which no one in their wildest dreams had imagined. And, as regards the 801 double-radial engine, it was the first engine, along with Sachse's specifications for simplification and handling, which made a German aircraft equivalent to the feared 'Spitfire' in terms of altitude at full pressure and speed, and even superior, as was later shown in the FW 190 fighter. But it was still a long way from being ready for production.

On 1 August 1940 Popp wrote to Lucht, the engineer-in-chief at the RAM in Berlin.

Of course the double-radial engine is a novelty for German aviation. Neither we nor the airframe or propeller makers could fall back on German experience. However, we tried to collate foreign experience when designing the engine, and I do not believe that either airframe or propeller makers have done this. The Americans, to mention just one example, have proved that the double-radial engine, as a system, has a prominent place. When the problems of the oil tank and the propellers had been satisfactorily resolved in America, there was clear evidence that our airframe and propeller makers were behind in this respect. It was not the engine system as such which presented an insoluble problem for these items.

Design on the 801 had only started in October 1938 under Martin Duckstein. The power plant consisting of propeller drive-gear, engine section, supercharger section and mounting points was not yet finished (an initial trial engine ran on the test bed in May 1939) when it was released by the RAM for series production in December 1939 – far too early. It was delivered in large numbers to the aircraft industry from the middle of 1940, but was essentially only ready for large-scale production from the middle of 1942 (as BMW 801 A and C).

Another two years passed before 'complete power plants' could be delivered – those in the aircraft types FW 190, making it the fastest mass-produced fighter in the world, reaching about 700 kph; the Do 217, a bomber and long-distance reconnaissance plane; and, as the BMW 801 TJ with exhaust-gas turbo-charging, for the Ju 388 which, together with a pressurised chamber, enabled its crew to fly for several hours at altitudes up to 11,000 metres. Almost all the letters of the alphabet had to be used to designate the various versions of the '801' which, by the end of the war, had been produced at between 20,000 and 21,000 units (the figure can only be estimated). To this needs to be added the fact that the average life-span of an engine at that time when there were aerial combats, bombing of airfields, etc. only amounted to six hours.

'You presumably know,' Heinrich Leibach said to me, when I wanted to know details about his command module, 'you did know that the 801, the one Sachse presented to the RAM, went straight from the drawing board into production?' (He had modestly declared to me that from the middle of the thirties all aero-engine factories, as well as the German Research Centre for Aviation, were working on petrol injection and single-stick operation.)

I nodded.

'Good. Then you will also know what that meant; that all the teething problems an engine normally grows out of on test appeared in series production! Sachse weeded them out with all the energy he could muster. Huge efforts were made. Just imagine! This did not take place in development, but in production, which the RAM had instructed should not be concentrated on one site, but distributed in various places, for example, in France, where many components were produced. This, of course, meant that it was quite some time before improvements (new design details and so forth) came about. And who was to blame? Sachse was quite clear on that. Not him. It was somebody quite different.'

'Who?' I asked. 'Milch?'

Leibach shook his head.

'Göring?'

'You won't believe it,' Leibach said. 'You see, the Americans began their raids at very great altitudes, dropping their bombs, and staying out of reach. The altitudes were between 10 and 15 km. How could they suddenly do that? Well, they had fitted their machines with exhaust-driven turbochargers. Previously, in 1940 (or maybe it was 1939), Sachse had suggested to the RAM that BMW should start work on this so-called high-altitude engine.'

'1939?' I interjected. 'BMW had sent a high-altitude engine to the front in 1918 when the First World War was almost over, allowing the Germans to fly a few thousand metres higher than the enemy. Udet won victory after victory in a Fokker fitted with this high-altitude engine, Max Friz's IIIa (yes, Friz's, the man who later built the famous R 32 motorcycle). Udet wrote a glowing report of it.'

'Udet?' asked Leibach. 'When?'

'In October 1918, when he was leader of Fighter Flight 4 in the Richthofen Squadron.'

'Listen,' said Leibach, 'this is the pure truth. During a discussion in Sachse's office (I still remember it as if it were yesterday), the door opened and his secretary handed him a telegram. Sachse read it, smiled, and said: "It says that I shall be threatened with internment in a concentration camp if I defy the order to stop all work on the high-altitude engine. Aerial combat will not take place at altitudes higher than 5 km. Signed Udet."'

'And in 1941 the Americans were already flying in at altitudes which we could not reach. It was not long after that that Udet shot himself.'

'Yes,' said Leibach. 'And the high-altitude engine was rapidly commissioned by the RAM, at Junkers, at Daimler and at BMW. But it came too late, along with the turbocharger which we developed to give high pressures.'

A second eye-witness to these proceedings was Wilhelm Dorls, previously the works manager at Allach. In 1982, a few weeks before his death, he confided to me that during a discussion with Udet, who used to land at Oberwiesenfeld more often than Popp liked (although BMW had the best altitude test facilities in the Reich), he, Dorls, had heard the Director of

Armaments say loud and clear that no aerial combat would take place above nine kilometres (just a bit more than what had been in the telegram to Sachse). For this reason, he was not interested in the 801, even if this were to reach twelve kilometres. No aerial combat above nine kilometres! And then he went off, leaving them all standing around, and probably went off to have a couple of cognacs in Munich. 'This was why the "801 i" was never built, let alone developed for large-scale production. When I came from Berlin to take over the Allach works in 1944, we were then supposed to build the "801" on the orders of the RAM. 1944! But it had not even been designed. The air ducts, sleeves, etc. needed on any engine had all provisionally been fitted, meaning that it was almost impossible to change a sparkplug. Admittedly, we had started producing individual parts, but we never built the complete "i", as the war was soon over. Then . . . let me think when that was . . . autumn 1944 . . . no, a bit earlier . . . a group captain came along, I think he was called Keudell, who was very interested in the high-altitude engine. His reconnaissance pilots had all failed to return from England because they had not been able to fly high enough. It doesn't bear thinking about – men had to die just because someone did not want to spend money on further development, and because he claimed that aerial combat could not take place above nine kilometres. Keudell, as someone in reconnaissance, almost wept: here was the engine which could have helped him . . . and it wasn't ready! What was the use of saying to Keudell: all right, we'll start building it now . . . it would still have needed years to be ready for production.'

The importance which the Americans attached to the 801 (until quite late in the war, they had assumed it was, if not a copy, then an imitation of the 14-cylinder 'Twin Wasp' engine which Pratt & Whitney had denied Popp) became obvious. In May 1945, they confiscated all documents, drawings, half-finished and finished parts for the 801 in Munich and at all transfer points (crankcase and gear production, for example, was at Markirch, near St Dié in Alsace, where it was carried out by concentration camp inmates in a railway tunnel in horrific conditions under the code name of 'Alsatian Special Cellars') and sent them to the USA before the other Allies could get their hands on them.

Nonetheless, it cannot be assumed that the 801 was the reason BMW was put on the blacklist. There was no rational reason for this. It was *one* aero-engine among many others, and even if the American Brigadier-General James E. Chaney, who travelled to England at the end of 1940 to learn about the general situation in the air war, had described the performance of German fuel-injected engines as being superior to English power plants, then it would have been absurd to blame this retrospectively on *one* factory which, moreover, had never once been the leading supplier of armaments to the Luftwaffe.

So what was it then?

Long before the war, it had been shown that speeds called trans-sonic (near the speed of sound) could not be reached with piston engines and propeller drives. The Italian Francesco Agello had held the world speed record since 1934, at 709.209 kph, established with a sea plane. It had only been developed with the record in mind, and so was nothing more than a 'flying engine', without any practical value. 'Utility values' were first developed by Heinkel and Messerschmitt, and anyone travelling to Augsburg by train will remember that here, between Buchloe and Bobingen, the test pilot Fritz Wendel established the absolute world speed record at 755.138 kph (on the first leg, he achieved 783 kph) in a Messerschmitt 209 V 1, along a three-kilometre-long test section, flying not very high, between about 30 and 75 metres above the railway embankment. This took place on 26 April 1939, when he flew along the measured section four times, twice in each direction. The record stood for 30 years. It was only in 1969 that the American Darryl Greenamyer was able to raise it to 771 kph, using a naval fighter plane from the Second World War.

A method of propulsion which would only come into effect beyond these values, had, at a time when aircraft flew at best between 300 and 320 kph, only produced theoretical discussions of jet propulsion. With the apparent, very late application of Wendel's world record, it was clear that the distant future had now dawned. Jet engines, which BMW had started developing in peace time at Milbertshofen and the Brandenburg Motor Works acquired in 1939, were the most revolutionary step forward since the days of the Wright brothers, when an engine-driven flying contraption had first taken to the air.

In completely secret trials, Heinkel managed to prove for the very first time, using a rocket drive developed by Wernher von Braun, that flight was possible without a propeller, using only a 'push from behind'. Combining highly concentrated alcohol and liquid oxygen, which was then ignited, he produced a thrust similar to an explosion lasting 30 seconds. Soon after this stationary test on the fuselage of a He 112, which was manned and anchored to the ground, Heinkel's attention was drawn to a young physicist called Pabst von Ohain. Hans Joachim Pabst von Ohain was the assistant to Professor Robert Pohl at the physics department in Göttingen University, and was involved on a new type of drive for aircraft (using thrust, without a propeller). Heinkel took him on immediately. This was when that breathtaking development, which literally brought about the 'crossing of the threshold', began at that specially equipped camp in Marienehe near Rostok. As Heinkel said himself: 'We worked without the knowledge of any official body on the development and construction of the first turbine or jet engine which, a year and half later, still in the strictest isolation and following a series of failures after which I required all my willpower to persevere, ran for the first time on a September night in 1937. I shall never forget the way in which Hahn, who had spent almost every day and night on his feet, just like von Ohain, shouted out in joy to me that night at 1 a.m. The engine had got underway for the first time. Fuel for the combustion chamber was then provided by hydrogen and not, as later, by benzine or crude oil. And for a quarter of an hour I heard for myself, for the first time, with my own ears, that extraordinary howling and whistling noise which shook the whole shed, and which has become commonplace for any of us nowadays who has been in a jet aircraft.'

271

But there was still a long way to go before they could make that engine fly. In order to keep spectators away, tests took place in the first light of dawn, initially with an He 118 which took off with an ordinary engine until the pilot switched on the jet engine. 'This was the first time we saw the bluish flame shooting out of the engine into the air. The He 118's speed immediately increased with a jolt.' Heinkel had had a second improved power plant fitted to an He 178, which had been developed purely as a jet aircraft and finally, on Sunday 27 August 1939 (four days before the outbreak of war), it was ready between three and four o'clock in the morning.

On the day when the first jet aircraft in the world flew with the Heinkel He S3B engine (a year and a half before the English Gloster E 28/39 with a Whittle engine), Captain Erich Warsitz reported:

> The machine was towed out for take-off. As Heinkel had built this airplane completely off his own bat, and without informing the RAM, we could not have shown this machine previously, even on company land, as this would have broken the secrecy. Heinkel wanted to present the RAM with a finished airplane. This was why I had been forced to forego the normally indispensable roll tests. I just tested all the rudders for operation, checked the turbine at various speeds, as well as pump pressures, temperatures and quite a few other things, before giving a sign to the fitters that they should pull the cockpit canopy across. After a run-up of about 300 metres, I quickly gathered speed. It was wonderful how I could hold her on course with the brakes. Then she took off.
>
> Time and again I tried to retract the undercarriage. But something was not quite right. The main thing, though, was that she was flying . . . my air speed indicator now showed 600 kph, but there was no way I could fly faster, according to my instructions from Herr Schwärzler. So I had to throttle back.
>
> I had now been in the air for six minutes, and had to prepare to come down. The turbine obediently responded to my throttle lever, although one fuel pump was out of action, as I saw on my instruments and as we were later to establish on the engine. While flattening out, I almost overshot, but could not fly round again due to a shortage of fuel, and so I had no choice but to sideslip, otherwise I would have rolled into the Warnow. Sideslipping was always very disagreeable to me in a new machine, quite apart from the fact of being so close to the ground. The machine landed smoothly, without bouncing, and continued rolling in the same direction it had landed. I was able to bring her to a halt immediately in front of Dr Heinkel and his group.

It was still only 4.30 a.m. when Heinkel rang up Udet in his Berlin flat. Still half asleep, Udet replied: 'Well, fine, congratulations, then. And to Warsitz, as well. But first, let me catch up on my sleep.'

Did Udet not understand what had happened? Did he not know that in the previous year two experts from the RAM, Helmut Schelp and Hans Mauch, had undertaken a tour of all the German engine companies to interest them in developing jet engines? Many had declined. But at BMW they had listened. The people they met here were the director Sachse and Dr Kurt Löhner and, at the Brandenburg Motor Works (Bramo), the director Bruno Bruckmann and Dr Hermann Oestrich, who declared themselves ready for development work.

Hermann Oestrich had been working since 1931 as the group leader for thermodynamics at the German Research Establishment for aviation on the project of 'prospects for jet-propelled airplanes with special reference to exhaust propulsion'. Under Oestrich's leadership the famous BMW 003 jet engine came into being at the BMW works in Spandau. This was the engine described by Allied commissions and experts after the war as being the best German turbo-prop engine in its specific performance figures and design details.

When Oestrich began work on the first pre-tests in collaboration with the engineer Hermann Hagen, anyone who had previously only built piston engines was entering unknown territory. They gained their first experiences using a pre-test appliance, constructed out of the turbocharger from a Bramo 323 piston engine, a segmental combustion chamber and an exhaust turbine. They rejected the ram-jet process, despite the fact that it worked, and decided on the turbo-propeller system, fitting this with an axial compressor – which was admittedly more complicated than the radial compressor engine, on which Ohain was working, but had the advantage of having a small diameter. (As Heinkel had explained in his memoirs, the radial compressor deflected the air flowing in axially near the hub in a radial direction, and accelerated it outwards, while the axial compressor conveyed the air through several rows of wing-like vanes, which were mounted one behind the other, with some standing still while others rotated, in an axial direction under a constant rise in pressure.)

By the middle of 1939 the engine had been well designed throughout. By the beginning of 1941, the BMW P 3302 test engine was beginning its first trials.

'Starting up went smoothly enough,' reported Oestrich, 'but further tests subsequently revealed various difficulties, such as vane failure on the turbine after a comparatively short running time. The welds between the rotor body and the vanes were difficult to produce perfectly. The combustion chamber also had very uneven temperature distribution and a high loss in pressure.'

Yet in November 1941 (the offensive by the German armies in Russia had come to a halt short of Moscow, as the first snowflakes were falling), the engines were fitted to an Me 262 V 1, but the machine was only ready for take-off on 25 March 1942. Did it actually fly on that day? No, it did not, because both engines failed at 50 metres off the ground due to vane fracture, and it was only the Junkers aero-engine fitted to the machine for safety reasons which saved Fritz Wendel (who had dared to take off) and his aircraft.

The Oestrich group now went ahead with a new version of the P 3302 engine. Four further engines were built (V11-V14), and the 'ring combustion chamber', typical of the 003, came into being. (As Dr Oestrich recalled: 'It was initially not at all clear how this volume was to burn the ten- to a

273

hundred-fold increase in the amount of fuel, which had been converted into one of the most modern available in terms of unit volume. The air left the compressor at around 85 m/sec. The rate of combustion of the gases in the tubes was normally between 2 and 5 m/sec, with turbulence. Areas of lower air speed therefore had to be created, in order to keep the flame inside the combustion chamber and prevent it from being carried out by the high gas speed. The slipstream was initially created by flat baffles, sixteen in all, which were sprayed from the front by sixteen fuel injectors assigned to each.')

A new, hollow turbine vane was developed, through which cooling air entered through a drilling at the foot of the vane. The initial test results were encouraging to Oestrich. The engine had considerably greater reserves, and the air throughput was 30 per cent higher for the same diameter of compressor. After the engine had been tested at low-level flying under the fuselage of a Ju 88 (this was in October 1943), the result was a standing thrust of 800 kiloponds (the output required by aircraft companies) and continuous running of first 20, then 50 hours. The maximum speed near the ground was 800 kph. On 4 February 1944, an Arado 234 V 8 took off from the wintry airfield at Brandenburg on the Havel on an initial test flight. This was a long-distance reconnaissance plane with four BMW 003-A-O in twin nacelles under the wings. Two months later, a test flight took place with the same engines in four separate nacelles. In September of that year, Captain Josef Bisping reached a maximum height of 13 kilometres in the aircraft with twin engines.

This had taken five years. Anyone reflecting on the fact that components occurring thirty years later in the most modern engines of the jet age were invented, developed and applied at that time (axial compressors, ring combustion chambers with secondary air mixing, axial, pressure-compensation plungers, those hollow turbine vanes and guide vanes made from sheet-metal with cooling inserts, the adjustable thrust-jet, single-lever operation) is faced with a problem. There were shortages of nickel, tungsten, molybdenum, and chromium, metals indispensable for the alloys capable of resisting high temperatures. In addition, there were countless difficulties. Overcoming them led (to name but one example) to those hollow vanes cooled from inside, which were no mere stop-gaps, but were to determine technological progress. Thousands of tests were necessary just to track down what was generating the vibrations which had led to fractures. It took a year to discover a method to measure vibrations during operation, by direct observation – a year in which Oestrich faced competition from the other German jet-engine developments. At Heinkel, this was the Ohain group, which was working on an engine of radial design, and a second group working with an axial compressor. At Junkers, technicians were developing the Jumo 004, under Dr Anselm Franz. This was a more conventionally designed engine, based on earlier developments under Herbert Wagner, which went into production and was delivered in 5,000 units to the Luftwaffe by the end of the war. And all these groups were in competition with BMW, not to mention those abroad who were now at war, about whom little was known except that they were feverishly building jet engines, too.

It was only this fear of the enemy which forced the Luftwaffe high command to give up their fear of the unknown, even if they were hesitant and only took one step at a time. They had to accept the radical, technological change which had happened and became clearer by the day. But it was too late, as was subsequently shown. When Heinkel had provided the proof, even before the war (on 27 August 1939), that jet propulsion was a reality and not a fantasy, even Ernst Udet thought it was little more than a gimmick. This was humanly understandable, considering that he, the old fighter pilot with his 'Pour le Mérite' [Germany's highest military award in the First World War], had achieved his victories with petrol engines. Even Field Marshal Milch was full of reservations, going as far as to forbid Heinkel from any further experiments after the Polish campaign, thereby stalling peacetime development in the grand illusion created by those days.

After the Battle of France, and in the belief that the war was as good as won, a so-called stop on development was even ordered, whereby all developments to do with flight technology, stretching beyond six months, had to be called off or at least interrupted, in order to release men and materials for those proven types of aircraft which were deemed to be what was needed for final victory (over Britain). This was a measure which caused Germany to lose its undoubted air advantage. Even as late as 15 September 1942, as Heinkel reported, Milch decided himself to downgrade the He 280 jet fighter, which had already been test-flown, and the rival Messerschmitt Me 262 'to the lowest level of urgency'.

However, that argument finally came to a head at a conference convened in January 1943 between leaders of industry and the Director of Armaments to whom Heinkel said that considering the present state of jet engines, there was not a second to lose. Something had to be done like inviting a committee from the Ministry on a visit. This would sort out the difficulties. 'It does not matter whether a Junkers or a BMW engine, or anybody else's, is fitted. Whatever the case, the machine will be ready for take-off by the middle of next year, with fifty, sixty or a hundred machines able to do 900 kph. The enemy could appear any day now.' That was when fear took hold, this time a much greater one than before. Accused by Hitler of inexcusable failures, Milch got ready to deploy the jet aircraft.

When it was then deployed (Adolf Galland, chief of fighter command, found words for jet propulsion that were as macabre as they were striking: 'It's as if an angel were pushing!'), it was supposed to measure up as a fighter, night fighter, interceptor, reconnaissance plane and bomber. It was supposed to make up for what conventionally designed airplanes could no longer offer, in spite of all the efforts of the aviation industry now directed from Speer's Department, and in spite of approximately 30,000 aircraft being produced in a Germany devasted by bombing raids, an output twenty times greater than at the height of the the Battle of Britain. (In Udet's time, 898 aircraft per month were delivered by German manufacturers to the Luftwaffe; with Milch, the average in 1943 was 1,700; Speer reached the highest figure ever delivered with 4,352 aircraft in September 1944.) What did that mean? What was undeniable (looking at it from the viewpoint of the war) was the fact that the Me 109, for example, which at the start of the air war had been greatly superior to every enemy fighter, given that it was also being built in large quantities, was no longer technologically up to its opponents by the fifth year of the war. It was faced with what men like Galland could only describe as a tragedy. The tragedy was that the jet engine, propelling a Me 262 twice as fast as the enemy's fighters (and still 200 kph faster than their best escort fighters), came too late. It was a type of propulsion which would 'provide us with an unimaginable lead if the enemy is to keep using piston engines' (Galland to Milch), and opens up 'completely new tactical possibilities'. It came too late, too late for production, for it to be produced in considerable numbers, too late for the front . . . too late altogether. This is a sentiment we are justified in thinking we have heard before – Udet had concluded his letter to BMW at the end of the First World War with the very same words.

This 'too late' was also in no measure altered by Heinkel's design of the legendary 'People's Fighter' He 162, realised in an incredibly short time (design work was begun on 24 September 1944, and the first flight took place on 6 December 1944). Fitted with the BMW 003 jet engine, it flew at a height of 6 km and a speed of 840 kph. Heinkel had mounted the engine above the fuselage, not fitting any tanks, but allowing the fuel to flow from hollow wooden parts on the wings, which had been specially impregnated for this. These parts had been produced at very small joiners' workshops in Thuringia and Wurttemberg, i.e. by cottage industry.

The Hitler Youth, after intensive courses to become pilots, were supposed to soar up into the skies 'for the defence of Germany'. Heinkel openly acknowledged in his memoirs:

This 'too late', however, only had a very limited connection with Germany's victory or defeat. Even earlier completion of our work (when in 1941 Germany enjoyed overwhelming military superiority) would not have altered the outcome of this war. It would have delayed it, and it would have created a respite in the air war – but a respite is all it would have been, because no technical development, however revolutionary, is restricted to one country. Quite independently of us, Britain followed the same path, even if they were a year behind. The numerous 'V-1 (flying) bodies', which never reached London, but broke up over the Channel, fell victim, amongst other things, to the British 'Meteor' jet airplane with a Rolls-Royce Welland jet engine. German development at this time may well have been far advanced, but it could never have essentially changed the face of the air war. It would only have encouraged the other side to employ twice as much effort, given their huge material and industrial facilities, to catch up with and overtake German development and its many obstacles. A respite from fighting does not amount to victory. Everything else is myth; comforting maybe, but far from the truth.

Whether it was far from the truth or not, when this 'too late' should have paralysed the hands of any reasonable person (easy enough to say, since who could afford to be reasonable), a group of technicians was working on a few secret projects which only had a limited connection with the 003 engine. They were at Allach near Munich, in an area sealed off by barbed wire and screens, where they were subjected to daily interruptions from air-raid sirens. These were the 'rocket people', headed by a certain Zborowski. Count Helmut Philip Georg Alexander Rudolf von Zborowski, calling himself simply 'Zborowski' as an SS lieutenant, was mentioned in a report from the BMW works council in evidence given to the denazification court in 1947: 'It was well known in the company that he had to leave his home, Austria, because of Fascist intrigues, and that he was already subscribing to National Socialist ideas in his youth. His appearance at the works showed that, both mentally and physically, he was completely convinced of these ideas. In the latter years, he was rarely to be seen out of an SS uniform.'

The director Bruno Bruckmann even went as far as to recommend him for a salary increase at the end of 1944:

> Herr Zborowski is the spiritual father of completely new kinds of weapons, which have been designed and implemented on his ideas in the development facilities created for this. All the development facilities were put under his control and, in a very short space of time, he has brought the appliances to a stage of development where their rapid deployment can be contemplated. Next to high engineering ability, the organisational skills demanded by the break-up of the company (which was brought on by the war) should be especially emphasised. Without sparing himself, Herr Zborowski has worked tirelessly to bring the task to fruition. For his special achievements, he has already been decorated with the Service Medal with swords, and now there is an urgent need for his salary. . . .

Was it this man, was it the rocket department he headed, was it their 'tests' at Zühlsdorf and Allach which had led the Allies to judge and condemn BMW?

Faust and Mephisto

Clad all in steel, where lightnings shiver,
The host, that realm on realm subdued,
They come, the trembling earth must quiver,
They pass, and thunder is renewed
(Goethe, *Faust*, Part Two, Act III)

What Goethe had in mind when he made Faust say the mysterious words as he turned to the leaders of the forces: 'Clad all in steel, where lightnings shiver . . .' has, it must be admitted, little to do with the vision that the jet and rocket era started in the Second World War. Yet, allusions can be made, if only tentatively. The old 'history of Dr Johann Fausten, the much learned sorcerer and black magician' acts upon Goethe's epic poem, in which the Faust saga turns to the tragedy of the human mind striving for truth, and human fate in general, even to this very day.

My Faust was thirty-six years old when, on 24 December 1941, he sent a secret command and control document to Mephisto, which promised the solution to five problems decisive to the war. Each of these problems (increasing the carrying capacity of aircraft, improving their peak altitudes, raising the maximum speed of U-boats and speed boats and, above all, the military application of rocket engines with liquid fuel for both aircraft and missiles) was a question of how to power the object, and he, Helmut Zborowski, had solved it. Whether this involved a new mechanical operating process, as he had already invented in 1939 to improve conventional piston engines (forced induction with simultaneous fuel enriching by injecting water with added methyl alcohol), or whether it involved rocket-assisted take-off devices, or pump engines, compressed air appliances, or his revolutionary differential plunger engine, or that adjustable power plant for the Me 163 B rocket-propelled fighter designed to fly beyond the speed of sound, then Helmut Zborowski could supply it. An SS Second Lieutenant and employed since his 'decommissioning from the SS Adolf Hitler Leibstandarte [regiment entrusted with safeguarding the Führer's life]' in October 1939 at the Spandau development department of the BMW Aero-Engine Works Ltd, he had here (or more accurately at the Zühlsdorf rocket works on the Brandenburg Heath near Berlin) researched,

278

developed, tested and finally so designed everything that existing weapons could be equipped with these facilities or adapted in next to no time.

The secret command and control document, covering thirty-six pages, was logically and cleverly drafted. It did not conceal the inventor's father (he was the 'famous Colonel Zborowski, one of the most decorated officers in the Austro-Hungarian Army and pre-war flying corps'), nor the mother ('the eldest daughter of Georg Schönerer, the champion of the pan-German concept in what was previously Austro-Hungary'). It also quoted applications for patents and test reports, tables and comparative values, which clearly showed that all these projects (whose technical details even a layman could understand) were no mere fantasies or rough sketches. Being head and shoulders above all previous systems, they could immediately be put into practice. An 'outlook' as to how far each individual project had been realised was added, from which the recipient could work out what he still had to do to get it working as quickly as possible, and to use those powers he had to put it into application. A striking monument to this was the use of a chemical substance available in unlimited quantities (in contrast to other costly fuels which had all but run out). This was something which was not without its hazards, but could be controlled, i.e. nitric acid, which would act as a source of oxygen.

After reading page after page of this report, and other items, which went back as far as 1944 and which are now stored on microfilm in the Institute for Contemporary History in Munich, I was left in no doubt that this had all really happened. In the Deutsche Museum, individual rocket engines made by Zborowski in the form of cross-sectional models are on display. But the fact that this man, who here resembled Faust in promising to be able to change German fate through his inventions, had also found his Mephisto, was new to me. Faust and Mephisto!

Mephisto came in no other form than that of SS Reichsführer Heinrich Himmler, to whom all these memos and reports on inventions were directed. It is a picture that will not leave me.

What kind of dubious arrangement had BMW got itself into again? The SS, smoking red nitric acid, combustion chambers which flew through the air, a restless inventor popping up here and there, risking life and limb in his experiments, mines, in whose tunnels deep *under* ground concentration camp inmates, literally living corpses, screwed together glider-bombs with sets of rockets designed to save a Reich *above* ground, whose fate the SS state with all its crimes had long since sealed. The end result of an industrial plant (even if it was only burdened in passing with such pictures of horror) facing a merciless sentence by the victors was not far off.

The question was all the more pressing. What was BMW really being charged with in its guilty implication with facts which were bound to affect every German, whether he was in a position to do anything about it or not (but at least causing considerable embarrassment)? When and where had it taken place, this testimony of guilt? Given that it had, could it have been foreseen? Could one have guessed what was involved or potentially involved with the contract given by the RAM to BMW in its development of both the 003 jet engine and rocket engines?

When Popp appeared before the denazification court in 1947 on a charge of being a skilful collaborator in the Third Reich, he passionately protested that he had opposed the purchase of the Brandenburg Motor Works (Bramo) as far back as 1938–39 (unfortunately in vain), knowing full well that expansion of aero-engine production would disturb the foundation he was trying to establish, namely having three legs to stand on (aero-engines, cars, and motorcycles). Yet Fritz Hille, his opponent on the board, had insisted on it, making it impossible to decline business from the Reich, which he could comfortably have avoided before by being able to show that he did not have enough capacity. That was no longer possible. Enlarged by facilities for expanding in size and scope on the Brandenburg sand behind Berlin, where Bramo possessed further works and sites, there had been no way back for BMW, forcing the company to do what he, Popp, had wanted to avoid.

Who would contest otherwise? Even if earlier statements by Popp (in his letters to the RAM) show the acquisition of Bramo in a completely different light. Here he had been the promoter of the merger, not its opponent. Yet this brought up quite a different question, and if Popp concealed it, then he knew the reason why. Here was a company at the top of the technological ladder, which, so to speak, had taken out a lease in conjunction with him. Could it shut itself off from a development, which (admittedly forced through by war) aviation had demanded? No, Popp was not the kind of man to be relegated to second or third place by others, just for him to stand idly by, watching everything that had been achieved now suddenly be given away to others, simply 'because of insufficient capacity'. A glance over the frontiers (when it was still possible to do so) left him in no doubt that the principle of thrust, produced either by jets or rockets, would enable speeds to be reached which broke the sound barrier. This would bring about a new era in aviation. To refuse to have anything to do with this was not on BMW's agenda, not even when it was politically expedient to make oneself small and keep one's head down.

So what had to happen, happened. After the first step (expanding the company), BMW was no longer in a position to deny the RAM its wishes, as shown by the contract to develop a turbo-prop engine and adopting rockets in its research programme. (Popp could only raise his old objection against the jet engine, saying that it was utterly wrong to let all the firms, even an outsider like Heinkel, have a go at it at the same time. In his opinion, an essentially new form of propulsion like this needed to be developed exclusively by a government body, such as the German Research Establishment for Aviation, naturally with appropriate consultation with the whole aviation industry. This concentration would, in time and after expenditure of considerable mental effort, undoubtedly lead to the one true solution and 'release the major capacities we need in the immediate future for even more important things. As regards the jet engine, my thoughts are therefore exactly the same as they were towards the 803 engine, i.e. it is not through false ambition that I can contemplate a possible, temporary advance for our competitors, since this problem is far from vital to our survival over the next five years.')

But back to rocket manufacture. As can be proved, the contract was issued in 1939, when the war was already underway, and probably at first only because the Technical Section, in time-honoured manner, wanted competition for another company; this time the Walter Works in Kiel which had already begun tests on rockets in 1935. But where could they find people who knew about rockets? There was no one apparently more suitable to spirit a rocket works out of the ground than an engineer, once employed at Milbertshofen on aero-engine production (this was in 1934), who had set up test beds in the Lüneberg Heath for the Gas Dynamics Department of the Aviation Research Establishment at Brunswick. Collaborating there with Eugen Sänger, the pioneer of rocket research, this man proved to be none other than Zborowski. When whole concrete foundations were poured into the sand for jet engines in the pine forest near the villages of Basdorf and Zühlsdorf, where the Niederbarnim Aero-Engine Works, now a part of the BMW group, were situated, just a few forest aisles behind Oestrich's test beds, only a few select people knew what was being developed here; it was like a witches' coven, where a handful of technicians and mechanics began to convert Zborowski's ideas into practice.

Even today a veil hangs over this place, just as it did when air-raid sirens were sounded over the rocket site, and artificial fog shrouded test beds, combustion chambers, mechanics and engineers in their sheds, making them invisible from above. These sites were never fully recognisable, even to those who let off the rockets and moved them around (people knew just enough to carry out their specific job, and that was it). This was how they remained in the twilight. Technical reports, stamped TOP SECRET, described combinations of weapons whose realisation was either never taken seriously or which failed for reasons that are still unknown. Old document files, filled to overflowing with these reports, refused to substantiate what was mere fantasy and what was reality. Names crop up: Kappus, Ristau, Wessel, a qualified engineer called Schneider is mentioned frequently, who, next to Zborowski, appears to have been the driving force. Technical terms abound: rocket-assisted take-off fitting, using hydrogen peroxide, with fuel delivered by compressed gas; glider-bomb propulsion using nitric acid delivered by a differential plunger; turbo-propeller drive for a high-speed torpedo (500 hp); rocket propulsion for a winged anti-aircraft missile, with fine tuning and able to resist spatial acceleration, as well as for a winged ship-to-ship missile, also using nitric acid, with a pre-set thrust programme.

On 30 August 1946 the Bavarian Motor Works gave a written testimonial for engineer H.P.G.A.R. Zborowski, to the effect that he was born on 21 August 1905 at Theresienstadt and from 1 September 1939 had been 'in the service of our company', working with his colleagues on various systematic series of tests, pre-tests, model evaluations and principle tests, and on technical reports and projects relating to the appliances and rocket fuels requiring development for the contract. He developed and tested the first nitric-acid combustion chambers 'in our company', after having built the first nitre high-pressure pumps and other equipment items. Hang on a moment. 1946? It sounded like a comprehensive report with nothing but successes, as if the sky over Germany had been swept clean by this machinery, the enemy's armada destroyed, the war not lost, but won.

A summary from the post-war period, dealing with the 'development of the rocket-manufacturing department at BMW', lists individual projects but confines itself to numbers, dates and abstract phraseology. Here and there places are mentioned: 'Zühlsdorf', 'Allach-Munich'; more than once sentences like these appear: 'P 3370 and P 3371 were stopped, later completely dropped from the programme, P 3372 was embarked upon . . .'. Became, succeeded, turned out to be, started up, had to be stopped . . . as if it were a piece of secret machinery, drawing a life-force from itself, without the aid of humans beings. At best it was human brain-power which a superior being had made use of and directed. And time and again, without giving a valid reason, and after countless experiments had led to something being ready for production and then finally complete and ready for deployment (at the expense of human beings who went up with it and were torn to pieces, at the expense of millions of marks, and with valuable, almost unobtainable materials going up in smoke), time and again, the stereotypical statement runs: 'Large-scale production was not started, because the RAM was no longer interested in the engine.' Or: 'Stopped because of a shortage of suitable workers and finally abandoned during 1944.' Or: '. . . did not get beyond the pre-test stage . . . put back . . . cancelled . . . stopped.'

Why was this? I could find no answer.

Who could give me one? Zborowski had already died. One of the test engineers from Zühlsdorf, Kurt Sohr, had written to BMW about a welfare matter (he had been badly burnt during a test in the war), in which he admitted his involvement, and noting in a PS:

Many of our writers have only praised the major successes and achievements of the Americans and Russians – space travel, missions to the moon, and other such undertakings. Unfortunately, what all these history books fail to mention is all the ground work contained in the many tons of files and drawings and complete rockets (secret command and control documents!) which were removed and evaluated by the GPU [forerunner of the KGB] and the Americans under the code-name 'Paperclip' after the war, when they rummaged through the underground works at Peenemünde, Zühlsdorf and at BMW in Staßfurt.

What was still missing could have been supplied by us at Zehlendorf in Berlin for a packet of Camel cigarettes.

Nobody tells this story, either because everyone has forgotten, or because they weren't allowed to know. He who pays the piper, calls the tune.'

I rang Sohr up. He came across immediately. 'You knew Zborowski?' I asked. The question had the effect of opening the floodgates.

'He would often turn up in the middle of the night,' Sohr began, 'on his motorbike, a gift from BMW. He lived at Lietzenburger Street in Berlin. He would wake us up by hammering on the door.

'"Listen, gov'ners" he would say in his Graz dialect, "lend an ear, will you, I've got something to show you." That sparked things off.'

'Sparked what off?'

'Well,' said Sohr, slightly surprised, 'a new test. It's all beautifully drawn on graph paper these days – ellipses, curves – but at that time, there was none of that, just a few sketches. Then it was off to the test station. We set about making parts straight away, we were out there day and night. When we fitted the parts and it broke up, we knew we'd gone wrong. There weren't any ready cook books for rockets, like you get today. Everything had to be tested . . . by Müller. He was my test chief (he later went off to America). Mucha, Elmar Mucha, conducted the "test". Then there were two other men from design.'

'And Zborowski?'

'Of course, Zborowski, he was the leading light, got things going, carried everyone along.'

'Did you know of his double role?'

'Double role?'

'Yes, he was an SS man, an SS officer, though not one of the top.'

Sohr nodded. 'We weren't blind, you know. He would turn up in uniform – the SS was an elite association in those days, many were there under instructions – but we made out we hadn't noticed anything. There we were in our old boiler suits, scruffy old clothes, and so on, with him there dressed to the nines in a black tailcoat and medals. Until one day he said: "Any of you gov'ners here a member of the SS?" We gawped at him. "SS? What's that?" asked one of us. That set him laughing! That was the last time he asked anything like that. It was only rockets we had on our minds, we had put up the buildings ourselves, even the test beds. The first were still made out of wood, with double walls and filled with sand, that Brandenburg sand which would all just trickle out when shrapnel hit it, just like an egg-timer. Udet once copped it; he was standing around when we were experimenting, when the combustion chamber broke apart . . . I stuck a plaster on his nose, he had to pay for a crate of beer, but never had any money on him. His chauffeur was cursing that he had to pay out seven marks fifty again, but my colleagues pressed me to take them off him. You don't trust yourself, as Berliners say, but I trust myself . . . and then we built up the concrete beds . . . and anchored the equipment, and then all sorts of projects got going – V 1, V 2. These weren't the V weapons, they were the test numbers: Test number 1, test equipment 2. And this nitric acid, which corroded everything, metal, rubber, skin, if you didn't wash it off with water straight away. We gradually learnt how to handle it . . . as everyone knows, Zborowski was all for nitric acid, it was his discovery, or if it wasn't, then it was a kind of obsession he had. In '39 he had had difficulty promoting it, this idea of nitric acid as a source of oxygen. It was simply that no one wanted to have anything to do with it, least of all the RAM. Until we discovered an autoreaction. It was pure chance, simply good luck. *Tempi passati*, as the Italians say. But I still remember the mechanic even today.'

'Which mechanic?'

'We had tested nitric acid on Zborowski's suggestion, for the thousandth time, and still the thing wouldn't ignite. We had put a little bowl with methyl alcohol (or was it aniline?) on the ground, with a pipette with nitric acid in it, thumb over the top, we'd always drawn it up like this, with our other hand covering our eyes (there weren't any protective goggles like today), we'd always put a few drops in, but it wouldn't ignite. We told the mechanic, who was wearing protective gloves, to wipe the bowl out. So he wiped it out with some waste cotton, something as simple as an old cloth . . . and suddenly it ignited, bright and red . . . almost burning his hands. What a miracle! Without ignition, on its own! We went at it with layers of cotton wool, saturating it with aniline, poured on some nitric acid. Nothing. Just yellow smoke, as before. Was it the fault of the waste cotton? How can I put it? That's exactly where the fault was! We sent it to the laboratory, and they discovered that cotton wool is chemically cleaned in production with some kind of substance . . . copper salt! A tiny trace of it, but enough to act as a catalyst, as the chemists say. Now we knew that it would react on its own. So I stood there with my motorcycle goggles (which I always wore) around my neck and not around my eyes because I was so excited. We'd made an invention. Sensational! All this trouble with ignition was over now. And what those people at the top of the RAM had refused to believe was now working. Nitric acid could act as a source of oxygen. We carried on testing until we had the right mixture, which admittedly stank to high heaven, like the stench of decay, really bad. We called the brew "tonka": tonka 93, tonka 250, tonka 500 – at least the components were obtainable: xylidine, aniline, and whatever else there was to ignite the fuel.'

'Did you know that they were also working on it in America?'

'Me? At that time? No idea. Zborowski didn't know anything, either. It was only much later that they came across it – in Pasadena, purely by chance, like us. There was talk of "hypergolene" – or hypergolene combinations, as they are known scientifically. That's always the case with inventions. Suddenly everybody has it. And amongst the eminent authorities which they had over there, for example, Kármán. . . .'

Sohr knew about this. This was Theodore von Kármán, the great aerodynamics expert and theoretician in rocket and space technology, who, while trying to use liquid fuels for rocket engines on tests at Pasadena, USA, in 1942, also opted (but later than Zborowski) for 'smoking red nitric acid', because it was much easier to handle than liquid oxygen.

With no knowledge of the German tests, they also encountered the problem of igniting nitric acid with benzine or kerosene, and came across the so-called 'hypergolene combination' due to a series of lucky breaks. A standard-bearer, the chemist Ray C. Stiff, had the idea of using aniline with nitric acid, to produce the gas pressure needed to deliver the fuel, meaning that extra tanks for this gas pressure were superfluous. The experiment was successful, the flame burnt entirely evenly. This meant that the problem of liquid-powered rockets had been solved.

'Yes,' said Sohr, 'just like us. In our case, the RAM were against nitric acid, but over there, the US Air Material Command was against aniline. They said it was too toxic. But it took only practical tests to convince the military, which was just the same in our case. But with one difference – they were just starting out over there, while here things were up and running; with liquid oxygen and hydrogen peroxide. There was now no way of changing everything over to nitric acid. There was no money, no resources, no stomach for it. If anything exploded, the motto was: play safe!

'Some would say: we need bombers; while others would say: we can do it with fighters. Some would say: with rockets; while others: without!'

'But wasn't rocket development stopped?'

'It was still going on, day and night. You couldn't imagine what we had set up in such a short time! Especially when you see today how long it takes to develop a piece of equipment like that. After the war, they brought me back to work on the Milan anti-tank rockets. I was there, watching the fiasco. It's incredible how much time the Milan needed – fifteen years! With us, it was a question of days! Each test bed had different groups working on different pieces of equipment.'

'The reports keep mentioning a water additive,' I prompted.

'That was for the gas-steam producer. There were three elements providing power for the Me 163 – methyl alcohol, nitric acid and then water was added, first to the steam-gas producer, which drove the turbine, this then delivering the other elements . . . everything was ready! Eisenlohr at the RAM (you can ask him, he's still alive) stood at the controls, looked at the pressure gauge and even flew the plane. The glider-bomb was also ready.'

'And was never built?'

'It was the same, project after project: filed in the bin! And nobody told anyone why. Just thinking about our rocket-assisted take-offs (I've still got the numbers in my head: P 3370, P 3371), and how they were stopped, then later struck off the programme is enough – propulsion for the glider-bomb with its differential plunger, 150 of these items were running on the test bed, and had been officially inspected before being thrown out. The power plants for torpedoes were postponed, then cancelled. The rocket propulsion for the interceptor, the rocket fighter, the Me 163 B, suffered similarly – it was stopped, taken up again, then finally abandoned.'

'Why?'

Sohr shrugged his shoulders. 'The equipment fitted with the differential plunger, Zborowski's stroke of genius, was something I worked on as well. It ran without pumps or any other form of drive. It only had a cartridge which ignited and gave off the gas. This gas ran behind a plunger, the same differential plunger with its outer surface greater than its inner one. In the cylinder, running inside it, was nitric acid, and there was methyl alcohol in the outer cylinder. And that's how we got the pressure differential. The pressure outside was 30 atmospheres, while inside it was 34, meaning that the fuel elements were forced into the combustion chamber through these 4 atmospheres. Then the gases left the combustion chamber through a butterfly valve behind the plunger. The gases acted all on their own on the fuel elements – it was wonderful!' Sohr said enthusiastically.

'And the differential plunger was never put into operation?'

'Well, yes and no,' said Sohr, almost embarrassed. 'It was used in the Walter device, which is now in the Deutsche Museum. Only the X 4 device, known as the pipe-snake, was built.'

'And what was that, the "pipe-snake"?'

Sohr said: 'There the fuel elements were in a pipe-snake – and were then blown out by compressed air. But every test produced different diagrams. Another problem. How come, why? Until we came upon . . . or rather I came upon . . . a glass-blower at the Neues Tor in Berlin. They were all there, hundreds of glass-blowers, wonderful people. There I had a glass snake made. I only described it roughly, but they made it very well, almost while I waited. We filled the glass snake with water, blown in by mouth, and what did we find? Well, we found that if we blew air in, the water column would rise right to the top – and fall back again to the right and left. Then we forced in some very small balls . . . made of a plastic called lupolen, for the nitric acid . . . they were only made out of leather for the other element (I recently gave one of these balls to the Deutsche Museum) . . . and look what happened. Expelled by a plunger, the fuel elements could no longer move away, meaning that they had to escape out of the front. A small detail, but these are the kind of things you cannot see on the drawing-board. We made some sketches, went off to the workshop, tested it – and it worked!'

'So the X 4 was built?'

'Yes, though not by BMW, but in the mine at Nordhausen.'

'By whom?'

'Under SS supervision, as it was called.'

'So that was that.'

'That was what?'

'Take a look at this a moment,' I said, opening out on the table in front of Sohr the photocopied documents which Zborowski had sent to his lord and master about the secret command and control document.

Sohr looked at everything carefully. Now and again he said: 'Mmm, that's right, that's right.' Or: 'That's when everything was ready.' Or: 'I was there at the time.'

Then he read aloud: 'Reichsführer! The development work on the new BMW power plant has now reached a stage that now . . . when was that?' he interrupted himself, looking at the date and reading 'Berlin W 15, Lietzenburger Street 12, 2 September 1943', before reading on: '. . . that now a start can be made on serial production of this unit. The engine, in contrast to normal piston engines, is designed as a gas turbine, by which forward thrust takes place through the reaction of the air and exhaust jet without recourse to a propeller.'

He bent over the lines which were difficult to read, and which the microfilm excerpt did not clearly reproduce, as if the original had been affected by heat or water. 'The following is underlined. Who did that?'

'Probably the Americans,' I said, 'when they found the documents.'

Sohr continued reading aloud, deciphering word for word: 'This engine enables speeds to be reached in the airframes which both Messerschmitt and

Heinkel have developed, and which are approximately twice those previously attained by piston engines. In addition, the possible chemical combination of these engines with rocket power plants provides for such high ascent speeds that the airframes fitted with them can happily combine short ascent times and high speeds with long periods of flight. Consequently, these machines provide the ideal engines for the home defence. . . .' He turned the page. 'The production of these engines has now come up against difficulties at BMW, as there can and should not be any justification for closing down existing works involved in aero-engine production just so as to increase production of the new equipment. The present state in the air war requires much more than that, not only that production of fighter engines should remain undisturbed, but that it should be increased to the maximum.'

Sohr pushed the papers away and looked at me. 'It's all correct. Just one thing, though. What's it got to do with the Reichsheini [Himmler's nickname]?'

Sohr read on: 'Reichsführer, I have this process to report to you, to provide you with clear information so that you can make your decision in due course. Your obedient servant, Zborowski, SS Lieutenant.'

'Yes, that was probably true, then,' said Sohr, and stood up. It was only then that I saw how small he was, 1.595 metres tall, the small Sohr, who had failed the medical inspection because he was not tall enough to be considered for the Wehrmacht. This was not the only reason why he became a rocket technician.

'It's very odd,' I said, 'that it never occurred to you that there was more to Zborowski than simply someone who was entrusted to come up with inventions which never got off the ground. Your Count must have been thinking much further, right from the start. Was he in the SS on instructions? Hardly. To further his career? Perhaps. But also as a means to an end, to push through his inventions. And so he forced these inventions, realised by BMW but declined by the RAM, onto the only real power that still existed, as far as he was concerned, however sinister that may have been – onto Himmler, the head of the SS.'

'So we were shopped twice,' Sohr remarked.

'Twice?'

'Once to the SS; nobody knew about that, no one at all, I can swear to that. . . .'

'And to who else?'

'To the British. It was the Abwehr captain we had, who hermetically sealed off the rocket site in Zühlsdorf. He was a man by the name of Illinger, and whenever we had father's day (once a week we were allowed home to our wives), he would calmly inspect all the safes in the compound at five in the afternoon. He naturally had all the keys, and photographed anything we had sketched and put in them. The Tommies knew everything being thought up at Zühlsdorf. We, in turn, learnt from Canaris that they knew everything. . . .'

'Then they also knew in England that the RAM abandoned all the Zborowski equipment as soon as they were ready, and that they never put them into effect?'

'Certainly. They could rest calm about that.'

'And Zborowski? Wasn't he very depressed when he saw engine upon engine being rejected, that everything was a waste of time?'

'We never noticed. He was always an optimist; at least, that was the impression he gave. When the raids got heavier (probably because of Illinger's report to the Tommies), the whole rocket department was moved to Allach, and then from Allach to Bruckmühl near Rosenheim. At Allach in 1944, our Count built entirely new test beds.'

'Was he popular?'

'With us certainly. He stuck his neck out, just as we did.' (Sohr had, as I knew, been to many outside tests at Peenemünde, and on his twenty-fifth visit there, he had literally taken off with the rocket – he still carried the marks from it on his face and hands.)

'The story in Munich was that Zborowski was supposed to have charged around on a bicycle fitted with a small machine gun after the capitulation.'

'I knew nothing about that,' said Sohr. 'After my accident I was transferred to the Oestrich people, the jet engine group. I was virtually immobilised, my hands were in plaster.'

'That was in 1944?'

'Yes. When I got better, I tried out plain bearings for the Me 262 fighter instead of ball-bearings (Kugelfischer had been completely destroyed in the bombing), and then I went to the potash mines at Staßfurt, down to the third level. This was where I came across the documents.'

'Which documents?'

'Well, the design drawings for the jet engine, which I snatched up when I saw that it was all over. But that's another story – which Zborowski had nothing to do with.'

'You never saw him again?'

'Yes, I did,' said Sohr, 'after the war. The French had immediately got him back to work again; he was based in a little château near Paris.'

'Rockets again?'

'What else? From Paris he was then brought back to Bonn, which is where I met him.'

'So he was never arrested as a war criminal?'

'No,' said Sohr, 'only me.'

'You, "small Sohr"?'

'It's always like that. The big fry are allowed to go, while the small fry get hanged. Well, as you can see, I didn't actually get hanged, but. . . .'

That was indeed another story, and it also provided information about the status of war criminals. Judged on Eisenhower's decree, every German rocket technician was one – an edict which possibly explained why BMW was put on the blacklist. As regards Zborowski, it was preceded by an episode which no chronicler can ignore if he is looking into the question: what was it really like? Was it genuinely like that? Trying to get to the bottom of things.

A few days after 20 July 1944, when Stauffenberg failed in his attempt on Hitler's life, Zborowski made an appointment to see Krafft von

Dellmensingen, the head of the legal department at BMW. He wanted to see him privately, not on business.

Krafft was extremely surprised. Privately? He had only met Zborowski twice. Once with Hille ('Be careful,' he had warned, 'never say a word more than you have to. We can't be sure that Z. is definitely on our side.'), and then at the test beds in Zühlsdorf, when Zborowski was presenting one of his time bombs to the BMW directors. There he had been modest, polite and showed no trace of arrogance, because he was absolutely sure of his subject. Now, meeting for the third time, he said that he knew that Krafft was soon to marry Princess Lippe in Vienna, if he was not mistaken, and he wondered if he could place an SS car at the couple's disposal for the journey to Vienna. He said it would be a pleasure.

Krafft thanked him, but declined the offer, saying that he had been able to get couchettes, because he preferred to travel at night because of the air-raids, etc. He thanked him again. But he very much wanted to know who had told Zborowski about this, because no one outside his closest family knew about it. Zborowski came straight out with it. It was from Bendler Street in Berlin, the conspirators' headquarters, where he had been ordered by the SS Reichsführer after the events of the 20 July, in order to, well . . . sort things out. It was there that he had found a note amongst the papers and letters which had been confiscated from those under arrest or already executed. It said that Krafft was to marry Henriette Lippe, specifying time and place.

Krafft had to think on his feet. There were three possibilities. Firstly, Zborowski wanted to boast about his connections at the top: look here, you little director, look at the fantastic man you've got here. Secondly, Zborowski was fishing for information: what do you know, Krafft, about the assassins' circle? (Krafft knew nothing at all, and was mystified about who could have named him.) Thirdly, since his name had been mentioned, should he now be warned by a BMW employee, with as much caution as possible (given that we stick together, as it were, in BMW!)? All three possibilities were considered. Krafft somehow felt confident about all three. And so, turning a deaf ear to Hille's warning: 'Not a word more than you have to, for God's sake!', he now asked who was still being hunted beyond the circle of known assassins and their accomplices. Whereupon Zborowski quoted him eleven names, as if he were reading them aloud, which Krafft memorised, although he did not have a particularly good memory. As it would have been too dangerous to commit them to paper, he repeated them to himself syllable by syllable without moving his lips.

Immediately after Zborowski's departure, he sent for Dr Keßler, one of his closest colleagues, whom he could assume was close to the assassins' circle. (Keßler was related to the Dohrns, who had played a role in the White Rose trial of Hans and Sophie Scholl for high treason, and had encouraged Keßler to persuade as many eminent people as he could to speak up for the family.) Keßler appeared, went pale as he learnt of the eleven names, had them repeated to him once more, thanked Krafft, and left without saying a word.

On 14 August Krafft was married. Back in Munich, he called for Keßler.

Keßler revealed that he had warned all the eleven people and that he himself was a member of the Kreisau circle, being close to the Jesuit priest Alfred Delp, who had unfortunately been arrested and was now facing execution. He said that he must assume that sooner or later further investigations about members of this group would point to him in person. It now appeared equally certain that if Zborowski had quoted a twelfth name, it would have been Keßler's. Had it been omitted by chance or by design? Whatever the reason, Krafft now explained how from today he would be sending Keßler on a series of courier assignments throughout the Reich, firstly to Lower Franconia, where he was to deliver commercial documents of a purely factual nature to the chairman of the supervisory board and member of the Deutsche Bank, Hans Rummel. Keßler was then to travel on to Würzburg, which was not without its element of risk, as daily bombing raids were turning the last remains of Germany's pride and glory (Nuremberg and others) into dust and ashes. At BMW in Munich, they were therefore confident that they would not see Keßler again, at least not for the time being.

Keßler set off. They lost track of him in Würzburg, as an envoy sent after him was able to confirm. This was on the very evening when the city was obliterated by the Royal Air Force Bomber Command. Had Keßler managed to escape the air raid? There was no evidence of that. Krafft then ordered a ceremony in honour of Keßler's memory, and 250 mourners assembled in the conference room on the directors' floor at BMW. Krafft himself read the funeral oration. Three days later (Frau Keßler had just received the first payment of her widow's pension), Gestapo officers appeared at her husband's former place of work at the BMW works at 76, Lerchenau Street to arrest him. There they were told by Krafft that his colleague had lost his life on a business trip, probably in Würzburg.

A few days after the end of the war, a man claiming to have belonged to the legal department at BMW asked a GI on guard about the former director of his department in Milbertshofen, once he had worked his way through the mounds of rubble at Works 1. He was about to say 'Herr . . .', but the GI did not understand him. But Krafft, who like all the other directors and managers who had been detained was now busy answering the Allied Questionnaire, glanced out of the window which overlooked the main gate. He turned to the investigating officer in the room and said: 'Sir, invite that man down there in. He belongs to the company. Question him. If he tells you his name is Keßler, then you will be dealing with someone who's risen from the dead.'

Nobody in the company, including Krafft, knew that Keßler had entered service as a forester for Prince L. near Würzburg, and had been able to stay hidden. Krafft first learnt of this when he saw Keßler again. A Jesuit priest, a brother in the same order as the arrested and executed Father Delp, to whose circle Keßler had belonged, was a blood-brother of Prince L. He had provided Keßler with a hiding-place.

Krafft von Dellmensingen never learnt whether Zborowski omitted the twelfth name because he knew that Keßler was not far away. Perhaps he did not know Keßler at all, and all that Krafft had done was have 'second sight'. When we spoke about this, he told me that it was not beyond the realms of possibility that his visitor had been determined from the outset to warn Keßler. He even said that the longer he thought about it, the more it seemed possible. 'Which does not mean,' he concluded, 'that I am saying that Zborowski was a secret resistance fighter. All I'm saying is that inventors are contradictory beings. God and the devil are the same to them. How does Mephisto put it in *Faust*? 'A little jet of fire I have in store, to lift us from the earth, with strength to soar!' Nothing came of it. Why not do something that will please God and save a human being at one and the same time? A lot of things were possible in the Third Reich.'

As the War Drew to a Close

At the end of March 1945, the Allied armies had advanced as far as central Germany, with the German Army Group B encircled in the 'Ruhr Basin'. On 1 April the teleprinter at the Wehrmacht High Command entered the following about the unchanging situation into the logbook with the prosaic dryness of a legal document: 'At Kassel further enemy tanks. The 6th Tank Corps advancing on Eisenach.'

On the same day Hitler received SS General Karl Wolff in his bunker deep below the Reich Chancellery. He said to him: 'There is no point now in abandoning defence. We must hold out. We can resist the Russians in the east for another two months, and we must also hold the Italian Front. During this time there is bound to be a break in the alliance between the Russians and the Anglo-Saxons. Whichever of them manages to get to me first will be the one with whom I will ally myself against the other.'

On 4 April the teleprinter noted in the logbook: 'The situation is worsening in the Thuringian Forest on Army Group G's flank. Gotha, which the enemy reached by motorway, has been lost. 300 tanks advancing on Eisenach.'

Two days later, on a bright morning, with the light of spring lying over Wartburg Castle, the first American tank rumbled through the largely destroyed and frightened town, turned off through the underpass, leaving the old streets behind it, and sped up to the 'race track', with ruins all around. The works gate appeared, with BMW's management building close to collapse, and in front of it, a small group of people waving a white flag. Zero hour had come. At last, thank God. And the chief engineer Albert Siedler, whose task it was to direct the demolition squad to blow up anything still half standing, heaved a sigh of relief. Nobody could put him up against a wall anymore for not obeying orders. His look on leaving, as a free man simply going home, once more reflected the aftermath of war: shattered windows, broken-down walls and rubble. Rubble had replaced the repair shop, the compressor and transformer stations, the boiler house. . . . Only the old factory chimney from 1895 had survived all this devastation. But what remained could perhaps be patched up again – the body-making plant, the mechanical workshops, the halls for engine and motorcycle production, the design department, the spare parts department, the forge. But what was all this to him, to this man who, years ago, light years ago (seeming, as it did, so far away), had transferred motorcycle production from Munich, and had assumed control until that had had to shut down? With bombs falling all around, the factory had been transferred to a potash mine 450 metres underground at Abterode on the Werra so that it could produce items still being ordered from BMW's general store. These were gears for tanks, adjustment gearing for jet engines, rockets, high-explosive bombs – using British, French, Russian, ethnic German prisoners-of-war. What was all this to him now?

By four in the afternoon he had already discovered what it *did* mean, when a jeep picked him up – the free man who had simply returned home – and brought him back to the factory. There was no investigation. He was told to start work again, with twenty men who had also been dragged in or who had just simply rolled up. They were to establish a pool of vehicles by bringing together all those standing around and getting them going again, as well as to start up the printing shop, not for posters calling on people to hold out, nor for instruction manuals (desirable as that might have been), but for appeals by the town commandant to the local population. Life goes on.

Life goes on, as Sohr, the rocket technician, said to himself. Weeks ago, when it was still winter, he had left Staßfurt (from the 3rd level of the potash mine) and with his wife, who had followed on from Berlin, reached the small community of Leimbach, a desolate village in the Harz with an abandoned munitions plant in the forest. There, they told him, you will set up tests for plain bearings which can no longer be done safely here. Everything now depended on plain bearings. Production never got off the ground. No courier ever showed his face bearing instructions or wages when they were due. Well, who gave a damn. But if you spot black dots moving beyond where the main road to Eisleben runs, and these are not German, but Sherman tanks of the 6th American Armoured Division, then start thinking where to hide the plans! Sohr had brought with him from Staßfurt a complete set of the drawings for his plain bearings on the 003 engine – probably the last design documents in existence. It was doubtful whether the German U-boat which, as Sohr knew, had sailed with them to Japan, had ever reached its destination at Kobe (at least, nobody ever heard of it again). Near the abandoned factory and linked through passages, there was an old and, as Sohr discovered, empty munitions bunker, which was clearly visible from his accommodation in spite of its being well-camouflaged in a hollow in the ground. Here, Sohr said to himself, is just the place, and he proceeded to wrap up the drawings in two old SS coats left behind by the fleeing guards, to protect them from moisture. He then hid them under some slabs in a drainshaft at the entrance to the gallery.

On 18 April the Americans appeared outside Leimbach, and an inhabitant shouted to Sohr: 'They're on their way!' They did not come. The little birch wood and the earthworks in front of the settlement did not concern them because they were working according to the map, and the map did not show anything. Fine aerial reconnaissance, thought Sohr, if they did not know what was hidden here! 'Go and meet them,' his wife said, 'give them the thing!'

'What, just to get in their good books?' he said. 'What do you take me for – a traitor?'

Three days later, shots were heard. Sohr sprang out of bed, grabbed his trousers . . . Outside GIs were roaming the countryside and firing at bunkers and earthworks.

Sohr attracted their attention. 'The bunker!' he shouted. 'Are you mad?' He did not mean the empty one where his plans were hidden, but the mound a few hundred metres further on. It was still full of explosives and arms, long abandoned by the guards, and could have gone up at any moment.

'Come on!'

'I'm coming!' said Sohr, pulling his trousers up. When he was put against a tree and threatened by soldiers excitedly waving their arms about (showing their MP bands), he demanded an interpreter. They got him one.

'You – owner?' said one GI, who made out he was about to throw the lighted cigarette in his hand into the bunker.

Sohr threw himself to the ground and took cover.

'Get up!'

Well, now they believed him.

'I not owner!' he said. 'Technician.' He rummaged in his briefcase for his documents. The interpreter glanced through them, and paused. Sohr immediately understood why. 'Test engineer in R-research' was what he found written there. He was immediately asked: 'What does "R" mean?'

Sohr said: 'Rocket.'

'You're under arrest,' said the interpreter.

And that was how a man found himself guarded by two GIs who had been posted in front of his house in Leimbach, a village in the Harz, in the back of beyond (they thought they had caught a potential war criminal). But even a detainee had to stretch his legs, and taking a stroll, which he would make seem as innocent as possible, was bound to come close to the gallery entrance of the empty bunker one day.

At the same time, a second man appeared whom the Americans were more friendly with. He was pushing a pram with a little boy in it. The man was called Buske, Alfred Buske, and Sohr knew him well. Buske had been his superior, having headed 'tests' with Dr Oestrich. Nobody knew that around here. Buske had come down with his family and found accommodation in the nearby village of Großörna. He got on well with the American area commandant, as he spoke English like a native. He had told the latter of his dearest wish to leave Germany, to leave this Europe and go to America. But how could he get there as a German? Buske was no dreamer, and the captain was glad to hear his story. Perhaps with a gift, which the Russians, who must already have reached the Elbe, would have been just as keen on as the Americans. How about the drawings? Buske told Sohr that the company to which they belonged and for which he, Sohr, had put the drawings to one side, was finished, and that Germany was finished, too. He asked him what they were worth to him. Just think, man, he said, they can help us both; me to get to America and you to get free!

And so after Buske had promised to repay the favour by putting in a good word for him with the Yanks, Sohr, within sight of the GIs guarding his door, lifted up the slabs, reached for the first bundle of drawings on the top and stuffed them under Buske's little son's bottom in the pram. 'Come on!' called out the voice of one GI, and Sohr, replacing the slab, quickly did what he was told.

The next day, the game was repeated. Buske appeared with the pram and received a further bundle of design documents. This was good material, thought Sohr, coming, as it did, from head office.

And so this went on for an entire week, with Buske pushing his pram and son back and forth until the drainshaft was empty, and he had got what he needed.

Sohr waited and waited, hoping against hope. The GIs did not move from his door. Sohr felt ill at ease. That Buske . . . he's left me here to stew in my own juice . . . how simple it would have been to have burnt the whole lot. Now the Americans have them, and as for me. . . .

Sohr's wife came back from the village where she was allowed to go now and again to exchange food, with the news that the whole area, Thuringia and the Harz, was to be handed over to the Russians. What would have happened then, thought Sohr, if the drawings were still under the stone slabs?

What an extraordinary thing human conscience was, he thought! Why did I feel duty-bound to think of the company first, and not of myself? When I did think of myself, where did that lead me? And then he thought: better the Americans have them than the Russians. How was that?

Sohr's wife had also heard something else. People in Großörna were saying that Buske had not got further than fifty kilometres west on the motorway. Just before Hanover the American lorry had stopped, Buske, his wife and his little son had been forced to get off. Their furniture and belongings had been handed down to them. Then the Americans had driven off without saying goodbye, taking with them the design plans of a German wonder-weapon which Buske had handed over to them, plans, though, which had not been able to change the course of the war.

By that time the Americans had long since reached the town of Staßfurt near Magdeburg. There, in an undamaged potash mine (Sohr had assumed that it would be blown up as he had seen the fuses), the complete BMW 003 jet engine fell into their hands, to use a military expression. In less military terms, officers from the US Army Technical Service had immediately interviewed Dr Oestrich and his closest colleagues, who had been working on the 003 engine in the completely dry and spacious halls of the disused potash mine since October 1944. They had learnt everything, as it were, 'on site' and at first hand, and wanted to know about the state of development on German jet engines. A report about this stated: 'An 003 engine had to be presented to the Americans in various states of loading. They were very impressed.'

It was only when the operator on the Milbertshofen long-distance switchboard received no answer to her question 'Eisenach – Eisenach – Can you hear me?' (only hearing a rushing sound, rather like the strange rushing a child can hear when it puts a shell to its ear), it was only at noon on 8 April 1945, that Kurt Donath, engineer and works manager at Milbertshofen, knew that the biggest mistake BMW had made during the war had been to transfer motorcycle production to Eisenach. With Eisenach gone, the basis, the last item of the 'civilian sector', was lost – even if motorcycle production had served the war effort. Whenever the Americans decided to take Munich (there was no question of them not doing so; it was all a question of time), they would have a factory at their disposal which was purely producing armaments, and lacking any justification for a private company designed for peaceful production. The war had only deflected it from this purpose. What that meant was clear to any realist (even if he only had a vague idea of the Yalta Conference, where the Big Three had divided up the world and had decided that Germany would be dismembered).

The loss of Eisenach, as Kurt Deby – who, as the chief engineer at that time, was the right-hand man to the board member Max Wrba and 'dogsbody' in Milbertshofen – had told me, this loss had been 'like a rift which went through us all. It was like a fissure which had opened up between them and us – something which could not be bridged, although no one knew at the time that we would ultimately end up in two halves; we in the west, they in the east.'

Three days later, at 14.00 hours on 11 April, with the precision that the administrative machinery still showed in the last days of the Reich, the Tilly order was received at the works. (This was an order from the Führer for a 'scorched earth' policy, requiring the destruction of 'all military transport, news, industrial and supply installations, as well as assets within the Reich which could be of use in any way to the enemy in the immediate or foreseeable future which might further his war effort'.) This led both Donath in Munich and Siedler in Eisenach (who had fortunately been able to put this behind him) to face the question: what would things be like following another new beginning? Would it not be better to blow up the last remaining installations, instead of keeping them (which might cost one one's life) in the hope of benefiting from the 'enemy's', meaning the victor's, mercy, and being able to count on his magnanimity?

The order was signed by the 'Gauleiter and Reich defence commissar'. An 'executing directive' issued by the Army High Command, from Field Marshal Wilhelm Keitel, however, provided for a ruling by the Reich Minister for Armaments and War Production *vis-à-vis* the Party and Reich defence commissars, as to how the order should be prepared and carried out. The minister was Albert Speer, who, known to be a reasonable man, applied this by practically annulling the Führer's 'scorched earth' policy. Yet no one knew exactly where he stood if he kept to it. (Speer's courageous statement: 'We should not destroy what generations have built up before us. If the enemy does this, thereby eradicating the German people, then he will bring the whole guilt of history upon himself!' was only made known after the war, when the victors held their trials at Nuremberg. Speer answered Hitler by saying that it would not be necessary to have consideration for the basic positions which the people needed for their existence at the most primitive level; on the contrary, it would be better to destroy the things themselves.)

Already, by the end of March, the Munich Gauleiter Paul Giesler had demanded just this, and Dr Ammann, head of the test department at BMW aero-engines and 'Abwehr appointee', drove with his most dependable colleague, the Viennese development engineer Josef Krauter, to the Gauleiter's office, to talk Giesler out of the destruction he had ordered. The timetable was still to be established, but this was a venture to which they themselves attached little hope. As expected, Giesler rejected the argument that the work sites should be kept intact, simply resorting to the formula that the Americans should 'in no circumstances find operational plants'. What did that mean – destruction? Giesler avoided the word as much as his visitors did. They reassured him, to the extent that he tried to give the impression that he had all the power necessary to insist categorically on the orders being carried out; namely, that everything would be complied with as ordered, but with the proviso that the worst could be avoided, if only at the last moment. Above all, Ammann added, he was concerned about the prototypes of the most recent aero-engines, the TL 003 turbo-prop engine, as well as the latest version of the BMW 801 engines, whose premature destruction (if, as hoped, the enemy was to be repulsed) would inflict immeasurable damage on the Reich and its ability to win the war. And so, with deceitful complicity, they agreed on a position to their mutual advantage – the Gauleiter had not been forced to take back a single word (countermanding his order would have cost him his life), and Ammann, without having to be asked, could issue the word 'paralysis' instead of 'destruction' to a group of people he trusted and whom he had posted to the bunker at the south gate. Whatever paralysis meant, it could include removing fuses, opening valves, dismantling drive motors and the like, or 'combing' the halls, cellars and stores. In the fifth year of the war there was much which, abandoned and forgotten, had no importance for the war at all – quite the contrary. On one occasion, the search troops came across climbing boots for mountain soldiers, and Ammann immediately fitted out the remaining workforce with them. Then, in order to put his words into practice (no one was left in any more doubt that Munich was soon to fall), he summoned representatives from the RAM and Gauleiter's office to the test track at the works. Here prototypes were lined up whose destruction he had offered to Giesler. Ammann had had petrol poured over them. They were then destroyed in an artificial fireball (a macabre sight, inasmuch as they had remained intact throughout the waves of flames spread by air raids) in front of official witnesses, without any of them having any notion of what was behind the bricked-up entrance littered with junk leading to No 2 cellar in the assembly hall, just to the left of the entrance – double copies of all the models (amongst them were even the originals, with the copies being set alight and incinerated on the test track), which Ammann had ensured were set aside and walled in.

The war drew inexorably to a close. The question still remained as to how anyone who had stayed alive up to now could come out of it unscathed. The important thing was to appear credible (even at this late stage) in one's motivation by the 'unshakeable prospect of victory', as the slogan went, and to have no doubts about final victory. A vital feature of this was recovering those outstanding debts which, for example, the Aviation Ministry had long owed the company. The commercial manager, Theodor Scholl, who had tackled outstanding debts with an iron hand, had received licence fees to the tune of 20 million R-marks for the 003 aero-engine delivered to Japan, whether it got there or not. This was shortly before the diplomatic services left Berlin, when there was still a Japanese embassy on which he could press his claim, acknowledged by the RAM. And just on the day when Eisenach fell, he had further recovered what had accrued to the company in the way of stop-loss charges for uncompleted aero-engines, which were usually only paid after delivery, once preliminary work had been done. His assistant, a young man by the name of Oscar Kolk, had therefore travelled to Dessau-Kochstädt, where the RAM, transferred from Berlin, was already working out of suitcases (at least those they had bothered to unpack).

But travelling from Munich to Dessau, which lies on the Elbe, was at that time no less arduous than in the following years and decades when, admittedly, Dessau still lay on the Elbe, but because it had been annexed to the Soviet-occupied zone it seemed more distant for a West or Federal German than anywhere in America. The Hermsdorf intersection, where the north–south motorway crosses the east–west one, was already closed due to the approaching front. Equipped with all the special permits and authorisations needed to pass through all the checkpoints without being challenged as a civilian (one in a car to boot), Kolk was obliged to make a detour via Franzensbad on the River Eger in the 'Protectorate' (present-day Františkovy Lázně on the Ohre in Czechoslovakia). So he arrived late at his destination after by-passing Leipzig. No expert at the Ministry was willing, or any longer in a position, to conclude any kind of business whatsoever. The order had already been given to evacuate the area around the Elbe and look for a refuge further south. So Kolk was fobbed off from one person to the next, with the last one being the first person Kolk had turned to. He was a lieutenant colonel who admitted that he had an additional dilemma. He said that his wife was here with him and he could no longer get her to Zerbst, where she would certainly be safe as her brother had a chemist's shop there. Kolk said that he knew the region, since before the war he had worked for quite some time in Wittenberg and places around it, and would gladly do him this favour if by then. . . . But of course, said the lieutenant colonel, no problems on that score, Kolk could bank on it.

The bridges over the Elbe had been destroyed. Kolk had to wait for hours until he managed to cross over on a swaying pontoon bridge erected by sappers. And everything worked out. The officer's wife, not for a moment disappointed that it was Kolk and not her husband driving her, was received amicably by the chemist in Zerbst, although he would have preferred to have joined Kolk in his car and driven away across the Elbe rather than to stay in Zerbst which, more than likely, would fall into Russian rather than American hands. Once he got back to Dessau-Kochstädt again that night,

Kolk waited until morning and was relieved to see the lieutenant colonel again. He received from him (fair exchange is no robbery, as the expression goes) a covered cheque from the Reich Bank for the required amount – 13.5 million stop-loss charges for the command module ordered by the RAM. It had been in production since March 1943, but when bombs destroyed this production at Milbertshofen, work was transferred to the company of Sachse KG in Kempten, to which BMW owed this sum.

Kolk immediately set off for home. In Františkovy Lázně, with its view far out across the Ohre, he covered his car, as swarms of bombers moved overhead. He could have saved himself the trouble; the bombers' target was the Egerländer Aircraft Works. Kolk knew it well, as BMW had delivered aero-engines there. Now they went up in smoke and flames in front of Kolk's very eyes. As early as the afternoon, Kolk was in Weiden near the Oberpfalz Woods when his car broke down due to rear axle failure. He went to a BMW dealer in Weiden, but the latter regretted that he could not help him as he had no spares. Kolk then turned to the Wehrmacht headquarters, saying that he was a courier on top secret 'Reich business' (he pointed to his breast pocket) and had to get to Munich. A foot soldier flagged down a big grey army lorry. The driver said that this 'Top Secret Reich business' was not good enough, as he had Reichsleiter Bormann's cook in his cab, and they were en route for Berchtesgaden, loaded with the Führer's furniture. 'It's good enough,' said the foot soldier, and Kolk, given a leg up by him, jumped over the tailboard, right onto the sofa on which the Führer was due to sit in Berchtesgaden – something which Kolk, now sitting there (as he continued to do until they got to the suburb of Freimann in Munich, where the lorry stopped and dropped him off) thought almost as unlikely as his ability to cash the cheque in his breast pocket before the end of the war.

A fortnight later, around 22–23 April, when Hitler had already declared his 'irrevocable decision' to stay in Berlin and fall there (i.e., put a bullet through his head), Kolk travelled to Augsburg to ask the RAM, which had, in the meantime, fled to Messerschmitt, to pay up again. Here he received, again in a covered bank cheque which the Deutsche Bank in Munich credited on 28 April (an historic date), the 50 million which the Reich owed to the works and which BMW had insisted on, without success till now.

The development department, which had moved to the Elsholz Castle at Berg on Lake Starnberg, did its bit for the 'unshakeable prospect of victory', by joining the local Home Guard after office hours – with one exception: Alexander von Falkenhausen who, as before, was responsible for design, testing, and development in motorcycle construction, and who had taken a furnished room in Ammerland, because his house on Raps Street in Munich had been destroyed in the bombing and was uninhabitable. The room was bitterly cold, but it allowed him to tell the people of Berg that he belonged to the Ammerland Home Guard, while he could credibly assure the people in Ammerland that the Berg Home Guard was responsible for him. This was how he avoided doing duty in both places, being missed and, he hoped, being killed, as things were still very much uncertain.

The safest thing for him to do seemed to be to drive towards the

Americans (who must have reached Nuremberg), and head for a crossing over the Danube. His wife and daughters were staying on the estate of his parents-in-law in Leonberg, a small town about 20 kilometres north of Regensburg. He reckoned that he could get there just before the village became the 'front'.

He set off on his R 75, the same motorcycle and sidecar which he had taken to very near Stalingrad in the early autumn of 1942 and through the steppes to the foothills of the Caucasus. The night was pitch-black, the road unlit. Despite this, the road was strafed by American fighter bombers, which roared from nowhere across woods, rivers and roads, as the remains of the German army in flight pushed south with its tanks, lorries and teams of horses and guns. To avoid being swept along (the stream of those in retreat grew ever thicker), he took to the minor roads, reaching Moosburg, after by-passing Landshut, in hours which nevertheless seemed like days to him. He crossed the Danube in the early morning and, without stopping, reached Leonberg, only to discover that he had arrived too soon. The estate was occupied – not by Americans, but by the SS.

Falkenhausen hid his motorcycle and side-car in the bushes and crept unseen through a back entrance into the castle. Here he lived hidden in a small room in a tower, from which, with the aid of binoculars, he looked out over the Lower Bavarian plain as far as Schwandorf, until the SS, who left their weapons standing around unattended in the courtyard (while placing two sets of guards on the cognac supplies they had hauled back from France), suddenly left the estate on one of the following days, 'clearing off', as the expression had it in those days.

Falkenhausen immediately left his hiding-place, and went with his wife to the outbuilding where, under junk, old horse blankets, halters, coachman's items and rusty ploughshares, his sports car stood on wooden blocks, untouched, just as he had left it. The car, a BMW 328, which he had bought for himself before the war, was in excellent working order, although it looked like a heap of scrap metal. There was nothing missing, apart from the wheels. Falkenhausen had thoroughly greased the rims and sprinkled talcum powder on the tyres, before burying them under the circular rose-bed in front of the outside steps in the late autumn, before the ground had frozen.

When country people return to their estate after any length of time away, the first thing they usually make for is the stables, where they can look at their cattle, check they are all right, slap them and even talk to them. This is what Falkenhausen did with his car, which he viewed as importantly as the future, whatever might happen to BMW. Even when he had been in Berg, he had worked on plans for it. If the works at Milbertshofen and Eisenach were to go under, he could, through this car (which for him was the most beautiful, the fastest, and most technically successful car in the world), save a development which was not yet over, despite appearances to the contrary, a development which would be revived, despite the simplicity and primitiveness of any new beginning.

A few hours later the first American jeep rolled across the bridge over the Regen on the edge of the village, and Falkenhausen, stepping out from the

300

Starting up Again

The undamaged works at Allach became a US-Army
supply and transport depot under German management

The first official production authorisation issued by the
victors to BMW for Works I at Milbertshofen

ORDNANCE PRODUCTION CONTROL
THIRD U.S. ARMY.

REF.NO. __XX - f3 -__   DATE __28 July 1945__

Subject: Authorization for production.

To   :   Bayerische Motorenwerke, Munich, Plant #1.
           (Upper Bavaria)

    1. You are hereby directed to start immediate production of the
following listed items utilizing present stocks of material on hand:

Reference on Reverse side

    2. A report in duplicate as of 1200 each Saturday properly
enveloped and addressed to:

THIRD ARMY ORDNANCE OFFICER
A.P.O.NO.403 U.S.ARMY
ATTN. PRODUCTION CONTROL

Demanded by the Times

BMW produced what the times demanded:
bicycles, saucepans, agricultural machines –
all made of aluminium components
retrieved from aero-engine production

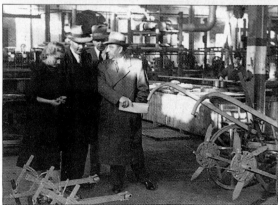

Below: Ludwig Erhard, then
still Bavarian Minister for
Trade and Industry, with the
American Secretary of State
Byrnes in Munich in 1946.
From left to right: the
Bavarian Prime Minister
Hoegner, Byrnes, Erhard
and General Clay

Above: Visit by the Bavarian
Minister for Trade and
Industry, Dr Alfred Seidel
(*right*), to BMW's
'Agricultural Machine
Factory' in 1946

Eisenach and Milbertshofen

BMW Eisenach: a Russian public limited company called Avtovelo

Above: The Eisenach prototype of the 342 model at the Leipzig Spring Fair in 1951. Wavering between the American example and staying loyal to the 'kidneys'

Below: Theodor Heuss, the first President of the new German Federal Republic (*right*) at the International Motor Show in 1953 with Mr McCloy, the US High Commissioner for the Western occupied zones, and the BMW trustee, Dr von Mangoldt-Reiboldt

Above: The assembly lines are running again

BMW is here Again

Kurt Donath, director at Milbertshofen since 1942, prevented conscripted workers attacking the plant and the destruction of the works ordered at the end of the war. The Allies appointed him as works manager

As early as 1946 BMW Eisenach was presenting its products at the Leipzig Autumn Fair

BMW Munich showed its first post-war motorcycle, the R 24, at the Geneva Show in 1948

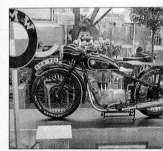

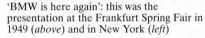

'BMW is here again': this was the presentation at the Frankfurt Spring Fair in 1949 (*above*) and in New York (*left*)

Back in Motor Sports

With Count Lurani as driver and H.J. Aldington as navigator, the Bristol 400, modelled on a BMW, took third place in the over-1.1-litre class at the 1949 Mille Miglia

BMW technology under a foreign name: Alexander von Falkenhausen on the race track in the AFM racing car, which he designed

Apart from Falkenhausen in the AFM, Karl Kling (shown here on the Hockenheim circuit in 1950) achieved the first major racing success during the post-war years in a Veritas

From Lorry to Luxury

All the US-Army lorries leaving Allach after being overhauled carried the BMW stamp of quality on the engine

BMW Milbertshofen, Gate 1, Dostler Street. A lorry loaded with motorcyles leaving the works

Dreams of luxury. *From left to right*: 327 coupé; BMW 501; Daimler-Benz 300; BMW 335 saloon

The 501 in its final form

Eye-catching, if not always taken
seriously: the bubble-car as fun for the
troops, a wedding carriage, a snack room,
and as a prop in a performance of *The
White Knight*

Ahead of its time? The BMW 600 'mini-bus' with a streamlined caravan on the way to St Gotthard

'The suppliers keep quiet. No one leaves us in the lurch.' Deliveries of the 700 at Wolfgang Denzel in Vienna

Permanent feature: the kidneys

The end of the 501

After the General Meeting

Left: Victory! 'The man in the brown suit', Friedrich Mathern, while the votes were being counted

Below: Three men vital to restructuring. *From left to right:* Board member Ernst Kämpfer, Assistant Secretary Dr Barbarino and Dr Hans Peter, President of the Bavarian Office for Industrial Investment

Right: Major shareholder Herbert Quandt and head of works committee Kurt Golda

Below: The new management board with members of the supervisory board. *From left to right:* Golda, Pollmann, Hahnemann, Dr Peter, Osswald, Dr Draeger, Gieschen and Wilcke

Renouncing the Air

Left: The Dornier 32 E helicopter with a small gas turbine made by BMW Power Plant Production Co Ltd

Defence Minister Franz Josef Strauß with a group of officers

Lockheed Starfighter F 104 G with General Electric J 79/11 A engines manufactured by BMW Power Plant Production at Allach

The high-wing Do 27 monoplane

Focke Wulff P 149 D SC 333

Reach for the Stars

From left to right:
Hofmeister, Fiedler, Wolff,
von Falkenhausen

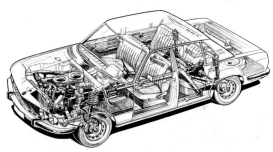

A cut-away drawing of
BMW 2500 and 2800

BMW 2000 CS coupé (*left*);
the 3200 CS Bertone coupé
(*right*)

BMW 2000 (*left*);
BMW 2800 CS (*right*)

The BMW 2000 tii Touring
(*left*); the BMW 1600
Cabriolet (*right*)

Above: De Gaulle escorted by BMW motorcyles

Left: The BMW R60/5 in its official version (*above*) and with sports handle-bars (*below*)

Klaus Enders and Ralf Engelhardt winning a world championship race for motorcyle and sidecar teams. BMW were victorious twenty times in a row

Above: Hubert Hahne in a BMW Formula 2 car (Brabham chassis) at Hockenheim in 1966

Below: Alexander von Falkenhausen in his attempt on the world record with a BMW 2-litre Formula 2 car on 22 September 1969

Above: Dieter Quester won the Formula 2 race at the Hockenheim circuit in 1970

Right: The pits at Thruxton, England, during the Easter Monday Race in 1970

Above: Paul G Hahnemann, a symbol of the sixties, Head of Marketing

Above: Gerhard Wilcke, lawyer and legal adviser to the Quandt Group, chairman of the board of BMW AG in the second half of the sixties

Left: Ernst Kämpfer with Karl Heinz Sonne, first chairman of the board in the Quandt era

Below: Presentation of von Kuenheim to the BMW directors in the presence of members of the Bavarian cabinet

Above: Eberhard von Kuenheim, chairman of the board of BMW AG from 1970

Golda speaks to the workers
at the works

Herbert and Johanna
Quandt accompanied by
works manager Dompert
and the new technical
director Koch, walking
through the new plant at
Dingolfing

Herbert Quandt and Eberhard von
Kuenheim

Built in 791 days: the tower at the BMW headquarters in Munich

bushes, directed them in. The next day his motorbike was discovered by resourceful GIs. An American officer asked him if he knew what the thing on top of the tank was; he meant the air filter which looked like a steel helmet welded on. Falkenhausen explained its function. The officer made out that he had not heard properly. But that's what it was, Falkenhausen said, it's what you need to get through any kind of mud; he had tried it out himself in Russia, as he tested everything he had designed himself.

A little later, CIA officers appeared and interrogated him. He willingly told them that series production of the machine had (unfortunately) been stopped, as far back as 1943, to the benefit of the Volkswagen jeep. He went on to tell them that he had developed a one-man tank, the 'slider', which the driver, lying on his stomach and next to an automatic quick-fire aeroplane gun, would drive by means of two steering levers. This small tank was not yet ready. The only one to be ready was the large, Panther tank, for which he had fitted a nine-cylinder, radial aero-engine, the famous BMW 132, because the Maybach engines had failed (they had never been properly tested). He had fitted a giant flywheel onto the propeller spigot with air vanes for forced cooling. The prototype, only recently finished, had been sent to Berlin, just in time for the Russians to be able to take delivery of it. He had just heard on the radio that they had got through to Berlin.

Some of the things Falkenhausen said were believed, others not. They certainly did not believe that the Alpine Redoubt at Berchtesgaden was only an invention by Goebbels. Of course it existed. If, however, a man like Falkenhausen who offered them true stories about secret projects now professed not to know anything about the Alpine Redoubt, then this made them suspicious and they wondered if they should believe him.

Yet they had to believe him after General Patton, whose staff took up quarters in the manor house, received no other information from intelligence sources, apart from what Falkenhausen had supplied (which included the fact that there had been no military resistance between Regensburg and Munich).

In addition, when the Americans finally set off to capture Munich, they left the R 75 with its eight forward, two reverse gears and differential lock behind, undamaged (they had already started racing on it). Leonberg, 20 kilometres north of Regensburg, with Falkenhausen and his family (which was able to move back into the manor house after Patton's departure); Leonberg, with the 328 in the outbuilding, whose four wheels were under the rose-bed, and the R 75, which would soon prove indispensable to farming, sank back into the humdrum way of life to which small towns are accustomed when not disrupted by war.

In the meantime, Kurt Donath had long since distributed all the food still stored in the works, had paid off everyone still in a position to claim wages, and had sent home the core staff, right down to the last few who had been assigned to fit fuses to the demolition chambers marked in the plan of the buildings. These had been ordered by the Reich defence commissar, and were subject to checking at any time to see that they were 'operational'. Donath sat with a few people, including the engineers Deby and Claus von Ruecker,

Bruno Bruckmann, head of aero-engine development, Dr Ernst Flatow, director of the personnel department with power of attorney, and the head chef, Widmann, in Command Bunker C at the south gate, and was determined not to open up to any party man banging on the gate. They just waited.

But the Americans took their time. They just would not arrive. Scouts reported that the armoured column leading the 1st Gaullist Army under General Jean de Lattre de Tassigny was approaching the Landsberg-Lake Ammer region from the west. On the other side of the Danube arc between Ulm and Regensburg, the 7th American Army under General Alexander Patch and, further east, the 3rd American Army under General George S. Patton, were marching on Munich. What could be believed in all this, and what could not? The *Völkischer Beobachter* reported that there was 'heroic resistance everywhere in the epic battle for Bavaria', and Wilhelm Dorls, as head of the Allach works on the edge of the city, had only one concern. This was that the installations still intact could still be the victim of stupid clashes at the last moment. These appeared inevitable since the Army High Command had ordered the enemy to be held up by a cordon north-west of Munich, in the region between the Glonn and Amper rivers. The last contingent streaming there could be seen with the naked eye from an office window – SS men, defence infantrymen, anti-aircraft auxiliaries, the home guard and the Hitler Youth.

On the morning of 28 April 1945, when it was still dark, the telephone rang in Dorls' shed (he had long since given up living at home and had moved into the works). 'There's a revolution in Munich,' reported the air-raid warden; it wasn't a rumour, Reich Radio Munich had just put out the password 'pheasant-shooting', and a Captain Rupprecht Gerngroß was said to have occupied the radio station, all command posts, the city hall, and so on. 'Eradication of the National Socialist blood-rule, removal of militarism, and re-establishment of peace' were the aims; he was calling for armed rebellion and for the population to unite.

Dorls immediately rang up all 'brown' people: the 'pheasant-shooting' was going ahead! Or, more specifically, golden-pheasant-shooting, with all local party bosses wearing the light brown uniform in the firing line, as well as factory bosses and company officials. He said that no one was to come to work, and that on this occasion they could stay at home. He then summoned a works meeting.

Here it was decided that no pass was valid without Dorls's signature, that factory security would be tightened up (almost everyone volunteered for this), and that the gates should be secured. Whatever happened outside, not a single shot would be allowed to land inside.

In addition, no machine would be destroyed, not a single litre of fuel would be 'spoilt'. The company only had blue dye which was harmless, although this would have appeased inspectors if added to aviation fuel.

Towards noon, those who had been warned turned up at the works gate, some wearing uniform with only the badge of rank removed. They said that the revolution was over, and that the rebels (or as many as had been apprehended) had already been summarily executed. It had been little more than a storm in a teacup. Dorls let the people in, pointing to their uniforms. One man said: 'Are we German men or not?' Dorls replied: 'You certainly aren't. Where are the three stars on your shoulders?' They all laughed. Even Dorls could not help laughing.

But that afternoon, as Dorls was discussing questions of capacity with his branch managers, the door flew open and an SS officer walked up to him with a written order in his hand. Dorls read it out: 'You must go immediately to Ebensee. You must bring with you all documents for building and equipping a new aero-engine works. Signed, Himmler.'

'Ebensee?' asked Dorls. 'Where's that?'

The officer looked at him in amazement. 'In the Alpine Redoubt,' he said.

Dorls gulped, tried to make a joke about whether anyone had noticed the war had been won. The officer looked at him icily, saying that he would very much appreciate it if such remarks, even if humorously meant, were left out. He urged immediate departure.

'He raised his arm, clicked his heels and disappeared,' Dorls later related. That he is still alive today to report this is due to the fact that, having initially decided not to leave, he then decided to do so the morning after. He said that an SS officer had appeared again. 'In the works we had a camp of SS prisoners who had been very badly treated, so I was only presuming that he belonged to those in charge of the camp. In any event, the latter said: "If you don't want to die, then travel to Ebensee."'

With these words, Dorls went on, he had succumbed momentarily to the same spectre as General Eisenhower, less because of any threat, than because of the certainty with which the man had said: 'Travel to Ebensee.' Although American troops were already east of the Elbe, Eisenhower had made his historic decision (admittedly all this only came out later) to let the Russians enter Berlin alone, as he was mainly concerned about southern Germany, where he wanted to prevent the Germans from withdrawing to the 'Alpine Redoubt', which he firmly believed in. Indeed, the SHAEFF [Supreme Headquarters Allied Expeditionary Force in France] intelligence service had put forward Goebbels's fairy tale about a last defence station for the Reich in the Alps as a fact to Eisenhower as early as 13 March. This reported that the ice-covered peaks were 'practically impregnable' and:

> protected by nature and the most effective of the latest secret weapons, the powers which have led Germany till now will live on and prepare for their resurrection. Weapons and munitions will be produced in bomb-proof plants, food and equipment will be stored in huge underground caverns, and a specially selected corps of young men will be trained in guerilla warfare, so that a whole underground army can be set up and deployed, leading to the point where they will liberate Germany from the occupying armies.

'Good,' said Dorls, 'whatever this "Alpine Redoubt" had going for it, I would get myself a little car (we still had got an old 1.2 out at the back in the otherwise empty garages), packed some suitable tools into it and drove off without any documents. These are the ones I knew by heart, so that if anything happened

303

I could talk myself out of trouble; secret command and control documents were too dangerous to have in a car. I went via Salzburg, nobody stopped me, to Ebensee, on a completely empty road. Shortly before arriving, I landed up in the ditch, with a broken front axle. I took my rucksack, everything I had was in it, as I had planned to survive on the road till the end of the war. I thumbed a lift (there were still many about here, driving around as if there had not been a war at all) and reached pastures near my destination.

'A group of Junkers technicians was already there (we greeted each other like conspirators). SS people and orderlies were scurrying around. What would happen now, I wondered? Everyone looked at me as if I knew more than they did. It was the most hopeless gathering of men I had ever seen. Watch out! No, it was not Himmler, but SS Colonel Purucker.

'He said: "Heil!" not "Heil Hitler!", even though Hitler was still alive. "Let's get down to business."

'The business was: how could an aero-engine works be set up in the Alpine Redoubt (I had not seen any)? I replied, because he was looking at me: "Herr Purucker, you cannot make engines out of butter!" And then went on: "You can milk cows here because you've got some; you'll probably also have concentration camp inmates to do the work. The only problem is that you won't get any aero-engines. Aero-engines are at the top of the engineering ladder; they can't be made just from will-power."

'A man from Junkers, their "group leader", whose name I have forgotten, said something similar, whereupon Purucker, looking more relieved than depressed, declared the discussion over, but wanted to continue talking with me and two others who had confirmed the "impossible". A bottle of champagne from my rucksack saved the situation. "Let's have a few drinks and call it a day." And that's what happened. Purucker joined us for a drink, and that was the end of that, as far as the Alpine Redoubt was concerned. But how did I get back? My car was in a ditch, so the Junkers people lent me a Fichtel and Sachs bike (hardly lent; rather gave), and because I had brought two suits with me, I put one on top of the other, picked up my rucksack, and trundled off to Munich via Salzburg. I spent the night in a farmhouse not far from Salzburg, where I took Himmler's order and dropped it down the earth closet. I had nothing to fear any more. I was not even frightened when I met an American tank (a negro jumped down and waved me through), or when I saw the wild shapes of rebelling foreign workers emerging from behind some woods. That was when I naturally lost my Sachs bike; as well as my rucksack, in which I had hidden all my cash in knotted handkerchiefs (this being what I had brought from Berlin when I had picked up everything before going to Munich). But because I had also wrapped up some cigarettes, they did not find the cash (in the end, they threw away the cigarettes, because they were used to better ones). That's how I got my rucksack back, leaving me to make my way on foot again. I first went to Zorneding, where I had a friend. Then to Milbertshofen. Don't ask me how. There was a GI standing at the gates. "Hi," he said, "who are you?" I showed my defence pass, the only document I still had. He wasn't interested. Speaking in English, I said: "I do engineering." He let me pass, and I went in.'

In the early morning of 29 April, Josef Krauter was in Hall 5, as on all the preceding days when he hoped they would finally come. Hall 5 was only half standing following the last air raid, but he had climbed up the steps on the chimney, from where he had a clear view to the north out towards Schleißheim.

It was cold. Nothing was happening on the streets and roads around Oberwiesenfeld. Artillery fire in the distance seemed to be unconnected with the clouds of dust being thrown up across the site. Krauter told himself that it would perhaps be better to climb down and go back to the bunker. Exposed points are favourite artillery targets, Ammann had said, and given he had fought through the First World War, he should know. The clouds of dust now moved forwards towards the chimney. Krauter suddenly decided to hurry, taking two or three rungs at a time. He slipped and fell, without hurting himself, and ran across to the bunker, certain they would come now.

They did not come. Towards noon the rumble increased, and in the afternoon it subsided. When everything was quiet, with not even the sound of an engine to be heard, he coupled up his motorcycle, in whose side-car he had packed tinned food, and waved to Hugo, his mate from development. Like him, he lived over in Moosach and they had arranged to go and have a look to see if everything was still all right over there, as soon as it seemed appropriate.

It was appropriate now. They raced out through the south gate, with their steel helmets on. A solitary motorcyclist met them on Oberwiesenfeld and greeted them. Krauter thought: he takes us for soldiers. So much the better. He suddenly realised that he was armed and Hugo, too, had a pistol on him. What for? Who were they supposed to shoot? Perhaps if not werewolves, then Americans? They did not believe that themselves. But the Americans might have believed it.

Krauter was later to recall that, from the very moment when they turned into Dachau Street, they had not thought ahead. Because as they turned in, a thin, bespectacled and very tall GI jumped down from a jeep, which was travelling down the middle of the road towards the city centre. Nothing resembling a machine gun was aimed at them, and all the GI used to stop the German motorcycle combination was a signalling disc. He explained politely (Krauter had spent quite a long time working in the States, and understood every word) that this was the advance party of the American Army, and asked them where they wanted to go. Krauter immediately replied just as politely, and in the best American the GI had probably had ever heard from a German, 'To my wife and children over there!' (pointing out of town, towards Moosach). He explained that he was a worker in the BMW plant, like his friend beside him, and insisted that both should be accompanied by an officer. With that he looked at his watch. By German summer time, it was exactly twenty past five in the afternoon.

By ten to six Krauter was back in the works. He could not believe it himself. Leaning on a wall in the Borstei district, a 2nd lieutenant, who was directing, via radio, the snaking army from invisible deployment zones in their march on Munich, had instructed the GI, after briefly and casually interrogating them

305

and cursing a bit (God dammit, he had a wife and children, too, and hadn't seen them for months!), to let them go.

At this, the GI accompanied them back to the crossroads. There they found that all the tinned food had been stolen from the side-car by fleeing civilians trying to make off with the booty. He took all the tins back from them, put them in the side-car, told both Germans to get back on, raised the signalling disc and let them drive off at full speed.

'And what were you thinking about all that time?' asked Ammann nervously, keeping back any further reproaches about 'all this incredible thoughtlessness', which could have cost both of them their lives.

'Not much,' said Krauter, putting his pistol to one side. 'If only I had taken along a white flag instead of all that stuff!' Then he explained how the 'situation' looked to the Americans, according to the 2nd lieutenant's radio message (if he had understood the words correctly). This was that the SS was dug in at Oberwiesenfeld, meaning that the 7th American Army was skirting round them so that they could flush them out once they had been encircled.

Who had dreamed up this fairy-tale of the SS being dug in? Krauter and his pillion rider had not seen a single SS man on their excursion. But who would believe them, even if they were to approach the Americans ten times with a white flag?

But Krauter could not get the white flag out of his head. Passive behaviour, battening down the hatches, everyone at diving stations (in the justifiable fear a Party man could order things to be blown up even at this late stage) was just as inadvisable as shirking all responsibility by fleeing. If virtually nothing moved in the factory, the Americans, distrustful as they were, would rather destroy everything themselves than take the slightest risk. Perhaps there were mines ready to explode just as they went through the gate? On Krauter's suggestion, Ammann had already had all the weapons collected up and stored away in three safes. The only sticking point was how to hand over the key. That night they still had not come; everything had been deathly quiet.

The next day, shortly before sunrise, Krauter had climbed up the chimney in Hall 5, as he had done on every day he had hoped they would come. It was cold, but it would not be long before the sun warmed the land. Reaching the top, Krauter felt how the sun caught him from behind, as it were, and permeated him. Its rays did not fall obliquely, but almost horizontally towards the north where he was looking. Then suddenly he saw something sparkling in the distance. It was like the glint of crystals, hundreds and thousands of them. But this was no marvel of nature, it was windscreens catching the sunlight. They were on their way!

What happened next is contained in a short report by Krauter, which says:

> In order to make provision for the easy surrender of the works, I obtained from Dr Ammann (this time) permission to contact the Americans as a peace negotiator.

So I marched alone with an improvised white flag through the good old south gate. In Lerchenau Street, outside what is today the 'Olympiastadion' underground station, I met the first jeep forming the vanguard.

There was a body search. I explained that the BMW plant would be handed over to the US Army without further ado. The next moment, I was sitting on the jeep's bonnet with two MPs in the back, and we made our way back, at walking pace, through the south gate and onto the open area above the bunker.

Military security was established. A command centre was set up. Dr Ammann and myself were ordered to the colonel. The colonel laid out a plan of the works in front of us (espionage had clearly done its job!).

Obviously the occupation proceeded very slowly. It must have lasted hours, with endless investigations, tapping on walls (looking for 'jumping torpedoes' which, according to intelligence reports, had been bricked in somewhere in the works. There were the weapons to be handed over. ('With howls of delight,' as Krauter's report expressed it, 'the Americans leapt on the German guns when the safes were opened. These were favourite souvenirs. One immediately helped himself to three Mauser pistols . . .') Indeed, it took the whole day before they dared go down to the bottom of the south bunker (security measures were constantly changing). Here is how Deby, who was sitting there, remembered it:

'It was on the evening of 30 April, just after the radio had broadcast the news, introduced with drum-rolls, that "our Führer Adolf Hitler has this afternoon fallen at his command post in the Reich Chancellery, fighting Bolshevism to his last breath in the name of Germany", that they appeared in the bunker, led by a half-Indian (as I later discovered), Captain Henry, who had followed the occupying troops with a special unit from the ATI (Aeronautical Technical Intelligence). Suddenly there was a sergeant standing next to me. Instead of a weapon, he was holding an open notebook. I looked at it. It contained a detailed plan of the works. But the plan was not quite right, as it did not show the transfers. Was it really possible that they knew nothing about the Cenobis cellar, and so on, that they knew nothing about where we had transferred our workshops, which had covered half of underground Munich, as far as Bruckmühl and Kolbermoor? It is remarkable how hope never abandons one. I was hoping that perhaps they would never discover everything that was there. "Where is the Herbitus equipment?" he asked. It took me a while before I understood him. "Well, I'll take you there," I said. "Come on," he said. So I took him there, because the Herbitus was so big that we had not been able to transfer it.'

'What was the Herbitus equipment?'

'The best we had to offer,' said Deby. 'A test bed for high-performance engines, which simulated altitudes previously unimaginable – 12,000 to 15,000 metres at minus 40 degrees Celsius! All the aircraft firms in Germany had carried out tests on it. The Americans cast their eyes over it. For them the war was not yet over and, once they got our Herbitus over to Tullahoma in Ohio in 1946 (as far as I know), they were going to test their own engines and jet power plants for use against Japan. If they had known all the things the Herbitus could do, they would have captured Munich much earlier.'

Shortly before Eisenach fell silent (as the telephonist at Milbertshofen expressed it), Goebbels, the Nazi Propaganda Minister, sent out an appeal to the troops streaming back from both west and east.

'The Führer has declared that this year will see a change in fortune. And it will come, even if we have to wait months for it. . . . The true quality of genius is its infallible consciousness and its certain knowledge of an imminent reversal. The Führer knows the exact hour when it will take place. Destiny has sent us this man, so that we can bear witness to this miracle, in this time of internal and external need.'

Goebbels was here thinking of the Seven Years War, of that dark year of 1762, when Frederick the Great declared to his ministers that if there were no change in events by 15 February, given the hopeless situation he was in, he would take poison. On 12 February the Czarina died, and the House of Brandenburg benefited from this stroke of fortune. At the Peace of Hubertusburg, the great European power of Prussia was confirmed in its possession of Silesia. The defeats at Kolin, Hochkirch and Kunersdorf were forgotten, and the victories at Prague, Roßbach, Leuthen, von Zorndorf, Liegnitz and Torgau turned misfortune into triumph. Prussia's hour had come. The Third Reich's hour would also come, Goebbels believed, bringing an end to need, and bringing triumph to the Führer.

Goebbels was firmly convinced that at times history liked repeating itself. In an uncanny way things seemed to confirm his view that he was not just clutching at straws. Shortly after his appeal, he visited the Oder front where General Busse assured him that the Russians could not break through and that the front would hold until 'the British kick us up the backside'. This was on 12 April 1945. That night Goebbels arrived back in Berlin. The Reich Chancellery (what was left of it), and indeed the whole of Wilhelm Street up to the Adlon Hotel, were a sea of flames. No X 4 (surface-to-air missiles) had been able to stop the RAF bomber squadrons from doing their demolition work. But when he entered the Propaganda Ministry on the other side of Wilhelm Square, which had still been spared from the flames, an adjutant rushed up to him on the steps (a cheap thriller could not have done it better!) and said: 'Minister sir! Roosevelt is dead!'

It is not known how Hitler took the news. One can only presume it inspired him. This was hardly the first time Providence had taken a hand in his and Germany's fate. The last occasion was on 20 July 1944, which he could show to Il Duce arriving at his headquarters shortly after the attempt. 'Here, right at my feet, is where the bomb exploded. Having been saved from the threat of death, I am now more than ever convinced that I am destined to bring our major joint undertaking to a successful conclusion.' And Mussolini had exclaimed, as he stared at the ruins: 'This was a sign from heaven!' Could heaven have meant Roosevelt's death to be anything other than a turning point, in the same way that the Czarina's death had saved Prussia? The fact that Roosevelt and Hitler had come to power at almost the same time in 1933 was not lost on the dictator, when he called out to Reichstag members on declaring war against America: 'It was then that the United States and the German Reich began a development which posterity will find it easy to make a conclusive judgement about as to the validity of the theories.' There is no question that, as regards Hitler and Roosevelt, posterity found it easy to make a conclusive judgement. Seventeen days after the supposed turning-point on 30 April at 3.30 p.m., Hitler ended his life, not as the radio announced: '. . . fighting Bolshevism to the very last' (meaning falling like a soldier in battle), but by suicide. The game was up. The Praetorian Guard, except Goebbels, had left him; Himmler, the 'most faithful of the faithful', had cleared off and was negotiating with Count Bernadotte in the Swedish Consulate at Lübeck, hoping to win him over as an intermediary for capitulation in the west. The plan was that Germany would continue to fight against the Russians in the east – the Russians, who were already at Potsdam Square and approaching the Führerbunker!

Just two weeks later, on 12 May 1945, after the unconditional capitulation had been signed by Jodl and von Friedeburg in Reims, followed the day after by Keitel in Berlin, Churchill sent a telegraph to President Truman, Roosevelt's successor:

An iron curtain is descending along the Russian front. We do not know what is happening behind it. There can be little doubt that the whole area east of a line from Lübeck through Trieste to Corfu will soon be entirely in Russian hands. Added to all this will be the extensive areas captured by the American armies between Eisenach and the Elbe, which, as I must assume, will also be incorporated into the Russian sphere of power when your troops pull out in a few weeks. General Eisenhower must take all possible measures to prevent a second mass exodus by the Germans to the west, should this enormous Moscovite presence decide to march into the heart of Europe. And then the curtain will descend again, down to a narrow chink, if not completely. The attention of our peoples will be directed towards punishing Germany, which lies ruined and impotent.

The telegram clearly expressed that the coalition which Hitler brought together (an alliance between two world powers diametrically opposed to each other in their philosophies) no longer existed, now that he was dead. It also showed that Goebbels's hope, based on the 'miracle' of Roosevelt's death, was completely unrealistic. Germany, in its death throes and in Hitler's image, held these forces together like an iron band, which, figuratively speaking, only came to the fore during Hitler's last days. The fact remained that nothing less than Hitler and his destruction really united them.

Divided into two spheres of power with irreconcilable goals, the world, Europe and, in its midst, a Reich (which as a state had literally been dissolved) now had to get on with the task of living.

PART TWO

THE TOWER

For which of you, intending to build a tower, sitteth not down first, and counteth the cost, whether he have sufficient to finish it?

Luke 14:28

The Victors and the Vanquished
1945–1951

The Allied Questionnaire

'The earth was not shaking, the stars were not falling from the heavens, no comet heralded it, Nature stayed silent, and nowhere were there any signs and miracles; at least not where peace had been so ardently awaited – in the hearts of men.' This was how Horst Lange, a German writer, had determined the arrival of Zero Hour, and if he said that it was finishing in exactly the same way as it had started, 'in quite an ordinary way (the apocalyptic signatures did not tell the whole story), beginning with hysteria and unassumed fear, and ending with exhaustion and quite perceptible fear,' then this meant that what was now starting in Germany came first and foremost from the removal of this fear.

What if millions had lost their homes in the east; or millions were worrying about relatives whose fate was unknown; or armies of prisoners-of-war were lying around on bare fields, tattered, starving and freezing? What if there were barbed wire and Allied orders, tanks and the even stronger military presence of the victors, whether they were Russian, American, British or French? Who was frightened by this any more? The fear had gone – and with this fear, something which breathed down every German neck, something called 'duty'. Whether he had been a party member or not, whether he had supported Hitler or not, even if he had been called a defeatist in believing for some time that Germany would lose, he had longed for nothing more fervently than the end. The burden, as a German, of having to belong to this state, for better or worse, whether through love or hatred, had stayed right to the end.

Now it, too, had gone. The state, a creation, made up of the lifetime contributions of generations, of their sacrifices and their diligence, had forfeited all personal responsibility for those things which transcend the simple bodily needs of its citizens. Reduced to nothing, the state had left a nation of 70 million to their own devices – and that was Zero Hour. A situation with no sense of history, in which the Germans were floundering about now that they were delivered of the Almighty 'Führer', knowing that they could live without him, had to live without him, were allowed to live without him, they were (absurdly as they might think), vanquished and yet free. They were free from bombs, no longer falling from the sky; they were free to breathe without thought of tomorrow.

313

What had happened could never be reversed, and what was to come, would come.

Kolk was sitting in the sun at the window in his flat in the Borstei when the doorbell rang. He had been expecting it. He opened the door. A lanky soldier in khaki stood before him. He was just as Kolk had imagined him, lanky, in khaki, even the Colt dangling at his belt.

'Are you Kolk, credit controller?'

Kolk nodded.

'Come with me.'

'Where to?'

'To BMW.'

'What am I going to do there?'

'Bit of work.'

This was absurd. It was like a script unfolding, one he knew.

'What should I take?'

'Just some clothes.'

'What about food?'

'You'll get that from us.'

Kolk let the neighbours know, so that they could tell his wife what had happened. She had been evacuated, but knew that he had got back to Munich safe and sound after his trip from Augsburg, where he had collected another cheque for 50 million marks. He closed the flat door, went downstairs with the soldier behind him. Was he afraid that Kolk might run away? Just as Kolk had imagined in the script, he got into the jeep, which (as expected) was outside the house, waved to a few children who were skipping around him, and was driven to the works, which was less than ten minutes away.

Here the script ended. His imagination could not have foreseen that a journey into the past would now begin. Kolk and all the directors, as well as their assistants, starting out on the journey with him, would have to be more thorough and exact than their memories allowed. The Allied questionnaire put before him evoked memories of what no individual (even if he were a superman) could ever have been faced with at the time when these events occurred. As these concerned the company and not individuals (just on the edge of things), Kolk had the impression that he was crossing a world which had finally disappeared – a jig-saw put together for one last time before being consigned to the dustbin.

They wanted to know *everything*. Yet every question they asked revealed that they already knew everything – from the firm's foundation, its aims, its successes, failures and achievements under the Kaiser, the Weimar Republic and Hitler's Third Reich, right up to the resultant and inevitable catastrophe. They wanted all the acquisitions ever made to be listed, saying who had financed them, which boards and banks had been involved, along with annual balance sheets. They also wanted to know what transactions had been made with Japan, directly or otherwise, or just planned. They wanted to know where individual items from the factory had been transferred, and which activities, personnel, working areas and site capacity were involved. They wanted to know when things had gone into production, and when they had not; and if they had not, why not. They even wanted to know what things had looked like in the bearing shell foundry, how much lead, bronze and white metal had been processed over how many hours per month by how many universal machine tools. They asked who had delivered these small-scale forged items, those gearwheel blanks (Beilhack in Rosenheim, Schneider in Aalen, Henningen in Metzingen, Krumm und Dowidat in Remscheid, Pettinghaus in Altenförde, Herder und Hammesfahr in Solingen, right up to Janischek in Brno, and Stör in Sagengottes) and, of course, they wanted details about large items such as connecting rods, propeller shafts and epicyclic gear carriers, which came from 'weapons forges' such as Krupp in Essen, Rheinmetall in Düsseldorf, the Tatra Works in Nesseldorf and the German Stainless Steel Works.

Presumably in all these companies, men such as Kolk had spent long hours hunched over the same questionnaires, listing in great detail the products which their firm had delivered to Munich, expecting to be charged with making false statements (should the details not tally) and sentenced by special courts and punished, feeling themselves under threat of provable discrepancies.

The procedure surpassed everything even the Germans had experienced of the bureaucracy of German public offices. What was the point of it all, with fifty or more per cent of production halls in ruins, plant destroyed, design drawings burnt, and a workforce scattered to the winds, no longer in existence? What was the point of it when the Allies' only intention was to turn Germany into a potato field? (Apart from the cession of East Prussia and Upper Silesia to Poland, the Saar and the areas between the Rhine and the Moselle to France, the conscription of a contingent of German workers to do reparation work for the victors, the internationalising of the Ruhr and the destruction of all major industrial and coal-producing plants, this was surely what the first announcements on the radio had intended? Or was the plan to start again on what had originally been produced here? Rumours were also circulating to the effect that this was now intended for the Russians, as well as the Germans.) Perhaps the Allied questionnaire was nothing more than an attempt to delve into people's consciences – if you tell us little lies, will you also tell us big ones? Or was this all part of the display dance of the victors, who wanted to know more than ten wise men could answer? Perhaps, Kolk thought, there was something behind it after all.

The opportunity to gain insight into an inexplicable process (never to be granted again) was without doubt a great attraction for anyone wanting to find answers to the following questions. Why had the Germans remained industrially on a par with, or even superior to, their enemies (in spite of supplies of raw materials being cut off, their own material bases being exhausted and, at least from 1943, their position being desperate on all fronts)? What was the secret, this secret which could not solely be attributed to their mad leader, but which, on the contrary, had first enabled him to unleash this war? Supported by a force which the 'National Socialist Idea' could not begin to explain, he was able to prolong the war for almost five years – five years in which the German armies had conquered half of Europe.

Kolk admitted that (while searching for an answer relevant to BMW) this question was no less interesting for him than for anyone else posing it from outside, even if it was only for reasons of competition. As in Lesage's novel *The Limping Devil*, who removes the roofs from Madrid's houses, allowing the reader to see what went on in thousands of homes, heads and hearts, the Allied questionnaire revealed what had gone on in the maze of economic and industrial life under dictatorship. Yet what did it produce? There was not much point in trying to disguise a single answer, or in piecing together the multiplicity of details which memory had dredged up to produce some kind of definitive picture.

'The general history', which was supposed to portray the firm's history, contained nothing more than what was in countless histories of firms all over the world. A man recognises that a need exists for something which he plans to produce. The trigger for this need is an invention. The fact that the latter could fundamentally change the present century was a consequence of all the industrial activity it had released – BMW included. Kolk was right to put everything he knew down faithfully. But what did he know?

That a certain Rapp, a simple motor engineer, had founded the Rapp Motor Works in Munich in 1913. His goal had been to build aero-engines. Many others were doing the same, so why should not he? People were flying. He had his own contribution to make, although he did not have much luck. War broke out, the one later to be called the First World War, saving him from bankruptcy. This man was no hero, rather an unfortunate soul for whom nothing went right, to whom nothing came easily, until finally (nobody was interested in his aero-engines in either Prussia or Bavaria) the Austrian naval flying corps placed an order. Was that it then? Yes, that was it. But only when the Austro-Hungarian Lieutenant Popp received the instruction in Vienna to 'look over' the order on behalf of the authorities, and only when he travelled to Munich did anything materialise. Without a moment's hesitation (to save the order and to save what was pompously called a 'motor works'), he gave the whole business (even if it only consisted of a miserable shed) a new name – BMW. The fact that the factory, put up when the war had been lost and when thoughts about aero-engines had been forgotten, grew into a firm whose real founder was called Gustav Otto (Otto, like the inventor of the four-stroke engine, whose son he was) may well be seen as a curiosity rather than as an important indicator one could proud of.

If Kolk thought about it soberly, then all this would never have produced anything else, in spite of its worthy founding fathers, without two other people – the man with the capital (a cut-throat, war-profiteer, an inflation-speculator, adventurer, and God knows what else), and a technician who was capable of directing fate through a simple invention which he called the 'high-altitude aero-engine'. Success, the magic word, appeared for the first time. But what had motivated Castiglioni, as the first man was called, to finance BMW (at a time when only risk, and certainly not profit, was the likely outcome)? The fact that, as a Jew, he could set foot in Bavaria and be tolerated (Hitler had not yet decided to become a politician) did not add up. And what had prompted Friz, Max Friz, the Swabian engineer, who had worked for years in Daimler's design office at Stuttgart, to apply for a job in the small dilapidated building of the Rapp Motor Works in Munich on Schleißheim Street? Was it really just because of the 50 marks per month by which Gottfried Daimler had refused to increase his salary? No, it was the attraction of being able to put an idea into practice at Oberwiesenfeld in the Bavarian capital with a firm which possessed nothing more than the name BMW and a white and blue propeller as its trademark. At Daimler, the idea would have collected dust in a drawer because nobody gave it a moment's thought. But this high-altitude aero-engine, the BMW IIIa, was to bring the Germans air superiority which would patently outstrip the enemy. This could be attributed to the greater altitudes they reached, even in 1918, the last year of the war. Ernst Udet alone, fighter leader in the Richthofen squadron, won thirty air victories with the new engine, an engine which only had one flaw; that it arrived too late, as Udet complained. The same Udet, who later became Director of Armaments under Göring.

Yes, thought Kolk, here was the 'general history' – a straight line leading from the First to the Second World War; was it not a conspiracy against the world (long before Hitler appeared on the scene), in which BMW played an active part by its continuous claim to have subscribed to technological dreams important to the motorcycle and the car, but which, in reality, had only one aim in sight? This was to acquire the pre-eminent role in air armaments, firstly by means of the best piston engine in the world, and then with the first large-scale production of a jet engine in the world, and finally by powering rockets which left everything on the Allied side standing.

Was this how it was? Still, thought Kolk, they might believe what facts and figures showed to be obvious in each answer column, for the questions which did not allow for any additional explanations. The fact that it was something else, or could have been something else, was of no interest to anyone. Germany had stopped playing a role in the international community, and he, Kolk, made no claim to show off his knowledge. And so he wrote away, as much as he could reconstruct, putting down what he knew, in part from memory (bookkeeping, along with the Hollerith department, had been moved out to Feldafing, where it had been sacked and set on fire by marauding conscripted workers), and in part from documents which a cautious person had stored away in safes. When the keys to these safes had not come immediately to hand, over-eager GIs had blown open the locks with their revolvers. They did not find much in the steel trays: only wage lists; unimportant notes; minutes from the supervisory board; a survey of all the machine tools and to which outside plants they had been taken – to the Hofbräuhaus Cellar/ the Franziskaner Cellar/ the Reed Mat Factory at Dachau (1,583), Bleichach (345), Immenstadt (244), Kempten (310), Kaufbeuren (243), Landshut (141), Stephanskirchen (172), Trostberg (376), in total 3,414 machines; and more of the kind, randomly offered information ('the Gnôme and Rhône Works in Paris initially built a greater number of BMW 132 engines, subsequently delivering parts for the BMW 801 up to June 1943 . . .'). All of this amounted to little more than fragmented references to things which had been known for a long time, and not to the great secret that the 'Joint Intelligence Objective Committees' were hunting all over Germany, in order to make use of information in the continuing war against Japan in the 'first systematic exploitation of a foreign country's brain-power'. They wanted to go beyond that, they wanted to be able to prefer charges on Germany.

If such a charge could be brought against BMW, then filling out the Allied questionnaire made no difference to it. So this was an open and shut case, and any remark, any reference to the fact that the company had not primarily been an armaments factory, but a civilian business (and should be treated as such), was only designed to give rise to doubt where facts spoke for themselves. An example of this was the licence issued to BMW by Pratt & Whitney, an American firm, to build the air-cooled radial engine. In 1928, there had been no thought of war, and the word 'armament' was quite legitimate. Should Germany renounce for ever what every other state in the world claimed as its natural right, not least of all America?

But there was nothing in the Allied questionnaire about that. Who was interested in whether all technical designs developed and offered by the firm had been at the forefront of progress in their respective fields; in whether BMW had remained competitive in this way, and only in this way, and was thought highly of and was more popular abroad than almost any other make? And how could that continuity which had twice existed, unlike anywhere else in Germany, be explained? Spanning three fields of business (aero-engines, motorcycles, and cars), *one* management, which barely changed, and *one* man, who had presided over this management for a quarter of a century, Franz Josef Popp – a rather unapproachable, conceited, foolish and obstinate man – had forced this continuity out of the epoch. And what an epoch it had been, with its gleaming 'Wehr' (as the army was called under the Kaiser in the First World War), and then a republic which, as Stresemann had once lamented to Briand 'had become paralysed in its black frock-coat, and took no account of the psychological needs of the masses', a republic which collapsed due to reparations payments, as well as being weakened by inflation and the Slump. And then it was finally forced from a Hitler with all his racial mania, from a deceptive new flowering of Germany, which called itself the Greater German Reich, and from its proudly proclaimed new military sovereignty with all its consequences, which had ended in the catastrophe of the Second World War. By virtue of this continuity, which seemed to be immune to all world disasters, BMW, after the revival of the aero-engine business, had moved from motorcycle manufacture to car production at the end of the twenties. They had acquired a small car with the purchase of the Eisenach Vehicle Works, the Dixi, an Austin Seven built under licence. They had gradually refined this car, which was extolled as being 'bigger inside than out', or rather a runabout which the increasing numbers of the less well-off could still afford, despite banking and company collapses and the already apparent armies of unemployed. They did this until that in-house, unmistakable BMW car was the result. It was still produced in small quantities, being avant-garde and functional, and having technological exclusivity combined with a sporting flair and practicality. It had conquered Europe's race-tracks and, with a clockwork reliability under the bonnet, had served a clientele which gave no concessions to mass taste and technical sacrifices (they were only worried about being able to drive it). They swore by BMW with a fanaticism that suggested they were dealing with their own egos.

Looking out of the window, staring onto the rubble of the works, Kolk reflected on when and why he had joined the company. Like most people who have ever come across BMW, he had had a crucial experience, which for him, the car fanatic, was called quite simply the '328'. It was a small, white racing car which, as a regular visitor to the Nürburgring, he had seen for the first time in 1936. No sooner did he read the advert: 'Proficient costing clerk required for company accountancy at BMW in Munich . . .' than he applied. He landed the job. When working on his first end-of-month accounting, he discovered, much to his astonishment, how the costs had been distributed, even the indirect costs: 80 per cent were booked to the limited company (meaning aero-engine) and only 20 per cent to the public limited company (cars and motorcycles). How come? He had thought he was coming to a car company, to *the* car company in Germany, and now he had landed up in an aero-engine factory. When he realised this, he was devastated . . . until he understood that everything he knew as BMW, as a car fanatic, was only possible this way; in other words, that a business which incurred huge costs could exist no other way. This was because money was needed to build the best cars and motorcycles in the world, because they were still built in very small numbers; money was needed to maintain a design and test department incessantly working on new models. Money, money, money. It was obvious that BMW would long since have gone bankrupt if the red figures (Popp's trick, which was as daring as it was practical) had not been covered up in the black, profit-bearing ones of aero-engine manufacture. Did this amount to deceiving the tax man?

Well, the tax man knew exactly what he was doing, when he approved this method of accounting, fully aware that one thing was not to be had without the other. It was now May 1940, and the 328 had taken part in, and won, the Mille Miglia in Italy. When the old team from car production now found themselves allocated to posts in aero-engine manufacture (like Friz, the creator of the R 32, who later managed the Dürrerhof plant at Eisenach; like Fiedler, his successor as chief designer; like the head of the racing section, Ernst Loof, who patched up bullet-ridden aero-engines at a repair shop in the Parisian suburb of Argenteuil; or Claus von Ruecker, put in charge of the engine test beds at Allach), when they all became armaments people, then it all came down to one thing, which was to keep their job, to last out until that distant day when they could take up their old work again. That would be the time when designs, which had been worked on in secret, could move beyond breaks in development and take shape, when people would realise they had not been lazy, had not been asleep, but rather had made car-making a virtue out of a necessity. Freed from the constraints of fashion and marketing, they had used the time to develop a car which was not stuck in the past but looked towards the future. Fully developed, years ahead of its time, it was supposed to herald a new start for the post-war works.

Dreams. They also had no business to be in the Allied questionnaire.

Kurt Deby, chief engineer at the Milbertshofen works, went underground. Immediately after the fall of the city, he had had to take the Americans to the undamaged Herbitus equipment. This was the altitude test bed in Building 100, on which Rolls Royce engines were then running. The test bed could simulate altitudes of between 15,000 and 20,000 metres. All the indications were that it was to be dismantled and shipped to America, which (judging by the observations of a US Army engineer) had nothing like it. Surrounded by American officers and with his ruler in his hand, the engineer was stepping around a bomb crater, measuring it and entering the figures in a notebook. What for? Was the crater to show how accurately it had been bombed? He was looking for clues. Where did the clue lead?

Only ever to aero-engines, thought Kolk. Only aero-engines; aero-engines which had been conceived and built here in Munich, built and sent in their thousands to the front. Everything else had been handed over to Eisenach, except for the design and test department for cars, which had remained in Munich. Even motorcycle manufacture in Milbertshofen had been transferred to Eisenach, in the Thuringian Forest, on the orders of the Reich Aviation Ministry, as early as 1942.

What value was there in the fact that, from the twenties onwards, all the inspiration for motorcycle development upon which BMW had created a worldwide reputation through Henne's records, had come out of Munich, and that those phenomenal cars of the thirties, even if Eisenach had produced them, had first emerged here? The company had become an armaments supplier, an armaments works. The investigators in the Allied questionnaire were only interested in establishing this fact, which was designed, Kolk was sure, to be used against BMW, awful as the balance sheet already was.

Works 1 at Milbertshofen had been destroyed. What was left of the workforce, numbering 14,000 at the end of the war? Works 2 at Allach, escaping lightly (with only 3.2 per cent of approximately 200,000 square metres under cover being destroyed, as Kolk discovered from the list of damage), had been looted or, more accurately, had been left open to looting (a vital concession by the occupying power to the freed conscripted workers, to the inmates at the concentration camp extension bearing the notorious name of Dachau). It must have seemed a miracle that nothing had gone up in flames there, and that pent-up hatred had not been released on the machines and fixed installations. Eighteen thousand people had worked in the Allacher Wäldchen, as it was still called. Where were they now? And Eisenach? If the works, initially occupied by the Americans, were to become booty for the Russians, it would be lost, lost for ever. The Spandau works, which had been half destroyed (with a workforce of 7,000 at the end of the war), had immediately been taken over by the Red Army on entering Berlin, and, according to refugees, dismantled. The same had happened to Zühlsdorf and Basdorf on the Brandenburg Heath, which belonged to the works at Niederbarnim. The Berlin subsidiary was also gone, totally destroyed by bombs. The other subsidiary in Vienna was subject to confiscation of German property in Austria. On top of that, Bischwiller in Alsace, where BMW had possessed a foundry, had also been lost, as well as a machine tool factory.

Those were the physical assets. They did not include all the losses known as intellectual property: drawings, patents, diagrams (much of it more valuable than any bricks and mortar); nor the people who had been 'BMW', who were now no more, and whose loss headed the list, and which, as always, no statistics could quantify.

Was there any chance at all of BMW surviving, however small it had become, of starting up again?

Only a fool could think there was.

Inside and Out

If, as Treitschke said, history were an exact science, then one could unveil the future of nations. But no one has managed it yet. And so it was that in all the misery that had afflicted Germany, the Germans were quite incapable of imagining their future, while the victors thought this future was calculable and that the calculation would come out right.

But things were already going wrong when, immediately after Roosevelt's death, a day after President Truman took office, Henry Morgenthau Jr, the Secretary of the Treasury, left the American government. He was the man closely associated with the plan to remove Germany, as an industrial region, from the map and to consign it to a state similar to the one after the Thirty Years War – that of a wasteground or, at best, grazing and arable land. (In the notes of Secretary of State Hull, an opponent of the plan, it was envisaged 'either to completely dismantle all industrial plant and installations which have not been destroyed by the war, or to remove them from the region and totally destroy them. All installations are to be removed from the mines and the mines are to be utterly destroyed.')

Nothing came of this. The 'OK, FDR, WDC', that famous note with which Roosevelt and Churchill had agreed to Morgenthau's plan at the Quebec Conference in 1944, had met with a resounding 'No' (which, however, still could not prevent Morgenthau's ideas from continuing to have some effect for the time being). Never fully announced officially, and consequently never expressly rejected by the governments (it was only on 3 July 1945 that Truman made a declaration on it), it had found its way into the American Chief of Staff's directives, with the 'JCS [Joint Chiefs of Staff] Directive 1067' determining the direction of American policy in Germany. It would determine policy right up to July 1947. During this time the military showed little concern over the question as to how long 'Germany could be transformed into a continuing workhouse', without this having repercussions on the economic situation in western Europe.

If one looks back today to those days with the hindsight of these dates and events, then much becomes clear in the contradictions thrown up both by the ambiguity of the occupation policy, and by the behaviour of the vanquished. With the occupation forces, views, orders, areas of jurisdiction, attempts to create order changed by the day (sometimes the carrot, and at other times

322

the stick; sometimes polite requests, other times cold rejections); with us, there was every type of justified or unjustified hope, which encompassed obsequiousness to composure, and indifference to subtle exploitation of even the slimmest hopes.

The word went out from Churchill to Roosevelt, saying that he did not want Britain to be chained to a corpse after the war. Yet he had agreed to the Morgenthau Plan in Quebec as the price for not having the Americans occupy the Ruhr, as originally planned. This was to be occupied by the British – not a bad exchange, as it involved excluding German competition from the iron and steel market, which was principally concentrated in the Ruhr. ('This is the heart of German industrial might!' Morgenthau acknowledged in his memorandum.) The result was that American (and not British) troops marched into southern Germany, which should have suited Kurt Donath, who was entrusted with managing BMW. Somehow he preferred Americans, either because they came from further afield and had never had to fear BMW, or because he thought they were more generous and less military-minded than the British masters (a misguided view). The Wild West methods by the 'Texas Boys' concealed administrative strictness, which was not to be trifled with.

War damage at Milbertshofen was heavy. About half of all buildings and halls, half of all works installations, half of all the precisely interconnecting units which covered the 300,000-square-metre site, had been destroyed. Donath thought that it would be better to raze ruins on this scale rather than rebuild them. Everything was therefore a question of submitting their usefulness to proof before any decisions were made. There was talk of Control Council decisions still to be made. What could be done to prevent everything being razed? 'You Germans are getting ready to plan for another war!' was how one US officer very bluntly put it to Deby, as he refused the request for an increase in the workforce, which had stayed behind as an emergency team on the site. Fully employed with patching up power cables, water and gas pipes, Deby's people did nothing but suffer, since a life without a kitchen, without ambulances, and without bars (which the GIs had installed first) was no life at all. It would have needed whole battalions of workers to clear things up, clear away ruins, remove rubble from the alleys in the works, and so forth. The question remained as to which plan should be followed and who would establish levels of urgency, in the same way that every ant is programmed to make its destroyed home operational again straight after a catastrophe.

The solution surprisingly emerged one morning after a night which had not passed off without incident. Two drunken soldiers of the American occupation forces had tried to steal a motorcycle hidden behind a supply of food (the last R 75 still intact at Milbertshofen which had, up to now, escaped confiscation by using food tins as an alarm). Deby jumped out of his camp bed, awoken by the clatter of tins, and sized up the situation (one charge against another!). He promised that if he let the soldiers he had caught go scot-free, and providing they kept their mouths shut, he would have their broken motorcycles repaired, since this had been the reason for the attempted theft. So this is what happened. A few hours later, there was a long line of vehicles in need of repairs (lorries, jeeps, appropriated private cars, motorcycles with and without side-cars) standing in front of the fitters, whose skill and sense of improvisation, set on a kind of work 'stage' out in the open, engendered respect and approval amongst the occupiers. In a trice, Donath received an authorisation to 'carry out repairs', and was openly assured there were no better mechanics. This was initially without any claim for any kind of reward in money or kind. Then, when more and more covered space was needed, just so that they could satisfy the most urgent requests, it became official. Machines and hand tools could be removed from the works site, which had been cordoned off, there were proper terms of work and skilled workers were allowed to fit new installations. This was how those who had been shut in (anyone inside was not allowed to go out, and anyone outside could not come in) were at least able to come into contact with the outside world again.

The spell had been broken. Even soldiers sworn to follow orders are only humans, after all, and humans change a climate, in spite of all the orders aimed to prevent this. With sixty skilled workers which Donath was able to employ on the strength of an official 'authorisation to carry out car repairs' (issued on 21 June 1945), the moribund site at Lerchenau Street took on new life, and hope also increased for those left outside (who were not allowed to enter the works as they had once been able to).

All this had been due not least to Alfred Böning, one of the leading engineers, responsible for many patents in motorcycle development under Rudolf Schleicher. Transferred to Allach as a 'team leader' during the war, he had been called back to Milbertshofen by Donath, not staying 'inside', but 'outside' (a man Donath described as his 'best horse in the stable') when the Americans arrived. This turned out to be a stroke of luck. As early as May (when the guards were in the process of changing), Böning had succeeded in speaking to Donath at the gate.

'We are founding a new development department,' Donath whispered to him. 'Rent some rooms somewhere, perhaps near the evacuation points at Cennobis Cellar . . . Hofbräuhaus . . .'

Böning shook his head, saying that it was unsuitable; he had already visited it and the place was crawling with GIs.

'And here – nearby?'

Böning nodded. He would do his best. At that moment the new guard appeared, Donath vanished and Böning set out on the hunt.

So it came about that, behind the walls of a vulcanising plant, not far from Lerchenau Street, under the eyes of the occupying power, and yet quite undisturbed by them, BMW ran a 'development department' in an office in which drawing tables could still be found. This was where the first designs came about quite independently of whether or not they could be produced. ('The idea of making a start was like throwing a stone into the water and making ripples,' Böning later said.) Little by little, the original staff trickled back, and just as you can't get a leopard to change its spots, they designed what the times demanded – bicycles, saucepans, agricultural machinery. They even worked on a motorcycle. Growing more confident, Böning then moved onto the works site through holes in the fence, once the Americans gave permission for the repair shop. He settled in Building No 11 on the fifth floor, and hid himself away under the sign 'NO UNAUTHORISED ENTRY. DANGER OF COLLAPSE!' The windows were blacked out as if in war time, and the stairs barricaded by junk.

Another course of action turned out less successfully. Fritz Trötsch also belonged to the world outside. As the works export manager and one of the few people who not only knew the victors' language, but also their mentality, he had reflected that Popp, the former managing director of BMW now retired to Grainau near Garmisch, now had his one and only chance to come back. The question remained whether that was also what the company wanted. Popp's successors could hardly object (they had, like most barons of the war economy, been sent to internment camps). There was no supervisory board which could be considered authorised to act. What about asking Donath? He was sitting inside, totally inaccessible to any of them outside (and had as much chance of coming out as we had of going in, as employees besieging the gate explained). In the crowd, Trötsch also noticed Fiedler, the chief designer, and Brenner, who had been in charge of after-sales service. They embraced each other. In those days nobody knew if anyone else had come out alive. Trötsch asked them both for their views.

'Yes, fetch him!' they said.

Trötsch cycled back to his house, jumped into his Lancia, a test car he owned (which the victors had forgotten to requisition) and drove through occupied Munich out to Grainau.

'It was like peace time,' Trötsch recalled, when he showed me photographs of that period. 'Nobody stopped me. Everyone thought that if I could do that, then I must have had it on the highest authority, even from Eisenhower himself!'

Popp could not believe his eyes when the Lancia pulled up outside his house.

'Nobody has sent me,' said Trötsch, 'but the three of us, Fiedler, Brenner and myself, think it's time you came back.'

The affair did not turn out well. Many believed that it had been a bold escapade, which completely under-estimated how things really were. But who really knew how things really were? When Popp received the instruction to go to Property Control (in Holbein Street behind the Angel of Peace, at the seat of the American military administration), he thought that they wanted to appoint him the Bavarian Minister of the Economy. He could not imagine it could be anything else. He felt a weight had been lifted from his shoulders. (In the end he had to show his Party disqualification document in person. The fact that he subsequently re-entered it was to be treated as a purely protectionary measure.) The times demanded capable men who could take decisive action. So he was extremely surprised when a military policeman came up to him in the corridor and, without even waiting for a answer to his question, 'Are you Mr Popp?', arrested him. They left Trötsch behind. The latter looked at him sadly as he went off. Popp was taken to the prison in Stadelheim.

325

'It was there that he sketched out the "Great Plan" with ruler and pencil on lined paper that I had provided for him,' Trötsch said.

'What was that, the "Great Plan"?'

'You had to keep it quiet – a motorcycle engine. That was what BMW was pinning its hopes on. After all, Germany had lost the war, and Popp felt that people would rush out to buy them.'

'After the First World War, BMW also built an auxiliary engine for cycles. There had not been the least rush to buy it. Had he forgotten that?'

'He must have forgotten it, like he forgot everything that seemed to have no future. He was quite serious when he spoke about its rescue, which is what his idea amounted to. Zipprich was already designing details (this was Erich Zipprich, the technician and war-economy baron, who had once sat on the board with Popp, and was now sitting in a cell next to him). Franz Josef Popp was firmly convinced it was his destiny to raise BMW to its former heights.'

Four weeks later, Popp's detention was changed to house arrest, and Trötsch picked him up from Stadelheim.

'Everything is ready,' he said.

'You mean the engine?' asked Trötsch anxiously.

'What? No, my memorandum!' Popp said slyly.

'You've drafted a memorandum?' asked Trötsch, who had become even more anxious.

'Thanks to your lined paper,' said Popp. 'It now holds all the evidence that BMW never became an armaments factory voluntarily. We were forced into it, and once in it, I was charged with sabotage. And rightly so! Yes, you're hearing me correctly.'

He actually meant that if Germany had possessed aircraft with insufficient performance to win the Battle of Britain, then he was to blame, and no one else. Obviously he had forgotten that his row with the Aviation Ministry had been a purely private affair. God could not have created two more different people than Milch, the Field Marshal, and himself – they could not stand each other. And jet engines, rockets – who had got BMW to 'do' all this, if not Popp? He had always been ambitious, and so saw beyond that. His memorandum was irrefutable, as he had realised in prison.

'You must have us build cars again,' he said, 'we just won't get started with motorcycles. You must, Trötsch. I shall see to it.'

'There's no question of "must", Herr Popp!' growled Trötsch. 'Quite the opposite. What's left of BMW is going to be dismantled.'

Popp raised a faint smile. 'Our works?'

'At least, that's what they're saying,' said Trötsch. 'Have you read what was decided at the Potsdam Conference? After the poison-gas industry, we come next on the list. See for yourself.'

'That's nonsense,' said Popp. 'Just my connections with Pratt & Whitney . . .'

He was incorrigible, concluded Trötsch and added: 'But I was, too. How could I have imagined that he, the great Popp, who had founded BMW and raised it to its heights, could assume its mantle once again? No, the Popp era was over – the epoch of an absolute rule which had determined the company's fate, together with all the good luck which had blessed the firm with all those technically gifted people such as Friz, Schleicher, Fiedler, von Falkenhausen, Böning and others. It was precisely as if Munich, BMW and technological progress had been synonymous. Popp believed that it could all be repeated. He believed in it, because he had never lost belief in himself. . . . Until they put him in front of the denazification court – the Germans, that is, not the Americans. He never got over it.'

Dr Max Wrba, formerly a deputy member of the board at BMW, also found himself in Stadelheim. As a war industry baron, he had been 'automatically' arrested. If Popp had gone to Holbein Street thinking that he would come back a minister, then Wrba had been allocated an office right in the lion's den, just a few corridors away from where Popp had been arrested. There, as the experienced administrator, he held the job of head of German personnel at Headquarters. He had not pushed himself forward, since his questionnaire stated that he had been a Party member from 1944. In spite of this, he enjoyed the full confidence of the military government – for no more than a fortnight. Then someone discovered that he was also on the list. So he was sent to Stadelheim, like Popp, but not before giving the Americans the best piece of advice in his life. This 'best piece of advice' concerned Allach and one man who, in turn, enjoyed Wrba's confidence – Wilhelm Dorls. As his former assistant, Dorls had proved himself in planning and, after an interlude as works manager at the Spandau aero-engine works, whose boss Donath he relieved (Donath never forgot this), had been appointed to head Allach on Wrba's suggestion.

When the war came to an end, working on the premise 'We must get safely through to the end', he had been able to prevent Allach from being sacrificed to the chaos of war. No machine had been blown up, no test bed destroyed, not a drop of aviation fuel spoilt as ordered by the Gauleiter's office. Whenever anyone asked him if he still thought that 'we would win the war', they received the answer, 'Don't you?' Ordered to go to Ebensee, a small place in Austria, shortly before the fall of Munich, Dorls was supposed to set up 'engine production of the BMW 801 for the so-called 'Alpine Redoubt' (refusal was punishable by death). There he had come across neither an 'Alpine Redoubt', nor the smallest provision for a factory. When he returned, he found Munich occupied, reported to Milbertshofen and heard from Donath that Allach was still standing. It had escaped the chaos of the last days, undamaged and almost as his plan had intended. No one had fired a shot. The Americans had marched through, and because they were not in the least concerned about the works, the population of Karlsfeld and Dachau had moved out 'for easy pickings', following the example given by released camp inmates ('displaced persons', as the conscripted workers were now called), along with detainees from the Dachau concentration camp who had survived the end of the war in the Ludwigsfeld camp.

When Dorls saw Allach again, he might well have imagined it had been visited by a plague of locusts – stripped of everything that could be moved, with kitchens, cellars and working quarters empty, furnishings destroyed, and doors and windows broken. Anything useful lying around (and with a monthly production of between 600 and 1,000 BMW 801 engines, there was plenty lying around) had disappeared to be bartered for cigarettes, schnapps, butter, flour and similar luxuries. They had been either carried or dragged away. But that was all pretty minor. Nothing had gone up in flames. As Dorls noticed to his joy, all the fixed machines were still in their place and all the buildings had remained unscathed, apart from a small amount of bomb damage. But for how long? The whole site had only token security, provided by a squad of ex-Polish prisoners-of-war acting as guards. It was an almost ideal spot for a depot, a supply and vehicle depot, which the US Army (Wrba had a reliable source) urgently needed for overhauling, collecting and redeploying its field equipment. (Within the 3rd American Army alone, twenty divisions had to be supplied!)

The fact that Allach had not yet been visited, in spite of searches for suitable sites (conducted with a magic lantern, one might suppose), was grotesque. With a surface area of over one million square metres, as well as its close proximity to Munich, the Allach Works, which had been landscaped with trees between the halls to provide camouflage, had escaped the military again, just as it had successfully escaped being seen from above during the war. Wrba wondered if this was because it suggested the idea of 'wood' and not 'place'. One only had to clear the trees, and there was a mass of space. Or was it that Allach was thought to be 'state property' (state property was regarded as booty, for which individual jurisdictions held sway), or was it that Allach simply did not figure on the list of Property Control, the all-powerful confiscation authority in the military government?

Be that as it may, Wrba's reference to Allach and to Dorls, who was his man, was entirely successful. The Americans gave their OK, Dorls demanded that guards should be placed at the gates to put an end to the thieving, and two days later, he received the order to completely overhaul large quantities of engines, axles and gearboxes for the US Army.

As early as 4 July, a few days after the opening of the 'repair shop' in the Milbertshofen Works 1, the American Army moved into Allach, with bulldozers, lumberjacks and concrete-laying gangs. Tree after tree fell (the army reported infestation by bark beetles and also put out poison for these animals when everything was done). While the last remains of the Allach Wäldchen were disappearing, an operation was undertaken, like the cleansing of the Augean stables, in which everything resembling wartime production, and which the looters had not been able to drag away, was removed from the halls – stacks of materials, half-finished aero-engines, aluminium parts, cylinder blocks, carefully protected stocks of precious metals, whose loss only weeks earlier would have cost the head of the guilty party. Carted to huge pits, everything was thrown in and covered with soil. At the same time, posters, newspaper advertisements and radio messages announced: 'Workers wanted! Accommodation available!' The army actually did up the abandoned, desolate houses of the Karlsfeld housing estate, and the camps on the Würm and at Ludwigsfeld, putting in new lockers, beds, chairs and tables from their stocks. All the refugee camps containing ethnic Germans who had been driven out of Eastern Europe and who were now streaming into the US zone were scoured for skilled workers, as indeed were the German prisoner-of-war camps between New York and New Orleans, from Fort Dix, Fort Devens, etc, right up to Alaska. These men, even if they were never skilled workers or were just claiming to be, were brought to Allach. Allach near Munich, Germany. There they were supposed to repair and overhaul 'Ordnance equipment', as it was officially called. In other words, they had to get an army which was materially exhausted ship-shape.

With the arrival of the 143rd Ordnance Base Automotive Battalion, directed by a man whom the Americans had made head of the Works Security (this was Schorsch Meier, who had once been a policeman and had brought the Tourist Trophy to Germany in 1939 after racing in Britain on a BMW), the Allach site was renamed KOD, the Karlsfeld Ordnance Depot. There was even a German works management officially appointed, headed by Dorls. Its job was to advise the American superintendence, meaning the army (later, every German branch and department manager had an American supervisor at hand). There is an authenticated story in which the chief cashier at Allach, shortly before the occupation of the works, examined the coffers, which contained exactly one million Reich marks. As he did not know what to do (his head, Dorls, was absent), he took the money home with him. When the KOD was set up, he brought it back, apologising that he had to return it without interest. He sat down at the table straightaway and paid out the first wages (basic hourly rate 1 RM, semi-skilled rate 88 pfennigs).

'Although it sounds like a tall story, it wasn't,' Dorls recalled, shortly before his death in 1982. 'Everything was simple. Man is a creature of habit. Wages! Work! There were mounds of gearboxes and axles which the Americans brought along. Yes, that's right, gearboxes and axles which had to be overhauled. And to think that we could redeem the costs for it, including 100 per cent indirect costs. So we thought, why not? If you think about the situation, it seemed like a joke, but it wasn't. I brought in Lorenz Dietrich on sales, and he just laughed: If we don't say what is "direct" and what is "indirect", we shall certainly earn enough. We all earned a good amount, always settled directly, with little or no expenses. Army is army, where the left hand doesn't know what the right hand is doing. Eveything went like clockwork. The Americans brought and collected the goods, and a little plate was attached to the reconditioned engines, saying "BMW". The GIs then insisted they wouldn't have anything other than these reconditioned engines, as they were better than brand-new Ford engines. Only once was there any trouble, and that did not come from the Americans.

'Two members of the public limited company's supervisory board appeared (there were only two), and made out we had taken the contract with the Americans without asking the board. "Which board?" I asked. They named Donath and Krafft, amongst others. I disputed their right to be on the board. "A board," I said, "must be engaged by the supervisory board, and the former must have the power to make decisions. Have you that power, as a pair? I don't believe you have." They hit the roof, and I quite literally said: "Damned lot! Just think of those people who had to die in the war because you people produced so much rubbish; and it's still going on! I feel like throwing you out of the window. Choose the skylight you'd like to fly through!" Well, they preferred to leave. Without saying a word.

'We had a completely free hand. It was only later that inspectors appeared, who stood beside the production lines and monitored quality. Our controllers checked the quality. This was the best and cheapest way to do it, given that just one day after I had signed the contract, requisition of the works was cancelled by the Control Council in Berlin. We were saved at the last minute!'

BMW (at least as regards the Allach works) had escaped by the skin of its teeth. But how were things at Milbertshofen?

Here, a works council had been formed by secret ballot under the supervision of the military government and the labour department. Its chairman was a Herr Denk, in charge of the tools store. Representing the small workforce of office staff (although separate or independent representative groups no longer existed), was a man who had played a role as long ago as 1933, on the last freely elected works council in the company. His name was August Kaiser.

'A manager called Herr Scholl,' it stated in the minutes of the first meeting between the works management and this works council, 'expressed his satisfaction that . . . an institution had now been created which would enable the workforce to bring wishes and complaints to the attention of the works management, and moreover, to co-operate in the reconstruction of the company through suggestions and such like . . .'

There it was, dated 3 August 1945: 'Reconstruction of the company.' There was no doubt that it would be reconstructed! And so that everyone immediately knew what a company was, Scholl went on to explain that, although the works were discharged of any obligation towards its employees as this was now a case of 'force majeure' (the occupation of BMW by American troops), both the supervisory and management boards (the first time both of them had been mentioned!) had decided to pay two months' wages and salaries in lieu of notice. The only payment which would be refused would be payment not made in lieu of holiday from 1944 for those on salaries above 600 RM ('and all this,' Scholl added, 'at a time of great financial strain requiring all the effort and commitment of the company and works management, and of each employee, so that the situation can be overcome in the interest of the works and the name BMW'). A decision from the Bavarian Ministry of Employment was pending with regard to holiday entitlement for 1945, and the former rights of employees continuing to work for the company. A sale of old furniture would soon be organised for employees injured in the bombing, and as regards apprenticeships, sixty apprentices had been accepted up till now, mainly apprentices from the second and third years, providing them with an opportunity to complete their indenture.

Works council, workshop for apprentices, back payment of holiday money. Did not all that mean that everything had more or less been straightened out, as one might expect in peacetime – even in Milbertshofen? Yes, the military government had, after several inspection visits, already approved 'drawing together production into two or three halls', and a plan for larger-scale production had already been submitted to the 'Production Control Agency'. It contained the request to grant permission for 'final conversion', to put a complete company together from the transfer plants. 'This will involve a total of 992 machine tools. Our monthly need for coke will be 400 tonnes, a further 400 tonnes will be needed to heat the building occupied by the 9th Air Force . . .' The request concluded: 'Our desire is to reach a middle level of industrial activity so as to enable the works capacity to be used productively. Signed: Donath. Signed: Deby.'

The day the letter was written and taken across by courier to Holbein Street was 28 August 1945. Everything happened that August. Atom bombs had fallen on Hiroshima and Nagasaki (6 and 8 August), Japan had capitulated (14 August), bringing the Second World War to a close. And the Big Three had ended the Potsdam Conference on 2 August.

Now to Factory Dismantling

The Big Three – Stalin, Truman and Churchill (who was only there at the beginning; Attlee took over after the surprising victory of the Labour Party in Britain) met on 17 June in the Cäcilienhof at Potsdam to establish their principles for dealing with the defeated country throughout the first period of control. 'Complete disarmament and demilitarisation of Germany and the elimination of every aspect of German industry which could be used for war production.' That was all too understandable. But another formulation was designed to destroy any optimism still left in the Germans for the future. 'The German people must be convinced that they have suffered total military defeat and that they cannot escape the responsibility for what they brought upon themselves, namely that their own pitiless conduct of the war and the fanatical resistance by the Nazis destroyed the German economy and made chaos and misery inevitable.'

Well-known sentences, thought Donath, but he was not worried. Even the statement that 'persons hostile to the Allied aims' (he knew nobody who was) were to be removed from public offices and positions of responsibility in important, private-sector companies, and the certainty of the obviously imminent elimination of the National Socialist Party and the arrest of war criminals did not astonish him. The only surprising thing was the sentence: 'The payment of reparations should leave the German people with sufficient means to be able to exist without outside help,' when elsewhere it stated: 'The dispensable production capacity in those industries which will be permitted is either to be removed or, if it cannot be removed, be cancelled, in line with the reparations plan recommended by the international reparations commission and established by the governments concerned.'

You did not need to be an economist to calculate what that meant. Food supplies were drying up in the Western zones. Germany was going hungry. The daily food ration was temporarily already below 1,000 calories. Its provisional aim, as General Montgomery had declared on 1 September, referring to the British occupation zone, was the allocation of 1,500 calories per day to the German population, although this quantity could not be issued everywhere due to distribution difficulties. The unusually bad harvest that year made the situation even worse. There was only one solution: to import food into Germany.

But how was this going to be paid for? From German investments abroad? They had been confiscated. From the proceeds of German patents? They were outlawed and available in the USA for a few cents per photocopy. From the revenue produced by the work done by German prisoners-of-war? That was just as rarely recognised as a method of payment as what German scientists and technicians, who had been taken abroad after the capitulation (amongst them, leading BMW people from rocket and jet engine research), produced for new developments. So there was only one way – to export goods. Feeding Germany thus depended on its industrial production – and this depended on the level of reparations, which the Big Three in Potsdam had not been able to agree about. There had only been the demand from the Soviet Union to receive, without payment or service in return, in addition to reparations from their own zone, 10 per cent of West German industrial plant which would not be needed for German peacetime armaments. This had been agreed upon. The report stated that the control council would set the details for the extent of the reparations.

It was autumn, and it was the last week of September. The August sun had faded the big, white letters which someone had written on the end wall of the Military Command Hall: 'DACHAU – BELSEN – BUCHENWALD CONCENTRATION CAMPS – I AM ASHAMED TO BE GERMAN'. On the side facing the residential quarters, the sketchy outlines could still be read saying: 'NO SHAME, JUST RETRIBUTION! SWASTIKA – CROSS OF DISGRACE!' Another inscription nearby announcing: 'GOETHE, DIESEL, HAYDN, ROB. KOCH. I AM PROUD TO BE GERMAN!' could no longer be clearly deciphered. The occupying power had removed a few posters which had recently been put up at prominent points in the town area, which denounced the behaviour of German women and girls, who were abandoning 'their honour for just a few cigarettes or a bar of chocolate' ('Beat them, cut their hair off, those American whores! Come on, everyone!').

On 27 September the *Münchner Zeitung*, the newsheet for the American army, reported: 'Lessons are starting for 2nd, 3rd and 4th forms at the Municipal Grammar School for Girls at St Anna Square, on Luisen Street, on König Square and on Teng Street.' There was a further report stating that the head of the military government in Munich, Lieutenant Colonel Walter Kurtz had died in the Schwabing hospital from his severe injuries, which he had suffered a few days earlier from sections of wall which had fallen into the courtyard at the bomb-damaged city hall.

None of this affected Donath very much. Finding a school for daughters had never worried him (his marriage had remained childless), and he had never got as far as meeting the head of the military government. He only knew him by name.

There was no mention of any decisions on reparations.

Then, that same evening, the news came over the radio. The announcer said that the Control Council had decreed confiscation of a series of German industrial companies as well as ordering their plant to be transported to the victorious nations as reparation payments by Germany. The Bavarian Motor Works AG, Works 2 in Allach, was also on the list.

Deby, who had heard the news with Donath, remembered later at the mention of the Bavarian Motor Works that they they had both become pale, but their pallor had immediately gone when they heard the phrase 'Works 2 in Allach'. This was because the Allach Works was not their business in the strict sense. It had its own administration and had always been an 'extended workbench'. The Americans had legally requisitioned it (in contrast to Milbertshofen which was treated as private property). Donath himself, as the person at BMW nominally responsible for Allach as well, had signed the requisition order – with the result that he no longer controlled Allach.

A 'record about how confiscation took place at the time' captures the mood of hope and fear. At first, nothing at all happened. A few days went by. It almost seemed that what had been heard was just a bad dream, of which the only remarkable thing was that a lot of people had dreamt it at the same time.

Then, as the works management entered the factory on Tuesday, 2 October 1945, they found, posted at the south gate and the entrances to factory buildings, a decree from the military government dated 1 October and signed by 2nd Lieutenant Moskowitz. All the company's assets, it stated, had been confiscated according to Law No 52 of the military government. Enquiries were made as to who had pinned it up. The duty officer in works security said that yesterday evening a police officer from the Milbertshofen station had been there. As he had pointed out that the decree involved Works 2 and that this was Works 1, the official had gone away, only to come back again about an hour later to put up the poster everywhere, in spite of the gateman's protests. At this, Donath immediately rang up the Allach works, where he discovered that confiscation notices had also been posted there. However, they involved Works 1. The 'record' went on to say: 'Herr Thomas was instructed to suspend all payments by the company for the time being. All managers in the company were instructed to refrain with immediate effect from making available any of the firm's property which could be let out, leased or sold and to break off forthwith any negotiations in this respect. Following this, the works management made an appointment to see the mayor, Herr Scharnagl, and were received by him in the course of that very morning.'

Scharnagl was not alone. Along with the deputy mayor, Dr Stadlbauer, a Professor Hencky, the head of municipal building and formerly works manager at IG Farben in Bitterfeld, was present. Scharnagl informed the gentlemen that, due to technical disruption, he had not managed to inform them personally about the military government's order, and that consequently, he had had the questionable confiscation notices posted at both works in Munich and Allach by the police. But that was not all. He asked whether the gentlemen would like to read another written order here, as he handed over the carbon copy of it from the Munich city military government, dated 1 October and signed by a Lieutenant Colonel Keller:

Headquarters of the Munich Military Government
1 October 1945
GMM/Bck

The Mayor of Munich,
Munich City Hall

1 You are instructed to begin immediately on razing the BMW factories 1
and 2 within the Munich city limits.
2 You are further instructed to pack all the works plant into crates for
shipment. A detailed inventory is to be made for each crate, and a carbon
copy of it is to be attached inside each individual crate.

On behalf of the military government:

Eugene Keller Jr,
Lieutenant Colonel, AUB, 0103324
Deputy District Commander

Scharnagl added that Professor Hencky would deal with everything else, as
the military government had appointed him to close the matter from an
administrative point of view.

So it was the end – and time stood still for a moment. Was that what
it was, the end? It is said that when Napoleon was faced with abdication
after Waterloo, he whispered the words: 'I did what I could!' words which
contained everything a human being can offer to justify himself.

Donath had also done what he could. Weighed down with responsibility
because he had not been in the Party, he had taken the blame, suffered
injustices, accepted humiliations, had put every ounce of effort into keeping
the firm alive, had consistently defended BMW, had thought up thousands
of ploys to wring out small 'territorial concessions' from the victors, and
never once to their disadvantage. He continued until obstinacy turned into
understanding, and prejudice into the readiness to help him (and through
him, the company).

'Would you be ready to accept a present?' he asked the commander of the
occupying troops, even before there was a repair shop. 'We shall give you
BMW and you can ran the shop as a sideline. Well?'

And when Donath laughed, he said: 'Why are you laughing? It's a
serious offer!'

Just as serious as packing up the works in crates for shipment, Donath
could have said. But there was no longer any laughing.

The unknown author of that 'record of how confiscation took place at the
time' certainly did not know what a remarkable document he was creating
when he was stringing together date after date, quoting meeting after meeting,
plea after plea (while refraining from any detailed descriptions, commentary
or dramatics). The position of the Germans could be seen here in needle-sharp
images, as if seen through inverted binoculars. Sometimes they were in one
grouping, sometimes in another, with positions changing from one minute
to the next. They were official and efficient in the city hall, and they went

335

home to stark private accommodation, with the faint whiff of conspiracy in the air. They worked in makeshift company offices where, without a break and with ersatz coffee mixed with a few coffee beans bubbling away on cylindrical stoves, they sat in front of the desks of the military officials with their 'Stars and Stripes' on the wall in the background. Here was the works management, doggedly trying to save what could no longer be saved (and everyone knew it), and a city council which, headed by the mayor, as the responsible executive body, was supposed to commit to death on behalf of the Control Council its dearest child from local industry (this being BMW – as much a part of Munich and Bavaria as the Hofbräuhaus). Even the appointed hangman was there. The fact that he was called Hencky (which sounds like the German for 'hangman' – 'Henker') was an omen about which he could do nothing. But the fact that he, as a former manager at IG Farben in Bitterfeld (and IG Farben was top of the victors' blacklist) and dismantling commissioner (as he was officially called) was not supposed to have any reservations at all about the legitimacy of wiping out BMW, clearly weighed him down. Beside him were men who must have been in constant fear because of their positions in the Third Reich, for although they had admittedly produced evidence of non-involvement, they could still get into trouble at any time. They could present him, the dismantling commissioner, with a secret agreement made with the Americans clearly showing that a society which no longer exists, does in fact exist. And behind him were the pro-consuls with the solid weight of power, which they played off against each other; sometimes bound by the Control Council's decisions, which left no doubt as to the legitimacy of transporting all the machines from BMW and leaving it completely dispossessed, and at other times striving to look after their own interests to the best of their ability, which even went as far as complicity with the Germans.

In fact, Dorls and Dietrich, the directors from Allach, had come to an agreement with Colonel Serren, in charge of the Karlsfeld Ordnance Depot, by which they would undertake servicing and repairs of 6,000 American army vehicles per month. If the numbers of machines at Allach were not sufficient for this, then plant from Milbertshofen could be brought across, together with financial resources from the public limited company (estimated at 6,683,000 RM!), although the dismantling commissioner had confiscated all the assets. That did not seem huge, even to the people at Milbertshofen (no one had any idea at the time that Allach would one day become the tuft of hair by which BMW would pull itself out of the swamp, like Münchhausen had once done). The confusion of the whole situation was shown by a list of twenty questions which the disconcerted works management pressed into the hand of the disconcerted dismantling commissioner, who ran with it from pillar to post. His job, in which he was not only obliged to be everything, but wanted to be everything (supervisory board, management board, works management, receiver, liquidator), had long since got too much for him.

The list had something of the awkward questioning adopted by young children when they wear out their mothers and fathers by countering what they know of the world and parental orders. Here that meant:

Shall we pay out the second installment on the trade association contributions (social security) for the Munich and Allach works amounting
to 300,000 RM due on 1 October 1945? We have taken out a one-off
loan by way of 50 million RM made by the German Aviation Bank,
half the funds coming from other private banks and which we have not
yet paid back. Shall we transfer the interest due on 30 September 1945?
We had to move out items of plant, stores and various installations on
the orders of the Ministry for Armaments and War Production. Shall we
pay the rents owed since then to the businesses housing them? Together
with the rents due after 3 October 1945? We are obliged to return the
buildings to their original state when we moved in. Shall we comply
with this obligation? Shall we pay the premiums for insurance policies
that have been drawn up? Shall we settle the telephone charges which
arose a) before the American army marched in; b) after the American
army marched in; c) after the assets were confiscated, given there is a
danger of the telephone being cut off by the Reich Post if bills are not
paid? Shall we comply with our obligations with regard to our suppliers,
whose businesses are either wholly or partly foreign-owned (principally by
America, Britain, Switzerland, Czechoslovakia)?

Shall we, can we, should we, must we . . . there was hardly anything which
was not asked. What it amounted to was whether obligations from contracts
of employment were valid, whether legally binding undertakings to manual
and office staff should be maintained or deductions made from wages for debt
repayment, death benefits, sickness insurance; and if so, where the deductions
were to be paid. They even asked if 'objects designed for private use, which
were of no interest for continuing the business, could be sold to company
employees, preferably those injured in the air raids'? They even wanted
to know if demands on the business with respect to the Reich, as well as
the city, (which resulted from bomb damage, transfers, looting, deliveries,
cancelled contracts and so forth) were still valid. Should a list be drawn up
and submitted, and if so, to whom?

In the meantime, requisitions were made for the sheer hell of it, this time
involving Allach, as later revealed. 'One morning three American officers, led
by Major Pedsel, appeared.' When it was pointed out that the signature on the
contract did not comply with the internal guidelines, 'the gentlemen from the
site inspection were not put off, but requisitioned the fittings from the offices
still in use at the time'. (A few weeks later the light fittings were removed
and even the electric wires were pulled out of the walls.) Hardly had the men
left than Colonel Silvey from the military government Property Control drove
up, had himself shown around bunker C by von Krafft, Schneider and Deby,
and declared that the vehicle parts department stored there was exempt from
confiscation (it was needed for the 'repair shop' which was to continue). He
also released the store of food housed in the bunker 'for catering purposes'.
Barely had he gone than the men from the American press drove up to take
pictures of the disarmament operations. Deby showed them to Halls 17 and
19, without making any reference to disarmament in general. But he made
four figures known:

1 At least 70 per cent of all the machines kept at BMW could be used for peacetime work.

2 The value of the machine tools presently included for removal amounted to 30 million.

3 The value of the test installations was around 15 million RM.

4 Around 1,000 men were involved in dismantling at Milbertshofen.

Was it really a thousand men? You hardly saw any. All you saw were machines and more machines – whole columns of gleaming, highly complicated shapes, which had left their stands and were now dismantled in thousands of parts, rolled out of the halls in crates. You may well ask who was doing this work. That was of no interest to American newspaper readers. German coolies did every bit of it, the main thing being that it was all paid for. Another primary consideration was that there was food in it for them (special rations), meaning they would roll up their sleeves, and then it was heave ho! And so they went to work, although not with a sledge-hammer (there was even one photo showing a worker taking a control mechanism apart with a pair of tweezers and magnifying glass!).

The fact that there were specialists at the works went without saying (Donath had employed them, he was glad to get anyone he could put to work again). Another question was . . . but let us not speak of tragedies. Let us speak of the co-operation shown by all, let us speak of the sense of reason which set the tone, reason which ensured everything went smoothly, reason in which everyone working there was applying himself for the inevitable. Dismantling a factory was nothing like eating sweets. Dismantling a factory was . . . well, what was it? Barbarism? There are worse things.

But it was bad enough. A thousand men doing their best to remove what they had lived off . . . ripping from concrete stands things which they would like to have lived off again . . . destroying the only things that would allow them to live again – their workplace, the factory; which meant their future, their life.

With Germany's capitulation, at Zero Hour, the fear which had been breathing down every German's neck disappeared. They were free of the bombs falling from the sky; they were free to breathe without thought of tomorrow. What had happened could never be reversed, and what was to come, would come.

Now a new fear was gaining ground.

By the Skin of our Teeth was the name of a play by Thornton Wilder then being widely staged.

Had we escaped by the skin of our teeth, people asked? Indeed we had. Then they asked themselves a second question, a question consisting of just three words: for what purpose?

What Happened in Eisenach

It is time to look towards the east. The same fear was prevalent here, where the factory was dismantled, too. And yet this was to happen in Eisenach, where the sign of BAVARIAN MOTOR WORKS PLC had been completed with the word 'formerly' – THE EISENACH VEHICLE AND ENGINEERING WORKS CO. LTD FORMERLY BMW – in quite a different way from over there in Munich, under the Americans.

Over there in Munich, things still seemed to be beating with a single heart. Connections no longer existed with over there, since on the night of 30 June 1945 the American troops had left Thuringia and Saxony with bag and baggage and 'cleared out',to use the military term. There were rumours that they would be leaving. How many rumours there had been which amounted to nothing! A few Germans who had been classified as 'bearers of secrets' had been asked if they would prefer going to the West when the Russians came. Albert Siedler who, as chief engineer at BMW Eisenach, ran a vehicle pool outside the works in a worsted spinning mill, was also asked the same question.

'Is it open to discussion?' he replied.

'No, but if the worst comes to the worst . . .'

All right, he said, he would go. He carefully cleared out his house, storing everything essential to life (even the curtains) in a lorry which had been disguised as a wreck covered with strips of old canvas and parked next to the garage at his house. He prepared two other lorries, one of them for Schaaf, the sales director (whose last position had been as the nominal head of the whole AG in Munich, but who had returned to Eisenach where his family lived), and another one for the two technicians especially valued by the Americans.

Then, on the morning of 1 July, when Siedler had just arrived outside his office, a GI roared up on a BMW motorcycle. He wanted to know if he could still have the cylinder heads he had been promised, explaining he needed them in a hurry. ('Still?' thought Siedler, and 'so early in the day?')

'Come on,' Siedler said.

'Nix come on,' replied the soldier, and pointed over to the stores, which stood beside the workshops. He said that there would be no one there to hand anything out, as the Russians were there.

Which indeed they were. Siedler rushed to the shed where the lorries were standing. The door was ajar.

'*Poschol!*' [Russian: 'Come on!'] a voice behind him called out, 'you here boss?'

'Yes,' said Siedler, bolting the door, although there was nothing left to be bolted in as the lorries which had been prepared had gone. 'Me boss.'

He turned around and looked into the face of a young lad in a khaki uniform. With his Kalashnikov slung around him, the Red Army soldier cheerfully waved to him. Then they went in.

The trap snapped shut.

Four years and 220 days after his abortive escape (this was now in 1950, and the Siedlers had nothing apart from what they stood up in and two small suitcases), Siedler was giving evidence at the Munich works in a kind of hearing which the works management had requested of him.

He said that on that day he had no thought of BMW. That had been pure treachery, especially as he had got on well with the Americans, and they and Schaaf and the others knew exactly what was in store for anyone who had made his mark as a 'capitalist lackey'. Yet he had not managed to get away from BMW. This had not been his fault, but rather the Russians'.

'Nobody thought it possible,' Siedler said, 'they were outspoken BMW enthusiasts, starting with the major who immediately wanted me to repair a captured car, a green BMW 321 (and of course, I repaired it for him), right down to the soldier who arrived on an R 12, asking me to overhaul it – and that was not captured. It came from Siberia. There, during the war, the Russians had built copies of our machines, including the R 71. It was immediately obvious that it had not been arc-welded (the everyday gas welding), because it had poor welds, and the gears had been incorrectly blanked off during welding. Later when there was civilian administration, I constantly had to show engineers who had worked out there in Siberia how, with con rods which had to be honed by hand, the twist was removed so that they didn't "screw themselves in" – a problem they hadn't been able to cope with.

'One day (this was in October), I was told to go to the Commandant's building. I let my wife know (many who were told to go there had never come back), and was locked in a cellar for quite a few hours. Then they asked me if I could build motorcycles, immediately specifying the number they required: 200 a month.

'"With pleasure," I said, "but with what? And from what?"

'"You don't want to do it?"

'"Of course I do," I said, "I'll do it." I knew that anyone refusing was a "saboteur".

'You must understand this distrust,' Siedler continued, '. . . it was worlds apart from the Americans who had more than they could handle. The Russians came from a country which was poor, a country that been impoverished by the war, laid waste by the Germans, to use a harsh expression. Yet this Thuringia which they had now moved into appeared to them like a land of milk and honey, although we, too, were up to our necks in rubble. But nothing seemed impossible here – BMW was like a nut which only needed to be cracked open.

340

'We had hidden the rest of our brand-new cars (undiscovered by the Americans) in the hay. They found them immediately, and my first job was to get them ready for the road. My second task was connected with the Studebaker lorries which America had supplied under the Lend-Lease Deal. They could drive them, but not repair them, as there were no spare parts. I did up twelve of the things for them, and they paid for that (which the Americans would never have done), not with money, but with tobacco (our eyes popping out of our heads) which a jeep brought from some confiscated factory.

'They viewed technology in the same way children did. The Yanks had smashed up three motorcycles which we had knocked together from spare parts – they would never have done that. Quite the opposite – I had ten Russians helping me put together anything that could be put together (their old skill, making one out of three). Then they brought tea, bread and millet. That was when we had millet gruel for weeks at a time, until my stomach (though not theirs) turned over. Then we only had cabbage, until I (but not them) . . . well. . . . So after half a day without food and light at the commandant's headquarters, they told me what my third job would be – building motorcycles, not military ones, but civilian machines.

'"How long will it be? When can we have the first bike?"

'"It'll take a year."

'"You mad! Six weeks!"

'I refused, even if that meant going back to the cellar or God knows where. But all they did was throw me out and give the job to another engineer, someone loyal to the party line, who promised everything provided he received such and such. Provided. . . . Well, he didn't get it, and six weeks later there was not a single motorcycle in sight. So I was again told to go to the commandant's headquarters.'

'Do you remember,' asked Siedler, looking over to Deby, who was occasionally taking notes, 'do you remember the large spare parts department, which we had at Eisenach?'

'Oh, that one. Was it still there?' Deby asked.

Siedler nodded. 'Yes, it was, along with all the spare parts for the R 35, that 350-cc, single-cylinder bike which had to be discontinued then in Munich, because the wheel shook.'

'Yes,' said Deby, 'we took it out of production, and I, I don't know why, kept the spare parts. Everything then went to Eisenach when motorcycle production was transferred.'

'That was my good luck,' Siedler continued, 'So I thought about it. "All right, then," I said, not mentioning that the machine shook. "Two hundred bikes a month, provided . . . provided I get enough machine tools."

'"Where from?" asked the Russians.

'Then I said, despite the fact the factory was being dismantled and everything had already been confiscated: "From the mine at Abterode."

'They immediately took me there, across the Werra. The mine was very near the zone border. They had me go down the ladders, it seemed like for ever, down 450 metres. There they were in the potash halls, our wonderful machines, all in pristine condition in the dry air, with not a spot of rust. I went along using a miner's lamp, painting an "X" on what I needed, and "BMW", "BMW" . . . also on those from Dürrerhof, which they had already razed. Here were the newest and best machines we possessed. They rang down after three hours to ask what I was doing down there for so long, and I rang back saying: "I need more time!"

'I had to select on the spot, without any documents . . . and make my choice from what was going through my head: lathes, grinding machines, drills . . . adding up to 220 items! Three hours later, they rang down again: "Hey, you sabotage, come out now!"

'When I came out, I didn't know whether anything was going back to Eisenach or what. They were always threatening sabotage, deportation. . . . What could I say? I got the machines (they were brought to the light on ropes) through the empty shaft. The lifts had been removed, but they wouldn't have fitted into them, anyway.'

'All 220?' asked Deby.

'Yes, all of them,' Siedler said. 'The rest went to Russia, where they never got to their destination. Tipped out of rail wagons into the snow, or looted, *nichevo* [Russian: 'Never mind.']. I was soon in a position to deliver the first motorcycles – the parts were all there, we just had to build the frames ourselves. The first machines were then taken straight to Moscow, to a test department and put through their paces. Then came the order from Moscow: "The R 35 motorcycle is to be built at Eisenach!" and so on, signed and sealed, which I hung up on the notice-board in the works. And I just went on building – 200, 250 motorcycles a month – until the spare parts ran out. That was no longer a problem then, as we could now manufacture the parts ourselves. And in between times, I also built the first cars!'

'When was that?' asked Donath, who had come back in again after being called away to the telephone.

'In October, I think,' Siedler said, 'when the workers' delegation went to see Marshal Zhukov at Karlshorst in Berlin. That was the seat of SMAD (Soviet Military Administration), headed by Zhukov.'

'Why did they go there?' Donath asked.

Siedler laughed. 'To bribe him. Eisenach was due to be dismantled, and only Zhukov could stop it. They drove up in a BMW 321 and handed it over to him. They said that it was the last car in existence at Eisenach (it really was!) and the workforce had undertaken to produce five cars of the same type within a week. "All right," Zhukov had said, "if you manage it . . ."

'We built the cars, working day and night. That was my fourth job. And the miracle occurred – exactly at the time agreed, the cars drove up in front of Zhukov's door. He then issued Order No 93 to the employees of the Eisenach Car Factory. Nothing like it was issued to Audi at Zwickau, which was dismantled right down to the last bolt. The order was for an annual production of 3,000 cars of the 321 type, together with 3,000 motorcycles of the R 35 type (we already had the authorisation). We immediately employed over 4,000 people. All the cars left in large wooden crates (wood for them was cut from the Thuringian Forest) in batches for immediate delivery to Russia, as reparations goods. Just imagine it,' Siedler said. 'Wooden crate after wooden crate, each as big as a weekend house, and a car in each one!'

'We also had crates as big as weekend houses,' Donath said. 'But ours had machine tools in, not cars, which we would have loved to build with these machines. We had a list of sixteen countries (when India was divided, Parkistan was added to it, making them seventeen), who rushed out to buy them. They even rushed out to buy the cooking spoons in our works kitchen. A few Greeks insisted on some water-raising machines; they were planning to use them to raise ships, but there had been a mistake in the translation, as these turned out to be the pumps under our bunkers which had stopped the ground water washing their base away. We dug them out, too, and hauled them off. But enough of that. Why did you leave Eisenach? You were the chief engineer in a factory with ...' Donath looked at his notes lying on the table, '... 7,000 people, 5,000 of them were technicians. Design and production was all under your control. And you were building cars. Why did you leave?'

Siedler looked nonplussed at the man, under whom he would have had to work here.

An official at the housing office had asked him the same question as he asked to see his refugee pass.

'I haven't got a refugee pass,' Siedler had said. 'I crossed the border at night, with my wife. Perhaps you know what that involves. There are barriers everywhere – tracker dogs, guards who open fire on the spot ...'

'Can you name witnesses?' interrupted the official.

'There is no way I can name the people who helped me or tell you where that was. They helped me, and their lives are just as important as mine. I would not dream of naming them just to get a pass. I shall not apply for one.'

'Then don't,' said the official.

Siedler replied: 'That was BMW over there, that was the reason why I stayed. BMW is here, too. What is wrong with running from BMW to BMW? Don't you see? No, you sit here on your fat arse and don't see a blind thing. You've written off what you call over there. You just want a bit of peace and quiet. You have your regulations.'

'Yes,' said the official. 'I keep to them. You haven't got a pass, and so I can't enrol you as an applicant for a flat, let alone allocate you one. You do not know what is going on here, and that here in the West things are done in an orderly way. You can't say to a person: "You're sitting on your fat arse" without missing your turn. That's what happens when you insult an official.'

Siedler broke off the argument. He wondered if he was now letting himself in for the same thing at BMW because the same question:'Why did you leave?' revealed the same lack of understanding as almost everyone had here. Were they blind? Did no one see that over there, even with such goodwill as he had shown, nobody was getting anywhere? Naturally he had heard what had happened here in Munich ... That Hoegner, the Prime Minister, had shown them the door when the works management called on him.

He said that he would not raise his little finger for armaments factories and war criminals. Siedler knew that the victors had even begun blowing things up, and had only stopped because some people had been killed. And also that BMW stood no chance of making a comeback, with the result that serious consideration was being given to the idea of acting as an agricultural co-operative and to changing the firm into Raussendorf AG, named after the founder of agricultural machinery, which could be produced alongside bicycles and saucepans.

This was all the more reason why he had pulled out all the stops to maintain BMW. But that was not possible without deliveries from factories in the West, which were working again. Now and again he had been allowed across so that he could procure pistons from Mahle in Cannstatt, sparkplugs from Bosch in Stuttgart, along with generators and even injection pumps for a sports car which the Russians had wanted to build. This was until the hammer came crashing down, and the demarcation line was sealed. He had had his own sparkplugs produced at a ceramics factory somewhere in Saxony, and pistons were turned at an old engineering works in Leipzig, but he did not know how. This was also the case for generators produced in Halle, while bodywork tools were 'acquired', meaning stolen, from Ambi-Budd in Berlin, although the factory was situated in the Soviet sector. This was done stealthily because there was no authorisation and production was being held up.

He had learnt a lot more, right down to design contracts he was given and which he ran off as if he had been doing them all his life. Yet he had always felt himself in exile, watched over, spied upon, threatened. He had never got rid of the threat of being picked up if something did not work, or if a mistake had occurred which was not his fault, or for sloppy work or something worse.

On one occasion, cars had arrived in Moscow without spare wheels. He was taken under heavy escort to the loading ramp at Eisenach where crate after crate was ripped open. This revealed that every car had its spare wheel in the boot as required. 'And how can they have flown away en route?' the Russians taunted. 'Perhaps the devil has taken them? But he has been abolished by our great Stalin. So, tell us who has been robbing us?'

Then Avtovelo, a Russian business, took over the works and a Russian counterpart was placed alongside every German, from the top of the company right down to the book-keeper.

But that did not alter anything, no matter how excellent the co-operation was. When there was a trip to the general meeting, a kind of supervisory board meeting, held at Askania House in Berlin, Siedler did not know when he entered the building (which was guarded by machine guns from nine in the morning) whether he would stand up to the inquisition (without food, without sleep, lasting for the most part until the afternoon of the following day), whether he would come out alive.

At the very first session, a young chief engineeer pointed out to him (he had never seen him before) that thousands of rims, which he had checked, had rust marks. Siedler lost his temper (that temper which is called Swabian;

Siedler was a Swabian) and counter-attacked by pointing to the other's omission: if he had found just a single rust spot, he should have informed him immediately, and added that he found it all underhand.

They withdrew for consultation and sat in judgement over him. Coming back, they announced: 'Siedler, stand up! The Strasser Engineer (Strasser Engineer was the leading engineer in the company) will receive . . .'

No, it was not punishment camp, but only censure for improper conduct: 'We hope and expect that this will not happen again!'

Siedler, whether in the right or wrong, sat down like a schoolboy. It was all the same to him; he only wanted to get away from here, wondering if anyone could stand this kind of roasting. On the one hand, the money was good, with quarterly bonuses, and never any material worries. On the other, in a situation where there were no technical communication difficulties at all, which was all the more incomprehensible, the policy was: 'You have to design, you have to build what we demand, and if you don't sign to say that you will comply with your obligations now, you will not see your home again. Sign here!'

First, 10 or 20 per cent of the salary was deducted as a penalty for each month which exceeded the time stipulated by the contract. If the engine ordered did not produce the required output, then the best one could hope for was to lose one's job, one's accommodation, the privilege of tuition for the children, leaving only the option of working as an unskilled worker.

He again opened his mouth and protested. He said that mental work could not be put on piece-rate. No viable car could be built on data which had been calculated purely theoretically, imposing such conditions as: so many horse-power, such and such an engine speed . . . and fuel consumption must not exceed 'X' . . . 'My chief designer and I will not sign that.' In the end, they had to sign it. But he had dared to retort to a Russian managing director, who was also a general in the Red Army (a friendly man, who liked him): 'It is immoral, Comrade General.'

'What is immoral?'

'To demand that I should put something into practice about which I am not one hundred per cent sure, or even if it will work . . .'

The general smiled. 'Don't you understand that? When you sign, haven't you got something of the design worked out in your head, perhaps already in the drawer? You do see that in the time we give you, you can produce the next genuinely new things – and you will do it. That, my friend is how we guarantee progress.'

No, Siedler thought, but did not say as much. The opposite was true – that was the sort of thing which inhibits progress. A system which drags out the utmost from human beings, puts them under constant pressure, keeps even the most competent in fear of not doing enough, is an enemy of progress. What is it really all for? Was it to chase after an obsession still called BMW, just to be able to build a car with this name? The cars which now left Eisenach were no longer going to the Soviet Union as reparation goods, but were being delivered abroad where they brought in hard currency – to France, to Switzerland and elsewhere. Wherever this name was known, it immediately aroused great interest. It also stopped the customer from seeing that BMW was really called Avtovelo, was really a Russian company, and that the white and blue circle no longer had anything to do with Munich and Bavaria, from where it originated.

Should he report this? Who could it be of interest to? What was this question supposed to answer? When they asked him why he had left Eisenach, should he have said that he was a silly fellow, like that colleague who had fled three months before him? The Russian general had interrogated Siedler, and Siedler had had to say something. The colleague, a friend of his, had not intimated anything. That evening they had chatted with each other, and then overnight he disappeared.

'Where to?' asked the general.

'He was from the Rhineland, so probably there,' Siedler said.

The general laughed and slapped his knee. 'Silly fellow! How can anyone be so foolish? What a silly fellow! In six months at the outside, we shall be on the Rhine, and then we shall have him!'

And so Siedler stayed quiet for four years and two hundred and twenty days from that day, which for him, as he then swore on his own name, was to be the last day at BMW. The first one would become part of his quite personal attempt not to let the old symbol die nor to become a traitor to himself.

He kept quiet and thought: silence, too, is an answer.

'No,' said Donath, 'I did not want to offend you. We are glad to have you here, Siedler. It's only that we cannot guarantee that you have come to BMW here. There is a court case in the offing. Eisenach claims the BMW name because it has demonstrably built BMW cars – and we have not. The cars are even going to be offered here in the West, in the Western zones. Despite having defects the owners are now complaining to us in Munich about. We are naturally refusing the complaints, along with the liability. And so the question is: who is BMW? If the court case for the trade-mark turns out in Eisenach's favour, then we have lost the BMW name. And with it, the last trade-mark we possess.'

A Trial

The trial was conducted by the provincial court at Düsseldorf, not against the Soviet business of Avtovelo, which had manifestly infringed the legal rights of the plaintiff, BMW Munich, by producing and marketing the 320 and 340 models, but against a car dealer based in Düsseldorf. He had imported the cars, allegedly from Switzerland, where they had arrived from the Soviet occupation zone (already called the German Democratic Republic, but not recognised as a state). The importer was certainly taken aback when he discovered that he was an accomplice in this infringement, 'because in the Western zones, the fact of infrigement could only be constituted on purchase of the cars', as was stated in the indictment. Things had been tackled in the right way – the customer might get the impression simply by using the cars that they came from Munich and were 'original BMWs'. Everything suggested this: the trademark, the white and blue circle with the initials BMW, the overall, unmistakable shape of the cars. In this way, said the lawyers, the Soviet company was promoting itself as the manufacturer with an item which did not belong to it, which was subject to international law on goods and fittings, and which, on top of this, because it was of inferior quality, resulted in numerous complaints, and was highly detrimental to BMW's reputation.

Naturally the dealer defended himself. He said that expropriation of BMW Eisenach, which had been the centre of BMW car production for ages (in fact, not a single car had ever been built in Munich), was based on a reparation order from the Soviet military administration, therefore from the Control Council, involving legal rights for fittings, trade-marks and patents for the whole territory of the Reich. In addition, the cars had not been put on the road in the Western zones, but in the Eastern zone. There had recently been an agreement concluded at Frankfurt dealing with inter-zone trade, which allowed the cars to be imported.

Those were the outlines of the facts, with the question as to whether the car dealer could demand a session of the Allied High Commission, because it alone could settle whether rights on trade-mark and fittings had passed over to the Russians with the expropriation, and whether a German (West German) court could or should decide at all on the effect the Soviet order had had on civil law.

Assuming that the dealer had been given permission – which he naturally claimed for himself – in all innocence, then the world had really been turned on its head, because anyone noticing these cars on the roads of the Federal Republic, or in fact travelling in them, must have concluded that BMW was back on the market with its earlier cars. Consequently, any faults and any complaints about them were attributed to a company which had absolutely no influence on production. If the former was a serious infringement due to the fierce competition already existing, then the latter (being liable for something produced outside the company) was the last straw. If there were no longer any quality control to cover the trade-mark (the excellence and quality of the product), then nothing had any value anymore, and 'BMW' was extinct.

There had once been a similar situation after the First World War. On that occasion, the Knorr Bremse company, on Popp's invitation, had moved into the closed BMW factory at Moosach Street, due to the effect of the Versailles dictat, initially as a customer saving BMW, but more and more as the owner, until finally something calling itself BMW emerged which was no longer BMW at all. Camillo Castiglioni, who had once financed the company, but then sold it, now bought back the only thing which seemed of value to him. The name, the trade-mark. He literally bought the BMW name from the factory, as he wanted nothing else than that white and blue propeller with the three initials around its edge, a symbol, an abstraction. BMW had started up again.

That was twenty-eight years ago, not quite three decades. These were decades which had changed the world more fundamentally than ever before. In technology, in natural sciences, boundaries had been exceeded which no one had thought possible, and mankind as *zoon politikon*, as a socially acceptable animal in the Aristotelian sense, could no longer cope. Naked aggression, a return to the Dark Ages, genocide, pillage, and revenge in preference to the law, had been his answers to the provocation, with the powers that be having only one panacea for pacifying chaos – division. States, countries, families, which had evolved over centuries, entire cultures were divided, separated from each other, split up, just like a tree split by an axe, and subjected to new ways of thinking, ideologies, with new orders being implanted which were artificial and inorganic.

The axe had also struck BMW, with branches being lopped off; thick branches at that. The trunk, though, stayed alive. But what did this life look like?

The order to pack up the works into crates for shipment, something which, to any expert, seemed just as monstrous as it was comical, had not proved to be the product of some unpragmatic bureaucratic imagination, but something serious and feasible. It was feasible, as long as the idea that this had something to do with reason was laid to one side. That tangled pile of sheet metal, which lay stacked up in the foundry ready for transport, would never again fit into any other foundry, whether it was nearby in Belgium, or far away in Pakistan, or had just been erected on site. There would never again be any use (or only limited use) for those things which, built in and anchored firmly on site, were not simply ripped from their foundations, but also from their very function. This was the case with a special drilling machine which occupied a quite specific place in the finely-tuned production flow of highly complex aero-engines. It would have been better to blow up and destroy all these pieces of equipment on site. Often they did not even reach their destinations, like, for example, the ship bound for New Zealand which, fully laden with goods worth millions, hit a mine off the coast and sank.

This whole dismantling operation had been senseless. Not being feasible from one day to the next, it had dragged out for years – nineteen hundred and forty-six, nineteen hundred and forty-seven, nineteen hundred and forty-eight, nineteen hundred and forty-nine – one has to write out the years just to get an idea of the time involved. It was still going on in 1950 when the currency reform had long established stable conditions again in the country, when east and west had long been separated, when there was a Federal Republic of Germany and a German Democratic Republic, integrated into mutually hostile power blocs, and the zone-based economy had almost entirely been forgotten. Designed as punishment and compensation, then carried out more by accident than desire, it brought nothing of value to either the victors or their allied states. It rather produced the opposite. It was absurd not to contest that. While it freed the vanquished from machines which had, in the meantime, become very antiquated, it weighed down people who had to make use of this antiquated equipment with non-sellers which were ready for the scrap-heap. Originally designed to set a precedent, this dismantling now demolished every piece of confidence that had been won, despite all the goodwill produced by this intelligence. It humiliated and demoralised the Germans.

Any German at BMW entrusted to carry out the procedure was still able to walk through Halls 17 and 20 in 1946 and 1947, where thousands of machines were waiting to be transported away. It was 'like walking through an overgrown forest'. This was how an eye-witness expressed it:

> The only three-tonne crane that we had in the works hovered overhead, lifting the gigantic weights (which often weighed double its capacity) at one end of them. Something was put underneath, the crane swung to the other side, then something was put underneath, and so on and so forth. Work progressed centimetres at a time. We thought that it would take years to clear the halls. That whirring of the grab . . . I can still hear it today . . . I can still picture the scene when everything was finally transported away from those halls. They stood there, starkly bare, and we walked between the destroyed foundations which stuck up out of the floor like grave stones. It was as if we were walking through a cemetery. No one had wanted to do this terrible work. The employment office allocated people to us who were queuing up because they needed ration cards, and only anyone proving he had done work would receive a card. I was also queuing up (I had been fired because I had not been denazified), and reported for the 'wood job'. 'Wood job' was the nickname for doing this work at BMW. So I was back at the works. The test track, that giant oval which even camouflage netting had not concealed from above, had

already been blown up in the war. After the occupation, the Americans had thrown into the gaping craters anything they could – machine parts, propellers, cupboards, bedsteads, bicycles (junk in their eyes, but precious objects in ours). They were covered with earth and the ground levelled off. Now all this was dug up. Somebody found a cracked wash-basin, another person an old bicycle frame. There was also a lot of firewood amongst it all. Tags were given out so that it could be divided up fairly, tags called 'barter pennies'. Before the currency reform, they were more valuable to us than a wage, which could not be used to buy anything, because there was nothing to buy.

The most absurd things happened in Allach. A kilometre-long baggage train consisting of nothing but confiscated machine tools left the halls through one gate, while through another, a second baggage train, also a kilometre-long, rolled in with almost identical machines, absolutely brand-new, from far afield, with some of them even coming from the United States. The same military office which had ordered them was arranging to have the dismantled items taken away.

But some strange things also happened in Milbertshofen. In view of the fact that BMW would one day build cars again, Deby, acting on his own with money from the Marshall Plan (but for his part he claimed that it was with the board's consent), had bought in the USA something which was not available in Germany. These were two enormous Chillingworth presses, the most modern kind of pressing tool for car panels available. After they had been unloaded in Hamburg and put on a train, they went through a series of adventures crossing the country which was now called the Federal Republic. Diverted along local lines (they could not go through any tunnels), they arrived in Milbertshofen at the same time as those crates, as big as weekend houses, were also leaving the works with dismantled goods.

'A bit of horse-trading was going on at the time, too,' Deby recounted in his old age. His voice was already rather rough, he often interrupted himself and asked for patience, as looking back to the past was a joy for him, as with most old people. But whole sections sometimes slipped away, which annoyed him; but that could not be helped. Nevertheless, he could still see that time clearly before him.

'For example, an Englishman came along and wanted high quality light metal. I took him to the stocks. "Help yourself, sir," I said, not especially cheerfully. He thanked me, and then released machines which were on his list and were supposed to go to England. Not exactly the best machines were there, but at least they formed a basis on which we could start again. Immediately a Dane came along with the same wish – what was I supposed to do given that Claimes, the American officer who supervised control, was there? Either they went to him, or, if they knew any German, to me – and I had a bad conscience. 'Mr Claimes,' I said . . . Claimes shook his head, asking whether I was afraid. He said that he had seen and heard nothing, and I swapped something again. This was until the Russian delegation appeared, which Claimes could not escape from. There was a general with a lot of gold on his shoulders, accompanying officers and a female interpreter. They wanted to see the wind tunnel, which was probably listed due to a translation mistake – there was none. I immediately knew what they were looking for – the Herbitus equipment.'

'That had been confiscated by the Americans,' I said.

'Yes, that had been transported to America,' said Deby, 'and the Russians knew that. Now, as the better caretaker I had become, I knew every corner in the works, and I led the delegation round. Led them astray? Perhaps. Anyway, I carefully left out Building 10 (Claimes was watching me with his binoculars), as this was where the Herbitus was. I dodged awkward questions, pointing to this and that, and letting them have a look here and there. But they were not interested in the halls, in any single machine tool. They spoke scornfully of 'Grandmother'. They only asked: 'Where wind tunnel?', and I replied: 'There isn't one!' This was also true. After they had gone, Claimes came up to me, visibly relieved, and embraced me. I was very shocked; 'no fraternisation' had not yet been repealed. And Claimes did not stop with that gesture – I could stick some more 'tags' (with the designation 'works stock' – I always had some in my pocket) on a row of machines, which were supposed to be going to God knows where.

'That was when, as you know, we started up again with motorcycles in literally empty halls – after dough-kneading machines, saucepans, hot-plates and all that stuff. Coils were turned out from sections of steel which were somewhere around. Quite a lot could be made from things like that.

'We were very poor, but not unhappy. As a car factory, we had not got a single car. Nor any motorcycle belonging to the works.

'When we began to build motorcycles again, only 250-cc bikes were allowed. We were loaned machine tools from a machine association set up by the Ministry of the Economy, just things which had been picked up but were still intact, and which could only be distributed to plants which were not subject to reparations – so *not* to Kugel-Fischer, *not* to BMW. The fact that we were able to get anything was due to my friend Günter, formerly a manager at Allach, who worked in the Ministry and was later sent to Minden to work in the economic organization of the bizone. Of course we were asking for trouble. After he had managed to arrange these loans for us, Günter became the leading figure in materials allocation, and so we received quotas for iron, tyres and so forth, which we would never have seen otherwise.'

It was at this time (this was January 1947, when the deliveries of dismantled goods from the victorious powers first really started to recipient states) that the *New York Herald Tribune* portrayed the situation in Germany to its readers. 'Is there a new German nationalism in the making?' the introduction went, before going on:

After almost two years occupation, the archetype of the 17 million Germans living in the US zone is that of an unrepentant cynic who grovels in front of his victor, shrugs his shoulders when democracy is mentioned, and views a new war as a possible solution to his present problems. Impressed by

American power, he dutifully despises Nazism, and pretends to subscribe to democratic ideals. Yet the only real balm for his bitterness and humiliation is an obstinate belief in his own superiority and the final triumph of the German race.

If we open the Munich city chronicle written at the same time as this article appeared in the USA, we can read:

9 January 1947: A board with 'Bread sold out' would be put up at many bakers, even in the early hours of the morning. The reasons for the shortage of bread were the lack of flour, 'bulk-buying' using the supplies of bread coupons left over from public holidays and difficulties at the mills and bakeries through frost, fuel shortages and power cuts.

The so-called 'Temple of Honour' at König Square situated beside the former Brown House has been blown up. The foundations have been kept and are to be used for some building work planned.

120 basement flats are currently registered with the municipal housing office, together with hundreds of other squalid lodgings, shed housing and half-destroyed accommodation.

13 January 1947: After an announcement by the Bavarian State Chancellery, the American military government has issued the authorisation stating that Germans may again fly flags with the Bavarian provincial colours of white and blue, although not in the vicinity of the United States flag.

14 January 1947: The City Council has decided upon the renaming of seventy-seven streets and squares which were named after regiments, branches of the services, army and troop leaders and victories in past wars. In future, there will be streets named after, for example, the National Socialist victims Fritz Gerlach, Sperr and Caracciola.

16 January 1947: The second of the two Temples of Honour at König Square has been blown up.

18 January 1947: At a huge mass rally at the Krone Circus, the new expurgation minister, Alfred Loritz, spoke of denazification, and promised an increase in the number of denazification courts from 200 to 300. He repeated his view that most Party members after 1933 had not joined voluntarily but had been forced into it.

23 January 1947: Before the war, there were 23,000 vehicles in Munich, but today the figure will not exceed 10,000. There are 3,500 applications for registration, which have no prospect of being approved.

27 January 1947: The premiere of Goldoni's *Servant of Two Masters* took place in the 'Theatre of Youth'. Under the direction of Georg Kruse, the leading roles were played by . . .

1 February 1947: The *Süddeutsche Zeitung* issues the remark in its editorial section, We have no more coal! We urgently request people to refrain from visiting us! The editorship is now situated in the boiler house, entrance by Door II.'

It was freezing cold. A second cold snap hit the city at the beginning of January, with temperatures as low as minus 26 degrees. Classroom temperatures sank to between minus 4 and minus 6 degrees, with outside temperatures of minus 18 degrees. Lessons were only given for half an hour per day and class, and the occupation costs amounted (as the Finance Minister Kraus announced to the provincial parliament) to 723,674,800 Reich marks for the period between May 1945 and January 1947, with costs for foreigners amounting to 187,998,600 RM. Collapse was imminent.

The fact that things somehow continued was connected with an event which, although not easily recognisable for the Germans, was announced in a speech given by the American Secretary of State James F. Byrnes in the autumn of 1946. It promised the complete revision of the post-war policy previously adopted by the Western Allies in their occupation zones. Byrnes's words included the following: 'If Germany . . . is not to be administered as an economic unit in the way planned and called for at the Potsdam Conference, then modifications will have to be made to the industrial level set by the Allied Control Commission.'

What did that mean? Just a few weeks earlier, in order to settle Soviet objections, Byrnes had been ready to increase the length of occupation in Germany from twenty-five to forty years, alongside its complete demilitarization. Now he was saying: 'While we shall insist that Germany follows the principles of peace, of good neighbourliness and humanity, we do not want it to become the vassal of any one power or any group of powers, or that it should live under an internal or foreign dictatorship.'

Was this the break with the Soviet Union, the final collapse of the war coalition? Did this mean that whether they wanted it or not, they now saw Germany as a future ally without whom nothing could be done? At least it was the end of the sentence for that part of Germany occupied by the Western powers.

'The American people,' Byrnes concluded, 'want to give government back to the German people. The American people will help the German people find their way back to an honourable place amongst the free and peace-loving nations of the world.'

As early as 1 January 1947, the American and British zones were merged into the bizone, followed shortly afterwards by the incorporation of the French zone into this union. Then, on 7 July 1947, Byrnes's successor; George Marshall, spoke to students at Harvard University.

His words went down in history. Marshall invited the European countries, including Germany, to work out a programme which would provide for economic regeneration through co-operation – with the full financial backing of the USA. (Between the years 1948 and 1952, raw materials and goods, credits and grants adding up to 13 billion dollars were distributed from the 'European Recovery Program', shortened to ERP. Out of that, 1.24 billion dollars flowed into the area later to form the Federal Republic, which meant a credit of almost 400 marks per head of the population in the first three years of reconstruction – from 1947 to 1950 – while in the area occupied by the Soviets, rather more than this sum per head of the 17 million Germans who lived in the 'zone' were withdrawn as reparations over the same period). The Marshall Plan, in direct contrast to the Morgenthau Plan, brought dismantling operations under public scrutiny – but they were still continued, partly because Marshall believed that Germany's still unexhausted industrial capacity would be of benefit to others by surrendering closed factories, and partly because of the British, for reasons of competition.

BMW had had a first inkling of this, even before the decisions from the Control Council came into effect. A British officer drove into the Karlsfeld Ordnance Depot at Allach and curtly demanded to see the German Georg Meier. But Schorsch Meier, head of works security, had already spotted him (his job involved refusing entry to anyone who had nothing to do with the KOD) and knew who he was.

'Mr Craig!' he called out. The face underneath the stiff cap with the braiding (instead of the chequered sports cap) was none other than that of the former racing director of Norton, the British motorcycle manufacturer. That sports cap gave Craig the appearance of the so-often weary detective Sherlock Holmes, especially when there was a pipe under it, whose smoke obscured the English countryside. Even his pipe was there. But Craig neither took it out of his mouth nor stretched out his hand in greeting, nor did he slap his former racing companion on the shoulder in the amicable way he had previously done. Instead he said to his interpreter, whom he had brought along (although he could speak good German, as far as Meier remembered), that he wanted the design drawings of that racing machine handed over immediately, the one on which Meier had ridden on the Isle of Man. (This had been in 1939, when the latter had carried off the Tourist Trophy to Germany.) Meier believed that he had not heard right, and said that Mr Craig must surely want to take some time going round the factory, as he was already expected there. No, he definitely wanted the diagrams right away, unless they had been sent to America. And what about the racing machine? His machine, was Meier's amazed reaction! He said that, like all the company's racing machines, it had been transferred during the war ... to Berg on Lake Starnberg. There British soldiers, acting more quickly than Craig, would probably have confiscated it. (Meier was lying here; he had picked it up himself from Berg in 1943, and hidden it in a hay barn on the Karlsfeld estate.) As for the Tourist Trophy, a smaller version of the original, which was one metre tall and which had been taken to Vienna for security reasons, was his own private property and Craig was not going to have it. Then he told him he would have to continue with his duties.

'Goodbye, Mr Craig, hope to see you in better days!' he said and disappeared.

Craig, beside himself with anger, immediately drove over to Milbertshofen, where he shouted at Donath to send Trötsch, the former export manager. He now repeated what had happened with Meier, except that Trötsch (he had been in and out of Norton's racing team and become friends with Craig) believed that this was an act which Craig was putting on for him. This was until he could no longer doubt the seriousness of the situation. They drove to Berg Castle at Starnberg where the design diagrams were supposed to be in a safe. Craig thought this was a piece of subterfuge, took out his pistol, laid it on a table and demanded that the diagrams were handed over 'once and for all'. Trötsch said that it had been like a bad dream for him and, until today, he had never understood what Craig had intended by all this. It was absurd to try and discover the secret of Meier's supercharged machine from the diagrams, and Craig should have known that, if anyone did. Anyway, the drawings were handed over to him, not with gnashing of teeth but almost indifferently, coolly (which was perhaps to be expected). Later, when Aldington, head of the Frazer-Nash Company which was a genuine friend of BMW's, appeared in the works to make a specific request supposed to establish future co-operation, the incident was buried. Aldington formally apologised for Britain and promised to return the diagrams – a promise for which he requested some time, and one which he kept when they saw each other again at the Geneva Motor Show.

It was here, at the first motor show after the war, in March 1948, that the R 24 was displayed under the glare of spotlights. It was a motorcycle of 250 cc which the management at Milbertshofen had decided to build, although everything needed for it was still lacking. Trötsch was the only one who knew it was little more than a dummy. When the invitation to Geneva landed on his desk, he was keen to accept it immediately. Donath had thought him deranged.

'What are we taking there, then? A diagram?'

No, Trötsch said, reminding Donath of a trip to Nuremberg in the first year after the war: the tyres on the Lancia had gone (the selfsame Lancia with which Trötsch had picked up Franz Josef Popp at Grainau), and a BMW dealer in Nuremberg, 'one of the old school', had helped him out and done more besides. He had let them have an old burnt-out motorcycle which they had discovered on a scrap-heap.

'We then put it in the back of the car, if you remember. Well, I've had it done up by people outside. The basic components are missing. But what does that matter?'

Trötsch had then taken the machine to Geneva, and Aldington described to him how it took some of his colleagues' breath away, with just one of them blurting out his feelings.

'Just look at these presumptuous Teutons,' he is supposed to have said. 'They're already back in business!'

Two months later, in May 1948, the improved version (the cylinder and cylinder head had been turned on a horizontal boring mill, which the firm of Krauss-Maffei had loaned the company) was displayed at the Export Fair in Hanover, and obtained advance orders as a semi-finished product (with a gearbox, minus its gearwheels and crankshaft). These were better than anything which they could have hoped for in their wildest dreams – 2,500 motorcycles!

Faith moves mountains, as the Bible says. Nobody knew how series-production was going to be started for this seemingly astronomical number. All they had were empty halls, in which machine tools were only figments of the imagination, and where there was no steel other than what was on licenced permit. They only had men who were able and willing to work. At that time, it was illegal to have anything which could not be obtained legally. The economy acted accordingly and overcame bottle-necks by paying excessive prices (above all for machines which were indispensable) or by compensating, which meant bartering. Finished products were consequently withdrawn from the market, but transformed into their real equivalent. Both methods were against the law, both were denied to BMW. This was because BMW was run by a trust company, and Dr von Mangoldt-Reiboldt, the general trustee officially appointed by the military, would have risked his neck if he disregarded legal requirements, especially since he was employed in an important economic department of the High Commission in Paris. On the other hand, his role as a kind of managing director made him responsible for preserving the essential character of BMW.

The situation, with full order books, was more serious than ever before, when an unprecedented act of solidarity between friendly motorcycle companies, who were flourishing, brought unexpected help. NSU in Neckarsulm and Zündapp in Nuremberg ceded almost half their iron allocation to BMW, and the machine distribution office for Bavaria (which arranged for Bavarian firms who had been spared from factory dismantling to give up old lathes, machine tools and finishing tools) loaned or gave these to the hard-pressed works.

This was how things got underway, which, in all modesty, could be called 'production'. But the orders did not hide the fact that the subsistence economy then in force set limits on people's willingness to work. Every day Donath felt that simple encouragement was no longer enough to produce an incentive for work. Ground out, as if by millstones (caused by the eagerness of investors to seize assets, and the attempt from above to block access to the commodities market through bans, confiscations and the command economy), any hope for better times had been reduced to zero, no, *below* zero. The black market was booming and destroying any incentive to do anything at all. The rule of law no longer prevailed, and finished goods only produced money with which there was nothing to buy.

Something had to happen, the German economy had to be restructured, money had to be converted into real purchasing power, and the prices on official markets had to be equated with the true value of goods on offer.

A currency reform was essential.

Nobody knew at the time that the banknotes used for a new Deutschmark, whose appearance was so embarrassingly similar to the American dollar, had been printed long ago and stored in New York and Washington bank safes. They had been printed as far back as 1946, which was why there was nothing printed on them which identified an issuing bank or anyone at all responsible. In contrast to this, it was no secret that the Russians possessed the German Reich Bank's printing stocks in Berlin, and frustrated every attempt by the Western Allies to get rid of the surplus of 'dirty' banknotes, which were estimated at around 300 billion. They printed as many notes as they wanted and let them flood the Western zones. That was bound to have consequences. It was clear what a specific, new currency only valid in the Western zones would mean – the final split, a 'Great Wall of China' right through the middle of Germany! And so the currency question was postponed, from week to week, from month to month, until there was no longer any dispute that the Russians' Reich mark notes, which continued to be printed in unlimited quantities (they insisted on printing at least half of the future new German money in Leipzig) had long belonged to the munitions of a state of war, which one could well describe as a war of nerves, or as an initial skirmish in what was later to manifest itself as the Cold War.

Nonetheless, the Allies hesitated about tackling the currency question, until the last chance for negotiating with the Russians had been exhausted. Time and again, German specialists and financial experts had been invited to provide their own solutions under the seal of extreme secrecy. Finally, a German 'General Staff', calling itself the 'Special Unit for Money and Credit', moved into a few confiscated villas at Bad Homburg. Entrusted with working out the ways and means for the currency reform, based on the 'four zones' (quite pointlessly, as it later turned out), this group boarded a bus fitted with frosted-glass windows on 20 April 1948. This bus was to take them, accompanied by a certain Mr Tenenbaum from General Clay's staff, to an unspecified place. The fact that this was the American air force base at the former Luftwaffe airfield at Rothwesten near Kassel was not difficult to guess when they got out, because they could see the Habicht Forest with the Hercules monument on the Wilhelm Heights rising up into the sky.

Protected from the outside world by barbed wire, the conclave began. There was nothing left to change, as everything had been worked out to the last detail, as far as the German experts could see. Devaluation was based on a rate of 10 per cent, which in reality only amounted to 6.5 per cent, because part of the money was frozen in fixed deposit accounts. Fifty marks (raised at the last minute to 60 marks) set aside as the amount per person, for rich and poor, every man, woman and child. On D-day everybody could initially change 40 Reich marks into Deutschmarks (the remaining 20 RM later), and everybody was put on a par with everyone else. (A delusion, the Germans objected. It amounted to complete dispossession of the poor and old. They asked if the latters' nest-eggs, which had been wiped out at a stroke, could not be fully revalued. If increasing fortunes were envisaged at the same time as a falling rate, then that would not cost a penny more. That would be a social, as well as the planned capitalist, solution, which once again only favoured those who possessed something. But the objection was ignored.) Everything the German commission had to do (admittedly working day and night) was purely a matter of procedural technique; formulas were devised, referring to German administration reforms, texts were drafted, and so on and so forth. Whenever anything was ready, it immediately went by plane to London, where the printing work was carried out. By Saturday 19 June, it was finished. And it felt almost like war time again, when a special broadcast went out. A peculiar tension lay over Germany when the voice of the Allied announcer was heard from the loudspeakers that evening. With an obvious American accent, he announced in German the order for the currency to be converted.

D-day (the following Sunday) produced hours of waiting outside the offices which were to make the pro-rata payments, but also the suspicion that the new money would soon not be worth much more than the old. In Ingolstadt, an old lady took her life because she was afraid that on the day after she would become a burden to her children, and in Augsburg, a worker received considerable attention when he lit his pipe with a 10-mark note.

Then, the next day, things were quite different. Shop windows filled up overnight, there was white bread, there were flans and cakes in the bakers, vegetables and lettuces in the markets, nails and screws again in the hardware shops. Radios were available at electrical shops, bicycles were on sale in cycle shops and even cars were on offer, which actually got sold (the 40 Deutschmarks had suddenly multiplied in the hands of individuals).

Would the currency 'hold'? Everywhere there was a lack of the most important things – damage had to be repaired, and raw materials supplied. Where from? Gone was the old money from the time when any goods on offer had been hoarded. Now that they could again be acquired at normal prices, there was still no credit (the whole credit system had been brought to a standstill), and there were just as few reserves. Yet wages had not sunk, but had finally regained purchasing power. But could businesses pay them? The prime costs (strictly calculated) could only be partially passed on to the consumer. If the prices were too high, then the item was immediately beyond people's means. At the same time, anyone with possessions here in the West who acquired 'preferential treatment' (but what did this mean, apart from the official explanation that the war had spared him?) looked to the system of compensation with which the state planned to follow up the reform. Now that money was scarce and worth something again, the question was whether there should also be compensation paid for lost possessions in the East.

All these questions quickly brought people down to earth again after the euphoria which the 'day after' had produced. Once again, anyone who had any savings was caught out either if he had a small post office or bank savings account, or by insurance policies, or the possession of industrial debentures. The majority of savings, nine tenths of them, were wiped out, which amounted to wholesale deception, while holders of assets, owners of real estate, dealers holding stocks of goods in reserve, agricultural and industrial producers, and even shareholders were not only spared, but even given presents. Immediately after D-day, on which everyone was equal for one deceptive moment, their assets, which had been saved from the war and collapse, were increased without any help due to the immediate effects of economic resurgence. It was as if a good fairy had unlocked a magic mountain accessible to them alone. They only had to go in, and the treasure was theirs.

No, there could be no question of the unavoidable sacrifice being distributed equally across the board to everyone. Only by coupling the currency reform *and* the compensation system (therefore providing an immediate issue of the wealth held by those owning money and assets), only implementing both measures in one go would have made this possible, would have created that social balance which was vital for a new order. But the Western Allies had refused this. Even the so-called Dodge Plan, a 50 per cent mortgage on property, on means of production and supplies, as well as a property tax, which was to amount to 90 per cent of the value of the estate available, had found no favour in their eyes.

If the D-mark had thus been created according to foreign law, then everyone who came to feel the harshness of its social impact had to admit that in comparison with the consequences of inflation in the twenties, this was nevertheless bearable – bearable after the huge sacrifices which Hitler's war had demanded from every single person, and in view of the present revitalisation which was noticeably going on all over the country.

The real disillusionment was still to come. Most people had not thought about it when, immediately after the West German currency conversion the counter move, an East German currency reform, took place. It appeared only natural. Now there were two German currencies – a good one and a bad one. So what? The fact that a currency wall finally divided Germany, the fact that it would result in two German states, two defence alliances (one being NATO, the other the Warsaw Pact), and that this was bound to mean the separation of a common German consciousness, was clear to only a few. And yet nothing was clearer than when, on the night of 23 to 24 June 1948, the Russians blocked all passenger and goods transport from Berlin to the Western sectors, as well as electricity supplies from the Eastern sector of the city and food supplies from their zone. A day later, as stated in the history books, General Clay, the real head of West Germany, took the historical decision to establish an air lift. The Berlin blockade had begun. The West had decided to hang on to the city, come what may. The Cold War had started.

What America's interests were in the fight for Berlin had been made clear as early as April by Clay in a telephone conference which he conducted with the Washington Defense Department, in which he used the following imploring words: 'If Berlin falls, West Germany will be the next. If we intend to keep Europe from communism, we must not allow ourselves to move from this place. In Berlin, we can swallow humiliation and pressure, which do not lead to war, without losing face. If we leave, we endanger our European position. If America still does not understand us, still does not comprehend that the die have been cast, it will never recognise this and communism will overrun everything. I believe that the future of democracy requires that we stay.'

A scene in Marshal Sokolovsky's headquarters at Potsdam on 3 July, shortly after the Berlin blockade had begun, shed light on the Soviets' intention. It was after the Soviets had declared that the Allied Command no longer existed, that the three Western military governors went to see the Red Army marshal. They were received by accompanying Soviet officers at the city limits.

Clay reported on the last meeting of the old alliance:

We were taken directly to Sokolovsky's outer office, and then into his study. There he greeted us politely, but coldly. Robertson [the British military governor] expressed his concern about the deterioration of our relations, which had reached a peak in the blockade, and said that we wanted to reach an agreement about the currency question which would put everything back in line again. Sokolovsky interrupted him to declare in a forceful tone of voice that the technical difficulties would remain for as long as it took until we had buried our plans for a West German government. That was his first confession as to the real reasons for the blockade.

The decision of the Americans not to give in to this attempt at blackmail led to the first defeat which the Soviets had to acknowledge after the end of the war, and to that German-American solidarity which determined West German policy from that day to this. The blockade lasted 300 days, and when it was broken off on 12 May 1949, Berlin was no longer what it had always been, even for Clay – a symbol of a display of Prussian power, which had inevitably led to Hitler's dictatorship. It was more a place of freedom for the Western world, in which it could find its bearings.

Every day 4,500 tonnes of freight were necessary to supply the two and a half million West Berliners and the Western garrisons in the encircled city with coal, food and, the most essential, consumer goods. Even in the worst of weathers the American and British aircraft carrying these loads tried to find their way day after day, using radar to reach the West Berlin landing strips at Tempelhof, Gatow and Tegel. Factories – 3,619 – were closed down. There was electricity for two hours a day in varying parts of the city, but most of the time people sat in the dark with their dried potatoes and dried vegetables – POM, as the American potato preparation was called. (But, as the Berliners would say, better to eat POM than be raped by a COM!)

Work had also had to be suspended at the BMW Spandau Works which, like those in Munich, had been producing saucepans, agricultural machinery and even a few machine tools since 1947. On 17 December 1948, Harald Wolf, the Spandau Works manager, succeeded in getting through to Munich by telephone at four o'clock in the afternoon. He asked if Munich could send him some spare parts via the air lift, because although the factory was idle, they still wanted to use the time to overhaul a few machines.

'I cannot reach anybody,' the telephonist said. 'The gentlemen are all in Hall 17.'

'What's going on in Hall 17?' Wolf asked.

'Don't you know?' retorted the girl in amazement. 'The top brass are here, the military government and so on. There's champagne, they've even sent some across to me. Hold on a moment, the press people are just coming . . .'

Wolf heard her calling out to them: 'Hall 17. Hurry up, the party has just begun.'

'Which party?' asked Wolf, flabbergasted.

'We're delivering the first motorcycle,' said the girl, 'we're all in high spirits . . .'. Here the call was cut off.

'They're all in high spirits in Munich,' said Wolf to his secretary and replaced the receiver. 'Can you understand that, Frau Kummer?'

Frau Kummer, a native of Munich and otherwise always ready to explain Bavarian quirks, did not hear the question.

'But I can understand it,' Wolf said. 'They're really going at it in Munich. The first motorcycle. Hopefully it'll work, too.'

That was three years, two months and seventeen days after the officially ordered end, enabling 17 December 1948 to be described somewhat emotively as the beginning of BMW's second life. The works consisted of 1,227 manual and clerical workers. With regard to Wolf's worry, the motorcycle did run.

A few days later, on 23 December 1948, the following appeared in *Motor Cycling*, the leading British motorcycle magazine, under the title, 'The Eagle has Two Heads':

Reconstruction work by the BMW (Bayerischen Motoren Werke) at Munich, says the BETRO Overseas Intelligence Service, has progressed more quickly than had been anticipated. The company has already started mass production of its 250-cc motorcycle, originally scheduled to begin next January. It is expected that 500 machines monthly will be produced. The first 250 machines are likely to reach the market in January, at an expected selling price of about 1,600 Deutschemark. At the official export rate this would be approximately equal to £120.

That German industry should be assisted to recover as rapidly as possible was a policy laid down early in the peace. The sooner the victors could relieve themselves of the responsibility for sustaining the vanquished, the better it seemed to be. The main thing was to ensure that the Germans concentrated on the arts and sciences of peace instead of war.

But there are two kinds of war at which they have shown themselves to be adept – military warfare and trade warfare. So long as the occupying Powers remain across the Rhine they may prohibit the former and restrict the latter to internal economics, but a time will come when German industry will seek to sell beyond its own frontiers. In other words, Britain, whose very life now depends on her exports, may, in the not far distant future, find herself in trade rivalry with those same German industries which are now being encouraged to revive and prosper.

The article, written by Graham Walker, spoke further of the 'mixed feelings' with which this was greeted, although there was no doubt about the capacity 'of our own products which could meet this kind of competition and beat it'. He concluded: 'What disturbs us is the thought that, while our own motorcycle industry has to fight its own battles on the world market with a rather unhelpful government, the Allies seem to be fostering a cuckoo in the export nest. We would be happier if we had an official assurance that, should he stretch his wings, they will at least be clipped.'

The following year, in May 1949, Mr Arthur B Bourne, the editor of another trade journal with the very similar name of *The Motor Cycle*, visited the Bavarian capital and the BMW works at Milbertshofen as well, obviously to see how the wings could be clipped. He reported to his English readers:

Once inside the barbed wires, as it were – industrial police at the entrance, a bar across the gateway (US air-lift vehicles are repaired there in large

numbers) – I was whisked into the big office block. There was not a
soul in the long corridor upstairs. What a contrast this must have
been with war and pre-war days. I was taken to the chief engineer,
and soon we were roaming the great factory. Immediately following the
war, BMW produced pots and pans, bakery machinery, air compressors
and agricultural machinery. Just think of it – BMW making agricultural
machinery! Now they have ceased all except this last: that may have
stopped by the time this is published, and, other than their work for the
US Army, they are concentrating on motor cycles.

'All the machine tools,' Bourne then explained to his friends, 'were taken
as reparations. Now what a change: battery after battery of brand-new tools
of the latest type. "Surely," I suggested, "you are going to be even better
equipped than pre-war?" The reply was, "I would not say better, perhaps,
as well as."'

Bourne could not judge that (he had never been to Milbertshofen before
the war), but he was in no doubt that here there would soon be a motorcycle
factory which was no less modern 'than any other one'. With the diplomatic
answer of the German chief engineer still in his ear, he established: 'Whatever
may have been the case at this factory, other factories which I came to know
were not unhappy to receive loans to replace machine tools which had been
dismantled for reparations.'

He asked his British readers: 'Would you be unhappy to have the facilities
for installing new tooling based on your production programme, while your
competitors in other countries received your old machines?'

After this digression, he returned to the BMW factory and described
what was going on there under the ironic heading: 'Excellent Laboratory
Equipment'.

They showed me new testing machines for determining the properties of
materials and for checking the dimensional accuracy, hardness, etc., of
finished components. I did not wonder at their pride. And production,
which is concentrated on the 250-cc shaft-drive, unit-construction single,
is no hole-in-the-corner affair. They were making 50 a week when I was
there, and production only started last December (not January this year,
as I told at the Geneva Show). A total of 800 were working on motor cycles,
mostly their old, skilled men, they said, and by the middle of the year it
is hoped to produce 1,000 a month. Damaged shops are being rebuilt,
and as these are ready, and new plant and equipment received, there is
switching around; for instance, a new building laid out for line assembly
was scheduled to come into use last month.

Except for the usual accessories and for cylinder castings, the factory is
self-contained. Their foundry is for light alloys only. Tons of material is
available in the form of stacks and stacks of old BMW light-alloy aircraft
cylinders – the only articles, they say, which were not removed as reparations. At present, the crankcases and gear-box housings are sand-cast,
but later these, like all the other light-alloy parts and components, will
be die-cast. Incidentally, both shaving and grinding are used for finishing

gear teeth. They prefer the former method, they say, because it is cheaper and at least as good.

Bourne reported as if he had been on an expedition to a distant country which had been transported back into the Stone Age by a mysterious catastrophe. The natives were now beginning to handle technology better than ever before, although they had to start from the beginning again. 'Two test rigs for gears appealed to me,' he noted with the dryness of a researcher.

In one a complete gear box is mounted and then driven, at speeds which can be varied by an electric motor – driven under whatever load is desired, since there is a friction brake mounted at the output end. No guessing whether the box is quiet on all ratios: no queries later regarding the excellence or otherwise of the gearchange – yes, and no having to strip an engine-gear unit out of a completed machine. The other test rig is used to drive the assembled shaft-drive units. Does the shaft run true? Is the drive silent? I also noticed that the man assembling the shaft drives was using blue on the teeth – engineers, blue, presumably – to check for perfect meshing.

Pre-war, the 250-cc single, they pointed out, was regarded as an unimportant model in the range. Now it is the only model – 250-cc is the maximum capacity allowed the German industry except for Horex, who are making 3,000 three-fifties for police and other official uses. Consequently BMWs are trying to make the machine as good as any they have produced.

Two imported changes have been effected, both of technical interest and practical value. First, there is the new cylinder head. This is of light alloy with better port angles, a thick web arranged right across the head between the inlet and exhaust valves, and hexagon steel pillars which run up from the cast-iron cylinder barrel, clear of the light alloy, and carry the rocker spindles. In the past the rocker spindles were mounted in the light alloy head; with the new arrangement there is not the same variation in valve clearance. If and when permission is granted for the reintroduction of the R51 500-cc transverse twin, these new heads will be used. Next there is the new gear box. This aims at providing a better gear change and a factor of safety adequate for sidecar work. Presumably the gear box would also be used on the even-torque 500-cc twin. A major feature of the new gear box, is that on the input shaft, inside the box, is a spring-loaded cam-type shock-absorber. I had been told that the latest two-fifty was more flexible; here was a reason. But the kick-starter still operates in a plane at right-angles to the wheel-base of the machine. My remark that I had been hoping that they would alter this brought forth the reply that for normal use they thought the arrangement was probably better – that it was largely a case of what one was accustomed to.

The wheel of history can never be turned back. An unalterable process to which human beings and powers are subjected constantly wrings decisions from them. Designs, made as if for eternity, come to nothing, and new conditions arise. Bound to the spirit of the age, freeing people from prejudices, it summons those who were only recently enemies to act afresh. Never turned backwards, but constantly looking forwards, this process goes on inexorably and changes the face of the age.

Under the slogan: NO ECONOMIC MIRACLE WITHOUT THE D-MARK, people in the Western zones were astonished to note the immediate abolition of price controls, and the fact that the inflated economic bureaucracy (seen by the population at large as a real scourge) was deprived of power. Its demise brought a breath of personal freedom into households and businesses. This had not been caused by the Germans, but by the 'enemy'. With the feeling in boardrooms and materials offices that the Allies were still firmly resisting further reductions in restrictions on economic life and trying to hamper what currency and tax reform had set in motion, they had to wonder if the Allies had not thought things out far enough in advance.

No, you can never turn anything back. Even confiscated assets were suddenly 'free'. At BMW these included that 'collection against a background of scorched earth' which Oscar Kolk, formerly assistant to the board and now re-employed as a crate maker with the US Army in Allach, had undertaken just a few days before the capitulation. No one referred anymore to his adventurous journey along the Elbe to Dessau-Kochstädt, where he met up with the Reich Aviation Ministry 'on its transfer' from Berlin with its offices of packed and unpacked cases. There he was able to ask at the cash desk, with such good timing, that the sum which the Reich owed BMW for long overdue stop-loss charges poured into Munich on covered Reich mark cheques from the Deutsche Bank as late as 28 April 1945 – 63.5 million marks! Even if the decimal point were moved one place to the left, this was, after devaluation, still an unimaginably large amount of money with which Donath could do business.

But how to do business? He had decided to build motorcycles, but the production decision – Motorcycle – was not a free decision; it had been assigned. There had been no choice. Motorcycles were how they had begun after the First World War, when things were finished with flying for the time being, meaning the building of aero-engines. So things started up again with motorcycles. Few people in an impoverished country could afford to travel on four wheels. Two wheels were possible, however, were realistic, and the boom in German motorcycle factories proved it. Here, to hang on did not mean to fiddle about; here it meant to get to grips, making the worldwide reputation, which BMW had acquired with the essentially unchanged R 32 on which Henne's world records and Schorsch Meier's race victories had became legend, the driving force for a new upward trend. Schorsch Meier, who was in charge of works security at the Karlsfeld Ordnance Depot (i.e. the Allach repair works), had wheeled out his old racing machine, which he had hidden in a hay barn on the Allach estate, and had so stage-managed racing that he got the masses on the move and excited, even the American army of occupation. Hundreds of thousands went to the Solitude to see the motorcycle battle between BMW and NSU.

Against this background (which has only been briefly sketched here, although it helps make subsequent success more understandable) there were already 400 BMW dealerships by the beginning of 1949. In the course of that year, almost 10,000 R 24s were produced and sold; in 1950 the figure had already grown to 17,061, of which over 3,000 went for export. (This was particularly surprising because complete patent drawings for earlier BMW products were to be had abroad. In the USA they were available for 10 cents per drawing. Spare parts could be copied everywhere without a licence. Switzerland even copied a whole 750-cc machine under another name with startling similarity and used it as an army motorcycle).

Nevertheless, things were on the up at Milbertshofen. The restriction on cubic capacity to 250 cc, decreed by the military government, had been abolished. Now the long-planned R 51 with 500 cc could be put into series-production. It featured the famous telescopic, rear-wheel suspension, and the R 24, now named 25 and also fitted with rear-wheel suspension – which had previously been left off for cost considerations – came on to the market. There was also an R 67 on offer with 600 cc, and a sports version, the R 68, known as the 'fastest series-produced motorcycle in the world'.

Still, Siedler (a man who came from foreign parts, from Eisenach, which had become completely alien to him in the course of the following months) had cause to remember Donath's words: 'Who is BMW? If the court case [a court case for the trade-mark] turns out in Eisenach's favour, then we have lost the name. And with it, the last one we possess.'

All the initial successes could not gloss over the fact that he was right. Was BMW an enterprise without entrepreneurs, asked the press? They said that the plant facilities at Milbertshofen, without mentioning those potential facilities at Allach, were relative to the firm's assets, which were nowhere near being used to full capacity, with a present production rate of only 1,500 per month. The most valuable of the company's assets, its outstanding brains, had been allowed to go to other firms, and the once exemplary sales organisation had in the meantime become involved with other firms. In contrast to what many hard-hit conglomerates (AEG, Siemens and ball-bearing industries) had created, where little by little they almost reacquired their old significance in the tough enterprise environment, BMW had been passed by.

Now they reported a request for state help. Motorcycle production alone could hardly keep the main works at Milbertshofen, which had a book value of 40 million marks, going, let alone the entire business with a share capital of 100 million RM! The company even went as far as to complain that there were no resources available for expanding production. It was precisely this, the provision of resources, which is a top priority of business, and not the job of the state or the trade union. That is what gives meaning and value to the free enterprise economy, namely that it releases forces which overcome difficulties through tireless work, and achieves results which a cumbersome state apparatus is not in a position to do. What are they waiting for, concluded the Philippic?

Donath referred in vain to the Auto Union, with whom he had had discussions, but unfortunately all to no avail. The Ingolstadt-based company had decided to take up an offer in Düsseldorf, and not to locate in Allach. That got all the critics' hackles up: why, of all people, should the Auto Union, which had re-emerged from much more difficult circumstances than BMW, realise at Allach what BMW obviously could not (although it owed it to itself and the world) – namely, to build *cars* again?

Even the trial over the trade-mark no longer stuck out as an argument. It had come to a close with mountains of files and documentary evidence which the plaintiff and the defendant had expounded. On 17 November 1950, judgement was pronounced by the provincial court at Düsseldorf, where both sides were only represented by their lawyers. It stated: that the expropriation of Eisenach did not comprise a loss of trade-mark and patents; that the headquarters of BMW had always been in Munich; that the legal business rights had not been acquired by the Soviet company of Avtovelo, even if development work was said to have been carried out in Eisenach; that patent No. 633 031, involving the car types 321 and 340, could only be used by BMW Munich; that the distinguishing features resulting from the design, which is unquestionably a part of motor cars and which marks out one's own car from other cars, is conferred in the absolute on BMW; that the legal rights have been indisputably infringed by Avtovelo; and that the plaintiff's trade-mark may not be used by others.

To sum up, it stated that BMW Munich retained its name and trade-mark and consequently had won more than just a court case, ensuring that there could never again be a dispute about what the firm's past and present stood for.

So what was Donath hesitating about now?

Veritas versus Milbertshofen

At the beginning of 1946, thought had been given in Alfred Böning's 'design department' (Building 11, 5th Floor, NO UNAUTHORISED ENTRY) to a two-litre car – with sights set on America, where any car under 2.5-litre cubic capacity was not a car. Böning spoke of markets which had to be penetrated. The extravagance of such dreams was nourished by a find which Deby's people had made in the rubble of Works 1 – this was a pontoon-shaped, streamlined car which had gone up in flames. Its main feature was the cut-off rear quarters known as the K-line, as developed by the aerodynamics experts Reinhard von Koenig-Fachsenfeld and Wunibert Kamm for BMW. It stemmed from the legendary 332 prototype range and, mounted on the 326 chassis, had been built in only a few examples at the beginning of the war. Donath immediately had the car measured (there were no design drawings, as they were in Eisenach or, in what amounted to the same thing, Moscow).

Working for weeks and screened from curious gazes, a select group of old foremen and fitters restored the fossil, in a kind of euphoria which came over them. They not only worked on the outside, but on everything under the bonnet. There is a photograph with Deby standing in hat and coat in front of the finished car (the front garden bushes recognisable behind him show that summer was over and that this was early autumn). Theirs was not a victory pose; a timid smile around eyes and mouths expressed scepticism rather than joy. Perhaps he already knew that the car, which had just been on a test drive, would remain an exotic memory. There was no question at all of it going into series-production. Neither production facilities nor raw materials were available for it, and there was just as little likelihood that the military government would grant authorisation for its manufacture.

Yet the reproduced model was to bring about something in Donath which was more than just the first stage of an apprenticeship, as he claimed.

As a fanatic of precision, he had always viewed aero-engine manufacture as the *non plus ultra* in the 'wide-ranging field of combustion engines operating with closed combustion chambers'. ('Their precision and weight limits per hp became models for many engineers which have come down to us today', was how he had written about it in a study entitled: 'The air-cooled radial engine in Germany'.) Now he saw that what was valid for aero-engine manufacture was equally valid for car manufacture; in fact, it depended on it.

The recognition was absolutely new for the outsider Donath. He recognised that this factory, where he had been brought as an aero-engine man, could only produce cars in this way. These were cars which were to be the envy of others like them in the world. The latest example of this, and one to set the trend, was the 326, fitted with a prototype model on its chassis.

In 1936 this car, when it had been presented at the Berlin International Motor Show, had given a completely new image of the car. Although the components inside it (engine, gearbox, rear axle and suspension) had only proved to be further developments on tried and tested units, the effect on its new body, made by Ambi Budd (box sections, welded in a unit with the body!), was described by one critic as being 'as modern as tomorrow', in comparison with the conventional frames which up till then used tubes. It was therefore the antithesis of what was *fashionable*; a car with all-round solidity in design, road-holding, economy and fittings, which revealed previously unknown qualities. 'Safety in driving, without the need to worry about the state of the road . . .', 'backseat ride as good as the front . . .', were the judgements in the trade press, with even the engineer Ganz writing in the much respected *Motor-Kritik* that it ran so quietly 'that any incidental noise, such as a rustling sandwich wrapper, for example, came across disagreeably inside'.

Reminiscences like this cannot be shrugged off. Anyone dreaming of a new car in the midst of ruins, cleared-out halls, and within earshot of the victors' orders, must have said to himself: 'It is better for us not to build anything than remain subject to the demands imposed by the past.' Someone once put it that the little bit which BMW brought in the way of novelty need not imply that BMW was stagnating. The complete opposite was the case. That little bit had always shown the work done on basic details. There was no future without this obvious truth.

Fritz Fiedler, the creator of the 326 and the last technical director, had been refused entry into the works as a former baron of the war economy. So he did not waste too much time humming and hawing when an offer reached him from the Bristol Aeroplane Company in Filton, England, to do there what could not be done in Germany – to prepare the design and series production of a large car. The offer came within the framework of 'reparations' as well as 'old friendship'. The former head of the BMW licencee for Britain, Frazer-Nash, none other than Aldington, had been appointed to head Bristol Aeroplane. Immediately deciding to build sports cars and so put Britain in the lead in post-war Europe, he had struck a kind of secret deal with Donath. As the two men expressed it: we shall receive from you, by way of reparations, the design drawings for the BMW 327 and 328, which survived the war, and you will have the right to profit from subsequent development of these cars by us, meaning that you will be able to obtain the engines and chassis parts developed by Fiedler from us in England, as we once did from Germany.

Indeed, the faithful copy of the BMW 327 Coupé then came off the production line at Bristol Aeroplane in the spring of 1947 under the name of the Bristol 400. Fiedler had increased the engine to 85 hp. And so a pure BMW copy, which cost £2,375, immediately became *the* British sports car.

Admittedly, Donath could do little with it once Fiedler had fulfilled his contract, if anything at all (as soon as you have served your purpose, they have no further interest in you). A utility car was what he needed, not a souped-up sports model. So it was quite all right by him when Bristol gave him the push. No, things were not at all right now! He also claimed that Aldington was hiding behind a 'higher authority', denying that he had ever given any firm undertakings.

In fact, only Fiedler had followed up the offer, which had never been put down in writing. The other old colleagues and designers in the development department had never fully trusted the affair, and (like Ernst Loof and Hans Schaeffer, who had also both been invited to England by Aldington) never heard anything about it again. So what had happened to the 'old ones', those who from their safe positions in the war had longed for nothing more ardently than the day when things would start up again. Alexander von Falkenhausen laboured away on the estate of his parents-in-law at Leonberg, south of Regensburg, in his own company, AFM (Alexander von Falkenhausen, München); Donath had let him know that there was no job for him in the works, even as a detailed checking engineer. Schleicher, too, was left out of it, at Berg on Lake Starnberg. Above any suspicion of having been a Nazi, he had stayed 'out' of his own volition, not willing to accept subordinate roles which he had also previously avoided. He now ran his own company in the former test department (whose machine tools were not part of those set aside for dismantling, enabling him to acquire them cheaply). Max Friz, who had fled from Eisenach, had gone to Tegernsee (he too had no desire to fit in). This was after he had had to justify in writing why a technician, whom the leadership of the Reich had appointed to be a baron of the war economy, had not been a party supporter or beneficiary of this party to which he must have belonged. All the other ones were ekeing out their existence at Allach on fixed term work.

Dorls kept them going. Appointed the German manager of the Ordnance Depot, he issued them with small jobs, thoroughly approved by the American Army who profited from that, and even invested his own money in the 'crew'. With Lorenz Dietrich at his side, who looked after commercial affairs at Allach, he had assembled a development department here, the like of which was not to be found in any other car company in the world. This consisted of a handful of men who, free from the onus of deadlines, drafted plans and brought them to the design stage, put forward hypotheses, building whole planning ranges into them, only to reject everything again until they felt they had found the solution. They then brought BMW back down to earth, to the here and now, from the clouds of technical imagination. It was here that bread and circuses were not to remain a pair for much longer, with the designs of tomorrow being determined by them.

None of the people Dorls had gathered around him had contracts. But bound, linked by the common intention of not letting their technical inheritance perish, they looked upon themselves as a kind of brains trust, whose existence was well known to Donath, but with which he did not know what to do. This was either because he was unsure when dealing with car

369

matters, or because *his* people were sufficient to him for the little that was feasible.

Then there was something to be wary of. Was it not summed up in the idea of Franz Josef Popp quite openly meeting up with the 'crew' and discussing things with them? Although under house arrest, he was allowed to leave his place of exile at Sandizell Castle near Schrobenhausen (where he had found a shelter with friends) with special permission from the Allies. He was preparing his return to the works. Those concerned wanted reliable information on that. This was not an unfavourable prospect, given his good connections with the banks.

As absurd as this was (everyone knew about Popp's difficulties with the works council, which had excluded his return once and for all just because of certain official speeches which Popp, as a business leader, had made in the Third Reich), it was clear that old frictions between Dorls and Donath did not exactly augur well. Donath, formerly works manager at the BMW Aero-Engine Works in Spandau, had, due to insufficient use of capacity, been relieved by Dorls in November 1942 following a board decision (namely by Popp's successor, Hille, and the BMW group leader Zipprich), and transferred to Munich. In Berlin, the skilled planner Dorls had succeeded where Donath had failed. Without having to expand factory space or install additional machine tools, he had been able to increase production to 300 aero-engines per month. Under Donath, the figure had been 100 engines, a third of this! If, after the catastrophe of 1945, this could be seen more as a virtue than 'a lack of vision in what could be technically achieved' (a reproach which had deeply offended Donath), then Dorls's statement remained valid – namely that a company, regardless of whether in war time or peace time, would inevitably go bankrupt if it only produced a third of what it was capable of.

Reproaches like these survive world disasters. And the very first meeting between the two men in the time 'afterwards', when the army of occupation had made Dorls head of the Allach works, was a renewed affront for Donath, who was now acting as head of Milbertshofen. Immediately before the Control Council's decisions came into force, imposing total dismantling on BMW, Dorls had taken upon himself, without getting a decision from the board, to make an arrangement with the Americans which saved Allach, and with it, BMW. That was not forgotten. There was also the fact that Erich Zipprich, once jointly responsible as the group leader for the insult levelled at Donath, was appointed head of the technical team at Allach.

Released from Stadelheim, where we had last met him in the cell next to Franz Josef Popp, he had literally been picked up by Dorls off the street and seated at a design table. Dorls saw him as someone capable of throwing a project that was only a vague idea the night before onto the drawing board and working it through in detail by the following morning. He had, as a natural technical prodigy, found his way back to the task life had assigned him.

Beside him, and responsible for everything involving styling, was Ernst Loof, formerly head of the racing department at BMW. He was convinced that the future of BMW, however great poverty might be in post-war Germany, lay in leisure, in motorsport, and *not* in sets of wheels which others should and could produce much better, given their greater experience in the field.

Then there was the technician Schaeffer; the designer Rech from Alexander von Falkenhausen's old test department; the engineer Knoch; Leibach, who had developed the command module; and the practical expert Niedermeyer for production technology. Nothing but excellent people who did not consider themselves irreplaceable, but whose work was nevertheless worthy of praise.

In Milbertshofen, nobody seemed to have noticed any of this. The high spirits enjoyed by the 'crew' were quickly brought down to earth with the feeling that 'they do not want us!' But how flattering it was, too, to be respected, and therefore ignored (the fate of many an elite group), not to be used, but quite the opposite, to be patently debarred, leaving them asking the question as to what was going on there. So a separate company grew up from the team which wanted to remake BMW from BMW, which bore the informative, confessional name of 'Veritas'. Working with Georg ('Schorsch') Meier's help and reputation as racing driver (he had had enough of his security job and had long wanted to work for himself), they started at Kaufbeuren, where the refugees from the whole town of Neugablonz in the Sudetenland, famous for its glass-making, had been resettled in old labour service sheds. Veritas soon moved into a closed engineering works at Hausen, near Sigmaringen, and later to Rastatt-Muggensturm.

Veritas made new sports cars out of old BMW ones – principally from the 328 type, which was generally known as the Mille Miglia car, and which Loof, tearing around the country, bought up wherever he found one. The firm flourished. It was soon offering to put its own designs into production, creations from the design office run by Dorls at Caslano in Ticino. With the chassis made of light, steel tubes (engines and transmissions received overhauled components from 328s which had been checked very thoroughly), they bore the old ensign, the white and blue propeller with the three initials BMW at the front, above the characteristic BMW kidneys, without Veritas having being authorised to do that by the company. This led Donath to prohibit the firm from using the BMW trade-mark by law (Sigmaringen was in the French, and not Soviet, zone), as he was to do to every other private motorist in the West who fitted it to his home-made car just because there was an old, genuine BMW engine under the bonnet.

Not least because of this prohibition, which threw up a lot of dust, Donath had got himself into a tight spot. He knew the gossiping, to the effect that he had blown his whistle on that unique development group out of envy, and that, instead of being grateful for its existence, had only caused problems for it. The rumours said that BMW could easily have renewed its old sports car tradition, would have been able to have that start in car manufacture which was long overdue, if only. . . . Yes, he knew what was being whispered and murmured there, those people who said that the company was not going the right way forward because the second team (and not the first) was to be found at Milbertshofen, that time-wasters and no-hopers, theoreticians as

371

opposed to practicians, ditherers and not decision-makers had taken all the posts. Having framed their 'clean bills of health' on their desks ('clean bills of health' were the denazification certificates with the entry: 'Not affected') they pointed their fingers at those people who probably had good reasons to stay away from the works, and Donath, however good their specialist qualifications might be, wanted to have nothing to do with them.

Like fine rain penetrating soil, this mention of the 'second team' had seeped in, making relations uncertain and poisoning work.

Donath was not suffering from a superiority complex. He was all the more hurt to be constantly called into doubt. Assuming that all those who had made BMW great were once again to move into the works, with Popp as head, would they be able to realise *more* than he, Donath, with his 'second team'?

Who knew or wanted to know that everything that was technically feasible, whether thought up by first-rate or second-rate people, had come to nought, if the production facilities, providing for profitable, large-scale manufacture, had been lacking? What had there been then? A few old casting patterns, retrieved from transfer points in the Allgäu, had been used for manufacturing exchange components. They had got things started, enabling the first 500 engines for the 326 (to get the workshop running) to be built according to the old drawings, and without an in-house foundry. There was only *one* furnace for small test parts and the iron castings came from Esslingen, where Böning inspected them. It was just as unlikely for Dorls to conjure up an aero-engine works at the 'Alpine Redoubt' (which had never existed), as it was for cars to be built in empty halls, especially as the capital to be invested (despite being repeatedly mentioned) only ever existed on paper.

There was therefore a need to ask somebody who really possessed what the firm did not have itself. In practice, this meant merger. Which of the car makers were considered? Donath had travelled to see Simca in France, where an attractive, four-door, one-litre saloon with curved mudguards had been brought out. BMW could have the licence, but not the presses. His next journey had been to Ford at Dearborn in the USA. Perhaps they would allow joint manufacture with American Ford lorries for Western Germany, which might then result in car manufacture. But Ford wanted either to buy BMW or have a diesel engine built. Then Donath had discussions about merger with the Auto Union (at some time before the question of moving to Allach came on the agenda). But the people at Ingolstadt had just as little money for that as BMW, and the two-stroke DKW (or '*Das Kleine Wunder*', 'the little miracle') was too much of a barrier to the concept of the sporting and technologically demanding car which BMW had and did not want to give up. How would it be if they co-operated with Adler, which up to now had also only produced motorcycles, and whose people had suggested setting up a joint bodywork factory which would lighten the burden of investment costs? That also failed due to finance, after divided production had been considered, which would probably have left BMW with building only large, two-litre cars once more.

So everything depended on Allach again. That Allach! Donath had always been against that 'extended workbench', that 'bloodless body'. Created by the war, and much too big for rationalised peacetime production, BMW would surely be destroyed if it let itself in for using Allach as a production site. Nobody could talk him out of it, even if the press described Allach, hypocritically in his view, as 'an asset which could not be estimated high enough for the old name'.

At least there was one thing he could not dispute; that the 'extended workbench' had saved BMW, it alone and nothing else. And even a child knew that they were presently living from the business brought in by Allach, and not from their own products.

Palace Revolution at Allach

November was called the great moulting season, that month in which the day of repentance and the Sunday before Advent are commemorated – man pauses and looks around him; he does not look to the future, but to the past, he reflects upon himself.

In November 1949, two Americans provided special cause for this. One of them, Paul Hoffmann by name, the US administrator of Marshall Plan funds, did not have too much to do with Munich and BMW. In Paris he had declared to the representatives of eighteen European countries receiving help from his fund, in plain and (as was emphasised in the commentaries) carefully chosen words, that Europe would have to have made decisive progress towards implementing a customs union by the beginning of the following year, or face a catastrophe. The US Congress would probably require proof of an assimilation of the national European economies, before it approved further resources. The other American was a soldier. He was called Robert E.L. Masters, a lieutenant colonel, who had announced, as the new head of the Karlsfeld Ordnance Depot at Allach near Munich, that the American Army would have to reduce repair work, meaning that there would be substantial redundancies.

Both announcements spelt disaster. The first one, which put the writing on the wall, sprang from the view that Europe could only be saved as an entity. If it was not, its individual parts would pursue the old game of national statehood to such an extent that each individually, or all of them collectively, would perish. There was no alternative to the second. The works at Allach employed 7,300 men. What would happen, what could be done to prevent them being put on the streets? The end of the repair business had been set. The Amercans wanted to close Allach on 1 April 1951. What then?

When 1,300 workers were made redundant in June 1950, this was followed by a flood of memoranda, protests and declarations, drafted by the Allach works council, the trade unions and the parties. (They all argued in favour of maintaining and further concentrating American Army work in Allach, as no army in the world could manage without repair work.) This was accompanied by the fact that Milbertshofen, with just 2,700 employees, did not take them on! The story was that Donath was very much against it. He himself, now signing as responsible for the board, remained silent.

374

Two weeks later, when the summer had just begun in European latitudes, North Korean armed forces marched across the demarcation line on the 38th parallel into South Korea. After the unsuccessful Berlin blockade, the basic conflict which split the world had suddenly changed from a 'cold' to a 'hot' war. The affair of the redundancies was suddenly pushed into the background, into the geo-political background, although the two events were not seen to have any connection to BMW. But such a connection could be made.

While the bulk of the American troops in Germany, which was a divided country like Korea, were stationed along the Rhine, their supply depots and bases lay up to 300 kilometres in the direction of the East – that direction from which an attack could come. Should it be kept away from camp administrators and technicians? So re-deployment was necessary.

It was as if Masters, the new head of the Ordnance Depot, had predicted it! Immediately on taking office as 'a strong personality, who could not come to terms with collaborating as equal partners' (as was moderately stated in the work's councils memorandum about it), he had fired the technical manager Hundt, who was just on his way to the USA in the hope of acquiring a licence to build American excavators. He wanted to manufacture them in a part of the Allach production halls, if the army left. Masters's predecessor, Colonel Smith, had thanked Hundt on his departure for the excellent way 'in which you and the BMW II staff have co-operated with my office'. This had been a co-operation which, in the last few months, as he emphasised, had led not only to production being doubled, but also to continual cost reduction, not least of all due to prudent workplace allocation. It had even led to considerable profits. And now Hundt, as Masters had decreed, was denied entry to the works!

Even the BMW trade-mark, the white and blue propeller, upset the new boss. He could not see what it was doing on all those forms, drawings, lists, tables and other printed matter which the depot sent out. Unmistakably stamped on each date plate, on each repaired engine, each lorry and each tank assembly leaving Allach, in Masters's eyes, it belittled the performance of his own people, who ran the largest repair shops which the US Forces could boast of anywhere in the world. This was the jewel in the crown of the US Army and, if anything, the American star should acknowledge that. This was how the German works management received the instruction to remove the trade-mark, a measure which was in no way directed against the company of BMW as Masters led them to understand. BMW was, as before, the landlord of the Allach complex, but not the operator of the works – that was the army, and make no mistake about it!

The fact that his ban was a slap in the face to all those who, as BMW engineers and skilled workers, had helped Allach gain its fame for the army, counted for little. The highest command posts gave Allach their highest acknowledgement, a fact which not only made a significant imaginary difference, but a very tangible one, in the form of promotions. Masters had also counted on that (in fact, he was soon appointed to the rank of colonel), and so something happened which, in view of the situation in the world, was a joke – America banned the use of a trade-mark, over whose right of ownership BMW was involved in a court case against the Russians, who were very keen to have it for their works in Eisenach.

The 'whole direction' did not suit Masters. The fact that a victorious power like the USA gave a German works management a free hand to carry out contracts, whose costs were determined by Germans alone, annoyed him just as much as the explanations which the German works team found for criticisms made by the inspection authorities over defects. They said that there were insufficient technical documents (in fact there were often none), and defective drawings which the army had made available constantly needed to be laboriously reworked, if not completely reproduced.

The American personnel had changed many times over, technicians from the fighting forces being followed by experts who quickly grasped the advantages of German working practices. Time points and bonus systems, which were unknown to the Americans, were introduced. It was only when new people from the USA, who had had no special training, tried to compensate their lack of technical knowledge through bureaucratic overzealousness, that there were disagreements. Masters blamed the Germans for them. He also did not accept the difficulty of having to match the works and level of personnel at the time with the repair jobs ordered and carried out on engines and gearboxes, which were always done under the pressure of knowing that everything might come to a speedy end. Everyone knew full well that once engine assemblies had been thoroughly overhauled once or twice, the stage would inevitably be reached in the foreseeable future where a thorough overhaul would be unprofitable, or even made unworkable by material fatigue. Therefore Allach had become, from the outset, a business on a fixed-term contract.

Donath suddenly felt the wind blowing in his face. His refusal to take on the workers made redundant amounted to exactly what the Americans had suggested, which was to put everyone still employed for the time being at Allach on 'direct hire' immediately under the army. That meant no social contributions, and the cancellation of all legal claims which the workforce had acquired from the work it had done up to now. To escape similar claims, Donath set the condition in the event of taking someone on that only a new contract of employment would be available which precluded 'special privileges and contributions made over many years as elements of old contracts'.

How did he arrive at this? BMW had no moral or legal right to dodge their responsibilities. There was no doubt that Allach had saved BMW. While there might be some doubt as to whether use of the Allach works by the army did not also result from the failure to enforce the razing of Works 1, it was clear that nothing would have been possible without the repair contract, even if this had never been signed by the US authorities. (In international law, an army of occupation was under no obligation to conclude a contract with the occupied nation.) This contract had helped Milbertshofen start up again after all its plant and machines had been dismantled. Admittedly, the army had ordered that Allach was not to work for profit, but depreciation, rent and maintenance costs were entered in its accounts and were paid off by the parent public company (the yearly cost was 3 million marks, just to maintain the enormous facilities), not to mention the main item – employment of thousands of workers who had been faced with nothing. Most of them were ethnic Germans, whose origins from various European countries and diverse social strata inevitably led to certain tensions. But immediately after the currency reform, they at least formed a core staff of skilled workers which BMW could fall back on, whenever further expansion might be needed. Had Milbertshofen never considered this? It was not Masters's job to rack his brains over this. He was most distressed at the prospect of the army leaving here and taking him with it. To put down facilities like these in one go, he would at best have to go to Ford at Detroit (the halls at Allach were called Villers Rouge after Ford's kilometre-long production line on the River Rouge). He did not understand why the public company, which owned Allach, regarded the works as a 'bloodless body' (a creation which, in its proportions, exploded everything that BMW would find feasible). Were there not dozens of German industrial companies which, if BMW could not make any use of it themselves, would definitely rush out to acquire it, and move in as tenants (just like the army)?

Indeed there were, and the vital moment, of which Popp had dreamed in the twenties and then once again in the thirties, in order to merge with Daimler-Benz and form a large, common, south German car company, had never been so close as when the Swabian car company (at just the moment when the Allach crisis was reaching its climax) again took an interest in BMW. Here were just the halls they needed! They were not thinking of cars, but of an agricultural tractor called the Unimog, which had all the prospects of being a great success. The designer Friedrich had developed it for Mercedes through Böhringer at Böblingen. But there was not enough space either there or in Gaggenau, at the Mercedes lorry plant, to be able to put the Unimog into series production. When Dr Haspel, the head of Daimler-Benz and friend of Popp (he had been let back into his office after the usual automatic detention as a baron in the war economy), then appeared at Allach, the ideal production site had admittedly been found, but the question could not be answered. Nobody knew when the Americans were going to leave. A conversation with the 'authorised representative of BMW AG for Allach' (there was nobody else other than the technical director Hundt, who had been dismissed by Masters) then provided Haspel with a solution that seemed just the thing they were both looking for. At Milbertshofen, motorcycle production only took up a fraction of the halls; most of them stood around unused. How about setting up Unimog production in them, even if only at first for pre-production runs? That would also help BMW, and not cause any delay. Little by little, based on just how quickly or slowly the army withdrew from Allach, the operations could be transferred there.

But Donath did not want to know. Haspel had made an even bolder suggestion. Not only could production of the Unimog be allocated to Milbertshofen, but the entire manufacture of Daimler-Benz diesel engines could, also. Unaffected by this proposal, Donath continued to shake his head, saying that even if, in Haspel's view, such a stroke of luck (after a lost war, with all the consequences that that had!) only came up once in a century, Mercedes should not hold out too much hope for it. Yet the two works could never again complement each other so advantageously with regard to production sites: here, where there was an abundance of space; there, where there was a lack of it; here, where skilled workers who would have to be made redundant (and that could be very soon!) were to be found in numbers; there, where the management did not know where to find them; here, where there was a complete lack of capital to put things back on their feet; there, where contracts would roll in for a production which could not be carried out. There seemed no better time to him, in which to grab the opportunity with both hands while the going was good. Donath said no. Haspel asked if Donath was a bit worried that Mercedes might swallow BMW up. He assured him that this was absurd, because, in contrast to earlier agreements, BMW could do whatever it pleased with production. This did not ultimately mean that a merger was perfectly possible. (If a merger were of mutual advantage, as had earlier been planned, unfavourable circumstances had unfortunately continually prevented it.) Why not? But Donath continued with his refusal, and Haspel went back to Untertürkheim in Stuttgart a deeply disappointed man.

According to the minutes of an eyewitness, who had been on the sidelines of the negotiations:

> All of us in Allach were dumb-founded when we heard about it. To think we let such a wonderful opportunity slip through our fingers! Was Donath blind? The only possible conclusion was that he, a brilliant technical theoretician who belonged in higher education, now wanted to show qualities he did not possess: entrepreneurial determination, cool-headedness, vision. But a leopard cannot change its spots. In a cloak-and-dagger operation, we at Allach had once had to fetch some machine tools (not so much 'fetch', as 'steal'). Immenstadt lay in the French zone, and the transfer plant, where they were, was occupied by Moroccans. But we needed them, and they belonged to BMW. The army had supplied us with lorries, drivers, GIs. Donath told us we couldn't go. We went all the same. Everything went well. Donath threw a fit. He said he was personally responsible to the Control Council for every confiscated bolt, and told us we were an added liability . . . because the machines, as part of the reparation agreements, belonged to the French and not BMW! For administrators it does not matter what they administer. The main thing for them is that things get administered. Without knowing or wanting to know, they are powerless to represent anything other than a principle. The principle defines them, and not any venture associated with risk.

But in Milbertshofen, other interpretations were also disseminated because it was known that something was happening in the 'car' business. If Donath's 'no' had been determined by this, then it put a completely different perspective on it all. After all, who is happy to show his own hand? Bearing in mind old feuds with Mercedes-Benz, was it not a clear question of vision to anticipate and avoid subsequent feuds? The Swabian

'Big Brother' had always been concerned about production arrangements, the mood had always become icy when BMW had got anywhere near the big league. How could BMW push ahead with a new car in this class, as Donath intended, when Mercedes regarded this as its own domain? The Swabians working from Allach, or even sitting in at Milbertshofen, would have nipped in the bud any attempt at such 'trespassing'.

Nevertheless Hundt did not abandon the hope that he could still win Daimler-Benz for Allach, even if Milbertshofen was against him. Bearing in mind the brief issued to him by the general trustee, Dr von Mangoldt-Reiboldt, 'to take the Allach works beyond the period of American confiscation and to study every possibility for preparing it for subsequent civilian production', Hundt wrote to Haspel on 29 October 1950:

> The news now seems to have penetrated as far as the BMW management board, via the bank and the supervisory board, that Daimler-Benz is an interested party for the Allach works. The management board has withdrawn the previous plan involving Allach in future car production, and is now trying, with the support of the work's council and the union, through direct representations to Mr McCloy on behalf of the Americans, to achieve the release of at least one large hall covering 35,000 square metres. It is certain that Daimler-Benz in Bavaria would be received with open arms by the regional and municipal offices, as well as by potential employees.

Haspel did not bother to reply. Instead, he wrote a letter on 4 December 1950 to Rummel, the chairman of the Daimler-Benz supervisory board, in which he expressed his misgivings that, even if BMW was presently striving to this end, they would not get the Americans to leave the works, 'because before that, a great number of other time-consuming questions will have to be answered'. He felt that these answers would depend on 'our subsequent decisions'. He would find it imprudent to support 'efforts to this end' before these essential problems had been cleared up. He concluded: 'On our side, we would like to draw particular attention to the fact that in this respect we have no desire at all to offer any guarantee.'

That was the final refusal.

And how did the palace revolution at Allach turn out? As the King of Prussia had once had to learn that there was a Supreme Court in Berlin, so the victors were now forced to recognise that 1950 was not 1945. Their re-education process to shape democratic reforms had brought about a change in Germany which they now had to accept, even if it had changed to their disadvantage. Works councils and trade unions had (at the same time as they were appealed to by the highest occupying authority, Mr McCloy, the US High Commissioner for the Western occupation zones) grasped the bull by the horns and produced what was 'public knowledge'. Initially this took place at a works meeting to which radio, press and the provincial government were invited. (After all, the Bavarian ministers for employment and the economy came along and promised solutions). Then, to much razzmatazz, a rally was held at the Krone Circus.

Even if nothing more was said than had previously been on offer in an internal memorandum, the decision to make things public showed unmistakably that a new quality of responsibility had grown up in the land of the vanquished. Neither a military government, which wanted to (and had to) work with the Germans, nor a works management were protected from public complaints being directed at them, which, after all, involved *everyone*, not just the people directly concerned. That was new, however moderately expressed. These new features were that the workforce had decided to take its fate into its own hands, and that it no longer wanted to be a party to anything which would make it the toy of this or that interest. They wanted to participate at future consultations regarding the fate of the works and its workforce. And finally there were to be no claims by the firm on Allach if it refused justified demands by the workers and no longer wished to fulfil obligations incumbent on it after the army had gone. Allach, the buildings, the works, belonged to BMW in the same way that they, the workers, did.

The calls did not go unheeded. Even before they had been heard, Donath had indicated that the intention of the board of management to pull out of the Allach works was not shared by the supervisory board (now headed by the former general trustee, von Mangoldt-Reiboldt), and that the decision had been made to take over the duties as the contractual partner for the workforce at the Allach works. Even the military government was now giving way, and so the storm in the tea-cup ended more quickly than anticipated (in view of the world situation with the war in Korea). The Allach 'mutiny' could not have been described in any other way. Mr McCloy himself had probably been responsible for the decision which brought Allach the assurance from the army that, after abolition of 'direct hire', the repair works would be maintained for five more years.

Six months after the obvious failure of Daimler-Benz's attempt to settle in Allach, Donath invited the Federal German press, the provincial government, the gentlemen from the former military government with their ladies, and the usual dignataries, including a few film stars (who not only cast a few beams of light on the sparse glamour of a car launch of those days, but could also have a multiplying effect as customers) to the 'Bayerischer Hof' on Promenade Square in Munich. This took place on 13 April 1951, but Donath was not superstitious. He stepped up in front of the circle of guests and said:

'Our technical fate lay on the two pans of a set of scales. On one side was our choice to continue building our old models from our former works at Eisenach, and on the other was having our former products copied in another European country. As the pointer on the scales, we no longer possessed anything, and so we became nothing more than the indicator of our former quality. What else was left for us, from a technical point of view, than to try and put the scales back into motion? What that meant was that we had to follow new paths.'

Then he pulled away the white linen cloth almost as if he were unveiling a monument. And what appeared was indeed more like a monument than a car. A kind of safe was presented in solemn black. It was mounted on wheels, like a frozen wave in which everything was encompassed. The panels curved with a curvature that seemed endless. People attending the unveiling had the impression that Donath was not pulling off a linen cloth, but a shroud, giving greater cause for weeping than cheering. As it was, those standing around seemed immediately to agree that what they saw was rather less of a technical novelty than an extraordinary baroque creation (only possible in Bavaria) which combined ease with the heaviness of the earth.

Indeed, the name 'Bavarian baroque angel', as the car was known when it appeared on the road a year and a half later, intimated such sentiments.

Walking a Tight-rope
1951–1960

An Angel's Trickery

1950 marks the midway point of the twentieth century. The world, and with it Germany, was moving towards the year 2000, and anyone now in middle age would not reach it. If he held a position of responsibility, he was all the more haunted by the thought of how it should continue – with or without him? Did he still hold some influence over events, should he allow himself to be carried along as before, or should he attempt to control events himself, no matter how small his field, to the best of his ability? But where was the general development heading, which provided the reality of tomorrow?

The Englishman George Orwell had shown in 1948 a vision of this reality in his book *1984* (he had simply reversed the year), which he wanted his readers to understand as a 'positive incentive for reflection'.

'If we do not look ahead, we cannot be aware of anything in our present situation. Whether it is 1948 or 1984 – it is the feeling we have of an era, with all its implications, that is important, the here and now.'

Smith, the hero of Orwell's vision, lives in London, the chief city of Airstrip One, the third most populated of Oceania's provinces, one of the authoritarian state structures made up from the Empire and the former USA. It is constantly waging war. The watchword of the only party proclaims that anyone who controls the past controls the future; and whoever controls the present, controls the past. Or as Orwell's Smith says: 'All that was needed was an unending series of victories over your own memory. "Reality control", they called it: in Newspeak, doublethink.'

And a friend of Smith's working in the research department for Newspeak at the Ministry of Truth says enthusiastically: 'In the end we shall make thoughtcrime literally impossible, because there will be no words in which to express it . . . The whole climate of thought will be different. In fact there will be no thought . . .'

But the Germans had already put behind them the situation being propagated as a warning in this notion of the future. It had caused them to lose their identity. They lived from one temporary arrangement to another, each of which certainly gave the impression of being Germany, but which actually was not. All their endeavours and successes in both West and East, to provide a balance between West and East were, as a German journalist wrote in 1950, like those efforts of a family carrying brand-new furniture into a burning house. Nothing useful that would show the way forwards would result from this, nothing that could make universal involvement worthwhile. There they were, standing in front of a wall, before which problems seemed insoluble. It left them with nothing but the vague hope, faced by this wall, of releasing new forces within themselves which might take them forwards into the future.

No road had gone past the point leading to a divided Germany – conclusively, as far as this word is valid in history. There was little approval, no one cheered, neither in the state called the Federal Republic of Germany, nor in the other called the German Democratic Republic. What Karl Jaspers, the Heidelberg philosopher, said in a speech in 1945 applied to both places:

'Let us not speak cheerfully of "break-up", let us not for a moment fall into the trap of false pathos, feeling that things will now become all sunshine and light, that we would be exemplary people under happy circumstances. Many a person fell into the trap of just such an illusion in 1918 and 1933. This self-intoxication, which was simply destruction running its course, is now denied to us. All we can do is take our disaster upon ourselves and do what is still possible, that being hard work, as far as we can see, with little hope of immediate happiness.'

This was just as valid now. The Germans in occupied Germany remained protected from self-intoxication, while destruction was running its course. They did not think much of socialism, and anyone living in the Western zones had registered all those freedoms and concessions granted by the Western victorious powers with a sobriety bordering on scepticism. These ranged from the Marshall Plan and its blessings to the announced 'support for the German people to rebuild a state able to maintain itself with peaceful aims and be incorporated in the European economy'. This was how a new guideline from Washington was issued to General Clay in the middle of July 1947, which, from the spring of 1945, replaced the directive JCS 1067 from the Joint Chiefs of Staff.

So the course had been set.

'Anyone occupying a territory also imposes his own social system on it. Everyone introduces his own system depending how far his army can penetrate. Nothing else is possible.' This is what Stalin is supposed to have said even before Germany had capitulated, as reported by Milovan Djilas, one of Tito's comrades-in-arms and a subsequent opponent. Standing in front of a map of the world with the Soviet Union coloured in red, Stalin said: 'They [the Western powers] will never accept the idea of such a large area being red. Never, never!'

Now there were two German states, and there was no turning back.

What slightly perplexed the world, but most of all those affected by it, was the fact that the Germans in the three Western occupation zones had given themselves a constitution which embraced all the lessons from their history. They called this the Founding Law. The birth of this Law at Herrenchiemsee in Upper Bavaria went almost unnoticed by the general public. The landlord of the Castle Hotel had lived through it as a young man. When I looked him up (he was the only eyewitness still alive, apart from the reporters and the typists), I calculated that this must have been around forty years ago. What would he remember?

The sun was harsh, it was January, the Föhn wind made the mountains seem so close that they looked as if they would fall into the lake.

'It was as calm as it is today,' he said. 'The currency reform had just taken place. Only the previous Sunday the island had been packed with people. Later it felt as if we had been cut off. There was no money (apart from the amount paid to everyone, 40 marks, which was too precious to spend on a visit to the Ludwig Castle and a light ale. We were wondering whether we should close the pub and the hotel – we had already laid off the staff.) Then they turned up. Eleven elderly gentlemen (or that's how I saw them, as I was only in my mid-twenties then) moved in. The convention began.'

A couple at the neighbouring table, the only other guests that day, were listening quietly. You could see it in both of them, the way they were transported back to the past, to those turbulent times. Convention made them think of convent – monks had once lived in the monastery nearby, which was also known as the 'Old Castle'. The King of Bavaria, currency reform, the 'Founding Law' . . . what were all these things to do with this place?

'Did you or anyone have any idea what the men were here for?' I asked.

'Not at first, it only drawned on me gradually,' the landlord said. 'Firstly, there were eight gendarmes from Prien, along with two special branch officers. That was odd in itself. And secondly, there were the journalists. There were only two telephone extensions here, and everything was put through from the Prien exchange. You can imagine what it was like after the meetings! Everyone wanted to be the first.'

It had been Hans-Ulrich Kempski from the *Süddeutsche Zeitung* who had explained what it was all about. Quite a big thing, he said.

'The constitution depended on what was decided in the convention. Not the Bavarian one, but the German one. A state would emerge from nothing, a model state, not a nation-state, a federation of German provinces, although quite a few people, most, in fact, were still against it. One thing was for sure – we weren't going to get far without laws. And you need a constitution to make laws. This was what was intended to come out of here. The outcome would determine the state, and whether it could function as a democracy. . . . That's how it was, more or less,' said the landlord.

'That was the first time I realised what Herrenchiemsee meant. If something reasonable comes out of this, then these men here would be making history, I thought. And I thought of the Bavarian Party, which had rebelled in Prien. Something of the local lynching customs had seeped through. As you know, they smashed in window panes, set things on fire, raised hell. . . . So we had the eight policemen, and the gentlemen who were meeting in the Old Castle, right next door, Room 7. Whether they were Prussians or not, they were peaceful people. Constitutional lawyers, as they were called, more professors than politicians. Süsterhenn was among them, a minister from Rhineland-Palatinate, Theo Kordt from Bonn, and a professor Brill from Hessen, I think. There was also a man from Berlin, the chairman of the city council, Otto Suhr, although he should not have been there officially as it was only for the eleven provinces in the Western zones. A professor had also come from Kiel, representing Schleswig-Holstein, called Baade, a friend of Carlo's – yes, that's right, Carlo Schmid. Look here, Carlo Schmid gave me this book. It's got a dedication.'

He handed it to me, a book made of wood-pulp paper, now a bit yellow. I read the title: *A Roman Diary*. Then inside: 'To my dear Herr Huber at Herrenchiemsee. Carlo Schmid. 14 August 1948.'

'A valuable document,' I said. 'Take good care of it.'

'You think so?' asked the landlord. 'Nobody's interested in what happened here. It's all been written down, though,' he said, pointing to a second book which he had brought along. This was the *Report on the Constitutional Convention*, which had been published by Richard Pflaum of Munich under American licence (US – E 172).

'And everything is true,' he said, 'and written so clearly that anyone can understand it. Quite something!'

He opened the book and read: '"Article 1: The state exists for the sake of mankind, and not mankind for the sake of the state. The dignity of human personality is inviolable. Article 2: All men are free. Everyone is free to do that which does not impinge upon others within the limits of public order and common decency." So there you have it. They then put up a plaque. Come along, I'll show it to you.'

We went out and, after barely a hundred yards, he pointed upwards. Chiselled into the stone and so small that it could only be read with binoculars, the following inscription was built into the wall below a window on the first floor of the Old Castle: 'IN THIS BUILDING FROM 10–23 AUGUST 1948 SAT THE CONSTITUTIONAL CONVENTION WHO PREPARED THE FOUNDING LAW FOR THE FEDERAL REPUBLIC OF GERMANY.

'Was it set high up on purpose?' I asked.

'I don't think so,' he replied. 'People are only interested in the Ludwig Castle. Everyone who sets foot on the island wants to go there. It's a ten-minute walk. The guided tour lasts an hour and a half, then it's back down, the ship's already arrived, and then along come the next lot.'

He was probably right. A voice called out from the hotel: 'Herr Huber. Telephone!'

'Just a moment,' said the landlord. 'Would you like to go up on your own? You shouldn't miss it. The corner room on the right, Number 7. I've had it unlocked. By the way, it's the same room where Hitler, when he was released from the Landsberg Fortress, received money from the Bechsteins; Bechstein, the piano-maker, and his wife.'

'What money?'

'Oh,' said the landlord, 'a trivial sum. Just four million. It allowed him to rebuild the party. That was what got everything going.'

'That's not just a tall story?'

'I wasn't there,' the landlord said, 'but it happened up there, in Room 7. It's a fact. There's no getting away from it. Anyway, it's a place for reflection. Have you got the book?'

I nodded.

On reaching Room 7, a darkly-panelled room which was not very big but which comfortably provided enough space at one table for eleven men (twelve, if you include the man from Berlin), I opened the book, almost curious to see if that 'dignity' they had intended to resurrect had been transferred into the text which the Parliamentary Council in Bonn were to receive immediately after the discussions at Herrenchiemsee. The preamble began like this:

> The concept 'Founding Law' is ambiguous. In common usage it can designate a constitution, meaning the legal framework and the basic standards of a state. However, it is just as possible that, in making a particular reference to this designation (instead of the more accurate word 'constitution'), the provincial chief ministers wanted to express the view that the task of the Parliamentary Council should not consist of creating public order for a state in the full and strict sense of the word, but for a sovereign entity, which lacks certain features which are peculiar to those states in the full sense of the word.

I put the book down. From the windows of the room, I could see the magic of the landscape before me: Frauenchiemsee with its cupola, and its Carolingian archway, built by King Ludwig the German in 860 A.D. (Not far from there was the car workshop belonging to Willi Huber, who was called the 'man with the golden hands' at BMW because of the stylish sports car bodies fitted to 328 chassis which he hammered out on leather bags.) There lay the herb-filled island with its bushes and meadows, with the ring of mountains behind in the blue gleam of the Föhn, and I could almost hear Carlo Schmid say that the state structure whose birth had just been introduced here on Lake Chiem, should not be of more than a provisional nature. He was saying that a 'Western state' could not be a state at all, because it would lack the independent authority as long as the occupation continued. A true state must establish the limits of its effectiveness on its own, and should not be influenced in its construction by external forces. In addition, all doors towards a subsequent all-German institution must be kept open, and he therefore pleaded for a concept of a 'Western state' to be dismissed from the outset. The word 'dismissed' rang out in the circle around him, with Pfeiffer, the Bavarian minister, also using and applauding it. Carlo Schmid continued: The creation of a *de facto* state would constitute an act of outspoken separatism, and could, no, would definitely be the cause for creating the counterpart of an East German state. Moreover, there could be no talk of a constitution. A genuine constitution requires people to mount the barricades and they should not obtain the permission of a military government first. Bravo! the cry went up all around him, with Suhr, the man from Berlin, saying that a dash of Berlin air would be very beneficial to the work in hand for finding a provisional constitution, which they wanted to call the Founding Law. All eleven agreed with him, including the man who was not nominally supposed to be there, but was.

Down below, on the drive leading to the King's Castle, known as the

Bavarian Versailles, I spotted the couple from before. They had been on their tour. What had both of them seen? Probably not history in its popular version; that had been trapped in the Ludwig Castle like a fly in amber. But had my couple been told that the proclamation of the Imperial German Reich, to the explicit humiliation of France, had taken place in 1871 in the Hall of Mirrors at Versailles, which had been the example for Ludwig's magnificent hall? Two years later the fairy-tale King bought the island, beginning work on his copy a further five years later. Building went on for seven years, then the money ran out, and the following year he took his own life on Lake Starnberg. What kind of vision did he take with him? Was it that he had brought something to a conclusion, over and above the bed chambers, the magic table with its monstrous mechanics, beyond the hall of mirrors, 'Meicost-Ettal', as he called his undertaking (that was the metathesis of the Sun King's words: '*L'état, c'est moi!*')? Fortunately, nothing came of it all. Although he had not intended it, German history was present in his architectural copy. On 28 June 1918, the fifth anniversary of the assassination of Archduke Franz Ferdinand, the peace treaty with Germany, the 'Dictate of Shame', was signed in the Hall of Mirrors at Versailles, where King Wilhelm I had been proclaimed the German Kaiser. 'Bring the Germans in!' Clémenceau had growled, and the two German delegates were let in like criminals through a small side door, despatched to the far end of the table and, after signing, let out again through another small side door. An eerie scene!

But who knows this, or wants to know this when they are being hustled through Ludwig's wretchedly splendid copy of the Hall of Mirrors, over there in the Castle? But here, in view of the events associated with the state in which I lived, they welled up in front of me, along with that scene portrayed by the landlord in which Hitler is said to have received his money from the Bechsteins at the very same place where the Founding Law came into being.

Was this a paradox of history, an accident, or an inevitable outcome?

The couple had now reached the Old Castle. They had no time to look up at the stone plaque which said: IN THIS BUILDING SAT . . . to look up at where I was standing, behind the window.

The boat was already waiting.

Theodor Heuss, the first President of the new Federal Republic of Germany, announced, as he spoke on the threshold of the second half of the century, that he had brought no message full of promises.

'We are entering the new year with a strange mixture of feelings . . .'

These words expressed quite accurately what people thought and felt. Facing the population was a parliament with 'subdued sovereignty' (Heuss), but which was democratically elected. It was a population which, under the occupying powers, had lost its ability to act and take decisions independently. For more than four years, it had been guided (politically, legally, economically and culturally) by foreign hands, had been subjected to foreign directives and was used to behaving accommodatingly, just to survive. Anyone kicking against the pricks would quickly lose his post and be punished. The Western powers had also reserved the right to control all foreign affairs for *their* Germans, to codetermine modifications to the Founding Law, legislative measures, provincial constitutions, and so on. They had also stipulated that they were to be informed about agreements of any nature affecting trade and commerce, so that they could be stopped if necessary. Was that supposed to be democracy, self-determination? Anyone who believed this had learnt nothing, and if re-education had not been thought up for the greater good of the victors, but actually to change the outlook of the Germans for the better, then the role of their model pupils did not suit the majority. The census of 13 September 1950 revealed around 47,500,000 Germans living in that state which was now strangely, unusually, called the Federal Republic of Germany.) There was just one thing, though – the question of how the Western democracies would adopt West Germany; not so that they could interfere, and not just for reasons of self-preservation. In the interests of all sides, it was vital to get rid of the idea of the *vanquished*, and to become partners.

To do that, there was a need to 'sweep away the rubble of history', as Heuss had called for. Germany's contribution to peace could only lie in stabilising and democratising internal relations in such a way that no hint of revenge would materialise, and in a way that would allow the world to regain its trust. This was above all to be done through the economy. If the country's own efforts to get things going again were successful, then the future was not lost.

This was a modest future, as people at BMW also felt. But nobody went around with head hung low. The first car had appeared, and unrestrained applause followed the prophecy of doom at the Bayerischer Hof that the linen cloth was a shroud. At the 1952 International Motor Show in Frankfurt, hordes of people surrounded the black solitaire from Bavaria, as they had once done for the 326 in 1936. It attracted lay people as well as experts. The former were people who saw this object as something which went far beyond the purely practical. It was a very accurate indicator of the way forward, at a time when no one gave any thought to economic miracles. The latter, working in the trade, and with their background knowledge, wondered how BMW planned to build such a car.

No car had never come off the production line at Milbertshofen. They had only ever come from Eisenach. Now this first post-war car from BMW (appearing six years after the exodus, and twelve years after the development work suddenly stopped at the beginning of the war) was not simply a continuation of where things had been left off, not simply a continuation of 'big', limited edition, 3.5-litre 'motorway cars'.

If Böning had simply copied one of the test models from the 332 range or just improved it slightly, then a semi-modern vehicle would still have appeared on the market. But this '501', called the Two-Litre Car, wanted to be more than that. It contained features which development had brought forth in the design which had gone on during the war outside Germany, principally in the USA.

In a test report about the new BMW 501, Helmut Werner Bönsch (later to be a director of BMW) summed it up as follows:

Fifteen years' progress could not simply be ignored. America had created a new standard for space and comfort, while European car manufacture had learnt to combine high performance with flexibility. A car which was to continue largely unchanged for the next eight to ten years (and the enormous investment costs of a new model demand this time scale) must be geared up to this standard. What were the reasons for the astonishing successes of the Lancia Aurelia? What had the big American cars learnt in the last few years about road-holding, quietness of operation, seating design and streamlining? BMW could not ignore these questions, and so one after another of these cars was examined with the system developed independently in Munich. Using such methodology, three years' development time could be greatly compressed, resulting in the most successful synthesis of American and European automotive technology which I have ever come across.

This was already shown by the configuration. The engine was no longer mounted behind but across the front axle, producing a completely different weight distribution. With the centre of gravity moved forwards, the car had better straight-line driving qualities, and by fitting the rear seats in *front* of and *over* the rear axle, old faults were overcome. This meant that there were no more vibrations, as the passenger compartment and the road had been separated. As the engine weight had been pushed forwards, the 501 had acquired double wishbone front suspension, while the rear banjo axle was mounted on the parallel link system. Naturally, there was also torsion-bar suspension at the front (the 326 had only had it on the rear), and a steering-column gear change, which was obviously necessary because the car was fitted with three front seats – as in America, too.

What the pundits then noted was that the fully synchromesh gearbox was not bolted directly onto the engine, but connected by a universal-jointed intermediate shaft which ran under the front bench-seat. From here there was some complicated linkage to the steering column. As there was no straight-through connection between both front axle suspension units, each component formed a separate assembly which could be mounted individually and checked on its own. This was also possible with the chassis. With their facility for being mounted on two triangular mounting brackets, like on the edge of a pair of scales, the torsion bars could be very accurately set through adjustment bolts.

Another admirable feature was that the unusually stable box-section frame had been retained. This had a narrow front section and a wide central section, both connected by tubular cross-members. This was done for safety reasons as clearly illustrated with comparative drawings in the brochure. The fact that the engine was mounted on remarkably thin supports was not a mistake which a lay man might imagine, but an indication of the car's nominal breaking points. The suspension was designed to break up in a front-end smash, with the engine then dropping down and preventing the passengers from being crushed by it. The sales department also stated that this chassis was no heavier than the one on the 326 and, as a result, was light enough to be powered even by this engine, the old tried and tested six-cylinder, which could scarcely be bettered.

All this seemed to prove the resourcefulness with which the designers had gone about their work. On the one hand, in making a virtue out of necessity (the engine was available, so why design a new one?), they stinted on nothing which was likely to be part of the future. As it was, anyone knowing that the 332 developed during the war sported similar design features (but who knew that?) would have been able to contradict Donath's statement about the new ways the company was going. But what was the point of denigrating the successes which the designers had achieved? These designers were, in order of importance: Böning (overall designer), Böning (chassis), Böning (front-axle design) and Böning (steering-column gear change). What? Had Böning made everything himself? No, not the body. He had turned that down, his hallmark was not on that; it was too bulky, too heavy. That was Peter Szimanowski's work. Coming from Horch with its propensity for things heavy and bulky, Szimanowski could not be talked out of baroque styling, even if it had something of the shape of a Buick about it, which he openly admitted. But as he said: why not? Anyway, sketching by hand (the 501 had never been in a wind tunnel), he had created the most streamlined and yet stable body shape available at that time, and had received Donath's approval; the latter relied on Fiedler.

Back from England, Fritz Fiedler was on the board as a technician, which was more a nuisance to him than a pleasure. As a designer who worked more by inspiration (in contrast to Böning, who had to produce everything through 'perspiration'), he had too many ideas which, as he said, only spoilt any benefits he got from being on the board with all its responsibilities. With the 501, however, he had overall responsibility as director – and not as a designer – and had given his agreement, in spite of all the shortcomings which had been dictated by circumstances. All in all, he was satisfied. Items which had been tried and tested with BMW had been kept, and a new vehicle created which set international standards. Being both solid and extravagant, it could expect to find customers for whom both features, the demand for quality and the out-of-the-ordinary, had always gone hand in hand.

The fact that the car cost 15,150 DM (at a time when a middle-ranking office worker took home a salary of 350 DM a month) might just have surprised anyone who had not noticed that, even in series production, this car would require a great deal of manual work. From this point of view, its price was perhaps too low rather than too high. Excluding exports (which never count greatly when a new model is launched), it was an easy matter to estimate how many people were able to afford the car, and consequently how many cars could be produced, and how much profit might be left with its manufacturer, provided that the promised technical refinements stood up to the luxury which the car offered externally.

Anyone thinking that way was not wrong. If he asked anyone who needed to know more details about it, then he received a meaningful smile, which confirmed all positive suppositions. It confined all the negative ones to the realms of the absurd, whence they did not re-emerge. This was where they belonged, indeed.

The reason for this was that everything regarding the reality from which the Bavarian baroque angel originated was absurd. What its production was supposed to provide was absurd. Not worrying about market shares was also absurd (market shares which others had already taken), as was making sales solely on the old BMW image. In all the problems immediately surrounding the 501, subscribing to the point of view unanimously represented by management and supervisory board was also absurd. (It is not we who sell the car who are lucky, but the customer who owns it.)

By all accounts, this was not some kind of black humour, but the serious view of everyone involved with it in the works. In view of the long delivery times, many a wealthy, and also patient, customer may indeed have been fortunate when he was at last able to take delivery of 'his' 501. But time and again, eyewitnesses spoke of the 'inexplicable and unjustifiable arrogance by BMW which spoilt everything'. This might well have been appropriate for someone like Popp, but certainly not his successors. Hanns Grewenig, the sales director employed on the suggestion of the Deutsche Bank and a man who, at the very least, was still afflicted by this conceit, had already said at the launch of the 501 at the Bayerischer Hof: 'BMW cars should be the visiting cards of German society!' What had he meant by that? Were those old BMW drivers, who were now completely uncatered for between motorcycles and large cars, not entitled to the same visiting card as the few big shots at whom the 501 was aimed?

In a memorandum entitled: 'The situation of BMW public limited company and the resulting measures', it was reported six years later: 'BMW could only have competed in the market of a medium-priced utility car when this was produced in large quantities. At that point in time, the company did not think it could finance the major investments for such large-scale production.' As if concerned about not offending anyone, the text continued: 'It is open to question whether acquisition of such resources would have been possible at that time by a firm which had been badly hit by total factory dismantling and which, in addition, had been robbed of the most useful part of its production capacity by the confiscation of the Allach works.' If this showed polite reticence about what things were really like at Allach, then at least there was an unmistakable reproach: 'The market research would certainly have revealed at that time the dangerous limitations on the market for this expensive and comfortable car.'

Was the author so sure of himself in saying that the management board, even without having conducted market research, would not have known this? To be able to tackle the very question: 'Why not make a smaller vehicle?', as well as to cover themselves should anything go wrong, the supervisory board had approved development of an intermediate model at a time when a decision to build the 501 had long been taken and its design had progressed far beyond the pre-planning stage. Böning had been able to present it in a surprisingly short space of time. His blueprint, which was completed up to a prototype stage, showed a mini-car which, externally modelled on the 327 type, somewhat corresponded in size and configuration to the Italian Topolino. It had 'flair', benefited from air-cooling with automatic intake control and simply suspended front and rear axles. The drive-train (a two-cylinder horizontally-opposed engine), taken from the R 51 motorcycle, was trouble-free, economical and tried-and-tested.

The little car was rejected out of hand, before there was any evidence as to whether the public would like it or not. The management board objected that the doors and roof would require presses, which the firm did not have, and the expected quantity, between 300 and 400 per day, was over-optimistic. All this, admittedly, had been known some time before.

Even Grewenig's attempt (if the policy was now to stay with large cars) to preclude inexperience and to opt for a pontoon shape and monocoque construction (elements which he felt were where the car's future lay) failed. He had placed the corresponding work with the Italian stylist Pininfarina and Giovanni Michelotti. Michelotti's design was immediately rejected, although Pininfarina's was only rejected after some hesitation when a finished model of the car (scale 1:1) was rolled out. No, was the answer. There was nothing in it and nothing that suggested a BMW, which is what the customer wanted, and nothing in it, even in passing, that continued the old line.

Nobody had any more illusions as to how strong the 'upward' trend was in the fifties. Customers who had only recently been contented with a moped, a scooter or a motorcycle, turned to the small or mini car, as if they were being secretly impelled. People wanted to be protected from the elements, which was understandable, but at the same time (and this was the *real* reason), they wanted to prove they could afford a car after so many cheerless years. So the 'car' immediately came to signify the next rung on the upward ladder: the mini-car owner wanted a small car; and the driver of a small car wanted a mid-range car, with the mid-range driver wanting a big car.

The fact that those responsible at BMW adamantly flouted this market principle, believing that BMW could turn this sequential progression on its head and start by building large cars was, leaving aside the arrogance of top management (ignorance was almost inconceivable), due more to underestimation than overestimation of the company's own resources. Donath considered it an outrage setting up mid-range-car production on the company's own resources. The coffers were empty, and the core workforce could only gradually be trained in car mass-production if they were to maintain BMW quality at the same time (and Donath was determined not to make any cutbacks on this point). On top of all this came the Korean War. That had created disruption not only for the Allach Works. Materials were in short supply, there were again quotas for iron and steel, and if there had not been patrons at Minden, on the Economic Administration Council, like Deby's friend Günther and the assistant secretary Wenk, then BMW would never have received enough raw materials for its motorcycle production – so what hope was there for cars which the company was thinking of building? The car industry was allocated its quotas based on last year's registrations, and everyone watched like Cerberus to see that the allocation system was respected – according to which BMW should have received nothing at all.

The outcome of it all was to maintain the old Popp principle (as the first and last managing director of BMW, Popp had raised the six-cylinder engine to become the standard), and to transfer it to the post-war period – produce little (so that we can maintain our quality), sell expensively (there are still people about who have the money), instead of the reverse, i.e. producing a lot (which we cannot hope to do) and earn hardly anything from it (because the prices have to be low due to the competition). Certainly, there had been a slight change now – under Popp, BMW had never lived off cars, as it had never lived off motorcycles, but had depended solely on aero-engine production, which alone had provided for the finances of that modular system of car production which had marked an entire era. But the car had once been there, and it now provided for grants, securities and (supported by these and the old BMW confidence) bank loans.

But then, everything happened which must not happen to a car company with a new model. This ranged from the inexplicable situation in which twenty-one months passed between the launch and delivery to the first customer (it was only in February 1952 that twenty-five pre-series cars were built, with series production starting in October 1952, admittedly the same year!), to manufacturing difficulties, 'resulting from insufficient design co-ordination with the practical production conditions', as the body-builder Baur in Stuttgart complained. He had chassis after chassis, complete with fitted engine, delivered to him by lorry, which, once the body had been fitted (whose components had been pressed out in Milbertshofen) were then transported back. 'Continued modifications, fiddly inspection conditions,' Baur noted. 'Our late returner to Munich,' the press mocked, as example No.1 was joyfully handed over to its purchaser (in December 1952). When a press shop measuring 5,000 square metres was set up, with the help of ERP (European Recovery Program) loans, in which were installed the two extrusion presses which Deby had bought in the USA and which were unique in Germany, outside contracts had to be taken in, because capacity was not being maximised. The reason for this was that the car was not going down well with the public: the engine turned out to be too weak, or rather, the car too heavy.

Even before the series was ready for delivery, Donath knew that with its imbalance between engine power and weight, the 501's performance was hardly up to that of the comparable Mercedes 220. So he set about work himself, as he had some knowledge of combustion chambers, and designed a new cylinder head, which, although it increased output from 65 to 72 hp, also ruined the higher engine speeds because of the increased compression ratio. The result was warranty costs which ran into millions (subsequently, every owner of a 501 was supplied with a new engine at a flat-rate of 1,000 marks, regardless of the state of his car). And so they decided to take the bull by the horns and offer a higher output engine 'which should not interfere with the harmony of the chassis specification, either because

Unbound joy: The cover of a special edition of one of Germany's leading magazines, published to mark the occasion of Germany's reunification in October 1990

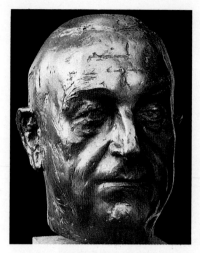

'He was no dictator ordering his subordinates to make reports; he was no prince holding court, nor a man tempted to create a sphere of influence for despotism in which only his will counted. There was nothing of that.

'He was much more a man who did not want to be judged solely on the successes of a product, nor only on the figures from profit-and-loss accounts and from balance sheets, but on the consequences which his decisions had on human beings. These were the consumers, the customers, just as much as those directly answerable to him, including those dependent on him and working under him. They transformed his investments directed at the business world into market results.'
– part of Eberhard v. Kuenheim's speech at the memorial ceremony for Herbert Quandt who died on 2 June 1982

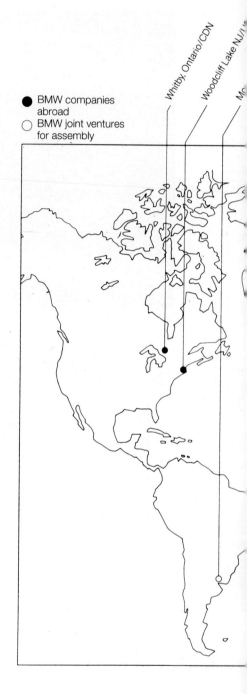

● BMW companies abroad
○ BMW joint ventures for assembly

Whitby, Ontario/CDN

Woodcliff Lake NJ/

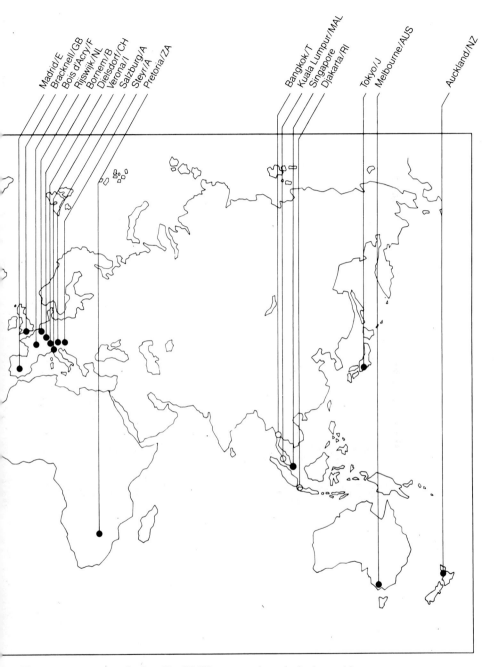

Madrid/E
Bracknell/GB
Bois d'Arcy/F
Rijswijk/NL
Bornem/B
Dielsdorf/CH
Verona/I
Salzburg/A
Steyr/A
Pretoria/ZA

Bangkok/T
Kuala Lumpur/MAL
Singapore
Djakarta/RI

Tokyo/J
Melbourne/AUS

Auckland/NZ

'If you are strong enough, then, like BMW, you can also exist in the world
market with an annual production rate of half a million . . .'

'We have never joined in the race to offer the fastest touring car in the world. We are, however, followers of achievement-oriented society, and we are not ashamed to admit that.'

'Even if the performance you provide, because your customers want it, is based on seduction?'

'Then everything would be seduction, transcending mere human need.'

'There will be further demands, even in comparison to what other manufacturers are putting on the market. New models are pacemakers. We can live for some while longer on the momentum of these pacemakers.'

– FROM AN INTERVIEW WITH EBERHARD V. KUENHEIM

A new chapter in aviation technology for BMW – BMW-Rolls Royce GmbH at Oberursel. Here Sir Ralph Robins, Chairman of Rolls Royce plc, (centre) talks to Eberhard v. Kuenheim at the 1990 International Aviation Show at Hanover

In February 1991, a European association of car manufacturers was founded in Munich. The chairman of the BMW management board, Eberhard v. Kuenheim, is seen signing the founding charter

'Today, more than 750 million passengers take off every year in one of more than 7,500 passenger jets currently being used all over the world. That means around 1,500 people at any one time. In addition, there are 14 million tonnes of freight. On top of that, there are still almost 2,000 propeller planes still flying, belonging to the fifty largest airlines alone. It has been calculated that in the next fifteen years, air traffic will double again. This will result in new aircraft being ordered from around the world. More will be ordered than can be delivered. At the beginning of the nineties, the order books of the aircraft manufacturers registered 3,000 orders.'

– FROM AN INTERVIEW WITH EBERHARD V. KUENHEIM

'And the man at the top – what is his secret?'
'The man at the top spends half his time in the political domain. He makes speeches, drafts the texts for general meetings, cuts a figure at Bonn, Brussels and Paris. The other half of the time, which is non-routine (although if you don't have routine, you cannot do anything), is mainly spent on a few, high-powered groups who have the skills to think, prepare and formulate, so that the entire nucleus of the problem can be whittled down to two sides of typewritten paper. Armed with documents which I don't have to check or read in advance, I can fly off to appointments, and just read them on the plane. When I get off at some place or other, I am better prepared than my counterpart in the negotiations, an advantage which often proves decisive . . .'

– FROM AN INTERVIEW WITH EBERHARD V. KUENHEIM

Eisenach: BMW is not building another car
factory here, but a factory for tools to
produce car bodies. The very day before
German unity was consolidated, 2 October
1990, the Federal Minister of the Economy
laid the foundation stone for this new BMW
works in Thuringia

Below: The new Federal citizens are now
buying West German cars, too. Dealers are
setting up shop. Melkus was the first

of its greater length or its increased weight' (test report), but which was 20 kilograms heavier than the six-cylinder. Initially fitted with a 2.6-litre engine and later with an optional 3.2-litre engine, which in turn had the option of 120 hp or, in a 'super version', of 140 hp, it was the first V-8 cylinder car in the world fitted with a light-metal engine block. This was called the 502, whose performance invited comparisons with the Mercedes 300, but which cost 4,000 DM less. Externally it was barely distinguishable from the 501 and was only comparable to the Mercedes 220. Public opinion was divided – some said it was an unhappy mixture of progress (light-metal engine), of excessive luxury and conspicuous lack of foresight – in short, a flop; while others said it was an all-round, modern design of a 2- to 3-litre touring car with sports versions, and gave it a genuine chance in the market place.

Did it have any? Unfortunately not. What emerges in a series-produced car by way of defects is due to insufficient development work, which is almost impossible to catch up on. Costs rose to gigantic levels and would have made the company (if it had continued, and not abandoned, the project) end up jeopardising not only its product, but its very existence.

BMW did not give up. 'It is not the big car, its design, its high price, etc., which is causing this dilemma, but simply its shape, the baroque shape,' the sales staff said. But Szimanowski, the best body-stylist in Germany at the time, had set his mind on it. As nobody had sensed the difficulties it posed, he had received a free hand once the supervisory board had given its say-so. A free hand! The front wings needed three or four pressing operations so that they did not rip. That was the same with the rear lamp sections. Everything was round, the mating parts in the bumper area were all round, which required an enormous amount of matching-up work, and this was difficult to check. Pressed panels try to spring back to their original shape if they are round; they become deformed from the original diagram. Only experience makes people aware of that, and very few had such experience.

So there must have been some joy in 1953 when a sixth of those cars actually purchased was set against the planned sales of 25,000 cars per year. In total, of all the six- and eight-cylinder cars produced (including the sports variants, 503 and 507, requiring huge investments, but failing to bring the hoped-for business in America), 23,400 examples were sold at home and abroad. Each example took a lot out of the firm, and it suffered a loss of 76 million marks, an amount which exhausted everything which the motorcycle business had brought in as return, everything which disposals (part of the Allach site) and rents (from the US Army repair works at Allach) had brought in and continued to bring in. BMW, with the help of all bridging loans from banks, state securities, convertible loans, etc., kept itself above water until that black day in December 1959 when the firm faced bankruptcy. That was a high, a very high price to pay for learning the vital lesson that products must match the market and that, whatever the firm's prestige, a start had to be made with a small car which would take up the slack of the motorcycle business (which was finally dropping off) and which could provide the first rung for a comprehensive model range.

The Egg

It was to Geneva, the city of Calvin, Rousseau and the League of Nations, the venue of countless peace conferences which had continually offered new, but false hopes to the twentieth century, it was to the shores of Lake Geneva that a man called Eberhard Wolff travelled from Munich in March 1954. He had been a development engineer for a number of years at the Bavarian Motor Works, with varying success. Glad for once to be able to poke his nose out, even if only as far as Switzerland, and given limited travelling expenses and the order to have a look around, he had the strange feeling that there was something in the air. But the air was leaden and heavy, winter had descended again from the Jura mountains, freezing any exhibition fever that might have prevailed. Wolff's destination was the Geneva Motor Show.

As the turntable for the international car trade and motorcycle sports world, this show had acquired a certain reputation. This was due not only to the fact that it opened its doors in March, when the first stirrings amongst customers were felt (and it took place every year, while other shows came round every two or three years), but also to the fact that Switzerland, which had no car production of its own, was dependent on imported vehicles. This made the place attractive. All the major makes exhibited here, as well as the minor ones, who felt that they had some chance of outstripping others. There were not only internationally famous designers, but also quite unknown inventors, who contributed to the show's flair. This was the place to see what they had devised for models which were as yet untested and quite unproven. Half-forgotten firms, as if commanded by fate, made themselves known again. BMW had sent its first post-war motorcycle here, and although it was little more than a dummy, the Germans went home with full order books.

That had been a few years ago, and while Wolff might care to remember that this had started the revival in his company, he also had to admit that BMW had nothing new to counter the slackness in motorcycle business which was now clearly perceptible.

Other manufacturers had certainly no less trouble in shifting their motorcycles, but they had not gone as far as considering a merger to get a small car off the ground. This was the only way to resist Volkswagen (which continued to run and run), an undertaking from which Popp had once shrunk.

398

Donath's persuasive words had got nowhere. It was only recently that he had presented a plan for a large car plant designed solely to build this small car. This he had done to the head of the Zündapp Works, Hans Friedrich Neumeyer (whose father had belonged to the co-founders of BMW AG), to Gerd Stieler von Heydekampf of NSU and to Richard Bruhn, who had often stood by BMW during and after the war, and who was now in charge of Auto Union. They all cried: no, hands off! In any case, our hands are tied, either because we are developing a small car ourselves which is due to appear in the near future (as Bruhn announced), or because we at Zündapp and NSU want to stay with small motorcycles as we have already invested too much in them for us to be able to redirect the investment now.

So again nothing came of it. Was there no light at the end of the tunnel? No sooner had Wolff entered the show, a giant hall whose stands, nonetheless, had the intimacy of a small room, than Wolff's eyes fell upon BMW's stand. Here, next to the old revamped R 24, on whose testing he had collaborated, stood the new 'luxury steamer from the Isar'. Admittedly it was only a prototype, but series-production of the 502 had been announced for that summer. With its super engine, created by the designer Ischinger working day and night (there was talk of his having done it in eight weeks), it amazed many a visitor, who was only able to distinguish it from its better known stablemates by its slightly larger rear window and the tiny 'V8' inscription on the boot lid. But simply opening the bonnet revealed its secret, the first light-metal, V-8-cylinder engine in the world. Anyone taken into Ischinger's confidence and able to see him at work was enthusiastic to the point of rapture about this engine's technical beauty, not to mention the logic of its configuration, which had been dictated by the need to compensate for the 501's heavy kerb weight. As Kolk was later to proudly point out, this engine seemed to have the same architecture as a master builder would give to a cathedral: the structural engineering, the crank case, the valve-gear. Wolff knew that the special machine tools which Böning had specifically designed for the eight-cylinder engine would probably 'make' around twenty engines a day, although they could not be utilised to anywhere near full capacity because the production facilities from the other factories needed on this car were, at best, only adequate for twelve engines per day. How was the company supposed to live off that, always assuming that this expensive car now costing around 18,000 marks could find any buyers?

Yet that should not have prevented Wolff from having his point of view. At the company he was reputed to have 'foresight' and certainly did not adhere to the foolish NHE-viewpoint (the German initials for *Not-our-invention*). He never shut his mind to new ideas, even if they sometimes came from outside. And was it not his job to 'have a look around'? So it was in this mood that he started his tour, with senses sharpened rather than blunted. He did not need to walk very far. Just a few aisles away he discovered an object which appeared just as strange as it was practical. On the one hand, although it looked like a scooter, it could not simply be called a motorcycle in disguise, while on the other hand, with its four wheels it had features of a car – although it was no longer a car.

399

So what was it then? Wolff went up to it. An egg? Yes, an egg, he thought, an egg on wheels, which BMW would do well to incubate. But something made him start back. There was no access from the side, as the door was at the front, taking up the whole of the front panel. If you opened it, the steering wheel and its column moved away and upwards and you were instantly in your seat. If then you stretched out your hand and pulled the door to, clunk!, you had the steering wheel, gear lever and brakes at your control, as if they had always been there. You had nothing but a clear line of vision in front of you. There was no bonnet, though that also meant no protective areas, which car drivers feel they should always have in front of them. (In reality, Wolff thought, these areas provide no protection at all, since they tend to move inwards in a crash and so endanger drivers even more.) Wolff's engineering mind started ticking over: abandoning side doors meant that a vehicle of this size had a shorter wheelbase, at least 300 mm shorter; the shorter wheelbase meant weight savings. Weight savings reduced production costs, which would naturally also affect other parts, principally the frame. The shorter the base formed by the latter, the higher, at constant stability, its bending and torsional strength. And that was notwithstanding the vehicle's manoeuvrability resulting from the narrow rear quarters. Nipping into a parking space at right angles to the traffic flow would present little problem, and would allow the occupants to step out directly onto the pavement. Even parking at an angle was possible, because the thing (what *was* its name?) would not stick out beyond other cars parked along the kerb.

But, Wolff thought, as he got out of the egg again, who in Munich would realise this, who there would be ready to hatch this egg? Nobody would ever do it. Even if it were to keep to the specifications claimed by the manufacturer, and promised to become a winner, the answer would still be no. Wolff thought of the designer Hofmeister, who continued to dream of the mid-range car, not without cause. Hofmeister had set about the first blueprints (a 4-cylinder car with double wishbones, rigid rear axle and monocoque body. But would anything come of it?). He also thought of Grewenig, who would say that it was better to go to the food market if it was eggs one wanted and not cars. Yes, they were bound to be against it with their elitist illusions, claiming that before long the company would land up with a bicycle with an auxiliary engine, as the firm had done in the dim and distant past – the 'Flyaway', the 'Flink'; that is what they were called, weren't they? But they also knew that they had run out of time, that something had to happen quickly. Just as when you are up to your neck in water, a saving hand is welcome in any shape or form . . . even one looking like an egg. Its name in fact was the 'Isetta Motorcycle-Coupé' – a name which could be kept by the manufacturer under licence, as the head of the company, Rivolta, personally confirmed to Wolff. He also said that he had gone to Geneva looking for interested German parties. This was because the Isetta, with its front door, had not been greeted with much approval by the Italians, whose obsession with small cars had been nurtured by Fiat.

Wolff listened, but suddenly felt he had not much time to lose. He interrupted his tour, and immediately returned to Munich, where the unexpected happened. He was able to persuade Donath and Fiedler to pack their bags straight away and go to Milan. There they quickly agreed terms. As Rivolta was prepared to sell body presses together with the licence, as well as having nothing against a more powerful engine which the people in Munich wanted to fit, there was nothing to stop immediate production . . . and all doubts as to whether the egg on wheels was suitable for BMW or not were nipped in the bud.

What had produced this change of heart? Anyone in the company still able to remember the days of the little Dixi, immediately turned their thoughts to that. That began on the day when (even before Eisenach had been acquired by BMW) a hundred Austin Seven cars had been unloaded in the yard at the moribund factory, were jeered at by sceptics, and accompanied by snide remarks. This lasted until the incredible victory in the Alpine Rally by the team of Buchner/Kandt/Wagner, which, driving the BMW 3/15 hp, a car which had inauspicious beginnings, had crossed the most difficult Alpine passes without a hitch. It was there that they had beaten international competition with nothing but best times over 2,500 kilometres. The egg was also manufactured under licence, just like the Austin Seven which, flowering into a BMW and quickly making people forget its foreign origin, proved to be the great hit even during the Slump. Why should not the egg also become a great success? The times were similarly as hard as those at the end of the twenties, and the desire of the masses to acquire a set of wheels at an affordable price was similarly great and indisputable. At that time there was Messerschmitt's bubble-car, which was becoming an ever more common sight on city streets. (It was a three-wheeler, more like a covered motorcycle than a 'true car', with its perspex cover giving the effect of a light aircraft cockpit mounted on wheels. It was mockingly referred to in the vernacular as the 'man in aspic'.) There was the Fuldamobil, a kind of side-car without a motorcycle, and later, once the Isetta appeared, Heinkel and Hoffmann bubble-cars, not to mention the Zündapp Janus, which was also making a name for itself. Then there was the Goggomobil, made by the Lower-Bavarian, agricultural-machinery factory of Glas, which was a genuine small car. All of them offered protection from the wind and rain, and had clearly roused the motorcycle industry from its slumber. As Werner Osswald wrote in *Auto Motor und Sport* in 1954, 'everywhere in technical and sales offices there was a lot of activity, with each firm wanting to outstrip the other, living in fear that they had come too late for their share of the rising cake'.

That included BMW, too. But no one in the company, from Donath through to sales, saw the Isetta as a car. They agreed it was just a stop-gap. That was all. That was the only reason they had been able to opt for it. It was not a car, so it could not disrupt the course they had set themselves.

So they got down to work. And fitted the four-stroke engine from the R 25 to the egg, whose two-stroke, twin-piston engine produced all of 9 hp, now making it 3 hp more powerful. A new gearbox was also designed, and with its price of 2,250 DM, the Isetta managed to undercut the competition offered by any small car on German roads. Then they waited for the reaction.

They were quite astonished when no one burst out laughing, when the press did not criticise it but praised it, saying: 'Look how the "egg" fits into the firm, as once the Dixi did; in no way does it disturb their programme; quite the opposite, it reinforces and supports it.'

Everyone was delighted, saying that it was this that had been missing all along. At only 2.30m long the Isetta fitted into almost any parking space. Its maneouvrability, even if its narrow, rear track might be far removed from usual BMW charm, was extraordinary. Its fuel efficiency (3.5 litres or 81 mpg in town) was unbeatable. Moreover, it could be driven by anyone holding a class IV driving licence (prior to 1 December 1954 this could be acquired without a driving test). And, as the company established, it was not something to be shrugged off, since anyone overtaking it, and still hearing the characteristic whistle of his 502, could only smile and raise his eyebrows at the same time. Leisurely chugging along, modest, reliable and steady, fearlessly climbing any mountain, it had absolutely no effect on its stablemate. In fact, the owner of the latter learnt to respect it.

Picture stories commissioned by the company reflected its popularity. The first picture shows thirteen horses pulling a Roman chariot. At the command of the charioteer (a crack of the whip), the horses and chariot stop and regroup. In the second picture the horses are transformed into the engine block, the chariot into the Isetta's body and the Doric column becomes a petrol pump from which the Isetta is sipping. Actually sipping! We already know how much: 3.5 litres! The heading on the poster is: DRIVE AND SAVE. Another picture story is entitled: YOU DRIVE LIKE YOU SIT. Two fat, jovial men are standing in front of a closed door. They can hear the noise of a pea-whistle coming through the keyhole. One of them is looking through it. The other one also wants to know what the whistling is. Taking it in turns to peep through the keyhole they both recognise three people (a father, a mother and a child), who are practising getting out of a wooden box fitted with wheels at the command of a fourth person, the driving instructor, the one with the whistle. On a plaque behind the man with the pea-whistle can be read: DRIVING SCHOOL. LESSONS OFFERED TODAY ON HOW TO GET INTO SMALL CARS. Both men look at each other blankly. One taps his forehead. Laughing, they both let themselves down onto a sofa which can comfortably seat two people. The sofa fades into an Isetta in which both the fat men drive off with as much comfort as if still sitting on their sofa.

It was presented as a runabout, a rickshaw, a club chair on wheels, a self-propelling travel bag and a dogsbody. As with Pirandello, where six people were looking for an author, the BMW advertising department had twelve people looking for a vehicle (a worker, a country doctor, a foreign office official, a lady in evening dress going to the opera, a midwife, a lady skier, a petrol pump attendant, a councillor, a female press photographer and a housewife), which indeed they found. It was the ideal fulfilment of their wishes. This was the BMW Isetta Motor-Coupé, whose economy had beaten all previous requirements ('Two adults and a child can travel about 230 kilometres for all of 5.80 DM!').

Anyone in the company thinking that the hard times were over had another think coming. With nearly 13,000 Isettas produced, which the dealers took and sold in 1955, the profit was meagre – too meagre to cover the losses brought about by the big car. In order to increase demand, improved specifications were devised and fitted. The spring travel was increased on the front axle from 30 to 80 millimetres to reduce road shocks. A new knee-operated locking lever was fitted, which closed the weighty front door firmly and almost soundlessly in one go. The output from the engine, which had a capacity of 300 cubic centimetres, was raised to 13 hp, making a top speed of 85 kph a 'certainty' – in fact, as a 'survey of all the small cars on the market' showed, the Isetta could now (with two people aboard) offer more flexibility in fourth gear than the much more powerful Volkswagen. It made use of aspects from trade and industry. Fitted with a backward-folding soft top in place of the perspex rear window (enabling a small load area to be fitted), it became a convertible and a delivery van at one and the same time.

It also kept up in the sports field, boldly mixing with the participants at the International Alpine Rally, where Max Klankermeier had left the road on a bend and turned over during the night descent from the Großglockner Pass. After he had secured the back window (which had been forced out of its mounting) with a rubber band, he was able to continue and, together with the other two Isettas, was able to complete the Lesachtal stage from Heiligenblut to Kötschach via Lienz on the Drau (travelling at an average speed of 41.4 kph, while the heavy cars were doing 52.1 kph). Driven by Paul Schweder, with Ann Botschen as his navigator, it drove nonstop from Etna in Sicily to Northern Sweden, a distance of 2,947 km, at an average speed of 60.1 kph. As a precaution, Hoepner, the head of the press section, wanted to accompany the 'Matchstick Rally' (the participants joked that they could only keep their eyes open with matchsticks) in his 502. But even before he had had a good look around Etna, Schweder was already off and away. Then, while his passport was being checked at the Brenner Pass, someone asked him: 'Why are you pushing to the front?'

'I'm in a hurry,' he said.

'Me, too,' said the other person, who turned out to be Schweder.

'While they were filling up in Munich,' Oscar Kolk, now in charge of the company's home-market sales, recounted, 'we quickly examined the tyres on both vehicles. The Isetta had lost nothing, not even a millimetre. We had to put four new tyres on Hoepner's 502. Then the journey continued.'

That was in 1957.

But as early as January 1958 demand had dropped off, in spite of all the advertising ploys which now included verses such as: 'It may sound dreadful /Waldi' (that was a dachsund which ran around beside an Isetta) '. . . but it's dearer and taxable.' But none of this had any effect any more. People wanted a proper car, something which Hans Glas from Bavaria had offered with his Goggomobil. When, every Saturday, new Glas verses appeared in the newspaper, a real poetry competition broke out:

> *Space travel is not yet possible.*
> *Anyone waiting for it, waits in vain.*

403

> *For the family not prepared to wait.*
> *The solution is clear: Goggomobil.*

or:

> *I want to carry you in my hands,*
> *You often hear fathers say.*
> *Which for mothers soon became too much;*
> *The solution is clear: Goggomobil.*

As part of the duel between Isetta and Goggomobil, Glas was able to exhibit at the Frankfurt Motor Show his 'GoggoRomeo' (as the BMW people described the sports version of the Goggomobil, which was also called in the vernacular the 'Refugee's Porsche'), while BMW with its Isetta could not. It was strictly assigned to motorcycles. Nonetheless, in order to be able to show it to people at the Motor Show, Kolk put one on a pedestal in front of the main gate (as a raffle prize for every 250,000th visitor). With over a million visitors the firm gave away four Isettas as an advertising stunt. Everyone could see it there when they joined the throng of the show and again when they left. Back in 1955, Kolk was claiming: 'People are snatching them out of our hands.' Two years later there were piles of them for as far as the eye could see. The firm's future depended on whether it could come up with a car. Unfortunately only the 600 came out of it, which was not a car but a kind of microbus (with the Isetta's front door making it a totally unsuccessful hybrid).

Why did they stick to their principle, when it was clear that the Isetta had had its day? It could only be explained by the courage of a man who had put all his eggs in one basket and who could no longer go back. Investment after investment had been made. Everything had been scraped together just to build new halls, install new production lines and set up new presses for the agreed export objective of 40,000 Isettas throughout the world! What were they to make of the shock news that the French manufacturer of Isos under licence in Paris, who supplied the Benelux countries and Spain, had declared himself bankrupt? Benelux and Spain are not Germany, where the Isetta, as the cheapest vehicle for first-time motorists, would remain viable. 'The competition continued to make the mistake of abandoning such a vehicle too early,' Wolff, who had discovered the 'egg' in Geneva, reminded the new managing director at a crisis meeting in the autumn of 1957. His view was that quantities had to be increased, thereby making the Isetta cheaper and so defying all the prophecies of doom. Was he right?

Nobody knew. All they knew was that the 600 was not hitting the mark. 'Come over to BMW, it could make your fortune!' had been the slogan used in newspaper advertisements as late as summer 1956, showing that optimism was still unbroken. Yet just a few weeks later, in August, the 'Committee For Large-Scale Redundancies' at the South Bavarian provincial industrial tribunal approved the application by the Bavarian Motor Works AG in Munich to issue 600 workers with redundancy notices. It was all a mystery. Just in the period from January to July, 15,000 sold Isettas had left the production halls – then overnight the factory yard was overflowing with unsold vehicles. Any ploy to make them tempting to the dealers failed (this included a circular offering them the chance to stock up while the going was good, as there was a major export order pending; first come, first served).

What was the reason behind this? The Metall trades union had achieved an 8 per cent pay rise which could not justify any rise in price (by 200 DM). The other production costs had certainly not risen. Quite the opposite, they had fallen. Was it the announcement made by other firms that they would soon be bringing out cheap, small cars which had made people planning to buy a car hesitate? Was it the Suez Crisis and the fear that petrol would become scarce? Now there was the hybrid, for which Grewenig had applied for (and received) 7 million marks' worth of loans secured by the Federal Government, whose Economics Minister was Erhard, a native of Bavaria and the inventor of the social-market economy.

From a sales point of view the 600 was certainly a hybrid. But anyone calling it that failed to see that, in their attempt to make a genuine four-seater from the Isetta, its designers had come across something whose importance they themselves (and automotive engineering in general) were only to recognise much later. When Schleicher, who at that time was back at work in the company as an 'adviser', stood beside Fiedler at the drawing board (the exercise was to bring the Isetta's narrow rear track into line with its front one by increasing the wheelbase by around 70 cm), they both had to choose from several designs.

'We tried a rear axle using trailing arms!' Schleicher said. He hit the nail on the head. The invariability in track and camber, the exactness in steering, the excellent wheel arrangement (independently sprung wheels) and the minimal tendency towards oversteer were the advantages of this new axle mounting, which, initially fitted to the 600, was to further prove itself on the 700. As a rear axle with semi-trailing arms and a high-mounted pivot point (for vehicles with the engine at the front driving the rear axle), it fully achieved its objectives. ('Mercedes also had to fit this type of axle,' Schleicher was to say in his old age; 'then Bob Lutz introduced it at Ford with the large Opels following suit. BMW had had it almost fifteen years earlier: the best swinging-arm axle available, guaranteeing outstanding driving qualities.')

Yet despite what the 'big Isetta' notched up in the way of innovations, the public still turned it down. Nothing mattered or had any success: not the side door fitted in addition to the front entry (the former provided easy access to the rear seats), nor its spaciousness or its power of acceleration. Both were the result of the 'world-famous, twin-cylinder, horizontally-opposed engine, tried and tested over decades in umpteen thousands of BMW motorcycles', as an advertising brochure expressed it. No interest was shown in either its extremely low fuel consumption at increased engine output or the tax concession for road traffic (based on use between home address and place of work), designed to stimulate sales of small cars, any more than the fact that folding the back-rest produced a spacious load area. When the company decided to lengthen the chassis (which was not particularly cheap), it looked even more like a micro-bus. People wanted to sit in a car with doors on the left and right. They felt more 'at home' in Glas's tiny Goggomobil (which many saw as the 600's gravedigger) than in the BMW creation which had always been seen as an emergency solution, however technically progressive and superior it might have been.

'As the human frame is the criterion by which any small car design must be guided, we have again chosen a front door as the ideal means of access,' the company announced when the 600 went into series-production in December 1957. A few weeks later, when the big Isetta was standing around in large unsold numbers on the works site, they realised that the sentence was not valid. You could not determine human beings just by their build; their desires and longings also counted. As well as their prejudices.

Who better than Popp to have known that? But Popp, however much he would have liked to do so, was no longer in a position to give advice. He died in Stuttgart on 29 July 1954, almost unnoticed by the world, a world which had meant nothing to him without BMW. At Sandizell Castle, where he had gone to stay with friends after his detention, he had written the following in January 1946 with his own brand of sentimental pathos: 'Driven from my place of work, separated from my family and my own home, deprived of my freedom and exiled to the sanctuary granted by my good friends, my thoughts, as they have so often done in my life, turn to the serene words of Leonardo da Vinci: "ANYONE WHO CANNOT DO WHAT HE WANTS, MUST WANT WHAT HE *CAN* DO."'

His successors had good reason to remember that.

The Stuff that Dreams are Made of

In a drama, characters and events interacting with each other move towards a peripeteia. The same was true for BMW. On one side was the cautious Donath (Donath Cunctator, as he was known), who was still trying to save whatever could be saved (but what was that, given that the large car was draining every single asset?), and on the other was the ambitious sales director Grewenig, who felt the trouble lay in insufficient export business. With his sights on America, he implored the supervisory and management boards to build a sports car. This would be the way they could not only revive the success of those glorious days of old, but also achieve profits which would prove their salvation.

A third figure was the BMW importer for North America, Max Edwin Hoffmann, known to his friends not only in New York, but throughout the world, as 'Maxie' and 'the baron of Park Avenue' (which was where he had his business).

'He is the Duveen of the motor business,' a specialist of many years' experience in imports once said of him, 'a great entrepreneur. He has tremendous vision, loves cars, and he's a fantastic salesman.'

Hoffman visited Munich on his first trip to Europe, rediscovered his old love of BMWs amongst the ruins, continued to stay in touch and, when the V8 came onto the market, imported thirty 502 saloons in one go.

'I had no difficulties with them,' he told Fiedler, when he reappeared at the works in 1954. 'But dealers had difficulties. BMW's time had not yet come in the USA. Now it has come.'

The fourth player was Ernst Loof. We last met him at Veritas, the company which Donath finally closed down when (at the expense of scrapping all the assembly installations) he took over Loof's Veritas shed at Nürburgring, together with a dozen people. This was everything that came under the name of the 'BMW Research and Development Department, Nürburgring Branch' and was concerned with small orders involving detailed trials on the 501 at the Eifel race track. Loof had continued to eke out his existence here, still consumed with the car designer's dream of creating the sports car which, as the former head of racing at BMW, he had always wanted to do. The dream faded. In the meantime he had become a seriously ill man. Then fate cast him one more chance. He knew only too well that it would be the last one.

407

The announcement that reached his wooden house on the Nürburgring came right out of the blue. The supervisory board (in Donath's absence, as he had gone to take the waters at Bad Kissingen) had given the go-ahead to build a fast two-seater car. Loof knew what their targets were: Mercedes, whose 190 SL and 300 SL sports cars had already gone into mass production, and America – with Hoffmann's belief that he would have no difficulty finding buyers for the car between Florida and New York, which would inevitably help BMW break through into America.

Loof immediately sprang into action. He met Grewenig in Munich. Grewenig denied knowing anything about such design work as only Donath could issue such an order, and he was in Kissingen. Loof dashed out of the office and rushed over there. He went straight to Donath who, pale with horror, had received the same news a few hours earlier by telephone from his Milbertshofen office. It was this order which now prompted Loof to implore him: 'Give me the job. I'll get cracking on it!'

'Good,' said Donath (the same Donath who had always shot down Loof's plans with as much refinement as severity). 'Build the car. Build it by hand. The factory will supply you with the engine and chassis from the 502. We won't fit a six-cylinder engine, as Hoffmann wants, but take the eight-cylinder engine which is now ready for production.'

Overjoyed, Loof set to work. The bodywork was manufactured in aluminium by Baur at Stuttgart, and when Hoffmann appeared in Munich, he and Fritz Fiedler travelled specially to Stuttgart to see the miracle.

Hoffmann said politely but firmly: 'We'll never be able to sell that; it's too ugly: the flat dashboard and the unattractive shape . . .' He went on to say that he would ask Italian designers to produce some blueprints. Just as he was about to set off for Italy, he decided to fly back to New York instead, remembering the stylist Count Albrecht Goertz, a German who had been living in New York since 1937. Hoffmann sketched out for him on a piece of paper what he thought the car should look like. When Count Goertz put the first detailed sketches in front of him, he immediately realised they were on to a winner. The sketches were sent to Germany, and ten days later BMW Munich were on the line to Park Avenue. They asked if Count Goertz could come to Germany. Goertz went. Time was short. The prototypes were supposed to be ready by the next international motor show. It was to be a slim and yet spacious coupé of the Grand Tourer type to be called the 503, which would also be developed as a convertible, and as a touring sports roadster which BMW wanted to call the 507.

Soon a mock-up of the 507 produced in the works to the scale of 1:5 on Goertz's design was shipped to New York. But Hoffmann did not like it.

'Too high, too angular, more like a Thunderbird than any fundamentally new design,' he complained, having a clay model made which he sent back over the Pond. Embittered by the rejection of his prototype, which the supervisory and management boards also found 'disappointing', Loof decided to go to Neuenahr, to a beauty contest, where he won a gold medal for his model, along with the 'Golden Garland' for line, shape and fittings. This caused Grewenig to have a fit of anger when he learnt of it from the following lines in the trade press: 'What possible point can the tactics of the BMW management have in showing the prototype of its long-awaited sports car at a beauty contest, only for it to be quickly taken away again and enveloped in a mysterious cloak of silence?' That meant 'curtains' for Loof, whom Grewenig now forbade to go any further with the car. This was a setback for Donath who had commissioned the vehicle, which was not inelegant, required simple production technology and, above all, was not expensive to produce.

It was in August 1955 on a beautiful, mild summer's day in New York that Alexander von Falkenhausen, the designer responsible for the 507's chassis development, handed over the car to Maxie Hoffmann at the Waldorf Astoria. The *Süddeutsche Zeitung* said of the car that it gave the impression of having combined the gutsy power of an express locomotive with the playful elegance of an English greyhound. It went on to describe its 'three-metre-long bonnet, pale yellow pigskin seats, sparkling fittings, gleaming paintwork, discreet chrome, a cross between an aeroplane and a car, a jet fighter for the motorway, a technological and design miracle'.

Hoffmann was enthusiastic as well. Was there any truth behind the rumours that the story had begun at the Waldorf Astoria, where Goertz's creation had just triumphed? How did it begin? Well, designer stories begin like all stories. It started shortly after the war when Goertz was parking his car, a car which had an unusual body (Goertz had designed it as his first car in 1938), in front of the Waldorf Astoria behind another car belonging to Raymond Loewy. Loewy was the doyen of US designers. When Loewy was about to drive off, he noticed Goertz's bodywork in his rear-view mirror. Goertz became his pupil.

Design is about the understanding of dreams. This means being capable of dreams, even if you are not stimulated by the stuff dreams are made of Goertz had travelled a lot: a few times around the globe; five years in the American Army during the war, half of them in the Pacific; and four or five times a year between New York and Brunkensen near Hanover, where he helped his wife manage the estate she had inherited from her father. A temporary farmer and livestock owner, he had nonetheless remained a designer, determined to establish identities which he felt the key industries had lost, especially the car manufacturers. As they never greatly varied from the norm, their products resembled each other; they were blurred faces, with no 'identity'. Although the 507 did not have the characteristic kidneys, he had a resounding success with it, with one critic exclaiming that it was a brilliant achievement from Count Goertz following his return to America. By this he meant BMW, which had created a vehicle whose 'high level of design would rise by a factor of two in relation to its waiting times' – even though you could tell that it had not been nurtured on Bavarian soil. A special issue of the *Kölnischer Rundschau* announced at the 1955 International Motor Show that 'barely had half an hour elapsed from the time when the grey sheets had come off the BMW models than a murmur went through the hall to the effect that the BMW people had even beaten the Italians'.

What was not in that article, because it was not known, was the following.

The BMW importer Maxie Hoffmann had pulled out. The 2,000 cars ordered by him (he even spoke of 5,000), whose sales he linked with the guarantee that the purchase price would be 12,000 DM per unit, were nothing more than paper. Corvettes and Thunderbirds, cars offering about the same performance as the 507 at a fraction of the cost, had just appeared on the American market. So the American dream of the sales director Grewenig had turned to dust. The asking price would not even cover the prime costs, not even in large-scale production, for which there was neither the factory nor the necessary machine tooling available to produce such high quantities.

Yet the company stuck to its decision to put both cars into series-production. And it manufactured only individual parts for which, it must be said, no effort was spared. Each car ready for delivery was driven by the test department for another 100 kilometres following receipt. If anything in the car's running noise suggested any discrepancy, it was taken to pieces like an aero-engine and put back together again. In order to guarantee a speed of 220 kph required by the management board, Falkenhausen had had the motorway between Munich and Ingolstadt blocked off. Photoelectric beams were set up just before Eching, which he and the official from the Technical Monitoring Agency, holding a stop-watch beside him, crossed at 220.1 kph after a ten-kilometre run-up (thank God the drag factor values were right and the Continental racing tyres, inflated to 5 bars, held out!). The 507 was later to reach 223 kph effortlessly, and Hans Stuck Senior raced it on mountain rallies past Jaguars, Ferraris and Mercedes 300 SLs.

But who had the money to afford one? And so, in the absence of customers, only 253 examples of the 507 (list price of 25,000 DM, soon to be increased) were built, while rather more example, 412 in fact, of its 'sister', the 503 (list price 29,500 DM) were built. In 1959, just four years after production started, the 507 was discontinued. But wherever it appeared (at the Copacabana, in Hollywood, on the flower-filled boulevards of Nice, in short anywhere frequented by its customers), it turned heads, amazing people (to quote Count Albrecht Goertz himself in an 'epilogue' to his creation) at 'how much ingenious skill, how much dynamic force from the 150-hp, eight-cylinder engine was concealed under the bonnet, with its turbine-like suppleness and flexibility. Style and technology were combined in successful harmony.'

Ernst Kämpfer, who joined BMW in 1958 as the new head of finance, knew how much this harmony, produced by the combined style and technology in the 503 and 507 'dream cars', additionally cost the works. He was later to say:

As long as it was all paid for by the Reich Aviation Ministry, we could afford to mess about. The Dixi had come to the end of its day, so we brought out the BMW sports car, which proved very popular. At that time, very small quantities made little difference, and the fact that nothing resulted from the turnover it generated did not stop the firm continuing to exist. And continuing to exist well, under the premise that we appeal to individualists, people who are ready to pay a lot of money for a car. Just look at how this premise was like plantain forcing its way through tarmac surfaces. Sports cars! BMW had always built sports cars, on top of its utility models. Their interior dimensions have never been as successful as Mercedes cars. The slogan of 'bigger inside than out' was even applied to the micro-bus, the 600. In addition, BMW was accused of never offering a car suitable for a chauffeur. Was that a good idea? It was for individualists such as doctors, lawyers, actors and so on, including the respectable middle-class. Unfortunately this is not good for the coffers, or rarely so. BMW has no fleet customers, has no car suitable for a chauffeur. And that is wrong. However bad the times may be, once a firm has committed itself, it just sticks to it. It's established that our directors' cars are sold with between 100,000 and 200,000 kilometres on the clock. So they get sold after this distance. Even if the car has half broken down, the car is disposed of and a new one is bought – come spring, summer, autumn or winter. The individualist thinks quite differently. He thinks: 'Goodness me, it's February already; I'll just wait until May.' If times are bad, he just does not buy anything, meaning that cars become objects which live into old age.

Was that anything new? Not at all. Such thoughts had also inspired Grewenig, resulting in a vehicle next to the sports car at the International Motor Show about which the Zurich newspaper *Die Tat* wrote: 'With the BMW 505 we can speak of true luxury.'; and the Berne magazine *Automobil-Revue* said: 'This time BMW has no sporting pretensions. This official limousine on an extended BMW 505 chassis has the outer lines of a Ghia, and internally the discreet luxury of top-of-the range German cars.'

It was not for nothing that the Swiss papers praised the vehicle. It had been designed by the Swiss body-builders of Ghia-Aigle and built in just two examples. They were fitted with a glass partition between the driver and the rear seats, an intercom to the chauffeur, a bar, a wrap-around (American) panoramic windscreen, and included everything which the standard-production car did not have. This 505 had been designed with a view to Bonn, and beyond. Firms who prided themselves would not want to take second place to the prestige requirements of ministries. With the end result that when the car was driven up to Adenauer, he enjoyed the test drive, but his hat was knocked off his head when he got out – the car was too low for him. So the car was limited to the two examples.

Renouncing the Air

When, after the First World War, the Germans were trusted enough to have 'flying allowed again', incomparably better conditions existed for it in the defeated country than after 1945. Admittedly Rathenau had spoken of scientific murder being perpetrated on Germany, admittedly arbitrarily adopted 'definitions' ensured that there were further delays and restrictions after the ban on 'manufacturing and operating aircraft' had been lifted. But the old flying spirit lived on, and anything forbidden in the Reich, such as training pilots and testing aeroplanes, was possible in Russia, where the Reichswehr and the Red Army co-operated to make up for deficiencies in military aviation as well as to practise civilian flying and introduce new technology.

How different things were after the Second World War. The German aviation industry had been totally decimated. Anything which was still operational was dismantled and sent abroad. Along went designers, inventors and scientists. Some of them went voluntarily, as there was nothing for them to do there. Gone were their research institutes, laboratories and test stations; as were their manufacturing secrets, production and organisational methods, and business experience. And all their patents were expropriated without compensation, and could be used freely in the victor states by anyone wanting to have them, on condition he was not a German. The expression 'flying is allowed again' sounded like bare-faced cynicism. How? With what? Yet on 5 May 1955, almost ten years to the day after the unconditional surrender, the oft renewed 'ban on manufacturing and operating aircraft' came to an end. Germany, the part called the Federal Republic, got its air sovereignty back again.

As early as 1948 Franz Josef Popp had summed up the situation when he maintained in his memorandum that 'no modern economy can in future do without aviation, just as it cannot do without other means of transport. This applies just as much to the military. The ban on civilian aviation in Germany is a measure against civilian competitiveness.'

The victors did not dispute this. There was no logical reason to see the ban as anything else. When Popp demanded it lifted, he was thinking of his company and the foundation upon which he had established it, which he wanted to see continue in the future, with the aero-engine as

412

the centre of production while continuing the manufacture of cars and motorcycles. Whoever was assigned the task of getting BMW back on its feet again would have to stay true to that, even after his death. He could see no other alternative, and he was not the only one. Donath (being an aero-engine man) and others had never given up the plan. The only question was when, yes when, they would be able to carry it out. This 'when' would be the decisive factor in the future. And so nobody racked their brains about 'how'. It was ready now. But how did things stand?

If you consider that the Federal Republic had long possessed the status of an ally when the ban was lifted, that it was a member of NATO as well as the Western European Union (having gladly given the commitment not to produce any nuclear, biological and chemical weapons on its territory), then Popp's early assessment had a doubly macabre effect.

Three days before the end of the war, Dorls, the director at Allach, had been ordered to the Alpine Redoubt to set up an aero-engine works on green meadows (in fact, that was all he found there). He was to do this without people, without materials, without machine tooling and without technicians. Was anything different now? How was a country, which had to some extent been removed from the cutting edge of aviation technology to the Stone Age, to take over defence contracts which gave overwhelming importance to airspace – airspace in which supersonic aircraft and ballistic missiles were operating!?

In 1944, at the height of the war, an American air marshal with some insight had said: 'Twenty years ago pilots, pilots and yet more pilots formed the backbone of the airforce. The backbone of the next airforce will be scientists – people who think in terms of technology.'

If this were right (and in 1955 nobody had any doubt it was), then the demolition of the German aviation industry only played a minor role compared with the loss of scientific and technological know-how.

The story goes that Archimedes set fire to and destroyed enemy ships moored at Syracuse with a burning glass. One would be quite justified in taking this fable with a pinch of salt; the reflection of the sun's heat using a 'force' powered by a concave mirror could never have set fixed bodies alight.

However, it is beyond doubt that if Archimedes had not died in the surprise attack from the land (as subsequently happened), the Romans would have taken him into custody as the inventor and given him a 'good grilling', as happened again after the Second World War when the Allies pursued analysis of scientific ideas for military applications by all means possible.

In September 1944 the aerodynamics technician Theodore von Kármán, who had studied at Göttingen and had been the founder and principal at the Aerodynamic Institute of the Technical High School at Aachen, was summoned by Henry A. Arnold, head of the Army Air Corps, to La Guardia airport in New York. The air marshal was on his way to the Quebec Conference, where Roosevelt and Churchill were meeting. Now, at the stop-over, he let Kármán, the scientist, into his thoughts concerning the post-war period. He said: 'We have won this war and it is no longer of any interest to me. I do not think that we should waste time discussing whether we achieved victory through simple force of numbers or through superior quality. Only one thing should interest us – the future of aviation and the future conduct of air wars. Where are the new inventions such as jet propulsion, rockets, radar and atomic energy leading?'

Kármán listened in fascination and accepted Arnold's suggestion to go to the Pentagon and establish a group of scientists. Similarly, while the battle for Berlin was still raging and the end of the war was imminent, he took up Arnold's second suggestion, which was to go without delay to Germany and establish on site, and at first hand, how far the Germans had actually got with their scientific research.

As predicted, this was how the 'Scientist Collection Programme' by the American airforce began. Its code name was 'Operation Paperclip', and involved people who were not unlike grouse-shoot beaters, or worse. Both the army and navy, as well as the secret services, scoured Germany using special technical commando units in the search for their prey. There existed genuine 'shopping lists' for sought-after German scientists, and the armed forces representatives behaved, as Kármán said himself, like 'buyers at a slave market', often helpless to stop French intelligence officers beating them to it. (Two of the latter forced their way into the Wittelsbacher Hof at Bad Kissingen, where, guarded by US sentries, 120 German specialists were living with their families. They went up and down the quarters and persuaded some of them to live in France before anyone caught up with them.) This inevitably wreaked havoc on German science, as Kármán rightly feared. In spite of this, operations were continued (a second undertaking by the US Air Force was aptly named 'Lusty' as it hunted for German scientists in aircraft manufacture). As a result, millions of documents were examined, put onto microfilm and assigned to an information control centre, which later became the 'Department of Defense Documentation Center'.

In 1952 the 'Arnold Development Center' was opened by President Truman at Camp Forest near Tullahoma in Tennessee, on a military site covering 16,000 hectares. Here BMW's Herbitus altitude-testing equipment had been sited. The centre's star attraction, however, was a wind tunnel built on the model of the largest wind tunnel in the world (which was never completed). Kármán and his people had tracked it down in the Ötztaler Alps during their 'grouse beating'. It had been designed to operate close to the speed of sound, at 0.9 Mach. (At Kochel the American experts had also come across a small wind tunnel which was still being built, designed to simulate speeds of up to seven times the speed of sound. They also found drawings showing flight paths to New York; this was the first indication of the possible practical applications of intercontinental flight.)

Amongst BMW technicians, the engineer C.K. Soestmeyer, who had collaborated on building the Herbitus developed by Helmut Sachse, had landed up in Tullahoma, while others found themselves at Dayton, Ohio, or were employed at the Aerospace Research Laboratories on the Wright Patterson Air Force Base. Professor von der Nüll, who had been in charge of the Institute for Aerodynamic Bodies at the German Research Establishment for

Aviation in Berlin, took over the project management for gas and air-supply turbines at Garret AiResearch in Los Angeles. Helmut Schelp, the man from the Reich Aviation Ministry, who had once been part of the BMW team developing jet engines, was also there; later he went to Phoenix where he worked as a chief engineer. Bruno Bruckmann, head of development for the entire BMW engine manufacture, joined General Electric at Cincinatti, Ohio, where he got the J 47 jet engine deployed in Korea operational. Also at General Electric was Peter Kappus, last heard of as head of the staff section for pre-projects at BMW, now conducting investigations into the application of particular forms of power such as the 'lift-fan' and the 'aft-fan' jet engines. The Junkers people, who had once developed the Jumo 004, worked under Dr Anselm Franz, in an all-German engineering group at Avco-Lycoming in Stratford, Connecticut; the *New York Times* credited them with 'pioneer work with jets' in an article in 1954.

They all had long-term contracts. When these expired, most Germans accepted offers from the American aviation industry which provided for continued work as 'advisers' even after their retirement. Nobody had any desire to return to Germany.

Only Dr Hermann Oestrich, who had developed the 003 jet engine at BMW, and eleven of his colleagues, had preferred to stay in Europe. The French Aviation Ministry, in its efforts to catch up on the years of interrupted development in aviation technology, had made a substantial offer. This offer was as tempting as it was generous to the O (Oestrich) group which had temporarily reassembled in a Dornier subsidiary at Lindau-Rickenbach on Lake Constance. Under the designation of ATAR (*At*elier *A*éronautique de *R*ickenbach), they were supposed to develop and build a new jet engine for French military aircraft. As the 'Groupe Technique Voisin' with the O group at its centre, the first prototype drawing sets were delivered as early as June 1946 to the company of SNECMA (*S*ociété *N*ationale d'*E*tudes et de *C*onstruction des *M*oteurs *A*éronautiques), as the parent company based in Paris was called. At the beginning of 1948 the first of the six V-power plants were running on the test bed at Villaroche, the test centre not far from Dammarie-les-Lys (Seine et Marne), where the German technicians were to move to in 1953. In 1948 Dr Oestrich took French nationality and was later awarded 'Knighthood in the French Légion d'Honneur'. After the Federal Republic was in a position to have 'flying allowed again', most of his colleagues returned to West Germany, either to work in the aviation industry, which was emerging from nowhere, or to be lecturers at High Schools, where they were welcomed with open arms.

Helmut von Zborowski, the 'Rocket Count', was also among them. Released by the French from a prisoner of war camp, the former SS officer had designed and developed the famous 'Beetle' coleopter for France at his 'Bureau Technique Zborowski' based at Brunoy (Seine et Oise). This was a vertical take-off which, as a 'circular-wing aircraft', caused quite a stir. The fact that Zborowski was once again to play a role at BMW, albeit a temporary one, was something that neither he, nor those who were to appoint him to head the subsequent BMW power plant production, could ever have imagined. But what would have been seen as a snare to any other mere mortal did not apply to inventors, even if they served the devil – in other words, their complicity in Germany's past. There was no power on earth which felt it could do without geniuses (whether they actually were geniuses or just thought they were). And neither the United States, France, Britain, or even the Soviet Union, turned their noses up at them.

When war broke out in Korea, a Russian airplane, the MiG 15, inspired wonder (and horror) in American fighter units. There was only one plane on the American side which was up to fighting it: the American F-86 Sabre Jet with its swept-back wings.

Theodore von Kármán related in his book *The Whirl Lane* how America took up the challenge. In it he described in detail how he discovered a secret installation in 1945 at a pine forest near Brunswick, close to the village of Volkerode, which had eluded the secret services. This consisted of 56 buildings, erected below tree-level, which hid research installations for ballistics, aerodynamics and engine technology. Of course he was especially interested in the aerodynamics building. And, sure enough, he discovered on a desk the model of an airplane, 'the like of which we had never seen before. Its wings were swept back, like an arrow head. Georg Schairer [Kármán's companion] was as excited as I was when he saw the model. It heralded a new type of ultra-fast plane.' It had only been a few months earlier that a similar development had been discussed.

As Kármán knew, the Germans had given the order to destroy all documents of predetermined security classifications once they had received a specific code word. Piles of ashes proved that the order had been carried out. He was certain, however, that they had not had enough time to destroy or get rid of everything, and it was highly likely (as with all bureaucratic organisations) that there were duplicates. But where could the plans be hidden? There were literally thousands of hiding-places. Kármán asked the German director Dr Hermann Blenk where, but he said that he did not know.

'I had a sergeant with me who had been assigned from the intelligence service,' Kármán went on to say. 'Frank Tchicherin was of Russian extraction, being related, in fact, to the first Education Minister in the Kerensky government in Russia. As we were going to our car, I said in English (which the director understood): "Listen, Tchicherin, we're finished here. I think we can now tell the Russian Intelligence Service that they can take over." The Russian Intelligence Service was in fact nowhere to be seen. But I knew that the Germans were afraid of Russians and that this would scare them.

'I was right. The next day Blenk rang up Tchicherin and showed him a dried-up well shaft. He looked down it. The shaft was full of papers. Amongst them were descriptions of the swept-back wings and numerous wind-tunnel measurements, which clearly showed that the swept-back wings had superior flight properties at subsonic speeds. These data were the first of their kind. Schairer quickly wrote to his colleagues at Boeing in Seattle, telling them of his find and instructing them to stop work on the Mach-1 aeroplane, which they had designed with straight wings.

'He recorded the material on microfilm and used it on his return to Seattle to design the B-47, the first American bomber with swept-back wings. A footnote stated that "the American F-86 Sabre Jet, deployed in Korea, was also based on documents captured from the Luftwaffe in 1945".'

It is futile to reflect what would have happened if Kármán's suggestion to inform the Russian secret service had not been a ploy but something he had been serious about and intended to carry out. But the Russians really had no need to wait. It is not known exactly where on German soil they came across the same design documents. One thing is certain though – they got their hands on some, and from these plans German designers developed and built in Russia the MiG 15, which found its counterpart in the American F-86 Sabre Jet.

The fact that the American swept-back aeroplane proved to be a match for the MiG 15 ensured that the military balance was still maintained (at least in the eyes of the US military). However, as Kármán mentioned elsewhere, a special unit was immediately formed at the Pentagon for research and development under a Deputy Chief of Staff, a fact which showed 'the importance attached by the airforce to research.' Kármán summed it up by saying: 'It is tragic that the enemy has to prove time and again the value of scientific investigation.'

In the summer of 1954 the German 'specialist' Karl Prestel returned home from the Soviet Union. He went to Augsburg, where he took shelter at his brother's. Before he had properly woken one morning, a man knocked on the door. He identified himself as a member of the American secret service, the CIA. He knew all about Prestel: that the latter, as 'chief designer' (he used the Russian term) had been in charge at the BMW Works at Staßfurt, called OKB 2, and had got the 003 engine running in the shaft complex at the former potash mine in 1946 and, following orders, had given the engine a greater thrust. 'But we didn't reach 1,100 kiloponds, as ordered,' Prestel interjected, 'we only reached 1,000 kiloponds.'

'All the same, that was a 25 per cent increase over the standard version at the end of the war,' the American said. 'Would you be prepared to come to Frankfurt for a fortnight? As our guest?'

'Is that an order?' Prestel asked.

'A request,' said the American politely. 'You'd be doing us a favour like some of your other colleagues.'

Prestel had nothing to hide. He was not too worried, either. He did not hold any secrets, or the Russians would not have let him go to the West. In Frankfurt he came across familiar faces: Dr Scheibe, formerly the head of testing for aero-engine development at Junkers (like Prestel, he had been appointed 'chief designer' at Dessau by the Russians), and Dr Vogts, who had got engine specifications at Junkers back on its feet again (all the documents had been destroyed there, too). At the interrogation, which took place in a relaxed, almost cheerful atmosphere, it seemed doubtful to Prestel whether the 'old news', which he and his colleagues were asked to elaborate on, could have been of any interest to the Americans in 1954. Was not all this history, their talk, for example, of what had been the cause of the constant fracture at the vane foot on the turbines? At full loading, the turbine vanes had become longer and longer, had brushed against the housing and had naturally been damaged. They had discovered that the fault lay in the material (admittedly the Russian experts had precise details of the German material, but not the technology behind its production). Or when they discussed the development of the 3,000-kp engine that had taken up two full years and that, on taking over the Jumo-012 concept, they had found that a combination of the 'ring combustion chamber' (BMW) and the 'single combustion chamber' (Jumo) produced an astonishingly good, smoke-free exhaust? Were any of these details still important? Apparently so. Also, a 6,000-hp propeller engine developed from the Jumo 022 had received specific modifications after it had been cleared for series-production, once it had successfully completed 100 hours run-in on a government-run test. Which modifications were these? The counter-rotating propeller had been replaced by a simple four-blade propeller, the welded housing had been replaced by a cast housing, amongst others. Was this the Kuznetsov NK-4 engine? It certainly was, to be found on the Antonov AN-8 and -10 and the Ilyushin Il 18 transport planes. And the NK 12? We had simply doubled the 022 engine with power output running to a common propeller gearing. Only a thorough understanding of the technology could tackle the vibration faults. The trial carrier had fallen off. As a result an engine was only developed in one unit, with 12,000 hp. This was the NK 12, which was put on the test bed at the beginning of 1953. Was it successful? Well, Nikolai Kuznetsov ran the collective, the best man the Russians had.

Prestel had to smile to himself at all these questions (and the answers he gave). Whenever they gave a new job to the German collective, the Russians had always responded in the spirit of what the Soviet Aviation Minister, Comrade Khrunichev, had said to the head of the collective, Ferdinand Brandner, in Moscow in 1948: 'We know that in technology, everyone does his cooking with water, like the Americans. You don't need to explain everything to the Americans, since they're not going to copy anything from us. All they want to know is which types, and what quantities of each type, we intend to build. But they will never find that out.' In fact Prestel had never found that out either. The only thing he did know was incomplete work, which had not been proven.

During the evenings they talked about more human issues. Prestel recounted how, in 1945, when he was in charge of clearing rubble at Spandau, he had driven to Staßfurt 'out of curiosity', to pick up a few personal effects. A certain Schilo, the director at Spandau, who had previously been at Bramo (The Brandenburg Motor Works), had touchingly dispelled Prestel's fear of being abducted by the Russians. All he had heard was that Dr Oestrich and his people had been taken to Munich by the Americans immediately after Staßfurt had fallen. Presented with the choice of going either to France or to the USA, most of the Oestrich people were said to have chosen France. Only individual components were available from the 003 engine, which the Americans had confiscated and transported away, along with all the design documents. Since German technicians had managed to fit the remainder together (an undertaking with no other purpose than to make themselves popular or, better, indispensable), the fear of possibly being taken to Siberia vanished. The redesigned engine had even been made to run without reference to drawings, there were good rations and the Russians asked for detailed plans as to how the Germans envisaged a complete development works.

'This was naturally the hope amongst the 2,200 men whom we re-employed, including irreplaceable skilled workers. This hope, not least for BMW, was something we attached to our reports. Nobody doubted that the company would be set up in Germany, a plan which took definite shape in our heads in the warm summer evenings when countless ladybirds would bang against the window panes. (The summer of 1946 saw an epidemic of ladybirds, making work impossible if the windows were not closed.) Autumn came, and with it October, and the cooler weather. I had just made the last arrangements for running the large 018 engine ... it was set at 6,000 kiloponds, and we were all finished and happy that we had done it. I went to bed. Then, while it was still dark, at about 4 a.m., somebody called out with an obvious Russian accent: "Get up!" A Russian officer, accompanied by his female interpreter, was standing in my bedroom. I managed to jump out of the window. Russian soldiers were running back and forth below. Our villa (that's right, my wife and I were living palatially in one of the few remaining directors' villas) had been surrounded by soldiers who had forced their way into the house and filled the whole building.

'"My wife stays here!" I shouted.

'"No here. Wife comes with."

'We offered no resistance, no protest. Four weeks later, it was now winter, we arrived at Upravlenchesk Gorodok (which meant something like 'small, self-governing town') on the Volga, 20 km from Kuibysev on Lake Stau. There were 250 technicians from BMW (engineers, designers, skilled workers), about 50 from Askania in Berlin and around 350 "specialists" from Junkers at Dessau, who had been dragged from their beds on the night of 21 October 1946, exactly as we had been at Staßfurt. We then spent eight years on the Volga, until shortly after Stalin's death.'

'And you never came home?' asked one of the Americans.

Prestel did not answer at first. Then he said: 'They constantly asked us what we wanted. They told us that things were good for us there. And that we could go home, by train, by plane, any time we wanted, when Germany was Soviet.'

'And that's what finally happened,' someone jokingly interjected. 'You're back home again.' They laughed.

'I'm not so sure any more. It's like a foreign country,' Prestel said.

He could not explain it any more clearly than that, and did not want to. It was no concern of the Americans. In all the triumph of having survived, he felt a dull pain inside him. Where did this pain come from? He was not a political animal, he was a technician. But he was also a German, and if the disagreement between the victor powers had lead to a West German and an East German state, then he knew where *he* belonged.

A year before, the Germans living in the 'zone' had tried to rebel. He had only just learnt of this. He knew all the squares and streets where they had marched, the large factories from where they had advanced to the centre of Berlin. These were the Henningsdorf Steel Works, Siemens-Plania, the Oberspree Cable Works, Johannisthal, the Oranienburg Rolling Mill, Weißensee, Strausberg, Rüdersdorf, Mahlow and Velten. On leaving Strausberg Square, they had moved along what was now known as Stalinallee (he had lived in the neighbourhood), in the direction of Alexander Square and Leipzig Street, with the Russian tank columns following them. They had taken down the red flag from the Brandenburg Gate. Berlin was burning, this time not because of what fell from the sky. Enforced and conscripted labour, as well as material dissatisfaction, was probably the tinder-box. But then there was a real uprising, an event which showed that political ideals for freedom were still alive and could not be obscured and removed by propaganda.

People's behaviour here seemed all the more incomprehensible to him, with their sense of acquisition directed purely at things material, with their practical understanding which lacked any pride in being German (but 'pride' only approximately expressed what he meant). Was it that the fear of being identified with Hitler was also a curse? Was that the reason they were so efficient? What was it that made them blind to the true reasons for having suffered again as Germans? What was their explanation for thinking that this and their diligence had made them the envy of everyone? Their 'efficiency' had discarded all the calculations, all the predictions as to how long it would take to transform the sea of rubble into a habitable world. It had also thrown out everything which had existed in the way of understanding, concern and warmth towards others. He still remembered very clearly Zero Hour, the feeling of being truly free in the midst of the utter misery which could overtake people. What was left of this freedom? Was this why he had turned down the Russian nationality offered to him? Three times he was asked, three times he said 'no'. And it had grown harder to justify this, to ignore all this goodwill, harder than trying to avoid being sent to Siberia, as was frequently threatened.

The feeling of now being like a beggar at the door (for he had no possessions and had to ask for each and every thing), was one reason. What weighed more heavily upon him was the feeling that, as a technician, he was faced with nothing.

Whatever he and his unfortunate colleagues had been given to provide technical solutions at Upravlenchesk Gorodok (and he had put all his expertise into it, his imagination and his enthusiasm to puzzle over and test what he had created) was never used. The Russians were only interested in *how* what was made was made. They were only interested in the method, not the result. When they had found out how the Germans explained, calculated and designed something, when they saw that there were instruments which could first test the function of individual components before they were put together, when they found out why they had not got this or that to work, and when they then discovered how it was to be operated, that they could do it for themselves, they cancelled all projects and discarded the toil of umpteen years. Once they had done that, they sent the Germans home.

Finally at Sovolovo, a hundred kilometres north of Moscow, where the remaining group to which he belonged had been transferred, they had pursued a project on a civilian aircraft which Professor Baade at Dresden and Pirna in the GDR wanted to realise in a proposed aircraft factory which would have its own engine manufacture. The Austrian Ferdinand Brandner was due to take over engine development, with Prestel in charge of testing, as before. Both turned down the offer. Brandner returned to neutral Austria. Prestel went to the West, because a high East German Party functionary, who wanted to enlist him for Pirna, took pity on him: he had been an apprentice at BMW.

In 1954, in the same year as his homecoming, Prestel was asked to go to BMW at Milbertshofen. He came across Helmut Sachse in the boardroom. They knew each other well, as Sachse had built the command module, which Prestel had helped develop, at his own factory in Kempten in the Allgäu.

'So the old team's back together again,' said Sachse. 'Want to join us?'

'Join you in what, and where?' he asked distrustingly.

'We have founded a research company here, and I'm offering you the job of head of testing.

'Why?'

'Its exact name is the BMW Research Company for Power Plant Production. Don't worry, it's nothing illegal. They're building up the Bundeswehr. There'll also be a Federal Defence Ministry. And an "Office for Defence Technology and Procurement", which, once the clauses lapse, will issue contracts. They plan to order turbo-propeller engines from Daimler-Benz, but they don't seem that keen, so BMW could be in the running. The board has agreed. We are thinking in terms of a small turbine, 50 hp, for driving pumps.'

'Nothing military?'

'Once bitten, twice shy, as they say,' Sachse said.

Then he explained that they would only win back their lost connections to the aviation industry if they could find people here who could develop and carry out production contracts. Initially these would be extremely modest. They would need people with the practical experience (and here he looked cheerfully at Prestel) that Russia had managed to acquire.

'But there you are too late,' Prestel said and told him about his interrogation at Frankfurt. 'As we parted,' he concluded, 'the Americans made it known to us that we late-returners from the Volga had saved them millions, in terms of what they now knew.'

'In addition to the millions which "Paperclip" brought them!' Sachse let slip.

'What was "Paperclip"?'

'That, too, was a kind of deportation, American-style. Some of our people are still over there. They're happy to stay, they've got permanent contracts. Some have even become Americans. But now you're here, Prestel. What do you say to us developing and producing a trainer plane engine?'

421

'Alone?'

'With foreign firms, highly efficient ones, naturally.'

'Who are you thinking of?'

'Rolls Royce, for example. We would manufacture at Allach. The US Army are finally leaving, or will be by the middle of next year. They've already given notice. In addition, a few test beds are still at Works 1 here. Shall we have a look at them?'

'I already have,' Prestel said. 'Before I came up, I had a look around. They'll do for the time being.'

The idea behind the BMW research company had been well thought out. Sitting on the advisory committee, Herr von Mangoldt-Reiboldt and Herr Donath stated that BMW had decided to re-establish the old structure back at the company. In addition to motorcycles and cars, power plants for aircraft were to be built. But there was a catch to it. They said there was a clause listed under the conditions laid down by the Bonn Defence Ministry stating that there must be a strict division between power plant production and the parent company with respect to both administration and finance.

Sachse said that he had foreseen that. Naturally power plant production must be independent, not exactly separate, but . . . Everyone knew that the AG was making losses on big cars, which profits from motorcycles and the Isetta range did not cover. Since the war, the company had not paid a single penny in dividends, which had already prompted many shareholders to get rid of their shares. The result was a loss of confidence. And he did not need to elaborate on what that meant. Admittedly, the car business was not his concern. This was not unconnected with the fact that the mid-range car, which all the world was crying out for, required enormous investment. This would not be generated from rents, like those which the US Army still paid at the time. Where would it come from, then? Once you could see the wood for the trees, it was as plain as daylight.

What was as plain as daylight, asked the gentlemen?

Well, Sachse said, taking money from one big kitty, provided there was still something in it.

He did not stipulate how much that might be, but made it clear that, when someone is up to his neck in water, desire knows no scruples when it comes to falling back on money which had originally been put into the kitty for quite another purpose – put in by the Defence Ministry, by the Economics Ministry, put in by those foreign partners whom he had already enticed into 'power plant production'.

In fact, what Sachse had already achieved was not inconsiderable. It was designed not to reduce desire, but to increase it. The small turbine he had spoken to Prestel about had been developed up to the production stage. An in-house combustion-chamber test bed had been built for open combustion, and test beds at Allach, still available from the days of rocket development, had proved large enough to take an air-supply fitting (comprising two Demag radial compressors) and the test piece. (By the end of 1956, combustion tests were being run with this facility; there was little that needed to be changed.)

422

Contact had also been made with Rolls Royce. Sachse had concluded a deal whereby BMW would be able to carry out maintenance at Allach on the engines of aircraft (purchased in America and Canada) for the new German Luftwaffe. The project with the trainer plane also seemed to be going well. Discussions about it had been held in Bonn. A discussion had impressed itself indelibly on Leibach, who had been present. It took place between the subsequent Chief of Staff of the new Luftwaffe, Air Marshal Johannes Steinhoff, and his advisor, Group Captain Horten. When all the details had been cleared up, Air Marshal Steinhoff said to Horten: 'How fast is the new plane supposed to be?'

'Just under Mach 1,' (meaning just below the sound barrier) Horten said. Then he added: 'Sir, if we can fly at Mach 0.9 or just under 1, wouldn't it be a good idea if we had a trainer plane that could also fly just above the sound barrier?'

'Quite right,' Steinhoff said. 'But you know, Group Captain Horten, once we get to 1.1 or 1.2 Mach, then we might as well go to 1.3 or 1.4.'

Horten replied: 'You are right again, Sir. But if we're flying at 1.3 or 1.4, we might as well go on to 1.6 Mach.'

And so it went on, with the gentlemen reaching Mach 2 (double the speed of sound) within a quarter of an hour. So Sachse was not surprised when he heard that he should submit a tender for a 5-tonne power plant.

There was just one stumbling block − namely that the strict division between BMW AG and BMW Power Plant Production was an irrevocable condition.

And so something happened which might have been desirable had BMW been allowed to keep it. This was its aero-engine production, which now fell offside. The whistle blew for a free kick. But when it came to be taken, there was no one (to keep with the metaphor) to pick the ball up. The players had left the pitch.

How that came about could be explained just as much by human intolerance as by the desperate financial state of the parent company. On the one hand, there was the waning motorcycle and Isetta business with its minimal sales revenue (profits from the big car did not bear thinking about), while on the other, there was a whole new production subsidiary represented by Power Plant Production.

By the end of April 1955, the AG took the first step away from this course, when it decided to sell part of the Allach works: two large production halls, a small power station, business and ancilliary buildings, workers' accommodation and other buildings (520,000 square metres, over half the Allach site). It had been acquired by MAN (Maschinenfabrik Augsburg-Nürnberg AG) for a purchase price of 21.5 million DM. Added to that, there were a further 8,500 square metres, with a third production hall leased to MAN, whereby the latter would erect workshops on BMW land for the new (or revived) BMW Power Plant Production Co. Ltd, as the parent company had no money to do this.

Was this complicated? Not in the least. It was like cutting the Gordian knot. The army had gone, the site was free, but much too big to be used sensibly for in-house production, even in the long term. It would have been quite irresponsible not to have given up parts of the works, which, with no long-term use, would have placed an intolerable burden on the company's financial development.

Sachse saw that as well. But he was far too used to independence to fall into line and be dictated to, a situation which, when BMW appointed a new man to head the company, then endangered, if not completely wrecked, the co-operation which had been started with companies abroad, principally with Rolls Royce. He continued to press for independence, as well as separation which the new managing director Dr Richter-Brohm was to refuse him, just as his predecessors had done. The fact that Richter-Brohm had received a rebuff from the Bavarian Finance Ministry, from which he had sought help when looking for a 20 million DM loan, only confirmed to Sachse which way the wind was blowing. (With regard to auditing, the AG, as the sole owner, categorically refused to put two representatives from the Bavarian provincial government on the supervisory board of Power Plant Production Co. Ltd.) Yet was that the reason why (many years ago) Sachse had given up working at the Reich Aviation Ministry, was that the reason why he had thrown in the director's job at BMW during the war, only now to go under with the AG? What is more, they did not like each other – the 'new man' who was supposed to save BMW (without, in Sachse's opinion, having any idea about BMW), and he, who had done everything to give BMW a basic structure again. His request not to have his contract renewed pre-empted his inevitable dismissal.

Sachse's successor was the Austrian Ferdinand Brandner. He struggled against the contract lying on his desk, because it 'was supposed to bring in something against the large sums of money which my team and I were capable of giving without additional costs, on the basis of our eight years' experience in Russia.'

Brandner's book *A Life between the Fronts* goes on to say:

> Our lobbyist introduced me to the influential people of the Bonn Defence Ministry on the Hardthöhe. At this first and only meeting in the ministry, I explained my standpoint with regard to the draft contract. I was embarrassed at the sharpness with which my refusal was greeted. They put it to me that I should forget my past and my time in Russia and learn to think like a European. Unfortunately at that time I had no notion of either the personal links amongst managers of German aviation or amongst the public offices of the new Federal Republic of Germany. I had completely forgotten that Germany was a defeated country. Old personal relationships were fostered internally, and externally everything was done to comply with what the former enemies now demanded as 'selfless' friends of Germany. As an example of this, aerodynamics had been removed from technology manuals for ten years after the war, to bar entry to young Germans who wanted to go into aviation science. So the FRG became a land of copiers in the aviation world, with large-scale, artificially cultivated free-wheeling in technology and science.

It was in May of 1958 that Brandner was summoned by Dr Richter-Brohm to a management meeting at BMW. Richter-Brohm informed him that he had received a note from the Bavarian Industry Association, to the effect that he could not remain managing director of Power Plant Production Co. Ltd, because he was not a citizen of a NATO country. It included information from the NATO Control Office saying that he consequently had no prospect of obtaining the 'security clearance', and would not be admitted to development discussions at the Office. Therefore, as long as he remained the managing director, BMW would not receive any development work. For these reasons, Dr Richter-Brohm then declared, his position had become untenable, and as sorry as he was . . . The Office had expressed its preference for the qualified engineer Helmut von Zborowski to be his successor, who at the time was negotiating with the Federal Republic over a coleopter project.

'He was, like me,' Brandner later wrote, 'an Austrian.'

The subsequent course of history lead right to that fateful day in December 1959, when the new man, the managing director Dr Richter-Brohm, sat like a defendant on the management panel at the shareholders' meeting and was made responsible for decisions which he had in no way taken. One of the shareholders called out: 'Why did you sell Allach?' And the coal-merchant Nold who, just like Richter-Brohm, would later claim that it was he who had saved BMW, spoke of the 'jewel in the BMW crown', the Power Plant Production Co. Ltd, which had slipped from BMW's hands.

In the Hand of the Banks

The expression 'highest state of alarm', a concept which the Germans had become familiar with during the war, was no less valid for industrial undertakings, when the annual balance sheet showed a considerable deficit. The 1956 balance sheet revealed a deficit of 6.5 million DM for BMW – after the receipt of 4.8 million DM from revenue in rent and assets from the Allach works had been converted into liquid assets, as the company report revealed. This meant a loss in real terms of 11.3 million DM.

As the share capital amounted to all of 30 million DM, this triggered off the 'highest state of alarm'.

But the real figures, which an annual balance sheet does not show, made plain just how things really were for the company. With a loss of 60 million DM up to now from car manufacture (that was 38 per cent of the car turnover achieved up to 1956, meaning that the company had paid out between 4,000 and 5,000 DM on each car delivered!) and interventions on capital assets, whose proceeds had melted like ice in the sun (21.5 million DM from the partial sale of Allach to the Maschinenfabrik Augsburg-Ñurnberg, 14 million DM as revenue from rent at Allach, which the Americans had in the meantime left), would push BMW over the edge, unless a miracle were to happen at the last minute.

We know how difficult it is to change something at the head when the limbs are failing. Who was the head? Without doubt, Dr Hans-Karl von Mangoldt-Reiboldt. Initially taken on by the Allies as the general trustee, the Deutsche Bank had delegated him to head the supervisory board. The supervisory board monitored the management board, and he was equally responsible to all those to whom the company belonged – namely the shareholders. The Deutsche Bank, pooling about half of all BMW shares in their vaults, was probably aware of how valuable Mangoldt-Reiboldt was to them in terms of reputation and connections. He had been the first German to chair an international body, becoming President of the European Payments Union, as well as President of the Directorate of the European Economic Agreement. (As the representative responsible for the Federal government at the European Economics Organisation in Paris, he was involved in all discussions when Europe was on the agenda.) Did he have time for Milbertshofen? Hardly. Dr Robert Frowein, assigned by the bank to act as Mangoldt-Reiboldt's deputy (he was based in Frankfurt), was a man who held other posts, so he did not conduct this as his main business. The only thing Frowein understood was that it was his responsibility to act when there was something that could still be saved.

On a previous occasion, it had been the Deustsche Bank which had directed BMW's fate. At the end of the twenties its director, Dr Emil Georg von Stauss, had helped BMW into car manufacture. On Stauss's behest, and with his bank looking towards a merger with Mercedes (Stauss had a seat there on the supervisory board, as well as at BMW), BMW bought the moribund Eisenach Vehicle Factory and took over the little Dixi (which was soon to prove a stroke of luck).

While history might repeat itself, nothing turns out *quite* the same. There was now neither a Dixi nor a Popp. The latter never lost sight of the fact that dependency encourages greed; he was a man who declined co-operative deals. The result was that there was no merger with the Swabians and no bank dictating to BMW. The fact that the bank, the Deutsche Bank, was controlling and employing new men, need not, however, be seen as a misfortune. It would have been a misfortune if it had held power. Bankers, whose business is determined by risk, are not entrepreneurs. Bankers want to make profits, and businesses to whom they grant loans must flourish – that is what they rightfully come to expect. If a business does not flourish, their patience becomes limited, as does their involvement. If things go downhill for the object of their support, they will try to 'turn it around' – with the help of the shareholders who have to carry part of the losses. As a last resort, it has to be sold off.

But things had not quite got that far. In his determination 'to put BMW back on its feet', Frowein replaced the old management board, with one exception – Heinrich Krafft von Dellmensingen. Donath was given early retirement. (At the end of the party given in his honour, the strain of years showed itself when, sitting on his chair with his face buried in his hands, he wept like a child. The lively Grewenig, taking retirement for the 'sole reason' that he had reached the required age, comforted him.) Grewenig's place as sales manager was taken by Ernst Hof from the Henkel company – but would he be able to sell cars? ('If he finds any cars!' some people mockingly predicted. Later they would say: 'And he travelled from court to court . . .'.) Frowein appointed a man to chair the management board and gave him the select and approved title of 'managing director', a man who had the reputation of having what it took, although he was new to the business. His name was Dr Heinrich Richter-Brohm.

He had tracked him down at Pintsch Bamag AG, a solid family business, which Frowein's man had had to leave because, as the new chairman of the management board, he had wanted to double the share capital immediately and put 'everything on a broader basis'. He had also left Kampnagel AG, a Hamburg engineering firm, on the grounds that there had been friction 'due to restricted freedom of movement'. Before that, he had researched and implemented restructuring operations at smaller companies as a kind of 'trouble-shooter' for South German banks. He had also collaborated on the liquidation of IG Farben, and, shortly after the war, had risen to the lofty heights of managing director at the United Austrian Iron and Steel Works (Vöest AG), a subsidiary of the former Hermann Göring Works – only to be knocked off his pedestal when he was remanded on subsequently unjustified accusations by the state government of violating currency regulations. He was a self-willed, awkward, but nonetheless self-assured man, with undeniable stature, who did not necessarily enjoy the luck of the times. Yet, according to Frowein, he possessed everything which BMW now needed: circumspection, vision, authority, staying power, knowledge of human nature and, above all, the determination to take full measures while quick to renounce any half measures.

The picture he portrayed of himself when he joined BMW corresponded to everyone's expectations. Anyone seeing and working with him might justifiably have believed in reincarnation. Was it not old Franz Josef (God rest his soul) standing there, the very image of Popp? Six foot three inches tall, duelling scars on his face (admittedly, Popp did not have those), his desk always neat and tidy, down to the current document at hand. He had everything worked out, was brief in expression and clear in speech (after all, he was the son of a Prussian officer), and used language lightly peppered with Berlin idioms, not unlike Popp, who liked to remind people where he came from when he used linguistic borrowings from his earlier days in Vienna. Like anyone insisting on the title of managing director (he had stipulated that in his contract), Richter-Brohm was also touchy, even arrogant, 'to the point where he would throw a fit', as thoroughly well-meaning people stated. On top of this, he was fearless. In 1934 he was said to have personally beaten up a Nazi works cell official, and thrown him out of the window because the latter had accused him of having a relationship with a Jewess, and during the war in Prague, where he had run the Bohemian-Moravian Engineering Works, he had thrown the police out of his brightly-lit villa, having his man-servant give the message that the 'managing director does not wish to comply with the blackout'. It was an impressive scene – no blackout (for which there were probably good reasons in war time).

Upon his arrival in Munich, where he met the gentlemen of the management board, which included Herr von Mangoldt-Reiboldt, he said to the latter, whose office was next to Heinrich Krafft von Dellmensingen's: 'Please move out. We can't have two managing directors. You are the chairman of the supervisory board. Your place is not at head office.'

Equally unambiguous was his question when he politely asked what the company planned for the next few years.

'How do you mean?' asked Mangoldt.

'Well, its programme.'

'There is no programme.'

'How come? Do you really think you can manage with the eight-cylinder car and the small Isetta?'

'We have no choice.'

'But surely you must have thought about what you were going to do in the future?'

The only answer they gave was that they had been forced to live from hand to mouth. No programme, no programme. No, this was worse than anything he had expected.

As a newcomer to the business (something he himself disputed as, under his management, the Bohemian-Moravian Engineering Works had primarily built lorries and cars), he went to Turin and there looked around Fiat, where his father, the Prussian general, was well remembered. (Thanks to him, the Reich army's heavy artillery had always procured its tractor engines from Fiat.) Substantial market research, which Fiat had conducted for many years while BMW had basically never contemplated such work, gave him a stark picture of sales prospects inside the international car industry. After that, his mind was made up.

This resulted in his first work, a study covering 133 pages describing how 'the present failures, which have produced the almost desperate financial situation, must be changed from the ground up'. His suggestion for saving the company was a completely new, mid-range BMW car which he conceived as follows: 'A 1,600-cc engine giving 80 hp in the standard version. This will give the car exceptional liveliness (acceleration capacity). As the engine will be designed with an extremely short stroke, its output can be increased without much extra work, should sales prospects open up for that.'

An annual production rate of 24,000 vehicles was planned, with 16,000 being sold at home and 8,000 abroad. Based on production planning, 13,000 vehicles were to be sold at home and 6,400 abroad in 1959. (He calculated that that meant a turnover of 300 million DM and a balance sheet profit of 14 million DM.)

Ambitious words. Richter-Brohm was no less ambitious at the annual general meeting at the end of 1957: 'Finance has been arranged for the new production programme designed to fill the gap between the Isetta and the big car.'

Was this really the case? When Ernst Kämpfer was on a visit to BMW in December 1957, before taking up his post as the new head of finance (he had been brought in by Richter-Brohm), he was told that the mid-range car was at the run-up stage prior to production.

Fate decreed that he should go round the works with a man from Ford, whom Richter-Brohm wanted to employ as technician on the management board (the last technician on the board had just been sent home, leaving them with none!). They looked in vain for a mid-range car; Kämpfer, who had always worked in the industry, had keen ears, and the man from Ford had sharp eyes. What they discovered was . . . precisely nothing! Not a single bolt from a mid-range car! On his return to Richter-Brohm, Kämpfer said he had learnt that procuring tools for a new model would take at least a year. It was not simply a matter of having no tooling – none had been ordered! There was no engine ready, no bodywork, nothing! Richter-Brohm cut him short, saying that he realised this, but everything was now nearing completion. And financing? That had also been dealt with.

Was this the highest state of alarm? Well, Richter-Brohm was not too bothered, he had Frowein as a base, whose word was unwritten law in the banking world. This meant that 35 million DM would be available for the mid-range car, shared out amongst BMW's banks (in addition to the Deutsche Bank, there was the Dresdner Bank and the Bavarian State Bank).

'In Frowein's presence,' as Kämpfer remembered, 'they sat round like well-behaved children at the dinner table. Nobody said anything. Yes, yes, we'll join in! But there were no written records, no binding declarations. That did not matter in Frowein's way of doing business. Only one day in 1958, Frowein went into a flower shop in Hamburg and dropped dead of a heart attack. And then everyone declared: 'We haven't committed ourselves to anything. We refuse to have anything more to do with it, we won't pay a single penny.'

This was followed by the Krages affair. Compared with the hopes and expectations which the wood-merchant from Bremen temporarily stirred up at BMW, as the major private financier, it ended in a miserable fiasco (apart from the fact that a convertible loan for 15 million DM came out of it, guaranteed by Krages, since it could not be handled on the market). Krages resigned, subsequently relinquishing his supervisory board mandate in February 1959. In the same way, every attempt by the 'Prussian' Richter-Brohm, infamous for his arrogance and conceit, failed to obtain that state security from Bavaria which his predecessors had not taken up (with no apparent reason, as it had been offered by the Bavarian state).

We know the reason for Bavaria's refusal to Richter-Brohm, or can surmise it. It was Richter-Brohm who had frustrated the Bavarian request to have two representatives from the province on the advisory council of the Power Plant Production Co. Ltd subsidiary at Allach (and with it, NATO armaments contracts for the Federal Defence Ministry amounting to 300 million marks for the development of jet engines, which the Allach subsidiary was due to receive, on condition that the money flowed into the latter's coffers, and not to the parent company's). If what Richter-Brohm is supposed to have said was true, when he told his friend and patron Frowein about it – 'Why do we need two Bavarians on the advisory council? I've got rid of them' – then no one was surprised.

He had also got rid of the Bavarian plan to put a native Bavarian, the retired director of Shell, Ernst Falkenheim, in the chair of the supervisory board as 'administrateur délégué', with special power of attorney. What was behind that? What was the state trying to do in the free market economy? He, Richter-Brohm, had had enough of state planned economies, being mindful of the time he had been remanded at Linz. 'We shall solve this problem in the private sector!' he pronounced.

But how could this be achieved, now that Frowein was dead? Without Frowein, the supervisory board was just a torso, there was no guiding hand, a role which Richter-Brohm wanted for himself. He now had to negotiate individually with each bank, and each one knew that the financing (scarcely maintained as it was) for Richter-Brohm's promised break-through could only be effective if the required sums of money flowed in at the right time.

'Only this can bring about an improvement in profits within a relatively short space of time,' as the General put it to the general meeting in April

1959. In other words, his 1957 production plan had remained unfinished, with the mid-range car being relegated as a potential *deus ex machina*, although anyone being shown the prototype could scarcely deny that it had consigned everything known about the mid-range to the shadows, no matter which country it came from.

'With its modern flowing lines, in no way reminiscent of the well-known, big BMWs, it has a sports car feel about it, right down to small, useful features. In short, beauty, spaciousness and comfort add to the sportiness of its engine. It is a car one can safely predict will stand a major chance of success,' Heinz Kranz wrote in *Automobil Technik und Sport* in July 1959, firmly convinced 'that not only here, but throughout the world, there will be many thousands of enthusiasts who would jump at the opportunity of a sporting BMW 1600 in the price range below 10,000 DM. With sufficient production it could conform to the usual price considerations on mid-range cars, and yet offer performances way above them.'

What was that supposed to mean, the banks asked? One of their representatives on the supervisory board, Ernst Matthiesen from the Dresdner Bank, relinquished his mandate shortly before the above-mentioned general meeting. Falkenheim also withdrew his consent, to become chairman in place of Mangoldt-Reiboldt. Krages had also left, and the most important point of the general meeting, namely electing the supervisory board, had to be removed from the agenda. When it was already too late, the Deutsche Bank acted and appointed at the official company registry a man from its own management board, Dr Hans Feith, to be the deputy supervisory board chairman (the chair itself had remained empty).

Who still knew his way around? Well, Feith did. There was only one way out for him – abandon illusions (and for him the mid-range project *was* an illusion) and seek a financially powerful group, on which BMW could rely. Where was such a group? First there was Ford (he negotiated, but the negotiations failed), then there was General Electric (he negotiated, but the negotiations failed; at a visit by the president of the company the latter had to wait 25 minutes, which Feith was later to deny). And then there was the British car maker Rootes (who made their interest in purchase conditional on a visit to the Munich works, although this did not actually come about). And finally there was Daimler-Benz, whose director Dr Zahn swooped down on Feith's offer at the very first discussions in the Deutsche Bank building at Frankfurt. And no wonder, since, as a representative of the Deutsche Bank, Feith also sat on the board of Daimler-Benz. The situation was all quite clear to Richter-Brohm.

'Feith just wanted to sell BMW to Daimler from the outset,' he later said. 'For him, there was simply no other alternative.'

According to Richter-Brohm's plans when he joined, the BMW 600, the micro-bus, was supposed to bring in part of the money for the mid-range project. The public had turned it down, and so nothing came of this 'bridging operation'. (In October 1959, production of the 600 was finally stopped, meaning that the 8.9 million marks, which its run-up costs had amounted to, had been spent. But that had not been Richter-Brohm's fault.) However, the situation where no one wanted to buy the unloved vehicle, produced an initiative which itself did not come from the works (and, in fact, could not come from the works).

And so at the great speed with which events were approaching some sort of catharsis, there was a delaying factor. Everyone knows when it occurs – somewhere near the middle of the last act. 'Gentlemen, I have tact. No one dies at the beginning of the fifth act,' the mysterious passenger calls out in Ibsen's *Peer Gynt*, and the play goes on. Whether it just postponed the catastrophe, whether hope of reversing the inexorable course of events was only an illusion, only the possibility that everything might still turn out differently, keeps us enthralled and renews our hope. It is as if we can see the night-darkened landscape lit up by lightning, making everything as clear as daylight. Therein lies the solution.

Was it Krages who promised this? Scarcely had he leapt onto the stage than he withdrew to the wings with his sack of money, which he was afraid of losing, on his shoulder. He also had the feeling that the people were alien to him, as well as the whole issue at stake, which he had always found a little frightening. If he could not double the money in his sack, he would rather stay in wood, which he understood, or (as he in fact did) put it into chemicals.

But another man appeared on the scene. He was not a man with money, and yet he was also no out-and-out fool. Neither was he a prince from the East. Yet he came from Vienna (where feelings were easier, more elegant), and he had ideas to offer. He was an entrepreneur (as far as he could be proved to be such, as the BMW importer for Austria), having been a technician. Both features had produced in him a unique blend of inventiveness, idealism, and enthusiasm for motor sport (he was also a successful racing driver) and an attachment to the project which bound him to BMW and BMW to him. At least he saw further than anybody else, and recognised the point at which the scales could be brought back into balance. He was Wolfgang Denzel.

Working with a small, in-house development group, he had developed a body for a new, small car based on the BMW 600's chassis, which would free the car from its associations with the micro-bus and make it into a genuine vehicle. At the end of March 1958, Richter-Brohm issued the contract, and four months later presented the finished prototype at Lake Starnberg. Kämpfer remembered the event in the following way:

> There was a plot of land on the road to Possenhofen, falling steeply away, and right on the shore of the lake was the car under a tarpaulin. All the people were standing sixty or seventy metres up the slope, and when the tarpaulin was pulled away, everyone was flabbergasted. Nobody had expected what they saw, no one had believed Denzel capable of it. All the technicians could find fault with were a few minor details. The plot of land could not be seen from the road. All the technicians and the sales staff from BMW were there. It was white, on a green lawn; a fine car, a real blessing after the 600! The fact that this blessing came from outside (and not from within) certainly had something to do with the famous wood which could

not be seen for the trees. But it also had to do with the fact that a mid-range car had been planned with everyone's thoughts centred on it. No one had thought of a small car, certainly not by further developing the unfortunate 600, which Black, the technical member of the management board, still thought of as the last word, and planned to build in huge numbers. But now there was this. It had been Denzel's idea to make a proper car with only minimal expenditure on the micro-bus, with the idea behind it of making up for lost time with this (little) car, and so make the money to bring out the mid-range car, come what may, if at all possible by the firm's own means, a car whose manufacture had been stopped by the banks.

To justify their position, the development department later (in 1960) tried to prove that, after all attempts to enlarge the Isetta had failed in 1955, it had designed and drawn up a four-seater car 'with a transverse, water-cooled, rear-mounted, 4-cylinder engine in a body compatible with the latest design'. The management board had approved this model in the summer of 1956, but had then decided on the lengthened Isetta, which appeared under the name BMW 600. However, it was admitted that Denzel in Vienna had been issued ('due to existing connections both with Herr Michelotti as well as the Italian body-builders Vignale') with the contract by the chairman of the BMW management board (meaning Richter-Brohm) 'to draw up the first prototype for a small car of the 700 class with a conventional body shape. According to a memorandum signed by Fiedler, Wolff, Böning, von Falkenhausen and Hofmeister: 'As documents for building this model, Herr Denzel was supplied with design drawings for the body shape, as well as all the parts and components to be adapted from the BMW 600 in the form of drawings (see appendix: design sketch of 7 November 1957).'

This was followed by the remark that 'due to the dimensions laid down in this sketch specifically to establish body height, this vehicle had already been planned with a monocoque body'.

The sketch showed the outlines of a vehicle which was strikingly similar to the Denzel coupé – or vice versa, which begged the question as to whether Denzel had simply carried out the company's requirements. So it did not make much sense that everybody was so dumbfounded at the presentation on Lake Starnberg. ('Nobody would have thought Denzel capable of it . . .'.) And had not the monocoque body, whose fitting Denzel had been most proud of, also belonged to the design contract, borne out by the sketch?

Something was not quite right there. When I asked Denzel about this, he smiled benignly.

'In the end,' he said, 'was I responsible for the sketch? I don't want to accuse anyone of forgery, only . . . it wasn't like that. The coupé and the limousine were developed in Vienna. Why was that? Well, because Richter-Brohm used to turn up there every Friday evening or Saturday morning – at Wattmann Lane, sometimes, too, on my yacht in San Remo, looking for advice and relaxation, and I had a certain influence on him. That was understandable, because here our Viennese design team worked efficiently, productively and quickly on new, unconventional ideas, while over there there was a 'court clique' with all its squabbles, which made his life difficult. On top of that, there was this Black, who was later suddenly to disappear.

'Damn it, Denzel,' he complained, 'what am I supposed to do? Everyone just designs for himself, what he wants to design. And everyone thinks that he can do that just because he believes this Richter-Brohm knows nothing about cars.'

'I regularly advised him to hold development discussions with him in the chair, to give direction which had been missing up to now, and would continue so if he did not give it. He knew how far I was involved in it . . . BMW was his, as well as my, future. As an importer, I had nothing, only BMW, and when the firm was still struggling, I had been sent to see Maxie Hoffmann in the USA, to make connections with certain Jewish-American banking circles. But Hoffmann kicked me out, and did not once invite me out to lunch. (Two years later he rang me up in Vienna: 'I'll offer you such and such amount of money, if you can reacquire the BMW franchise for me!' And a year later, when he didn't reacquire it, he wanted to initiate proceedings against BMW.)

'I also negotiated in Detroit and New York with, amongst others, American Motors. But Roy Chapin, their vice-president, was a ditherer; at first he didn't want something, then he did. When he came to Munich (we sat in the park opposite the bombed-out War Ministry, it was a summer's evening, and I shall never forget it), I laid down this condition: "All right, provided you don't spoil the essence and design guidelines at BMW (I was principally thinking of the monocoque body). You must stick to that!"

'Chapin shook his head, and even now, when things had got as far as they had, he again refused. (If he had agreed, he would not have done that badly out of it, by today's standards.)

'But that was all behind me. Time and again I had drummed my plan into Richter-Brohm – first to build the small car, and then with the money it would bring in, build the mid-range car and completely give up the 600 (of which Herr Black wanted to build 400,000). Even the 60,000 which had been built by then were too many. That was until one day Richter-Brohm was on my yacht, wanting to sail to Corsica and throwing the rope off while I stood on land. That was when I got the idea in my head, I'd even brought my Italian designer from Turin to stay with me . . . I called out: 'You can't go sailing now, doctor, just because you've decided there's no work for us!'

'Then he called back: 'Do what you like!'

'And, although he couldn't hear me any more, I shouted after him: 'Thanks for the contract!'

'That, and nothing else, marked the beginnings of the 700.'

Full of enthusiasm at what had come out of the 600 chassis fitted with a trailing-arm rear axle, Schleicher had then immediately put in an application to have the car built. This was while he was still on the shore of Lake Starnberg.

'Yes, while still on the shore of the lake, the management board took its decision to build. Minutes were drawn up, containing the clause which stated that no one was allowed to change even the smallest detail on this design.

Then all the interested parties stepped up and signed (even Hofmeister, my main opponent in the 'clique'), and I received, as if selling a horse, a contract and money. Until then I had been working completely off my own bat, preparing for the possibility that this or that might be criticised, and that perhaps both prototypes might even be turned down flat. Working alone meant putting the last few pennies we had in Vienna into a project which Richter-Brohm could have said at any time that he wanted nothing to do with.'

Relieved, Denzel went to Turin and, as agreed, ordered all the moulds, cut-outs, panel and wooden models for the prototype. It was quicker to have them produced there than anywhere else in the world. He arranged transport, paid for everything, including customs documents and road haulage, and took off for the sea, alone once again after so much sweat, worry and stress.

A radio message a few weeks later off the Algerian coast shattered all his dreams. From the next port, he rang Munich to find out why he had been asked to call them. Kämpfer informed him that the models had not arrived, everything was held up, every day was costing money, and delays in production were inevitable. Denzel immediately broke off his journey, and discovered in Vienna that Fiedler (no less) had declared to his chief engineer Hubert Stroinigg that the models should stay where they were, as BMW no longer needed them. Was it some misunderstanding? Or, as Denzel suspected, a plot by Hofmeister wanting to gain time to push through a rival model he had developed? (Denzel had seen it in Munich as a plaster cast, a cross between a Goggomobil and a 600, after it had been inspected and rejected by the board.) Whatever the reason, three precious months had been wasted – three months which could have put the car on the market earlier to prove its sales potential.

Much depended on it. No one would have doubted BMW's future, no one would have been able to spread tidings of imminent bankruptcy to the shareholders. Faced with this, they would have been prepared to accept Flick's ultimatum and let themselves be talked into believing that their firm was on the line.

Then, by September, the BMW 700 coupé started to roll off the same production lines from which the 503 and 507 prestige models had done six months earlier. Michelotti had given it its finishing touches, with both the press and public cheering and celebrating it 'as the most sporting and fastest of the small cars currently offered on the German market'.

Only the initiated knew that a supervisory board meeting had had to be interrupted three times to give the representatives time to negotiate with their head offices over the 2 million marks needed to introduce series production. Then finally, the head of the Deutsche Bank, no less, Herr Abs, gave instructions for the loan to be made without any form of security.

'What the polo pony is to horses, the BMW 700 is to cars!' was the judgement of a Munich newspaper. At the 39th International Motor Show at Frankfurt on 17 September 1959, where both the coupé and the saloon were presented, orders poured in – 15,000 cars from the home market, 10,000 alone from the USA.

The home market demand was centred on the small 700 saloon. It cost 4,900 DM (the coupé cost 5,200 DM) and bore the unmistakable features, as did the coupé, of Michelotti's design and Denzel's hallmark on the body, as before. And yet, things were different. Usually, a four-seater was built first and then, in order to raise its status, the much more expensive coupé. This time it was the other way round. The four-seater had, so to speak, been 'back-developed' from the coupé – for the family.

Schleicher had given the signal for this on Lake Starnberg. When speaking up for the Denzel design, he had noted only one fault, namely that there was only enough room for two people, and perhaps a dog in the back. A short time later, Helmut-Werner Bönsch, famous as a trade writer and technician especially concerned with motorcycle manufacture (he also ran a freelance engineering and consultancy office at Altbach on the Neckar) joined BMW. Struck by the despondency and uncertainty which he found at the works, he quickly pushed through some radical changes and (as is vital in a car factory) demanded independent checks. Naturally, design had to be checked by testing, and naturally series-testing had to be able to confirm or reject the results from the test department. Naturally, new items of information, which arose through differences in manufacture, needed to be incorporated. None of this occurred. Instead, unproductive, costly parallel work was the rule, from design right down to sales. Exchange of information, obviously the first requirement for any success was unheard of, and made any sensible course of work impossible. This even affected the supply industry, which received separate, contradictory orders from one department to the next.

Bönsch was no Hercules, who could immediately grab the malaise by the root and tear it out. But when the Denzel coupé burst onto the scene in the middle of his reform plans, encouraging everyone to think that this car would be their salvation, he demanded (or Richter-Brohm suggested this in a document) that a saloon should be built mirroring the coupé. Only the saloon would be capable of converting customer enthusiasm about a vehicle (which was finally up to BMW standards again) into the willingness to buy a practical utility car. And so Hofmeister got to work (at the time when Denzel was cruising off Algeria) and built, in less than three months, a saloon which was then to stand at the Motor Show next to Denzel's coupé, unchanged down to the smallest details. Michelotti had also been won over to design the body for it. By virtue of its air-cooled, horizontally-opposed engine of 700 cc developing 30 hp, thanks to its exemplary road-holding, its monocoque body with frameless doors (until now a feature only reserved for luxury cars), it proved to be a real favourite, next to the coupé with its two carburettors and 40 hp, and brought back that bond between customer and vehicle which the company had not had since the war.

But what did that count for a few weeks later? At the beginning of December 1959, the management board of Daimler-Benz AG at Stuttgart-Untertürkheim sent out a circular to its 63,000 employees which revealed a completely new situation:

In the last few weeks, an opportunity has arisen from outside which had to be subjected to conscientious examination. Over the last few days, you will have followed how the Bavarian Motor Works AG (BMW) has been trying to find its way out of its protracted crisis. In the last few months, it has become clear that this business is no longer in a position to gain a firm footing by its own means. In economic circles and amongst the public in general, the view has found favour over quite a long period that a link between the famous Bavarian car company to Daimler-Benz AG could provide a way out. As BMW and the Bavarian state turned to us for co-operation in restructuring the Bavarian Motor Works AG, the supervisory and management boards could not keep this fact hidden from our company.

Such assistance in restructuring would enable our company to make use of the free capacity of the Bavarian Motor Works AG for our benefit, and thereby fully employ the workforce, which amounts to about 6,000 employees. We could thus reduce our delivery deadlines in the most economical way after an appropriate run-in period. The general meeting of the Bavarian Motor Works AG taking place on 9 December 1959 has still to approve the restructuring plan which is known to you through the press.

Here it was on paper, for all the world to see, that BMW was facing bankruptcy. The solutions imposed upon the owners (meaning BMW's shareholders) were either to agree to a restructuring programme (given in the form of an ultimatum), which amounted to selling the firm, or to declare bankruptcy, which amounted to losing all their investments. If, however, Mercedes were to take pity on the Bavarian company, then it would certainly not be for reasons of maintaining the famous name. To put it frankly, BMW was much more likely to become a parts supplier for the big brother in Stuttgart, whose production capacity, on its own admission, 'was no longer sufficient to fulfil the growing interest of the market in our vehicles'.

By 'production capacity', the layman might think of machine halls, workshops and production lines. But Daimler-Benz mainly thought of personnel no longer being available in Swabia. They had delivery deadlines of between twelve and eighteen months and were faced with the problem of who and where to build the 180 and 190 types to meet demand. At Milbertshofen there was not only unused factory space, but also 6,000 skilled workers (now worried about keeping their jobs), all to be grabbed in one go. The cost of this was worked out by one alarmed shareholder and immediately put before BMW's management and supervisory board. He wrote that 'in the capital-intensive car industry, every position has a value of 20,000 DM. This alone justifies a rate of 400 per cent, based on the invested value, and if Daimler-Benz includes the installations created by the shareholders' capital, along with the invaluable core staff (given full employment) in its production expansion, then installations and core staff are worth considerably more.'

Had Feith overlooked this, he who had greeted Daimler-Benz as a saviour? On the restructuring balance sheet presented, there was no mention at all of this figure, and if valuations were made, they were derisory. The forty-five current patents and sixty-one patents pending registered by BMW were valued at just one mark!

Another shareholder asked how this could be justified. His answer was that there was little justification in the statement that Flick could put the investments needed to acquire BMW into building a whole new factory.

'Was that supposed to frighten us, as if issued by the German Association for the Protection of Bond Holders?' he wrote imploringly to the BMW management board as late as 4 December, five days before the general meeting.

'It is, of course, possible to build production facilities of corresponding dimensions with a lot of money, just as it is possible to acquire the most modern and productive machines, etc., etc. However, it is not possible to acquire, with nothing other than money (not even a lot of money), the core staff needed for these halls.'

Psychologically, this shareholder, who happened to be employed in the wood business, did not see any difference between creeping around a rail waggon full of boards valued at between 5,000 and 6,000 DM (which he would gladly have had) at an Upper Bavarian sawmill, and a giant business creeping round a giant object. 'In both cases, all possible efforts will be made to hide the fact that this object is desperately wanted, because otherwise the price would be driven upwards.'

And so this is what happened. If Feith, the eager champion of restructuring through Daimler-Benz, was negotiating with other 'partners' and continued to negotiate, he knew better than anyone else what everyone was gambling on – 'time', so that they could acquire the object of their desire still cheaper than had already been offered, at a time when the latter's owner was up to his neck in water.

Now Daimler-Benz, the most reliable partner and a German one to boot, had received acceptance of its bid – for a 100-million DM contract, which was immediately to be placed with the company at Milbertshofen. That was not all, Feith said. There was also a guarantee to pay a 6 per cent dividend over three years, along with a cut in the share capital by 2:1, meaning that each share valued nominally at 1,000 DM would, from then on, only be worth 500 DM! It was a question of sink or swim. The shareholder had to bear the loss. On top of that (the root cause of the indignation), there was no legal recourse to an option on new shares. These were taken over by a bank consortium, together with Daimler-Benz, which included the right of pre-emption for the new boss.

'The skat hand has been bid up to the limit. The game will end either in a *null ouvert* or a *grand with fours*,' Feith said to the press when he announced his plan to restructure the company.

But this was before the suspicion could gain ground that Feith might have put forward his proposal to save BMW, not for the good or bad of the company (whose supervisory board he chaired), but for selfish or even outside interests. Neither did it take account of an ultimatum by which the shareholders were supposed to agree a reduction in BMW's share capital from 30 to 15 million marks without an increase levied through the issue of new shares. It also ignored the dubious aspects of what was without doubt a questionable restructuring. Faced with Hamlet's question of '*to be or not to be*' (at a time when economic and industrial life had merged into a state which had long been called the German economic miracle), all those involved had to reflect carefully on what they wanted to say to their shareholders at the general meeting summoned for 9 December 1959.

If they were to conceal anything, put a new interpretation on events, or give the merest hint that those sitting up on the panel regarded the rights of small shareholders as having no value and those of the banks and big shareholders as having every value, there would have been an outcry, the like of which economic history had never seen in the post-war period.

So everyone awaited the day in tense expectation, including a number of directors from Daimler-Benz who, along with their colleagues, had taken over some suites in Munich hotels the night before. They were finally to take control within twenty-four hours. And after twenty-four hours the ultimatum issued to BMW for Daimler-Benz to restructure the company would expire.

A Day in the Life of BMW AG: 9 December 1959

Snow was falling, the head on the Bavaria statue on the Munich Theresienhöhe was already white, and care was needed as the snow was beginning to turn to slush on the road surface. Everyone approaching the Little Congress Hall at Exhibition Park had his own thoughts. The time had come to divide humanity into two groups – the losers and the winners. This meant two camps, determined by fate to be one or the other. That was the way things had always been, and today was no different. The losers would lose, the winners would win; the former had to bow submissively to it, the latter were only to keep up appearances that nothing yet had been decided and that the last word had not yet been spoken. And so people streamed in through the glass doors, well aware of which side they belonged to. The losers were in the majority (small shareholders, dealers, company employees), while the winners were a small clique which as far as possible wanted to remain anonymous. They were bank representatives, proxies from major shareholders, even the shareholders themselves, and advising lawyers. The former were sceptical to the point of despondency, wondering what they were really doing there. The latter were eagerly expectant to the point of high spirits, ready to be conciliatory if it came to negotiating unimportant procedures. There was a willingness not to stand out as obvious victors in the arena.

The hall filled up slowly, stewards ticked off names and the investments they had. They directed people to the right and to the left; there was no seating order. Only the press, raised up on one side, had preferential seats, from which they could work out who 'recognised' whom. These included a BMW director who recognised a man from Daimler-Benz, whom he had met in the works the day before; there was a brief greeting. Then a representative of the 'Association for the Protection of Bond Holders' recognised a long-standing shareholder who had transferred his voting rights to him (they whispered a few words to each other). Then a BMW dealer recognised a dealer from the other side. They waved to each other, saying: 'Naturally, everything will stay just as it was!' But who really believed that?

There were two tables on a kind of stage, one covered with a green cloth, and the other with a black cloth. Behind them were eight empty chairs, a scene which some of the men who were to sit on these chairs might have found eerie. Despite that, it looked like any other general meeting. Nothing suggested that anything could take place other than what was planned, or that there was any tension in the air. Nothing suggested that the losers, although the die had been cast long ago, might succeed in turning on its head everything they had previously grown accustomed to, exercised and experienced. Others had decided to give validity to the Morgenstern dictum of what must not be, cannot be. They were to do this by stubbornly trusting the voting machinery whose cogs were merciless in their crushing of all emotions. They believed that the meeting would break up no later than the early afternoon, and that the evening papers would report what the article writers, certain of the outcome, had already written the previous evening; namely that the general meeting had followed the proposals made by the boards, apart from insignificant opposition from a few minor shareholders who had refused to understand that it was *they* who would have to foot the bill.

Two men, who had met each other in the foyer half an hour before the meeting started, were also of the same opinion. One of them, a coal-merchant from Darmstadt called Erich Nold, had been the only shareholder to register public opposition, and the other, a man in a brown suit who had a more youthful appearance than his age would suggest, was a lawyer, who had come from Frankfurt with a mandate from the BMW dealers. His name was Dr Friedrich Mathern. Both knew each other (Nold had once engaged Mathern on some property business), and both said: 'Fancy meeting you here!' The former was happy to have a comrade-in-arms in Mathern, who had a good reputation as a lawyer. The latter was far from displeased, and nowhere as surprised as his exclamation might have suggested. Nold never missed a general meeting at a larger company. He was both famous and infamous, notorious as a 'provocateur', an 'instigator', even a 'rabble-rouser', when he felt that necessary. As a result, he was feared. He was treated as a professional opponent (which he was not at all), and did not mind a bit of fun now and again. He was, at any rate, skilled in putting life back into sterile balance sheet figures.

He was quick to admit that this time he had not come to Mathern to save anything, but (in anticipation of the programmed demise that had been decided with the certainty of an 'amen') 'to tell it to them again'. By them he meant principally the Deutsche Bank, whom he felt shouldered full responsibility. As he now represented a range of shareholders, they had at least the right to speak their minds frankly, even if, as their last hope, he had to disappoint them. That was why he was here.

Mathern was familiar with Nold's story. The reason why Nold frequented general meetings and asked awkward questions could be traced back to a long-standing grudge. Nold's father had owned over 100,000 DM-worth of BMW shares, which the banks had sold at a rate of 35 per cent after his death in 1946. This was how the young Nold had learnt about fear, so that he could put the fear of God into others. His creed was that shareholders are co-owners, board members are only company employees and, as a result, shareholders' employees. Yet how did they react to this? The fact that they were monitored by the supervisory board had no effect (according to the

Share Act of 1937 based on the Führer principle and still in force) on the situation, where they established rates for the capital administered by them (i.e. the dividends) at their discretion, and could refuse the shareholders any insight into the company's revenue and could interpret any rights granted to the shareholders by the Share Act so that they met their own interests. Nold had found out that the shareholder, who was allowed to enquire about the success of his business once a year at the general meeting, had a practically unlimited right of information, which no one could take from him. This was in spite of the practice adopted by administrations to draft the agenda as briefly and as vaguely as possible. So, by asking his questions, he had become the bugbear of large public companies. If he ever once queried directors' fees and saw one of the high and mighty laugh conspicuously when driven into a corner, he would say:

'If you want to laugh, go to the cinema! You are here to answer my questions. If you don't, I shall get the law to force you!'

This would make the big man do what Nold demanded, leaving the public with mouths agape.

Erich Nold was certainly no grumbler. But was he to be taken seriously? Mathern listened in amusement to what he had on his mind. Nold told him about how on the previous evening, while staying at the Catholic Hospice (all hotels in Munich were fully booked) with a share adjuster friend of his, who was himself a BMW shareholder, he had found a bible on his bedside table. And then something extraordinary happened. Although he was not a religious man, not a church-goer, he had picked up this bible and prayed aloud.

'What did you pray for?' asked Mathern.

'Well, quite simply, that God would let the miracle happen and save BMW.'

Mathern's jaw almost dropped. 'And did you ask him how?' he said.

Unperturbed, Nold continued and said that he had subsequently spent a quiet night, and had repeated the prayer on waking up. Then he had gone to Theresienhöhe with his companion, Dr Josef Kübel, early enough to have a look at the list of those due to attend. Only reluctantly was he given this, and only after threatening to make a fuss if he were refused. All the illustrious names he read there had both encouraged him and discouraged him. The 'Protective Association' which swore by the Deutsche Bank and, as a result (despite all its misgivings), by restructuring, was represented by 3 million votes. Then the thought had come to him that he had to 'turn them around' – and now here, like a blessing from heaven, was Dr Mathern standing in front of him.

What was Mathern supposed to say? Was he supposed to say that he was here in the name of the dealer network, just to voice protests, however ineffectively. The matter should not be allowed to pass off without trace. Admittedly he had no voting slip and so no right to speak (dealers dealt in cars, not shares), and in order to get onto the list of speakers he would need at least one proxy share. So he would just have to stay silent and do without the funeral oration. Nold immediately said that he could help. He had enough votes to provide speaking rights, even if not enough to force an adjournment.

'Here you are!' he said.

Mather gratefully accepted the voting slips which Nold handed to him. He was amazed to hear that the coal-merchant himself only possessed 1,100 DM-worth of shares, and that, because he had proposed to show opposition, trusting shareholders had transferred voting rights equating to around 800,000 DM to him.

'A nominal 800,000,' said Mathern, and Nold added that there were some more held in strong-rooms at the banks. In total, that made 3 million!

'Good to know that,' Mathern said. 'But even that won't go very far. There is nothing we can do to change it.'

At that moment, as Nold was later to relate, as the subject turned towards saving BMW (something he often liked to talk about), an idea came to him from God as a result of his prayer of the night before and, again, of immediately on waking up on that morning of 9 December. The idea was to supply Mathern not only with voting rights so that he could speak, but also to make an offer which would render the decisive point in the agenda (and with it the restructuring) superfluous, and make an adjournment unavoidable. If the Protective Association were then to see that things were going quite differently, it would turn around and oppose merger with Daimler-Benz. So he suggested to Mathern that the latter, as the dealers' representative, might like to ring up the company of Gutehoffhungshütte at Oberhausen right away – to which, as everyone knew, MAN (Maschinenfabrik Augsburg-Nürnberg) belonged. The latter, already owning part of Allach, had its eye on BMW Power Plant Production, and was prepared to buy this 'jewel in the crown' – at a considerably higher price than had already been offered. The managing director at Oberhausen was Hermann Reusch, an opponent of Flick and consequently against the Daimler-Benz offer. If there were a successful attempt to get a new bid from Oberhausen and Augsburg (which was highly likely, given the fact that Power Plant Production had had the commitment confirmed from the Federal Defence Ministry for 300 million DM-worth of Starfighter orders), and if the news arrived while speeches were being made, then this alone would be enough to save BMW.

Erich Nold wanted to do his bit, as well, and put on his jester's cap and bells to hold up the meeting until the new offer was on the table. He was confident he could talk the hind legs off a donkey. Accustomed as he was to heckling, he would paralyse supervisory and management boards (by reading out letters, shouting until he was hoarse, without quite going as far as to get himself thrown out) – in short, he would organise such a spectacle that Mathern would have enough time to act behind the scenes.

Nold's 'rescue operation' went according to plan, as he later admitted. He had tacked together a little book and had given it to Mathern, 'just in case they didn't succeed'. It was his commentary on the rights of shareholders, which he always carried around with him. In this commentary, he had underlined every paragraph which referred to strong possibilities for contesting the balance sheet, in case the latter were to prove incorrect, which he thought it was here. Then he entered the room while Mathern was on the telephone.

Was this what actually happened? Any chronicler would find it difficult to dismiss evidence as pure fantasy. But equally he should not use it as an unconditional basis for his reconstruction of a day which was to decide so much. So he had to ask himself whether, if he had been there himself, he would have recognised the truth in the battle of wits which occurred so quickly. On one side was an unmanageable opponent, who seemed hell bent on raising the temperature of the meeting to boiling point, and on the other was an administration making a great effort to justify what it thought was legally right, and yet had no answers to the dilemma as it claimed. In between, there were excited people applauding and calling for the public prosecutor to 'withdraw the motion!' (one turned to Richter-Brohm and shouted: 'Stand up, you scoundrel, if you want to speak to us!'). Anyone at the end of the day who suspected, after twelve and a half hours of a general meeting (which was usually over after one or two hours) that this had been stage-managed might be forgiven for thinking so. But it seemed equally impossible that anyone could have directed an event like this.

Only Mathern could have done. He had stayed silent three or four hours, in constant contact with the dealers who supported his position, who confirmed to him that things were not over for BMW yet. Three days earlier, he had flown to London on their behalf, and there had negotiated with the Rootes company. He had established links with American Motors, and had again spoken to Ford, where, in their attempt to acquire a greater share of the German market, they had only been interested in a mid-range car and in the purchase of Milbertshofen as a place to produce it. He had also gone into the idea of scraping together all the dealers' money, along with dealers' banks and savings accounts, in order, so to speak, to keep the company as a family business, and head off any outside influence. He thought this had some promise, but rejected the notion of dealers as owners. That was no basis for the company. But if this 700 which Denzel had brought from Vienna continued to go down well (there was nothing to suggest it would not), then he could. . . .

Having looked at it from all sides, Mathern felt more and more strongly that this 700 could bridge the financial gap to the mid-range car. It was more than just clutching at straws. This idea finally matured into a plan headed by Mathern at the Aschauer Post, where the dealer opposition was in permanent session. It would be absurd to imply that he had stage-managed popular anger like a demagogue, that he had stage-managed a scene which was threatening to disintegrate into chaos, just so that he could roll out his rescue package in a high and mighty way. That was not in his character, on all accounts, not the way he did things. It was not Mathern's style to inspire fear, just so that he could achieve certain objectives. It was equally inconceivable that he had let himself be guided by Erich Nold, whose voting cards had enabled him to ask leave to speak.

This is what Nold might like to have believed, given the way things transpired. Mathern, who died in 1968, never gave away any clues. Nobody can deny the fact (the minutes show it) that Nold, then at the age of 31 and in full possession of his faculties, chose to play the role of the jester. But Nold's tomfoolery alone was not enough. He and Mathern must have sensed

444

this immediately. It was to set in motion a dialogue of cautious rejection and indignant refusal.

What was at stake was the BMW make, nothing less than its value, and that this value received no mention in either the restructuring proposals or in its justification by the supervisory and management boards. The stated book value, the announcement that half the share capital had been lost (given that the available visible and hidden reserves had been used up to compensate for the loss in the past few years), could not indicate what 5,500 skilled workers were worth, nor what BMW had meant to its shareholders for many years, in the war years and the post-war years. This had been a kind of gold standard, considered as safe as Fort Knox.

Come what may, BMW shares were never called into question. They had resolutely kept their rate. It was clear from the many letters which deed holders had written to Nold so that they could transfer their voting shares (Erich Nold read them out one by one as resolutely as a rock amongst the breakers) why the BMW shareholders had forgone any dividend for years, without so much as batting an eyelid or raising a murmur. They clung with unbounded trust to 'their' firm. And if the banks, as had first happened in July 1959, warned of purchase of BMW shares, then they viewed this more as an indication of the consolidation of the AG, rather than its winding-up and dissolution.

A general meeting had never passed off as smoothly and unproblematically as the one of the previous summer, which had closed the financial year of 1957. In one and a half hours, after a blunt portrayal of the situation by the management board, the shareholders had issued 'approval' (certainly at the balanced result), and that was that. (A supervisory board meeting at the Süddeutsche Bank the night before had gone over the question till midnight without coming up with an answer to the question as to what they should do if the shareholders rebelled.) It was unbelievable the way no one protested, and how everyone showed reason and understanding. And the rate kept up. By the middle of August, people were paying 188 per cent, a few days later, between 250 and 300 per cent for a BMW share, and on 24 August, its rate had been established at 400 per cent. Then it fell back to between 350 and 270 per cent.

The banks again recommended disposing of the securities 'at such favourable conditions', since consideration had to be given to the possibility of the share capital being consolidated. But still there were new buyers. (Were they really new?) None of the drastic consequences people were warned of occurred – such as a reduction in capital and a subsequent increase in capital, with no legal recourse to an option on new shares. No scare words such as 'cold expropriation', 'disregard for shareholders' rights', 'empire-building' had effected any change in the impending decision on restructuring as it was now presented. When there was talk of BMW shares, the image conjured up was of sturdy men in coarse woollen jackets keeping possession of their shares and storing them in the wardrobe, since they felt that was a more secure place for them than any safe. If it had been appropriate to decorate the congress hall with banners, as political parties are wont to do, then a kind of 'confession of faith' would certainly have made itself known, if it had been up to the shareholders. 'Joe the Ox', or Dr Josef Müller, the CDU member of the Bavarian Parliament, had once referred to it. He said:

'I believe that the Wittelsbachs will always remain the highest authority in this land; Munich will always have the reputation of a city of art; and BMW shares will always be traded over the odds, regardless of what happens.'

Despite all the mistakes committed, it is understandable that an administration might feel that the company could no longer be kept afloat through its own means and would have to be restructured. However, the fact that with a share capital reduced by a half and simultaneously increased by 70 million marks, the shareholders had no legal recourse to an option on new shares, which were to be awarded just to the chosen strong man of German car companies, Daimler-Benz AG, appeared to those concerned as treason. No, it was more than that – it was fraud.

A man asked to speak. He was a small shareholder called Backmann.

'Herr Richter,' he said, speaking into the microphone, 'you will hear no fine words from me – just plain speaking. May the Lord protect me from my friends.' He bowed at the table with the members of the supervisory board. 'I can protect myself from my enemies.'

Then he set his sights on Richter-Brohm again.

'There was once a fitter from America,' he said, 'who opened a car company at Dingolfing. Take a look at the company. And what have you produced? I would be ashamed if I met this fitter. Let's admit it, we need the public prosecutor. Yes, that's the only answer.'

The man who should have been ashamed of himself, Dr Heinrich Richter-Brohm, did not change his expression as he gazed into the seething cauldron that the general meeting had now become. Whose fault was it, his? Everyone in the room knew which side they stood on and that, according to the statutes, he was obliged to represent the decisions of the supervisory board, and that he was not allowed to oppose it.

'Ladies and gentlemen,' he asked, 'would you have shown any understanding if my colleagues and I had abandoned ship at the time? The company's situation would have got into deeper water without leadership of any kind.'

And he enlisted support by saying that, however bitter it might have seemed to all the shareholders that day, if they were initially to suffer a loss in the nominal value of their possessions through the rescue process (by Daimler-Benz AG), then the strength and reputation of this partner and its immediate willingness to help out with both money and orders, justified the assumption that their BMW shares would acquire a value in the not too distant future which would compensate for today's loss.

'Let's hope so,' a heckler shouted to Richter-Brohm. And he looked at those responsible for the debâcle, looked at the supervisory board table. The person responsible started to speak.

'The chairman of the management board has just given you an overview of the Bavarian Motor Works's past . . .'

'Who do you think you are?' the heckler interrupted. 'What's your fine name, then?'

'My name is Feith,' said the addressee. 'I am the chairman of the supervisory board at the Bavarian Motor Works. I was appointed supervisory board member by the Munich company registrar. I am also a management board member at the Deutsche Bank.'

For a moment it went as quiet as a church. Was that because people already knew that the Deutsche Bank also represented Daimler-Benz and that it had a seat on its supervisory board?

'Aha! So you serve two masters! You shave two customers at one and the same time!' someone called out from the side.

Laughter rang through the hall. If a film director had been following the scene, the camera would then have zoomed in on Richter-Brohm's nervously twitching jaw, expecting a smile to appear on his face. However, Richter-Brohm's face remained implacably serious. He took hold of his pipe again (a shareholder had called out that he should do them the favour of taking it out of his mouth, which is what Richter-Brohm had done), and relit it. Whichever way the business now went, he was under no obligation to anyone.

But was that really the case? Not far away from him, at the end of the black-covered table on the podium, sat the works council chairman, Kurt Golda, as a member of the supervisory board. It had only been yesterday that both men had had a detailed discussion, and he knew the tension with which Golda anticipated his 'justification' and how it might now disappoint him. Did Golda sense that he, Richter-Brohm, had thought long and hard about it? They had met in the rooms of the Deutsche Bank on Promenade Square. They had always got on well with each other, the man from the workforce and the managing director. A feeling of trust united them. Golda felt that in the interests of his main aim, namely securing jobs, Richter-Brohm's model policy was essentially right. He had fully approved the 'white paper', which had the mid-range car at its heart, when Richter-Brohm had presented it to the supervisory board. In fact the entire supervisory board had approved it. At the same time, he had objected to the fact that the same supervisory board had left Richter-Brohm in the lurch when it had been required to grant the necessary finance for just such a mid-range car, after they had denied him this twice.

'Tell them this tomorrow. Tell them that we, the workforce, will be with you through thick and thin, as will the shareholders if they discover the true reasons. Tell them that we know that it is not your fault if the mid-range car project is not getting off the ground, but rather the fault of the supervisory board, along with the banks.'

Richter-Brohm replied that he did not believe the banks would let down the supervisory board.

To which Golda answered: 'No! They are letting *us* down. Tell them that! Even if you have to stand up against the supervisory board!'

Richter-Brohm asked if Golda knew what that meant, and, without batting an eyelid, Golda replied: 'Of course! You're putting your job on the line, resigning. But then all hell will break loose. If only every-one could see (not just the small shareholders) that here is the man who can take the necessary steps, a man who'll put us back on our feet again!'

It was all right for Golda to talk of resignation! That meant abandoning everything which contractually bound him to the company. He would then have no right to a pension. He knew exactly what Golda was thinking, namely that the responsibility of a man heading a company must be solely directed towards the good of the company, and by extension, to the jobs it could offer, and not to any shabby claim to a pension. All the others on the management board had covered themselves, even if they had to go. It was known that one of them had even secured a contract with Daimler-Benz, and made no bones about how things now stood. Daimler-Benz had then firmly decided to let BMW disappear from the scene, not least because of the mid-range car which they saw as competition directed against them (just as once before, when a planned merger had failed!).

Richter-Brohm did not delude himself on that score – his 'white paper' was known in Stuttgart. Nonetheless, he kept by his decision to fall into line and, in Golda's eyes, to prefer the 'mess of pottage'. Golda had to understand. Richter-Brohm was certainly no superman, and no one had ever taken him for one.

Admittedly, his darkest hour would not be turned into victory. But at least history would be made in this hour of truth. He followed, almost with a sense of pleasure, the present tussle between a man from the table below at the front (immediately in front the management and supervisory board tables on the podium) and Dr Feith.

'Who is that man?' Richter-Brohm asked his board colleague, Kämpfer, the head of finance, who was sitting on his left.

'A coal-merchant from Darmstadt,' the latter said. 'He regularly appears at general meetings and kicks up a row. If Feith doesn't stop him from speaking right away, he won't know what's hit him.'

But Feith, after continuous interruption from Erich Nold, leant forward and raised his hand, and went on to give the information asked of him.

'The company has been unprofitable since the currency reform,' he said. 'Its insolvency has reached proportions which can only be described as dangerous. Even the current programme for the company does not guarantee any sustained profitability. In fact, it will bring the certainty of further losses!'

'Aha!' shouted the man from the lower table.

Richter-Brohm slightly, but unmistakably, shook his head, something which did not escape Feith.

'Of course,' he went on, 'this raises the question as to how these losses came about, and . . .' (with a sideways glance to Richter-Brohm) '. . . whether the administration was at fault here.'

'A higher authority!' was the answer from below, a remark even heard at the back, which set everyone laughing.

'Naturally this question has to be carefully investigated!' assured Feith, which prompted Nold to interject: 'Where's the investigative report, then?'

'Herr Nold,' Feith said calmly, like a teacher compromising with an impertinent pupil, 'it will be your turn to speak after me. I am sure you would welcome not being constantly interrupted. Perhaps you will allow me the opportunity to present the administration's point of view.'

This point of view was well known. But why had the administration withheld a report which had been commissioned from the German Audit and Trust Company? Was this really due to a shortage of time, as Feith maintained, and not to cover up any possible 'serious dealings and omissions' contained in it, which had justified claims for compensation? It was precisely this that the report would clear up, namely which facts had led to the mounting losses. Other questions were whether, and how far, the proposals on the 1.6-litre car had failed because the banks had not made the required funds available. And whether the costs for this programme had been entered in the usual accounting procedure for this type of company. Feith confessed that, without knowing the outcome of the investigation, the general meeting was incapable of exonerating management and supervisory boards. As a result, the administration was withdrawing point 5 on the agenda (the aforementioned exoneration) quite voluntarily. This immediately led people to suspect a new plot.

Oh, what a miserable game, thought Oscar Baldauf, the company's head of personnel, a small, unprepossessing man, who, fired by the Allies, had rejoined the company during clearing-up operations. As an employee, he could not ask to speak, and it was clear that he took this badly. In the *Süddeutsche Zeitung* the day before, an article had appeared entitled: 'How BMW has driven itself into a cul-de-sac'. Like many others, he had the newspaper folded open on his knees. A shareholder, a Dr Haufel, now admitted that he felt this picture was far too mild.

'You can always turn round in a cul-de-sac. BMW is not in a cul-de-sac. It has fallen into a sewer with a raging water-flow, a sewer with such steep and smooth walls that the poor wretch cannot climb out by itself. Someone comes along with a pole and holds it out to us, leaving us to wonder whether the pole is good enough, and whether we wouldn't prefer a more comfortable lifebelt! Are we really in a position to say in the same breath: what's more, I want someone to tell me who's going to compensate me for my wet suit!'

No, my friend, you are mistaken about the suit, about the lifebelt, Baldauf thought. We're in a bad way, no doubt about it, but what were things like when the 501 came out, when we felt ourselves responsible to the customers in pre-war times? It was only when the car was finished and in production that we noticed how scarce these customers had become. Sewer, smooth walls . . . who held out a pole to us then – the banks?

Our chief bookkeeper was a man called Holzinger. Friday had always been pay day, and the coffers were empty. On Wednesday, then Thursday, and as late as Friday morning, he went with me in my motorcycle and sidecar as we drove around. I waited below, and he went up to the condemned man's chair in the lobby of the banks. We scoured them all, but each one wanted 'securities' and we had none, apart from ourselves. And whenever we got back home, our wives asked us if we had received our pay, and if the miracle had happened. We said that yes, the children could hang the little BMW flag out of the window (the pennant they owned) as a sign that there had been a miracle. It was not through religious teaching that they understood the concept of the miracle, but through BMW – and that was every Friday. And it was only once (Holzinger and I were not yet back) that the people had to wait more than half an hour for their pay. That was no laughing matter. Nobody had more than 20 marks in their pockets, and at the end of the month they might have had as little as 20 pfennigs.

The shareholder went on speaking. 'We must be level-headed when it comes to finding the limits of what is appropriate,' he said. 'The fate of the company has been entrusted to all of you, in a very small way because of the situation, but to a large extent through the power of your voting slips.'

Baldauf wondered to whom it had been entrusted. To Holzinger, to me, to every worker. Now this man was saying: 'If things go wrong for you, you can have no claim against third parties. This claim is all the less valid if the party concerned is a competitor.'

He chose to end on a very banal note: 'Do not reject the restructuring proposal and make it still cheaper for those people you're trying to find beyond every bush and hedge!'

Baldauf wondered that people could speak of 'still cheaper' when it was so cheap already, and reflected that they were talking about their lives.

But the words spoken died away, so that finally the business, the restructuring, could be dealt with, leaving it unclear as to who the people were who could be found behind every bush and hedge. Did that mean Flick? Or his backers, who were also present in the hall?

Dr Kübel, Nold's companion, asked to speak and said: 'There are bound to be contracts with Daimler-Benz in existence. Why isn't the wording of all the agreements made plain to us? As a conscientious legal man, I refuse to pass firm judgement on a restructuring plan or accept it without knowing all the sub-agreements.'

Now Feith opened out again. 'There are no secret treaties with Daimler-Benz,' he said. 'There has only been agreement over one basic arrangement dealing with a 100-million DM contract for 1960.'

So now people knew, and what they did not know, they could only presume.

It was 12.30. No headway had been made. Outside, the snow continued to flutter down onto the Bavaria statue and the Congress Hall. People in the overheated room looking out of the windows began to grow more and more weary. But nobody bought Feith's story, in which he said that he had conducted every transaction in the interests of the shareholder.

'Those weren't transactions, they were sell-outs!' Nold exclaimed. 'It's just a piece of theatre, doctor! You carry the moral responsibility, even if the voting turns out in your favour. You up there are a dictator, Herr Feith! You have no reason to smile, let alone laugh.'

The subject kept coming back to the new share option. Calls went up asking why it had not been 1:1. Why could the long-standing shareholders not be given free or additional shares without voting rights?

One voice, drowning all the others, shouted: 'What are 5,500 skilled workers worth?'

It was the voice of the coal-merchant from Darmstadt again, and Kämpfer had been right to suggest that if Feith allowed him to speak unhindered, he would not know what had hit him.

But Feith knew what he was doing. A taped transcript which the newspapers printed in excerpts two days later captured the turbulent highpoints of the day. For some unknown reason, the tape-recording was destroyed. Thanks to the article, one of the key scenes has come down to us:

NOLD   I have made a petition to the administration. I would ask that this petition is read out, so that the general meeting knows what I have requested.

SHOUTS   Read out the petition, or can't you read?

[*Dr Feith hands over the petition so that he can read it out himself.*]

NOLD   With reference to my announcement on 10, 12 and 26 November 1959, in which I stated my opposition and which I hereby enclose, I repeat the petitions contained in it: postponement of the resolution of the administration's proposals until the report of an independent expert investigator is available as per paragraph 118 of the Share Act – definitely not a trust, because, in my view, trusts cannot be trusted . . .

DR FEITH   [*interrupts*] Herr Nold, point of order. This is a factual discussion. If you are going to be offensive, I shall remove your right to speak.

NOLD   . . . So that the shareholders are in a position before the general meeting itself to investigate the administration's proposals and make the correct decision, I would ask the agenda to be widened in accordance with my counter motions. At the start, I declared to the administration that summoning the general meeting did not comply with the legal requirements. Most of the shareholders do not have this report from the trust company available to them, so they are in no position to come to any decisions at this important juncture. Everything you want to decide here today is a botched-up job, like Flick's trust company . . . [*Lively applause.*]

An interesting parallel case can be cited. A year ago, the Henschel Company was in the same position as BMW is today. Yes, they said, the firm is in such and such a state. There had to be an adjustment at 4:1, due to the bad economic situation, etc. But today, after Herr Semler has successfully sold his bread rolls, the Henschel Works has had a ten-fold . . .

DR FEITH   Herr Nold, I have told you that this a factual discussion. If you are going to insult anybody . . .

NOLD   I am proposing that you adjourn the meeting for a short period so that those present can get a bite to eat, and be able to follow what I have to say.

[*Applause and great amusement. Nold speaks with the administration.*]

DR FEITH   After your explanations . . .

A SHOUT	Lunch break!
NOLD	I ask you to call a lunch break.
DR FEITH	Herr Nold, you have leave to speak. Please carry on.
NOLD	I will start reading and then continue after lunch.
	[*Nold reads out longish reports from the magazine Der Spiegel and excerpts from dozens of letters he has received. After a certain period, increasing unrest at the meeting is detectable.*]
SHOUTS	Stop, Herr Nold, you are doing us no service whatsoever.
NOLD	Just let me finish speaking, so that you are not suspected of . . .
DR FEITH	Herr Nold has leave to speak.
	[*Nold continues speaking. After a while a shareholder interrupts him.*]
NOLD	Give me your name, I would like to know the gentleman's name.
THE MAN	But, Herr Nold, you know me.
NOLD	I don't know you. Who are you?
THE MAN	My name is Dr Siara.
NOLD	Dr Siara, an attorney from the Deutsche Bank, am I right?
	[*Commotion in the room.*]
DR SIARA	I request that Herr Nold's speaking time is limited to a quarter of an hour.
DR FEITH	Herr Nold, you have leave to speak.
SHOUTS	Stop, stop!
NOLD	Go and buy yourself a Coca Cola!
DR FEITH	We have no intention of doing that. Herr Nold, you have leave to speak.
NOLD	I must do my duty here as an amateur collector of voting slips.
SHOUT	Point of order! I request that Herr Nold is prevented from speaking.
SHOUT	I request that this is not done. He is obliged to carry on reading.
DR FEITH	Herr Nold, you have leave to speak.
NOLD	I have the instruction to read it out. That may last another half hour.
	[*Lively dissent.*]
DR FEITH	Herr Nold has leave to speak.
	[*Nold continues reading out. A shareholder requests that a bell is rung when Herr Nold is finished. The hall is gradually emptying.*]
NOLD	I must stand by my duty, and by my duty I shall stand.
	[*Great commotion, people are calling out simultaneously. Nold does not let himself be put off and reads on. He is interrupted by constant shouting of: 'Enough, enough!'*]
NOLD	Mr Chairman, it is impossible to continue speaking. I must ask you to make a break.
DR FEITH	You cannot have a break. You have leave to speak.
NOLD	There is no way I can carry on speaking. I am physically and mentally incapable of speaking further. I am constantly being interrupted.
	[*Nold goes back to his seat. The room fills up again.*]
DR FEITH	Herr Nold, you should not have been interrupted.

452

[Dr Feith answers the questions asked by Nold. Nold asks additional questions; this results in new controversies and sometimes heated arguments. Answers are refused to part of the questions, as they were not on the agenda. Finally, the chairman of the supervisory board gives Dr Mathern leave to speak.]

Had Feith scored a victory? All the indications suggested he had. Nold, the main opponent of the restructuring plan and of the sale to Daimler-Benz, was 'out for the count'. Physically and mentally drained, as he himself had to admit, he was hanging (to use an appropriate metaphor) 'on the ropes', and nobody paid any more attention to him. Even those for whom he had fought and from whom he had elicited applause and, at times, set against the 'mighty in the world', now admitted to themselves that they were not better off, but worse off, than before.

The room, which had almost been talked empty, had filled up again. How was the person now walking to the microphone (nobody knew him) supposed to light a spark of hope from the ashes? The only thing people knew was that he spoke as a representative of the dealers, and that he would defend the latters' interests, which did not necessarily include those of the small shareholders. To apply for an adjournment, this time in the name of the dealers, would be absurd. Just that morning, Dr Will of the German Association for the Protection of Bond Holders had fought in vain for that on behalf of the shareholders, exclaiming the emotive words: 'Crashing out of the skies, we are today clinging like grim death to the Mercedes star!' The best they could hope for now were some concluding words.

Yet now, without any dramatics, this man (what was he called?), Dr Friedrich Mathern, gently demolished the respect of the 'saving Mercedes star'. Was Daimler-Benz saying it wanted to replace 50 per cent of the capacity? Yes, 50 per cent, Feith stated.

He asked whether it was right that 25,000 examples of the 700 had been ordered some time ago for the home market, and not quite 5,000 examples for abroad? The management board table answered that it was right, and that confirmation was not linked to an inspection requirement.

A shareholder called out: 'Which gentleman have we just been listening to?'

Dr Feith said that it was Herr Kämpfer, a member of the management board of the Bavarian Motor Works. Applause rang out, and he emerged from a corner where he had stayed silent till then.

Mathern did not let up. He asked if the price for the 700, naturally based on sufficient production, had been calculated for sales to produce a profit. Feith said that it had. In any event, account needed to be taken of the fact that a few extra costs would arise for the run-up in 1960.

These questions, raised in a bland and matter-of-fact way, made people prick up their ears. What was this Dr Mathern after? What was behind the question as to whether contacts had been made with MAN over a possible sale, and whether in October the British car company Rootes had shown interest in entering into discussions with BMW, and what had subsequently transpired? Then, while thoroughly agreeing with the necessity of restructuring, there had been his comments on the Reichs Court decisions, which had certified the immorality of these measures – at such increases in capital going to the benefit of third parties (in similar circumstances to here). Even the question of property, premises and buildings with a book value of 13 million DM interested him. With a fire-insurance value of 44 million DM already, they would have had an estimated value of at least 30 million DM. With the present employment situation, namely full employment in German industry, this had been estimated too low rather than too high – with all the halls and machinery, and with the capacity of between 5,000 and 6,000 workers employed within them. In addition to this, a new question emerged, in which he asked if he could hand over a majority shareholding from this company to third parties, to outsiders. And was the administration (he now believed implicitly that no effort was too great for them) quite certain that it had really negotiated the best purchase price at Daimler-Benz? A firm like this and a man like Herr Flick, whom he valued, even admired, were not disposed to get rich out of a corpse. They had no need of that. In conclusion, he had to say that he was astounded at how little confidence the administration had in its own company.

The climate had completely changed. Not once had the 'man in the brown suit' (as the papers called Dr Mathern the day after) attacked the gentlemen behind the committee tables. He had made them think that that was all. But Mathern had not finished yet. He now said that he had spoken with a number of dealers. They said that they were even more convinced they could reach the stated figures. He was, too. Then he said, with unconcealed scorn: 'Naturally, we would do well not to work on the figure of 25,000, which has been named by competent people, as that would mean that for the coming year 30,000 examples should be taken as sold, implying an additional 130 million!'

Someone laughed. Mathern continued unperturbed.

'If it was now possible to work this year (meaning 1958, which had been signed off) *without* the 700 and *without* operating losses, then why, oh why, do there have to be losses for next year?'

In the applause that greeted him, he called out to Feith: 'And here we are told that continuing the company is absolutely impossible, unless additional orders are also coming in without money!'

By that he meant Daimler-Benz, as everyone in the hall knew. But did they also know why Feith was nodding? Mathern had hit upon his basic motive. Because of the orders which Daimler-Benz had assured him of, he had taken on the role of promoter. Without guarantees of work for the lame company, any restructuring was pointless, given the inappropriate model policy. But still he stuck to it. He had also not liked the fact that the shareholders had no recourse to an option on new shares, and that it was quite simply a condition. Now he had to take the blame for it – and listen to what this Mathern was proposing, in his quiet way, a proposition which held everyone in suspense, down to the last listener, including Feith himself.

This struck at the heart of the matter.

Mathern said: 'When an administration has to come before its shareholders to announce to them that they have again lost some of our money and that half our capital has gone, they tell us they want new money, but they stop us from giving it to them because it will probably also be lost. So my view is that this decision should be left with the shareholders who have made sacrifices up to now just to get as far as they have done.'

He broke off for a few moments.

Then he continued: 'To use a simile, is this not like telling a Christmas goose shortly before it's slaughtered that it is going to be eaten by a refined family?'

The minutes state here: '*Laughter and lively applause*'. As Wolfgang Denzel said when he described this scene to me twenty years later in Vienna, Mathern's words had left him quite dumbfounded. Until then, no one had rightly known what was really going on in the interested parties' Chinese puzzle. People resigning themselves to the situation, high spirits, Nold's exaggerated play on words such as 'you can't trust a trust', together with the occasional bare-faced cynicism on Feith's behalf, for whom everything had run its course (as the agenda provided for) – all this had created a state of tumultuous bewilderment which Mathern's words about the Christmas goose dispersed at a stroke.

Heinrich von Kleist wrote a famous essay entitled: 'The Gradual Composition of Thoughts in Speech'. In it he speaks of 'extended tricks' for producing his 'idea on the workshop of reason to gain necessary time'. Mathern's simile of the Christmas goose was just such a trick. If, as Kleist says, 'language is not a shackle like a brake-block on the mind's wheel, but more like a second wheel running parallel to it on its axle', then reading the minutes of the subsequent hours clearly reveals how this second wheel gripped, and how, overrunning any resistance, it carried the speaker, who was simultaneously thinking about all the complicated facts of the case, to the real purpose at hand. On the subject of MAN's offer, which had resulted 'not wholly without initiatives from colleagues here present' and from himself, he said: 'This offer still stands and states: we shall pay 30 million in cash. I have expressly made sure of that once again and it says: to be paid straight into the company.'

So it was full steam ahead! He excluded any lengthy discussions which might have thrown everything into doubt again.

'I may well not have negotiated the last purchase price. But are we not like a man standing up to his neck in water? At least, that is how it is portrayed. This man has to eat something. He still has a diamond ring, although we cannot be quite sure that it is not just a pebble. Without evidence to the contrary, the price of 30 million seems to me an utterly fair one, although it could be adjusted slightly.'

The wheel gripped. And it continued to grip with every new revolution.

'Now comes the next question: what is Daimler-Benz doing, what are the banks doing? I am one hundred per cent convinced about this, and I believe that our chairman will give it his wholehearted support. I do not regard our German banks as robbers and rogues. I know that they are fully aware of their economic task. I do not believe, either, that Daimler-Benz will say that because you are making one last effort to drag yourselves out of the mire, we shall withdraw our offer. It is also not the case that they are going to turn round and say something different tomorrow. The company wasn't built in a day.'

He said that quite incidentally. The wheel gripped. And while it was gripping, he discarded the images and made some solid proposals. These contained the willingness of the shareholders to sell Power Plant Production Co. Ltd to MAN for 30 million immediately, or for an amount still to be determined. That would initially mean money would be handed over and the loss would be made good. He calculated it stage by stage.

'From the sale, we shall then have a balance-sheet profit, after deductions, of between 12 and 15 million DM for contributions towards the system of compensation. From the reduction in the share capital, we shall have a book profit of 15 million DM, making a total book profit of 30 million DM. This will allow us to offset the loss and will give us a capital value of 15 million DM and a reserve value of the same amount. Then we shall begin to be quite a respectable company again.'

Was the Christmas goose back again? No, it had vanished into thin air. People were now going to the meal table themselves – to find what exactly?

'It is quite clear to me that the other 30 million will also have to come in. And if we've got a balance sheet like this one, and shares can be issued *with* an option on new shares, then nobody can fail to take advantage of this option on new shares, or at least sell this option. Then the capital requirements would also be covered.'

What was still missing? Yes, that's right. Somebody would have to take the company to the meal table (with no master of ceremonies to entertain them). This was no pleasure outing, but much more like hard work, as it involved organisation so that people could carry on living. Mathern was of the opinion that 'this task should be entrusted to someone who would take the time to do it'. He was careful not to say that the administration had done it badly or wrongly, he did not mention the chairman of the supervisory board who worked in an honorary, or almost honorary, capacity. He glanced around at the panel, looked at Feith, and Dr Feith said: 'I believe that's right.'

Then he sought out Erich Nold, who was back in his old chair in the auditorium, and laid his hand on him.

'I shall make a suggestion, although it won't quite agree with Herr Nold's wishes or ideas. I propose Dr Johannes Semler as the right man for the job. I do not believe that Dr Semler has done such a bad job at Henschel. In fact, he has worked well. Naturally, I, too, am at the board's disposal, inasfar as I can be of use.'

The wheel gripped. Applause showed it. Everything which this Dr Mathern had said had appeared quite incidental. And now he said, quite incidentally, 'In addition, I request adjournment of the remaining resolutions.'

Was that possible? Well, it *was* possible, if this room deemed it possible – and the administration followed the proposal 'without lengthy voting or similar tomfoolery being necessary'. If they had not done that (for the first time, Mathern raised his voice), he would have contested resolution of the balance sheet, because of the errors it contained.

Feith had gone pale, something which was visible in spite of the lamps he was sitting under. Outside, darkness had already enveloped the Congress Hall, his paleness showed how profoundly he knew. He felt like Siegfried, with his vulnerable spot not protected by his calloused skin. He knew the Share Act, which states that inaccurate balance sheets can be contested. And the balance sheet *was* inaccurate. It was inadmissable to include all the depreciation costs for the 700 model (development costs, tool-making costs, all the other possible run-up costs) in the year's overall loss! Of course, they should have been shared out over the years to come, at least over the next year. But everyone, including himself, believed that this car had no future.

What was to be done? Make up for time. But how could this be done? By wearing down the enemy. But how was he to be worn down? By destroying his credibility publicly. And so, as the applause subsided, Feith said: 'Herr Mathern, as a lawyer, you are an excellent representative of MAN.'

But faced with the boos round the room (were they directed at Mathern or Feith?), Mathern simply retorted: 'Ladies and gentlemen, I take that as a compliment. There is no reason to boo.'

There was, indeed, no reason to boo. This view was shared by a shareholder sitting in the back rows. Yet he tried to find out where the catcalls were coming from – either from the shareholders approving Feith's insinuation, or from all the others disgusted by it. He knew exactly in which corner of the room the proponents for restructuring were sitting, and his heightened sense of hearing (he had an eye complaint and was practically blind) told him the true measure of things. No progress was being made. How was it to continue? Feith had not been convincing, unlike Mathern. Our shareholder was now wondering on which side *he* should stand.

To a certain extent, he had to feel affiliated to the 'strong partner', which Dr Mathern had apostrophised as the 'refined family', as he himself held a not inconsiderable number of this 'family's' shares. And what was more, it had been he, in conversations with Friedrich Flick (with whom he sat on the supervisory board at Daimler-Benz), who had invented the design for a planned increase in capital (together with the resulting 75 per cent participation of the Swabian company in BMW). For him that represented the sure way of saving the company.

The only thing which disturbed him about it was that Flick could not decide to give a binding undertaking to have at least *one* car model continue in production under the BMW name in the new business. He knew Flick. No one could later talk Flick out of anything he had not expressly confirmed. And if Flick's plan of a large car group, which he wanted to form around the Mercedes star (possibly including Auto Union and Maybach), were to become reality, then BMW would be a small cog in it which would not be allowed to upset the balance. But it was already causing some upset – with new losses before the old ones had been paid off. And every new model of necessity initially brought new losses before it became profitable.

Looked at this way, there was no denying that our man was taking part in consuming the Christmas goose, but the thought of delighting in this bit of wing or that bit of neck was anything but pleasant to him. The Christmas goose (to retain the metaphor, which was still in everyone's mind's eye) also belonged to him, although to a lesser degree than would justify him sitting down at a refined family's meal table. But he was undeniably the most positively committed shareholder in the Bavarian company.

Almost unnoticed, even within the circle of his closest confidants, he had begun by buying smaller and larger parcels of shares and convertible debentures in the company concerned (the wood-merchant Krages from Bremen had helped him acquire them). He did this with all the risks which are always part of an inner commitment, because cars were his love. His ambition was rooted here in the desire not only to see the money he was putting into BMW go to work, but also be used to bring a potentially creative influence to bear on the company and its products, a wish which had been denied him at Daimler-Benz. There, there had never been the slightest chance of him having any effect on the business, either in its product or in its commercial policy. The heirarchy was too rigid, model development was an impenetrable erratic block, and it was the mighty Flick who determined the main developments, if anyone did. This was not the case at BMW, where an entrepreneur was involved in quite different conditions because of an obviously incompetent top management, or, at least, one at odds with itself. One which was also, in the technical area, patently indecisive. Here, everything cried out for a 'strong hand'. And that could well be his.

It is time to refer to him by name. This major shareholder was called Herbert Quandt, and he had come here from Bad Homburg, where he had directed the widely diversified family business of the same name with his brother Harald. He had not come with any great joy, but was certainly able to get approval for his own restructuring plan, with the majority of the shareholders present. He felt that the wind was now changing.

As early as the lunch break, he had sat down with Kurt Golda and his closest adviser and his company's major-domo, Dr Horst Pavel, along with Feith, for a brief consultation. He valued Golda. Occasionally, the chairman of the works council (an extremely unusual event) had come to him at Bad Homburg, or had telephoned him, in the full knowledge of who the secret purchaser of BMW shares was, which Krages had entrusted to Quandt after securing the transaction. Concerned about guaranteeing jobs threatened by potential bankruptcy (his main concern), Golda had put his cards on the table and had entrusted and 'secured' decisions already made to Quandt, whom he saw as the future main shareholder. Now Golda had once again stated that if the ultimatum were complied with, it would be over for BMW. In the interests of the workers, he would have no other option but to consent to become a supplier, which is what the company would sink to. If only you, Dr Quandt, would. . . .

But Quandt forestalled him. He said that nothing would be possible without Daimler-Benz, as the 700 was still only a vague hope, which in no way altered the fact that he, Quandt, had nowhere near the required means. . . .

He had therefore persuaded Flick to consider this restructuring plan, although the latter had been quite reluctant to do so; he would in future, when dealing with Flick, ensure that BMW would not go under.

He had the feeling that Golda did not believe this and that Golda's silence was a slight on his own ability. If other blows were to follow, might he possibly start wavering? Good God, he thought, just imagine if I dared offer the shareholders restructuring from our own resources? Outside in the room, Nold was still reading his letters. Throughout the economy, there had never been a time when shareholders had stuck so closely to the company on which they had set their hearts and minds in its hour of need. Quandt felt he would like to have rewarded this, but he quickly dismissed the idea as pure romanticism. Who had ever given *him* anything? There was too much at stake. He had his own company empire to think about. In worrying about his own business concerns, he wondered if he had not taken leave of his senses, now that complete strangers suddenly seemed more important to him.

Inspired by Mathern's words, he now realised that 'loyalty', an incalculable concept in economic life, *was* calculable here. Its greatness, which his restructuring model had ignored, was a real concept. Why was this? Why had the management and supervisory boards, with the overwhelming trust that had been expressed, completely missed this crucial moment? And if they had missed it, why had *he* missed it, the originator of this concept?

He calculated. What Mathern planned seemed to him amateurish. The man also had nothing to lose. No, if . . . it would have to be done in a different way. Provided the meeting rejected Daimler-Benz. But, despite all his cunning, Mathern was no longer in a position to achieve that. Spellbound, Quandt stared out at the room which was flickering into life again. What was going on there?

Well, what was going on was that a kind of bloodthirsty mood was taking over. Still impressed by the attempts at rescue or enquiries about them (which were unfortunately in vain), the public did not feel inclined to include Feith's declarations in this offer, being disinclined to give credence, or even just to listen to the fact that Daimler-Benz AG had pressed itself on BMW, or that this had come about only after difficult negotiations. Mathern had reported on these attempts and enquiries in his casual way, reporting about his weekend excursion to London as if it had been a men's night out. He told them about having breakfast with Lord Rootes, head of a car factory producing 1,300 cars a day, when the lord had expressed his regret at not having had an opportunity to look closely at the Milbertshofen Works.

Back in the room, the public was crying out: 'Resign!'

A dealer indignantly asked: 'Has anyone even considered thinking of getting in touch with us dealers and saying to us that we must forego profit on so many cars? We would have done it! And now, we've got a pistol at our heads!'

Even a telegram, which Feith read out after a request to take a break (for consultation), had no effect. It came from the Federal Defence Minister, and contained the declaration that his ministry 'could only put through a proposed contract with a value of 300 million DM for Power Plant Production

Co. Ltd, if there was an advanced and financially strong partner for Power Plant Production Co. Ltd.'. That was aimed at Daimler-Benz. But was not MAN such a partner? The question kept coming up (Erich Nold's voice was clearly audible).

'Ask us if we are ready to take over the shares!' (Cries of 'Bravo!' rang out). 'You are there for us, and not for the Deutsche Bank. Why do you hold back from asking us?'

This went on until Feith, vainly struggling against a chorus of voices demanding 'Resign! Resign!', said: 'The administration moves that adjournment be rejected.'

'Which adjournment?' asked Mathern, 'Point 4 on the agenda? Adjournment of the whole meeting?'

'The motion in front of me refers to adjournment of the general meeting. I move its rejection,' declared Feith. Then he called to the boisterous room, saying that everyone who wanted to see the general meeting adjourned should vote 'Yes'.

For this they needed a majority of all votes. In the room there was a share capital of 20,744,400 DM represented by around 1,000 men and a handful of women. If he got more than 70 per cent of them, Feith had won. The voting produced 70.5 per cent of the capital entitled to vote. He heaved a sigh of relief. So, after nearly ten hours debate, adjournment was rejected, meaning that the proposed restructuring plan could be regarded as adopted.

But anyone believing that the day of the dealers and their spokesman Mathern was now over, would be wrong. Late that very afternoon, Denzel telephoned Roy Chapin, Vice President of the American Motors Corporation, and discovered that in the States it was quite illegal to write off a product prematurely, regardless of whether its success was proven or pending. And, breaking the silence imposed by his lawyer, the Viennese importer had publicly turned to the head of marketing in the company, and called out in the hall: 'How far ahead has the 700 been sold out?'

'Two years,' was the answer.

'And how far ahead in the export market?'

'Three years,' came the reply.

This immediately caused him to turn towards the podium and shout: 'These are the people who dare to question the value of this product and write it off!'

And Dr Schwinner, Denzel's lawyer, stood up, declared the figures in the accounts supporting the balance sheet to be inaccurate, and tried to get the board to announce the correct figures straight away. Of course, the board did not do this.

Here Mathern joined in, and if, as Kleist believed, language is not a brake-block on the mind's wheel, but rather more like a second wheel running parallel to it on its axle, and if it had now brought the speaker to his central purpose, then Mathern was home and dry. He took a little book out of his pocket and held it up high, so that everyone could see it. If we recall that morning, Nold had slipped it to him before the general meeting started. It was Beck's commentary on the Share

Act. Mathern flicked through a few pages, and then found the page he wanted.

'According to paragraph 125, section VII,' he said, 'the votes from 10 per cent of the share capital are sufficient for adjournment if the balance-sheet resolution is contested. And we contest it.'

He had found out that the development costs for the BMW 700, together with the costs for producing the tools, had been completely written off in contravention of all tax law, and as a result had shown a loss. 'Although,' he added, 'production of the new car had scarcely begun and proceeds could only be shown from the start of next year.'

What followed ran as smoothly as clockwork. People thronged round Mathern, and quite a few who had raised their hopes too soon also pushed towards the exit. Baskets were handed around, a notary was called to supervise counting the voting cards. That produced 6,236,100 DM-worth of votes for Dr Mathern. That was far more than he needed.

The minutes stated what Dr Feith said, as he stopped the general departure for a few minutes.

Dr Mathern has received the 10 per cent minority according to paragraph 125, section VII. As a result, point 4 on the agenda, resolution for share capital reduction, etc., is adjourned. (*Lively applause.*)

I can confirm that points 1, 2 and 3 on the agenda have been completed. Point 4 has been adjourned. The administration deletes points 5, 6 and 7 from the agenda, and will bring them up at the next scheduled general meeting.

(Voice from the back. 'Where we shall be so cosy together!')

'I believe that the general meeting has gone on for so long that everyone must feel rather exhausted.'

'Not at all!' countered a single cry again. It came from Nold.

Mathern had reserved the final words for himself. It stated in the minutes:

Ladies and gentlemen. You applauded. The required majority for adjournment has been reached. Whether this applause was justified is something which only time will tell. The vital question remains (and here I would very much like to have a clear answer from the chairman) what is now being planned on the part of the administration. If the intention is now to let the next three or four weeks elapse before summoning a new general meeting without anything being done, then our vote here has been a waste of time.

Feith replied. 'Dr Mathern, the administration will naturally make good use of the next few weeks.'

There was a shout. 'Thank you, Dr Feith'.

This marked the end of the 39th general meeting in BMW's history. It had made irrelevant the ultimatum expiring after 24 hours, which Friedrich Flick had put on his bid. The thanks addressed to Dr Feith, however ironically they

461

may have been meant, were directed at a man who, on taking his place as chairman of the supervisory board at the black-covered table on the morning of that day, must have known that he was letting himself in for a completely new type of responsibility, which the law assigned to the shareholder. For the first time in the history of German shareholding, shareholders were able to decide themselves the fate of their company. Now they had decided.

Dr Feith suffered the consequences of his defeat. He resigned on 31 January 1960. As did Dr Heinrich Richter-Brohm, when this was suggested to him by the supervisory board. The company fulfilled its contractual obligations to him.

Practically all the other members of the supervisory board, including representatives of the major banks, also handed back their mandates. The company was now completely rudderless, without a supervisory board, which had to appoint a new management board. (According to paragraph 89, section I of the Share Act, the regional court could appoint new supervisory board members if there were only a minority of members on the supervisory board for 'longer than three months', as prescribed in the Share Act or in the firm's articles of association.) On 1 February, a whole series of supervisory board members were appointed by the Munich company registrar, including Mathern, and a previously unknown lawyer called Gerhard Wilcke.

He was the legal adviser to the major shareholder, Herbert Quandt.

Anabasis
1960–1972

Anabasis (Greek): climbing, especially on a journey
or a campaign, to a higher-lying region.
Meyer's Larger Conversational Dictionary, 1904

Quandt

The Quandts, descendants of a Dutch rope-making family, had settled at Pritzwalk in Brandenburg, and had achieved considerable fortune when the 'second major blow' of his life befell the industrialist Günther Quandt – his wife died. Professor Silex from Berlin, who had examined and was treating his nine-year old son, Herbert Werner, for poor eyesight, told him that the retinas on both eyes were healthy again, but scars remained which would probably impair his clarity of vision for ever. As he wrote in his memoirs, Quandt's doubt as to 'whether Herbert's eyes would ever recover sufficiently to enable him to handle life's difficulties' led him to act immediately. In the Easter of 1919 Herbert, together with his brother Helmut, who was two years older, was transferred to the Arndt Grammar School in the Dahlem suburb of Berlin. This provided a child who had been advised not to read, with a private teacher who did not use books or other written material. The aim was to enable the child to pass the normal school leaving exams. The best doctors, such as the Privy Medical Officer, Count Wiser from Bad Eilsen (who had achieved great success with his unorthodox teaching methods), had been offered jobs at Arndt – although they still worked on the basis of 'mnemonic acquisition of material'. An unusual self-confidence developed in the boy, similar to the one a human being can easily lose if he is left to rely solely on his memory to make his way in the world. In 1929, Herbert took his school leaving exam as an 'external candidate' in front of an officially appointed teaching staff in Potsdam. He decided to work with his father, and not in agriculture, although it had been planned that he would later take over the Severin estate at Parchim specially bought for him. He wanted to become an industrialist like his father.

It was in 1960, on one of the first cold, bleak days in January, that the assistant head of the Bavarian Finance Ministry, Dr Otto Barbarino, was travelling from Munich to Stuttgart-Untertürkheim to arrange a last 'attempt to save BMW'. With him was the Permanent Secretary Guthsmuths from the Ministry of the Economy, who had asked Barbarino to join him. They were to make their presentation in the presence of Könecke, the managing director of Daimler-Benz. Barbarino did not think much of this. After their dramatic departure from the general meeting on 9 December 1959, he did not think Daimler-Benz was a suitable partner for BMW, even if acceptable conditions were to be applied once tempers had cooled. What were 'acceptable conditions'? Daimler-Benz wanted to produce in large quantities and without delay in Milbertshofen. That could only happen to the detriment of the 700 model, whose recently launched coupé required all free capacity – which was just what the people in Stuttgart wanted to take over in Munich. It was not for nothing that the Deutsche Bank had played down the sales success of the BMW 700 at the Theresienhöhe. This car had been a heaven-sent blessing – it was exactly the product which could provide the financial bridge on the way to the mid-range car, provided . . . well, provided what? This again raised the question of the partner, which the company needed, and to which the province of Bavaria would give full agreement. There was also the question of how much expansion there should be to provide for an increase in the share capital, without which nothing was possible.

Barbarino from the Finance Ministry was certainly ready to commit all the necessary securities and injections of capital, as long as they did not go overboard. The province of Bavaria, which had managed to absorb incredible numbers of refugees from the East into local industry, into agriculture in both Upper and Lower Bavaria, and into its towns and communities, wanted to keep BMW – at any price. This was not only because of the jobs offered by Milbertshofen, but also because it identified Bavarian economic policy, as a kind of state symbol, and because it was simply 'Bavaria' (which held no connotations of provincialism). There were other reasons why the 'Prussian' Richter-Brohm, in hinting at this in a stream of new ventures at the Finance and Economics Ministries, did not get a look in. There were other reasons why he may often have given the impression of turning a deaf ear as soon as anyone who was brash and domineering came forward to state their demands. This lay in the absence of a truly strong hand which was needed to drag the shattered company out of the mire, and for which Barbarino did not see Richter-Brohm as suitable. It also lay in the absence of financial backing, and a necessary commercial structuring. Where was this backing? When Krages emerged and established contact with Barbarino, it was quickly revealed that here was not a man who pursued industrial concepts, expanded them and took risks. He was simply a collector of share packets. There might also be a concept in that, but it was of no use for BMW. The Bavarian state, with no interest in private speculating, would have to 'keep itself out' if it did not want to get itself into a mess.

Fine, that was all in the past. How should things proceed now? Should they continue with a supervisory board, which did not direct, and which made commitments it did not keep to? And should things continue with a management board which was suddenly caught out, even if its ideas pointed technologically in the right direction? Well, we are going round in circles, thought Barbarino, and my dear Permanent Secretary, as you must be aware, every door has been closed to us here in Untertürkheim, after we spent three fruitless hours exchanging points of view.

The telephone rang. Barbarino had the strange feeling that it was for him. Könecke, the host, irritably let it ring. He had given the order that calls should not be put through.

The phone stopped ringing. Well, where were we? We have said all there is to be said. The secretary appeared at the door.

'Dr Barbarino, it's urgent,' she said, 'a Herr . . .' She gave his name.

Barbarino nodded, although the name did not ring any bells. There must have been some mix-up. However, he got up, apologised, followed the secretary into the anteroom and closed the door, just to be on the safe side. The conversation lasted a matter of minutes. Suddenly Guthsmuths and Könecke were standing next to him and saying goodbye.

'So 5 o'clock, Hotel Zeppelin,' Barbarino said and hung up.

'You've still got something in mind?'

'Yes,' said Barbarino, 'something quite unexpected.' And he smiled gently.

Outside, Guthsmuths asked, 'What's happening at 5 o'clock?'

'We have not come to Stuttgart for nothing,' Barbarino replied. 'Quandt wants to discuss things with us.'

'Quandt?' asked Guthsmuths. 'I thought it was a Herr Lindemann. . . .' That was the name he had understood and noted down.

'An assumed name,' said Barbarino. 'Quandt is in Stuttgart. Somebody told him we were here, exactly where we were. Did you know that Quandt is almost blind? He was nine years old when he nearly lost his sight. Quandt once told me that an old teacher, to whom he had been very attached, was called Lindemann, or something like that.'

When they met in the 'Zeppelin' at the agreed time, Quandt was already at the table. He hoped they understood his ploy, saying that he had his reasons for making sure that not everyone at Daimler-Benz (where he sat on the supervisory board with Flick) should learn of his presence here. Provided that the Bavarian state would support him over the next few years, he would be ready to buy the rest of Krages's packet and, as far as he could, acquire the majority shareholding in BMW. Guthsmuths and Barbarino exchanged glances. Then they declared that the government had a vital interest in maintaining BMW. Subject to approval higher up, they would gladly give the assurance to do everything in Bavaria's power to further Quandt's plans.

'That suits me,' said Quandt, getting up and holding out his hand ('roughly in the direction where I was sitting opposite,' Barbarino was later to recall. 'So I was the first to grasp his hand, a very firm, manly hand. I let go of it, and then Guthsmuths shook it. We had the feeling that here was an agreement with the kind of validity you wouldn't find anywhere else in the world. We travelled back to Munich full of relief.').

Quandt was later to repeat his statement that the decision to branch out into BMW had been linked to a longer decision-making process. After the failure of the general meeting, he had spent a lot of time debating whether he would not be better off disposing of his BMW holding and come away with a black eye, meaning a loss, rather than getting further involved. That would require all the power at his disposal, being the only obvious way to achieve command. He did, however, gradually acquire the courage to do it.

Golda, the chairman of the works council, tells the story quite differently. After the meeting, at 11 p.m. on that 9 December, they sat down as a very small group – there was Quandt, Dr Horst Pavel (his confidant and committee member in the so-called four-man council in the Quandt family empire) and he, Golda. Quandt was very agitated. That Mathern! he would say, all that rhetoric, and that impeccable diction of his! And did he not know, did he not sense for a moment the *kind* of constructive solution he was getting involved in, that there was certainly a major shareholder whose shareholding was more than sufficient to undermine the administration's proposals, even to undermine himself? The reason for this was that Daimler-Benz's concept, as known to the men, came from Quandt, and that he, and nobody else, had introduced and suggested it to Daimler-Benz and the Deutsche Bank. As late as that morning, he had considered it the only reasonable and feasible solution. How different everything looked now! Overwhelmed by the confidence of the small shareholders, their courage, their willingness to take risks, impressed by this rare 'spirit', he had recognised that there was more at stake than just keeping a business above water, i.e. protecting it from bankruptcy. So he had decided to be the driving and determining force behind restructuring – with all the means at his command. Whether he would succeed was doubtful, but he'd give it a go.

Had Quandt's memory played a trick on him? Unaccustomed to making quick decisions, never giving way to any uncontrolled outburst of feelings, and always allowing things to mature slowly, was he now trying to prevent himself from thinking that the situation was anything else (or could ever have been anything else) than what it was? Even on the occasion of the 20th anniversary of the historic BMW general meeting, he looked back at the events of 9 December 1959 in front of a small, invited circle. He was adamant:

'The shareholders did not want to take the safe, reliable way without having any other possibilities or solutions. But for me that meant that the year 1960 arguably contained my most difficult decision. A difficult decision both for BMW, of course, and for me and my family, who would have to risk the consequences. To a certain extent, I was at a crossroads, deciding whether I should give up my white-and-blue possession with certain losses, or whether I should lay myself open to single-handed involvement with all the associated risk, risk which I would have preferred to hand over to the financially strong business of Daimler-Benz with its very good reserves. The decision I then made in the first six months of 1960 might well have been compared in this circle to a song without words. Through my decision, I then, so to speak, forced myself to find happiness.'

Happiness! This was the first time he had spoken about it (this was in 1979, three years before his death). He still distanced himself from it, did not trust the concept, qualified it with a 'so to speak'. It was as if the concepts on which others build their lives had no value for him. He was a man whose whole life was portrayed as the single consequence of coolly taken, carefully considered strategies, which exclude any incalculables. There was no place for 'happiness' in all this.

The Quandts were numbered amongst the country's super-rich – their industrial possessions, which had been decimated in 1945, had been regrouped and had risen up as gleaming new companies. But was that 'happiness'? It could also be a strain, a burden, a 'duty', under whose weight the popular conceptions of happiness melt like snow in the sun. To this extent, Quandt had never been a 'happy man', and the inheritance from his father, which he and his half-brother Harald had assumed, had not been a burden to him, though neither had it really fulfilled him. Administering in order to 'multiply' what has already been acquired, and also to taste 'power' through concern for revenue and additional profit (power, the exquisite fare of the rich) had been imposed upon him rather than his actual desire. It was true that he loved life, and that he was no ascetic. But his passions (horses, fast cars and power boats) were escapes rather than actual privileges he enjoyed. Then there was always his eye complaint, which he so masterfully disguised that people meeting him for the first time would never suspect he was nearly blind. However, it was always there, veiling the joys of the world from him. If he pierced the veil surrounding him, then it was only because of the abilities which his will to overcome his handicap had developed. He effortlessly mastered what others can only master if they have texts and tables from which they can retrieve statistics at any given moment. He spoke English and French, had in his head every share value for his installations, knew all the difficulties and advantages of his companies, knew whom he could rely on and whom he could not. Nobody could fool him. His day began early, like that of the farmer he had never become, and ended in the evening or at night.

Was that happiness? As Nietzsche put it, if there is an inkling of happiness in the feeling that power is increasing and resistance can be overcome, then perhaps it was. But Quandt was no longer a young man, and there was a key event which precluded him once and for all from such feelings of happiness. In 1943, when the war economy was running at full stretch, he travelled, at the age of thirty-three, with his father from factory to factory. Much had been destroyed, decimated by air raids. New plant had to be installed, and old plant re-equipped for higher production. Not only were repairs necessary, but improvements had to be made, and everything was needed in the shortest possible time. They dashed frantically from place to place. But no less frantically were new factories being built, existing ones expanded, completely new production facilities developed, and ever greater numbers of people employed (in spite of the difficulties of finding them). What materialised in one place was lost in another.

On the night of 23 December 1943 the Pertrix factory complex at the Niederschöneweide suburb of Berlin was 70 per cent destroyed. Six weeks later, it was again running at full steam. But was the use of it? Transfers were made from the West to the East, and (when the earth was being scorched in the East) back again to the West. Nothing came out of this, nothing at all ... except the discovery that human beings wanting to survive can tolerate mental and physical strain which the good Lord had not apportioned to them when he created them.

Anyone surviving this would of necessity wonder what he was supposed to do with the 'power' attributed to him – economic power, that is. He was rich, to be sure. But did that make him another person? The wealthy would always regard themselves as different; this was the reason why any simplistic revolution, which allows all property distinctions to continue, must inevitably degenerate into new tyranny. This is what is stated in the first communist manifesto written (long before Marx and Engels) by Joseph Fouché in the middle of the French Revolution. Quandt considered this arrant nonsense, the claim that anyone simply having more money than others must be different from everybody else. And what about tyranny? He lacked the drive, the desire, as well as any opportunity (or any reason) even to become a tyrant in his own economic domain. Money does not release one from responsibility – quite the opposite, it consigns one to it. He was also consigned to it, and, like everyone, he had discharged it with Harald. He had mended what had been broken, and so, over and above his father's inheritance, he had occupied himself as a businessman, breaking new ground, while still keeping to the spirit of the Quandt company doctrine – which was to produce consumer items for the masses, such as batteries, small-scale appliances and pharmaceutical articles. These were all first-class products, nothing of world-shattering significance, but products we still regard as indispensable.

Günther Quandt had said about his father that he had been 'thoroughly open-minded to modern equipment'.

'But as a result of everything he created from scratch, he almost exceeded his own limits. There are people whose forte is perseverance, and there are others who constantly strive to break new ground; for these the future cannot come quickly enough. Both types are necessary and serve as a complement to one another. If there were only persevering natures, then the world would be condemned to stand still; if there were only people constantly wanting progress, tradition would be broken and mankind would lose its best feature.'

After extremely successful years in business, Günther Quandt did not disown his father when he acquired his 'multi-coloured possessions' during the inflationary period. These possessions formed the basis for the Quandt empire. He had always remembered his father's warning: 'Loans? Keep away!' and, even if he did not apply this very much, he had always borne his father's advice in mind, which was to 'keep to factories which one man can oversee, from a technological, commercial and financial point of view. Only then will you find true happiness.'

It was as if this advice, as old-fashioned as it might seem, also guided the hand of the third generation. When Herbert Quandt, the grandson, decided to restructure BMW, he believed he was up to the managerial task because of these three conditions. He had to admit that he was not a technician, though he channelled all his energies into the product – cars. His mastery of commercial acumen was second to none; and financially. . . . well, he was not going to put anything at risk that was not 'in it', and he certainly would not sacrifice the family's interests just to save a shattered business.

On the other hand, what he was letting himself in for was not some business game. There was much more to it than that. There was a dimension to consumer goods represented by the product 'CAR', which other consumer goods did not have – its value-added quality. It was not something people hid – they measured themselves against it, and, in turn, were themselves measured by it.

Seen like this, the brand name, the image of BMW, was worth every risk.

In the middle of December, a few days after the general meeting (at which BMW had preserved its independence for the time being), Quandt asked the head of finance, Ernst Kämpfer, to come and see him in Frankfurt.

'How are things with the 700?' he asked him.

'It can go into production in the spring,' Kämpfer replied.

'In spite of all the debts you have?'

'The suppliers keep quiet. No one leaves us in the lurch.'

'Amazing,' said Quandt. 'And Bosch?' He knew that Bosch only ever supplied cash on delivery.

'Even Bosch,' Kämpfer assured him. Immediately after the general meeting, he had had to give a television interview, in which he said that if anyone were to exploit his monopoly position, he would shout it from the rooftops. . . . They then ate humble pie.'

'And what do you think of the car?' Quandt wanted to know.

'I drove here in one. You can keep it here. A reasonable vehicle. Four seats, plenty of room. But it still has a motorcycle engine which we have "tweaked up" to 700 cc's. But it runs like a one-litre car, and looks attractive. A BMW from top to toe. It is in every way the equal of the coupé which Denzel developed in Vienna.'

'And the saloon,' Quandt asked, 'who built that?'

'Milbertshofen,' said Kämpfer. 'It has a bit of Vienna, and a bit of Turin in it – Michelotti drew the top section.'

Quandt wanted to see the miracle right away. Seeing is believing, thought Kämpfer. But how would he actually see it?

But he did. Quandt went around the car, gauging it, touching it here and there, the bonnet and rear section, making out its contours through touch, opening its doors, and sitting inside.

'Thank you,' he said, 'I shall drive it. I believe you have another example. Drive it to Nallinger at Daimler-Benz. Do it discreetly, on my behalf. Is that all right?'

Kämpfer returned by train, and came back to Stuttgart the next day with the prototype (there were no others). That evening, Nallinger rang up Frankfurt.

'Dr Quandt? We have just been on the test track. Go ahead and build the car, although I have to admit I wouldn't let any of my family travel in it, given the tank is at the front. But otherwise it's a good vehicle. You can make something out of it. It's a taste of things to come. It'll give you time to develop a mid-range car.'

'This was the signal for Quandt to go to the company registrar,' Kämpfer said later when he spoke of the time he still had to spend at BMW. 'We still had hardly any supervisory board members – but Quandt would have quite a few appointed, including Wilcke.'

A Brief

In all his undertakings, Quandt could be said to have the gift of always putting the right men in the right place.

As his biographer Treue said: 'As others hear music, so he, the music lover, heard modulations of voice. He drew conclusions from changes in volume, speed of delivery, and from the pauses between question and answer, a capacity which was just as useful in the context of discriminating between leading figures, as it was in everyday conversation with high-level employees, visitors and participants at meetings throughout the world.'

This supports the legend, but only partly explains the 'phenomenon' that suggests an innate ability. He was already exploiting this in his thirties. Given power of attorney by his father at Pertrix-Chemie AG, he had been mainly concerned with the personnel department when, in 1940, he joined the management board of the battery factory, the heart of all Quandt enterprises. It was in personnel that he saw the 'key position in the business'. Here he developed that sensitivity for being able to judge people, the gift of finding the 'right' man, and, in addition, the resilience to persist, once he had believed he had found him, until he had won him over.

What attracted Quandt to Gerhard Wilcke, his legal adviser for many years, was something which the latter was (understandably enough) least able to explain. Wilcke was a lawyer, a man whose whole life revolved around his profession, so that anyone only coming into fleeting contact with him took him to be a born advocate, something which only his outer appearance intimated. In reality, his appearance belied a profound artistry in him, which Quandt probably sensed immediately. This polarity, which suited him, corresponded to Quandt's own nature. Moreover, Wilcke, born in or near Berlin, was, in coming from there, closer to the 'Brandenburg'-born Quandt (the Berlin way of life came to the fore again) than the latter cared to admit. Educated between 1925 and 1933, Wilcke had had business experience at Schering, and then at Philips. There had then been a short interlude in 1945 as the mayor of Alt-Wolfsburg, followed by employment at the Lower Saxony Ministry of Education and the Arts, before he settled down as a lawyer in Hanover. An offer from VARTA, the main business concern of the Quandt group, led him to move to Frankfurt after the currency reform, where he subsequently had his chambers as a lawyer and legal adviser in Hansaallee.

It was shortly before New Year's Eve 1959 that, casually glancing out of the window, he saw two men getting out of a small car below, which looked remarkably like a BMW (he was immediately struck by the 'kidneys' on the radiator). He knew these men. When they had enlisted his services in the past, they had always made *him* come to *them*. They were Herbert Quandt and (yes, he was not mistaken) his confidant on the four-man council, Horst Pavel.

Wilcke was just about to leave for South America on business, on behalf of the Quandts. He had agreed to do this despite a spinal injury which caused him some trouble. Everything was arranged. The visit, he was sure, must be for other reasons. However, the lawyer was more than a little surprised when he heard what Quandt and Pavel wanted from him. Reflecting upon who their man could be to prepare an undertaking which was not without its dangers for the Quandt group, and especially (in Pavel's words) for Herbert Quandt himself, they had come up with the man who had provided many years of proven and commendable legal advice. They asked him if he was prepared to represent Herbert Quandt's interests for restructuring BMW in the company's supervisory board still to be formed. Dr Feith, the previous chairman, had resigned.

Then Wilcke was told, in Quandt's usual straight style, what was planned. The plan was to reduce the share capital by half to 15 million DM, which would make good the losses in capital assets (set at just this amount). Then there would be an increase beyond the former share capital (30 million), which would require finding a German or foreign party interested in the car business. As a way of obtaining further money, 50 per cent of the (at present) wholly owned subsidiary of Power Plant Production Co. Ltd would be disposed of. This would not cause any major difficulties, as the firm possessed a rather large contract from the Federal Defence Ministry. Quandt said casually that it would bring in a billion, and the rest would be found.

'Where is this going to be handled?' asked Wilcke.

'Munich, of course.'

'How long will this take?'

'We're thinking in terms of three to six months,' both men agreed.

Wilcke neither shook his head nor nodded. He knew how every client underestimates the time he quotes to his supplier. But it was not his business to raise any misgivings. Was this a brief – yes or no? They knew him – and knew that he would see it through to the bitter end. A full-time job, of course. And a change of place (at least, provisionally). But it was also a brief which not everyone would resolve, and not everyone would be entrusted with. Even if it were to require twice as much time . . .

When he declared his willingness to undertake it, he did not realize that it would determine the rest of his life.

When Wilcke reached the management floor in Dostler Street at Munich-Milbertshofen on a winter's day in the middle of January 1960, he was more apprehensive than he had ever been before. The acting management board chairman was either not there, or was pretending not to be there. Wilcke stood around in the anteroom. Then the personal assistant took him to 'our head of finance, Herr Kämpfer'. Herr Kämpfer was very pleased to see him, accepted Wilcke's offer, declaring his willingness to study it and show it to his colleagues as well (and, thought Wilcke, mention it over the telephone – probably with his negotiating party, the 'free state' of Bavaria. He ticked himself off for not having been clever enough to go there in the first place). He asked when he could come back. In an hour, Kämpfer replied.

No, said Wilcke to himself, this was really not the right way to start. Granted, he had not expected a fanfare reception. But people certainly knew he had been sent by Quandt. It occurred to him that this Kämpfer had claimed to have already concluded a contract with Daimler-Benz before the controversial general meeting. That was what the so-and-so had said. Or had he?

The weather was uninviting, cold, snowless. Could this be Munich in winter, without snow? Well, it can happen sometimes. Wilcke turned up the collar on his overcoat and went out onto the street. The works were over there. He had looked it up for himself on the map; it was a large rectangle with fences around it, shielded like a fortress, with its gates providing the only points to spy on what was going on inside.

He went off, with the determination of a spy trying to discover something through the back door when the front door has been barred to him. But all he could discover was tranquillity, leaden, oppressive tranquillity – and this was on a working day! Was this where cars were already supposed to be leaving the line? The first 700 coupés would soon be leaving the factory, as Quandt had enthusiastically said. Where? Was it here? (Wilcke did not know at the time that the pressing shop, just like the basic assembly plant, screened by halls and yards, was in the centre of the site). There was hardly a sound. Now and again there was an electric vehicle which went humming by behind the fences, then a few workers moving nonchalantly across the site. And that was it! And Wilcke suddenly thought he had been rash to allow himself to be taken in so easily.

Accustomed to systematically examining the files, which any lawyer will do when he takes on a case, the whip of time had picked him up like a spinning top and immediately spun him towards its centre. After Feith, almost half the supervisory board, including the representatives of the major banks, had resigned their seats. Without a supervisory board required to appoint a new management board, the company was hanging in mid air.

According to paragraph 89 section I of the Share Act, the regional court could appoint new supervisory board members, if 'there were only a minority of members on the supervisory board for longer than three months, as prescribed in the Share Act, or in the firm's articles of association.' Who would the company registrar appoint? Quandt's right of recommendation as a major shareholder was limited, having, in addition to Wilcke, decided on Dr Johann Semler. Semler was an independent auditor and provided excellent credentials, as the president of the Association for the Protection of Private Bond Holders, to be the 'restructurer'. The favoured candidate from the acting management board, as Wilcke suspected, was Fritz Aurel Goergen, regarded as an entrepreneurial thoroughbred. Recommended by the Hessian Chief Minister Zinn (Goergen had rebuilt Henschel in Kassel), he was also an experienced technician. He had already had the company examined by business experts in order to implement new types of production at BMW (he was thinking of gears, which could be produced on many of the existing and under-utilized machines, without major re-tooling).

What had Semler got in his favour? He had successfully restructured Henschel before Goergen arrived there. He was not lacking in courage. On one occasion, he had made himself unpopular with the Americans with his 'chicken feed' speech (he had been the chairman of the Bizone Economic Council), in which he severely criticised the contradictory American economic policy with regard to Germany. His successor was Ludwig Erhard. His authority was indisputable. But the wind was blowing against him, as he had been the one to recommend the unsuccessful Daimler-Benz package for saving BMW in a report to the shareholders. The employees' representatives on the supervisory board (besides Golda, there were two other representatives from the works council and a man from the trades unions) would, not least because of that, vote against him, and for Goergen, when the election for chairman came up. If Goergen were voted in at the top, that would mean a fraternal feud within BMW after successful restructuring, even if that were to meet with Quandt's approval. Wilcke was under no illusions. Having Quandt and Goergen together was not desirable. Both wanted to act as entrepreneurs, and were bound to get under each other's feet. Having accomplished the Herculean task of building a strict business organisation and profitable production, Goergen would never agree happily to the idea of being the man to pull chestnuts out of the fire for Quandt. And Quandt, who wanted to be the entrepreneur, but was not one yet, would never accept the demands for power-sharing which were bound to result. It was far better for them to keep their hands off! Everything ultimately depended on this election, all the more so as the company was about to conclude a contract with the free state of Bavaria, which would make the province (through a capital investment amounting to 50 per cent of the capital of Power Plant Production Co. Ltd), to all intents and purposes, the other partner in the subsidiary company. Admittedly, Bavaria was anxious to put ten million DM down on the table straight away, but, as Quandt and Pavel immediately saw, BMW would suffer irreparable damage, firstly because no buy-back clause would be inserted, and secondly, because the shares had been set far too low. (General Electric, as Quandt had instantly discovered, was prepared to bid considerably more for a participation, as it was interested in following the Starfighter contract issued by the Federal Defence Ministry.) So, working feverishly, Quandt, Pavel, and Wilcke put together a parallel offer. Would the management board still consider it at all, so soon before concluding the agreement with the Bavarian government?

Well, Quandt had not sent a man like Wilcke onto the battlefield for nothing. Used to negotiating, he would not deviate from his practice of putting his cards on the table – this had always proved to be an advantage, and never a disadvantage. Things would not be different now. The fact that he represented interests (we all represent interests!) only carried limited weight. The better offer would count. He was ready to accept it if the opposition were equally willing. Apropos the opposition, is that what it still was? Weren't we all in the same boat? The state of affairs (nothing needed to be glossed over) was serious enough.

And so, once he had returned to the management section, Wilcke showed all the insight required of him, weighing up other points of view, refuting them and founding his own theories. He said impartially from the beginning that there had been an 'entente cordiale' between Strauß, the Federal Defence Minister, and Quandt, and that, without doubt, the Federation, by awarding a major contract, would prefer to entrust the fate of Power Plant Production to Quandt than to anyone else. Should the tables turn, then so be it. A supervisory board was an independent body, whose members represented interested parties, but also had a conscience. Nobody could buy this conscience. Nor his conscience, either.

And so he managed to make people suspicious with what initially seemed a scornful refusal of their offer. They wanted to include the right for reacquisition in the contract, and promised not to agree to anything which might damage managerial solutions for the future, whether they had been drafted by Quandt or by others.

What annoyed and disconcerted Wilcke was precisely the displeasure which affected him in his initial enquiries within Bavaria. He swore to himself that this would not happen again. When the first supervisory board meeting had been summoned, he travelled to Munich a few days beforehand, to get to know the lie of the land in Bavarian ministries and public offices. He even looked round the offices of his legal colleagues who had been nominated for the supervisory board, swotted up on lion-maned business practices.* He learnt that the Bavarian colours are white and blue (and not blue and white). He learnt of the connections that existed between state and city. He discovered that the Abbot of Andechs, Hugo Lang, joined in the politics of the free state by speaking powerfully outside his ecclesiastical jurisdiction. But he also discovered how the weights were stacked in relation to BMW. There was a greater leaning in the Ministry of the Economy to Herr Goergen, but in the Finance Ministry, it was to Herr Semler (and this was simply because the major shareholder had proposed the latter). Dr Barbarino often declared that the mess of the past decade could primarily be attributed to the lack of leadership in the company. What BMW was missing was the 'strong man', who possessed both financial acumen, as well as sufficient courage, to become an outward-going entrepreneur.

The question remained as to whom the supervisory board would elect. Then a piece of news came to Wilcke's aid and a realisation that there was likely to be a majority for Goergen. The press stated, on the day before the election, that Goergen wanted to bring the American aircraft company

---

*Tr. note: The symbol of Bavaria is a lion.

United Aircraft into the BMW business. It was later shown that there was not a word of truth in this. But Goergen failed to deny this, and the Bonn Defence Ministry had firm agreements with General Electric, and not with its competitor United Aircraft.

Now behold Wilcke the negotiator! Faced with a seemingly hopeless situation (the majority of the supervisory board members were for Goergen), he declared (Semler and Goergen had been sent out to wait at the door) that there was clearly some suspicion against a representative of a major shareholder which he had to overcome. However, he could do nothing other than argue for Semler. Why? Well, Semler would be neutral, would take their views into consideration and act as a representative of all the shareholders, and not just for one section, the Quandt group included. Incidentally, it was in no way striving to acquire a majority shareholding in BMW, and that in neither car nor power plant production did it possess its own facilities or developments. As a result, it was also not in a position to be able to offer a feasible, technical approach. As restructuring was not only a financial, but also a technical problem (in his view, the technical part even prevailed), there was most likely a need, in the absence of a technician on the management board, to form a technical works committee whose chair Herr Goergen (Wilcke knew no one better) should take over.

It was not expressed unconvincingly. Mind you, Wilcke continued, without raising his voice, the decision as to who would restructure the company was dependent on the Starfighter contract, and he had the feeling that Bonn would make the award to the Power Plant Production subsidiary dependent on a supervisory board chairman guaranteeing . . .

A furore erupted. There were cries that the election was the business of the supervisory board alone, that it was of no concern to either Emperor or Pope, and that they, the board members, were elected people. Wilcke tried to pacify them, claiming that Bonn had never said *who* the supervisory board should elect. They had just hinted at the thinking applied by the customer to the recovery of the sick man at Oberwiesenfeld, if the one or the other candidate were to be elected. He stated once again that it was obvious that only the Federal contract would enable 'restructuring by the company's own means.' If this failed to materialise, everyone might just as well go home there and then.

So was Semler the right man? Certainly, argued Wilcke. And so Semler was voted in unanimously. Goergen and Semler came back in, and, as the defeated candidate, Goergen was the first to congratulate the elected candidate, during which, as Wilcke described in a report, he 'behaved sportingly'. (At the next supervisory board meeting, however, Goergen resigned the chair of the technical committee, which was thereupon wound up, speaking of the 'greatest conspiracy of all time.' Soon afterwards he also resigned his supervisory board post.)

Had Quandt won? We shall see. In any case, the restructuring could begin, and people could read in the press that it was now up to the BMW administration to examine all the possibilities for restructuring. The Quandt group would then decide on the best one out of the emerging solutions, provided that BMW would continue to build cars with the white and blue trade-mark, and (no longer on the agenda) that Power Plant Production Co. Ltd would remain a subsidiary of the AG.

The Restructuring

Anyone trying to follow the confusion surrounding the restructuring of BMW would gain something out of it, provided he was sufficiently patient. Comparisons with the game of patience played with dice are indeed appropriate: 'Back to B, if position R is taken. Poker bids are being made on square E till it makes your eyes water, and a delaying tactic on F (missing a turn twice). Unreasonable conditions on G, which the challenger cannot accept, without losing face. Advance to O . . .' The picture portrayed is not dissimilar to an ant-hill whose inhabitants move with secret messages, making their apparently aimless way past the ruins of the catastrophe which has overtaken them.

A look at the disaster area a few days later shows that things have already changed. Obstacles have been cleared away, new paths are recognisable, without it giving any indication as to how building will continue, whether it will be abandoned or whether the directives from the secret command post will be enough to save it.

This is what it was like here, too. Enquiries, conjectures, exploratory discussions, and orders were issued to all four points of the compass. Telephones rang, telexes chattered away; a state of feverish activity had taken hold of everyone, whether they were at the top or on the side – assistants, secretaries, messengers, detail designers at the drawing board, workers on the factory floor, all of them constantly kept abreast of the most recent developments of the restructuring by press and radio, looked to the 'top', where three men (when not openly conferring inside the company) were constantly on the road. These were Semler, who, as the neutral authority, determined the main direction of the attack; Wilcke, who ran the restructuring committee, though obliged to represent Quandt's interests in all that he did; and Kämpfer, the man on the management board. After Richter-Brohm had collected his hat (in an amicable arrangement; meaning that he had left the company), he, as the first amongst equals, determined daily production, directed marketing (meaning sales), and made sure that both activities went smoothly to attract all-important investments. With the desperate financial situation, this proved a juggling act in its own right. He was present at all the decisive negotiations on restructuring, and was the very man who often produced the final outcome by calculating the most intelligently, and arguing the most rationally.

A fourth man from the Quandt group, Dr Horst Pavel, Herbert Quandt's confidant and trustee in the so-called four-man council in the family empire, as well as being a friend of Wilcke's since the thirties, was the promoter who directed and guided all negotiations, who calculated and determined what Wilcke had to do next, and who in turn obtained Quandt's approval.

From the start, all four of them knew that they had to proceed on two tracks to get the ship underway again – keeping the jewel of Power Plant Production Co. Ltd within the AG (anyone wanting to have the daughter must marry the mother) and, at the same time, ensuring that any suitor from the car business putting down his card would at best be satisfied with half (never more than 50 per cent) of the total.

First of all, Wilcke sounded out the field at Daimler-Benz. He secretly met Dr Zahn, the head of finance for the Swabians, on neutral ground at the railway station at Ulm. The atmosphere was as one might find in a waiting-room. Zahn, the real promoter of Daimler-Benz's involvement at Milbertshofen still thought that there were some points of common interest, and Wilcke knew that he would have to abandon his primary goal, as Zahn had been rankled by it. His goal was that BMW should become the important achievement of his life, because the Deutsche Bank had made that ill-fated decision to submit the restructuring package not to the administration, but to the shareholders to vote on.

'Yes, yes,' said Wilcke, 'and that was quite right. Mercedes would always be stuck with the accusation that it had killed off BMW!'

After a pause, he went on to ask what would happen if BMW were prepared to deviate from the cast-iron law and grant Daimler-Benz 51 per cent. The supervisory and management boards had empowered him to make this proposal, 'provided that we (he was already using we) are left with our independence.'

But the signals indicated a different track, and the signalman was none other than Flick himself. In March 1960, Wilcke had another meeting at Frankfurt with Könecke, the management board chairman of Daimler-Benz AG, and handed him a revised offer. But Flick, who had not got over the refusal, gave an angry 'no', to the disappointment of both management boards. Three years later, BMW's disappointment changed to very great satisfaction.

Even the American Motors Corporation was interested and sent a whole team of experts across the Pond. They arrived in the hope of building the 'Rambler', which was a small car in American terms (a car which had not succeeded), as a mid-range car for Europe. They made their calculations, flew back, made further calculations. But the calculation (made in the USA in US dollars, and in Germany in D-Marks) left too wide a gap when set against the costs and achievable prices of the German competition. This applied equally to the method of production. American Motors wanted a cheap car, while BMW preferred better quality cars, and consequently, as justified by performance and fittings, a mid-range car which would naturally cost more. However, they 'liked' each other and left nothing untried. As late as August 1960, when the engagement was well and truly over, Kämpfer and

Wilcke visited the American Motors' factories on Lake Michigan. It brought tears to their eyes. They were taken aback at just how much automation there was, feeling that, especially in bodywork, Milbertshofen was the poorest of relations. And yet on closer examination, what need was there to feel ashamed of the numerous panels and their often primitive finishing (for example, on joints and edges, as the layman Wilcke had noticed)? We were streets ahead in comparison! To give that up would mean the end of BMW.

And what about Ford? Courted by Richter-Brohm as early as the previous year, only the price was really of any significance. Kämpfer had then set it at 180 million! Without batting an eyelid, Ford had immediately accepted it. But for what reason? They had wanted (and still wanted) to take over the firm's name, the trade-mark – in fact, the entire Milbertshofen works. On the other hand, they would leave the AG with Allach, Works 2, with all its paraphernalia, as well as power plant production. The AG could then call itself what it wanted, provided it was not BMW. The offer was still valid – and was filed away, with the understanding that the matter was closed.

There then followed discussions with Chrysler, with Rheinstahl-Hanomag, with Simca, with Fiat at the five-star hotel Baur au Lac near Zurich, and also with Rootes in London, as a continuation of those contacts which Mathern had entered into there, immediately before the 'coup' at Theresienhöhe. Herr Borgward from Bremen also appeared on the scene, a self-made man, the creator of the extremely successful 'Isabella' and the owner of the Lloyd and Goliath Works.

As Wilcke remembered: 'He turned up with rather a large number of colleagues, including the director Wilhelm Gieschen, who the following year was to transfer to the BMW management board. The resident group in the BMW boardroom at the time did not comprise the members of the party. After one fairly cursory visit round the factory (we called it then the "50 cents tour", as opposed to the "5 dollar tour" which we had offered the Americans), the discussions started. It emerged from these, after both sides had expounded their interests (but not during the explanation itself), that Borgward intended to take a lease on the Milbertshofen works, in order to introduce expansion for his own production facilities and, alongside that, keep the capacity to build BMWs as well, inasfar as that were possible. All of this seemed a curious plan. The realisation that we needed a considerable amount of new resources to proceed with our restructuring, and that a regular rent could never reach the amounts of money required, seemed not to have dawned on him. He obviously had no idea that his business, just nine months later, would be in a more serious financial situation than ours would be. Our viewpoints were too disparate to make further discussions appear sensible.'

It was almost like the fairy tale in which the king presents his stubborn daughter with suitor after suitor, all of whom were rejected owing to the wilfulness of the beautiful princess – or rather, they got themselves rejected when she set each in turn the same insoluble riddles. They did not lose their heads as in Turandot's time; on the contrary, they kept them, and it was the princess's head that was at stake. And yet did she really keep saying 'no'?

The secret quickly came to light, and we shall let Wilcke speak now, as the 'king' receiving suitor after suitor.

'There was always a change of heart when we declared that no participation in the BMW share capital could be tolerated if it exceeded 50 per cent. This did not come out immediately; it often only emerged later when the delegates had spoken with people, such as their major shareholders, their supervisory board, or their general management board. Viewed with hindsight, this appeared quite understandable. Yet if the question is put today as to where we got our confidence from which enabled us to insist throughout on this requirement, despite our unfavourable negotiating position, then there were probably two determining factors. These were that we again had a major shareholder with solid finances, allowing everyone, even the sceptics in the background, to be confident of building. And there was our confidence in our own technological potential, which grew from negotiation to negotiation, since almost every interested party showed particular interest in the state of our development, especially in engine production.'

That was probably it. There was an ever increasing self-confidence, faced with which even pessimists had to admit, on meeting the lawyer Wilcke, that not every powerful influence was harmful. It was scarcely conceivable that, under the aegis of a major shareholder, the former BMW management could have squandered away millions. The suspicion was certainly still great as to whether Quandt, who was still also a shareholder at Daimler-Benz, only wanted to increase his shareholding influence by being active at BMW. Flick definitely set the tone at Daimler. Yet Flick's example as the man who had just acquired the Auto Union (DKW) for his car empire, could not be a justification for Quandt to behave in a similar way. Would that mean using BMW as a means to an end, whereby Flick's majority would be disputed? There was a lot to be argued for that (as shown in Semler's initially seriously considered plan to have co-production of 'certain components' at Daimler-Benz for the future BMW mid-range car, which would undoubtedly mean granting participation in the BMW share capital to Daimler). Yet there was more to be said against it, above all Quandt's willingness to invest fresh capital in BMW to a more than adequate level. This would not only be done, as he had announced, by having recourse to an in-house rights issue for recently acquired shares, but also, more importantly, by taking over under-utilised surpluses of such shares on the stock market. Anyone wanting to do that, as the press said in its attempts to assist him, probably believed in his own luck.

That self-confidence also persuaded the Bavarian banks to give up their strict refusal (which they had politely but firmly applied) when Wilcke had continued in his attempts to obtain loans for production costs. But loans for running costs are not loans for investment, in the way that they had been refused to Richter-Brohm. The refusal which Wilcke, as Quandt's representative, had been faced with, not only at the Deutsche and Dresdner Banks, but also from a man such as Baron von Tucher, the chairman of the Bayerische Vereinsbank, and someone known to Wilcke for his loyalty, was initially so adamant that it led him to think there might be some conspiracy. This was a suspicion which, upon closer inspection, was quite unfounded. Quandt's connections with the Bavarian banks had always been good. Granting loans for running costs to a Bavarian industrial business, which was also picking up, was nothing extraordinary. So what was this resistance supposed to mean? Finally, Wilcke and Kämpfer, calling in their 'deserved right' after ever more negotiations, managed to have BMW granted 25 million, '25 million and not a penny more'. There was just 10 million missing now (the estimated running costs showed 35 million) and a security should guarantee that. With this security, which was never taken up, it was far from being one of the major banks which stepped in – it was the free state of Bavaria which guaranteed it. This was brought about through the provincial institution for financing reconstruction and through its president Dr Hans Peter, who had also helped BMW previously. (Later, when the resurgence of BMW was no longer in doubt, the banks queued up, which, in view of earlier humiliations, 'created a great sense of satisfaction' for Wilcke.)

There was no way of avoiding a strong partner. If he could not be found in the car business, then why not in power plant production? The company had always been borne up by aero-engines. Even if Power Plant Production Co. Ltd, which it had re-founded, had not, for good reasons, been seen again as the hub of a major and vital branch of production capable of supporting the Bavarian Motor Works, and had been side-lined (the reasons for this were explained in the chapter 'Renouncing the Air'), there was no possibility of it remaining on the back lines of Quandt's chessboard. The forward moves they made had, as we know, been determined by that huge contract from the Federal Defence Ministry, which had only been a theoretical proposition before. This involved copying the power plants for the Starfighter, called Project J 79, whose licence the Germans had acquired for their Federal Luftwaffe from General Electric (USA), the most important power plant producer in the world after Rolls-Royce and Bristol (both British).

As early as the general meeting of 9 December, which Wilcke had attended as Quandt's representative, his attention (as the sober observer) had been attracted by the great interest of MAN (Maschinenfabrik Augsburg Nürnberg) in the 'jewel', which Mathern had again made much of. It was quite clear what was being planned. A counter offer, designed to alarm the shareholders, would first check-mate Daimler-Benz, so that if it did not actually save BMW, it would at least provide an initial breathing space. It was a question of wait and see. At that time, Wilcke had not doubted for a moment that restructuring by Daimler-Benz would be carried out, and the question of what MAN wanted had been irrelevant to him. If Daimler-Benz made the running, it would be over once and for all through other people (naturally, only once there was acquisition or a participation in the 'jewel'). Only now did he understand what was involved. Although he did not belong to the supervisory board, but spoke up for MAN again through shareholders' letters, as the representative of shares to the value of 3 million DM, Mathern had prophesied at one of the many conversations on the subject that it had by no means been ruled out that the limited company (meaning the subsidiary) could one day be worth more than the entire company in its present form.

The fact that MAN was making increased efforts towards power plant production was known all across town, outside of which, on the works site at Allach acquired from BMW in 1955, it was building its vehicles. Right next to it was Turbo Engines Co. Ltd, which it had founded as a company concerned more with research and development, and which maintained close connections with the British power plant company, Rolls Royce. Rolls Royce built 55 per cent of all the power plants used in aviation throughout the world, and MAN had been awarded the job of developing a power plant suitable for vertical take-offs, a far-sighted goal into the future for both military and civilian applications. The question was not a new one: why should not a common future be envisaged for both companies, given that they both lived, so to speak, back to back at Allach? BMW AG let people know that this was fully open to discussion. They only thing was, though, that the daughter could not be had without the mother. MAN was asked why, given that they had been building vehicles for ever and a day, they did not want to become partners in a car company. Yet things did not drag on for very long. A counter offer was made. In fact, a very good one.

It was no secret where it came from. It was from General Electric, the issuer of the licence for that Starfighter contract whose acquisition for the BMW subsidiary, Power Plant Production Co. Ltd (the means to achieve restructuring) was a matter dear to the heart of the major shareholder Quandt.

It was against this background that Pavel and Wilcke negotiated, and found themselves torn between two suitors. In General Electric's favour was the fact that only *one* partner needed to be dealt with (with MAN, in addition to General Electric as the licenser for the contract to copy the engine, there was always their competitor, Rolls Royce, to consider). A second plus point was that General Electric appeared willing to co-operate on restructuring the parent company without further ado. It was still unclear as to how they would do this, but they held out the prospect of a loan of 40 million DM in exchange for a 51 per cent majority holding in the subsidiary (a requirement which MAN also imposed). Their aim was to establish a BMW in Munich their all-European centre in the field of jet engines.

MAN was a more complicated affair. Here there was the need to confer with the provincial government in Bavaria and Bonn. A clause in the contract between BMW and the free state envisaged that if the investment in Power Plant Production provided by the province were to be passed on (the first money to have flown into the restructuring coffers), then MAN, independently of the re-acquisition right sought for BMW by Quandt, should be the preferred partner. The free state of Bavaria, which was particularly supportive of the old industrial businesses and their many traditions on Bavarian soil, wanted this. Such was the case with MAN, which was older and richer in tradition than BMW. Bonn, too, with the Bavarian Strauß as Defence Minister, had in this respect secured for itself the right to be consulted through financial participation when the Federal Republic of Germany acquired 2 per cent of the Power Plant Production shares in a trust.

All that was more annoying than gratifying, but it might serve as the starting-point for avoiding that 51 per cent which MAN had originally demanded and which, as we saw with the suitors from the car business, had so frightened Pavel and Wilcke, that it seemed as if they were selling themselves to the devil by accepting it. The fact that MAN (instead of a genuine participation in BMW, which it could not yet decide upon) wanted to guarantee a genuine restructuring loan to the mother, just in case the latter should supply it with the daughter (to run for ten years at a favourable rate of interest, even being interest-free for the first two years), was something which persuaded Pavel and Wilcke (appointed to give away the bride) that, all things considered, this was the better offer, however much they valued the 'clear and elegant negotiating style' of the Frankfurt-based lawyer Dr Rudolf Müller, representing General Electric.

The bottom line was a purchase price of 22.5 million DM. If the loan confirmation were calculated in, then it would be a good equivalent for the shares in Power Plant Production to be transferred.

It was planned that the deciding 51 per cent would later be offered for sale to MAN when both companies (BMW Power Plant Production Co. Ltd and MAN Turbo Engines Co. Ltd) had been merged. Even the purchase price had already been set. A packet supplement of 2 million DM was to be added to the nominal value. (Mention was still made of the fact that General Electric had reduced its purchase price amounting to 21.7 million DM by 3.8 million DM at the last moment. Both offers had been subject to deadlines. However, they granted a loan for the same amount to cover this. They had long moved away from the initial figure of 40 million DM.) Pavel and Wilcke had also negotiated with Bristol Siddeley, the third possible partner in the field of jet engines. There had been mutual visits to London and Munich, and discussions about solutions which amounted to Bristol, with its long attachment to BMW, considering taking up 25 per cent of the share capital to be raised in BMW AG. Throughout May 1960, the Bonn-based Bristol delegate rang Wilcke in Munich almost every day. Yet by 1 June (the deadline for submitting tenders), there was no proposal on the table which the supervisory board might still discuss.

In the marathon negotiations with MAN, which dragged on at Nuremberg into the night of 31 May, the partners came to an agreement. Now, as a result of the concluded contract, the Federal Defence Ministry issued the major contract for copying the Starfighter GE-J 79 engine. This proved to be an ill-fated plane, whose rate of loss in peace time was equal to many an air battle in the Second World War. But that is another story.

If we compare the BMW restructuring with the three phases of a space rocket taking off, then the first phase (lift-off) had been achieved. Those responsible for restructuring had separated themselves from half of the share capital of the largest subsidiary the AG possessed, at a price of 37 million DM in round figures.

The second phase (leaving the earth's atmosphere) proved the decisive one. For those responsible for restructuring, this meant finding and transposing that technological concept with which the mid-range car sank or swam. Was BMW capable of that? Was the old engineering spirit still to be found in the company?

The third phase (entry into orbit) was of a purely financial nature. This involved legally restructuring the shares by consolidating the capital and increasing its value again, meaning that the company would be provided with around 50 million DM of new resources. Together with the revenue from phase 1, that was 87 million DM, exactly the sum which investments came to for a new model range.

No sooner was BMW 'out of the woods' with this model range than the company would again find links with the other car manufacturers in Germany, who had raced far ahead of the company in the preceding decade, such as Volkswagen, Daimler-Benz and those already belonging to the Americans, Opel and Ford.

To catch up with them was the aim of this restructuring, which was about as modest as it was mad.

Later, when the banks (impressed by increasing interest payments at BMW) tried to make up their lost ground, one of the bankers, at a banquet to which they had invited leading BMW people, said as he turned to Wilcke: 'A remarkable firm, this Bavarian Motor Works. When, in the defeat of war, the car industry started up again modestly building small cars, BMW built a big one. When all of them went over to building mid-range cars with ever increasing engine sizes, BMW built a small car. The fact that they were successful, in spite of this, must be the seventh wonder of the world.'

What he was referring to was the BMW 700, which (and this was the *real* wonder for Wilcke) had initially appeared as a coupé and only then as a 'small saloon'. This had turned all known rules on their head. The coupé *and* the saloon had, at a time when Kadetts, small Prinzes, Taunus 12 Ms and Arabelles were seen on the streets, literally kept the company above water by their sales success, and bridged that hazardous period which the mid-range car needed for its run-up.

To retain the metaphor, if the concept of a countdown is applied to this run-up, then those responsible for restructuring had to start from a date which, at the earliest, would be fixed in 1963, that D-day when the projected mid-range car would be ready for production.

Crossing the Rubicon

In the model room of the works there was a prototype, dating from Richter-Brohm's times, which had never been put into production because the banks had refused the resources. Every so often Wilcke would go past it, accompanied by Semler or Kämpfer, whose disparaging remarks, as a layman, he did not understand. The car seemed quite acceptable to him. Borgward immediately dismissed it. On a visit to Milbertshofen, he had driven it a few times around the yard (the yard was not very big). He claimed that it was no Isabella, and so should be left where it was, and not given a second's thought.

But it was not this judgment by Borgward which led to its rejection. The car had been technologically superseded. Just to alter the rigid axle mounted on leaf springs would have required considerable re-designing. The car would have become too expensive, making it cost more than 9,500 DM, and that was a lot of money – too much money to be able to compete with the mid-range cars of other manufacturers. By the end, a considerable amount of money had been shelled out for it, as with the large cars (still produced at a rate of three per day). So the answer was no. Faced with all the lost time which that would cause, Kämpfer suggested designing two mid-range cars, a 1.3-litre model with four cylinders, and a 1.8-litre car with six cylinders with extensive rationalization of their components. But even this idea was thrown out. Everything depended on finding the right price.

The break-even point (the point in the calculation which marks the profit threshold, in which revenue is equal to all fixed and proportional costs of the product) was for BMW to be found at an annual turnover of 240 million DM (halcyon days: two decades later, it would be way above ten times that figure!). In order to achieve a monthly turnover of 20 million DM, two basic models were required – the small car (at a low price) and the mid-range car, which would have a price level above Opel and Ford, whose quantities it could never match. If the company kept to the countdown and the calculation was to add up, the mid-range car had to be 'up and running' by 1963. Could that be done? Faced with this deadline, any large factory would have capitulated. But at BMW, apparent weaknesses would be turned into strengths. The company was small, and therefore more flexible than any large car factory, whose much greater automation imposed levels below which production could not fall. With a much lower requirement in materials, the suppliers could also be quick, punctual and accurate. And as regards technology (designing, developing and testing), everyone employed on it stood 'at order arms' (to use a military term), prepared, if necessary, to turn night into day.

Kämpfer had always been amazed how a car was produced in a car factory (at least at BMW). With the simplified mind of a businessman, this is how he saw it:

'The technicians set to and started tinkering about on one thing or another. Over here engines, over there bodies. Someone makes something in the model room. Then one day, they get together and go to the management board, saying that they have got something to put forward. Then there's a great hullabaloo, as happened with the big car. Technicians always want to produce something they're happy with. . . . still more hp. . . . better performance. . . . the weight still isn't quite right. . . . It's all been established how many kilos it can weigh, this new, unique car, this lightweight, thoroughbred dream of a car. It was only then that the prototype was on its feet, but weighing much more than planned. Weight costs speed, meaning power and fuel. But it is hopeless trying to get the car to lose weight, more hopeless than any slimming courses for humans, where at least the basic concept is still generally valid. But with cars, the effect comes from the shape. . . .'

He had learnt that under Richter-Brohm, when the staff had fallen back on the 503 for the mid-range car. The 503 as a coupé and convertible was the epitomy of a dream-car, but, being predominantly handmade, it was, at 32,000 marks, unaffordable to the general public. The management board thought that if they were to put this on the streets as a mid-range car (and that must be feasible in production), then people would dash out to buy it. So it had been reduced to a mid-sized format using a pantograph, and when the management board viewed the plaster-cast result in the model room, Kämpfer admitted that 'while they made sure that people weren't ecstatic, everyone was still unreserved in their praise.' Then the creation was exhibited out on the yard. The impression was devastating. Outside, the car gave the impression of looking like a toy. No one could imagine it would be marketable.

As the man in charge of finances, Kämpfer had now offered the marketing department, by way of a trial, something which had previously been the technician's business – to determine what should be built. He told them: 'You have the customers' ear, and you know what can be sold and what cannot!'

This went down just as badly with the salesmen as it did with the designers and technicians. Kämpfer was soon to sum it all up by saying: 'One side is disgruntled because they weren't able to complain about not being asked what they needed, and the other side, deprived of power, would have to come up with ideas which did not immediately imply debt, even taking into account the materials.'

He also instituted the practice of always having all the management board assemble in the model room whenever a model, or even just a modification, was on the agenda. There it could give its approval or justify its rejection. The new car was fitted at the front with MacPherson-type struts, and, combined with a modified rear suspension using semi-trailing arms taken from the 600, provided exceptionally good road-holding, together with Alex von Falkenhausen's revolutionary 'turbulence chamber' in the engine. These made the vehicle innovative (in spite of all the inevitable faults which the 'criminally short development time', as described by one of the directors, would result in). With an overhead camshaft, the engine with its 65 hp was limited to 1.5 litres (the management had wanted this, with an eye on Mercedes). But the engine block had been so constructed as to hide the fact that it could be increased to 1.8 litres without reworking.

Fiedler had envisaged an engine block made of light metal. But Falken-hausen insisted on cast-iron, to avoid bearing failure and piston seizure, which in his view were inevitable, and could lead to the premature end of not only the car, but BMW as well. But he did not force it through, even when he threatened to hand in his notice.

Robert Pertuss was persuaded to transfer to the management board as the technical member from the Karmann company in Osnabrück, where he had spent four years building bodies. Pertuss had been the works manager at Henschel during the war. He was familiar with machine-tool production, but lacked practical experience in car manufacture, although he knew how bodies were built – the Karmann Ghia, something the experts felt was never to achieved again, had come about under his direction. So his principal concern was the body shape of the new car, for which he envisaged a wide radiator grille, as fitted by most other manufacturers. This met with Herbert Quandt's opposition. Quandt insisted, to put it bluntly, on the 'kidneys' – an intrinsic characteristic, by which BMW was distinguished from all other vehicles. It had always been like this, and would remain so. This was the first time that Quandt, as the major shareholder, got involved in product fashioning, an event whose symbolism no one who experienced it could deny (since it involved a symbol). With a recognition that he was increasingly taking on risks, the entrepreneur's will had shown its desire here to have an effect on the product that was deemed to be marketable. There was more to it, as he wanted to avert irreparable damage. (Indeed, the 'kidney' soon proved to be indispensable. Quandt was right to hold firm; his instinct had not let him down.)

Wilcke had also been profoundly impressed that this almost blind man had recognized something which had stayed hidden to the full-sighted experts. Quandt was crazy about cars. Since his youth, he had been fond of fast sports cars, admiring BMWs above all else. Long before coming to work for Quandt, Wilcke himself had driven a BMW 328, and he could understand what attracted men to it, even someone like Quandt, who had never personally been able to take the wheel of one of his cars. The legal adviser did not know that this love went deeper. It was only now that he realised it was directed at the make, at the genuine admiration for the complicated interplay between, on the one hand, engineering skill, styling, and sporting flair and, on the other (given premium engine technology), a very accurate knowledge of humanity's secret desires. This was what fascinated the man (who was his client) to the point of passion. And Wilcke understood that this provided the reason for deciding to cross the Rubicon (Wilcke was a classics scholar, and thought in such metaphors). This was where 'restructuring through in-house resources' took root, a venture Quandt now wanted to undertake.

This meant managing without a partner from the car industry (MAN was not this partner). It meant being completely at the mercy of the smallest hiccup in production or sales, which was what Richter-Brohm, less than a year ago, had cited as the reason for those losses. There was certainly no such crisis in sight. Yet one could occur at any time. Would everything then collapse like a house of cards? In other words, were they not putting everything at stake? In the meantime, the general meeting was approaching.

They viewed it calmly. The shareholders would probably agree to the two major points. These were, first, the intended reduction of the previous share capital by the ratio of 4:3, from 30 million to 22.5 million DM (the plan the year before had been to reduce it by half!), and second, the increase in the share capital (from 37.5 million to 75 million DM, which was to be done by issuing new shares at a rate of 140 per cent). They expected these to be approved. To do this, they hoped to offer long-term shareholders, as well as holders of convertible debentures, a rights issue of 1:1, something they had been excluded from at the unsuccessful restructuring offer in December 1959.

The prospect of remaining participants in the future of BMW rested on the administration's decision to keep the company as an independent, mid-sized car business. At a planning meeting, Pertuss, as the technician responsible, had given an unreservedly positive answer to Semler's question as to whether the programme under consideration could be realized with the company's facilities. The press shop, the foundry and everything up to the paint shop, final assembly, quality control, etc, everything was right, together with the space needed for a daily production of 350 cars. The machines and installations were on site. Any new buildings and acquisitions would be within the limits of the resources brought in by the increase in capital.

'Of 50 million DM?' Semler asked.

'Let's say, with a limit of tolerance of ten per cent,' answered Pertuss.

Semler said nothing.

It was somewhat later (the meeting had been interrupted for lunch) that he let the cat out of the bag. He said that it would be doubtful that BMW could continue if it limited itself simply to car and motorcycle production. He argued for the 'second support', by which he meant power plant production. The contracts with MAN did not preclude that, and at Allach, buildings could be put up over a good 30,000 square metres on the land still held by BMW.

That was old hat, according to Pavel and Wilcke. In long discussions, including those with Quandt, no one had felt the slightest inclination to take BMW back into the armaments business. The chapter was closed, and

491

if Golda, the chairman of the works council, had worriedly asked Wilcke if there was any guarantee that BMW would remain a car factory and not be converted into an armaments business, then this clearly showed that management and workforce had decided not to let that unfortunate connection arise again, a connection which had almost cost BMW its life. The shareholders would understand the truth of the statement which says that history does not repeat itself and that comparable events cannot re-occur.

There was quite another question, which was whether the firm would stick to its intention not to aim for too many mid-range cars. How disastrous the attempt might be to go over to producing large numbers of cars with insufficient resources was becoming evident at Borgward. What it came down to was how a medium-sized company would continue to exist in Germany. If there were a corresponding desire to shake up BMW, then, according to expert estimates, around 150 million DM would be required (the kind of money which could not have been realised even with Semler's 'second support').

In America, cars were being built, even big cars, which quickly altered in line with rapidly changing fashion. Even machines which were expensive to produce quickly paid for themselves. They were all standardised, and the low standard accelerated turnover. Although this principle had leapt across into Europe (Opel and Ford), production of individually recognisable cars had been fully maintained in Germany, with Daimler-Benz as a prime example, which could fairly claim to offer 'high-class series production'. Even at BMW they were returning to old concepts (based on long observation of what was going on around them, which had delayed the restructuring proposals). They were returning to special orders, to the individually produced car. The customer appreciated the value of this, as the 700's sales figures proved. Those responsible for restructuring were more than happy with Kämpfer and Wilcke, being immune from the worries which built up for the big boys in the business due to the pressure of large-scale production.

The question remained of finding an issue syndicate. According to the Share Law, a bank or a group of banks takes over the new shares to be created by means of the increase in capital, with the obligation to offer these to the shareholders at a rate determined at the general meeting. BMW's main bank, the Deutsche Bank, had declined to co-operate in this, following its declaration that the new issuing conditions glaringly diverged from those which 'their' man, Dr Feith, had proposed in December 1959 with the now famous rejection. What was to be done? The Quandt group had to swallow the bitter pill, and implement the capital increase itself through an in-house reception syndicate, which would guarantee subscription to all new shares.

That was easier said than done. Like the sheriff in the famous western *High Noon* who ran from citizen to citizen asking for their support, so did Pavel, and then Wilcke likewise run from bank to bank. They came up against a curt refusal in one place, and half-hearted acquiescence in another to take part in a kind of a limited involvement on the reception syndicate, without showing themselves in public. They found, literally at the last minute (this was twenty-seven days before the general meeting summoned for 1 December

1960; the enrolment deadline had already expired), two 'highly reputable' banks who were willing to share the risk. These were the Dusseldorf Bank of Trinkaus (whose director, the banker Rudolf Groth, had been friends with Wilcke since 1937), and the Frankfurter Bank in Frankfurt (where Pavel negotiated with the chairman of the management board, Dr Janssen).

The risk, which the Quandt group took over as the syndicate management, theoretically lay between 0 and 39 million DM (three quarters of 52 million), from which Quandt calculated that he would have to take on around 10 to 15 million DM. He did not consider that a misfortune, as the new shares would increase the authorised capital upon which a partner's eyes would first alight, one whose appearance was getting more and more likely, one who could possibly be won over. As Quandt had undertaken to hold the assembled shares at BMW's disposal for up to three years, the administration was at ease. What more did it want? No one was predicting just how many of the new shares would be taken up. The only thing that was certain was that the company would also actually receive the financial resources produced by the increase in capital as a result of Quandt's acceptance to take on all the unsubscribed shares.

When the 40th general meeting of the Bavarian Motor Works was opened at 10 a.m. on 1 December 1960 in the Congress Hall of the Deutsches Museum, it was clear that it would go down in the annals of German economic life. No German public limited company had ever increased its capital and implemented a rights issue without an issue syndicate. But no one was surprised. The last general meeting, if you remember, had already borne the hallmark of the unexpected – the passing of the balance sheet by the shareholders. Wilcke had constant recourse to remember that. If the balance sheet had not been passed in the customary fashion, the meeting could not have been adjourned and the decision would have had to have been taken, even after twenty hours on the go. The shareholders would finally have said 'yes' to Daimler-Benz.

The fact that they now accepted the restructuring concept without any issue syndicate with the overwhelming majority of 17,301,500 of all the votes cast (18,073,800), i.e. 95.73 per cent, showed that this time they trusted the administration's proposals. In contrast to the marked reluctance to take risks shown by the Deutsche Bank and other leading West German banks, they were once again ready to share the risk of a come-back by BMW, whatever the circumstances.

This happened although the coal-merchant Nold also wanted an adjournment (justifying this through Quandt's convertible debentures, which could discriminate against the other shareholders). Another objection came from a Dr Prein, who claimed that his overall view led him to think that a business student passing his finals could have made this restructuring proposal just as well. He would go as far as to say that if an economics student in his second year were to hand in the proposal as a seminar paper, his professor would give him a friendly pat on the shoulder and say: 'Young man, you will have to do better than this!' As Wilcke later remembered, it was as if a small terrier (Prein was the chairman of the Association for the Protection of Small Shareholders, a registered society in Frankfurt) were barking at a well-groomed great Dane (i.e. Dr Semler, who was facing Prein not only as chairman of the supervisory board at BMW, but also as the president of the Association for the Protection of Bond Holders).

Even the question of the partition of Germany came up; which conditions for participation would apply if assets in the East were to return to the domain of BMW, and whether there would be 'improvement certificates' for the shareholders. Dr Semler replied that this meeting could not possibly vote on that.

And so it went on, for seven and a half hours. Then the doors of the large conference room at the Deutsches Museum were opened, people streamed outside, a few reluctantly, but most with relief. Anyone who had come from out of town would cast a glance at the Isar, before continuing into the city centre and looking for his hotel. The Isar was covered by green spume, which made him forget it was already December.

Wilcke waved at his driver in the throng of people and cars driving up. On other occasions, he would have driven himself, but he had been unable to for several weeks. He swayed a bit. His back operation was still affecting him, and sciatica was causing him trouble, as it had done to old Fritz, about whom he, the 'Prussian' in Bavaria, had frequently had cause to think recently. Under the effect of powerful pain-killers, which made him feel that they not only relieved the pain but also deadened the mind, he had spoken only once, as he could not get up from his seat on the supervisory board panel. He was afraid that the same thing might befall him as it had with Richter-Brohm when the shareholders cried out: 'Stand up, if you want to speak to us!' Nothing of the kind had happened, but then how could it? The atmosphere had been entirely defused, and if an occasional aggressive remark had come out (as when Nold shouted to Semler: 'Who's stopping you opening your trap?'), the meeting had more hissed than applauded. At the election of the supervisory board, Wilcke had again been confirmed in his job, as well as voting in the indisposed Mathern, who was now his partner. Good, he thought, feeling a little bit happier now, it's over with.

Dr Semler, also re-elected and now the chairman of the supervisory board again, had declared before the election that election to the committee was a temporary arrangement for two years. He himself had wanted to relinquish his mandate but, as he had not managed to find a suitable person for the job, he would be a candidate again, although he wanted to be known as a proxy.

With the comforting news that 3,100 cars of the 700 type sold in December had exceeded the expected sales figure, Wilcke had travelled for a cure to the Wallis at the beginning of January. Consequently, he calculated that the turnover for 1960 amounted to 238 million DM, 8 million more than planned. In 1959, the turnover had been 170 million, and in 1958, it had amounted to around 195 million. Wilcke had stipulated that there were to be no telephone calls, no letters from work, nothing from the Stock Exchange, and nothing about how the new shares were being subscribed. For once, he wanted to know nothing for the entire three weeks.

494

On his journey back at the end of January, accompanied by his wife, he stopped off for lunch at Kempten, and bought himself a popular daily newspaper. It contained the news that Dr Semler had just taken on restructuring the Borgward works near Bremen on the request of the local Senate. Semler had already issued press statements in Bremen which clearly showed to Wilcke that both activities were irreconcilably opposed.

So they were going to have to part company with Semler. But the shareholders had only just re-elected him. What was the position with his responsibility towards share ownership? If Semler left, upon whose head would it be? Implementation of the share issue was in full swing.

A few weeks later (the subscription deadline ran until the middle of February), it was revealed that the new shares had been subscribed to a par value of 37,405,300 DM, which no one had thought possible. Only 94,700 DM needed to be taken up by the reception syndicate at a rate of 150 per cent for unsubscribed shares, from which a further 45,000 DM could be issued to those entitled to participate within an extended deadline.

With that, 52,509,470 DM in total flowed in as a result of increasing the company's share capital.

Quandt was entirely justified in considering himself proved right. The willingness he had shown to take a major risk had been overwhelmingly rewarded by the share and debenture holders. Quandt knew that that was not due to him. The shareholders had, to put it rather emotively (even the legal adviser Wilcke could find no fault in that), remained true to BMW.

Hahnemann Comes

BMW had stronger ties with the fate of the Borgward Works than people in Munich admitted. Even the man responsible for restructuring called from Munich to the Weser (this was Dr Semler) did not have the slightest idea that the success of one restructuring (this had by no means been completed at BMW) could be determined from the outcome of the other, at Borgward. But that was certainly the case. The collapse of Borgward unexpectedly coincided with the rise of BMW – not through additional purchase as in Schapiro's times, when Popp acquired the Eisenach Vehicle Factory, but through the availability of highly qualified technicians and businessmen who yearned for new responsibilities and whom Quandt immediately took on.

How this could have happened is a lesson in its own right.

There had been mass redundancies at Borgward. The reason for this ultimately lay in the figure of the firm's founder and proprietor. (There was an economic boom at the time, and West German industries did not know where they could get their workforce from.) More of a designer and researcher than a businessman, the skilled fitter Carl F.W. Borgward had hardly left any time for running his company, and had almost as little interest in it. Everybody knew that, locked up in his model room, he moulded piles of warm plasticine, which would soon take shape as cars and be put into immediate production in his works. But they disappeared again as quickly as they had emerged – without any regret from their creator, who raced from one new design to the next. They might quickly emerge again in altered forms, in a modified version and under a new badge. The cars attested to 'development', and were received warmly to the point of enthusiasm by the customer. But Borgward's strength (his complete independence) had not been able to hide his weakness. Despite initial successes with an eye-catching model, he had never managed to obtain that strong position in the market-place for the latter, which alone would have allowed for further experimenting, and which would have borne up the firm (there were three firms to which he had treated himself).

For reasons of raising capital, Borgward, now at the age of seventy, had finally accepted the proposition to turn the Borgward group, wholly owned by the family, into a public limited company – too late, as it now turned out. This was because favourable conversion facilities, which the law provided for up to 31 December 1959 (and which Flick, as well as Quandt had made full use of in their groups of companies), had been missed. The right moment had now been irrevocably lost.

As early as 1954, when raw materials had long been freely available on the open market, Borgward had left everything as it had always been. Instead of combining marketing, advertising and after-sales service, all three (with three times the costs) were run in parallel. It was a similar situation in administration. The dealers, who as a rule were only allowed to represent one of the three Bremen-based makes (Borgward, Lloyd and Goliath), looked around for rival products. This was because they were unable to help Borgward customers climb up the social ladder by supplying them with cars which came from the same company and which very probably marked the way ahead. Nevertheless, Borgward had managed up to now without outside help. Using his suppliers' money (he was not upset by his reputation of being a bad payer), his wide range of models, which consumed profits, had never become a threat to his existence. He was even considering expanding. If possible, that would be to Munich (we have heard about his visit to BMW), where he seriously proposed manufacturing his new Isabella, saying that there was no reason not to market it as the BMW Isabella. Last of all, he had ventured into the top of the range (like BMW with its 501 and 502 baroque angels) with his new 2.3-litre Borgward (with air suspension and automatic transmission). As always, he was not concerned, and failed to consider what was involved in applying a style which would have frightened off even someone like Grewenig, the former head of marketing at BMW, despite this being something very close to his own heart. Borgward expressed it quite straightforwardly:

'We are targeting our 2.3-litre car at the driver with sporting pretensions, because he is still the one who finds pleasure in driving. That is the car's strong point. The car is not a chauffeur-driven limousine, but has a sports character. Sports-minded drivers will gain more pleasure from it than from a Mercedes.'

It was bound to go wrong. It had gone as wrong for Borgward as it had gone right for BMW, if we remember Flick's ultimatum on the 9 December 1959. Facing comments referring to the bankruptcy of the Bremen-based company, Nordwolle (its collapse had shaken one German bank after another during the Slump), were cries from connoisseurs of the business. How can someone like Dr Borgward, who must know his trade, have his vast resources of energy channelled as an employee of second class administrative boards? Indeed, the Bremen Senate had set up the issue syndicate, which had appointed Dr Semler as chairman of the supervisory board, the same role he had had at BMW. Seen by the press as an 'ill omen' for the industry, he had first of all subjected the coffers, accounts and stocks of cars to inspection like an honest auditor, and had immediately declared to the public that the situation at BMW had been far from hopeful before his appearance in Munich. The differences in the tastes of European customers made it entirely possible to keep Borgward's specific characteristics.

Quandt was upset. However, he had gone with Wilcke to Bremen following an invitation by Semler to consider participating in the purchase of the

Borgward works. He inspected all three works with Wilcke next to him. The man showing him around was not unknown to Quandt. He had impressed him when Borgward had visited Milbertshofen with a group of technicians. This man was the chief engineer Wilhelm Heinrich Gieschen, right hand man of the car manufacturer Carl F.W. Borgward. Kämpfer wanted to discover why Gieschen had always sat on the other side of the table, opposite Borgward, and had never done any more than accept the latter's jobs, 'a man who did not take control, although he could have done, given that he had the whole production process under him . . .'

This was how Gieschen remembered his conversation with Quandt and what subsequently transpired:

'I said: "Our best technicians here are leaving. Herr Schicken, our chief car designer is going to VW, Büchner from the development department is doing the same. . . ." Quandt asked:

'"Can't they be encouraged to stay?"

'I said: "That I don't know."

'That evening, Quandt rang me up at home, wondering whether he had been mistaken, as he had a strong feeling that I also wanted to leave Borgward.

'"Yes," I said, "that's quite possible."

'The next day we met in Hanover.

'"How about coming over to BMW?" he suggested.

'"That would be like jumping from the frying-pan into the fire," I replied.

'Then he sent for a file.

'"Just have a look through this. You will see how I have restructured things, and what remains to be done."

'I saw that he had acquired a majority shareholding, had also bought Krages's shares, and was having difficulty working with Pertuss. Soon afterwards, I travelled to Bad Homburg. Wilcke drew up the contract. Quandt wanted to provide me with the best lawyer in contractual law in case Semler would not let me go. But that was not necessary. When I handed in my notice, Semler was very angry, but could not deny that he no longer consulted me on important decisions concerning technology (Semler had no idea of technology). He had always acted over our heads, and I gave this as the reason for handing in my notice. Naturally I said nothing about BMW, and anyway that was none of his business.

'It was now October 1961, at the time of the BMW general meeting, the second after the failed one of 1959. There I was, sitting up there on the podium. All I saw below me were peaceable shareholders. I was amazed that there was no mention of paying a dividend. Then Semler came in, still the official chairman of the supervisory board, saw me on the management board panel, next to the supervisory board members, and asked:

'"What are you doing here, then?"

'"Well," I said, "I am now on the management board of BMW." He had known nothing about it until then.

'Next to me was sitting Paul G. Hahnemann. We did not know each other well then. That very day we sat down together in private, alone for three days, without a telephone, and with no one disturbing us. I asked, in the spirit of the meeting:

'"What can you sell?"'

'And his question was: "What can you produce?"'

'Simple as that. We got on with each other immediately. He was just as happy following me as he was leading me (and vice versa), ten or eleven years later. There had been an entire era between those dates – the finest I could have wished for as an engineer. I was also in charge of construction. I built the tower, or rather, he planned it and executed it, through thick and thin, with all its refinements. My God, what an era we were in for!'

Just as Gieschen had come from Borgward, so had Hahnemann come from Auto Union, 'that once proud Auto Union, which had not only been involved in racing, but had also been Daimler-Benz's No 1 competitor in seeking the customers' patronage.' This was how Hahnemann expressed it whenever the subject came up. He would certainly have added without a moment's hesitation that, as the head of marketing at the new Auto Union, he had intended to do everything other than re-establish the status quo.

What he later presented as his subsequently famous 'Niche Theory' could already be discerned here. His marketing strategy, which he was to develop at BMW, had also been largely formulated by that time, as shown in the parting advice he gave to his colleagues at the 'once proud Auto Union': 'Go to a scrap-yard and get yourselves the old radiator grille from an Audi, with its upright figure "1" on the radiator cap. Then build a modern car around it with a four-cylinder engine. If you retain front-wheel drive and call this vehicle an Audi, then you've got it made!'

Just as with BMW, Auto Union had started up again with motorcycles in the West, where it only had a few service points left (all its factories, along with the famous names of DKW, Audi, Wanderer and Horch, had been lost to the Eastern bloc). At the same time, it had also got the old two-stroke DKW going again, which, as the DKW Junior, DKW Jeep for the Federal Army, or even as a sports coupé designed to reach 150 kph, only vaguely hinted at the former two-stroke model. Efforts were also made, wherever possible, not to overstretch themselves, and make similar mistakes to those which the large company of Horch and, it must be said, BMW made. However, the two-stroke engine remained an insurmountable obstacle for exports, and there was a lack of money all round. Yet, when Daimler-Benz bought Auto Union at Flick's instigation, this proved to be neither salvation nor solution – in spite of the fact that the two-stroke was certain to die, and that a four-stroke would take its place in the mid range, and despite the fact that the old production facilities (the casemates at the old fort in Ingolstadt and the former Rhine Steel Works in Dusseldorf) were no longer sufficient. Although a new factory had already been built at a time when Daimler Benz was acquiring Auto Union, and although the associated administration building had been ready for occupation shortly afterwards, Daimler-Benz refused to incorporate the company, insisting that the two firms ran side by side. This resulted in two marketing departments. In short, the parent company did not take its child to its breast, where it would have been nourished. In the midst of the quarrels which also disgruntled Flick (he was always disgruntled when losses occurred, and they were naturally occurring), Hahnemann received a call from Quandt.

What was he to do? Hahnemann was bound by contract, and Flick did not want to release him. An understanding between the Flick and Quandt groups not to entice away each other's managers entitled him to do this. But Quandt had got it into his head that he was going to have Hahnemann, and he knew how he was going to do it. Just a few weeks earlier, he had rejected Semler's offer to go to Borgward at Bremen. He had a feeling that his life's work was to be in Munich. Moreover, he had something against northern Germany. He said that 'the girls were too different. Then there was the accent. I'd also been recommended (no less than six times) to try that famous north German stew, being told it was a feast fit for the Gods, as my landlord's daughter still lived in Munich, where I had studied in 1931. As a native of Strasbourg, I was an out-and-out southern German – and now very keen on Munich. In a nutshell . . .'

In a nutshell, Hahnemann explained, he would hand in his notice, so that he could join Borgward. No one could stop him from doing that. Thereupon, Quandt, still in Hahnemann's presence at Bad Homburg, where both were negotiating the procedures, reached for the telephone, rang Flick in Dusseldorf, and arranged Hahnemann's release. Flick said that it would be absurd to lose the man to Borgward, but that was better than losing him to BMW, something which he, Friedrich Flick, would have found very hard to accept.

This was how BMW came to Hahnemann, or how he came to BMW, whichever way you look at it. He did not go to the Borgward group, which, at that time, in early 1961, was quite overwhelmed with the remnants of its stocks, not to mention 15,000 Arabelles standing in their yards. Their sale, which Hahnemann was considered for, would have brought the money necessary into the coffers which Semler had requested from the Bremen Senate. As we know, it was in vain – Borgward disappeared. And yet Borgward lived on in Munich through its many technicians who followed Gieschen. He was accompanied by Monz, head of purchasing, who was won over by Quandt, as well as complete plant facilities which Milbertshofen took over from Bremen. There it was joined to Auto Union, forming a second group with people whom Hahnemann had enticed to his side.

'How many were there?' I asked Hahnemann in his office at Friedrich Herschel Street in Munich, long after his departure from BMW.

'Oh, let me think a moment,' he said. 'At least fifty. Perhaps as many as a hundred. It was like a buy-out. What's more, I loved Auto Union, I learnt a lot there. I was never disloyal, nobody wooed me away. They just came along, it wasn't my fault, it was BMW's. It was like the gold rush, with people staking their claims – everything had to be staked out, as there was nothing there, nothing. What's more, cars had never been built in Munich. The test beds were silos for aero-engines. The halls were aero-engine halls.

The machine tools were tools for aero-engines. I didn't know that everything had been dismantled. It seemed to me that what had been put in again had only been put in for that, and not for cars. They knew a lot about that, but nothing about cars. I even wondered whether the few they did build could fly! Such as the 501 and 503. Then there was the 700 lying around in large numbers. Well, I sold them, quickly. How I did it is something Kolk can tell you about one day. We had to shake things up, literally everything. And we only achieved results if we resorted to drastic measures. With a few men – Gieschen, Mons, Kolk, Osswald, and fine men such as Falkenhausen, for me the best engine designer in the world! And Wilcke, when he became managing director, looked over it supportively. Supportively, because he didn't need to understand anything about cars. He cleared the ground, said yes whenever he understood the situation. And no when it appeared illogical to him. Never yes and no. And he said yes more often than no. And he never had any bad luck, anywhere. I often used to say, loud enough for him to hear: "Here comes the chief telephoner!" But he'd turn a deaf ear. I felt a bit ashamed. I never knew that he knew I was ashamed. Only much later when we had bought Glas did he tell me. And only after he had told others. It all started . . .'

It all started with the story which Kolk was to tell me.

'Do you know who brought Hahnemann to BMW?' Kolk asked, even before we had sat down.

I nodded.

'Quandt, of course, with his famous feel for things.'

'No,' said Kolk. 'Quandt was interested in technology, not marketing. He had no idea what could be done through marketing.'

'And who did then?'

'Mathern.'

'The lawyer Mathern, who scuppered Daimler-Benz's plans?'

'Yes, that's right. It wasn't just that he caused the general meeting to break up. He was the one who gave Quandt the tip, via Wilcke, and implored Hahnemann: "You're not going to Borgward, but to BMW."'

'Did he know him?'

'Both were interned in the same camp after '45, and had shared the same bread and water. There's no stronger bond than sharing bread and water. That was at Freiburg airport, under the French. They had locked away anyone who had a name and rank, and was above a certain salary level. Managers, university professors, scientists, high officials, party bosses, "dignitaries", and SS Hahnemann had something like the role of a "sarge" at the camp, and Mathern, who wanted to leave Germany and go with his wife and children to South America, was fed up. Mathern played the piano for (amongst others) the gendarmes in their quarters outside the fencing where they had their dinner. One evening, he said he had to leave the room. And he simply disappeared. They thought he had gone back to the camp. In actual fact, his wife was waiting for him in a car. Hahnemann then delayed roll call next morning. He repeatedly had the men numbered off, until he knew that four and a half hours had gone by. That was the time they agreed the Matherns needed to reach the border.'

'And they got away?'

'Yes, via Genoa to Brazil. Mathern returned in the fifties, became a lawyer again, advanced his career in Frankfurt and then. . . . well, you know the rest. Denzel brought him in to represent the BMW dealers. When the shareholders tried their rebellion, Mathern was the hero of the day. Then, in Dusseldorf, he saw Hahnemann again, who had just received the brief from Semler to go to Bremen. Mathern said: "Are you mad? You're going to BMW!"

'Hahnemann had asked: "How do I get to BMW?"

'Mathern answered: "I am on the supervisory board there. It's a disgrace that Semler (he's the chairman of our supervisory board) wants to bundle you off to Borgward." That's how it happened.'

'That was in early 1961. But Hahnemann only joined BMW in autumn.'

'Yes,' Kolk said, and we sat down. 'There were problems. Nobody wanted him. Golda, the whole works council took the offensive, most of the supervisory board were against him, and he was even turned down on the management board.'

'Was his reputation that bad?'

'They knew that he had been involved with Daimler-Benz, since everyone knew everyone else there. He wasn't to our liking, trying as he did to sell BMW (and here I use his own words) "from under our arses". There was some truth in it. This came out (he hadn't been with us a fortnight) when I took him through the works. Practically every empty spot in the yard had been taken up by the 700 range.

'"Why aren't they at the dealers?" he asked.

'"The dealers can't take any more," I said. "The home market is saturated."

'"Why?" he asked.

'You really should have heard how he came out with that "why". Although I had a clear conscience (I was marketing director for home trade, and so I was responsible), I felt blood rushing to my head, but still managed to keep my cool. I asked if he perhaps knew that the prototype for the 1500, the new mid-range car, had appeared at the Frankfurt Motor Show. He did not reply. And I continued, saying that anyone considering buying a 700 had shelved his intention of buying from the very moment the prototype appeared.

'"We have taken 2,000 advance orders for the 1500 in the first ten days after the show," I said. "Unfortunately, it is still a long way off being ready for production."

'Hahnemann still didn't say anything. I explained that the 700, even the 700 Sports, which was called the "skilled workers' Porsche" had undoubtedly saved the company, but even with its new chrome strips, it no longer provided the bridge we needed.

'Finally, Hahnemann said that he knew all that. What he did not know was betrayed by Kämpfer's worried expression. The latter was afraid of the balance sheet, as the end of the financial year was approaching. Hahnemann had asked him what monthly turnover he needed to balance it. Kämpfer replied: "20 million!"

502

'"That makes 60 million to the end of the year," Hahnemann said. "And what if I got it for you?"

'"Then I would call you *Sie** for the rest of my life."

'That was our conversation.

'On the very same day, Hahnemann set to work. He had the list of importers brought to him, and asked which one was the weakest and thus the easiest for the company to dispense with. He was told the importer in Copenhagen. He immediately sent a man from the export department (the head of export had just gone to the USA) by plane to Denmark. The latter came back the day after, delivering the importer's refusal to take the thirty or forty cars foisted upon him. This made Hahnemann pick up the phone to terminate the contract on the spot, and had all the other importers rung up one by one and made sure they were "honoured" with fixed quotas. His subordinates said something to the effect that there was a new man on the job who was acting a bit crazy. All they could advise them was to take the cars if they wanted to keep their contracts. Most of them already knew about the clear-out. No one rebelled. And so that same evening the thousands of cars in storage were sold, and Hahnemann had 6 million "in the bag". (That was another of his stock expressions.) He then presented it to a flabbergasted Kämpfer.

'That was his opening act, and it opened up the doors. It opened them upwards, to as far as Quandt, to whom Hahnemann's style had such little appeal; to the supervisory board, which immediately dropped any ifs and buts; to the management floor, where Kämpfer was not the only one to be dumbfounded; and down the stairs to the middle managers and senior office staff, of whom I was one. And it inspired the design department and technical services, especially Gieschen, as well as Monz in purchasing, who, having initially gone from Borgward to VW, was now with us. There was no one it did not reach, not least those whom it most concerned – the dealers. They all felt that a new wind was blowing, and that it was blowing in their faces. They may well have felt that unpleasant, but for BMW it was beneficial. And what was beneficial to BMW was beneficial to them as well.

'When Hahnemann arrived, his amazement at what BMW had become was the same as our amazement at him. For him this was not a firm, it was "the real dregs", as he was later to admit to me. What had most amazed him was that we were so proud of combining the "dregs" with our performance. Thank God it was our, as well as his, fortune. It seemed unlikely that he could have done the things that he did with us with anyone else. Or that he could have expected from anyone what he expected from us, as well as from himself. He spared no one, least of all himself, even admitting mistakes when he happened to make them. He never pushed anything aside. He identified himself and showed solidarity with the "dregs" – and through that, he won us over, overcame our scepticism.

'Before the war, he had been schooled by General Motors, had learnt about

---

* Tr. note: 'Sie', meaning 'you', is used when addressing superiors, or when a speaker wishes to demonstrate respect.

cars at Opel, which was the "elite high school" of the world, working his way up, just like Nordhoff and Stieler von Heydekampff. General Motors had unquestionably invented and implemented everything which could only be found in its most basic form (or not at all) at BMW – after-sales service, spare parts department, marketing school. We lacked all of those, we were a small car factory. And if the trade press described our dealer network as "inner-tube patches", they were right. Alongside a few proper dealers, there were small workshops representing us. The company enjoyed a great reputation amongst them, something which had not escaped Hahnemann either. He immediately saw what could be made of them, just as Gieschen saw what could be made out of the "antediluvian" machinery.

'What essentially happened to BMW with Hahnemann on the marketing side was what had once happened to Popp on the technical side with Friz. He was the one who had put his design drawing for a high-altitude aero-engine into his leather briefcase because Daimler-Benz had rejected it. He had then worked with men like Schleicher, Böning, Fiedler and von Falkenhausen to create the BMW image. Starting with the R 32 in 1923, this image was now just forty years old.

'Hahnemann discovered what it was worth when he invented his niche. This niche was nothing more than the sentence which, I think, came from *Der Spiegel*:

'Anyone transferring from a Mercedes to another make is taking a step down, while anyone going from Mercedes-Benz to BMW is taking a step *across*. Not a step *up*, let me say!'

'So BMW could never get into the area covered by the Mercedes-Benz image, but, on the other hand, it had to do all it could to achieve parity. Although this was a contradiction in itself, it was nevertheless the reality. The niche was to be found here in such terms as "youthful" and "sporty", but also with "manoeuvrable" and "high-quality finish". This was something a small manufacturer could take up without upsetting a big one.

'Hahnemann was, above all else, a psychologist.

'He had seen that nothing had been able to ruin BMW – no serious mismanagement at the top or a strange set of wheels like the Isetta. Or, in fact, anything at all. What counted was (how can I put it?) simply how the consumer conceived what he wanted to buy. The decisive factor was not what it was like, but what the potential customer thought it was like.

'Hahnemann staked everything which BMW would now become on this premise. The ineradicable image was the pre-condition to that. The fact that technological imagination was not an illusion was due to the first-class engineers (which there had always been in the company), whose telephone lines in the design offices were always directly connected to his marketing department. They might well laugh about his niches when Hahnemann propagated them like some itinerant preacher. But it came to stay for almost a whole decade at BMW. Or, more accurately in retrospect, it came to "overstay".

'But it is well-known that anyone leaving the town council is wiser than when he went in. I, too, came to believe, although at first only gradually, in the validity of "Niche-Paul's" theories, as the press was soon to call Hahnemann. But I have never been a man of theory, either. The niche idea was, I grant, never a theory for Hahnemann – just a means for turning fiction into practice. Force also played a part. He used it ruthlessly. Only rarely did he miss. When, in 1971, this force ran out of steam, the tower was already up. It marked the end of the pioneering age.'

This was one version of the story, and when Kämpfer, on leaving in 1963, told another version, it did not contradict Kolk's. However, it shed some light on events from the viewpoint of a management board member, which made quite a few things more understandable.

'My experience of Hahnemann was limited to the early years,' he said. 'Things got off to a good start. I flew in from New York, where there had been a lot of trouble, and after a night flight, Herr Wilcke was already waiting for me at the airport.

'"What's wrong?" I asked. "Are you bankrupt?"

'"No," Wilcke said, "but you must come immediately to Milbertshofen. There is a supervisory board meeting. Herr Hahnemann will be introduced to you there. We want to make him head of marketing today."

'"We?" I asked, thinking that Mathern was behind all this.

'"Quandt wants it," Wilcke said.

'"I can't decide that quickly. I'd like to speak with my people first."

'Wilcke understood that, as did the supervisory board in the meeting. Hahnemann was *not* appointed. That only happened at the next supervisory board meeting, which was in September 1961.

'This had been preceded by the statement that I had to go into marketing. Export sales into countries like the Netherlands, France, Belgium, etc were in a muddle.

'"We need management in marketing, with everyone just doing what he is supposed to do. I am no salesman. . . ."

'"But you've shown you can do it," everyone said, "you've been doing just fine."

'How badly I had been doing was something I saw when Hahnemann came.

'Right at the beginning, he told me (and others) that he was a scorpion.

'"How nice," I said.

'He replied: "Nice? Listen to a story my wife made up, not me."

'The story went like this: A scorpion was sitting beside a stream, and, on the other side of the stream, a frog was croaking. The scorpion said: "Come along, take me over to the other side, you won't come to any harm!"

'"I refuse," said the frog, "you'll do something to me."

'"I won't do anything to you," said the scorpion, "I won't harm you."

'So the frog swam up, carried the scorpion across the stream to the other side, but scarcely had he got his feet on land than he felt a sting.

'You said you wouldn't do anything,' bemoaned the dying frog.

'The scorpion said: "Well, what did you expect from a scorpion?"

'This is how Hahnemann presented himself to anyone he would have dealings with, so that the latter would immediately know the type of man he was. If that did not hit home (as it did not with me), and you did not let yourself be immediately intimidated, then you got on well with him. That is what was to happen now.

'As a financier, I allocated the budgets – with necessary control, of course. He went through the roof, saying that he could do whatever he wanted with the advertising budget.

'"You cannot do that," I said, "without a counter-signature from me."

'He immediately accepted this, without so much as a murmur – and used it as an argument at quality control, which he so insisted upon, and with which his philosophy stood or fell.

'At that time, planning had been completed for 1963. This was the year I left, and the mid-range car was supposed to bring something in by that time. I had always been rather sceptical, but now saw how Hahnemann did it. He had representatives come from all over, and said to them: "The price will be such and such. If you don't like it, you can lump it!" That's how he got it through! Wherever I noted in my monthly report that this or that had not gone right in sales, Hahnemann said to his sales staff: "You will make it up next month. The plan will be fulfilled!" And so it was!

'When I was already working for the Max Hütte steel works, I went to see Wilcke again in Munich.

'"Do you know, Kämpfer, what we have just decided?" he said. "We want to reach a turnover of a billion marks."

'"But how do you plan to do that at Milbertshofen?" I exclaimed (Dingolfing had not been acquired then). "That's just wishful thinking!"

'It was not wishful thinking. As many as several billions came out of it – but they would not have happened without Hahnemann, given the great motivator that he was.'

An analysis using market psychology (the first that BMW had ever commissioned) revealed how strongly the BMW product was determined by what the consumer conceived of it. The analysis was conducted by the market researcher and psychologist Dr Bernt Spiegel. He advised that the 'niche theory' developed by him should be applied to BMW.

The subjects had been handed small cards on which were marked the names of car makes. They had to match up these cards with other cards, which had statements such as: *State-owned company* or *partially state-owned company* or *company with a major state shareholding*.

The subjects did not know who had commissioned the survey. They had indicated that they had no economic or political bias. They spent hardly any time on the question as to which was state-owned. The majority of them thought Daimler-Benz was. This was in spite of a long-running discussion, fully covered in the press, about a state-sponsored restructuring of BMW, together with radio broadcasts about government loans, possible government assistance or the company being taken over by the Bavarian state. None of that had stuck in their minds. Yet nothing of the sort had been broadcast about Daimler-Benz, despite it being considered initially.

In a lecture to the Nuremberg Academy for Marketing in 1968, Hahnemann described the products which had created images in people's minds, as well as those which had not, with regard to BMW. The successors to the Dixi had proved quite ineffective, although many people still remembered them well. It was not they that had been consigned to oblivion, but that their association with BMW had. The situation was similar for all those Isetta models of only a few years ago. The 600, the micro-bus, had not stigmatised BMW as a make. From the 700, only the small sports coupé version was accepted as something approaching the BMW image because of its sports successes, its compactness, and its engine's beefiness (as one subject stated: 'You know the one, the little tinder-box . . .'). Even the large cars of the fifties had done no harm to BMW, although neither had they left much behind that was considered typically BMW. They were stated as not being really BMW. BMW was something quite different. In contrast, the pre-war models of the 326, 327, and 328 kept being cited time and again. Hahnemann said:

'Based on this research, we discontinued the Isetta and the BMW 600. The big models, and later the BMW 700 range as well, had to go the same way. Against this, a car had to be developed in line with the customer's image of BMW, and in direct line from the exclusive BMW pre-war models.'

On the question of what was 'going to die' and what was soon 'to be dead', he was unapologetic:

'Quite a few members of the administration cannot come to terms with the idea that the management board wants to do without its flagship. This is the car which causes quite a stir and amazement on motorways and wherever it appears.

'The fact that this model had been a long-term source of major losses had possibly been ignored, as had the mocking remarks by the competition, which had long dismissed the car as the "old-fashioned, baroque angel" or as the "baroque teenager". The car died like the old farmer in the story who, having withdrawn from public life years previously, had become a kind old granddad, whom the young people of the village were glad to see and liked a lot, because his pockets would be stuffed full of sweets which he generously handed out at any time. Then he died. Just was not there any more. He was soon forgotten, leaving not the slightest trace behind him. The same fate befell the large BMW car. After its death, the image faded. As did its aficionados, apart from a few exceptions (such as the Bavarian provincial authorities, who were now distressed at having to travel across holy Bavarian soil in cars of foreign origin). This shortcoming would soon be healed, though. They certainly knew that we would put a six-cylinder car into production in the course of that year (1968), a car also designed to suit government officials.'

He finally mentioned a marked 'German feature', which, brilliantly encapsulated in the Mercedes image, exhibited authoritative 'German national' features. In contrast, BMW incorporated more than just the 'non-American', the refined, the unfashionable, more than what was technological and prosaic. The subjects gave classifications such as 'keeping its value', 'for people who want to keep their car for a long time', and 'no frequent model changes' which had become typical of BMW cars.

This revealed that the agitator in Hahnemann controlled his craft just as much as the marketing psychologist in him; he had been an Opel main dealer for fifteen years before he went to Auto Union. As someone always concerned with defining differences and mindful of the psychological 'gap in the market' in which BMW had to operate, he could not put off the host, in whose niche he was sitting. But neither could he put off the guest, whom he might entice away from him. In a seemingly harmless way, he attributed assets to the big brother which the latter had not the slightest interest in hearing about – and made it blatantly obvious to the customers, who had previously accepted attributes (like those mentioned) without comment. He had never forgotten the words of the telegram, which he found on his desk: 'All the best to the eminent company of BMW. Daimler-Benz AG. Dr Joachim Zahn.' He knew Zahn, the head of finance at Untertürkheim, who never missed a chance to assure everyone that the Bavarian Motor Works had undoubtedly achieved considerable success at the level of a refined workshop, but could hardly be described as a car factory. This is how he believed it would remain in future, too. Such views put Hahnemann on his guard.

There was little room for manoeuvre, and irony is a delicate little plant which he cherished and protected. If he spoke of the 'beautiful and tasteful elegance' which characterised BMW cars, he omitted to say that they also had a pompous elegance. Anyone wanting exhilaration in which the ideas of 'sportiness', 'maneouvrability' and 'dexterity' played a simultaneous role, had simply to forego a more 'semi-official' calibre, not to say an official one. Only when Daimler-Benz, which had previously shown refinement in ignoring the pin-pricks, examined Hahnemann's theories point by point in an internal brochure without fault or favour (as they professed), and brought technical evidence to the contrary to bear, did he take up the gauntlet and say openly what distinguished BMW cars from a Mercedes. He said in his own style:

'If a businessman has made something of his life in Germany and has to show his neighbour he is something, he can only drive a Mercedes. If, however, he has made something of his life, but feels not the slightest need to show off, then he can buy himself a BMW.'

Amazed and not without respect, the people in Stuttgart followed Hahnemann's ideas on public relations. He put questions to the customers in large adverts.

The first question was: '*Do you have any reason to doubt the integrity of a car company?*' There was a second question a few weeks later: '*Are you certain you were sold your car in all good faith?*'

At first sight, these adverts all seemed the same: a big picture (a car, recognisably a BMW, in motion or parked, a 'beautiful' photo) with the caption underneath and the white and blue BMW logo, followed by the text. Caption and text were always a surprise.

ALONE
Twenty-four hours at Spa in Belgium.
The toughest trial between the best touring cars in the world.
Only the quickest can keep up.

508

Only the safest come through.
And only the most reliable finish.
Here are the races which BMW cars have won:
1964, 1965, 1966

Another caption was called THIRD PARTY INSURANCE, with the text underneath reading:

We have given the BMW good brakes
So that you never get too close to the driver in front.
Unfortunately, we cannot oblige the driver behind
To drive a BMW as well.
His bad luck.

Then, when the six-cylinder came out, there was a presumptuous, self-confident, advert, but one not without charm:

PRIVATE CIRCLE
The BMW 2500 has only two competitors in appearance, comfort and performance – itself and the BMW 2800. It will be out in the new year.

And underneath, based on a song, which the whole world sang in the thirties, and which had become a catchy number: 'To Paris for love's sake. . . .', there was SHEER DRIVING PLEASURE (this had occurred to Lummert, the head of advertising – he was later to come up with the slogan: 'The new class').

None of this had been produced off the cuff – however much Hahnemann liked it when anyone thought it was. It was much more the case that everything was 'custom-made', calculated to the last figure, psychologically always directed at people (that also meant 'big brother') and never pitted against a vague opponent. This explained why everything hit the mark, entertained and had verve. Even when things went over the top, they aroused curiosity as to what was behind it all. Was it a company or a person? People soon had a name for him: Mr BMW. The competition smiled somewhat forcedly over that. That suited Hahnemann.

His strategy was extremely simple. Stark, bare figures distinguished it. Apart from the results produced by the market research (how does a car buyer view BMW? What conceptions does he have of a car made by BMW?), they laid down his approach, and dictated product and marketing considerations. Here was the key expression guiding him – 'unpretentious exclusivity'. And over there was the goal into which he would have to introduce it. In the meantime, there was much personal risk. It is not the right moment to quote Hamlet's soliloquy, yet failing was part of it, and he would fail, along with everyone who was associated with him.

But the goal was no mere figment of the imagination. Price is related to size – who could afford a car costing more than 9,000 marks? People earning 10,000 marks a year? Hardly. 20,000? Again, no. 30,000? That's a bit more like it. How many people were there in this income bracket in the Federal Republic? 480,000 was what the market research had revealed. Around 450,000 of them used cars, but only 300,000 of them comprised this type of customer (buying cars every two or three years). What was happening with the others? They drove cheaper cars.

In 1964, 145,000 units were sold on the home market in the price category above 9,000 DM. If the reserve of 40,000 customers were added to them, those using cheaper cars but not having to do so, together with the 20,000 drivers who entered the upper income bracket each year, then the calculator was working overtime on its sums. Calculations included the customer reserve with a potential for being activated, set at an annual figure of 40,000 drivers, although that could differ. No, that was taken as the lowest limit which we could reach and which we had to reach. So it was a matter of rolling up our sleeves and getting on with it!

Strategy! According to Moltke, this is the application of sound human reason to the art of war, but it also includes 'a system of temporary assistance'. This meant improvisation, managing with conditions, accepting diversions, taking cunning ways out, but never (the marketing strategist Hahnemann hammered it into their heads), never making cuts – cuts which could bring into question the goal itself (and here that meant the product), endanger its quality and might shake the customer's belief in the absolute superiority, reliability and technical merit of what was being promised him. In the meantime, as we have already heard, the prototype of the 1500 had aroused expectations which, in amongst all the jubilation they provoked in the factory, were to produce cold sweat on the foreheads of the technicians who had to get the car ready for production in a short space of time, given the pressure of the sales orders. One of these technicians was a certain Gieschen who had overall responsibility for technical services. *How* were they to fulfil the unconditional demands of the marketing department? After all, they wanted to have a car up and running with no teething troubles, a product which set new standards and which had to determine and ensure BMW's future for the sixties, if not the seventies, in line with those unforgettable cars of the thirties!

'Deep down, but nonetheless there, is the longing in the heart of the German car buyer for high-quality, which can only be imperfectly fulfilled by value-for-money, mass-produced cars,' was what the leading German car magazine wrote when the premiere of the 1500 was brought forward at the International Motor Show. It left no doubt that this was the car which fulfilled this longing.

When, eleven and a half months later, on 25 August 1962 (premature for anyone in the know), the lines for series-production were finally starting up, Hahnemann knew what was in store for him. The car was *not* ready for production, and there would be (in fact, there would have to be) an avalanche of complaints. As indeed there was.

He did not blame anybody. Everyone had done his best. But what normally took four to six years (that was how long a car generally took to reach series production), even the most experienced technical group could not produce in two. That could only lead to a 'shit car', as Hahnemann put it, an undeveloped object, built, moreover, in halls where a car had yet to be built (he did not accept the 700). That was asking too much, even of Gieschen, he thought; Gieschen, who was responsible for production, and with whom he got on extremely well.

According to the statutes of the Association of the German Car Industry (the VDA), a vehicle presented at a motor show must enter series production within six months at the latest. If it did not, there was the threat of a high penalty for breach of contract. Before the chief technician from the VDA appeared at the works to type-approve it, Gieschen had had a section of track producing 700 coupés cleared, and had twenty, handmade 1500s planted on it. Workers were transferred there, who busily went about the last little jobs.

'But you're not trying to tell me that that is series production?' laughed the tester.

'Certainly is,' Gieschen maintained. 'How big then is series production at Porsche?' (The rate there ran as always at between twenty and fifty cars at the most).

'Are you Porsche?' asked the tester.

'No,' said Gieschen. 'BMW. That's also why pressings don't look like pressings here.'

'And why cast-iron blocks look like aluminium ones!' the VDA tester mocked, well aware that a row had almost been started as to whether the engine should be made from light metal or cast-iron. (Even on the eve of the show, there had been a last minute decision to go for a cast-iron engine, as von Falkenhausen wanted, and the shiny aluminium engine on the prototype had been coated in grey paint.)

They were just able to avoid a penalty for breach of contract, but the defects which were to appear when the first cars were delivered (to enthusiastic approval from the trade) exceeded their worst fears. The steering was out of synchronisation with the chassis suspension, final-drive units seized, con rods snapped and came through the side of the crankcase. Hahnemann's scorn knew no bounds. He almost felt as if he were one of the competitors when he spread the story around that if he saw a Hamburg-registered 1500 in Munich, he was tempted to donate a candle in St Peter's so that the driver would get home safe and sound. In the meantime, he courteously and amicably accepted every need to give credit where credit was due. However bad the car might be, he could not deny that the boys were good. Then he acted. A staff of twelve people was formed, headed by Helmut-Werner Bönsch, to examine the type and range of defects. They reached the grand figure of 124, of which 120 were minor matters (the majority were invariably the same, and could be remedied in next to no time), with only the remainder requiring major modification. We can do it, said Gieschen. But he was beside himself that final approval was to be taken away from him and placed under marketing. But that was precisely the point of it all, as Hahnemann declared.

'Even God has someone to check on him – the devil. All you have is us, something we can both be thankful for.'

And he was right. If he had to accept that the car had more faults than a dog has fleas, there was still no reason why production defects could not be cleared up very quickly. Hahnemann resignedly accepted the fact that cars rejected by quality control blocked up production halls, that chaos reigned all around, and that the telephone lines were buzzing with failures to meet delivery deadlines. His controllers went unrelentingly from car to car with their checklists in their hands, rejecting anything that was defective, and so returning costs to the company which the customer would otherwise have had to bear. In turn, the company passed them on to production, whether Gieschen wanted it or not. It was the job of production to get to grips with them, as it was Hahnemann's job to sort out the price, which, originally promised at 8,500 DM, had blown a hole in the calculations and had to be set at almost 1,000 DM higher. A crazy price! said the industry. Comparable Fords and Opels did not even cost 7,000 DM. Hahnemann agreed. At the same time, he knew that this was the test. If the customer accepted the price, then he also accepted the added value offered by BMW: exclusivity, sporting pretensions, technical innovations (as offered by no other car in the upper mid-range). On top of that, it boasted quality, which was now ensured by rigorous control. This was the added value which determined the niche in which BMW could operate.

And as this was applied, and there were no protests against it, the theory of a low basic price was then refuted. Everything making a car desirable and something people wanted to drive was to be added to this price and accounted for in the costings. It was a delusion which achieved the opposite of what was intended, and one which the customer would never forgive. In addition, it confirmed the validity of Quandt's old demand that a BMW must show its value in its price. If you, as he once implored his management, want to make a good return with a good car (and we must make a good return, otherwise we cannot build a good car), then its price must be high. Or the clientele, whom we value, will not buy it. If Auntie Lizzy can buy the car, then our clientele will not.

As was now shown, there could be no 'ifs' and 'buts'. Hahnemann vigorously rejected Quandt's opinion that the car might cost considerably more than 10,000 marks. There are magic boundaries which cannot be crossed. The 10,000-mark boundary was one of these. And the niche (Hahnemann never got tired of repeating it) was not a 'gap', not a 'sector', and was certainly not to be evaluated materially – only psychologically.

The question was: how long could they keep the customer's goodwill? This raised a second question: how were things to proceed? The small cars, including the Isetta, as well as the big car, could be continued. In the customer's opinion, the 1500 had fulfilled its promises and hit the bull's-eye. But measured against what other manufacturers were offering *below* it (Opel and Ford) and *above* it (Mercedes), the euphoria over the sales success should not be allowed to hide the fact that everything depended on a model range which had only just got going. Only a model range could fill the niche. Only a model range could break into and occupy the gap in the market at the edge of the niche.

Hahnemann called this 'the new class' (with the 1800, then with a sports

512

version acquiring the initials TI; the company presented both models in the autumn of 1963). Were they the 'expected, further developed' models? A car with only minor external changes from its predecessor (the 1800 differed from the 1500 in that it had a full-length chrome strip and hub-caps, more comfortable seats, and a rather more luxurious passenger compartment) is generally not regarded as being that much different. It was a BMW. At any event, this is what the customer thought, though God knows why. It only had its 90 hp (the 1500 had just 75 hp) to make it into an 'experience', into a 'four-door sports car' (this was not Hahnemann's claim, but the tester's). And the TI (Turismo Internationale, a widely used standard expression) immediately became known, with its metallic paintwork in silver (the only version available), as the 'silver-grey understatement'. Was this because, with its 20 extra horse power and its two twin-choke carburettors, it could accelerate from 0 to 100 kph in 10.5 seconds and reach a top speed of 170 kph? Others could do the same. Hahnemann shrugged his shoulders. That was just how things were with cars – provided they were BMWs. How else could it be explained?

Yes, provided that this was the case. And that meant not having image and model policy poles apart, but having them homogenous, so that the two were brought together, so that the right hand always knew what the left hand was doing. It also meant being able to take vigorous action against an ever changing background. This included new supervisory boards, new management board chairmen and colleagues. But management demands remained the same, which, in an extraordinary procedure for an AG, were issued by the major shareholder, Quandt.

The New Class

The myth of the phoenix, which rose from the ashes, certainly applied to the free part of Germany, to the Federal Republic, and was a definite sign that the patient had recovered. Anyone looking back from the eighties at the year 1960 could see it clearly represented by the fact that the workers were much better off than they had ever been.

'They had achieved less than the self-employed, but certainly just as much, if not more, than civil servants,' was how a contemporary report referred to it (Fritz Richert in *Monat*). 'They belong to this state. They recognise it, as it does them. Many workers will become office staff and will no longer have or arouse any feelings of resentment (if not in themselves, then in their children). The share of wages in production costs will continue to fall, and any argument against higher wages will pale into insignificance. The trades unions are rich, they put their money to work like capitalists. They have also got used to the discreet silence of property owners. There is barely any more controversy about the economic reform, with only food prices causing annoyance. Although the workers are nowhere near as well off as those envying them believe, it does, however, seem that there is nothing more that the political parties can promise the people.'

The report continued: 'Have the Federal citizens really got so much that all they can be offered now are rolling heads, like Salome? The proponents of social policy respond with a "no" to this question, and demand "ownership for all". They are more dissatisfied than the broad sections of society who are directly concerned. This is because the catchword (along with the desire for employees to have a greater participation in the increasing prosperity than has happened up to now) does not stem from the huts of the poor, but from the typewriters of the thinkers. They feel that the workers who have finally become state citizens should also become fully-fledged citizens of the economy. . . .'

In spite of all the cutbacks contained in it, there is a balance sheet which is worth looking at. How had it come about? A considerable social upheaval had taken place. Where? When? What was it to be put down to? Which forces had brought it about? Could it be sufficiently explained by the 'German situation'?

The fact that a country like the Federal Republic could rise from being a state receiving aid to the second largest industrial nation in the Western hemisphere within two decades must certainly have had something to do with the motivations which losing a war inspires in people. This is the time when people stare into the void, when people are certain to face the initial stupidity of the victors in their desire to dismantle everything that remains. This enabled the Germans to acquire new technology almost out of necessity, which replaced destroyed production facilities. And it certainly meant that the Federal Republic was reflated by American economic aid and, for the time being, released from that burden which America, Great Britain and France had to carry with regard to armaments and atomic weapons. It was not for nothing that the upturn in the German economy dated from the outbreak of the Korean War. Freed from the need to produce armaments, but also from foreign competition which was obliged to switch over to producing them, the Germans arrived on the world markets 'ready for business'. Even German partition played its absurd part in the economic miracle, entailing technicians, researchers, highly qualified skilled workers and commercial staff coming from 'over there' and contributing to it. But was that enough, could it all have 'gelled', if there had not been the conditions for it, which were to be found elsewhere? Created after the period when things were more real (such as the currency reform, the division of Germany, the Federal Republic, its incorporation into the West, and Erhard's social market economy), the Germans benefited from what they had counted on least of all. As the German historian Fritz Sternberg expressed it from his home in New York:

'We in the Western world (including those in the Federal Republic) are in a process where the increasing majority of people will achieve the living standards of the middle classes. The USA started it, and the process has continued in Europe. It is by no means over. It is going on in front of our very eyes.'

Sternberg cited the fact that in the USA, which had not been a theatre of war for a single day in the Second World War, *new* factories had been built in the three years, from spring 1942 to spring 1945, with a production capacity which was about half as great as the capacity of the total number of factories built in the USA from 1842 to 1942. In the Federal Republic, on the other hand, as Sternberg pointed out, factories and towns had been most severely affected by the war. This was why there was a quite a marked increase in production after the currency reform, just so as to make up for what the war had destroyed. But people did not stop at that in the fifties. Just as in France and Italy, a large, new production apparatus was built, which the USA, on the other hand, had already built during the war. This resulted in a growth rate throughout the decade of the fifties which was incomparably greater than that in America.

It is against this background that we should look at what was happening in Milbertshofen. Those cars, which were developed in an incredibly short space of time in the thirties and which established BMW's reputation, were now associated with features other than models. These included pace of development, the pioneering approach, the technological climate, partly determined by the same people (von Falkenhausen, Fiedler, von Rücker), and the type of interplay between the company and its public, all of which were quite similar to the thirties. Like then, there were incentives to produce new types of car, which the market immediately accepted. Diversions, forced by necessity, lead surprisingly from defects to the objective. Limitation on the choice of resources became the overriding virtue. The situation was often explosive to the point of becoming disastrous, with everybody going as far as their abilities and capacities would take them. If expectations were lowered, there were over-extravagant reactions (Falkenhausen would leave, if. . . . 'Good,' Gieschen abruptly declared, 'then leave. If you leave, then I will, too.' Falkenhausen stayed.)

The person bringing all this under control and who created, as it were, the right firing order for their explosions, the person who calmed them down and urged them on, clipped their wings and brought them together, directed and led, was Hahnemann. This was the man whose marketing ideas determined the product, set run-up deadlines and quantities, reversed production principles if a model had to be out sooner than planned, deprived advertising people of their sleep. Anything and everything he tackled was in the interests of marketing. If somebody did not like what was happening (such as the stipulation to the dealer network that cars would only be released from the factory against an open cheque), he made it clear that this was not just bloody-mindedness. He explained that this was the only way things could be done, and told them why it was being done as it was. He argued that production planning and planning in the marketing department were one and the same thing, acting like communicating tubes to each other, and that both called for a third condition. This was company planning. For the moment, at least, that was to be found in marketing. He vigorously ruled out export policy, which any world-class company was entitled to, but not BMW, as yet. (As was stated in the company's announcements: 'We export to 136 countries in the world.' Amongst these, as Hahnemann ascertained, were countries like Ghana, Uganda, Kenya and Chile, with annual intakes of between two and ten cars, an unparalleled effort.) Even the branches maintained in America and Canada ran at a loss, at a major loss. He closed them down, so that he could use that investment better to cover the home market, and (equally important to him) the neighbouring European countries. He set up 'importer centres' which were accountable only to themselves (such as Thodoroff in France, Fleischmann/Sodi in Italy, Moorkens in Belgium, Grewe in Holland, Blackburn in England, Hübner in Switzerland, Söderström in Sweden, Denzel in Austria, and Ere Juri in Finland). His policy of 'home market first', with the EEC and EFTA (the European Free Trade Association) countries in second place, was where he would operate and where BMW's fate would be decided. He told his staff that since they had to operate here, they *would* operate here. The old statement that half a car factory is on the outside (outside at the dealers) is certainly a truism, but one which nobody heeded. Except Hahnemann. Yet however curtly he behaved, when he motivated lazy people, stirred up even the most lethargic and got them to join in (often turning refusal into spontaneous approval, as well as dismissing those with whom 'nothing more could be done'), he only did this because there were men supporting him who unquestioningly looked after the strategic implementation of his concept in their own field of responsibility. (This concept stated: build what the customer needs, and build it so that he can pay for it; at the same time, make sure it's a decent car.)

They were only a few in number, but they were all men of his age, with no significant generation gap. They were all around fifty (the only one who had reached sixty-five was Fiedler, but he was part of them, and they were reluctant to let him go). There was no scheming, because there was no fear between them, and each of them was a 'pro' in his own area.

There was Monz, the head of purchasing, a man who was as monosyllabic as his name, who said to anything which was outside his jurisdiction: 'Not my cup of tea!' Yet in his own area, he had grasped how to make a materials economy out of simple purchasing. This meant including the whole accessory industry in the supply of in-house technology, and earning money without being productive, by limiting stocks to minimal levels. This was done not by haggling over purchases (he only had to lift up his little black book from his purchasing days at Volkswagen to receive the same rebates on bulk orders), but by saving high interest payments on stocks.

Then there were the four 'sovereigns' in development: Alexander von Falkenhausen, aristocratic, inflexible, stubborn, modest, quiet, an engineer who had already made BMW motorcycle history. He was no ordinary man, but a man of high calibre, as they say in the trade. Then there was Alfred Böning who still mourned Donath a little, as the man who had once entrusted him with the development department (where he had lost his pre-eminence since Falkenhausen's return). He always felt slightly aggrieved, because he claimed he was not sufficiently respected. But in reality, he was an indisputable designer recognised beyond BMW through hundreds of patents. The third man was Eberhard Wolff whom we know from the Isetta. Wolff was *the* man in testing, who got on best with the fourth man, Wilhelm Hofmeister, the company stylist and successor to Szimanowski. Denzel found Hofmeister an evil spirit, as he felt he had messed up his 700. Hahnemann openly expressed his doubts on this, as he saw in Hofmeister something approximating to the technological conscience on which he could always rely, if the others started arguing.

Every one of them was an individualist to the core. There was no love lost between them, all four were difficult to manage. Claus von Rücker as head of development (at one time, in the thirties, he had been in charge of motorcycle testing under Schleicher, and Quandt had brought him back to BMW from Porsche), and Bernhard Osswald, now representing development on the management board, both had a few stories to tell about that. Bönsch, too, found things difficult with these four. He ran a department which fell between technology and marketing, answering directly to the management board. Until then, no such department had existed throughout the German car industry. It was called 'value analysis'. Here every model of car produced was 'sounded out' part by part, to see if it could not be produced more cost-effectively without entailing any reduction in quality requirements. This might involve the simple replacement of a solid chrome strip (costing 48 DM) with a hollow one (costing 5 DM).

And then there was Gieschen, who, to Hahnemann, always seemed like Sisyphus, rolling the boulder up the mountain, never grumbling when it rolled back down again, bracing himself again to try and accomplish the impossible. It was Gieschen who was trying to make a car factory out of installations which had been bombed to pieces and only partially cleared, in addition to making car workers out of men who had never worked on a car before, and sometimes not even on a piece of sheet metal. As the 'technician with the grease rag' (as Kämpfer amusedly still regarded him) he was a master of improvisation, who had become the irreplaceable counterpart for Hahnemann's marketing skills. Being both systematic *and* creative, but without knowing to what extent inspiration played a part, and without even knowing whether or not he possessed it, he built up the factory stone by stone, thereby bringing about the 'new class' and everything that resulted from it and which took shape in the tower.

At his side was the irreplaceable Paul Volk who, coming from Auto Union, had acted as the works manager at Milbertshofen since 1963. It was Volk, in conjunction with Siedler, the man from 'over there', who successfully brought off production and manufacturing. And that meant thorough organisation based on the formula which had come second nature to him after twenty years of making cars. It was not a formula known throughout the world. When he studied engineering, his professor had written it up on the blackboard, which always happened if someone had been particularly proud of the achievement he had acquired. There it stood then: N A:T. And that was all. The pride soon wore off, though, because work (A) only becomes output (N) in the unit of time (T) in which someone does the work. This is what determines the extent and pace of industrial growth.

It could not be anything else, even at BMW. The search for an explanation as to how it was possible to combine production *and* construction (simultaneously dismantling all the outdated plant and installing the newest, the most up-to-date processes, e.g. electrophoretic painting using an electrolytic immersion tank, which was only at the testing stage at Daimler-Benz) was to be found in Volk's 'formula', whose rigorous application in production allowed Gieschen's goal to be reached faster than the others. This meant that they could go ahead, much further ahead, in the market. (Boldness and risk, so closely related, were god-parents: so as not to endanger the planned increase in quantity, the first-phase pressing shop had to be expanded. Higher up, where the concrete sheds were being linked via pillars, work continued in the small halls nestling below. How the pictures resembled each other! In the twenties, the wooden hangars of the Bavarian Aircraft Works, formerly Otto, had been built over in concrete in a similar way, on Popp's instructions, while production had continued.)

In the meantime, five main departments formed the skeleton of the new marketing organisation – home market, export sales, spare parts procurement, after-sales service and distribution, and (the most important for Hahnemann) marketing. Here were assembled market research, sales statistics, sales promotion, advertising, press and public relations. Each was an entity in its own right, a string on which he played, with the sounding-board of seventeen districts into which he had divided up the Federal Republic. There were about 1,000 dealers in these seventeen districts (brought together in three zones). About 500 of these had a sole BMW franchise. It is worthwhile making a comparison. In 1964, there were 7,500 main dealers and 17,000 service points (including the repair garages run as a subsidiary business by the dealers) for *all* the makes and firms within the Federal area. These figures are needed to quantify the significance for BMW in the sixties of the expression that 'half a car factory is on the outside'.

The new branch in Berlin, acquired in a surprise coup, was presented as a showpiece in the midst of this. The old branch ('the one we've had the longest,' as Hahnemann said) bordered Daimler-Benz's factory-owned franchise on the banks of the Salz river. When Vancura, 'our man in Berlin', a native of Vienna, who always knew what was what, let Munich know that the main Ford dealer in Berlin had overreached himself, and that his showrooms and workshops in Moabiter Hütten Street were up for sale, Hahnemann saw that this was a once-in-a-lifetime opportunity if he could acquire them immediately. There was no time to consult management and supervisory boards. If the old BMW complex could be sold to Daimler-Benz at almost the same time, then a brand-new branch could be set up in the modern building put up only a few years earlier. Subtracting the proceeds from selling the old property to Daimler-Benz, it cost the company a total of 1.8 million DM. This was a price which forced Dr Karoli, the chairman of the supervisory board, to show admiration for Hahnemann's buying and selling skills, but also prompted him to say that he and the committee he chaired would like to be asked in advance next time. Hahnemann replied that that would be done as a matter of course, provided that 'poor BMW' could afford to do it at all. That could mean forking out considerably more for such opportunities if they were not to be completely missed (they could not be had without making snap decisions).

Hahnemann invited the wives to the first major dealer meeting (Gieschen had made available for it the recently completed engine-production hall 140). Hahnemann asked what a dealer would be without his wife standing at the cash desk, running the bookkeeping and making sure everything was under control. It was only then that he took up his theory of 'home market first', which had priority in everything the company planned to do. This was supported by four company-owned branches between Hamburg and Munich, as well as (not insignificantly) by the small dealers, even if their workshops at present were still shabby to the point of delapidation. Each of them could, should, and had to consider themselves as branches, with the plus point of having invaluable self-initiative.

He said: 'If you knew what now confronts us, what is now in store for us. . . .'

He spoke for the first time of his concern that production (as one of the halves of a car factory) was still lagging behind the marketing organisation (as the other half 'outside'), to such an extent that 'our cars are being sucked onto the market as other large companies would like to see, but in vain.'

'If this should happen,' he then said, 'never forget where the whole secret of the car business is to be found – in this cardboard box!'

He pointed to an attractive present, in what looked like an expensive wrapping, and had it raffled off. The wife of a main dealer won it. When she opened the box, she found a pair of dirty old shoes, which had disintegrated under the sweat of feet. Hahnemann held them up (Kolk had wrapped them up) and said:

'These are the worn-out shoes of a car salesman who grew old gracefully!'

Applause. Reflection. Sober comprehension. People continued to talk about these old shoes for quite some time. When the market collapsed, which almost brought the car business to a standstill for a few months after the oil crisis in 1973, a dealer in Westphalia wrote confidentially to Hahnemann. He said that if the items had already wandered off to the rubbish bin, he now had a pair of his own to show him.

'My life has revolved around BMW,' said Hahnemann twenty years later in an almost philosophical digression, in which he reflected on what he had done wrong.

'My principal mistake was not to do what was psychologically necessary for a management board having a major shareholder; namely, live in perfect harmony with him. Boyish defiance, I suppose. I often set myself against him. One example was the question of pricing. We could have done it more diplomatically.

'Quandt had said: "You're not used to it, and do not know what is acceptable."

'I said: "Am *I* responsible for it or are you?"

'Quandt had replied: "That's just it. I am not your management board chairman, nor your supervisory board chairman. I am just the major share-holder, but I'll say this – if, at the next general meeting, I see that you have given away money, next year on the balance sheet, then I'll be after you!"'

Hahnemann had replied that Quandt was perfectly entitled to do that. However, he knew that the price which Quandt wanted was excessive. Everyone had said he was mad, claiming he would not be able to sell the car.

'Then there was the general meeting. Best result for years. Dividends for the first time. In his joy, Quandt invited us all to the "Four Seasons". Toasts were made. There was much praise. I kept silent. Somebody asked where Hahnemann was. I was here. He raised his glass, that almost blind man was trying to catch my eye. And what did I say? "Dr Quandt, you told me you would be after me!" Was that the right thing to say? No, it was quite the wrong thing to say.

'But it was not the wrong thing to say when we had a fight with VW. (Once again, this involved co-operation, not marketing; co-operation with other car companies.) The occasion for it, as happened frequently in such rows, was an essentially reasonable consideration, similar to the one exercised over many years between BMW and Daimler-Benz, in spite of all the disagreements between us. This involved the exchange of technology and, if log-jams occurred, of basic production of gears, cylinder heads, gearbox parts, etc. What was on offer for VW and us was intended to be reciprocal. At that time under Nordhoff, 'development' over there was in a mess (ours was first class), while in the areas of production and after-sales service, it was the other way round (VW could not be beaten on that).

'"You over there and we here, are the last night watchmen. So let's have a chat with each other," I said.

'But there was nothing to talk about. As was intimated, the only thing to talk about was purchase.

'This talk took place at Fritz Mathern's house in Bad Homburg, just round the corner from Karinhall (as those in the know called Harald Quandt's residence). There we met: Lotz, the managing director at VW, Rust, his supervisory board chairman, and on our side, Mathern, Karoli, who was already supervisory board boss, and myself. So we talked about purchase. How much do all those proud BMWs add up to? 700 million, a billion?

'Rust called out: "Bring us Herr Quandt! You are not the right negotiating partners for us!"

'I said: "Herr Rust, you have completely misunderstood us!"

'Rust, Mathern and Karoli thereupon left the room, leaving me alone with Lotz. So that he did not appear too tall (at 1.92 metres, he was tall enough to be in the Guards), we got him to sit on the lowest sofa. Lotz said:

'"What are you really after, Hahnemann? Earlier this year, Daimler-Benz brought out the new S class, and our new model is coming out in the middle of the year. And then you won't sell any more cars!" There were just the two of us.

'I replied: "There's one thing you should bear in mind, Herr Lotz. When it comes to showing off, I win hands down!"

'Lotz then made a speech in Vienna, where, in answer to a journalist's question, the expression cropped up: yes, BMW would suit VW nicely. After that, my telephone did not stopped ringing. Our dealers and importers wanted to know if they should invest as much as a single mark in BMW, now that VW was taking over the shop. Well, I then rang up Simoneit, editor-in-chief of *Capital*, and asked for an interview, which resulted in the headline: "Herr Lotz, where are your billions?"

'When Quandt read that (and the adverts which I issued saying: "Now we are the smallest. But the length of the production line is not a guarantee of a make's quality!"), he sent for me.

'He said: "You cannot do that. I get on well with Herr Lotz. He had rung me up. You are endangering VARTA, and VW is our biggest customer in the battery trade!"

'And what did I say?

'"VARTA is not my responsibility – BMW is!"

'Quandt accepted this. He was not annoyed. On the contrary, he was calm, almost cheerful. Then he said:

'"If anything like this happens again, don't forget that I am the major shareholder. I, too, can fight. All you need do is let me know. It would have been very easy for me . . ."

'"No," I answered, "if somebody grabs me from behind the bushes, and holds a knife to my throat, then I am hardly going to ring up the general staff first and ask them what I should do! Not having a knife myself, I'd kick him in the stomach!"

'Quandt accepted that. Was it right or was it wrong? This time it was right. That was the last time such a subject was discussed.'

On 15 February 1962, appointed by Quandt, Karl Heinz Sonne, PhD, took over the chair of the management board at the age of 48, its youngest member. He had had seventeen years' experience in management in a public company, with seven of them spent at the top. He worked for 'the largest filter and dust-extractor factory on the Continent', Concordia Elektrizität AG, a member of the Quandt group of companies, whose turnover had had more than a six-fold increase from 6 to 40 million under his reign. Quandt, as he thought, had made the right choice.

He had made it all alone, and Sonne's appointment struck Munich like a bolt of lightning. They were most surprised at the choice of successor to Semler, chosen on Quandt's suggestion to be chairman of the supervisory board. This was the former honorary professor at the Munich Technical High School, Adolf Wagner. He had just announced to a press agency (which had broadcast the news) that Kämpfer, someone whom he got on well with at work, would soon take over the chair of the supervisory board as the most important man currently at BMW. A harsh, discordant note.

Wagner had a supervisory board mandate at Flick's Maximilianshütte Steel Works, and had industry experience as the former head of the Upper Silesian Steel Works PLC at Gliwice, which had once been amongst the most important suppliers to the vehicle industry. After the war, he had belonged to the Daimler-Benz supervisory board like Quandt. He was not just anybody. With verve and commitment, he had trained himself on the subject of BMW, but had soon also noticed how Quandt 'constantly meddled' in Munich. He found it unacceptable that minutes went to Quandt even before the supervisory board had received them. Then Quandt would keep conferring individually with management board members, summon them to Homburg, appear openly in person on the works site, to get a picture for himself of the progress being made in building new production lines and halls, or would speak to Hahnemann about pricing. Wagner did not like any of this, as BMW was ultimately an independent public company and *not* a Quandt business.

Kämpfer, as well, did not like coming across those financial reports which he wrote for examination by management and supervisory boards when they were reproduced in 'Quandt reports' which Wilcke regularly sent to Homburg.

He said to Wilcke: 'It's mad for Quandt to keep on meddling here with his 10 per cent.'

Wilcke stayed silent. He was a legal adviser and one of the few who really knew how high his principal's financial commitment really was, as well as the corresponding risk. Yet he arranged a conversation in which (meeting privately at Kämpfer's house in Söcking) he challenged Quandt with the prospect by saying:

'You want to govern – and cannot even credit me as head of company finance.'

'We've got the bank's votes,' Quandt replied. 'You don't need to concern yourself.'

Kämpfer immediately declared: 'I feel responsible to *all* shareholders, and not just to you.'

Then Sonne came along. Quandt again looked for Kämpfer.

'You know why I have sent him here?' he said.

Kämpfer replied: 'He comes from your group.'

'Yes,' Quandt said, 'I have put such a lot of money and commitment into BMW that I definitely need someone I can confide in.'

He then came out with the reason why he had not taken up Wagner's proposal to make Kämpfer the managing director, saying:

'*You* feel responsible to *all* the shareholders!'

Kämpfer drew the consequences from that and handed in his notice. He had received an offer from Flick to take over the 'Max-Hütte'. Even Wagner, maintaining his protest, resigned as the supervisory board chairman – in a spectacular way, a day before the general meeting at the end of August 1962. There the announcement was made that, in association with a second large shareholder Dr Jacques Koerfer (with 8 per cent of the shareholding), Quandt had, in the meantime, come to represent 25 per cent of the capital increased to 60.3 million DM.

The Essen-based auditor Dr Hermann Karoli was chosen as the new chairman of the supervisory board, again on Quandt's proposal.

And so everything seemed to have straightened out again, and would probably have remained so if Sonne had not suddenly resigned, after less than three years in the job. The disappointed Quandt was later to say:

'Although he was a clever, hard-working chairman, he did not feel fully at ease on the committee with the men he worked with. This led him to cross over to Herr Henle in the Ruhr early in 1963. *Der Spiegel* had already suspected as much when it published an article entitled 'Sonne und Wind'.* It stated that Sonne had resigned for 'climatic' reasons, by which readers might understand both the Föhn wind (causing a lot of trouble to the new resident in the foothills of the Alps after a year), as well as the unusual operating climate at BMW.

In fact, nothing had been changed in the collegiate principle, as the person appointed to head the management board had discovered. It maintained that every member of the management board, fully responsible in his field, was always bound by the overall agreement on decisions outside his jurisdiction. In this way, Sonne had remained managing director without authority. The

---

* Tr. note: A play on words, meaning 'sun and wind'.

fact that he was also acquiring specialist knowledge in the car industry (he had described himself in front of the press as the 'most expensive apprentice' in the German car industry, receiving full training in the car business at Block 54 in the development department) did not move anyone on the management board to concede him anything more than figure-head duties. Yet there was much respect at what Sonne introduced as a skilled management expert. In addition to the 'value analysis', there was the so-called 'covering contribution account', in which the costs and profit were calculated per model, distributed across all the 126 variants in the BMW car range. It was soon established that there were no earnings at all to be acquired from variant 100 onwards, and that there was only a surplus of 50 DM at best on variant 1. Shortly after Sonne's arrival, Kämpfer had presented him with an expected financial loss of 18 million DM, probably to indicate that things could not go on like this. Sonne had the calculations checked, and found that there was still a deficit of 13.8 million. He remained forever sceptical.

However, that play on words of 'Sonne und Wind' was entirely appropriate. When Sonne became convinced that better chances were to be had elsewhere (he joined Klöckner-Humboldt-Deutz as managing director of a business which bore no comparison with BMW in terms of volume and range), the wind of time had given him the reputation of being an entirely successful manager. This was because, at the end of his three-year term of office, BMW had found its way out of the woods, due to the circumstances already mentioned.

'Herr Sonne' was how an internal memo began from MAN's managing director, Ulrich Neumann, to the Augsburg Works dated 11.2.1965. 'Herr Sonne has told me that he will be giving up his activities in Munich from the beginning of April . . . He was very cheerful and light-hearted on the telephone. This is probably due, not least to the fact that he can extricate himself from BMW and from the quarrel with MAN in so fortunate a way.'

Quarrel? Differences of opinion about the future of BMW Power Plant Production Co. Ltd had indeed turned into a bitter row between the contractual partners, in the course of which a kind of power struggle developed. In the contract of 1960, in which MAN received 50 per cent of the shares in Power Plant Production (whereby half the 'jewel' belonged to it), BMW had declared itself ready to transfer a further shareholding, the deciding 51 per cent, to the Maschinenfabrik Augsburg-Nürnberg. (The purchase price was to be the nominal value and a packet supplement of 2 million DM.) This would come about if the two companies of BMW Power Plant Production Co. Ltd and MAN Turbo Engines Co. Ltd operating at the Allach site were merged.

The planned merger was left in no doubt. Even its timing was fixed, at which two conditions would be fulfilled. Firstly, MAN Turbo would have to conclude their current development contract for a jet engine designated MAN RR (Rolls Royce) 153, and secondly, an appropriate production contract would have to be issued for this or another engine to MAN Turbo. When asked when it would be ready, Wilcke had invariably given the same response to the shareholders at every general meeting (as they followed the further growth and prosperity of the BMW subsidiary with amazement and satisfaction): not yet, let's just wait and see. We shall only do it, indeed, we can only do it when there is a balance in the contracts issued.

MAN insisted the conditions had been fulfilled. BMW contested this, saying that the contract had been broken off, but never concluded. Was the reason behind this somewhat like the mother's desire to buy back the daughter, just to stay 'in mid air' (something which had been re-considered), so that they would not simply limit themselves to cars and motorcycles? It all seemed to fit in. Power Plant Production had increased its turnover ten-fold within four years (something which MAN, with its half ownership, was naturally not unhappy about), and had only really become a 'jewel' after its miserable beginnings at the end of the war. (In order not to be solely dependent on state contracts, in other words, military planning, which could quickly change, it had built considerable quantities of Lycoming piston engines under licence from the Americans, which were fitted to the Dornier Do 27 and the FWP-149. There was also a gas turbine and a jet turbine engine developed for civilian applications, the former being used as an aero-engine and auxiliary aero-engine, while the latter was used as an auxiliary drive for gliders, and as a stationary engine.) And yet there were no grounds for thinking of 're-acquisition' – if only out of loyalty towards a company which had shown solidarity in supporting BMW's restructuring by guaranteeing generous credit, beyond its own interests, to the point where restructuring might not have been possible at all without it. Wilcke had never forgotten that. No, no – there had to be 'balance'. Even in evaluating the land, premises and buildings, their positions were miles apart. Dr Karoli, the chairman of the supervisory board at BMW AG, who conducted the concluding negotiations with Wilcke (Sonne had already gone), explained the importance which Power Plant Production had had for BMW over the decades, and that an appropriate price must also be agreed if such a jewel were to be given up. At times, there was mention of 70 million DM, at other times, between 50 and 55. In fact, it was not only the property which had meanwhile increased in value. There was the 'production skill' as well, enabling it to produce practically any conceivable power plant.

The agreement finally came about at Hanover on the night of Thursday 28 April 1965. MAN had acquired and submitted a preliminary contract for manufacturing the Rolls Royce 'Tyne' engine under licence. BMW sold all its shares in Power Plant Production Co. Ltd for 30 million DM. On top of that, there were around 17 million DMs-worth of loans written off, all the shares in BMW Engineering Spandau Co. Ltd in Berlin (owned by Power Plant Production) and land and buildings owned in Munich. The bottom line produced a purchase price of 54.4 million DM in total and the fulfilment of Dr Karoli's wish to have the name of BMW removed forthwith from the future company title of Power Plant Production Co. Ltd.

Opinions were divided at the works. The sadness of parting (which almost reached consternation) was etched on many faces; old memories were revived, and, as people said, traditions could not be discarded like shirts. 'Renouncing the air' was now sealed, and the chance had also finally gone of somehow getting down to business with the revitalised armaments industry (through the Power Plant Production subsidiary), if only loosely. *Tempora mutantur* – times they are a-changing. Had they not already changed? And had not a Bavarian industrial policy long since agreed that the important consideration was to allow branches of the economy with a bright future to grow and develop in the agrarian land of Bavaria? One had only to think of Siemens at Munich and Erlangen, of Messerschmitt-Bölkow and Krauss-Maffei. In addition, a whole computer industry was emerging, while at Oberpfaffenhofen, there was the German Research Establishment for Aviation and Space. All these enterprises could not be separated from armaments considerations as implied by new technologies – in the way, for example, they furthered space travel. *Tempora mutantur* indeed. And in those times, BMW (which had often burnt its fingers) had frequently switched course. It was not called Bavarian *Car* Works, but Bavarian *Motor* Works, which had been the way to move from aero-engines to motorcycles, from motorcycles back to aero-engines, and from both to cars. They now stayed with the latter, and probably wanted to stay there, too. But they did not want to lose face with regard to MAN, and be in a position of someone in breach of contract. (Wilcke subsequently said about it: 'There was just no other way of doing things.')

However, the chairman of the works council, Kurt Golda, felt unrestrained joy. A heavy burden had weighed on him – now at last, he could lay it down. It had found its roots in a few sentences which the works council at the Spandau Engineering Works had addressed to the Federal Minister for All-German Affairs, Dr Rainer Barzel, at the beginning of 1963. It was a kind of cry for help, which pleaded that it was completely incomprehensible that the parent company, the Bavarian Motor Works AG in Munich, 'is capable, in our situation, of failing to make provision for use of the small workforce to capacity'. They said that the management's measures and the dismissals planned by company staff had led to serious disquiet amongst the workforce. This workforce had not only kept loyal to BMW AG during the seventeen years of reconstruction, but had made the Spandau works operate as a successful business in the most unfavourable conditions. Now they had been put out to pasture. In other words, this meant that 'hundreds and thousands of foreigners can be given bread and work at our parent company amongst others, although there is not the will to keep a handful of Berlin employees in work, despite the fact they fully deserve it.'

Golda sat down and wrote the following letter to his colleague, the chairman of the works council Fritz:

Dear Willi,

At the last supervisory board meeting on 15.9, the following report was agreed by the management or the supervisory board, which I can now convey to you privately and confidentially. Herr Wilcke introduced his report by stating that Spandau has a surface area of 137,000 sq. m. Of these, 33,000 sq. m can be used. The workforce amounts to 231 people. The turnover for 1964 was 5.4 millions, including 3.2 million from motorcycles. A loss of 33,000 DM resulted.

In the meantime, Herr Gieschen presented the following report to the supervisory board after his visit to Spandau.

The overall impression was positive. The intention therefore is to transfer all motorcycle production to Spandau. To ensure full capacity, spare parts production for models being discontinued (BMW 700) is to be set up. Both activities are only feasible if the present workforce can be increased from 250 to 1,000 men. Management and supervisory boards are clear that investments of between 10 and 15 million DM will have to be undertaken by 1968.

The second person with a load off his mind was Hahnemann. The way in which Spandau had been consigned to a miserable existence, from what one could gather from the outside, had always depressed him. It was difficult to reconcile the two. The Berlin branch, recently acquired so favourably at Moabit, stood there in its splendour, while Spandau, as the former parts factory, which had once boasted the best apprentice training facilities in Germany, was going to the dogs! So he was happy to be able to abandon that area of 'aircraft propulsion', which he knew little about, based at Allach with its military contractors. He had never felt quite right when he had driven out to Allach as the AG's delegate to Power Plannnt Production. All these complicated turbines, whose technology he had not the slightest clue about! On one occasion he had got too close to a test bench and had almost been blown away by the air-stream. And what was meant by 'twin-shaft twin-ram engine'? What was meant by 'continuous thrust-convector control'? This part was made here, and that part in England. Then there was 'that General Electric, who treated us like the dregs, with its tolerance levels increased three, four-fold against those supplied by the American factories. You never knew whether the waiter talking with you at dinner might not be a spy . . . No,' he had urged Sonne, 'let's sell the silly clown – let's build cars, they're more solid. Perhaps one cannot earn quite as much money with them, but they're all well made, and they do at least have a future.'

So he did not shed a single tear at the deletion of the letters BMW from the name of the future company in which Power Plant Production was involved. Nor did he mind when MAN Turbo Co. Ltd (as it initially continued to be called) was re-registered in June 1969 as MTU Motoren- und Turbinen-Union München GmbH. He only pricked up his ears when he heard that it had now 'combined the aviation activities of BMW, MAN, Daimler-Benz and Maybach'. Daimler-Benz as well? Well I never! Indeed, with the immediate transfer of its power plant development to Munich, Untertürkheim had obtained late entry to Allach (in order, fifteen years later, in February 1985, to acquire half of MTU, with right of pre-emption straight out of MAN's possession. This was not exactly chicken feed, being more than half a billion DM, just as it had not been chicken feed for MAN either, when they had had to shelve out for half the shares in Power Plant Production from BMW AG in 1965.)

So far, so good. Or was it bad? A few weeks after the sale of the Allach works to MAN in 1965, the annual general meeting of BMW shareholders took place in Munich. As the *Süddeutsche Zeitung* wrote, 'this unanimously approved all the required business, including the dividends increased from 6 to 10 per cent; cf. the theme of the day.'

Under 'theme of the day' was written: 'With its surprising decision at 10 per cent, does BMW want to take the wind out of the sails from some opposition or other, who had perhaps taken offence in the equally surprising sale of half of BMW Power Plant Production? Certainly the price was good. But with its sale, the second foundation of BMW has gone.' A sentence further on stated: 'BMW rates immediately rose on the stock market.'

On Sonne's resignation, the supervisory board delegated Gerhard Wilcke to the management board, and made him its chairman on Quandt's wishes. This was in spite of the fact that he had never run a business, although he now knew his way round BMW like no one else. If the decision might have been dictated by the pressure of time, then Quandt, too, might not have viewed his choice as the ultimate solution. But it proved a wise choice. Wilcke was practically a proxy for Quandt, but enjoyed enough authority, and got on with everyone with his unwavering, tolerant approach. He did not speak on a subject he did not understand, but did what he thought was right. He reduced Quandt's role more and more, although the latter refused to have anything to do with a desire for direct management (which sometimes led the commanders to play at being artillery officers). There were other things in the 'main business' of life for Quandt to do than just be involved in BMW. He was approaching his sixties, and his creative restlessness was abandoning him.

Good Luck and Glas

There was a man who was associated not only with BMW but also with Hans Glas's agricultural machinery factory in the Lower Bavarian town of Dingolfing. We have met him many times before in our story. In Munich, on Dachau Street, where it runs into the city centre, he had set himself up as a motorcycle and car dealer in the fifties, in hastily erected sheds in the midst of bomb sites. This was after there had been nothing more for him to sort out at the furthest end of the same road on the outskirts of the city, at Allach. (He had been head of the German works security at the Karlsfeld Ordnance Depot. There had been a fire. If there were ever to be a fire again, the Americans said, his time would be up. He had replied that there would definitely be another fire, and so chose to leave there and then.)

Georg ('Schorsch') Meier (who else could it have been), started as a bicycle dealer. He marketed the Imme, an ingeniously designed small motorcycle from Immenstadt, which unfortunately had production faults and did not find favour with the customers (the manufacturer had skilfully managed to link Meier and other dealers through shares). But immediately after that, one of the first vehicles in Meier's showroom was the Goggo, a scooter (somewhat modelled on the Italian Lambretta), which Andreas Glas, the son of the founder, manufactured and managed to sell easily. When demand fell and people wanted four wheels and a roof over their heads, the dealer and manufacturer pondered together as to what kind of engine could propel such a vehicle. The dealer immediately suggested a BMW engine (in the meantime, he had started selling BMW motorcycles, principally the R 24), went across to the works at Milbertshofen and was never, for the rest of his life, to forget the tone with which he was sent packing. The director's assistant said:

'My dear Herr Meier, you cannot possibly imagine that we would hand over our high quality engine to a Lower Bavarian agricultural machinery factory!'

The elderly Glas, when he heard of this, grumbled: 'BMW? Never. We'll do it ourselves!'

And he was to be proved right. His Goggomobil became the darling of the masses, beat the Isetta hands down, and Glas went from strength to strength. By 1966, the Glas agricultural machinery factory in Lower Bavarian

Dingolfing had produced about 300,000 Goggomobils . . . and would have continued producing and selling them had it not been for. . . .

Yes, what was to be done? thought Meier on an August day during the fateful year of 1966. It had become clear to him that by however much BMW went up, Glas continued to lose ground. Dealers viewed such tendencies coldly, but Meier did not. This was because he owed his post-war success to Glas, and less to BMW, and had always represented Glas *and* BMW. With Hahnemann's arrival and the desire for single franchises, he had told him: never without Glas! So he was one of the few BMW main dealers who still sold another make – and that was in Munich, at the seat of the company! This continued when Glas ventured into proper cars which found a market beyond the Goggomobil. They were not bad cars; quite the opposite, they were very respectable ones! On the other hand, Meier knew, remembering the example of the 501, just how quickly a manufacturer's resources can be eaten away when his ambition stretches beyond the means at his disposal. And now nothing was selling, apart from the Goggomobil. Joy gave way to deep depression. Quite apart from unrewarded daring, his reputation as a dealer depended on cars which could be sold and not left lying around. Drechselmayer, a supplier to Glas based at Geisenhausen and a friend of Meier's, was in the same trouble, but even more so, given that 90 per cent of his business depended on Glas.

'Confound it! What are we to do, Schorsch?'

'Yes, what?'

'Go and see Anderl,' advised Drechselmayer. 'Have a chat with him, he'll listen to you.'

'And what if he won't?'

Something occurred to Meier. The year before, he had met Hahnemann at the Frankfurt Motor Show. On the lefthand side of the BMW stand was the successor to the 503, the hard-top coupé designed by Nuccio Bertone in Turin, called the BMW 3200 CS. On the righthand side, separated by a small aisle, was Glas's new 3.0-litre car, with bodywork also designed by an Italian, Pietro Frua, which the scornful had already christened 'Glaserati'. Hoepner, the head of public relations at BMW, bumped into Hahnemann and said:

'Anderl Glas is standing over there. He would be pleased if you were to congratulate him.'

Hahnemann went across and Meier heard the following conversation:

'A stylish car, I congratulate you, it looks beautiful, a real winner. But, Anderl, if you had asked me, I would have taken you to a big room at Milbertshofen and shown you nothing but files, files of complaints about Bertone! If the car's mechanics are built here, and the body is brought from Italy, it turns out a disaster! Why? If anyone has an accident and needs a new door, then it will take three months to get there (from Italy!), and then it never fits! It'll be a centimetre short in one place, and two in another. As they're hammered out on wooden tools, no two items are the same.'

Glas said nothing. Then Hahnemann said in his calm, gentle way, quite without malice, almost cheerfully:

'But you imitate us in everything. You made your little Isar on the lines of the 700, you copied the 1500 with your 1700, and now it's our rocking horse, the Bertone! We've even put bankruptcy behind us, and now things are looking up for us. And you're probably going to copy us there, too! But if you get as far as you can down that road, give me a call! Milbertshofen isn't very far, is it?'

And Anderl Glas, taken aback, and yet never at a loss for words, said, without blushing:

'I'll do that!'

Recalling this, Meier drove to Dingolfing with his wife (the wives were always there) in his 507. As always, he was warmly greeted by the Glas family. They talked about the weather. Meier said that it was somewhat sultry. Yes, said old Glas, it certainly was. Tuesday was pay day, and he had no idea where to get the money from. This was a problem that had never occurred before. He had hoped for a state security, and he had received one, but had been refused a second. Now the game was up – not only with the latest model (it was to have been presented at the International Motor Show at the beginning of September), but with everything.

'Have you got any advice, Schorsch?'

Meier was amazed. He was later to say that, even when he had been a racing driver he had never reached his destination so quickly. He asked whether he should give Hahnemann a ring. What a good idea! both Glases, father and son, exclaimed as if with one voice. Why hadn't they thought of it before? If he were to do that, they'd never regret it.

'Saving face,' Meier continued, 'is just as important in Bavaria as it is with the Great Powers. Both Glases were saving their faces, but I had none to lose. So I rang up Hahnemann from their living room.'

Hahnemann had not forgotten the conversation any less than Meier, when he rang through. He said that he was speaking in the presence of the old and young Glas at Dingolfing, and that, speaking on behalf of the Glas company, it was over.

'It was a Friday,' Hahnemann remembered, 'the weekend, and, to be honest, I was exhausted. We had spent the last few days discussing just one subject: how to increase our capacity. Gieschen had innocently said that he could get the line to run a bit quicker. Using everything at our disposal, Milbertshofen turned out between 400 and 450 cars a day. We could have done with 500 or 600 for some time now. The factory was bursting at the seams.

'That evening Glas came round to see me. No, I mean we met at Schorsch Meier's place. I couldn't sleep that night. On Sunday afternoon, I went walking in the Isarauen. Problems have to be analysed if you want to solve them, I said to myself. But there was nothing to analyse, and I was all alone. I knew that none of my colleagues would ever dream of buying into Glas. Things were already going well for us. We had a turnover of between 500 and 700 million. Success makes you feel smug, and no one (I went through them in turn), no one thought that far, that we could contemplate bankruptcy at Milbertshofen, locked away as we were behind our walls, making 450 cars a day. Wages and costs, like everything, were rising and we *had* to expand production! As for Wilcke, well, I could get him on my side. And what about Karoli, chairing the supervisory board? He was an auditor, capable of doing everything I could not. We got on well. But would we this time? I weighed everything up. He would probably hesitate, or at least suggest sleeping on the matter. That meant putting it off. Once you started thinking things out, nothing ever happened.

'Sunday came. In the afternoon, I rang Quandt. I said:

'"We must buy Glas. We would get a few hundred thousand square metres of land. Worth it, at any price. We would get 4,000 car workers – people, who would hardly cost thousands of marks each to train fully. And . . . we would help the Bavarian state which would have them around its neck if Glas were to go bankrupt."

'Quandt said: "I see. See it through the management board. If it goes wrong, I'll back you up."

'I said: "Glas needs five million immediately."

'Quandt said: "Speak to Pollmann (Pollmann was head of finance). I'll cover the amount."

'On Monday, I went to Pollmann, and received the cheque without anyone knowing about it. I gave it to Anderl Glas. That is how we came to be involved with Glas.'

Hans Glas, the eleventh, but not the last, child of the agricultural machinery manufacturer Maurus Glas, who had produced hand-operated threshing machines at Dingolfing since the turn of the century, had gone out into the world at the age of eighteen, after learning his trade in his father's business. He had gone to Toronto via the Berlin subsidiary of a large Canadian agricultural machinery manufacturer, and joined its parent company. When the First World War came, he had taken flight. As he was to tell his children later, everything seemed to have happened with as much complexity as consistency. Every country he struggled through, working from dishwashing to the production line at Ford in Detroit, or the Indian Motor Cycle Company, where he made it to works manager, had undoubtedly created the preconditions for what he was later to become when he returned to the Isar. After buying back the family business from the hands of the Saar-based concern of Stumm, which had collapsed in the Slump, he succeeded in doing something in the thirties which no one thought possible. This was to make the Glas agricultural machinery factory, one among many, and one somewhere in Lower Bavaria to boot (a region where there were only tracks across the field), into 'Europe's largest seeding machine manufacturer'. It survived the Second World War unscathed, and Hans Glas, sensing the advent of car ownership, overcame the post-war crisis. We know that, faced with the seasonal production of agricultural machines (for three months, the company worked night and day, and for three months it did nothing at all), he began production of scooters to start with, and then Goggomobils. What we do not know is that his son, Andreas Glas, returning home from the war without a scratch on him, was picked as an agricultural machinery engineer in 1950 to undertake a study trip to the USA sponsored by the Marshall

Plan – a country that lived, as it were, on wheels (his strongest impression was of the unemployed collecting their benefit money by car). He was sure that it would not take ten years for things to be similar in Germany. He was speaking at a present level of zero, apart from a few Volkswagens making their first appearance. If only one could get involved. . . . Andreas was then the one who 'sorted everything out', together with Karl Dompert, his childhood friend and war-time companion (both had served in the same Luftwaffe unit). Dompert took over the design department, headed technical development, and the result was the Goggomobil, whose 100,000th example came off the line in 1959. It was followed by further models which Hahnemann ironically described by saying: you have copied us in everything. Encouraged no more and no less by BMW than what was also true for other makes, they nonetheless pursued a quite definite goal. This goal was to conquer a niche, too, in a similar way to Hahnemann. In what appeared a presumptuous idea, Glas's plan was to occupy a niche above Porsche. There was, in fact, a yawning gap there, and Glas went for it. He would use high-performance engines, with bodywork from Turin. And finally he was to fill the gap with a big V-8 coupé using a 2.6 and later 3.0-litre engine, which was to have its debut on 1 September 1966.

When Glas was asked where he got the courage from, as well as ability, to venture this far, the expression 'complex and consistent', which had accompanied the life story of the old Glas, again became appropriate. It was complex in that the Class 4 driving licence, which enabled the Goggomobil to be driven without the need for a driving test, ceased to be available after 1958. Therefore, the people enjoying this privilege died away, and with them, the Goggomobil. It was thus time to launch a new vehicle. Would it be another small car? Henry Ford once said that only a large car factory could build small cars, and only a small car factory could build large ones – the former being built in large quantities, and the latter by hand. If this was true for America, then it was also true for 'the smallest car factory in Germany', as Glas called himself, not without pride. It was patriarchally run (the senior boss continued to produce his seeding machines), and self-sufficient, right down to an in-house butcher's shop. It had no debts, no outside capital, and was therefore free from troublesome interference by others. Above all, it had a group of technicians which caused many a recognised company to envy the resourceful Dompert. Ischinger, for example, had gone to Glas from BMW, as well as outstanding technicians and fitters from other well known companies, in order to achieve here what was impossible, or practically impossible, elsewhere. This was to solve and implement fiddly design problems with as much flexibility as speed, and without any bureaucracy, with the whole thing often being done from one day to the next. (When Helmut Werner Bönsch moved from BMW to Dingolfing to bring Glas products up to BMW quality, he gave the highest praise to Glas technology.)

Where the problem lay was in far too limited financial resources, which simply forbade greater investments (and Glas insisted on not getting into debt). These would be investments in test equipment (after all, the company was building high performance engines), in quality control installations, and machines for testing materials, together with all the costly technology for achieving quality which began in design, but was equally dependent on materials and their testing under the severest conditions. Was not all this common knowledge? Of course it was common knowledge, but it exploded those barriers with which no one was more familiar than the chief boss himself. When, in 1962, a merger was discussed (Quandt was present, as well as Franz Josef Strauß, in another attempt at combining Bavarian car companies into a union), Hans Glas turned it down flat, saying that it exceeded his resources and that he did not want to pit himself against the big companies. He consciously wanted to stay 'small': 'Stones we cannot lift, we should leave alone.' And: 'We'll sell everything apart from our own family.' Glas was a family concern. But had he not sold it now?

On his return from a trip to Dingolfing, Gieschen declared the following in Hahnemann's office:

'Insure to the hilt, then light the fuse!'

Monz did not make the trip at all. However, Hahnemann wanted to know what he, the head of purchasing, thought about acquiring Glas.

'Not my cup of tea!' Monz said.

Had Hahnemann expected anything else? Although Pollmann, head of finance, had written out the cheque, he viewed Hahnemann with amazement. He could not refrain from saying:

'Be it on your own head, then!'

'After an initial look at the files, Pollmann estimated the annual loss which involvement with Glas would entail would be at least two and a half million. He still did not want to talk about purchase. Four weeks later, he said that after close examination, it was no longer two and a half million, but seven, or even eight, million. And six weeks later, he said his people had now worked it out at thirty-six million DM. Was that annually? Yes, it was! Osswald, head of development on the management board, was already against taking over Glas, for reasons of image, claiming that they could not simply fit the old bangers with BMW kidneys and say they were now BMWs. Somebody wondered if they could do it to the Goggomobil. He asked him why he did not consider resurrecting the Isetta. Everyone was against it. Wilcke, who was more in favour than against, felt himself outvoted. Karoli was wavering. And what about Quandt? He had said to Hahnemann: 'See it through!' Nobody now, certainly not Quandt, needed to tell Hahnemann that twice. His office had become a relay station for Glas.

In the meantime, Glas had still not been bought. The agreement only came into force when a prospective state security was granted. There was still the possibility of withdrawing, and the objections of the faction against acquiring Glas were reinforced in proportion to the increasing problems. The patriarch Glas had succeeded in building cars in the Dingolfing halls, and good ones at that. But he had only done it for eleven years. As early as 1964, with a turnover of 154 million DM, there had been losses. In 1965, with all resources stretched to the limit and investment limited to the bare essentials, there had not been any profit. In 1966, with a planned turnover of 200 million DM, capital was tied up in the form of materials and of completed but unsold cars lying around in droves at the works. But the burdens continued, with 3.5 million due in interest charges alone. Any company, even if it is called BMW, had to fail, if all it did on takeover was to continue drawing the lines. It would certainly re-arrange production, but would leave everything as before, as the family naturally hoped. How could a fair solution be found without distressing the Glases? Of course, such efficient people as Andreas Glas and Karl Dompert had to be kept at their factory (they had been appointed as factory managers), but could they be expected to give up Glas as an independent car factory, just to treat and subsequently see their life's work as no more than a supplier for the manufacture of BMW parts? But even then, most of it would have to be torn down and rebuilt. Were there sufficient resources available for that? That was doubtful, even with a 50 million DM state security to cover liabilities and for investments at Dingolfing and the Glas company's engine works at Landshut. BMW had just reacquired the Spandau works in Berlin, and had set aside 50 million DM for rebuilding it. Motorcycle production was to be transferred there. Did this mean give up Berlin, about turn, and take motorcycles to Dingolfing? What was to happen with the Glas dealers and customers, who had received the assurance that Glas cars would continue to run with the BMW seal of quality, completing, as it were, the BMW range? There was already the four-door Glas car with its 1.7-litre engine standing across its bows. Not only did it serve as a competitor to the BMW 1600 and the four-door BMW 1800, but its sales were far too small to justify double production. In addition, BMW had quite a different image which Glas would distort here.

And what about the big Glas 8-cylinder? It looked magnificent, but was not sufficiently developed to be useful as the flagship for the combined company, especially as such a top-range product was expected from BMW. Should its production be continued or discontinued? Both solutions would swallow up new funds and new investments. If the first solution were adopted, production would have to be organised more efficiently if a profit were to result. If the second solution were adopted, the car would have to be brought up to BMW quality. And where was this to happen? Was it to be in wooden halls, which had already attracted protests from the factory inspectorate? Then there was a whole string of further unresolved problems. Just the models produced by Glas in larger numbers, apart from the Goggomobil, yielded minute, and frequently no, profits. There was no way of manufacturing the models which provided profits with more productivity, such as the coupé and the new 1304 CL saloon, which looked a very modern car with its fastback. Calculations had shown that just a corresponding improvement in production would cost millions of DM. Hahnemann had to keep struggling with all that, more than he wanted to. He sat on the newly formed supervisory board of Glas GmbH with Dr Peter, the representative from the Bavarian state government, Dr Sonntag, from the Bavarian State Bank, and Dr Karoli. Then he had enough, left, and had himself appointed (with immediate agreement) as the 'overall authorised representative for Glas'. He rolled up his sleeves and set out to cut the Gordian knot. The sword-swipe (meaning to continue with Glas as an independent company or as a supply factory) lay in selling everything which was unsold in stock. This alone would bring money into the coffers and ensure Glas's existence, until such time as it was clear what was going to happen, when plans and such like would be issued. The resultant wall of fog (nobody knew what would appear on the other side) was principally marked by uncertainty. Would BMW's image be transferred to Glas? Would the loyal Glas customers take it amiss, now that they were linked to a partner who up to now, in the arrogance and complacency they saw, had appealed to quite a different clientele?

It was a marketing problem. That was Hahnemann's business. In the meantime, the state secured loan had been issued by the free state of Bavaria, and Glas had been transferred into BMW's ownership for 9.1 million DM. To solve this, he set up (with Bönsch for product alignment, Dompert for production, chief engineer Balbaschewski for technology, and Hahnemann's assistant, Schaab, for marketing) a liaison office at the scene of the event, whose first and most important job was to re-work unsold cars to BMW standards and to subject cars coming off the production line to the quality controls practised in Milbertshofen and which were only too well known. No car at all was allowed to be delivered within the first three weeks. It was only after this period that each customer received his car, guaranteed to the 'new' production standards. In conjunction with this, mobile service units undertook operations to remove the major complaints at the dealers.

If Hahnemann solved this problem with the trusty Kolk at Milbertshofen, in a twinkling of an eye, so to speak, then the customers' opinion on Glas cars remained divided. A Herr X wrote saying that he was surprised that it was only in 1966 that Glas had 'crossed the great divide' ('from the experiences I've had with my Isar 600 and the 1002 coupé, the people should really have disappeared from the scene much earlier'). A Herr Y regretted that, as far as he was concerned, 'that was it!' ('What am I supposed to do in future with my 1004 at a BMW workshop? It was precisely the personal treatment which was important, something which made all Glas drivers warm to this make in the long term. There was no bureaucracy in Dingolfing.') And celebrities, including filmstars like Dieter Borsche, made some salient confessions.

'With my Glas 1700 TS, with which I was very satisfied,' Borsche wrote, 'I got the pleasant feeling that I wasn't driving a mass-produced car. . . . It remains to be hoped that Glas cars will continue to enjoy a very long life in the good hands of BMW. As long as there are individual characters, there ought to be individual cars, as well.'

As far as BMW was concerned, there was nothing which initially stood in the way of such hopes. How else could Gerhard Wilcke have disputed the claim in front of the entire Glas workforce (which had assembled in the large despatch hall at Dingolfing for the works to be handed over at 10.15 a.m. on 10 November 1966) that a flirtation, an engagement, or even a marriage had taken place between the two businesses?

'We have not got married,' he said. 'All BMW has done is adopt a new daughter in Glas GmbH.'

536

And the 'new family father', as he liked to be known as, called out to the Bavarian 'sovereign', Alfons Goppel, and Hans Glas, the senior head, saying:

'Just think of the merger before the last world war of Horsch, Wanderer, Audi and DKW to form Auto Union. Just as these companies continued producing their products as partners, so it is our desire to collaborate as partners here.'

No, nobody saw any need at all to upset Glas's design principle, although there was a desire to highlight the advantages of the merger. These were the deployment of larger financial resources for expanding and rationalizing Dingolfing, the greater economies of scale, which 'our purchase could achieve through uniformity and higher quantities, especially for Hans Glas GmbH', expansion and strengthening of both dealer networks and, last but not least, the widening of common bases, such as after-sales service and spare-parts procurement.

With so much optimism around, Golda, the works council chairman, lowered his expectations. He was the one who had found it most difficult on the supervisory board to vote for the takeover. The entrepreneurial risk seemed too high to him, and incompatible with the need to abandon social improvements over the next two years. But he was not the one to put the dampers on it. The future of BMW was at stake, the second big step forward after successful restructuring due to Quandt's willingness to take risks. This was just after people had been able to celebrate the 50th anniversary of the founding of the company in grand style, since the company had not survived by the skin of its teeth.

The fact that the Glas daughter lost her independence quicker than might have been expected, and willingly slipped under her mother's wings, had perplexed even those who had, from the outset, viewed Wilcke's optimistic promise as a non-starter. Had Glas got nearer bankruptcy than seemed to be the case? Or was the reason to be found in the increasing self-awareness of the mother who was no longer keen on 'partnership'? Admittedly, the AG had registered a slight fall in exports for 1966, but, measured against home market sales, that did not weigh particularly heavily. The company report for 1966 stated that it was remarkable that we could increase our home market registrations by 9,387 units or 27 per cent, while total registrations for the Federal Republic of Germany were, in 1966, around 0.8 per cent below the previous year's figure. Amongst many other German car manufacturers, exports had to make up for the fall in home-market registrations. In contrast, BMW was able to increase its share of the overall home market registrations from 2.5 to 3.2 per cent (1966). This favourable trend in sales for BMW even continued when our whole branch of industry had to accept marked losses in registrations for the last quarter of 1966.'

If one reads the company reports of the following years, then it becomes quite clear, as far as it tells us about Glas, where things were heading. In the restrained language which company reports always use, it was already stated in the report for the financial year of 1966 (the one in which the takeover took place) that acquisition of Hans Glas GmbH (with property totalling over 300,000 square metres, buildings occupying 63,300 square metres of it, and a current trained workforce of 2,750 staff) certainly 'guaranteed the necessary facilities for further expansion in our company. It will, however, place heavy costs on this participation, during the transition period prior to Hans Glas GmbH and its production programme being incorporated into our company.'

A year later, it stated: 'Hans Glas GmbH achieved a turnover of 110 million DM in 1967, compared with 165 million DM in 1966.'

And: 'Since 1967, our measures for the final integration of the works facilities at Dingolfing and Landshut have taken effect. In the course of these measures, we had to withdraw production from Hans Glas GmbH which, as before, consisted of cars, agricultural machinery, kit-carrying bodies for Bundeswehr vehicles. We have had to introduce periods of short-time working and also temporarily reduce the workforce until about autumn 1968. Part of the previous staff at Hans Glas GmbH is being prepared at our plant in Munich for its work at Dingolfing and Landshut.'

Finally, the report about the financial year 1968, which had just ended, speaks frankly of 'incorporation of Hans Glas GmbH into the business fields of BMW AG being concluded as planned. . . .' and succinctly states: 'Only the Goggomobil is still being produced from the former Glas production. In addition, we have converted all the Dingolfing and Landshut works facilities to BMW production. Components, axle parts, service-exchange and spare parts, as well as parts sets, are now manufactured there. The agricultural machinery business, including the Pilsting factory, have been disposed of to the partnership firm of Eicher Bros, Dingolfing.'

The reader must ask if what Wilcke announced at the takeover was therefore nothing but eyewash. It certainly was not. People really believed what they were saying. It was certain that stiffening the Glas programme, and making modifications which went deep into the structure at Dingolfing were essential. In turn, Bönsch, looking beyond his allotted task of quality alignment, saw, in the further development of Glas vehicles, a chance for BMW to round off and consolidate its own programme at the bottom end. The 1300, developed for Glas by Ischinger (whom Fiedler had once let go) and fitted with a toothed-belt drive for the overhead camshaft, was built specifically to do that. This engine, to which Bönsch attributed epoch-making significance, enabled the model range to be completed below the New Class (where the sports version of the 700 was still remembered) and the lost market share to be won back again. Hahnemann had nothing against that either. Yet the Glas people wanted to continue building the 1700, as everything at Dingolfing had been installed for that purpose. But it had a counterpart in the BMW 1800, and Bönsch did not feel that the toothed-belt drive had been sufficiently developed for the big V 8. It was only when he saw that the resources allocated by Milbertshofen were not sufficient for the vitally necessary quality alignment that 'our man at Glas', with all his admiration for Glas designs and their technicians, went back to Milbertshofen and threw himself into the preparations for introducing the six-cylinder onto the market. As a result, they were able to present the BMW 1600 GT at the International Motor Show as early as 1967, the fruit of joint work and proof of the true co-operation between both companies on design. This was a car which was about to take on Porsche. The coachwork, originally designed for Glas GT models, came from Frua. The front axle was also original Glas design, with everything else coming from BMW, while there was *more* Glas lurking in the new 3-litre Glas 3000 V 8. With a top speed of 200 kph, which BMW guaranteed, and as the first German mass-produced car fitted with transistorised ignition, it was presented by Bönsch and Dompert to the trade press at Rottach Egern in 1967 as well. Bönsch exorcised the critics, saying that this was 'not a dream-car' which lead an anaemic existence at motor shows, but a real Gran Turismo, which combined the manoeuvrability, safe handling and directional stability of a genuine sports car, in a unique piece of harmony in which freedom from tiredness was achieved through its comfort. It also offered the quiet running of a long-distance touring car. It had been built by engineers who were used to sitting continuously behind the steering-wheel for 1,000 kilometres.'

Was this just hot air? Perhaps it was a last desperate attempt to redeem the Wilcke concept. But the new V 8 was soon to disappear, stopped by the accountant's pen, even if it was allowed to carry the enamelled BMW emblem on the righthand side at the back, quite without ostentation. Even Dompert and Anderl Glas, who acted as company managers, were well aware that reality went against the dreams they harboured, and, when BMW had to decide whether Landshut or Dingolfing should provide the site for new plant facilities, it was Dompert who waged a major campaign for Dingolfing – and won it.

What lay behind this question of where to put the site went to the core of the reasons for acquiring Glas. These revolved less around the space acquired at Dingolfing (whatever its use might be) than the purchase of the 'staff potential' of 3,500 car workers, without which the necessary and planned expansion would be barred to BMW. If they now decided to build from scratch, then it seemed reasonable to do it at Landshut where the property department at BMW AG had been able to buy large areas of land (400,000 square metres) from the Glas motor works at an extremely favourable price. This was a green-field site, which did not require the razing of old buildings, and which was not beset by the restrictions of Dingolfing of where to build the new car factory. So the management board of BMW AG had already decided unanimously (right up to Hahnemann) for Landshut when Dompert squashed the plan.

With his passionate plea for Dingolfing, where he said was eminently more attractive, he put forward a study peppered with statistics, figures and evidence of every type to support his main argument, that the majority of the skilled workers were employed here (something over 3,000, while there were 450 at Landshut and about 200 workers at Pilsting). The study was based on the fact that the labour pool did not lie in the area between Munich, Landshut and Dingolfing (a catchment area which had anyway been exhausted by BMW commuters going to work in Munich), but between Dingolfing and Czechoslovakia. This was in the largely undeveloped and industrially unexploited area of Lower Bavaria, mainly in its eastern part, in which any number of skilled workers that were required (between 26,000 to 28,000) could be found.

Dompert's vote for Dingolfing was aided by the latent fear of the Bavarian state government over Lower Bavaria's exposure to fluctuations in its labour market. If the engine for its industrialisation broke down (and this engine was Glas), then the province would be faced with unforeseeable difficulties.

And so they decided on Dingolfing, reversing their previous decision. Not least of the reasons for this was that no communication problems existed here, unlike the headquarters in Munich with its Yugoslavs, Greeks and Turks. The question of long-distance commuters was also solved, as these now became short-distance commuters. Nobody any longer needed to spend the week in a caravan or in emergency accommodation outside the workplace, separated from his family and small-holding. Works buses brought the people in at five in the morning, and took them home again at the end of the shift, some going as far as the gates of Passau. Their homes mostly included a small-holding with arable land or a garden.

If one tries to give life to the sterile details from the company report, one looks in vain for any excuse to dramatise. Sale of the vehicles in stock had gone smoothly, as had the 'integration' of the Glas dealers into the BMW marketing organization, thanks to Kolk. But what about the workforce at Dingolfing, whose trust in Glas had been unreservedly transferred to BMW? Even the 'wave of redundancies', which provisionally affected part of the workforce, had not triggered off the paralysis feared by the rural community of Dingolfing. Hahnemann had left it up to each individual whether he should work in Munich until the new halls had been built and production was again running. Then the worker would be re-employed. That was a firm commitment. The employment office had promised unemployment benefit to those who did not want to work in Munich. Everything passed off calmly at a meeting with the Minister of Employment Pirkl, at which Golda also took part. Incidentally, very few indeed took up the offer of going to Munich. Almost everyone had at least one cow in the cowshed, had remained part farmer, and preferred to fend for himself at Dingolfing on the Isar and cut down on expenses rather than fill in the time at Munich (which was on the Isar, too, but not in Lower Bavaria). This was how this problem was also solved. And even the additional purchase of the land which BMW needed in order to implement the master plan proposed by Gieschen, was made step by step, however difficult the beginning was, after the heaviest stone had been moved out of the way. This was because that second agricultural machinery factory (called Eicher) lay 'in the midst', cutting the land acquired in two. It had to be moved and resettled on other ground (the Glas property at Pilsting was offered to them). Also 'in their midst' was that 'Müller', determined not to entertain any offer at all. In this he was so unlike his historical model, the Müller of Sanssouci, who had submitted to old Fritz. Success only came after Dompert and Hahnemann had jointly implored the mayor Heiniger to win him over. He also succeeded in getting further land purchases for re-aligning the boundaries of the future factory site, and had managed to reduce to half the prices demanded by the farmers when they tried to force them up. He himself acted as purchaser during this, but not before being able to work out what the trade tax (based on the land acquired for BMW) would bring in to his little town.

The columnist Morlock reported in *Der Spiegel* what answer he had been granted at Dingolfing in 1966 to his question: 'Will you continue to produce the Goggomobil?'

Morlock wrote that Anderl Glas drew a pencil line in his notebook which represented the limit of profitability.

'Here [his pencil pointed to a millimetre above the line of the paper] we'll carry on building it; here [pencil on the line] we'll carry on building it, and here [pencil one millimetre under the line] we'll stop building it for good.'

He was writing in 1969, when the pencil landed under the bottom line and the Goggomobil died. Because of new contracts with suppliers falling due, the price would have had to be increased by more than 4,000 DM, a price which BMW (the Goggomobil was the only Glas car denied the BMW emblem) no longer considered realistic. It no longer fitted into the line, in spite of all the admiration for its success (with a total of 282,000 examples built, it was the most successful of all German small cars, having roundly beaten the Isetta [16,728] and also the small Lloyd from Bremen [131,733], known as the 'sticking plaster bomber', and removing all its competition). No, it simply did not fit into the BMW programme, not even with its variants of 300 and 400 ccs, which Glas had brought out after the original model along with a coupé. Hahnemann had organised marketing through separate delivery depots, so that piles did not end up in stock and did not get into the showrooms of BMW dealers. Now he handed over the 'rest of the show', as well as all spare parts stocks, to a firm up in the north at Bremen, as if the purpose was to remove the 'Goggo-thing' to as far away as possible from its birthplace (there was still a possibility that someone at Dingolfing might want to build it again). This was how a sense of good fortune amongst the Germans (Goggomobil equalled the re-awakened need for mobility at a minimum cost) came to an end in an act of displacement.

If one were to look for a symbol which epitomised the end of the post-war period, then the death of this car would be it. The Germans were finally back on the map. At least, that is what they thought.

Reach for the Stars

We must return once again to the 'Judgment of Paris', that episode in which Hans Nibel, the technical member on the management board at Daimler-Benz and an undisputed expert in the area of engine manufacture, chose Rudolf Schleicher's engine at Sindelfingen in the autumn of 1932 from among the three designs put before him as 'Paris' by BMW. This was a six-cylinder engine made according to the American design principle (cast-iron block, 1.2-litre and, instead of a new carburettor, which would take too long to develop, fitted with two Solex carburettors; no need to worry about the cost – a Solex carburettor then cost a mere 7.5 marks).

With this engine, fitted into a body, and produced in the time-honoured way at Sindelfingen (a simple wooden-frame superstructure over which the panelling was stretched), Daimler-Benz had, so to speak, assisted at the birth of a car which, as the BMW 303, was presented on 11 February 1933, just a few days after Hitler's seizure of power, providing the proof that luxury and economy are not mutually exclusive. Nobody sensed that a whole programme would be founded on this car. All it did was fulfil the concept cherished by Popp, the then managing director of BMW, that a new BMW must hide more power under the bonnet than appeared to be the case, something which only a six-cylinder could satisfy. Weighing 200 kilograms less than any comparable model, and with 50 per cent more output than the previous, four-cylinder 3/20, the car was the first to sport the distinctive BMW 'kidneys'. This was not a product of fashion; it came about of its own accord. Fiedler had laid out the radiator grille in a gently curved shape and rounded off the corners to reduce drag.

Daimler-Benz need not have bothered about either. The new six-cylinder produced 30 hp at 4,000 rpms from its 1173 cc. So no danger on that score! As far as the continuing plans of an 'arranged marriage' were concerned, Popp and his friend Kissel, who ran Daimler-Benz, had always agreed to maintain a strict division of both companies' products. On this, too, they were in full agreement, with Daimler-Benz even having defined the engine. There was not a cloud in the sky – until autumn 1935, when BMW ventured into the 'big league' with a new 2-litre car, the 319. Alarm bells rang! Daimler-Benz refused further co-operation, initially justifying this by saying that all-steel bodies were not built at Sindelfingen, and then quite openly stating that they did not want to be suppliers for a product which could only be described as competition. This marked the break between 'star' and 'propeller'. Who could imagine that the fraternal feud between BMW and Daimler-Benz, many years after the death of both men (a 'thousand-year Reich' had been and gone, with the Federal Republic of Germany growing out of its ruins), would flare up again with acrimony over that six-cylinder engine, whose prototype Daimler-Benz had blessed thirty-five years earlier, not knowing that it was nurturing the viper at its own breast?

When Hahnemann, 'Niche Paul', emerged from his niche (one might also say he was stepping out of big brother's slipstream), he did this just as he brought about the succession of his New Class with the 2500, a six-cylinder car. The bigger car had not been designed as a competitor to Mercedes, he declared, but for BMW high-flyers. He knew full well that the two amounted to the same thing. Each car which BMW sold in the more demanding upper mid-ranges would cost Daimler-Benz a customer. In the price category over 15,000 marks, Mercedes had previously been out on its own. Opel, Jaguar and the big Americans, with their small scales of production, did not count. The only make which stood a chance here was BMW.

Nothing was more natural than to exploit this. The legendary BMW 327, which before the war was synonymous with automotive progress, experienced more than any other BMW its modern rebirth in 1965 with the BMW 2000 CS. This was followed a year later by the 2000 TI (120 hp, top speed of 180 kph), although both only had four-cylinder engines. After disposing of the old eight-cylinder car, as well as the expensive Bertone coupé, not to mention all Glas models which harmed the image (and which, anyway, could not be rationalised for production), nothing was more appealing than to resurrect Popp's old conception of the car as a 'big' vehicle – not as a monster in the prestige market (which was happily to be left to Mercedes), but as a six-cylinder car for the 'new type of driver'. H.W. Bönsch expounded on it as follows when he presented it to the press at Rottach-Egern in September 1968:

> Our model was neither a muscle-bound body builder, nor a stolid citizen. We were thinking more of a field athlete – temperamental, sinewy, fit, nimble-footed, agile, energetic, and entirely youthful.

To this advertising lyricism he added his own thoughts of the 'balanced car' (we shall see later how much this lyricism tormented big brother). The 'balance' should in no way be limited to design. It should rather contain a symbiosis, a communality between man and machine, in the midst of new traffic conditions:

> Habits and environmental influences have fundamentally changed in the last decades. No longer can we drive sentimentally along empty streets; every day we play an exciting game with an infinite number of variables, which presuppose a quickness of reflex (and a car reacting quickly to these reflexes), if we want to have fun in this game.

543

Marketing language, no doubt. People in Untertürkheim knew just as well as those in Munich that the sports side of life was closer to modern sentiment than bourgeois representation (this was the essence of BMW's secret of success). The only annoying aspect was that the cool calculation behind the marketing rested on the new car's technology. At Daimler-Benz, they were developing the Wankel engine (for very good reasons), which, in the NSU RO 80, had proved it could run more quietly than any corresponding six-cylinder engine. The new BMW six-cylinder engine ran just as quietly. This was the result of rigorous balancing of the crankshaft which, in addition to its twelve counterweights, had seven main bearings, so that there was no chance of any vibrations. And when the critical experts (as in *auto motor und sport*) praised the 'sonorous and turbine-like' running at all engine speeds ('the engine can reach 6,500 and even 7,000 rpm, effortlessly, without any sensation of power fade or valve bounce'), if they spoke of the cleverly thought out shape of the combustion chamber, even talking of 'combustion chamber strategy', which made the engine exceptionally versatile, and if they stressed the absolutely minimal fuel and oil consumption in comparison to the free-running ability and quiet operation somewhat similar to the rotary engine, then the Stuttgart competition justifiably felt alarmed. At the same time, the critics emphasised 'the latter's truly aged engine design'.

The very word 'competition' sent the people at Untertürkheim into a frenzy. They went on to read about the 'unobtrusive sovereignty' which the BMW 2500 provided its driver, its 'manoeuvrability' and its 'agility' bordering on the miraculous, due to its innovative steering geometry. Quite apart from the long waiting times, all this would make it decidedly easier for the customer to treat the star as a shooting star, and to swing towards the white-and-blue make. It was therefore understandable that they no longer wanted to remain silent.

However, people reading the Philippic issued as a counter attack (semi-officially in *Scheinwerfer**, an internal newsletter from the marketing department) reacted with emotions ranging from amusement to disappointment. Even the headline: 'We are looking forward to the white and blue competition' set people thinking. Really? wondered the readers in all innocence. And they went on to wonder what, in heaven's name, might have prompted the author(s) to propound the following:

'The expense in design required to put this new Big BMW on the road,' it stated frankly, 'amounted, not least of all, to a clear acknowledgement of the work and skill of *our* engineers and associates in design, testing and production. It serves as proof that the people in Munich are quite clear as to who they are competing against. And they are determined to rival our place on the market with products that are as similar as possible.'

The proof for the insufficiency of this intention was to be found in the attached photograph of the 'culprit':

'Evil minds, which do not include us, have accused the new Big BMW

---

* *The Headlight.*

of being barely distinguishable from a Mercedes if the front part of the photograph is blanked off.

'This is certainly exaggerated, although the car does not look bad. Certain styling features are to be found today with more or less variation on many cars.

'A much more interesting question would be whether the Big BMW is really a big car, or whether it is just a small BMW which has grown up a bit.

'What stood out to the *Stern* test driver B. Busch, for example, was that "it did not stand out". That can be an advantage, for people who like to understate their case. But it can also act as simple proof that this car is lacking what it should really have – both the size and appearance of the true big car.'

And so it went on, sometimes mischievous to the point of malevolence ('On the face of it, the BMW is undoubtedly manageable, but then that's what its impression gives, being comparatively small'), sometimes praising ('BMW has put a further sprinter on the road, for all to see!), and, time and again, disparaging ('We have undoubtedly had fun at times on a quick spurt, but overall, we have a higher regard for the athletic superiority of the decathlete, of the man who is both quick *and* strong, nimble *and* has stamina. In our opinion, this is how cars should be built.').

Hahnemann remained unmoved. 'BMW is a bride who grows more beautiful by the day,' was the title of an interview *Der Spiegel* conducted with him a year later (the expression did not come from Hahnemann. It was actually Karoli's answer to a small shareholder at the general meeting, where the latter wanted to know if a merger was planned and, if so, with whom). At the time of the interview (September 1969), demand for the BMW 2500 and 2800 six-cylinder models had risen so steeply that customers were having to wait up to 15 months for delivery – just as long as for a Mercedes 280. Nonetheless, Hahnemann assiduously denied the accusation that he had finally succeeded in making life difficult for Mercedes drivers in the fast lane.

SPIEGEL	How are people to see your big cars, if not as an anti-Mercedes car, a car, incidentally, which has exactly the same engine size?
HAHNEMANN	That's right, if you're only comparing product with product.
SPIEGEL	Was that accidental?
HAHNEMANN	Completely. It is the result of our niche policy, because the 2.5-litre BMW or the 2.8-litre BMW are different cars, which are interpreted and experienced differently from the 2.5-litres Mercedes or the 2.8-litre Mercedes. Our psychological market niche is particularly noticeable here, because both these cars do, indeed, have precisely the same capacity.
SPIEGEL	And that was not intentional?
HAHNEMANN	I repeat, no.
SPIEGEL	Well, we'd like to repeat to you that it really was an extraordinary accident.

HAHNEMANN   We never thought of Mercedes when we developed this car. It
            could equally well have been a 2.6-litre engine. We initially
            thought of building a 2.2-litre car. We gave that up to avoid
            giving the Mercedes people the impression that we wanted to
            drive straight into their class.

SPIEGEL   And so prevent Mercedes suspecting anything at all . . .

HAHNEMANN   . . . . We built the 2.5-litre engine, and that was that . . .

SPIEGEL   . . . . Exactly. . . .

HAHNEMANN   Above all, it was because every car needs an exact balance
            between machine and weight. It is not for nothing that we have
            become famous throughout the world. After all, we have built
            a remarkably balanced car. Daimler-Benz is probably still a
            hair's-breadth ahead of us in production. It is also simpler if
            cars are built heavier, as they are done at Stuttgart. But we
            can certainly take on any competitor when it comes to fine
            balancing.

This is what Hahnemann said, and showed himself just as economical with
the truth when he declared that he and his colleagues on the management
board worked in perfect harmony with Daimler-Benz.

'The peace between both our companies has never been disrupted, at least
not at management board level. We co-operate amicably with the Stuttgart
people. . . .'

'Amicable conversations over a decent meal?' asked *Der Spiegel*.

'No,' said Hahnemann, 'not even in the exchange of technological information. For example, we are studying ways and means of controlling deadlines.
We exchange engineers. What's more, the Stuttgart people often put their
test track at our disposal.'

The *Scheinwerfer* had alluded to just such a test track which BMW was
lacking: 'The work there does not radiate the heroic glamour which is
produced from the hard world of motor sport. Instead it guarantees success,
with the car ready for production and its testing *behind* it.'

Hahnemann had certainly countered with skill the open insinuation that
BMW still had its testing in *front* of it. But it hit him harder than he admitted.
The real question of principle was whether the business of racing could act
as a test bed for mass-produced cars.

Evaluating information from motor racing, rallying and road testing, and
using it as the basis for the mass-produced car was undoubtedly correct,
provided it was not turned into dogma. It was, indeed, indispensable for
'that car with sporting pretensions' as offered by BMW to the customer. Its
'active safety' included: road-holding, braking performance, and power of
acceleration. There was also the publicity value contained in them, as the
technological interpretation of the very high demands made in motor racing
were naturally of benefit to the mass-produced car, even if it had no need of
them at all. (But does the customer buy what he needs? No, he only ever
buys what he wants.)

On the other hand, the conclusions to be drawn from a failing in the vehicle, e.g. on a distinct curve or on a definite course, were only of value when further tests followed the exact analysis and removal of the causes, tests conducted under exactly the same conditions, which only a race track could offer and never a public highway. Certainly a racing or rally driver ventured to the car's limits at the decisive moment, although a test driver never established these limits. Nonetheless, if the desire was to develop a vehicle ready for production with scientific thoroughness, then a site was needed for this on which the necessary testing, measuring and assessing drives could be repeated as often as required (until the best result was produced). Daimler-Benz had just such a site, and (something which the *Scheinwerfer* did not mention) generously placed it at the disposal of the Munich people. This was not, however, a long-term solution. Interests affected each other too directly – quite apart from the fact that there was a desire not to provoke the host with the company's own achievements by saying things like: just look what we've got again in the crate. For this reason, BMW had very quietly made arrangements to buy a quarter of a million square metres of land at Aschheim on Lake Speicher, to install their own test track.

And had it given up racing? Phenomenal successes had been achieved. The technology of the 'Mille Miglia' 328 car from the early post-war years and the early fifties shone out unforgettably, even if it ran under different guises and names (Veritas). Then the 'mountain king', Hans Stuck (who, at 57, believed he had come to the end of his career) had enjoyed a glorious comeback in 'the most beautiful car in the world', the 507, at the Wallberg Race around Lake Tegern. He had even risen to the title of German hill-climbing champion on a 700 RS, whose two-cylinder, horizontally-opposed engine with its 85 hp produced speeds up to 190 kph. When touring car racing began in Europe in the middle of the sixties, Hubert Hahne then succeeded in becoming the first touring car driver in the world, in an 1800 TI, and two years later in a 2000 TI, covering the north loop on the Nürburgring in less than ten minutes. (The time of 9:58.2 minutes corresponded with an average speed of 137.2 kph, prompting a sports journalist to say that the BMW 2000 TI anticipated the year 2000.)

That was all right by the management board. It suited them that the two-litre engine of the 2000 TI (this time with 16 valves producing 260 hp) was fitted to a hill-climbing, soft-top called 'Monti' (in 1966, about eight world records were established using this drive gear alone, which became known as the 'Apfelbeck engine'), and it had nothing against it when BMW entered Formula 2 in 1967, in which drivers like Hubert Hahne, Gerhard Mitter, Dieter Quester, Jacky Ickx and Jo Siffert won victory after victory. If BMW drivers with sporting pretensions identified themselves in this way with a product and a producer, then BMW was something more than just a factory. It had become a piece of their lives, a part, at least, of their philosophy of life – not such a bad thing! Motor sport also taught people to do the right thing at the right time in critical situations. It then worked its way inside the company, something which one man proved time and again – this was von Falkenhausen, designer *and* racing driver at one and the same time. A business is like a human being. If it plays sport, then it is fully fit, able to be motivated and more able to perform. Hahnemann had a story or two to tell about that. Design departments (he had come across a few) which were run solely by accountants were nothing to write home about. Paralysed by bureaucracy, the product also became paralysed. As Jochen Neerpasch, the subsequent head of motor sport at BMW, once said:

'Anyone who has experienced the aura and atmosphere of a sporting contest and has developed solutions, ideas and organisational talent under their influence, has that ability for motivation which is the basis for a totally different attitude towards the car.'

This basis was everything. If it was lacking in a design team, then it was also lacking in the customer. In this way, 'motor sport', especially for a company which had long cared for the 'sports car', was an indispensable marketing tool, which could only act as a boomerang if defeats (not only in motor racing, but also on rallies), or even accidents and potential catastrophes (one only needed to think of Le Mans), knocked the god 'car' off its pedestal overnight. That is the time when the masses condemn what they have just been extolling.

This was the root cause for the ambivalent behaviour which the company showed when it immediately forbade world record attempts on the Hockenheimring in the summer of 1968 (they had already been registered at the ONS, the Supreme National Sports Commission for motor sport in Germany, and accepted by that body). The firm then sanctioned them – to the triumph of Alexander von Falkenhausen. Just to get his Formula 2 car moving at all, he had already conducted test drives on the works site, around the production halls. On 22 September 1968, it actually achieved the world record over 1,000 metres and the quarter mile from a standing start at the first attempt at Hockenheim. Admittedly, the Italians got it back off them again a fortnight later, but they in turn were only able to hold it until 15 December, when Hubert Hahne won it back for BMW.

The need to further one cause did not remove the duty to keep the other in mind. What the potential customer demanded remained the decisive factor. As consumer behaviour had clearly shown in the last few years, this was the comfort afforded by a BMW, in addition to the sporting pretensions it offered. In all three classes, BMW had had to quantify both components differently. It had reduced the small car's distinguishing feature, which was its marked sporting pretensions (for young drivers, that meant a hard suspension, as they had 'to be able to dash through the bends'), in favour of comfort in the mid-range cars ('with a temperament and an overall level of performance which is common with this size of engine from cars with outspoken sporting pretensions, but not from a very comfortable large saloon', as the *Automobil Revue* in Switzerland enthused). Then, in 1970, the company paid the penalty for the Big Car, with its renewed sporting pretensions, when they suddenly found themselves with 5,000 six-cylinder models left out in the yard. This was after a rate of growth of 85 per cent the year before. How had that come about?

'We made a mistake,' Hahnemann admitted, 'simply miscalculated. Instead of the 30 per cent, the market only produced 12 per cent. What's more, export business was bad, caused in France by a double currency revaluation and additional special taxes, and in Sweden, by new safety requirements.'

The real reason lay elsewhere. Those elderly gentlemen with youthful thoughts on sportiness and comfort had turned their backs on BMW, as summary questionnaires revealed. (A unanimous criticism was that the 'cabin finish ought to be considerably better, and greater attention should be paid to detail in an expensive car like this one!') Hahnemann and Gieschen reacted like lightning, allowing 'more comfort' to go into the six-cylinder car, but making sure all the time not to reach Mercedes levels.

Hahnemann reacted just as quickly to another reproach levelled against the advertisement which claimed that it had triggered off a potentially disastrous sense of superiority in many drivers. This he did by having a leaflet inserted entitled: 'Do we need that?' in every new car, to prevent road-hogs from being attracted. In the very first chapter entitled: DO YOU NEED TO HAVE CHARACTER TO DRIVE A CAR? was the sentence: 'Show me how you drive, and I'll show you if I like you.' Whether that also depended on the choice of car was left unanswered. However, this did not prevent Hahnemann from publicly confessing that he had received the answer from Herr Walter Scheel, Leader of the Opposition in the German parliament. After the latter had bought a six-cylinder model, he had asked:

'Herr Scheel, what exactly made you buy a BMW?'

Herr Scheel replied: 'As Leader of the Opposition, I can hardly drive an establishment car!'

However, he refrained from playing one image off against another, and refrained from saying any more about 'Opposition' (for which BMW was the symbol) than everyone already knew. The signs of the time (student unrest, demonstrations, and sit-ins throughout all the street events in major cities, in front of factory gates, and at universities and parliaments) showed that what was at issue was a basic protest by young people against their fathers' and grandfathers' generations, and by extension, against affluent society as a whole, for whom Mercedes, no less, represented the ultimate status symbol.

He said: 'The Stuttgart people have a lot to lose from all this. We're the late arrivals. Everyone knows about the bad times we had.'

Economy measures are an unmistakable sign of crises. In addition to the mounting, temporary piles of 'uncomfortable' six-cylinder cars (this was in October 1970), an event occurred which caused a few waves in Munich. No sooner had the BMW Formula 2 car emerged victorious at the Neubiberg Aerodrome Race than the fitters covered the car with black sail cloth – as a sign of mourning over a management board decision announcing withdrawal from race tracks and closure of the BMW racing department, 'because of the danger in today's Formula 2 sport and the ever widening gap between it and mass-produced cars.'

Were these economy measures? In reality, it was not only at the Bavarian Motor Works, but rather throughout the German car industry (after unusual rates of growth of between 20 and 40 per cent; it had been 20 per cent at BMW only the previous year) that costs had got out of hand. The company had admittedly been able to keep them under control through increased turnover. They had produced more and more, without, however, improving the system of production; in other words, without further rationalization, as was 'normal' in normal times. Now the penalty was to be paid; a 'general attack on all costs' was imperative.

Works drivers, engineers, and technicians (with von Falkenhausen at their head) wore a black armband, because their dearest child, motor racing, had fallen victim to the maxim of 'cost-cutting'. Here the company was only following in the footsteps of what had happened to big brother over in Stuttgart many years previously.

BMW turned its gaze on Mercedes again. In all co-operation plans harboured in Munich (Daimler-Benz was in no way disinclined to run a common factory for producing automatic gearboxes in conjunction with BMW), it was more than ever a case of remaining a dwarf amongst giants. VW, number one in the German car industry, had been quick to take every opportunity at that time to proclaim that there would soon be no room left for a number of a small companies – without realising that Wolfsburg would itself soon be heading for the greatest crisis in its history. As a 'small company' with a relatively small output, and a workforce which could bring in enough innovative skill within the shortest space of time, to counteract any swings of the pendulum caused by current trends, BMW was more flexible than any 'big company'.

The only remaining question was whether the company could absorb the 'downwards' thrust into the domain which BMW had tenaciously occupied if Daimler-Benz decided, for its part, to acquire 'sports pretensions', and thereby abandon its conservative image. But there was no one at Stuttgart who even dreamt about that. The customer's conceptions were too firmly linked to 'makes', and to what the makes supplied him in terms of 'self-esteem'. This was the iron ring which bound both customer and make together.

It was to take Mercedes fifteen years to break this ring. It was only in 1984 that Daimler-Benz drove, for the first time in its history, straight into BMW's market sector with its 190 range and its subsequent sporting pretensions. It amazed the car industry – and also proved to be a success.

At Homburg and Elsewhere

What is hidden behind production figures, turnovers measured in millions and the like is always a company made up of people. If the curve goes up, then many people want to take part in it, and when it falls, only a few do. In a total collapse, no one has been involved, and in a spectacular success, everyone has, after they had triggered it off or brought it about, once they 'had had a major say' and 'an important part in it'. On the one hand, circumstances of the time ensured that there were tendencies against which people were powerless, and accidents which no one could have prevented. On the other hand, each individual talent, skill, knowledge and undeniable capabilities made their presences felt precisely in this field, and were what shaped events.

Nothing is different in our story. Many people I spoke to credited themselves with having saved BMW on that fateful day on 9 December 1959. This was founded conclusively on an understandable overestimation of their part and a grotesque underestimation of the part played by others. However, it was Mathern alone who had gained the 'victory', just as it was Quandt who, working on this precondition, put BMW on the right road. Initially amazed that this proved possible, then more and more convinced that there was no other way, and strengthened by emerging success, he became increasingly sure in his decisions, decisions which were always related to personnel. After all, what can a man do without the right colleagues?

What were these decisions? He sent Richter-Brohm into the wilderness. That was understandable, as negative symbols cannot be used, especially in relations with the Bavarian state (however, Richter-Brohm deserved a better fate). Feith, the champion of the failed restructuring by Daimler-Benz/Deutsche Bank, which had even been Quandt's original thought, had resigned on his own initiative. What was there left for him apart from appreciating this and being respected for it? Mathern, by no means immediately 'rewarded' with a seat on the supervisory board, was only allowed to join it later, and was then appointed to an advisory committee to the supervisory board. Pushed aside, he left, fell ill and died. Kämpfer, a man who unconditionally supported the Daimler-Benz restructuring, stayed when the page was turned, like an old lion at its post. He pushed Quandt's restructuring through with Wilcke, loyally, tenaciously, but was not entirely one of Quandt's men, and so did not become managing director, although everyone, including himself, expected it. He left without regret. Sonne took over the chair. The fact that the person chosen had no experience at all in the car industry did not worry the distrustful Quandt. Sonne was his protégé, 'with a proven track record in a Quandt Group company.' When 'his man' handed in his notice, it was a body blow. Then Wilcke, who on his own admission had never been more than Quandt's legal adviser, became chairman of the management board, and therefore its 'general'. Devoted to the major shareholder, he was, as the lawyer with a firm grasp of things, the ideal proxy, who did not mind temporarily stopping the gap created by Sonne's premature departure. He went on to surpass himself in the role which he had never understood in any other way, and was, as the chairman of the management board (eschewing the title of managing director), totally involved in the company, which he ran to universal amazement. However, Quandt understood what he saw in him. An example of this happened in the middle of 1969, when Wilcke hinted to the shareholders that BMW shares were overvalued and selling bonds was therefore advisable. This meant that Quandt immediately increased his BMW packet on the stock market (he had sold off his shares in the oil and potash business of Wintershall to the tune of 125 million DM).

One man was connected with most of these decisions. He was completely outside the Homburg management circle and the advisory staff in the Quandt group. He had achieved his authorisation from open elections, and always related his mission: SECURING JOBS to the company itself. If it flourished, there were jobs; if it floundered, there were none. He operated on this simple principle, and operated in such a way as if the company not only belonged to the shareholders, but to the workers and to him, too. Kurt Golda, chairman of the works council at BMW AG, had been a simple mechanic in the business in 1956, when he was elected to this post. The question as to how Quandt came to show such unusual trust towards him should be answered by turning it round the other way: how did Golda, a trades union man, who exclusively represented the employees' interests, come to trust Quandt?

Each man had a key experience for the insights which moulded him. Golda's key experience took place on that 9 December 1959 when he saw how Quandt made a change to his standpoint within the general meeting. Moving from the 'salvation via Daimler-Benz' which Quandt himself had initiated, he had come to recognise that it was worth it, through the readiness of the shareholders to fight for the maintenance of their company while there was still no firm indicator to the future on the table. He then came to the conclusion that this was the time to get to grips with all the risks and their consequences. Golda saw it as obvious that such an entrepreneurial decision must not be turned down, but must be supported with all the risks and consequences which that involved, even on his side. This caused him to break down all the barriers which were customary between employers and employees.

Quandt knew very well how much of the inner peace within a company depended upon enhancing industrial relations, and that it was not irreconcilable opposition, but 'constructive co-operation' (as the Federal Constitutional Council had made incumbent on both sides of industry in its judgment on the Worker Participation Act) which supported the social harmony which the country and its people strove for and needed. If there were social harmony at work, then there was also harmony in society. So everything depended on the company, whose 'inner peace' was clearly a sham if things stayed with the manners and customs once found in social structures. These must be re-established, more than anywhere else in the technique used to apply them, where any persistence of previously acceptable measures would mean a step back.

Therefore Quandt sought dialogue, as did Golda. Both men conducted it not in the spirit of from 'keeper to keeper', but more like neighbours at the fence, sometimes like friends, especially when it was socially and politically awkward. This often happened when the management board had already issued a 'no' to Golda's wishes and ideas. As a result, Quandt got into difficulties more than once, but had always found a solution which satisfied both sides. An example of this was when Golda demanded a strengthening of the company by depositing reserves, as well as by demanding workers' participation in the success they had helped to create. (In the above-mentioned case, 20 million DM in the form of workers' profit-sharing flowed back from 60 million DM reserves, with dividends of 60 million DM paid at the same time.) It was the same with capital increases, where Golda's thorough research into the critical question as to whether the company could stand such an increase at par when paying dividends of 18 per cent, without reducing its power of investment, proved decisive in creating the response that it could! It was the same with management board contracts, whose renewal could have meant a weakening in the company. If Golda proved, from his way of looking at things, that there was no danger, and Quandt let himself be convinced, then he signed the document, or did not sign, as the case may be. This was the case when it came to marking out opposing positions, where each advised the other on a course adjustment to prevent the pursuit of one course which might prove disastrous. Even Quandt's tendency to compare his industrial plants with each other gradually disappeared altogether, perhaps to Golda's credit.

All this took place when both met in Bad Homburg or other places, at intervals unconstrained by regularity, agenda or taboos. If they could not manage everything, they adjourned to get some breathing space and then met again. Quandt certainly did this when faced with a Golda who was trying to weigh up Quandt's interests against those of the workforce. This would happen after Golda had made the observation (which calmed his conscience) that Quandt himself was only ever concerned with the company. This summed up the situation for both men.

Quandt knew that Golda had paid his apprenticeship money. He had started at Allach (joining BMW there in 1949, where, as a member of the works council, he had tried to persuade the management board to give up Milbertshofen and expand Allach as a modern plant – to no avail, as we know. He had moved to Hall 95 on Riesenfeld Street at Milbertshofen where he again started as a mechanic, was elected to the works council and became its chairman. Nothing was spared him: short-time work, mass redundancies, the necessity of deciding who it would be (you're going, you're staying). This inevitably brought the response: why me and not him? There was also the impotence of looking on as the banks, as model after model failed, simply reversed decisions which had already been taken by the highest body, the supervisory board, to which he himself belonged, without regard to closure and the fate of the workforce. They simply withdrew from any managerial responsibility. (Even when Golda protested and promptly caused the representative of the Dresdner to leave the room, and subsequently give up his mandate, what good did it do?) Quandt also knew of Golda's road to Damascus, when Richter-Brohm, on whom he had set great store, did not resign because his pension contract was more important to him than the workforce. The latter might have decided ten times over to get behind him and 'pull the thing through', but a world had collapsed there for Golda. He also knew of Golda's secret meeting with Könecke, the managing director of Daimler-Benz, shortly afterwards, and how Golda, as the representative of the workforce, had rejected the bait of a 'components factory' (which BMW could still become for Untertürkheim, as Könecke suggested, 'in the interests of maintaining jobs'), preferring to trust in Quandt. But had that been so certain?

In all these activities, Golda had never exceeded his mandate, but had used it in a way which let the businessman in Quandt recognize how closely social policy 'at the coal-face' and managerial decisions were connected with each other. He had reflected. Nowhere in the world was a major shareholder interested in internal questions concerning the workforce. That was a matter for the business, in which he had admittedly put money, but which otherwise had nothing to do with him. How was it that it had nothing to do with him? Was, for example, the problem of foreign workers only limited to the business? Was it not a social problem? How the business solved it also determined how it was portrayed, with its reputation and credibility depending on that. Quandt learnt from Golda the details of what steps had been taken to prevent second-class citizens developing. What rights did German workers enjoy in preference to Turks, Greeks and Yugoslavs? None at all. They were treated equally. What disadvantages were there for the foreigners? What was the reason for the token strike made by the Italians in the paint shop? (As Golda had been able to ascertain, extremists had been smuggled in from Italy and had tried to ignite the fuse. Golda threw out the ringleaders, which resulted in his windows at home being smashed in during the night.)

'And referring to Quandt,' as one of the people concerned said casually, 'I know that these people are all tuned in a particular way. I personally met Henschel, Flick and so on. They are all the same. They are all very sceptical, distrustful and so on . . . and always have an ear for anyone who tells what others do not tell.'

Here he was alluding to Gieschen, who, in long telephone conversations with Quandt, kept letting something appear through the cracks. These were things that the management board would have preferred to keep for themselves.

Golda was free of such suspicion (quite apart from the fact that he was not on the management board, but on the supervisory board). Quandt was also free of any suspicion, as he made no secret of the fact that he owed Golda a new vision on the world of work, in which 'humanising the workplace', profit-sharing, bonuses from payments into reserve, and so forth, were not simply gifts issued to one's negotiating partner. They were basic rights to which a company was just as bound to as to the rights of the shareholder (which were naturally taken up). This raised the question as to what the latter would lose if business fell off, dividends were not paid, and, in the worst case, bankruptcy loomed. It would be, at most, his stake, his share, but not, like the worker, his existence!

Karl Heinz Sonne was the first younger person whom Quandt appointed to the head of the most important province in his industrial empire, the autonomous company of BMW AG. He came from the Quandt empire, having proved himself and made it right to the top.

At this time (1965), a qualified engineer called Eberhard von Kuenheim wanted to transfer to the Quandt group from Hanover, where he had risen quickly at a tool factory from plant engineer to head of technical services and, as such, was the right-hand man of the company proprietor. He was thirty-five years old, and, although he felt this to be an act of ingratitude towards his promotor and patron, the firm's proprietor (which was inevitable, as he decided to break all the personal ties he felt he had), he sent a letter of application to Bad Homburg. He addressed it to Dr Dirk Cattepoel, head of personnel and responsible for Public Relations at Günther Quandt House, the headquarters for many industrial contracts and application facilities. He had got to know Cattepoel slightly as a result of a lecture in Hanover. He entered in his application details of where and when he was born, where and when he qualified, and his specialist knowledge in the area of automation. For a long time he heard nothing. Then, in the summer of that same year, he received an invitation to a preliminary personal meeting.

He set off immediately.

Leaving Behind the Troubled Years

Browsing through a collection of portraits of new men in the Ruhr industry after the war, I kept asking myself the same question: how had the businessmen, technicians and researchers reached their management positions? A leading industrialist had pinpointed in the preface four basic conditions for the man at the top:

1. A solid, firm, straightforward character (which rules out any corrupt practices) plus healthy ambition.

2. Intelligence.

3. Sufficient educational background to be turned into experience. Coupled with intelligence, educational background and experience provide for above-average performance.

4. A capacity for hard work, where a 48-hour week is the norm.

In addition, he cited the acquisition of knowledge extending beyond the business, as required by the ever more complicated nature of the economy, knowledge which could be obtained at company seminars abroad.

Without exception, men were presented in the book who had worked their way to the top. Quite a large number of these had distinguished themselves by succeeding in tough negotiations with the Allies in preventing the destruction of factory installations through total or partial dismantling. Was that sufficient? Certainly not. But it gave them something to project. Fritz Berg, for example, a manufacturer of iron and steel wire, had long been in the USA, spoke perfect English, and saved the local Altena on the Lenne when it was threatened by marauding, conscripted workers, through co-operation with the occupying authorities. He became mayor, then a short time afterwards, head of the administration of a Landkreis, but, above all, he was seen to be active where he could appear as a spokesman for trade associations. This was in the South Westphalian Chamber of Trade and Commerce and at iron, sheet metal and metalware manufacturers. In 1949, his hour came, and he made it to the top of the umbrella organisation for German industry which had previously been the exclusive domain of men from heavy industry, such as Duisberg, Krupp von Bohlen und Halbach, Wilhelm Zangen. (Reusch, managing director of the Gutehoffnungshütte company had, however, *not* been accepted by the occupying powers, although he had been an open opponent of Hitler in the Third Reich. They did not want to take any 'big boys', and he seemed too dangerous to them.) Another man, the director of a steel works, Rudolf Graef, developed a new process for producing quality steels without the need to use that rare, raw material of scrap iron (as at Siemens Martin Steel). Professor Haberland, managing director of the Bayer Works, saved the business community of the Lower Rhine after the war, in disarray after the dismemberment of the I.G. complex. He saved the four plants at Leverkusen, Elberfeld, Dormagen and Uerdingen from dismantling and further disintegration, thereby enabling German chemistry to contribute to the rapid developments in macro-chemistry throughout the world.

Others went in the opposite direction, not against the occupying power, but with it. Such a man was Heinz P. Kemper who was made the trustee of the Stinnes Group, which, in the absence of a governing board, had been declared American property. He was appointed on the strength of his knowledge of the American economy and managed to get the Stinnes Collieries out of Allied control, even keeping the whole concern together and returning it to German ownership. Alfried Krupp von Bohlen und Halbach, on the lookout for a man who could patch together the remains of his company into an organic whole, met Berthold Beitz at the house of a young sculptor. Beitz, in charge of an insurance company, had not the slightest knowledge of the profession and became Krupp's general authorised representative, standing all the current rules on their head. The Korean War in 1951 was another great moment in the careers of German industrialists. Willi H. Schlieker, an independent iron dealer in 1948 without any nominal capital, invented the coal-steel exchange trade with the USA, as the Ruhr steel works had no coke for their steel production facilities. He imported American coking coal, had it turned into coke, exported the steel produced with it and used the proceeds to pay for the imported coal. He put the accruing large profits into an old sheet-rolling mill which he bought up, tore down and rebuilt. As he was irked by the high seafreight charges which he had to pay for coal shipments from the USA to Germany, he bought three ships and opened a shipping company.

They had all recognised their moment – and acted. Thanks to the good luck brought about by atypical situations, with poverty behind and problems ahead (which did not frighten them because they were brave), they had risen up to their managerial positions despite obstacles which time had thrown in their way. They had succeeded not without possessing the four virtues (essential for anyone wanting to establish themselves), and certainly not just because of them.

A thirty-five year old man in a middle-management position somewhere below them could only dream in the sixties of all these men and the chances they had been offered. It was not much good to him benefiting from the majority of the above-mentioned basic conditions. Thousands like him possessed them, thousands found the domain they had mastered too narrow, and thousands like him felt the same unease and apprehension, in spite of their knowledge and their specialist skills (which had yet to be put to any worthwhile use). Above all, given that their engineering capabilities were only being applied in fits and starts, they would be left standing and grow old before things ever got started.

Herbert Quandt first heard of Eberhard von Kuenheim in the four-man council where the latter's praises were sung. Cattepoel had allocated him to Harald Quandt's jurisdiction as the 'staff member for technical questions'. In the Quandt group, that was all the engineering businesses going from IWK (the Industrial Works at Karlsruhe), Keller & Knappich GmbH, from Busch-Jäger to the Düren Metal Works PLC. The new man had also caught the eye of Gerhard Vieweg, the man appointed in his father's will to be Harald's guardian.

'Just imagine, he graduated as an engineer in 1954 and I graduated in 1953,' said Harald. 'At the same Technical High School – at Stuttgart!'

But they had other things in common. Harald, a paratrooper in the war who had been wounded and captured in North Africa, had, following his discharge, struggled along as a bricklayer, foundry worker and welder before going on to study. Kuenheim had been injured as a midshipman at the age of seventeen, escaping the war to emerge an orphan. His father had fallen to his death from a horse in 1935. His mother had been carried off and had died in a camp when the Russians reached the family estate at Juditten, 50 kilometres south of what was Königsberg in East Prussia (now called Kaliningrad). Then he went to work at Bosch on the production line producing refrigerators, car components and the like, until he could start his studies (with a 10,000-DM grant from Bosch). Both of them struggled through. One of them was the heir of a rich father (and son of Magda Goebbels, Günther Quandt's second wife), while the other was the scion of an old aristocratic family, who could trace his origins to 11th century Alsace and who had been granted at least four years of privileged education at one of the Salem public schools. That, too, was no picnic, no school for the sheltered sons of the rich: 'If a piece of classwork was due, the teacher set the work and then left the room. There was never any copying. We did everything ourselves, which amounted to pupil self-administration. Of course, the teacher still extended a protective hand over things.' Although there was some age difference between them (Harald was born in 1921, and von Kuenheim in 1928), both had been moulded by the same impressions and experiences, and both were passionate technicians, even if this word, with its sobriety, no longer seemed appropriate.

In 1967, when Harald crashed his turbo-prop plane, with fatal results, at Nice, this spiritual union ended. As von Kuenheim remembered ('it was perhaps two months later – Harald died on 23 September, so it was the end of November'), he was summoned to Herbert Quandt.

'He said: "Let's sit down, and you can tell me what you've been doing."'

'It was a Saturday morning, and Saturday had already become a day off. So around ten or eleven, he was alone.'

Kuenheim went on: 'Of course, I had wondered what kind of a man he was. In the Quandt company, we lived together in cramped surroundings, as if we were on a U-boat. So it was impossible not to come into contact with the commanding officer. I had seen Quandt (Herbert, not Harald) only fleetingly on one or two occasions, and knew that he was blind, almost blind, something nobody noticed about him. However, I had the impression that he was ignoring me, and was not keen for people to meet him. On the other hand, his life was in no way isolated. Everyone who knew him said that he was a very modern man. Anyone in daily contact with him spoke of his "loyalty" and his totally disarming humanity. If anyone, such as a secretary on holiday, or a person en route somewhere, had an accident, then he did whatever he could to help. There was also the other side to Herbert, a man who impressed the feeling of dependency on anyone who had let him down in this dependency (we are all dependent in some way). He would do this in a sharp, hard, not to say brutal way. Mind you, I never accepted the view that he rejected other opinions if he had first firmly established his own, that he was simply unable to accept other opinions despite obviously being convinced by them. Was it dangerous to contradict him? Then it was also dangerous not to contradict him, if your knowledge was better.

'Well, back to our conversation.

'He said: "Tell me about youself."

'We chatted a bit, about this and that, and where I came from. I also came from the country. He had always been interested in horses, East Prussian horses, and so he knew my name, since my father and grandfather had had quite a lot to do with them.

'Suddenly he asked me: "What would you like to do in the sector you are currently working in? You've got good ideas!"

'I had had some good ideas working in the switch division at Busch-Jäger at Lüdenscheid. We talked about how staffing arrangements were to be assessed, and about certain other firms.

'I said: "I would pull out of this sector. I would sell it, because there's no point staying in it." I then explained why.

'Quandt answered: "Nobody has ever said that to me, but I have always had the impression that the only thing I couldn't do was justify it."

'Then suddenly he said: "*You* do it!"

'So I left Quandt House one Saturday morning thinking: what on earth have I suggested? We then very successfully sold Busch-Jäger, the switch division, to BBC. It fitted in exactly, and they were also happy with it, given that they were the biggest in the field.'

That marked his arrival at Herbert's, in 1967, and von Kuenheim was now 'his' man. He took over the whole of the technical responsibility of the staff formerly allocated to Harald, now orphaned within the Quandt group. This was in place of Faber du Faur, who had died at Christmas, and whom he had been earmarked to succeed. In the summer of 1968, he received a telegram on Guernsey, where he had gone with his family on holiday, imagining that they could not be reached. It said: 'Come immediately to Homburg.'

Kuenheim went on to say: 'You can imagine how that pleased the family, especially the children, who were only little then. We left early for Bad Homburg, and there Quandt said:

'"So, listen, I've been thinking about IWK . . ." [that had already been Harald's problem child] ". . . and things look gloomy there. *You* go to IWK."

559

'I went, and was delegated to the management board for a fixed term, initially for three months. Early in 1969, we managed to bring the spinning aeroplane back under control – when I say "we", I mean principally Vieweg and myself, along with Dr Wökpemeier, who later went to Klöckner-Humboldt-Deutz.'

It was a textbook-style operation. On von Kuenheim's fiftieth birthday, Quandt expressed the facts in his own way, by putting personal feelings into colourless business German whenever things got 'solemn'. He said:

'We were not wrong. The signs of your effectiveness were very quickly recognisable, and (what was even more important) a mental transformation took place within the company management and even the whole workforce, a transformation which you specifically imparted to the men there.

'The task was certainly a very attractive one. You started straining at the leash again. "Contented heart never has enough." One day, Dr Cattepoel came to me with the news that Herr von Kuenheim would possibly be interested in Herr Gieschen's position (at BMW) when the latter retired. He said he wanted to apply in good time. So you and I came to have a conversation which I'm sure you remember in detail. Unfortunately I had to give a 'no' to your enquiry, because in the final analysis I could not act in my brother's domain simply as some kind of recruiting officer. I could not wholly deny having an interest in you (but that would be for a higher position). But before all else, I had to speak to Frau Inge Quandt (Harald Quandt's widow).

'I did not need to wait long until you were back with me again, and I believe further words are not necessary. On 1 January, you were appointed by consent of the whole BMW supervisory board to be chairman of the company's management board.'

When Eberhard von Kuenheim, at forty-one the youngest managing director in a major German industry, sat down at his desk in Oberwiesenfeld, he was aware of two things. The first was that the majority of BMW shares had belonged to Quandt from about the middle of the previous year (perhaps that was the real reason for Kuenheim's appointment; Quandt wanted to guarantee what had been acquired, and provide continuity now that the 'storm and stress' period was over). Secondly, there was the fact that the evolved heirarchy (with Hahnemann as the driving force in a management board which firmly stuck to the principle of collegiate responsibility) could only be forced open if he, the new chairman of the board, put himself in amongst them, and not above (and certainly not below) them. The fact that it had to be forced open if he wanted to lead was known to everyone concerned, as well as to himself. He was a man who was liked and respected wherever he turned, most of all by Hahnemann himself. Deeds were what counted, not just the will to lead. As long as he was a newcomer in the industry, they were in the lap of the gods.

Even before he took up office (Quandt had announced the news in September 1969, one day before the International Motor Show, where the news broke like a bombshell), the press wanted to know which 'wide-ranging expansion plans' he planned to put into practice. According to *Der Spiegel*, BMW production was to be increased from a daily rate of 600 to 1,000 cars in less than six years, with turnover rising from 1.1 billion DM (1968) to 3 billion. The figures had not come from him and he read them in amusement. He was equally amused at what he was supposed to have said in reply to a question on his leadership style and how he would guide the company into the eighties. The press had quoted him as saying: 'Sometimes you have to beat people into shape, and at other times, you have to sweet-talk them into it.'

The sentence could well have originated from Hahnemann. This was not Kuenheim's style of leadership and it would never be. But what was it like, then? Kuenheim knew nobody here. Any leader upon taking office brings, at least partially, his own team along, whom he was as familiar with as it was with him. With his team, he gained a foothold and planted his feet on firm ground. If he was not immediately tough enough to carry the company, he had the bonus of 'a period of grace' and the certainty that people would say: you won't fall down, and if you should start sliding, we'll be there to support you and hold you up.

The only person supporting *him* was Quandt – and a company in a unique position. In the 1966/67 recession, when the German car industry was shaken by depressed sales, short-time working and redundancies, BMW registered a sensational increase of 34 per cent over the previous year (with around 44,000 cars sold in 1966 alone). Since 1967, when there were still only vehicles of the new class, the turnover had increased to 870 million DM (in 1962, it had not amounted to 300 million). It went on rising, crossing the billion mark threshold in 1968, and it was still going up steeply in 1969.

The motorcycle had also been saved from depressed sales. As a means of transport, it had had its day, and the major names had disappeared from the market. Only BMW had pulled through, supported by the reputation which the horizontally-opposed machine had with the police and authorities, one which was not limited to Germany (de Gaulle's' famous motorcycle escort is an example). Although it was certain that the company could not live on the motorcycle business, it was equally true that it gave new life to the leisured society. A new model range, designed in 1969, matched this trend and secured expansion and investment at Spandau.

Then Hahnemann's basic principle that only half a car company consists of the production site itself, with the other half being the distribution and import organisation, was rigorously pursued. Sales, broken up into home market sales, exports sales, marketing, after-sales service and the spare parts business, had given a face to BMW 'outside' with a new department called 'dealer development'. Service engineers advised the marketing partner on the spot. The colleagues of these marketing partners were given in-house training at the schools for after-sales service, as well as for selling. The branches at Berlin, Hamburg, Essen, Bonn, Munich and Saarbrucken ran smoothly. The export marketing organisations were constantly improved through the establishment and expansion of import headquarters in Switzerland, Austria, France, Belgium, Holland, Sweden, Finland, Great Britain and the USA, and ran like clockwork. Business links were also made with the Eastern bloc, and importers were acquired in Bulgaria, Yugoslavia and Hungary. There was an assembly agreement with a partner in South Africa. (A BMW 1804 was built there using plant from Dingolfing. It was nothing other than a slightly modified Glas 1700 saloon, which Hahnemann had discreetly got rid of in this way.)

All this had the consequence of producing a run on BMW cars, and in turn, almost all models were ordered between three and four months in advance. This meant that the acquisition of Glas had been brilliantly vindicated. With the restructuring of the old plant at Dingolfing, the building of a parts warehouse there, the additional purchase of extra land at Dingolfing for a second car factory, and the expansion of Landshut as a factory producing plastic, other parts and service-exchange units, and, above all, with the acquisition of a catchment area for new labour as far as the gates of Passau, the confinement at Milbertshofen had at last been forced open and problems of a life-threatening nature as regards expanding capacity no longer existed.

There was also nothing for Kuenheim to do as regards the oppressive confinement in which administration, as well as marketing and purchasing, lived. These were divided over twenty offices within Munich, with an annual rent of around 9 million DM. This was apart from the additional costs for unproductive practices.

Construction of an administration building had already been decided upon and was imminent.

The project had been preceded by an invitation for tenders to which eight architects had been invited. Two of them, Professor Schwanzer from the Technical High School of Vienna, and Professor Henn, the company architect for the Quandt group, had been placed second and third. No first prize was awarded.

'I was fascinated by Schwanzer's model,' Hahnemann reported to the new boss. 'It was modern, had an association with the car (four-cylinder engine) and fitted excellently into the framework of the Olympic site. Henn's design was certainly very good from a works sequence point of view, but without any publicity value for our image. We already had a whole collection of sixties-style, high-rise blocks in Munich. However, Quandt was for it, which surprised me. But I knew that not only had the old Quandt been an architecture fan, but Herbert was one as well. He intimated from time to time how much he would have liked to have been an architect himself. Function and aesthetics belonged together in a construction, and formed a single unit. Viewed in this way, this meant that the Quandt group was also a piece of architecture. In spite of that (or perhaps because of it), he declined Schwanzer's design, saying, as he felt around the model:

'"That is a tower. What are we supposed to do with it?"

'I explained to him. He stuck to his "no". The fact that the tower actually got built is a story in its own right. Are you interested in hearing it, Herr von Kuenheim?'

'Very much so,' the latter replied.

The story, which was as pointed as any Hahnemann told, revealed that nothing is lost (even when everything appears so), because human beings are, in the end, just human beings. It deals with an inspired architect who, like most artists, was an extremely bad salesman for his subject, to such an extent that when he presented his project he could not win anyone over for it. Neither Quandt nor any of the members of the supervisory board, including Golda, the three-man advisory body to the supervisory board (which had been founded in the meantime), the whole management board under Wilcke – in short, everyone right down to Hahnemann let it be known that, should it come to a vote, they would be inclined to prefer Henn's 'worthy' design to Schwanzer's 'bold' construction (a monstrosity, someone said, however 'bold' it might be).

'Do you want the commission, professor?' the sales psychologist Hahnemann asked the unsure Schwanzer.

He said that of course he wanted it. Hahnemann said that he knew nothing about architecture, and so asked if the design was not an untried experiment where even the most minor thing might go wrong. Schwanzer pointed to tower-like buildings which he had erected in South America.

'Good,' Hahnemann said, 'then go as soon as possible to Ascona. Take your drawings along, make it look unintentional, and look in on Herr Koerfer. After Quandt, Dr Jacques Koerfer is our second most important shareholder. He is a very open-minded man when it comes to art. He's got a smart house, made entirely of glass and concrete, set in an old farmstead. In the entrance hall, you will see a Braque. Tell him how much you value it – it's worth a cool two million (I presume you appreciate Braque). No, don't try and butter him up. Get him to discuss it. K. is a clever, serious businessman, fond of art, not because it's decorative or for show, certainly not. He really knows something about it, and is active as a patron, too. Make it clear to him what the tower will be like, which, incidentally, we want to baptise "four-cylinder". Well, it's just a publicity idea, so tell him it's not from you! Then go immediately to Essen, and visit Dr Karoli, the chairman of our supervisory board. He has a fine house there. Give him my best regards . . . and from Koerfer, as well, who'll be really fired up at the idea. Once you've won over Karoli, you'll have it all wrapped up!'

And indeed it was. At the next meeting of the committees (Quandt had invited all those entitled to vote to Bad Homburg so as to make a final decision on constructing the administration building), Hahnemann said that Koerfer and Karoli had spoken enthusiastically for Schwanzer's 'unique model', so that one after the other they gave in, and Quandt, still hesitating, at last issued the planning contract. The 6.5 million DM it cost (Hahnemann calmed the still sceptical architect by saying: 'Quandt does not lay out 6.5 million for a plan which then comes to nothing!') proved that the tower was 'in the bag', even if the objection that open-plan offices had long been superseded, needed refuting by another demonstration of the Schwanzer 'segments' which the four-cylinder provided.

Hahnemann, the salesman of this idea as well, had devised the plan of having such a segment built on a scale of 1:1 at the Bavarian film city at

Geiselgasteig. There were Alpine meadows and mountain huts lit by spot-lights in front of the windows. It was a vision of Alpine folklore as is sometimes carried to Munich by the föhn under the white and blue sky. There was also an indication of the future Olympic site, which was sketched out in initial designs. A crowd of attractive secretaries, organised by the Bavarian film school, mimed the 'world of work' at desks and business machines, when viewing took place. Everybody was enthusiastic and now nothing stood in the way of building the tower.

In October 1971, Gieschen left. He had reached retirement age. Quandt gave a reception and made a speech. With Gieschen as an example, he praised technology, underlined its importance for the future of BMW, outlined the future which was now entrusted to younger people and, with regard to the preponderant place which technology had to occupy, said that they wanted to reach the eighties safely and still as an independent company. He spoke only of technology. There was no word of marketing, no word of the other half of a car factory 'outside'. In this, Hahnemann thought he detected an outright denial of that entrepreneurial spirit by which he, the marketing man, had increased turnover seven fold. The company was already approaching 1.9 billion DM and, with the Glas acquisition, this concept was the pre-requisite for the tower and all subsequent growth (Quandt had honoured this by having a bonus of 100,000 DM paid to Hahnemann for his services). But was something up? Gieschen went up to him, and reminded him of their years together, as they had joined 'the shop' at almost the same time. He said he had observed Hahnemann's face and got the impression that he dearly wanted to leave, too.

Hahnemann retorted: 'Without a successor?'

Gieschen did not turn a hair. Behind the joke lay the old scorn, poured on him when in 1968, on his 60th birthday, he had requested a successor from Quandt, who had appeared at the party. Quandt had retorted almost in amusement that he had never come across a member of the management board worrying himself silly about a successor.

'Do you know of one?'

'No,' Gieschen replied, 'it's not my job. It's the supervisory board's job to find one within two years.'

Then, in 1970, with Gieschen just 'en route to Karmann' (the coachbuilder at Osnabrück, who was working on a new BMW coupé), Quandt rang him one evening in his hotel. That was not unusual for Gieschen, as they often telephoned each other.

'A young man has applied to me. He was at Ford's. He is working at some shock absorber factory now.'

Gieschen knew the firm.

'He's called Koch. Have a look at him.'

Gieschen did so, and found nothing wrong with the young man. He took him through workshops and halls in his empire, asked him questions, had him ask questions in turn, and tested him at meetings whose chair he handed over to him. Then he suggested to the management board that Koch should be his deputy. This was based on the 'graduated plan for the submission of responsibility', just like the one he had taken over in stages over the previous ten years. Then he was to be considered for his successor. His domain did not include the design department run by Osswald, as well as the stipulation that he, Gieschen, would oversee the building of the tower until it was finished.

Now, with his successor, he was free of that worry. This was in contrast to Hahnemann, who, in defiance of divided responsibility, which served no one and disconcerted everyone, had always evaded the question as to who could replace him when he retired. Why had he evaded it? Did he regard himself as indispensable? Gieschen aside, he had never thought about it. Now suddenly, what was happening to him? Was he thinking of leaving?

He now looked across to Koch, toasted as Gieschen's successor. He was in his early forties, slim, vivacious, dexterous, one among many people who wanted to make something of themselves. And he had already become something, without connections. His notion was simple: go out, offer knowledge and skill, win people over (our Gieschen, who straightway sees, smells, tastes – thou art the true one!), while the likes of us, still proceeding according to the setting: 'Thou art the one for whom I am the only boss!', were still groping around in the dark.

This dictum was valid in general, as it was also valid for Hahnemann, under Kuenheim, who was now the boss. Kuenheim was left wondering if he was the right boss for someone who had been used to deciding the way things went. But the problem was not here, was not in the renunciation or seizure of power.

Wherever there had been points of contact with the new chairman, such as at press conferences, preparing the general meeting, presenting the new programme, discussing with dealers, right up to wide-ranging expansion plans designed to secure or endanger BMW's future, there were also two lifestyles in conflict with one another. The clash was latent, never open, and was not unnoticeable to outsiders, but it involved two diametrically opposed views of management and leadership, and two principles of style. Both of them, as logical as they were compulsive, lay in the character of both men, and both at the same time lay in a development which, with the end of the pioneer period (under Hahnemann), also demanded the end of spontaneous decisions created by the situation. This was the time when nothing had been left to chance, and the law of trade had been freed from the dictates of the market. What imagination, intuition and even instinct had previously achieved was now transferred into military-style planning.

This could not be brought about with 'leading from the front', as had been the case in the pioneer time. Its 'jargon', linked to Hahnemann's personality, his articulation, the 'curt tone' which he cultivated, the sloppiness with which he depicted not only himself but also the company, all of these ill befitted the firm as Kuenheim conceived of it. It spoilt it for him. It had nothing to do with the fact that he came from aristocracy, was a 'cool Prussian', as people accused him of being, with few facial expressions and gestures, a balanced and collected temperament, who did not smoke and preferred to drink tea with his visitors, was conventionally unassuming in his dress, and was a 'lord' in his demeanour, attitude and manners. The troubled years were over. It did not suit the company, in his view, to become something which it no longer was.

But what was it? In spite of acquiring Glas, the new buildings at Dingolfing and Landshut, the expansion of Spandau and so forth, it was only just on the threshold of becoming a large business. But it was still a 'small factory', without its own production facilities abroad, and one whose ability to produce returns was endangered by every decision taken outside the company. However, it was big enough no longer to have to devote itself exclusively to growth and, should sales and production contract for once, to interpret this immediately as misfortune. The basis was solid, demand was good (in 1971, around 172,000 cars would be produced, corresponding to a growth rate of almost 7 per cent, and, in terms of turnover at 1.85 billion DM, corresponding to one of around 9 per cent or more). What more could anyone want?

However, it was Hahnemann's gut feeling that the ups and downs of the years to come would depend on completing a 'product range' which at BMW (the 'niche time' could be forgotten) seemed to him far too narrow to counter a recession which was always on the cards. So as not to drive away the customer who wanted to stay with BMW, they had to be able to offer a smaller vehicle – not one of lower quality, but one in another class and costing under 10,000 DM. In addition, this would prevent dealers from taking on other franchises just to survive (this was one of the reasons why Borgward had gone bankrupt). Hahnemann came back to the old dictum which guided him, which was that half a car company lay outside, at the dealers. The other half, the production site, now had to prove its strength by making itself the 'right car factory'. The Dutch company of Van Doorne Automobielfabrieken N.V. at Eindhoven was looking for a partner, and offered, in whatever form this partnership might take, purchase or part purchase of its car factory at Aachen. Here was something to get into. The salesman Hahnemann did not see any difficulty in taking over the small, Dutch cars, fitted with belt drives. He would get rid of them on the tried and tested Glas recipe, and build that small BMW car in large quantities which (in association with the 700, which the customer had accepted) could lead BMW safely into the future.

The plan met with little approval from Kuenheim. It was not so much the purchase which frightened him off (the DAF Works were to cost 70 million DM), nor was it physical distance to Aachen, but rather the dangers of such a fundamental change in programme. There were unassessable costs and the unpredictability of the model to be produced. According to Hahnemann, Osswald, head of development, had already developed the 'small car' in the 'crate'. But had it been tested? There were also no results from market research to make its introduction desirable, or even just provide approximate guarantees. It was only the previous year, in autumn 1970, that Goppel, the Bavarian chief minister, had turned the first sod of Dingolfing earth at the new 2.4 works, while there was a large model of buildings standing in the yard. The press was present and Hahnemann boasted:

'That is how we are going to be able to turn out between 250,000 and 300,000 cars!'

That was a gigantic figure measured against the 140,000 cars which the company had just built. The 8,000 staff planned at Dingolfing, as was then mentioned (the whole workforce at that time was made up of 20,000 people!) also reminded Kuenheim of the 'quaking fear' which he had had to go through. Was Hahnemann already contemplating the 'right car factory' which BMW was to become? No, definitely not. What Hahnemann was presenting made no sense at all. So they would have to let Quandt decide the outcome. When? Immediately! Quandt fixed the meeting immediately for the day after, with the participation of leading supervisory board members, such as Dr Karoli and Dr Draeger.

Hahnemann was not well. A few days previously, he had had a serious accident driving to Dingolfing. It was not his fault, as the police report established, but his car was a complete write-off. He emerged unscathed, although his female companion had had to go to hospital suffering from severe shock. It weighed on him heavily. When, as agreed, he arrived at the Günther Quandt House in Bad Homburg around eleven, he was asked to wait. The men were still in discussion, which, the secretary added, they had been since eight o'clock.

Hahnemann waited. As his report for the rest of the morning stated, Dr Karoli and Dr Draeger (but not Quandt or von Kuenheim) then appeared and told him that the DAF acquisition was not on the agenda. They said that they had only spoken about him – the complaints there had been about him, his 'list of sins', and his future responsibilities. Product planning, like every other question affecting the company, had hitherto been determined by marketing. Quandt was now planning to abandon the collegiate principle and have Kuenheim act (and not only nominally) as managing director. In response, Hahnemann declared that he had no objections to that, except for the fact that all this, as was customary, should have been discussed *with* him (he had been specifically summoned here) and not'to his hardly unintentional exclusion. He therefore asked to leave, with the request that this was passed onto Quandt. Without speaking to him again, Quandt approved this, a document was set before him and he signed it. Then he called his chauffeur, drove to Munich, and cleared out his desk there before going home. He had decided to dismiss any attempt to get him to change his mind, whether it came from Quandt or anyone else.

That was all there was to the proceedings in Bad Homburg. There were no supervisory board minutes to confirm or deny this representation. But Golda definitely remembered the following taking place at Munich from the afternoon to the late evening hours on the following day (28 October 1971). He, Golda, had announced 'resistance by the employees' to Hahnemann's departure. Thereupon the supervisory board committee met in his office and earnestly discussed the problem of the possible damage to the company. They managed to reach Hahnemann (in hospital, where he was visiting his female companion injured in the road accident) and persuade him to come in. They decided not to hold individual hearings for Hahnemann

567

and von Kuenheim, or the time for reflection they requested, as the matter had to be cleared out of the way. After wrestling long and hard, the supervisory board committee came to a unanimous decision. This was that Hahnemann should stay head of marketing, should stay in the management board as before, and that there should be no sense of 'demotion'.

'To this, Herr von Kuenheim requested a further time for reflection, which we granted him, but limited it to a quarter of an hour. When the time was up, he entered, carrying a copy of the *Süddeutsche Zeitung* (for the day after – it had already been delivered that evening in Munich). The newspaper announced Hahnemann's resignation, saying that the supervisory board committee was in constant session and that the members of this committee were planning to resign their mandates if this resignation was not reversed. Even the works council was planning to resign. There was noticeable disquiet amongst the BMW workforce, and the mention of strike threats. There was no truth in any of this, even about the resignation. There was no way of establishing who had originated this false report, but there was no longer any way of preventing 'damage to the company'. It was now left to us, those people who had wanted to avoid damage. Quandt had been ready to take back the resignation, but now there was nothing left for him to do than to throw in the towel. The resignation stood. Hahnemann would go.'

A third report, based on what von Kuenheim could remember, confirmed Golda's portrayal of the events, at least from outward appearances. At the same time, it provided an insight into the inner drama of an event which decided so much. Kuenheim had been considerably unsettled by the objections of the committee, which alone was empowered to make a decision. If, as he had wondered, everyone up to Dr Draeger had a fundamentally different opinion, then how right was his? Undecided as to whether he should 'chance it' after the events at Homburg, he suddenly became aware that, within the solution to the leadership question reeled off in front of Quandt, something now appeared on the agenda which had previously not been there at all. It all now boiled down to the question: 'He or me?' The truth that only one person could govern, which was an old idea of both Quandt's and Hahnemann's, now became alarmingly clear to him as he faced the questioning – so clear, that in estimating his capacity for leading the company, he could now only perceive Hahnemann's continued presence as an uneasy compromise. Nobody, least of all the company, with whose leadership Quandt had entrusted him, would be served by that. It would be better, as he then decided, that 'I resign from the job I have been given.'

At that moment, Dr Draeger (who had represented Quandt's concept on the committee in Kuenheim's favour, as he had at Homburg, and had defended him against Dr Karoli's insistence on Hahnemann) went up to him, and said three words in private. These three words were allegedly: 'Stick at it!'

'My decision was naturally abandoned,' Kuenheim said. 'Draeger finally assured me that I was right. What then happened, the business with the newsapaper, was a farce. It was pure chance, not fate. Or perhaps it was irony. Irony sometimes makes the difficult things in life easier. In any case, the die had been cast. Hahnemann was going, and I was staying.'

The Tower

When, in the summer of 1970, the construction machines moved into Petuelring, to sink the foundations for the tower, only a few people knew what they had let themselves in for. Among them was the architect who combined the vision of a working landscape where people could also live with the true significance of his creation ('significant' had become a catchword, which he himself used guardedly). There was also his head of planning, who had to carry out the building of the tower within twenty-six months, exactly to the day (that is when the Olympics would begin). And there was Quandt, who, as before, was troubled by the fundamental question, whenever he thought of the tower. Is it appropriate? Is it BMW? As the majority shareholder, can I honour what its external significance promises?

He had felt its shape on the model. It was nothing but circular segments, in which linear work routines were to take place. How come, given that everything would take place in the circle? This went against the grain for him, just as much as the idea of the four cylinders being associated with the vertical layering of the floors. Were the floors then to be fins? A cylinder was hollow, and the associated piston went up and down – a far-fetched comparison, perhaps, to describe the lifts! Moreover, if the administration building were then to be called the 'four cylinder', it contradicted the six-cylinder which characterised BMW. And what about the other symbol, the four-leaf clover, which corresponded with the ground plan? It could at best be seen from an airplane. He could not get much out of the technological beauty attributed to the four overhanging arms fitted at the top. (They held the four columns, onto which the circular segments of the floors were suspended). Did they look like cylinder heads and valves? Well, at least they had a function, the most important in the whole construction, which was to draw off the suspended load into the supporting centre of the building's core running down into the ground. These were again reminiscent of pistons in motion – and yet there were none. The only thing our major shareholder could appreciate was the shortened construction time, together with its associated cost savings (core construction and outfitting overlapped each other, and the floors assembled on the ground were lifted into place). It was incredible that there was no scaffolding; at least none running the height of the building. But what else was there?

Amongst suspended buildings in Germany were the towers of the Marl town hall and of 'Finland House' on the banks of the Alster in Hamburg. Our tower, at 99.5 metres (it was not allowed to be higher than the twin cupolas of the Frauenkirche, which dominated the Munich skyline at 100 metres high) was the third construction of this type, the art of which was to detach a house from the ground, to make it appear to hover. At the same time, it gave an idea of what Winston Churchill had once expressed in a sentence which architects fondly quote: 'First we build the houses, and then we let the houses build us.'

The architect was Professor Karl Schwanzer from Vienna, whom Pevsner's dictionary of architecture judged to be the 'best Austrian architect of the 20th century'. He did not share this view. As always, the aim of his plan in anything he had built had been to eliminate chance. This meant excluding 'the unforeseeable through consciously controlled actions', with the requirement that the planner dared to try and control the future. In other words, this meant that anyone using one of the buildings he had designed should recognise it as his own, as something belonging to him. In addition, it should be unmistakably set in its environment, and moreover (as in the case of the tower), carry characteristics of the 'idea' which it served.

Schwanzer agreed with Quandt (to keep in with him) that he would defend the notion of 'engine', which he found absurd. He had asked a reporter:

'Am I then supposed to build a shoe-shaped building to house the administration of a shoe factory?'

But it was just as urgent for the company (an 'amorphous conglomerate' of industrial buildings stretching over a wide area) to create a visual point of reference, as it was for it to strive for a self-image, so that anyone who saw it just once would always be reminded of BMW. It would be 'a solitaire with the technological radiance of a utopia, rising up in splendid isolation.'

And so, what was to emerge in 791 days, a time-scale fixed by the Games, was no new gasometer, no administrative stump rising out of the usual suburban buildings which surrounded old Oberwiesenfeld more by chance than design. Instead, what soared up was rather a slim building, acting as a significant counterpart to the graphic lines of an Olympic tent city hovering by ropes and masts, as well as to the pointed needle of the television tower rising into the sky. One important reason for this was its circular shape. Schwanzer's architectural idea was to catch the spirit of the Games, and transfer it to the everyday life of the business and residential landscape behind it in north Munich, which had always had scant attention paid to it. Anyone living there suddenly found themselves in another city.

Every major construction is an adventure with calculable and incalculable risks. Due to its location (BMW was once again back at Oberwiesenfeld, where the Games were to take place), the tower had to be ready for the start of the world spectacle (summer 1972). So Schwanzer engaged the best construction people in Germany. Yet only a critical path providing for many jobs to be carried out at the same time could ensure that the building was ready on time. The unusual design meant that the building was not standing, but hanging. Suspended on a supporting cross with four arms (each of these arms measured 16 metres), storey after storey would be raised by hydraulic presses over 'steel tensioners' called hawsers. All eighteen had already been fitted with an aluminium façade and had been fully glazed on the ground. They were raised 20 centimetres at a time. They would then be lifted in unison over a final 14 metres, to bring them to their final position, leaving the space below them empty. While work could be done on fitting out the interior in the suspension house, it was also possible to erect the entrance building on the ground, as well as the 230-metre long, four-storey, low building which was linked to it. (Schwanzer had planned the roof as a recreation area. He wanted to put some plants here, to 'give back to nature what we have stolen from her' and 'let the wood grow right into the works.')

Combined with the technological risk of the tower was the aesthetic one – a concrete key, painted in silver, with a diametre of forty metres. Situated at the intersection of Petuelring and Lerchenau Street, and accessible via a pedestrian bridge from the Olympic site (thus directly linking the Games to the tower), it was designed to symbolise the 'inherent relationship of cars, roads and traffic'. It was also to house the BMW museum.

If the architect had merely had technological and aesthetic goals for his work in mind, then he would have produced only technological and aesthetic solutions – and evaded social and political questions. But it was just these that Schwanzer was concerned about. If he looked back on his guild, the artist, which is how he would have understood himself in the 19th century, had become the social reformer and technician in the twenties of the new century. It was only in the post-war period that the architect had risen to become the co-ordinator and planner of today's and tomorrow's complex environment. This was how Schwanzer saw himself when he determined that the inside of the tower should be 'an open-plan arrangement, which actually would not be one'.

As it was, up to thirty people were to sit in each of the four three-quarter circles or segments, which were anchored around the four-tube core on each floor. There would be 'as many as in a school class, the only community which most people remember all their lives'. A new working atmosphere would be created, which would be human, cheerful, happy, animating, stimulating and engaging. Schwanzer summarized it in his 'Thoughts after building':

The circular room forms an all-embracing shell which encourages broadness of thinking. From a spatial point of view, it is just as effective for encouraging concentrated points of reference from concentrated, confluent ideas. The group or team identifies itself with the space inside, as well as outwardly (through its transparency) with the Munich city panorama.

This is how he envisaged it:

Individual members of staff look up from their desk work and look into the distance. They nevertheless feel a sense of neighbourliness and attachment. With its structural conditioning, the team unit holds together, forms a team

572

spirit, and develops a desire for competition underscored by performance. The round room necessarily assembles people into a community, like the round table which offers equal, unprivileged places, and unites human beings "of equal opportunities" in a circle without preferences.

In order to eliminate risks here too, Hahnemann, in the same way he had induced Schwanzer, had had to set up a whole segment on a scale of 1:1 at Geiselgasteig, with which he won over management and supervisory boards to Schwanzer's idea. He had then had 2,000 people from his departments take two years to get used to the new working arrangements in the fully air-conditioned Dukek House on the Frankfurter Ring. Approximating to what was planned in the tower, it had air-conditioned, open-plan offices fitted with partitions (which were still new at the time). When the departments moved into the tower (without Hahnemann), people were 'used to it anyway', as the planning engineer Franz Joseph Fritsche remembered.

Fritsche, who had gained experience in the USA, knew what Phase 1 (the already fully-planned building) would impose on the company's planning as it moved into Phase 2, which involved fitting out the shell. A also entailed B. From the outset, Schwanzer had implemented his concept of 'entity' against the 'sections' used in conventional building methods. He was well aware what this would mean, as any delay or interruption in building would leave fifteen storeys simply hanging in the air, raised up within smooth shuttering looking like a silo. That would have been to the joy of envious observers who would then have mocked: 'Aha, flashy BMW have run out of money!'

'Striving for the best solution, for perfection, is inherent in human nature, although, at the same time, we carry with us imperfection as original sin. This stifles every attempt at perfection while it is still at the imperfect stage. But every attempt to push forward into the unknown demands the courage to deal with the imperfect, as well as the will to improve. The "state of perfection" is a piece of arrogance, which would spell the end. But what is there in human affairs that cannot be improved?'

Words of the architect. But the other kind of building which Schwanzer's design required (dividing up production into similar, rhythmically repetitious building processes with regularly timed operations) had already demanded new thinking. This meant breaking up old working practices, as were still to be found in the 'great forge'. Schwanzer spoke of the 'great forge' he had found over there in the works, which, if BMW was to survive into the future, they had to step down from. This future began with the tower.

Fritsche saw this entirely through American eyes. For eleven years, he had assembled large-scale buildings as a planning engineer for NASA (National Aeronautics and Space Administration) and for the US Air Force. These included rocket-launching bases, radar stations, underground installations in Georgia, USA, and in Adana in Turkey. They seemed to be more oriented in their organisational installations towards science fiction novels than to patterns of thought involving such bold, yet traditional, engineering technology. Entrusted with 'operations research' (the application of scientific methods using mathematics, statistics and logistics to determine optimum values), he had also been involved in laying out that secret airfield from which the legendary U-2 had taken off – a spy plane operating at altitudes which had previously been thought unattainable. The Soviets had shot it down over southern Russia or forced it to land (they kept silent about which), and exhibited the remains, along with equipment from the unfortunate pilot, Francis Gary Powers. They did this right in the middle of Gorky Park in Moscow, when I went for a stroll there in the summer of 1960. When I recounted this to Fritsche (he knew Powers and knew about the take-off of the long-distance reconnaissance plane), it occurred to him how small the world was, and also how close failure had been to success in the tower, where we now found ourselves, somewhere between the 15th and 22th floors (in one of those bays where it really seemed as if one was gliding in over the earth from heaven knows where). Anyway, he immediately spoke about it.

'Don't imagine I'm making it up,' he said. 'The fact that the tower did not fail (or, to put it more accurately, those of us on the tower) was due to two circumstances. Firstly, there was Gieschen, who was not a yesterday's man. Although as a car man he was not involved in building, he understood all the important innovations which our pre-planning had provided for and calculated in. For example, there was the service floor which carried the top seven storeys, while the lower ones as good as hung on it. Schwanzer laid it out in such a way as to structure the main body of the building optically, as well as to house the air-conditioning and technical paraphernalia, so that it did not all have to come up from below. That was one reason.

'The second was that tomorrow's man (I mean Eberhard von Kuenheim) thought sufficiently far ahead. There was no one who better understood the virtue of throwing away installations which still worked well, but which were now outdated. Kuenheim knew about that. He also knew that trying to persuade somebody to give up voluntarily what they had got used to would have taken years, and would mean losses in millions, perhaps billions, in missed opportunities. They would not be lost in the tower. Kuenheim acted and, by circumventing all the "service channels", made some simple decisions. In this respect he was like Hahnemann, with whom he had little else in common. He did this although data processing, micro-processors and the new communication technologies had only just begun to change the world. He did not act on people's minds, as nothing changes very quickly there. On the other hand, he was a powerful organiser.

'As a rule, I reported around six in the evening, once or twice a week, anything that was outstanding. It only took a night, at most, and then I got my approval – or not, as the case may be. If Kuenheim could not be won over, he was usually right. At that time, I had thought too much like an American. Sometimes I would say to him that he was too German. He asked why. I justified my view. He would say: "All right, you've persuaded me." Then on the next day, he would retort: "Not you again!" Then I would reply: "Of course!" But that was okay. I would add: "But of course, we could also . . ." but he would raise his hand to stop me, saying that he had had it checked, and everything was in order. What amazed me the most was that the powers that be kept quiet.'

'Was that connected with Hahnemann's fall?' I asked.

'I wouldn't rule that out,' said Fritsche. 'At first, after his departure, an absolute calm fell upon us. It was as if an engine which had powered everything had suddenly stalled. Would another start up? Perhaps I was one of the few who knew that it had started up a long time ago.'

Behind the green partition (there were no walls inside the tower), the intercom buzzed. Someone picked it up.

'Yes,' I heard the female voice say. 'Herr Fritsche is here . . .'

While Fritsche ('always out and about, always able to be reached') took the call, I went to the window. Down below, next to the dome-shaped museum, stood policemen, looking like little plasticine figures, with walkie-talkies. An armada of dark BMW limousines drove up the cobbled-stone drive from Petuelring at a stately, leisurely pace. They stopped, doors flew open one after the other, and men in summer coats, small, wiry, pliable figures headed for the main entrance, while casting their eyes around. Some looked upwards, as if the architecture was extending their necks.

'They're here,' Fritsche said behind me. 'I must go down. Are you coming?'

We went down, hurried past the exhibition of South African art in the corridor, and entered a small room in the training centre, controlled by the works security, which I had never noticed before. It was a kind of board room, where the interpreters were already connecting up their simultaneous interpreting equipment. Young women and waiters serving drinks could be seen through sound-proofed glass walls in a room containing conference tables. On these tables were mounted colourful pennants. Crowds thronged the doorway. Then they came in, one after another. Fritsche said:

'The one in the grey suit at the front on the left, with short, black hair, is Signor Ghidella from Fiat – unfortunately, Agnelli couldn't come. In the pinstripe is the boss of Renault, Georges Besse. Behind them are the Swedes, with Pehr Gyllenhammar from Volvo. Just next to him is John Egan of Jaguar. Ah, welcome Mr Perry. He's the head of Rolls Royce. He's the small fat one next to Breitschwerdt, the head of Mercedes, who's just speaking to Kuenheim.'

Everything went very quickly. As the host (and current president of the guests), Kuenheim went to the microphone, and started by welcoming everyone. Fritsche murmured:

'If a bomb fell now, the European car industry would be leaderless.'

As the man in charge of planning, he had rebuilt the conference room for this summit, and installed all the necessary technical installations for it. (I later learnt that this was the annual board meeting of the CCMC [Comité des Constructeurs d'Automobiles du Marché Commun, Common Market Committee of Car Manufacturers] which this time was aiming at an international solution to the catalytic converter problem.)

'You must leave now,' Fritsche said. 'It's a private conference. Things are going well. Will you wait for me? I'll be right back.'

As I waited, I remembered what he had said about his customer, the air force, when he had built aerodromes. He claimed that it was probably the best organised being in the world (he had actually said 'being'). He had always aimed to implant something of this into the tower. Had he succeeded? Was the tower a 'being', created through cold-blooded organisation? Was it alive – with the firm inside it? Fritsche had reported about the arguments which had taken place when the company had moved into the tower. The very fact that there were now no walls had shocked people (in spite of all the 'practice' beforehand). Established departmental managers had refused to move in, because everything could be overheard. They did not think that micro-technology (here to be used when people wanted to hear what somebody was saying) made the thickest wall as permeable as paper. So what was the point of having one at all? Fritsche had tried to win them over, saying:

'Just look, there's light everywhere, natural light, even on the centre column, with no works place more than 12 metres from the window. There are four team rooms on each side, without any doors or passages . . .'

On the day of the official opening, Schwanzer had taken the board members involved in the building to the room, as big as a cathedral, which was attached to the low building. The room was empty, but he took them up to four small cabinets painted grey in the middle of the room. Kuenheim asked what the meaning of all this was, in view of the enormous waste of space. Schwanzer pointed to the cable. It had still not been covered, and ran from the cabinets onto a second floor which was tensioned above the base floor, and from there they went outside to visual display units, whose 'inspirations' the cabinets stored. Kuenheim, who was still amazed, asked:

'And the enormous room around it?'

'It is waiting for millions upon millions of items of data which it can process and store, such as compounded decisions, which will compound into new decisions!'

This would have been the vision which he, the planner, would have had to project. But he did not project it, because he could not. Fritsche said:

'Nobody can project it. Anyone with any idea how great the flood of data would be, would be well aware that, in spite of ever changing computer generations (today something will fit into the palm of one hand, which only recently would have filled up the whole hall), EDP (Electronic Data Processing) has been around for quite some time now. There are other buildings in the city which have it, although if growth causes expansion, that'll be a problem the tower will have to handle. If the teams increase by just a few people (there were 1,700 working in the tower, and there are still 1,700 there, so it's not a variable figure), then they will press from the top to the bottom – and from the bottom back up again. Constant removals occurred, departments changed locations and moved out into rented buildings. So that we did not have to rent, we built the tower. Today ten towers would not be sufficient to accommodate everyone. Do you know the Alabama site? We are now building an engineering centre there, but the shortage of space (it's been planned for 7,000 engineers) won't be remedied there, either. Growth continues. From a turnover of 1.5 billion DM when the tower was planned,

BMW has grown . . .' (I knew the figure, having memorised it from the last company report, stored in my head, as it was in his) '. . . to 17.1 billion DM.' We both shouted it out at the same time.

We looked at each other, as if we had just touched the philosophers' stone. Then we burst out laughing. Laughter, Homeric laughter, one might say. We were laughing at ourselves, at the mystique of the big figure which, as with everyone else, had taken our breath away.

Shortly afterwards, I was speaking with von Kuenheim. He was talking about the tower and how he had moved onto the 22nd floor, still in mortal fear after the Dingolfing press conference (where Hahnemann had announced the goal of between 250,000 and 300,000 cars which the company planned to build). He said:

'In 1973, the works at Dingolfing were officially opened, and the foundation stone had been laid at the time of the press conference. It was November, and the major energy crisis had come upon us. There were speed restrictions and bans on Sunday driving. When we opened the works, we had orders for 2,000 of our cars and we could have done with 15,000. Then everyone was talking about us falling flat on our faces. The entire remainder of the car industry were then making redundancies, putting thousands of workers on the streets. But we said that we would start up the factory, since to have closed it would have totally undermined morale. Then mathematics came to our aid. We got to work on the running curves based on the drop in orders registered, and saw that we had come to a turning point. The curve was rising. We immediately decided to persevere. This was in autumn '73 and early '74, at the time of the major recession after the Yom Kippur War, when the Arabs would not deliver any oil and Rotterdam was paralysed. The others, Opel and VW, continued with their redundancies and had to pay out a fortune in compensation. But we saw the turning point. It was to the credit of the young Economics Minister Friderichs that he would not introduce rationing. It was his major achievement. Fuel became expensive, but nothing else happened.

'Hahnemann would probably have put it like this: "I can feel the spring coming." We used mathematics to analyse the curve and predict what things would be like. Of course, we could not be certain, either. We were left wondering if it was us, or the others, who were seeing things the right way. But, as a result, we got back to a flying start in 1974.'

Epilogue

Here my story comes to an end, but not the story of BMW.

At this very spot, events branch off. In their demand to be taken notice of, my vision becomes blurred. Unimportant events come to the fore, important ones stay in the background, and events which ultimately matter prolong their life away from public gaze.

At the same time, historical distance is curtailed, the distance which allows the historian (and story-teller) to be universally present but incognito, like Harun al Raschid – to view events and figures, as it were, through an inverted telescope, and to see things with the reader's eye. (Have I succeeded? This is something which will become clear when the reader, having got as far as here, reads these lines.)

But I am not worried about that. I would be worried if I had allowed myself to depict these events from the vantage point of the year 2000, from that imaginary distance. (Eberhard Von Kuenheim's rise to chairman of the board, matching the rise of the company, Quandt's death in 1982, Count Goltz at the head of the supervisory board, Quandt's heirs maintaining their loyalty to BMW, the large-scale company which BMW started to become, etc. . . .)

It is almost as if I knew what had grown out of that thing called 'the car'. It is an object whose mobility, I suggest, has been the cause of real movement this century. This is what has torn people from classes and strata, forced them together, mixed them up and changed urban landscapes.

It is as if I knew that the firm depicted here would, proudly and obstinately, continue to be called BMW, the Bavarian *Motor* Works (not *Car* Works, incidentally; a small difference, which the founders may not even have bothered to think about, but which might have been of vital signficance to the future). Perhaps BMW was wrapped up in a gigantic trust, in which battles, like those with Daimler-Benz, were artificially staged simply to ward off boredom.

These thoughts stop me in my tracks. Not because they provide a vision that rejects everything the company had summoned up in the way of creative energy, obstinacy, resistance, perseverance, far-sightedness and cunning, just to survive the century (the company also had its fair share of luck), but because I simply cannot believe it.

I acknowledge that there is a worldwide integrational process going on, involving the Japanese with the British, the French and the Swedes, not to mention America. Cars are built in common, engines, as well as anything else stuck under the bonnet, are supplied in exchange. Yet did BMW, as a medium-sized car company, intend to resist this? Invited to give an answer, I can hear someone on the 22nd floor of the tower [Kuenheim] calmly say, from the other side of historical distance:

'Every case of co-operation has resulted from the fact that one partner needed development help which the other could provide. If a company is developing positively, another one cannot help it. With sufficient strength, companies like BMW can exist on the world market with volumes of around half a million cars produced annually.'

'So no chance of any partnership at any time, in whatever shape or form?'

'No. Absolutely none.'

'Does this matter?'

'Not for the time being. Because it is not the big ones who eat up the little ones, but the fast ones who eat up the slow ones.'

I strongly suspect that there is a further question which cuts BMW to the quick – by the year 2000 there will be 44 million cars on Germany's roads. Where does a company which stubbornly insists on the strength and performance of its products plan to stay when it is likely that nothing will be able to move and that all the roads will be blocked morning, noon and night? And again, I can hear that same voice on the 22nd floor saying calmly from the other side of historical distance:

'It is not only us, but the car industry as a whole, which has offered products which the public wants. Otherwise, their and our phenomenal market success would not be explicable. At the same time, we fully accept our responsibilities to help find ways and means for better co-operation between private and public transport. We initiated this co-operation in transport management, as the experts say. Because it is only through co-operation, and not through opposition, that cars, buses and trains will come up with the best possible solution.'

'And what about the sporty image which encourages people to drive?'

'We have never joined in the race to offer the fastest touring car in the world. We are, though, followers of achievement-oriented society, and we are not ashamed to admit that.

'Even if the performance you provide, because your customers want it, is based on seduction?'

'Then everything would be seduction, transcending mere human need.'

'And what about overcapacity which, by the year 2000, will have reached 30 per cent throughout the world?'

'This has existed for years amongst all manufacturers who offer products similar to each other. Manufacturers with the capacity to give their products an unmistakable identity are not affected by it.'

'But what if the development of the product comes to an end, in the same way that the development of the bicycle came to an end?'

'We are constantly surprised when we arrive at new solutions, especially as a result of demands such as lower fuel consumption, higher incomes, and higher standards of living, which lead to a need for greater comfort in cars. The comfortable car in 1955 has become

quite primitive for today's conditions. There will be further demands, even in comparison to what other makes (such as Mercedes, Audi and the Japanese) are putting on the market. There will be demands for our revamped models and then, year in, year out, for new models, which will need to be pacemakers for three or four years in succession. We can live for some while longer on the momentum of these pacemakers.'

'Even if people outside are saying there's nothing new, and that there is no real innovation? Is that really true?'

'As long as people buy our products, the competition are welcome to carry on thinking that way.'

'I admit, it is a miracle. In the twenty, twenty-five years the tower has existed, there has been nothing but success. Every year, more and more people work for the company, there is greater turnover, and greater profit.'

'Yes, it's like asking for the moon. But the problem lies elsewhere.'

'And where is that?'

'It is not in improving the product. Provided the need is there, we can do that. No, we have to ask ourselves just what the political and mental environment for this product is like. What if we were to say that the car no longer has the status which it had in the seventies and especially the fifties and sixties? Or, going back even further, the status it had in the twenties and thirties? Quite apart from the condemnation it is currently experiencing.'

'So you want to change course. But in which direction?'

'That's the point. From time immemorial, we have never been frightened of changing course – from aero-engines to motorcycles, from motorcycles back to aero-engines, and via motorcycles to cars. Let's make it clear – we won't be going across into making shoes (although, of course, these will continue to be needed). We shall remain loyal to our technological domain. I admit that we would have gladly bought back MTU from MAN, but Daimler had the option to buy.'

'Thank God for that. Going back into armaments would have meant you had learnt nothing from the past.'

'Must aero-engines necessarily be "armaments"?'

'An old question which almost cost BMW its life once before.'

'Times change. Let's forget it. That was nothing. Our problem is twofold; no, threefold. Firstly, we are undergoing personnel expansion which will continue even when things get critical. Of all the problems we have in this company, 80 per cent are ones of personnel. Once we have solved the first 80 per cent, we can solve the rest. It's amongst these first 80 per cent that we find those who matter. They're not perfect, because they're human beings, thank God. If it were otherwise, none of us would be needed. But how can we get the best personnel in this country? I would be very reluctant to define the word "best". In a large company like ours, the average ability amongst our 60,000 people is similar to the average ability of our society outside the company doors. It cannot be anything else. However, we must make quite sure that the managerial level in the various departmental structures is higher than the average abilities of these people. That's the whole secret and key to our future.'

'And the man at the top – what is his "secret"?'

'The man at the top spends half his time in the political domain. He makes speeches here and there, drafts the texts for general meetings, cuts a figure at Bonn, Brussels and Paris. The other half of the time, which is non-routine (although if you don't have routine, you cannot do anything), is mainly spent on a few, high-powered groups who

have the skills to think, prepare and formulate, so that the entire nucleus of the problem can be whittled down to two sides of typewritten paper. Armed with documents which I don't have to check or read in advance, I can fly off to appointments, and just read them on the plane. When I get off at some place or other, I am better prepared than my counterpart in the negotiations, an advantage which often proves decisive.'

'You said there were three problems. What is the second?'

'In the car business, we are not big enough to ensure we can continue to stay a significant force, even with 1.4 or 1.5 per cent of the world market. And then there is the third problem. As people know, we are prospecting around the world. We are a small, but important group, and we are preparing to expand into other product areas which are in line with our business.

'Has this "being in line", as far as the product is concerned, any role to play at all?'

'I think so. Certainly for us. If it has not been remarked on before, we are not called the Bavarian Car Works, but Motor Works, which is much more telling, and our research and engineering centre, which is eight times bigger than anything represented here by the tower, has around 5,000 specialist engineers who are already working there on expanding into other fields. Those are the principles of the project.'

'What does that mean? New product areas?

'That means that after a break in the seventies and eighties, a new chapter began in mid 1990 for BMW in aviation technology.'

'I see.'

'As I have already said, times change. Nowadays, more than 750 million passengers take off every year in one of more than 7,500 passenger jets currently being used all over the world. That means around 1,500 people at any one time. In addition, there are 14 million tonnes of freight. On top of that, there are still almost 2,000 propeller planes moving about in the skies belonging to the fifty largest airlines alone. It has been calculated that in the next fifteen years, air traffic will double again. This will result in new aircraft being ordered from around the world. More will be ordered than can be delivered. At the beginning of the nineties, the order books of the aircraft manufacturers had registered 3,000 orders. On top of this will come the need for modernising power plants. Just over the next fifteen years, this would produce a market of around $1.6 billion.'

'BMW started with aero-engines in 1916–17. By the end of 1934, this branch of the company had been made independent as BMW Aero-Engine Manufacture Co. Ltd, which lasted until 1945. A research company for power plant production followed in 1954, from which BMW Power Plant Production Co. Ltd (the jewel) subsequently emerged. It produced, amongst other things, the Rolls Royce Tyne engine under licence. Yet although, or simply because, it flourished, it was abandoned in the sixties. And now, in a roundabout way, you want to resurrect it as a new BMW company?'

'The new company, BMW Rolls Royce GmbH at Oberursel, in which we are the majority shareholder with 50 per cent of the capital, has nothing, but nothing to do with the old Power Plant Production. It has nothing to do with the past, nothing to do with armaments, and so nothing to do with getting our fingers burnt again. BMW AG Munich (66,000 employees, turnover of 26 billion DM) founded BMW Rolls Royce GmbH, in conjunction with the British company of Rolls Royce PLC, Europe's largest aerospace business (in 1989 it had 64,000 employees and a turnover of 3 billion pounds

sterling). It intends to develop and build new power plants of the B700 generation (which will replace the high by-pass ratio engines of the Rolls-Royce Tay range) for commercial aircraft in the nineties and beyond.'

'My last question concerns German unification. BMW has not reacquired its old site at Eisenach, which the Russians had dispossessed. It has also not asserted any claims for possession there, not even hinted at them. Why?'

'This is a huge subject. When we built our branch at Regensburg, reunification was unthinkable. When we acquired Wackersdorf on unbeatable terms (the proximity of Oberpfalz to Munich, a ready-made infrastructure which left nothing to be desired, etc, etc), a plant at Eisenach, which anyway could not have been linked to the town of Eisenach and would have had to have been built from scratch in the vicinity, would have overtaxed us. In addition, there would have been no point in it, if you look beyond simple reasons of tradition. But we shall erect a supply factory for major tooling at Eisenach. One other, quite different matter is that the new BMW Rolls Royce company will extend its activities throughout the nine provinces of the country. Although between 10 and 20 per cent of all turnover will come from non-car business, the car will remain the centre of our activities.'

And so spoke the voice in the tower. If there was also an absence of historical distance in relation to the events which it briefly mentioned, then it had been preceded by the change which took place in the last third of this century. This had seen a movement from leadership at the front with sleeves rolled up in the sixties to military style planning for safeguarding the company twenty years later. And this was how and why BMW succeeded in breaking through to become a world-class company.

Acknowledgements

My thanks go to Horst Avenarius and his colleagues, who encouraged me to write this book. I must also thank my 'period witnesses', who showed me so much patience; without them, and their direct involvement in events, my story would never have been written. My thanks also go to a number of people who were subjected to the equally tedious and difficult task of checking, correcting and completing my text with regard to accuracy of technical details. These include Helmut Schubert of the MTU company (Motoren- und Turbinen-Union München GmbH), Heinrich Leibach, Josef Hareiner, Christoph Meyer-Mendel and Max Pöhlein. In addition, I acknowledge the assistance of the qualified engineer Kurt Graßmann, who undertook to check the chapter 'Renouncing the Air'. I am also particularly indebted to Hans Fleischmann. He led me along the difficult path of putting the events of a highly complex company history into the broader perspective of a time about which we know so little (despite it being our own).

When I visited Gerhard Wilcke at Murnau a year before his death with my almost completed book (I was concerned about some difficult legal passages from the restructuring period, which he had run), he said to me, as he glanced through the text: 'Scrub that lot out!'

I replied: 'But I can't. It's one of the most important passages – it's the section about you. It shows all your negotiating skill.'

Wilcke was unimpressed. 'My dear friend, the man in that office you quote, who gave me the information which then made me so confident, is still alive.'

I replied: 'I will cross out the office, but not the information. By the way, it was you who wrote down everything I used.'

Wilcke said angrily: 'But I didn't write it down for you!'

'For whom then?' I asked, taken aback.

'For history,' was his answer.

. So much for dealing with living people, who are naturally entitled to be protected until contemporary history becomes history proper.

The tape transcripts of all the interviews I made before I wrote my book have been handed over to the documentation centre of the Bavarian Motor Works and placed in its archives.

H. M.

INDEX

585